2010

YEARBOOK OF CHINA AGRICULTURAL PRODUCTS PROCESSING INDUSTRIES

中国农产品加工业年鉴

科学技术部农村科技司
中国农业机械化科学研究院
中国包装和食品机械总公司
食品装备产业技术创新战略联盟
编

中国农业出版社
CHINA AGRICULTURE PRESS

内 容 简 介

本年鉴较系统地记述了我国有关农产品加工业发展的方针、政策、法律、法规和规划等贯彻执行情况；有关领导、专家对发展我国农产品加工业的论述；本领域内相关行业的发展综述；简介了相关行业经济运行情况及名、优、特、新产品；登载了农产品加工业的国内外统计资料；记载了相关的国家标准、行业标准、专利以及本行业的大事记。本年鉴资料新颖、准确、科学、翔实，内容丰富，可供政府管理部门、协会、学会、中介组织、生产企业、科研教学单位的管理人员、策划人员、教育工作者和科技工作者参考。

《中国农产品加工业年鉴》编辑委员会

编　辑　部

主　　任： 赵有斌
副 主 任： 王国扣
编　　辑： 王国扣　付　涛
地　　址： 北京市德胜门外北沙滩 1 号 82 信箱
邮　　编： 100083
电　　话： 010－64882617
传　　真： 010－64862464　64862459
E－mail： cpfmchy@caams.org.cn

编辑出版说明

一、为紧跟我国农产品加工业发展的时代脉搏和大力宣传主旋律，在各级领导和行业专家的支持与帮助下，我们组织编辑出版的《中国农产品加工业年鉴》（2010）与广大读者见面了，其宗旨是为我国农产品加工业的发展起到桥梁和促进作用。

二、《中国农产品加工业年鉴》由科学技术部、农业部、国家发展和改革委员会、国家林业局、国家粮食局、中华全国供销合作总社、中国机械工业联合会、中国轻工业联合会的有关主管部门及农产品加工业相关协会、学会、科研院所、大专院校等，与中国农业机械化科学研究院、中国包装和食品机械总公司联合编辑出版。

三、《中国农产品加工业年鉴》（2010）安排了7个部分的框架内容，每个栏目名称基本未变，其中的内容和数据均以2009年的基本情况为主。但根据资料的获取难易程度也有部分2009年前后的情况，并保持每卷年鉴的连续性，其中的政策法规及重要文件、大事记和标准均以2010年的基本情况为主。

四、《中国农产品加工业年鉴》记述了相关方针、政策、法律、法规和规划等贯彻执行情况；记述了有关领导、专家对发展我国农产品加工业的论述；记述了本领域相关行业的发展综述；介绍了农产品加工业行业经济运行情况及名、优、特、新产品；登载了农产品加工业国内外统计资料；记载了相关的国家标准、行业标准、专利以及本行业的大事记。年鉴既述事，也记人，每年编辑、出版一卷。若干年后，不但可以见证我国每年的农产品加工业发展情况，而且将是系统、全面、可靠、翔实的史册和工具书。由于年鉴的权威性和正式的连续出版发行，将有益于国内外各界了解和研究我国农产品加工业现状与发展等情况，促进相互交流与合作；有益于各部门借鉴现实和历史经验，掌握全局，运筹帷幄，制定政策和发展规划，指导本行业健康发展；有益于社会各界沟通行业信息、产品信息，互相学习，取长补短，推动我国农产品加工业的发展和国民经济的腾飞。

五、本年鉴各部分所列数据，因来源渠道不同，不尽一致。全面的数据均以国家统计局提供的为准。本年鉴全国性统计数据均不包括香港、澳门两个特别行政区和中国台湾省。两区一省的相关数据，在年鉴的附录中列出。

六、为系统、准确、科学、翔实地反映我国农产品加工业现状，并力争办出本年鉴的特色，我们在编辑中继续突出了综述文章以当年国家重点抓的农产品加工业中的有关行业为主，全书内容以推动产业发展为主，国家标准、行业标准与专利以加工工艺、设备和相应的产品为主，统计数据以国家统计局经济行业分类为主，国外的统计数据以特点显著的部分发达国家和少数发展中国家为主等。

七、本年鉴的编辑、出版、发行等工作，得到了中央及各级相关部门、协会、学会、科研院所、高等院校、生产企业、社会团体的大力支持和帮助，谨此表示衷心的感谢。

目 录

编辑出版说明

第一部分 专题论述

以加快转变经济发展方式为主线 推动乡镇企业和农产品加工业科学发展 …… 3
提高认识 依法履责 扎实做好食品安全风险监测工作 …… 8
积极开展肉菜流通追溯体系建设 努力提高质量安全和供应保障水平 …… 11
加强和改善粮食宏观调控 切实保障国家粮食安全 …… 16
深入落实科学发展观 开创食品安全监管和消费维权新局面 …… 23
大力推进农产品现代流通综合试点 加快完善农产品现代流通体系 …… 32
抓住机遇 迎接挑战 推动我国农产品加工业持续健康发展 …… 34
强化措施 保质保量 完成食品安全风险监测任务 …… 38
落实生猪屠宰规划纲要 促进生猪屠宰行业健康发展 …… 41
加大结构调整力度 推进茧丝绸产业升级 …… 46
依靠科技进步 推进纺织工业健康发展 …… 49
齐心协力 扎实工作 推动绿色食品和有机食品持续健康发展 …… 53
明确目标 强化措施 推进无公害农产品及地理标志科学发展 …… 57
实践科学发展观 推动食品工业持续稳定发展 …… 61
转变发展模式 提升行业整体素质 …… 63
着力转变发展方式 完善绿色生态饲料工业体系 …… 66
中国肉类工业发展概况 …… 69
全国水产品进出口贸易情况 …… 72
我国造纸工业发展现状 …… 75

第二部分 相关行业发展概况

粮油食品加工业 …… 81
油料加工业 …… 85
大豆加工业 …… 90
淀粉加工业 …… 96
制糖工业 …… 99
蔬菜加工业 …… 102
茶叶加工业 …… 106
蜂产品加工业 …… 108
食用菌加工业 …… 112
乳制品制造业 …… 116
烟草加工业 …… 125
酿酒工业 …… 129
蚕丝加工业 …… 131
饲料加工业 …… 135
水产品加工业 …… 137
林产品加工业 …… 141
农作物秸秆加工业 …… 145
食品与包装机械制造业 …… 149
棉花加工机械制造业 …… 151

第三部分 政策法规及重要文件

全国生猪屠宰行业发展规划纲要（2010—2015年） …… 157
粮油仓储管理办法 …… 161
食品安全风险评估管理规定（试行） …… 163
2010年食品安全整顿工作安排 …… 165
餐饮服务许可管理办法 …… 167
餐饮服务食品安全监督管理办法 …… 170
2010年流通环节食品安全整顿工作方案 …… 175
食品添加剂生产监督管理规定 …… 179
食品生产许可管理办法 …… 182
关于认真开展农村食品市场专项整治行动工作方案 …… 185
全国奶业发展规划（2009—2013年） …… 187
农产品冷链物流发展规划 …… 192
餐饮服务食品安全百千万示范工程建设指导意见 …… 197
关于推进纺织产业转移的指导意见 …… 199
放心粮油示范加工企业和示范主食厨房质量安全管理规则 …… 201

保健食品审评专家管理办法 …… 204
餐饮服务食品安全监督抽检工作规范 …… 205
关于进一步加强乳品质量安全工作的通知 …… 208
国家粮食质量检验监测机构管理暂行办法 …… 210
食品安全国家标准管理办法 …… 212
食品工业企业诚信体系建设工作实施方案（2010—2012 年） …… 214
中央储备粮代储资格认定办法实施细则 …… 217
食品安全信息公布管理办法 …… 219
中央储备粮油质量检查扦样检验管理办法 …… 221

第四部分 国内综合统计资料

农林牧渔业主要产品产量统计 …… 227
表 1 我国主要农产品产量（2005—2009 年） …… 227
表 2 各地区主要农产品产量（2009 年） …… 228
表 3 我国玉米主产区生产情况（2008—2009 年） …… 233
表 4 各地区水果产量（2009 年） …… 233
表 5 各地区茶叶产量（2009 年） …… 235
表 6 我国农垦系统主要农产品产量（2008—2009 年） …… 236
表 7 各地区农垦系统主要农产品产量（2009 年） …… 237
表 8 我国农垦系统茶、桑、果、林生产情况（2008—2009 年） …… 238
表 9 我国热带、亚热带作物产量（2009 年） …… 238
表 10 我国棉花主产区生产情况（2008—2009 年） …… 238
表 11 各地区蔬菜产量增减情况（2008—2009 年） …… 239
表 12 我国主要林产品产量（2005—2009 年） …… 239
表 13 各地区主要林产品产量（2009 年） …… 240
表 14 我国主要牲畜饲养情况（2005—2009 年） …… 241
表 15 我国主要畜产品产量（2005—2009 年） …… 241
表 16 各地区奶类产量（2008—2009 年） …… 242
表 17 我国农垦系统主要畜产品产量（2008—2009 年） …… 242
表 18 我国水产品产量（2005—2009 年） …… 243
表 19 各地区水产品产量（2009 年） …… 243
表 20 我国沿海地区海洋捕捞水产品产量（按品种分）（2009 年） …… 244
表 21 我国沿海地区海水养殖水产品产量（按品种分）（2009 年） …… 246
表 22 各地区农垦系统水产品养殖面积与产量（2009 年） …… 249
表 23 我国按人口平均的主要农畜产品产量（2005—2009 年） …… 250
表 24 我国城乡居民家庭人均食品消费量比较（2005—2009 年） …… 250
表 25 我国城镇和农村人口人均食品消费支出情况（2005—2009 年） …… 250
表 26 我国人口增长情况（2005—2009 年） …… 250
农产品加工机械拥有量及农产品加工行业固定资产投资情况 …… 251
表 27 农业部系统农产品初加工机械年末拥有量（2009 年） …… 251
表 28 我国农产品加工行业固定资产投资情况（2009 年） …… 252
表 29 我国农产品加工行业新增固定资产后主要产品新增生产能力（2008—2009 年） …… 252
表 30 我国农产品加工行业 50 万元以上施工、投产项目数（2009 年） …… 252
表 31 林业系统森工固定资产投资完成情况（2008—2009 年） …… 253
表 32 林业系统各地区森工固定资产投资完成情况（2009 年） …… 253
表 33 我国农垦系统固定资产投资完成情况（2008—2009 年） …… 254
表 34 我国水产行业固定资产投资情况（2008—2009 年） …… 254
按国民经济行业分类统计农产品加工业现状 …… 254
表 35 我国农产品加工业全部国有及规模以上非国有工业企业主要指标（2009 年） …… 254
表 36 我国农产品加工业全部国有及规模以上非国有工业企业主要经济效益指标（2009 年） …… 255
表 37 我国农产品加工业国有及国有控股工业企业主要指标（2009 年） …… 255
表 38 我国农产品加工业国有及国有控股工业企业主要经济效益指标（2009 年） …… 256
表 39 我国农产品加工业外商投资和港澳台商投资工业企业主要指标（2009 年） …… 256
表 40 我国农产品加工业外商投资和港澳台商投资工业企业主要经济效益指标（2009 年） …… 257
表 41 我国农产品加工业私营工业企业主要指标

(2009年) …… 257
表42 我国农产品加工业私营工业企业主要经济效益指标（2009年） …… 258
表43 我国农产品加工业大中型工业企业主要指标（2009年） …… 258
表44 我国农产品加工业大中型工业企业主要经济效益指标（2009年） …… 259
表45 2009/2010年度制糖期全国制糖行业主要经济技术指标 …… 259
表46 我国食品和包装机械经济运行情况（2005—2009年） …… 259
表47 我国机械工业、食品工业、食品与包装机械行业经济增长情况（2005—2009年） …… 260
表48 林业系统农产品加工业总产值（2008—2009年） …… 260
表49 林业系统农产品加工业国有独立核算大中型工业企业主要经济效益指标（2009年） …… 260
表50 林业系统各地区农产品加工业总产值（2009年） …… 261
表51 我国水产品加工业发展情况（2008—2009年） …… 263
表52 我国水产品加工业加工能力、产量及产值（2006—2009年） …… 263
表53 我国沿海省、自治区、直辖市水产品加工业生产情况（2009年） …… 264
表54 我国乡镇企业规模以上农产品加工企业基本情况（2009年） …… 264
表55 轻工业系统农产品加工业分行业主要经济指标（2008年） …… 264
表56 轻工业系统食品工业分行业主要经济指标（2008年） …… 265
表57 我国食品工业总产值增长情况（2005—2009年） …… 265
表58 我国食品工业焙烤糖制食品行业主要经济指标（2008年） …… 266
表59 我国饮料行业主要经济指标（2008—2009年） …… 266
表60 我国酒精工业主要经济指标（2008—2009年） …… 266
表61 我国乳制品行业主要经济指标（2008—2009年） …… 267
表62 轻工业系统农产品加工机械重点企业主要经济指标（2008年） …… 267
表63 我国烟草工业主要经济指标（2008—2009年） …… 267
表64 我国纺织工业主要经济指标（2008—2009年） …… 267
表65 我国纺织服装、鞋、帽制造业主要经济指标（2008—2009年） …… 268
表66 我国皮革工业经济运行情况（2008—2009年） …… 268
表67 我国家具行业经济运行情况（2008—2009年） …… 268
表68 我国造纸工业主要经济指标（2008—2009年） …… 268
表69 我国新闻出版业产业基本情况（2007—2008年） …… 269
表70 我国130个书刊印刷企业（含其他印刷）主要经济指标（2008—2009年） …… 270
表71 我国62个印刷机械企业主要经济指标（2008—2009年） …… 270
表72 我国橡胶工业主要经济指标（2008—2009年） …… 271
表73 我国橡胶工业全部独立核算工业企业主要经济指标（2007—2008年） …… 271
表74 我国中药行业经济效益情况（2009年） …… 272
表75 我国农产品加工业能源消费总量和主要能源品种消费量（2008年） …… 272
农产品加工业主要产品产量 …… 272
表76 我国农产品加工业主要产品产量（2008—2009年） …… 272
表77 轻工业系统农产品加工业主要产品产量（2007—2008年） …… 273
表78 我国粮油工业主要产品产量（2008—2009年） …… 274
表79 我国淀粉产量及品种情况（2008—2009年） …… 274
表80 我国淀粉深加工品产量（2008—2009年） …… 275
表81 我国淀粉产量分布及生产规模情况（2009年） …… 275
表82 我国玉米淀粉生产规模情况（2008—2009年） …… 275
表83 我国部分淀粉深加工品生产规模情况（2008—2009年） …… 276
表84 我国食品添加剂主要产品产量（2007—2008年） …… 277
表85 我国饮料行业主要产品产量（2008—2009年） …… 277

表 86 我国牛奶与乳制品产量（2008—2009 年）…… 277
表 87 我国饮料行业各地区主要产品产量（2008 年）…… 278
表 88 我国烟草工业主要产品产量（2008—2009 年）…… 279
表 89 我国酒精工业产品产量（2008—2009 年）…… 279
表 90 我国酒精工业各地区产品产量（2007—2008 年）…… 279
表 91 我国各地区味精产量（2008 年）…… 280
表 92 我国焙烤食品糖制品主要产区产量（2008 年）…… 280
表 93 我国各地区啤酒产量（2008—2009 年）…… 281
表 94 我国罐头工业产值与产品产量（2008 年）…… 281
表 95 我国各地区白酒产量（2008—2009 年）…… 282
表 96 我国饲料工业产品产量（2006—2009 年）…… 283
表 97 2009/2010 年度制糖期糖料与食糖生产情况 …… 283
表 98 我国食用菌产量、产值、出口情况（2009 年）…… 284
表 99 我国农垦系统农产品加工业主要产品产量（2008—2009 年）…… 288
表 100 农垦系统各地区农产品加工业主要产品产量（2009 年）…… 288
表 101 我国森林工业主要产品产量（2008—2009 年）…… 289
表 102 各地区森林工业主要产品产量（2009 年）…… 290
表 103 我国水产品加工产品的主要种类与产量（2006—2009 年）…… 292
表 104 纺织工业主要产品产量（规模以上企业）（2008—2009 年）…… 292
表 105 我国皮革行业主要产品产量（2008—2009 年）…… 292
表 106 我国家具工业主要产品产量（2008—2009 年）…… 292
表 107 我国家具工业分地区主要产品产量（2009 年）…… 292
表 108 我国造纸工业纸浆消耗情况（2007—2009 年）…… 293
表 109 我国废纸回收利用情况（2004—2008 年）…… 293
表 110 我国各类造纸纤维原料所占比重（2008—2009 年）…… 293
表 111 我国机制纸及纸板主要品种产量（2008—2009 年）…… 294
表 112 我国纸和纸板消费结构情况（2007—2008 年）…… 294
表 113 我国造纸工业主要产品生产及消费情况（2008—2009 年）…… 295
表 114 我国纸和纸板生产、消费及进口量与人均消费量（2005—2009 年）…… 295
表 115 我国 136 个重点书刊印刷（含其他印刷）企业主要产品产量（2007—2008 年）…… 295
表 116 我国纸和纸板人均消费量与美国的比较（2005—2009 年）…… 295
表 117 我国橡胶工业主要产品产量（2008—2009 年）…… 296
表 118 我国人均主要工农业产品产量（2005—2009 年）…… 296
农产品加工业主要产品出口创汇情况 …… 296
表 119 我国海关出口农产品及加工品数量与金额（2008—2009 年）…… 296
表 120 我国农产品进出口状况（2008—2009 年）…… 298
表 121 我国海关进口农产品及加工品数量与金额（2008—2009 年）…… 298
表 122 我国畜产品进出口状况（2009 年）…… 299
表 123 我国主要粮食产品进出口情况（2009 年）…… 299
表 124 我国林产品进出口数量（2008—2009 年）…… 300
表 125 我国林产品进出口金额（2008—2009 年）…… 302
表 126 轻工业系统农产品加工业主要出口产品创汇情况（2008 年）…… 304
表 127 轻工业系统农产品加工业主要进口产品情况（2008 年）…… 305
表 128 我国淀粉及部分深加工品进出口情况（2009 年）…… 305
表 129 我国食糖进出口与贸易方式情况（2007—2009 年）…… 306
表 130 我国乳制品进口情况（2009 年）…… 306
表 131 我国乳制品出口情况（2009 年）…… 307
表 132 我国罐头产品主要类别及品种出口情况（2008 年）…… 307
表 133 我国罐头产品出口情况

(2007—2008年) ………………………… 308
表134 我国蜂蜜生产及出口情况 (2006—2009年) ………………………… 308
表135 我国蜂产品出口情况 (2008—2009年) ………………………… 308
表136 我国水产品进出口贸易情况 (2006—2009年) ………………………… 308
表137 我国食品和包装机械进出口情况 (2005—2009年) ………………………… 309
表138 我国鞋类产品进出口情况 (2008—2009年) ………………………… 309
表139 我国纺织品服装出口情况 (2008—2009年) ………………………… 309
表140 我国家具工业主要产品进出口情况 (2009年) ………………………… 309
表141 我国皮革工业主要产品进出口情况 (2009年) ………………………… 310
表142 我国纸浆、废纸、纸、纸板、纸制品进出口情况 (2007—2009年) ………… 310
表143 我国印刷机械进出口统计 (2007—2008年) ………………………… 311
表144 我国机械工业产品进出口情况 (2005—2009年) ………………………… 311
表145 我国中药行业进出口情况 (2008—2009年) ………………………… 311
表146 我国橡胶工业制品出口量与出口额 (2007—2008年) ………………………… 311
表147 我国橡胶工业制品进口量与进口额 (2007—2008年) ………………………… 312
表148 我国胶鞋产品进出口情况 (2008年) ………………………… 313
表149 我国主要胶鞋企业出口创汇情况 (2007—2008年) ………………………… 314
表150 我国天然橡胶、合成橡胶进口情况 (2006—2009年) ………………………… 314

农产品加工业部分行业与企业排序 ………………………… 314

表151 轻工业系统农产品加工业分行业主要经济指标 (2008年) ………………………… 314
表152 轻工业系统农产品加工业分行业进出口总额 (2008年) ………………………… 316
表153 我国农产品进出口额前10位省、直辖市排序 (2009年) ………………………… 316
表154 我国十大最具增长潜力白酒品牌 (2010年) ………………………… 316
表155 选入我国500个最具价值品牌的酿酒企业拥有的品牌 (2009年) ……………… 317
表156 我国啤酒产量20万kL以上企业 (2009年) ………………………… 317
表157 我国啤酒销售收入3亿元以上企业 (2008年) ………………………… 318
表158 我国葡萄酒产量前10位省、直辖市主要经济运行情况 (2008年) ………………… 318
表159 我国饮料工业20强企业 (2008年) … 319
表160 我国饮料行业按产量分地区前8位情况 (2008年) ………………………… 319
表161 我国瓶 (罐) 装饮用水分地区产量前5位情况 (2008年) ………………… 319
表162 我国果汁及果汁饮料产量分地区前5位情况 (2008年) ………………… 320
表163 我国乳制品生产企业销售收入居前列的企业 (2009年) ………………………… 320
表164 我国液体乳产量位居前列的企业 (2009年) ………………………… 321
表165 我国酒精产量9万t以上酒精企业和产量11万t以上燃料乙醇企业 (2008年) ………………………… 321
表166 我国味精产量2万t以上企业 (2008年) ………………………… 322
表167 2009年中国蜂产品行业第二批信用等级评价结果 ………………………… 322
表168 2009/2010年度我国纺织工业各行业“企业竞争力”排名前列企业 ………… 322
表169 2008—2009年获“中国驰名商标”的家具企业 ………………………… 324
表170 2009年中国皮革行业10强企业 ……… 325
表171 2009年中国真皮名鞋、名装品牌……… 325
表172 纸及纸板产量100万t以上的省、自治区主营业务收入 (2007—2008年) ……… 326
表173 我国纸及纸板产量100万t以上的省、自治区 (2007—2009年) ………………… 326
表174 我国重点造纸企业产量排名前30名企业 (2008—2009年) ………………… 327
表175 我国印刷机械企业实现销售收入前10名企业 (2009年) ………………………… 328
表176 我国印刷机械企业出口交货值前10名企业 (2009年) ………………………… 328
表177 我国重点造纸机械企业实现销售收入5 000万元以上的企业 (2008年) …… 328
表178 我国重点造纸机械企业实现利税总额500万元以上的企业 (2008年) ……… 329
表179 劳动生产率在10万元以上的重点造纸机械企业 (2008年) ………………………… 329

表 180 我国橡胶工业协会会员企业按销售收入排序（2009 年） …… 329
表 181 我国中成药按出口金额排序前 10 名企业（2009 年） …… 330
我国西部地区综合统计 …… 331
表 182 我国西部地区主要农产品产量（2008—2009 年） …… 331
表 183 我国西部地区主要农产品单位面积产量（2008—2009 年） …… 332
表 184 我国西部地区茶叶产量（2009 年） …… 332
表 185 我国西部地区水果产量（2008—2009 年） …… 333
表 186 我国西部地区森林工业主要产品产量（2009 年） …… 333
表 187 我国西部地区热带、亚热带作物面积和产量（2009 年） …… 334
表 188 我国西部地区主要畜产品产量（2008—2009 年） …… 334
表 189 我国西部地区水产品产量（2008—2009 年） …… 335
表 190 我国西部地区人均主要农产品、畜产品、水产品产量（2008—2009 年） …… 335
表 191 我国西部地区农林牧渔业总产值、增加值及构成（2008—2009 年） …… 336
表 192 我国西部地区林业产业总产值（2009 年） …… 336
表 193 我国西部地区林业系统森林工业固定资产投资（2009 年） …… 336
表 194 我国西部地区林业系统农产品加工业总产值（2009 年） …… 337
表 195 我国西部地区森林工业主要产品产量（2009 年） …… 338
表 196 我国西部地区农垦系统主要农产品加工企业产品产量（2009 年） …… 339
表 197 我国西部地区轻工业系统农产品加工业产品产量（2008 年） …… 339
其他 …… 341
表 198 我国食品卫生抽样监测情况（2008 年） …… 341
表 199 轻工业系统农产品加工行业十大质量品牌当选企业（2008 年） …… 342
表 200 我国农产品加工创业基地第一批名单（2009 年） …… 349
表 201 我国粮油加工行业首批获 AAA 级、AA 级、A 级信用等级企业（2009 年） …… 351
表 202 我国轻工业系统列入国家 500 强的农产品加工企业（2009 年） …… 352

第五部分　标准、专利

农产品加工业部分国家标准（2010 年） …… 357
农产品加工业农业行业标准（2010 年） …… 364
农产品加工业机械行业标准（2010 年） …… 366
农产品加工业轻工行业标准（2010 年） …… 367
农产品加工业国内贸易行业标准（2010 年） …… 368
农产品加工业出入境检验检疫行业标准（2010 年） …… 369
农产品加工业烟草行业标准（2010 年） …… 369
农产品加工业纺织行业标准（2010 年） …… 370
农产品加工业发明专利（2009 年） …… 372

第六部分　大 事 记

第七部分　附　录

表 1 部分国家（地区）农业生产指数（2007 年） …… 405
表 2 我国台湾省农业生产指数（2006—2008 年） …… 405
表 3 部分国家（地区）主要粮食作物总产量（2009 年） …… 405
表 4 2007/2008—2009/2010 年度世界粮食生产、消费、贸易、库存情况 …… 406
表 5 世界植物油年均生产、贸易状况（2005/2006—2009/2010 年度） …… 406
表 6 部分国家（地区）主要油料作物总产量（2009 年） …… 407
表 7 美国主要农作物收获面积、单产、总产量（2005—2009 年） …… 407
表 8 世界植物油主要国家（地区）年均生产、贸易状况 …… 408
表 9 俄罗斯主要农产品生产情况（2009 年） …… 409
表 10 部分国家（地区）籽棉、麻类收获面积、单产、总产量（2009 年） …… 409
表 11 部分国家（地区）烟叶、茶叶收获面积、单产、总产量（2009 年） …… 409
表 12 部分国家（地区）甘蔗、甜菜收获面积、单产、总产量（2009 年） …… 410
表 13 部分国家（地区）蔬菜、水果和坚果产量（2009 年） …… 410

表 14 部分国家（地区）苹果、梨、橙等水果产量（2009 年） …… 411
表 15 世界葡萄栽培面积前 10 位国家（2008 年） …… 411
表 16 世界葡萄主产国前 10 位国家（2008 年） …… 411
表 17 世界葡萄酒 10 强企业排名（2008 年） …… 412
表 18 世界主要葡萄酒生产国家（地区）出口状况（2006—2008 年） …… 412
表 19 中国葡萄酒进口量前 5 位国家分布情况（2008 年） …… 412
表 20 世界主要葡萄酒消费国的消费量（2007—2008 年） …… 413
表 21 世界食糖供求状况（2005—2009 年） …… 413
表 22 我国台湾省主要农产品产量（2006—2008 年） …… 413
表 23 部分国家（地区）肉类产量（2008—2009 年） …… 414
表 24 部分国家（地区）猪肉产量（2005—2009 年） …… 414
表 25 部分国家（地区）猪肉消费量（2005—2009 年） …… 415
表 26 部分国家（地区）猪肉进口量（2005—2009 年） …… 415
表 27 部分国家（地区）猪肉出口量（2005—2009 年） …… 416
表 28 部分国家（地区）猪、牛、羊、禽肉产量（2009 年） …… 416
表 29 世界主要贸易国肉类生产、消费及贸易情况（2005—2009 年） …… 417
表 30 俄罗斯主要畜牧业产品生产情况（2009 年） …… 417
表 31 部分国家（地区）鱼类产品产量（2007 年） …… 418
表 32 世界鱼粉产量前 10 位国家（2009 年） …… 418
表 33 中国鱼粉进口主要国家和地区情况（2008—2009 年） …… 418
表 34 部分国家（地区）牛奶产量（2008—2009 年） …… 419
表 35 部分国家（地区）乳饮料、酸奶和其他发酵乳产量（2006—2008 年） …… 419
表 36 部分国家（地区）奶油产量（2006—2008 年） …… 420
表 37 部分国家（地区）干酪产量（2006—2008 年） …… 420
表 38 部分国家（地区）炼乳产量（2006—2008 年） …… 421
表 39 部分国家（地区）全脂和半脱脂奶粉产量（2006—2008 年） …… 421
表 40 部分国家（地区）脱脂奶粉产量（2006—2008 年） …… 421
表 41 世界乳制品主要生产国家（地区）出口情况（2006—2008 年） …… 422
表 42 世界乳制品主要进口国家（地区）情况（2006—2008 年） …… 423
表 43 部分国家（地区）液体乳消费量（2006—2008 年） …… 424
表 44 部分国家（地区）乳饮料、酸奶和发酵乳制品消费量（2006—2008 年） …… 424
表 45 部分国家（地区）奶油消费量（2006—2008 年） …… 425
表 46 部分国家（地区）干酪消费量（2006—2008 年） …… 425
表 47 世界乳品工业排名前 20 强企业（2009 年） …… 426
表 48 部分国家（地区）蛋类产品产量（2009 年） …… 426
表 49 世界主要鸡蛋生产国市场占有率情况（2008 年） …… 427
表 50 部分国家（地区）蜂蜜产量（2008—2009 年） …… 427
表 51 部分国家（地区）羊毛产量（2008—2009 年） …… 428
表 52 我国农业主要产品产量居世界位次（1949—2008 年） …… 428
表 53 中国对日本农产品出口情况（2009 年） …… 428
表 54 2009 年中国与东盟各国农产品贸易情况 …… 429
表 55 2009 年中国—东盟主要农产品进出口情况 …… 429
表 56 2009 年中国与东盟各国主要农产品进出口品种情况 …… 429
表 57 俄罗斯主要农产品进出口情况（2008—2009 年） …… 430
表 58 美国主要农产品进出口情况（2009 年） …… 430
表 59 中国对新西兰农产品贸易情况（2004—2008 年） …… 431
表 60 中国与拉丁美洲及加勒比地区农产品

进出口情况（2005—2009 年） ………… 431
表 61　世界饲料加工业 30 强企业（2008 年） ………… 432
表 62　世界主要农畜产品最大生产国（2009 年） ………… 433
表 63　香港特别行政区工业生产指数（2006—2009 年） ………… 433
表 64　香港特别行政区主要加工食品及饮料出口与转口情况（2007—2008 年） …… 433
表 65　我国台湾省农产品加工业主要产品产量（2005—2009 年） ………… 434
表 66　我国台湾省农业生产及稻米产量情况（2004—2008 年） ………… 434
表 67　我国台湾省出口与进口商品分类（2006—2009 年） ………… 434
表 68　世界主要国家（地区）棉花产量（2009 年） ………… 434
表 69　世界和中国纺织纤维产量（2005—2007 年） ………… 434
表 70　世界主要国家（地区）化纤产量（2005—2007 年） ………… 435
表 71　世界主要国家（地区）合成纤维产量（2005—2007 年） ………… 435
表 72　世界棉花供求情况（2008/2009—2009/2010 年度） ………… 435
表 73　世界主要国家棉花耗用量（2005—2008 年） ………… 435
表 74　中国纺织品、成衣出口额占全球出口份额（2005—2007 年） ………… 436
表 75　世界纺织品、成衣出口国（地区）前 10 强（2007 年） ………… 436
表 76　中国纺织品服装出口前 5 位的主要市场（2009 年） ………… 436
表 77　中国等 4 国纺织品、服装产品占欧盟进口的份额（2005—2009 年） ………… 436
表 78　2009 年 5 国 4 种产品占欧盟进口总额中的比重 ………… 437
表 79　世界 20 大纸与纸板生产国家或地区（2008 年） ………… 437
表 80　世界与中国纸浆、纸及纸板生产与消费情况（2007—2008 年） ………… 438
表 81　我国台湾省主要纸品产销量情况（2008 年） ………… 438
表 82　世界纸和纸板产量排名前 10 位的国家（2008 年） ………… 439
表 83　世界纸浆产量排名前 10 位的国家（2008 年） ………… 439
表 84　世界纸浆主要净进口和净出口前 5 位的国家（2008 年） ………… 439
表 85　世界纸和纸板消费量与人均消费量前 5 位的国家（2008 年） ………… 440
表 86　世界部分国家废纸回收量及进出口量（2008 年） ………… 440
表 87　世界部分国家或地区纸和纸板净出口量和净进口量（2008 年） ………… 440
表 88　我国台湾省印刷业基本情况（2005—2009 年） ………… 440
表 89　我国香港特别行政区印刷业基本情况（2004—2008 年） ………… 441
表 90　世界主要国家天然橡胶产量（2007—2009 年） ………… 441
表 91　世界主要国家（地区）合成橡胶产量（2007—2009 年） ………… 441
表 92　世界天然橡胶和合成橡胶产量、消费量（2005—2009 年） ………… 442
表 93　世界主要国家（地区）橡胶消耗量（2009 年） ………… 442
表 94　我国台湾省天然橡胶和合成橡胶消费量（2007—2009 年） ………… 443
表 95　我国台湾省橡胶工业产值情况（2005—2007 年） ………… 443
表 96　世界橡胶机械生产厂商前 10 名排序（2009 年） ………… 443
表 97　世界各区域市场橡胶机械销售收入情况（2007—2009 年） ………… 443
表 98　2009 年中国农产品进出口市场排序情况 ………… 444
表 99　中国农村居民与部分发达国家消费结构情况比较（1990—2007 年） ………… 444
表 100　按营业额排序的世界最大 500 个企业中农产品加工企业（2010 年） ………… 445

Contents

Editor's Notes

Part Ⅰ Special Subjects Exposition

Focused on Accelerating the Transformation of Economic Development Pattern in Order to Promote the Scientific Development of Township Enterprises and Agricultural Products Processing Industry ············ 3
Improving the Awareness and Implementing the Responsibilities According to the Law to Lay Down the Basis for a Better Risk Monitoring on Food Safety ············ 8
Actively Developing the Retrieving System Building of the Meat and Vegetable Circulation, Make Great Efforts to Raise the Level of Quality Safety and Ensure Supply ············ 11
Strengthening and Improving Grain Macro Adjustment and Control, Practically Assuring National Grain Security ············ 16
Implementing Scientific Development Concept Deeply and Initiating the New Prospect of Food Safety Control and Consumer Safeguard ············ 23
Devoting Major Efforts to Push on the Comprehensive Experimental Place of Modern Farm Produce Circulation, Accelerating and Perfecting the System of Modern Agricultural Products Circulation ············ 32
Grasping Every New Opportunities, Accepting Challenges, Promoting the Healthy and Sustainable Development of Agricultural Products Processing Industry in China ············ 34
Tightening Measure and Accomplishing the Task of Risk Monitoring of Food Safety Pledged to Quality ······ 38
Implementing the Programming Outline of Live Pig Slaughter, Promoting the Sound Development of Live Pig Slaughter Industry ············ 41
Intensifying Efforts to Structural Adjustment and Improving the Upgrading of Pongee Industry ············ 46
Rely on Science and Technology Development to Promote the Sound Development of Textile Industry ········· 49
Making Efforts Together and Working Whole-heartedly in Order to Promote the Sound and Sustainable Development of Green Food and Organic Food ············ 53
Clarifying Objectives and Tightening Measures in Order to Promote the Scientific Development of Pollution-free Farm Products and Geographic Symbol ············ 57
Practicing Scientific Development Concept and Promoting the Steady and Sustainable Development of Food Industry ············ 61
Remolding the Traditional Industries and Enhancing the Total Industry Quality ············ 63
Making Effort to Transform the Development Mode and Improving and Perfecting the Ecological Green Feed Industrial System ············ 66
Development Situation of China Meat Industry ············ 69
National Aquatic Products Import and Export Trade Status ············ 72
Present Development Situation of China Paper Industry ············ 75

Part Ⅱ Development Situation of Related Trades

Grain, Oil and Food Processing Industries ············ 81
Oil Processing Industry ············ 85

Soy-bean Processing Industry ······ 90
Starch Processing Industry ······ 96
Sugar-making Industry ······ 99
Vegetable Processing Industry ······ 102
Tea Processing Industry ······ 106
Honeybee Products Processing Industry ······ 108
Edible Mushroom Processing Industry ······ 112
Dairy Products Processing Industry ······ 116
Tobacco Processing Industry ······ 125
Brewery Industry ······ 129
Natural Silk Processing Industry ······ 131
Feed Processing Industry ······ 135
Aquatic Products Processing Industry ······ 137
Forestry Products Processing Industry ······ 141
Crop-stalk Processing Industry ······ 145
Food Processing and Packing Machine Building Industry ······ 149
Cotton Processing Machine Building Industry ······ 151

Part Ⅲ Policies, Regulations and Important Documents

National Development Plan Outline for Live Pig Slaughtering Industry (2010－2015) ······ 157
Administration Measures of the Foodstuff and Edible Oil Storage ······ 161
Administration Stipulation of Risk Estimate for Food Safety (try out) ······ 163
Working Arrangement of Food Safety Rectification (2010) ······ 165
Management Method of Food and Beverage Service Permission ······ 167
Supervising and Administrating Measures for Food Safety of Food and Beverage Service ······ 170
Work Program for Food Safety Rectification in Circulation Section (2010) ······ 175
Regulation on Supervision and Control of Food Additive Production ······ 179
Administrative Measures of Food Production Permission ······ 182
Work Program on Earnestly Developing the Specific Campaign of Rural Food Market ······ 185
National Development Plan for Dairy Industry (2009－2013) ······ 187
Development Plan for Cold Chain Logistics of Agricultural Products ······ 192
Guidance of Constructing the Hundred-thousand-ten Thousand Demo-projects of Food Safety for Food and Beverage Service ······ 197
Guidance of Promoting the Textile Industry Relocation ······ 199
Administration Regulation on Quality Safety of Processing Enterprises for the "Relieved Foodstuff and Edible Oil" Demonstration and Wheaten Food Kitchen that for Demonstrating ······ 201
Expert Management Methods of Healthy Foods Evaluation ······ 204
Catering Service Food Safety Supervision and Selective Examination Work Specifications ······ 205
Notice on Further Strengthening Quality Safety for Dairy Products ······ 208
Administration Interim Measures of National Grain Quality Inspection and Testing Institutions ······ 210
Management Methods of Food Safety National Standard ······ 212
Social Trustworthiness System Construction Implementation Work Program of Enterprises in Food Industry ······ 214
Implementation Detailed Rules on Confirming the Substitute Storage Qualification of Central Reserved Grain ······ 217

Administrative Measures of Food Safety Information Promulgating ······ 219
Administrative Measures of Sampling Inspection on Quality of Central Reserved Foodstuff and Edible Oil ······ 221

Part Ⅳ Domestic Comprehensive Statistics Materials

Statistics of Production of Main Products of Agriculture, Forest, Livestock and Fishery ······ 227
Table 1 Yield of Main Agricultural Products of Our Country (2005－2009) ······ 227
Table 2 Yield of Main Agricultural Products in Various Regions (2009) ······ 228
Table 3 Situation of Production of Major Corn Production Areas of Our Country (2009) ······ 233
Table 4 Yield of Fruits in Various Regions (2009) ······ 233
Table 5 Yield of Tea in Various Regions (2009) ······ 235
Table 6 Yield of Main Agricultural Products in the System of Land Reclamation and Cultivation of Our Country (2008－2009) ······ 236
Table 7 Yield of Main Agricultural Products of Land Reclamation and Cultivation System in Various Regions (2009) ······ 237
Table 8 Production of Tea, Mulberry, Fruit and Forest Products in the Land Reclamation and Cultivation System of Our Country (2008－2009) ······ 238
Table 9 Yield of Tropical and Sub-tropical Crops of Our Country (2009) ······ 238
Table 10 Situation of Production of Major Cotton Production Areas of Our Country (2008－2009) ······ 238
Table 11 Increase and Decrease of Production of Main Vegetables in Various Regions (2008－2009) ······ 239
Table 12 Yield of Main Forestry Products of Our Country (2005－2009) ······ 239
Table 13 Yield of Main Forestry Products in Various Regions (2009) ······ 240
Table 14 Situation of Main Livestock Raising of Our Country (2005－2009) ······ 241
Table 15 Yield of Main Livestock Products of Our Country (2005－2009) ······ 241
Table 16 Yield of Dairy Products in Various Regions (2008－2009) ······ 242
Table 17 Yield of Main Livestock Products of Land Reclamation and Cultivation System of Our Country (2008－2009) ······ 242
Table 18 Yield of Aquatic Products of Our Country (2005－2009) ······ 243
Table 19 Yield of Aquatic Products in Various Regions (2009) ······ 243
Table 20 Yield of Aquatic Products of Sea and Ocean Fishery along the Coast of Our Country (According to Variety) (2009) ······ 244
Table 21 Output of Aquatic Products of Sea-farming along Sea Shore of Our Country (According to Variety) (2009) ······ 246
Table 22 Yield of Aquatic Products of the Land Reclamation and Cultivation System in Various Regions (2009) ······ 249
Table 23 Average Yield of Per Capita of Main Agricultural and Livestock Products of Our Country (2005－2009) ······ 250
Table 24 Compare with Per Capita Amount of Food Consumption for Resident Family in Urban and Rural of Our Country (2005－2009) ······ 250
Table 25 Situation of Average Food Consumption of Per Capita of Our Urban and Rural Population (2005－2009) ······ 250
Table 26 Situation of Population Growth of Our Country (2005－2009) ······ 250
Holding Quantity of Agricultural Products Processing Machines and the Situation of Fixed Assets Investment of Agriculture Products Processing Trade ······ 251

Table 27 Holding Quantity of Primary Processing Machines of Some Agricultural Products in the System of the Ministry of Agriculture at the End of the Yesr (2009) ······ 251
Table 28 Situation of Fixed Asset Investment of Agricultural Product Processing Trade of Our Country (2009) ······ 252
Table 29 New Increase of Production Capability after Increased Fixed Assets of Agricultural Product Processing Trade (2008－2009) ······ 252
Table 30 Number of Constructed and Put into Production of Agricultural Product Processing Trades with 500 000 Yuan (2009) ······ 252
Table 31 Situation of Accomplished Investment of Fixed Assets of Forestry Processing Industry in the Forestry System (2008－2009) ······ 253
Table 32 Situation of Accomplished Investment of Fixed Assets of Forestry Processing Industry in the Forestry System in Various Region (2009) ······ 253
Table 33 Situation of Accomplished Investment of Fixed Assets of the System of Land Reclamation and Cultivation of Our Country (2008－2009) ······ 254
Table 34 Investment in Fixed Assets of Aquatic Industry of Our Country (2008－2009) ······ 254

Present Situation of Agricultural Products Processing Industry Based on the Classified Trade Statistics of National Economy ······ 254

Table 35 Main Targets of Entirely State-owned and Above-scale Non-state-owned Enterprises of Agricultural Products Processing Industry of Our Country (2009) ······ 254
Table 36 Main Economic Performance Targets of Entirely State-owned and Above-scale Non-state-owned Enterprises of Agricultural Products Processing Industry of Our Country (2009) ······ 255
Table 37 Main Targets of State-owned and State Holding Enterprises of Agricultural Products Processing Industry of Our Country (2009) ······ 255
Table 38 Main Economic Performance Targets of State-owned and State Holding Enterprises of Agricultural Products Processing Industry of Our Country (2009) ······ 256
Table 39 Main Targets of Foreign Merchant Investing and Hong Kong, Macau and Taiwan Merchant Investing Enterprises of Agricultural Products Processing Industry of Our Country (2009) ······ 256
Table 40 Main Economic Performance Targets of Foreign Merchant Investing and Hong Kong, Macau and Taiwan Merchant Investing Enterprises of Agricultural Products Processing Industry of Our Country (2009) ······ 257
Table 41 Main Targets of Private Enterprises of Agricultural Products Processing Industry of Our Country (2009) ······ 257
Table 42 Main Economic Performance Targets of Private Enterprises of Agricultural Products Processing Industry of Our Country (2009) ······ 258
Table 43 Main Targets of Agricultural Products Processing Industry of Large and Medium Scale of Our Country (2009) ······ 258
Table 44 Main Economic Performance Targets of Agricultural Products Processing Industry of Large and Medium Scale of Our Country (2009) ······ 259
Table 45 Main Economic and Technical Targets of Sugar Making Enterprises of Our Country During the Sugar Making Period 2009/2010 ······ 259
Table 46 Situation of Food and Packaging Machinery Economic Operation of Our Country (2005－2009) ······ 259
Table 47 Situation of Economic Growth of Machinery Industry, Food Industry, Food and Packaging Machinery Industry of Our Country (2005－2009) ······ 260
Table 48 Gross Output of Agricultural Products Processing Industry in Forestry System

(2008 - 2009) …… 260
Table 49 Main Economic Performance Targets of State-owned, Independent Accounting, Large and Medium Trades of Agricultural Product Processing Industry of Forestry System (2009) …… 260
Table 50 Gross Output of Agricultural Products Processing Industry of the Forestry System in Various Regions (2009) …… 261
Table 51 Developing Status of Aquatic Products Processing Industry of Our Country (2008 - 2009) …… 263
Table 52 Processing Capability, Output and Output Value of Aquatic Products Processing of Our Country (2006 - 2009) …… 263
Table 53 The Situation of Aquatic Products Processing in Provinces along the Coast of our Country (2009) …… 264
Table 54 Fundamental Situation of Agricultural Products Processing Enterprises of the Scale above Villages and Towns Enterprises of Our Country (2009) …… 264
Table 55 Main Economic Targets of Classified Trades of Agricultural Products Processing Industry in the Light Industry System (2008) …… 264
Table 56 Main Economic Targets of Classified Food Industry in the Light Industry System (2008) …… 265
Table 57 Gross Output Growth of Food Industrial of Our Country (2005 - 2009) …… 265
Table 58 Main Economic Targets of Baking Food and Sugar-made Products Industry of Our Country (2008) …… 266
Table 59 Main Economic Targets of Beverage Industry of Our Country (2008 - 2009) …… 266
Table 60 Main Economic Targets of Alcohol Industry of Our Country (2008 - 2009) …… 266
Table 61 Main Economic Targets of Dairy Products Industry of Our Country (2008 - 2009) …… 267
Table 62 Main Economic Targets of Classified Key Enterprises of Machine Building Trades of Agricultural Products Processing Industry in the System of Light Industry (2008) …… 267
Table 63 Main Economic Targets of Tobacco Industry of Our Country (2008 - 2009) …… 267
Table 64 Main Economic Targets of Textile Industry of Our Country (2008 - 2009) …… 267
Table 65 Main Economic Target of Textile, Dress, Shoes and Cap Industry of Our Country (2008 - 2009) …… 268
Table 66 Status of Economic Operation of Leather Industry of Our Country (2008 - 2009) …… 268
Table 67 Status of Economic Operation of Furniture Industry of Our Country (2008 - 2009) …… 268
Table 68 Main Economic Targets of Our Paper Making Industry (2008 - 2009) …… 268
Table 69 Basic Condition of Journalism Industry of Our Country (2007 - 2008) …… 269
Table 70 Main Economic Targets by 130 Enterprises Printing Books and Periodicals (Including Other Printings) of Our Country (2008 - 2009) …… 270
Table 71 Main Economic Targets of 62 Printing Machine Enterprises of Our Country (2008 - 2009) …… 270
Table 72 Main Economic Targets of Rubber Industry of Our Country (2008 - 2009) …… 271
Table 73 Main Economic Targets of Whole-independent Accounting Enterprises of Rubber Industry of Our Country (2007 - 2008) …… 271
Table 74 Status of Economic Benefit of Traditional Chinese Medicine Trades of Our Country (2009) …… 272
Table 75 Total Consumption of Energy and Consumption of Main Energy Variety of Agricultural Products Processing Industry of Our Country (2008) …… 272
Output of Main Products of Agricultural Products Production Industry …… 272
Table 76 Output of Main Products of Agricultural Products Processing Industry of Our country (2008 - 2009) …… 272
Table 77 Output of Main Products of Agricultural Products Processing Industry in the Light Industry

(2007－2008) …… 273
Table 78 Output of Main Products of Grain and Oil Processing Industry of Our Country (2008－2009) …… 274
Table 79 Output and Strains of Starch of Our Country (2008－2009) …… 274
Table 80 Output of Deep Processed Starch Products of Our Country (2008－2009) …… 275
Table 81 Situation Distribution and Production Scale of Starch of Our Country (2009) …… 275
Table 82 Situation of Production Scale of Corn Starch of Our Country (2008－2009) …… 275
Table 83 Production Scale of Partial Starch and Deep Processed Products of Our Country (2008－2009) …… 276
Table 84 Output of Main Products of Food Additives of Our Country (2007－2008) …… 277
Table 85 Output of Main Products of Beverage Making Industry of Our Country (2008－2009) …… 277
Table 86 Output of Milk and Dairy Products of Our Country (2008－2009) …… 277
Table 87 Output of Main Products of Beverage Making Industry in Various Regions of Our Country (2008) …… 278
Table 88 Output of Main Products of Tobacco Industry of Our Country (2008－2009) …… 279
Table 89 Output of Products of Alcohol Industry of Our Country (2008－2009) …… 279
Table 90 Output of Products of Alcohol Industry in Various Regions of Our Country (2007－2008) …… 279
Table 91 Output of Gourmet Powder in Various Areas of Our Country (2008) …… 280
Table 92 Output of Baking Food and Sugar-made Products Industry in Main Areas of Our Country (2008) …… 280
Table 93 Output of Beer in Various Areas of Our Country (2008－2009) …… 281
Table 94 Output Value and Products Output of Canning Industry of Our Country (2008) …… 281
Table 95 Output of White Spirit in Various Areas of Our Country (2008－2009) …… 282
Table 96 Output of Products of Feed Industry of Our Country (2006－2009) …… 283
Table 97 Output of Sugar Crops and Sugar during Sugar Production Period 2009/2010 …… 283
Table 98 Output, Output Value and Export Situation of Edible Mushroom of Our Country (2009) …… 284
Table 99 Output of Main Products of Agricultural Products Processing Enterprises in the System of Land Reclamation and Cultivation of Our Country (2008－2009) …… 288
Table 100 Output of Main Products of Agricultural Products Processing Industry in the System of Land Reclamation and Cultivation in Various Areas of Our Country (2009) …… 288
Table 101 Output of Main Products of Forestry Industry of Our Country (2008－2009) …… 289
Table 102 Output of Main Products of Forestry Industry in Various Areas (2009) …… 290
Table 103 Major Varieties and Output of Main Processed Aquatic Products of Our Country (2006－2009) …… 292
Table 104 Output of Main Products in Textile Industry (Above-scale Enterprises) (2008－2009) …… 292
Table 105 Output of Main Products of Leather Industry of Our Country (2008－2009) …… 292
Table 106 Output of Main Products of Furniture Industry of Our Country (2008－2009) …… 292
Table 107 Output of Main Products of Furniture Industry in Various Areas of Our Country (2009) …… 292
Table 108 Situation of Pulp Consumption of Paper Making Industry of Our Country (2007－2009) …… 293
Table 109 Situation of Wastepaper Recovery and Utilization of Our Country (2004－2008) …… 293
Table 110 The Proportion of Every Variety of Raw Materia of Paper-making Fibre of Our Country (2008－2009) …… 293
Table 111 Output of Main Varieties of Machine-made Paper and Paper Board of Our Country (2008－2009) …… 294
Table 112 Situation of Consumption Structure of Paper and Paper Board of Our Country (2007－2008) …… 294

Table 113 Consumption and Production of Main Products of Paper Making Industry of Our Country (2008－2009) ······ 295
Table 114 Average Consumption of Per Capita，Amount of Import，Consumption and Production of Paper and Paper Board of Our Country (2005－2009) ······ 295
Table 115 Output of Main Products by 136 Enterprises Printing Books and Periodicals (Including Other Printing) of Our Country (2007－2008) ······ 295
Table 116 Compare with Average Consumption of Per Capita of Our Paper and Paper Board of the Country and the United States (2005－2009) ······ 295
Table 117 Output of Main Products of Rubber Industry of Our Country (2008－2009) ······ 296
Table 118 Output Per Capita of Main Industrial and Agricultural Products of Our Country (2005－2009) ······ 296
Situation of Export and Foreign Exchange Earned of Main Products of Agricultural Products Processing Industry ······ 296
Table 119 Quantity and Amount of Money of Exported Agricultural Products and Processed Products through Customs of Our Country (2008－2009) ······ 296
Table 120 Situation of Imported and Exported of Agricultural Products of Our Country (2008－2009) ······ 298
Table 121 Quantity and Amount of Money of Imported Agricultural Products and Processed Products Through Customs of Our Country (2008－2009) ······ 298
Table 122 Situation of Import and Export of Livestock Products of Our Country (2009) ······ 299
Table 123 Situation of Imported and Exported of Main Grain Products of Our Country (2009) ······ 299
Table 124 Quantity of Imported and Exported of Forestry Products of Our Country (2008－2009) ······ 300
Table 125 Amount of Imported and Exported of Money Earned and Spend of Forestry Products of Our Country (2008－2009) ······ 302
Table 126 Situation of Exchange Earned through Exporting Main Products of Agricultural Products Processing Industry in the Light Industry (2008) ······ 304
Table 127 Situation of Exchange Spent through Importing Main Products of Agricultural Products Processing Industry in the Light Industry (2008) ······ 305
Table 128 Situation of Importing and Exporting of Starch and Partial Deep Processed Products of Our Country (2009) ······ 305
Table 129 Situation of Importing and Exporting，Trade Method of Sugar of Our Country (2007－2009) ······ 306
Table 130 Situation of Imported Dairy Products of Our Country (2009) ······ 306
Table 131 Situation of Exported Dairy Products of Our Country (2009) ······ 307
Table 132 Situation of Exporting of Canned Products Main Category and Variety of Our Country (2008) ······ 307
Table 133 Situation of Exporting of Canned Products of Our Country (2007－2008) ······ 308
Table 134 Situation of Production and Export of Honeybee of Our Country (2006－2009) ······ 308
Table 135 Situation of Exported Honeybee Products of Our Country (2008－2009) ······ 308
Table 136 Situation of Import and Export Trades of Aquatic Products of Our Country (2006－2009) ······ 308
Table 137 Situation of Import and Export of Food Processing and Packing Machines of Our Country (2005－2009) ······ 309
Table 138 Statistics of Import and Export of Shoes Products of Our Country (2008－2009) ······ 309
Table 139 Export Statistics of Textile Products and Clothes of Our Country (2008－2009) ······ 309
Table 140 Situation of Import and Export of Major Products of Furniture Industry of Our Country

(2009) …… 309
Table 141 Situation of Import and Export of Major Products of Leather Industry of Our Country (2009) …… 310
Table 142 Situation of Import and Export of Paper, Paper Board, Pulp, Waste Paper and Paper Products of Our Country (2007－2009) …… 310
Table 143 Statistics of Import and Export of Printing Machines of Our Country (2007－2008) …… 311
Table 144 Situation of Import and Export of Machinery Products of Our Country (2005－2009) …… 311
Table 145 Situation of Import and Export of Chinese Medicine Trade of Our Country (2008－2009) …… 311
Table 146 Quantity of Export and Amount of Money Earned of Products from Rubber Industry of Our Country (2007－2008) …… 311
Table 147 Quantity of Import and Amount of Money Spent on Products from Rubber Industry of Our Country (2007－2008) …… 312
Table 148 Situation of Import and Export of Galoshes Exported of Our Country (2008) …… 313
Table 149 Situation of Exchange Earned through Exporting of Major Galoshes Enterprises of Our Country (2007－2008) …… 314
Table 150 Situation of Import of Natural Rubber and Synthetic Rubber of Our Country (2006－2009) …… 314
Sequence of Trades and Enterprises of Agricultural Products Processing Industry …… 314
Table 151 Main Economic Targets of Classified Trades of Agricultural Products Processing Enterprises in the Light Industry (2008) …… 314
Table 152 Total Amount of Import and Export of Classified Agricultural Product Processing Trades in the Light Industry (2008) …… 316
Table 153 Order of the Top 10 Provinces, Municipalities of Amount of Import and Export of Agricultural Products of Our Country (2009) …… 316
Table 154 The Top 10 Brands of Most Increase Potentialities of White Spirits of Our Country (2010) …… 316
Table 155 Brands of Top 500 Brewing Enterprises of Most Value Brands of Our Country (2009) …… 317
Table 156 The Enterprises with Annual Production of Beer Over 200 000 kL of Our Country (2009) …… 317
Table 157 The Enterprises with Sales Revenue of Beer Over 300 000 000 Yuan of Our Country (2008) …… 318
Table 158 Status of Main Economic Operation of Top 10 Provinces and Municipality of Wine Output of Our Country (2008) …… 318
Table 159 The Top 20 Enterprises of Beverage Making Industry of Our Country (2008) …… 319
Table 160 The Top 8 Situation with High Production of Beverage Trades in Various Areas of Our Country (2008) …… 319
Table 161 The Top 5 Situation with High Production of Bottles and Canning Brinking Water in Various Areas of Our Country (2008) …… 319
Table 162 The Top 5 Situation with High Production of Fruit Juice and Fruit-juice Beverage in Various Areas of Our Country (2008) …… 320
Table 163 Front Enterprises of Sales Revenue of Dairy Products Production of Our Country (2009) …… 320
Table 164 Front Enterprises of Liquid Milk Production of Our Country (2009) …… 321
Table 165 Alcohol Production Over 90 000 t Enterprises and Fuel Alcohol Over 110 000t Enterprises of Our Country (2008) …… 321
Table 166 The Enterprises with Annual Production of Gourmet Powder Over 20 000 t of Our

Country (2008) …… 322
Table 167 The Second Batch of Credit Evaluation Results of Honey Products Enterprises of Our Country in 2009 …… 322
Table 168 The Top Enterprises of Various Trades of Textile Industry with "Strong Competitive Capacity" of Our Country 2009/2010 …… 322
Table 169 The Furniture Enterprises of Winning "Chinese Well-known Trademark" (2008－2009) …… 324
Table 170 The Top 10 Enterprises of Leather Trades of Our Country (2009) …… 325
Table 171 Well-known Shoes and Dress of Derma of Our Country (2009) …… 325
Table 172 Revenue from Principal Business of Provinces and Autonomous Region with Output of Paper and Paper Board Over One Million Ton of Our Country (2007－2008) …… 326
Table 173 Provinces and Autonomous Region with Output of Paper and Paper Board Over One Million Ton of Our Country (2007－2009) …… 326
Table 174 The Top 30 Enterprises with Annual Production of Key Paper Making Enterprises of Our Country (2008－2009) …… 327
Table 175 The Top 10 Printing Machine Enterprises Realizing High Amount of Sales Income of Our Country (2009) …… 328
Table 176 The Top 10 Printing Machine Enterprises of Exporting Delivery Value of Our Country (2009) …… 328
Table 177 Enterprises Realizing Sales Income Over 50 Million Yuan of Key Paper Making Machine Manufacturing Industry of Our Country (2008) …… 328
Table 178 Enterprises Realizing Profit Tax Over 5 Million Yuan of Key Paper Making Machine Manufacturing Industry of Our Country (2008) …… 329
Table 179 Enterprises with Labor Productivity Over 100 000 Yuan of Key Paper Making Machine Manufacturing Industry of Our Country (2008) …… 329
Table 180 Order of Sales Income of Enterprises of Association Members of Rubber Industry of Our Country (2009) …… 329
Table 181 The Top 10 Enterprises of Export Amount of Chinese Medicine Industry of Our Country (2009) …… 330
Comprehensive Statistics of the Western Area of Our Country …… 331
Table 182 Output of Production of Main Agricultural Products in Western Area of Our Country (2008－2009) …… 331
Table 183 Yield Per Unit Area of Main Agricultural Products in Western Area of Our Country (2008－2009) …… 332
Table 184 Yield of Tea in Western Area of Our Country (2009) …… 332
Table 185 Yield of Fruits in Western Area of Our Country (2008－2009) …… 333
Table 186 Yield of Main Forestry Products in Western Area of Our Country (2009) …… 333
Table 187 Area and Yield of Tropic and Sub-tropic Crops in Western Area of Our Country (2009) …… 334
Table 188 Output of Main Livestock Products in Western Area of Our Country (2008－2009) …… 334
Table 189 Output of Aquatic Products in Western Area of Our Country (2008－2009) …… 335
Table 190 Average Output Per Capita of Main Agricultural Products, Livestock Products and Aquatic Products in Western Area of Our Country (2008－2009) …… 335
Table 191 Total Production Value, Increased Value and Components of Agriculture, Forestry, Animal Husbandry and Fishery in Western Area of Our Country (2008－2009) …… 336
Table 192 Total Production Value of Forestry Industry in Western Area of Our Country (2009) …… 336
Table 193 Situation of Fixed Assets Investment of Forestry Industry of Forestry System in Western Area of Our Country (2009) …… 336

Table 194 Total Production Value of Agricultural Products Processing Trades of Forestry System in Western Area of Our Country (2009) …… 337
Table 195 Output of Production of Main Products of Forestry Industry in Western Area of Our Country (2009) …… 338
Table 196 Output of Major Products of Agricultural Products Processing Enterprises of Land Reclamation and Cultivation System in Western Area of Our Country (2009) …… 339
Table 197 Output of Agricultural Products Processing Trades of the Light Industry in Western Area of Our Country (2008) …… 339
Others …… 341
Table 198 Situation of the Samples Monitor of Food Hygiene of Our Country (2008) …… 341
Table 199 The Top 10 Enterprises with Most Quality of Agricultural Products Processing Industry of the Light System (2008) …… 342
Table 200 The First Batch List of Start an Undertaking Base of Agricultural Products Processing Enterprises of Our Country (2009) …… 349
Table 201 The First Batch A、AA and AAA Grades Credit Enterprises of Grain and Oil Processing Trades of Our Country (2009) …… 351
Table 202 Agricultural Product Processing Enterprises Enlisted in 500 National Strong Enterprises of the Light Industry of Our Country (2009) …… 352

Part Ⅴ Standards and Patents

National Standards of Agricultural Products Processing Industry (2010) …… 357
Agricultural Trade Standards of Agricultural Products Processing Industry (2010) …… 364
Machine Trade Standards of Agricultural Products Processing Industry (2010) …… 366
Light Industry Trade Standards of Agricultural Products Processing Industry (2010) …… 367
Domestic Trade Standards of Agricultural Products Processing Industry (2010) …… 368
Entry-exit Inspection and Quarantine Trade Standards of Agricultural Products Processing Industry (2010) …… 369
Tobacco Trade Standards of Agricultural Products Processing Industry (2010) …… 369
Textile Industry Trade Standards of Agricultural Products Processing Industry (2010) …… 370
Invention Patents of Agricultural Products Processing Industry (2009) …… 372

Part Ⅵ Chronicle of Events

Part Ⅶ Appendix

Table 1 Agricultural Production Index of Some Countries (Regions) (2007) …… 405
Table 2 Agricultural Production Index of Taiwan Province of Our Country (2006－2008) …… 405
Table 3 Total Yield of Main Gains of Some Countries (Districts) (2009) …… 405
Table 4 Situation of Gains Production、Consumption、Trade and Stock in the World (2007/2008－2009/2010) …… 406
Table 5 Situation of Plant Oil Average Per Year Production and Trade in the World (2005/2006－2009/2010) …… 406
Table 6 Gross Yield of Main Oil-bearing Crop of Some Countries (Districts) (2009) …… 407
Table 7 Harvesting Area, Unit Yield and Total Yield of Main Crops in the United States of America (2005－2009) …… 407

Table 8 Situation of Plant Oil Average Per Year Production and Trade of Main Countries in the World … 408
Table 9 Production Situation of Main Agricultural Products in Russia (2009) …… 409
Table 10 Harvesting Area, Unit Yield and Gross Yield of Unginned Cotton and Jute of Some Countries (Districts) (2009) …… 409
Table 11 Harvesting Area, Unit Yield and Gross Yield of Tobacco and Tea of Some Countries (Districts) (2009) …… 409
Table 12 Harvesting Area, Unit Yield and Gross Yield of Sugar Cane and Sugar Beet of Some Countries (Districts) (2009) …… 410
Table 13 Gross Yield of Vegetable, Fruit and Hard Nut of Some Countries (Districts) (2009) …… 410
Table 14 Gross Yield of Apple, Pear, Orange and etc. of Some Countries (Districts) (2009) …… 411
Table 15 The Top 10 Countries of Cultivating Area of Grape in the World (2008) …… 411
Table 16 The Top 10 Countries of Main Production Countries of Grape in the World (2008) …… 411
Table 17 The Top 10 Enterprises of Wine Gross Yield in the World (2008) …… 412
Table 18 Exported Status of Major Wine Production Countries in the World (2006 – 2008) …… 412
Table 19 Bistribution Status of the Top 5 Countries of Wine Import Quantity of Our Country (2008) … 412
Table 20 Amount of Consumption of Major Wine Consumption Countries in the World (2007 – 2008) … 413
Table 21 Situation of Supply and Demand of Sugar in the World (2005 – 2009) …… 413
Table 22 Gross Yield of Main Agricultural Products of Taiwan Province of Our Country (2006 – 2008) …… 413
Table 23 Total Production of Meat of Some Countries (Districts) (2008 – 2009) …… 414
Table 24 Gross Production of Pork of Some Countries (Districts) (2005 – 2009) …… 414
Table 25 Consumption Volume of Pork of Some Countries (Districts) (2005 – 2009) …… 415
Table 26 Import Volume of Pork of Some Countries (Districts) (2005 – 2009) …… 415
Table 27 Export Volume of Pork of Some Countries (Districts) (2005 – 2009) …… 416
Table 28 Gross Production of Pork, Beef, Mutton and fowls of Some Countries (Districts) (2009) …… 416
Table 29 Situation of Meat Production, Consumption and Trade of Main Trade Countries of Our Country (2005 – 2009) …… 417
Table 30 Production Status of Main Animal Husbandry Products in Russia (2009) …… 417
Table 31 Gross Production of Fishes Products of Some Countries (Districts) (2007) …… 418
Table 32 The Top 10 Countries of Fish Meal Production in the World (2009) …… 418
Table 33 Situation of Main Countries (Districts) of Fish Meal Import in China (2008 – 2009) …… 418
Table 34 Gross Production of Milk of Some Countries (Districts) (2008 – 2009) …… 419
Table 35 Gross Production of Milk Drink, Yoghurt and Ferment Milk of Some Countries (Districts) (2006 – 2008) …… 419
Table 36 Gross Production of Cream of Some Countries (Districts) (2006 – 2008) …… 420
Table 37 Gross Production of Cheese of Some Countries (Districts) (2006 – 2008) …… 420
Table 38 Gross Production of Condensed Milk of Some Countries (Districts) (2006 – 2008) …… 421
Table 39 Gross Production of Whole Milk Powder and Half-Skimmed Milk Powder of Some Countries (Districts) (2006 – 2008) …… 421
Table 40 Gross Production of Skimmed Milk Powder of Some Countries (Districts) (2006 – 2008) …… 421
Table 41 Export Status of Major Dairy Products Production Countries (Districts) in the World (2006 – 2008) …… 422
Table 42 Import Status of Major Dairy Products Production Countries (Districts) in the World (2006 – 2008) …… 423
Table 43 Consumption Volume of Liquid Milk of Some Countries (Regions) (2006 – 2008) …… 424
Table 44 Consumption Volume of Milk Drink, Yoghurt and Fermented Milk of Some Countries

(Regions) (2006－2008) …… 424
Table 45 Consumption Volume of Cream of Some Countries (Regions) (2006－2008) …… 425
Table 46 Consumption Volume of Cheese of Some Countries (Regions) (2006－2008) …… 425
Table 47 The Top 20 Enterprises of Dairy Industry in the World (2009) …… 426
Table 48 Gross Production of Eggs of Some Countries (Districts) (2009) …… 426
Table 49 Share Situation of Main Eggs Production Countries in the World (2008) …… 427
Table 50 Gross Production of Honey Bee of Some Countries (Districts) (2008－2009) …… 427
Table 51 Gross Production of Wool of Some Countries (Districts) (2008－2009) …… 428
Table 52 Rank in the World About the Output of Main Agricultural Products of Our country (1949－2008) …… 428
Table 53 Export Status of Agricultural Products in China to Japan (2009) …… 428
Table 54 Situation of Agricultural Products Trade in China and ASEAN Countries (2009) …… 429
Table 55 Import and Export Status of Main Agricultural Products in China and ASEAN Countries (2009) …… 429
Table 56 Status of Import and Export Varieties of Main Agricultural Products in China and ASEAN Countries (2009) …… 429
Table 57 Import and Export Status of Main Agricultural Products in Russia (2008－2009) …… 430
Table 58 Import and Export Status of Main Agricultural Products in the United States of America (2009) …… 430
Table 59 Situation of Agricultural Products Trade in China to New Zealand (2004－2008) …… 431
Table 60 Import and Export Status of Agricultural Products in China and Latin America as well as Carib Regions (2005－2009) …… 431
Table 61 The Top 30 Enterprises of Feed Industry in the World (2008) …… 432
Table 62 Major Production Countries Producing Main Agricultural and Livestock Products in the World (2009) …… 433
Table 63 Industrial Production Index of Hong Kong Special Administration Region (2006－2009) …… 433
Table 64 Situation of Export and Re-export of Processed Food and Beverage of Hong Kong Special Administrative Region (2007－2008) …… 433
Table 65 Gross Production of Main Products of Agricultural Products Processing Industry of Taiwan Province of Our Country (2005－2009) …… 434
Table 66 Yield Status of Agricultural Production as well as Rice of Taiwan Province of Our Country (2004－2008) …… 434
Table 67 Classified Imported and Exported Commercial Products of Taiwan Province of Our Country (2006－2009) …… 434
Table 68 Production Volume of Cotton of Main Countries (Regions) in the World (2009) …… 434
Table 69 Production Volume of Textile Fibres in China and World (2005－2007) …… 434
Table 70 Production Volume of Chemical Fiber of Main Countries (Regions) in the World (2005－2007) …… 435
Table 71 Production Volume of Synthetic Fibres of Main Countries (Regions) in the World (2005－2007) …… 435
Table 72 Situation of Supply and Demand of Cotton in the World (2008/2009－2009/2010) …… 435
Table 73 Consumption Volume of Cotton of Main Countries (Regions) in the World (2005－2008) …… 435
Table 74 Compare with Export Volume and Proportion in World of Textile Products and Clothes of Our Country (2005－2007) …… 436
Table 75 The Top 10 Countries Exported Countries (Regions) of Textile Products and Clothes in the World (2007) …… 436

Table 76 Major Markets of The Top 5 of Exported Textiles and Clothes of Our Country (2009) ………… 436
Table 77 Compare with Import Volume and Proportion in European Union of Textiles and Clothes in China as Well as 4 Countries (2005 – 2009) …… 436
Table 78 Compare with Import Volume and Proportion in European Union of 5 Countries 4 Kind Products (2009) …… 437
Table 79 The Top 20 Countries of Production Countries (Regions) of Paper and Paper Board in the World (2008) …… 437
Table 80 Situation of Production and Consumption of Paper Pulp, Paper and Paper Board in China and World (2007 – 2008) …… 438
Table 81 Situation of Production and Sales of Paper Products of Taiwan Province of Our Country (2008) …… 438
Table 82 The Top 10 Countries of Paper and Paper Board Production in the World (2008) …… 439
Table 83 The Top 10 Countries of Paper Pulp Production in the World (2008) …… 439
Table 84 The Top 5 Countries of Main Net Import and Net Export of Paper Pulp in the World (2008) …… 439
Table 85 The Top 5 Countries of Consumption and Per Consumption of Paper and Paper Board in the World (2008) …… 440
Table 86 Quantity of Import and Export as Well as Recovery of Wastepaper of Some Countries (Regions) in the World (2008) …… 440
Table 87 Quantity of Net Import and Net Export of Paper and Paper Board of Some Countries (Regions) in the World (2008) …… 440
Table 88 Basic Condition of Printing Industry of Taiwan Province of Our Country (2005 – 2009) …… 440
Table 89 Basic Condition of Printing Industry of Hong Kong Special Administration Region of Our Country (2004 – 2008) …… 441
Table 90 Output of Natural Rubber of Major Countries in the World (2007 – 2009) …… 441
Table 91 Output of Synthetic Rubber of Major Countries (Regions) in the World (2007 – 2009) …… 441
Table 92 Output and Amount of Consumption of Natural Rubber and Synthetic Rubber in the World (2005 – 2009) …… 442
Table 93 Amount of Consumption of Rubber of Major Countries (Regions) in the World (2009) …… 442
Table 94 Consumption Volume of Natural and Synthetic Rubber of Taiwan Province of Our Country (2007 – 2009) …… 443
Table 95 Situation of Output Value of Rubber Industry of Taiwan Province of Our Country (2005 – 2007) …… 443
Table 96 Order of the First 10 Countries of Rubber Machinery Works in the World (2009) …… 443
Table 97 Situation of Income from Sales Rubber Machinery in the World Market (2007 – 2009) …… 443
Table 98 Order of Import and Export Market of Agricultural Products of Our Country in 2009 …… 444
Table 99 Compare with Village Residents of Consumption Structure in China and Some Developed Countries (1990 – 2007) …… 444
Table 100 The Agricultural Products Processing Enterprises within the Major 500 Enterprises (Based on Turnover) in the World (2010) …… 445

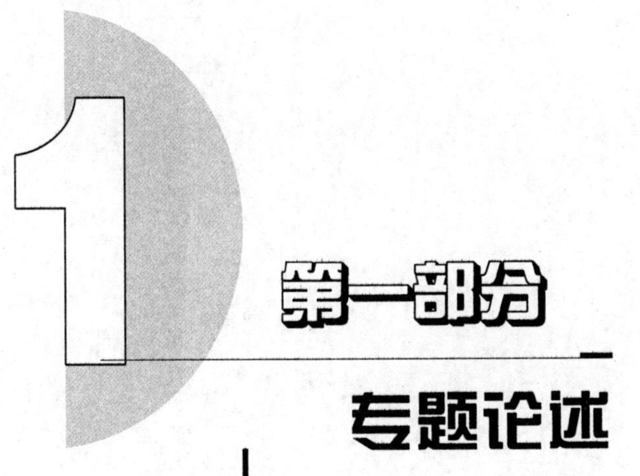

第一部分

专题论述

以加快转变经济发展方式为主线 推动乡镇企业和农产品加工业科学发展

农业部副部长　高鸿宾

党的十七届五中全会和刚刚召开的中央农村工作会议，对“十二五”和明年的农业农村工作做出了全面部署。韩长赋部长在全国农业工作会议上，系统总结了“十一五”和今年的农业农村经济工作，就贯彻落实中央五中全会和农村工作会议精神，全力做好“十二五”和明年农业农村经济工作进行了动员部署。今天我们召开会议，主要任务是以科学发展观为指导，深入贯彻落实中央精神和部党组的决策部署，总结“十一五”成就、经验，分析面临的形势、任务，部署“十二五”及明年重点工作，推动乡镇企业、农产品加工业和休闲农业又好又快发展，为促进农民就业增收和全面建设小康社会再立新功。下面，我讲三个方面的意见。

一、因势利导，多措并举，“十一五”各项工作取得重要进展

“十一五”时期我国乡镇企业、农产品加工业和休闲农业遵循经济社会发展的客观要求，顺应农民就业增收的新期待，加快结构调整、技术创新和素质提升，努力克服国际金融危机的影响，实现了平稳较快发展。

1. 坚持以“转型提升”为核心，推进乡镇企业质量效益稳步增长　通过调整优化结构、推进区域合作、培育产业集群、构建服务体系、强化技能培训、促进农民创业等工作，推动了乡镇企业持续健康发展。总量平稳较快增长，2010 年乡镇企业增加值预计达到 10.6 万亿元，年均增长 12.1%，年均拉动 GDP 增长 2.8 个百分点。效益稳步提高，实现利润总额 2.6 万亿元，年均增长 11.9%；上交税金 1.12 万亿元，年均增长 12.7%。贡献继续扩大，5 年间乡镇企业新增农民就业 1 556 万人，年均增加 311 万人，累计达到 1.58 亿人；年均支付劳动者报酬总额 1.48 万亿元，比“十五”期间增加 60%，对农民增收的贡献率达到 35%以上；5 年累计支农建农及补助社会性支出资金达到 1 400 多亿元。同时，乡镇企业自身素质和发展水平得到了新的提升。产业结构得到优化，第二产业中传统产业得到改造升级，新兴产业逐步兴起，第三产业所占比重比“十五”末提高 1.2 个百分点。产业集聚水平不断提高，近万个乡镇企业工业园区，完成增加值已占到全部乡镇企业增加值的 25.5%。区域发展的协调性进一步增强，中西部和东北地区乡镇企业增加值年均增速高于东部，所占比重比“十五”末提高 2 个百分点。从业人员素质显著提高，乡镇企业职工获得各类资格证书的人数达到 254 万人次，大中专以上文化程度人数比重由“十五”末的 14.3%提高到 22.2%，中高级技术职称人数比重由 2.3%提高到 3.5%。企业家和管理、技术、营销人员队伍逐步年轻化、知识化、职业化。自主创新能力进一步增强，有近 4 万个企业建立了技术研发中心，比“十五”末增长 50%以上。

2. 坚持以“优化布局、创新发展”为核心，做大做强农产品加工业　通过引导产业集聚、完善创新体系、加强技术推广、建设原料基地、健全标准体系和强化行业指导等工作，促进了农产品加工业的快速发展。2010 年规模以上农产品加工业产值预计突破 10 万亿元，比“十五”末增长约 1.5 倍。带动作用明显增强，加工产值与农业产值比例从“十五”末的 1.1∶1 提高到 1.6∶1，2010 年规模以上企业从业人员达 2 500 多万人，其中吸纳农村劳动力 1 500 万人以上，农民直接增收 2 800 亿元。结构不断优化，食品工业比重从“十五”末的 40%提高到 47%，方便、快捷、休闲和营养保健食品发展迅速，很多企业按照无公害、绿色、有机标准组织生产，形成了一大批名牌产品和驰名商标。产业加速集聚，初步形成了东北和长江流域水稻加工、黄淮海优质专用小麦加工、东北玉米和大豆加工、长江流域优质油菜子加工、中原地区牛羊肉加工、西北和环渤海苹果加工、沿海优质水产品加工等产业聚集区。创新步伐加快，以农业部认定的 200 多个农产品加工技术研发中心为依托，初步构建起国家农产品加工技术研发体系框架，一批共性关键技术取得突破，一批先进适用技术得到推广。

原料基地日益扩大，数万个领军企业按照公司加农户、龙头带基地等多种形式，建设了一大批规模化、标准化、专业化农产品生产基地，辐射带动1亿多农户。

3. *坚持以“引导、规范、服务”为核心，突出打造休闲农业新亮点* 休闲农业是我们的一项新职能。近年来，通过加强部门合作、完善相关政策、制定从业标准、培育先进典型、规范行业管理、打造服务平台等工作，推动了休闲农业的快速发展。据不完全统计，目前规模以上休闲农业园区超过1.8万个，农家乐达到150万个，年接待游客超过4亿人次。辐射带动作用明显，营业收入超过1 200亿元，带动1 500万农民受益。发展格局逐步转变，正在从零星分布向集中连片转变，从单一功能向休闲、教育和体验等多功能转变，从单一产业经营向多产业一体化经营转变，从农民自发发展向政府规范引导转变。发展氛围越来越好，农业部与国家旅游局签署合作框架协议，与国土资源部联合发文，规范了休闲农业用地政策，开展了示范县和示范点创建活动，启动了公共服务“进城入户”工程。休闲农业正在成为融合生产、生活、生态，横跨一、二、三产业的农业新形态和消费新业态，成为沟通城乡、拉动消费、富裕农民的朝阳产业、魅力产业和幸福产业。一些地方通过发展休闲农业，激活了一方经济、富裕了一方百姓、建成了一方乐园。

5年来，各地在推动工作中，因地制宜、大胆创新、勇于开拓，呈现出各具特色的新亮点。

1. *着力引导乡镇企业优化升级* 河北、山西、陕西、甘肃、内蒙古等地加快由资源经济向产业经济转变，产业和产品结构得到明显改善。江苏、浙江、上海、天津、广东、福建等地努力促进产业结构升级，先进制造、新能源、新材料、新医药产业得到较快发展。山东、辽宁、湖北、湖南、贵州、江西、安徽等地制定激励政策，培育园区经济，引导企业集群化发展，推动上下游产业衔接和企业分工协作。

2. *着力培育农产品加工业发展壮大* 山东、河南、吉林、内蒙古、河北、湖北、湖南、陕西等地依托农业资源，大力发展农产品加工业，在推动本地经济发展中发挥了重要作用。山东通过大力发展果蔬、水产品和肉类等加工业，已经成为我国第一农产品加工大省，产品行销国内外；吉林农产品加工业产值超过了汽车和石化工业产值，位居各行业第一位；河南、河北大力发展小麦加工，培育了一大批骨干企业；内蒙古大力发展乳品加工，努力打造“中国乳品之都”。

3. *着力推进休闲农业规范发展* 北京、江苏、湖南、浙江、四川、海南、江西、上海、湖北、福建、安徽、广西等地因地制宜，突出地域、环境、农业及民俗文化特色，出台了有针对性的扶持政策，制定了休闲农业发展规划。休闲农庄、农家乐、农业观光园区、农业主题公园、农事节庆等多种休闲农业业态蓬勃发展，涌现出一批各具特色的休闲农业品牌。

4. *着力加强公共服务平台建设* 江苏、山东、浙江、河北等地注重培育区域性担保机构，加大了小企业贷款风险补偿力度，缓解了企业资金紧张状况。北京、山西、海南、贵州、新疆等地搭建特色农产品加工推介平台，扩大了产品的知名度和市场占有率。辽宁、河南、湖南、宁夏等地通过举办农产品加工技术对接活动，有效满足了企业的技术需求，帮助企业与科研院所和高校建立了长期合作关系。天津、安徽、陕西、重庆等地积极实施蓝色证书培训工程，加强职业技能开发，并把促进农民创业作为一项重大的民生工程，在政策支持、项目推介、基地建设、创业辅导、公共服务等方面做了许多成效显著的工作。

5. *着力促进区域间产业有序转移* 上海、江苏、浙江、山东等地与河南、甘肃、吉林、黑龙江、贵州、新疆、青海、西藏等地建立产业对接平台，推进东西合作，加强了技术、资金、人才、劳务、信息等方面的合作与交流，促进了区域间双向共赢的良性互动发展。

“十一五”期间取得的成绩，是在我们积极应对国际金融危机的困难环境下取得的，是在资源环境压力加大和生产成本上升的背景下，通过优化结构、创新发展实现的，成绩来之不易，经验弥足珍贵，凝聚了全系统的智慧和心血，在此我代表农业部向全系统广大干部职工表示衷心的感谢！

二、分析形势，理清思路，明确服务“三农”、推进“三化”的重要任务

近年来，在我国社会主义市场经济体制和统筹城乡发展的基本框架下，乡镇企业面临的环境发生了深刻变化，通过不断的改革发展，自身内涵也发生了深刻变化。但是，乡镇企业与“三农”天然的内在联系没有变，对县域经济不可替代的支撑作用没有变。在今天的形势下我们讲发展乡镇企业，本质上就是要发展农村二、三产业。从“十二五”国民经济和社会发展的全局看，农村二、三产业在促进农民就业增收、发展现代农业、推进新农村建设以及统筹城乡发展中肩负着更加重要的任务。近年来各地的机构队伍进行了各种各样的调整，但不论叫什么名称，不论隶属于

哪个系统，我们肩负的任务是一样的，服务的对象是相同的。面对这个群体，需要我们加以引导和推动，需要我们开展相关的服务，需要我们为他们“鼓”与“呼”。因此，我们要统一思想，形成合力，共同为推进农村二、三产业发展做出应有的贡献。

“十二五”时期，经济全球化深入发展，国际产业分工进一步细化，科技创新孕育新的突破，我国经济社会发展呈现新的阶段性特征，农村二、三产业发展既面临难得机遇，也面对新的挑战。

从机遇看，一是强劲的政策推动。国家出台了加强宏观调控、扩大国内需求和强农惠农等一系列政策，加大了国民收入分配的调整力度，实施了区域发展战略、行业振兴规划，鼓励发展新兴产业，放宽了中小企业、民营经济的市场准入限制，这为农村二、三产业发展提供了强大的政策推力。二是有力的市场拉动。全球经济逐步回暖，出口恢复性增长；我国经济企稳向好，工业化、城镇化加速推进；人均 GDP 超过 4 000 美元，城乡居民消费结构不断升级；农业农村经济持续发展，粮食连年增产，农民收入稳步增加。这些为农村二、三产业发展提供了巨大的市场空间。三是现代农业和新农村建设带动。国家大规模开展农业基础设施建设，大力推进农业生产的专业化、标准化、规模化、集约化，为农产品加工业推进产业集聚，实现原料标准化奠定了坚实的基础；随着新农村建设的深入推进，农村基础设施和生态环境得到了明显改善，农村的生产、生活条件正在发生根本的改变，为休闲农业发展提供了有力的支撑。四是产业梯度转移促动。随着劳动力成本加速上升，以及土地、能源等生产要素供应问题日益突出，东部地区和城市部分产业正在加快梯度转移，这为中西部地区和广大农村发挥比较优势，承接产业转移提供了条件。五是新科技驱动。科技进步日新月异，新技术、新材料、新设备、新工艺不断取得新的突破，为农村二、三产业发展提供了强有力的科技支撑。

从挑战看，一是环境资源约束增强。环境容量有限的压力，国家严格的节能减排指标，要求农村工业特别是许多低端制造业必须调整提升。二是生产要素供给趋紧。农村二、三产业进一步面临融资、用地、能源等要素制约，企业缺资金、缺技术、缺人才问题突出，生产成本上升的压力增大。三是国际贸易不确定性增多。后金融危机时期，围绕市场、资源、人才、技术、品牌、标准的国际竞争更加激烈，受汇率波动和贸易保护主义抬头等因素影响，产品出口难度加大。四是企业自身问题比较突出。产业集中度偏低，区域间发展差距较大；产业链不健全，“小散低全”企业大量存在；大多数企业以中间制造为主，技术研发和营销能力弱。

综合分析研究，“十二五”时期既是农村二、三产业大有作为的重要战略机遇期，也是转型提升、创新发展的攻坚克难期。在这一大背景下，我们要特别强调加快转变经济发展方式问题。加快转变经济发展方式，是探索社会主义市场经济规律所取得的重大成果，是实现科学发展的必由之路。对于农村二、三产业而言，这一问题显得尤为重要和迫切。只有加快转变经济发展方式，才能有效应对挑战、增强市场竞争力，才能突破资源环境约束、实现可持续发展，也才能在发展中促转变，在转变中谋取更大的发展。因此，我们要下大力气推动产业结构向特色优势型和“三农”关联型转变，空间布局向产业集群和区域协调方向转变，增长方式向集约内涵型和创新驱动型转变，发展模式向资源节约型和环境友好型转变。

“十二五”期间，农村二、三产业总的发展思路和目标是：深入贯彻党的十七届五中全会精神，以科学发展为主题，以加快转变经济发展方式为主线，坚持把结构战略性调整作为主攻方向，把科技进步和创新作为重要支撑，把服务“三农”作为出发点和落脚点，把体制机制创新和对外开放作为强大动力，在促进农民就地就近转移上找出路，在提高农产品附加值上下工夫，在拓展农业功能上做文章，为农民就业增收、农业农村经济持续健康发展作出更大贡献。争取实现乡镇企业年均增长速度达到 10%左右，农产品加工业产值翻一番，与农业产值比值达到 2∶1，休闲农业接待人数和经营收入年均增长 15%以上。“十二五”期间，要在四个方面取得新成效。

1. 在促进农民就业增收中作出新贡献 农民问题的核心是收入问题，目前城乡收入差距拉大的趋势仍在延续。“十二五”期间，从农民收入增长的结构分析：受世界农产品价格水平和供求状况影响，我国农产品价格上升空间有限，通过提高农产品价格实现农民家庭经营性收入较快增长的难度较大；农村劳动力转移就业的结构性矛盾突出，转移难度加大，依靠农村劳动力转移就业促进工资性收入增长呈放缓趋势；国际贸易政策限制和我国国情、国力，决定了依靠政策因素促进农民转移性收入增长的幅度也不可能大幅增加。因此，必须拓宽农民增收渠道，通过大力发展农村二、三产业，延伸农业的产业链、价值链、效益链和就业链，提高产业和产品的附加值，促进农业农村经济稳定发展和农民收入持续增长。

2. 在建设现代农业中发挥新作用 推进现代农业建设，既是农业农村经济发展的内在要求，也是统筹城乡发展、加快全面小康社会建设、顺利推进国家现代化建设的迫切需要。但是，我国农业发展中存在

的生产规模小、物资装备差、产业链条短、农业功能单一等问题，已经成为发展现代农业的主要制约因素。因此，要通过发展农村二、三产业，进一步促使更多的农民从农业中分离出来，减轻农业的就业压力，为实现农业生产的规模化、专业化提供条件；要继续通过以工补农，以工建农的方式，增加农业投入，改善农业的基础设施和物质装备条件；要通过发展农产品加工业，促进农业产业化、集约化和标准化生产，健全现代农业产业体系；要通过发展休闲农业，拓展农业功能，提高农业效益。

3. *在推进工业化城镇化中担当新重任* 当前，我国已经进入工业化中期阶段，推进工业化、城镇化是“十二五”期间的一项重大战略任务，必须认识到，没有农村的工业化就没有国家的工业化，没有农村的城镇化也就没有国家的城镇化，推进农村的工业化和城镇化是重点，更是难点。因此，我们必须大力发展农村二、三产业，推进农村工业化，实现农产品和特色资源加工转化，支撑县域经济发展壮大。要通过推进农村二、三产业的集聚发展，带动农村人口、公共服务、基础设施向小城镇集中，使小城镇规模扩大、功能完善，形成产业聚集、市场扩张、人口集中的良性循环，辐射和带动周边农村，形成农村发展的内生动力，为新农村和小城镇建设提供产业支撑。

4. *在统筹城乡发展中开辟新途径* 我国城乡差距不仅表现在城乡居民收入差距上，也表现在城乡基础设施、公共服务和产业发展上。从现阶段看，产业发展是统筹城乡发展的关键，是工业反哺农业的重要载体。因此，要通过发展农村二、三产业，搭建起沟通城乡的桥梁和纽带，接受城市和大工业的辐射带动，吸引城市资金、技术、人才、管理等要素向农村回流，实现要素资源在城乡间的合理配置。要通过农村二、三产业的发展壮大，增强依靠自身积累推进农村社会事业发展的能力。通过农村二、三产业的协调发展，形成与城市产业分工明确、互为市场、互相补充、相互促进的产业体系，推动城市与农村共同进步、工业与农业协调发展。

三、开拓创新，狠抓落实，积极推进“十二五”和明年各项重点工作

新的形势和任务要求我们必须增强谋划力、执行力和创新力，采取切实措施，把各项工作落到实处。

1. *深入推进产业结构调整* 一要继续采取各项措施，引导企业向园区聚集，发挥集群效应，在集聚中优化结构。二要大力改造升级传统工业，推广运用新技术、新工艺、新材料和降耗节能技术。三要积极引导和激励企业自愿、自主开展兼并重组，培育一批大企业，提升中小企业专业化分工协作水平。四要着力支持有实力的企业发展新能源、节能环保、信息技术、生物技术等战略性新兴产业。五要结合工业园区配套服务和小城镇建设，发展现代物流、商务服务、工程服务等生产性服务业和家政、养老、社区服务等生活性服务业。六要高度重视技术创新，整合资源，搭建平台，做好技术的研发、引进、消化、吸收、转化和推广，培养企业核心竞争力，走特色化、差异化、可持续的发展道路。

2. *进一步促进区域协调发展* 一要进一步健全跨区域合作机制，继续开展全国性的东西合作经贸洽谈活动，在产业项目、技术、劳务、产品销售等方面开展对接。二要支持地区间、省间、市县间开展对口合作和交流，实现优势互补、互惠互利，促进区域经济协调发展。三要鼓励各地区从实际出发，找准产业功能定位，走各具特色的发展道路。西部地区要用好国家新一轮西部大开发政策，充分利用自身优势，重点发展特色优势产业，引进资金和先进技术装备，高起点起步，跨越式发展；中部地区要充分发挥承东启西的区位优势，积极做好产业转移的承接，建设一批承接载体，依托中部地区丰富的资源优势，重点发展资源型产业、农产品加工业和加工制造业；东部地区要发挥率先发展的经济优势，主动调整结构，“腾笼换鸟”，推动主体产业从劳动密集型向技术密集型转变，从低加工度向精深加工度提升，力争使高产业层次、高技术含量、高附加值的产业占据主导地位；东北等老工业基地要发挥产业和科技基础优势，围绕大工业配套和粮食加工等农产品加工业做足、做好文章。

3. *加快发展提升农产品加工业* 一要以提高我国农产品加工业的创新能力和整体技术水平为目标，进一步整合资源、集中力量，完善产学研紧密结合的技术研发体系建设，争取在重大关键共性技术的攻关、引进、集成和示范推广等方面取得实质性进展。二要以解决农产品产后处理设施简陋、工艺落后、损失严重、质量安全隐患突出等问题为重点，启动农产品产地初加工惠民工程，采取国家扶持、农民建设、农业部门技术指导和服务的方式，支持农民和专业合作组织建设产地储藏、保鲜、烘干等初加工设施装备，尽快提高我国农产品产地初加工水平。三要以发展农产品精深加工和提高资源综合利用率为目的，积极争取有关政策，支持农产品加工企业加快技术装备改造升级，培育壮大一批领军企业，树立民族品牌，保障产业安全，提升我国农产品加工业的发展水平和竞争力。四要以提升中小型企业的整体技术水平为核

心，搭建技术对接和推广平台，广泛开展先进适用技术、装备的推介活动。五要以服务政府决策和行业发展为中心，开展农产品加工重点行业、重要品种的跟踪研究和监测分析，发布行业信息，引导产业健康发展。六要以保障质量安全为目标，加强引导和监督，完善标准体系，推动更多的企业建立和完善农产品加工全程质量控制体系。

4. 努力实现休闲农业跨越式发展　休闲农业是横跨农村一、二、三产业的新型农业产业，是促进农民就业增收和满足居民休闲需求的民生产业，是发展新型消费业态和扩大内需的支柱产业。“十二五”是旅游消费向休闲消费转型的关键时期，而休闲旅游产品供给呈现结构性短缺，我国休闲旅游资源70%在农村，发展休闲农业面临着难得的历史机遇、蕴含着巨大的发展潜力和良好的发展前景，是一篇可以写好的锦绣文章，是一项一举多得的事业。我们一定要抓住机遇，把发展休闲农业作为解决“三农”问题的重要抓手，立足“富裕农民、改造农业、建设农村”，按照“转变方式、提升地位、引领发展”的思路，全面推进休闲农业持续快速发展。一要围绕农业生产过程、农民劳动生活和农村风情风貌，以城市和景区周边、山水牧特色区、少数民族地区和传统农区为重点，分类规划，因地制宜，创新模式，突出特色，整合资源，大力培育功能各异、特色突出、优势明显的休闲农业产业带、产业群，满足个性化、多元化消费需求。二要加强部门合作，在休闲农业公共基础设施、服务设施、安全设施、环保设施建设和从业人员培训方面形成工作合力，在财政、信贷、税收、土地等方面争取政策，为休闲农业创造良好发展环境。三要借鉴相关行业管理经验，遵循产业发展规律，结合各地发展实际和模式特点，制定休闲农业发展标准，规范硬件建设和软件服务，提升服务能力，增强发展后劲。四要深入开展全国休闲农业与乡村旅游示范县、示范点创建，做好中国最有魅力的休闲乡村推介、全国休闲农业星级评定等工作，着力培育休闲农业知名品牌，不断提升产业地位，引领休闲消费新业态的形成。五要加强人员培训和宣传推介，加快休闲农业“进城入户”公共服务平台建设，提升从业人员素质和社会影响力。力争经过5年的努力，通过休闲农业这一新型业态，把农业改造成快乐的产业，把农村建设成幸福的家园，把农民变成富裕的群体。

5. 大力支持农民创业　改革开放以来，一批又一批农民进城入厂，在为我国经济社会发展做出巨大贡献的同时，一部分农民增长了才干，提高了技能，积累了经验和财富，具备了自主创业的基本条件。从农民返乡创业热情高涨的现状和发展趋势可以预见，“十二五”时期是农民自主创业的高峰期。因此，我们要把扶持农民创业作为“十二五”的重要任务之一，加以谋划推进。一要积极争取政策支持，主动协调各级财政加大对农民创业的支持力度，发挥公共财政的引导作用，化解农民创业资金短缺的难题，还要推动有关部门在企业登记、金融贷款、税收管理、规费标准、市场准入、部门服务等方面降低门槛。二要抓好创业基地建设，采取政府引导扶持、鼓励多方投资的方式，充分利用城乡各类园区、规模较大的闲置厂房和场地、专业化市场等适合中小企业聚集创业的场所，建设具有滚动孵化功能的农民创业基地，为创业者提供场所，为创业服务打造载体。三要抓好创业服务，借鉴城市创业服务和高科技企业孵化器的经验和做法，从创业项目推介、创业辅导、技能培训，政策、法律、管理咨询，场地设施提供、证照办理、金融信贷，到产品检测、市场开拓等方面提供全方位服务。四要抓好典型引路，认真总结不同层面和类型的典型经验，进行示范推广，辐射带动农民创业向深度、广度发展。五要抓好规范提高，除在创业初期加强扶持外，还要注意帮助创办起来的企业解决生产、经营中的技术难题和管理难题，增强抵御化解市场风险的能力，提高创业成功率。

6. 努力提高从业人员素质　员工队伍素质一定意义上决定着企业素质。目前，不仅是一批有文化无技能的新员工需要进行职业技能培训，而且随着企业技术进步和产品升级，大量的在岗职工也需要进行适应性岗位培训。因此，加强从业人员培训是我们各级行政管理部门的一项重要职责任务。一要进一步开展蓝色证书培训，争取将蓝色证书培训纳入阳光培训工程，把农产品加工业、休闲农业相关工种纳入培训范围，扶持一批地方培训机构改善培训条件、提高培训能力，承接培训任务，扩大培训覆盖面，提高培训质量水平。二要进一步强化职业技能培训及鉴定工作，加强与有关部门、职业学校、行业协会配合，扩大培训与鉴定范围；在乡镇工业园区逐步建立公共服务平台，为中小企业开展培训与鉴定服务；鼓励和推动大中型企业自主开展培训与鉴定工作。三要通过组织西部地区企业经营管理人员到东部地区挂职任职和举办专题培训班，加快提高西部地区企业管理人员经营管理水平。四要开展证券融资培训，加强与证券部门合作，发挥他们的资源和专业优势，积极对有上市愿望的企业进行辅导，增强企业融资意识，拓宽企业融资渠道。

7. 积极营造良好发展环境　新时期引导行业转型发展，各级乡镇企业、农产品加工业、休闲农业行政管理部门要加强自身体系和队伍建设，建立领导支持、部门配合、协调一致的管理服务机制；要配合落实好国家促进中小企业、非公有制经济发展的有关政策；要深入实际，总结各地推进转型发展的经验做法、扶持措施，组织本系统、相关部门和专家学者研究提出推进行业发展的有关政策建议；要通过各种新闻媒体、举办重大活动、典型示范等方式，加大宣传引导力度，吸引全社会的关注和支持，进一步营造政策扶持、舆论支持、社会参与、行业引导和服务的良好发展环境。

（本文为作者于2010年12月23日在2010年全国乡镇企业与农产品加工业工作会议上的讲话，略有删改）

提高认识 依法履责
扎实做好食品安全风险监测工作

卫生部副部长 陈啸宏

召开2010年国家食品安全风险监测计划实施工作会议，目的是认真学习《食品安全法》，认真贯彻2010年全国卫生工作会议和全国卫生监督工作会议精神，进一步提高依法履责意识，扎实做好2010年国家食品安全风险监测计划的实施工作。下面，谈三点意见。

一、认真学习《食品安全法》，提高对食品安全风险监测工作重要性的认识

（一）严格把握法律精神，进一步增强依法履责的意识

食品安全风险监测制度是《食品安全法》确立的一项重要法律制度。《食品安全法》及其实施条例分别对食品安全风险监测制度的目的和要求做出了具体规定。《食品安全法》第十一条规定，国家建立食品安全风险监测制度，对食源性疾病、食品污染以及食品中的有害因素进行监测。《食品安全法实施条例》规定，国务院卫生行政部门会同国务院质量监督、工商行政管理和国家食品药品监督管理以及国务院商务、工业和信息化等部门制定、实施国家食品安全风险监测计划，并根据核实后的食品安全风险信息、医疗机构报告的有关疾病信息及时对国家食品安全风险监测计划进行调整。省、自治区、直辖市人民政府卫生行政部门根据国家食品安全风险监测计划，结合本行政区域的具体情况，组织制定、实施本行政区域的食品安全风险监测方案，并根据国家监测计划的调整及时调整省级监测方案。《食品安全法》还规定，国务院卫生行政部门通过食品安全风险监测或者接到举报发现食品可能存在安全隐患的，应当立即组织进行检验和食品安全风险评估。此外，还对监测信息报告、监测结果通报与处理等提出了明确要求。我们要认真把握、全面落实《食品安全法》的规定，认真履行职责，切实把法律法规赋予的风险监测各项工作做好。

（二）充分认识食品安全风险监测的重要性，进一步增强责任感

食品安全风险监测，是通过系统和持续地收集食源性疾病、食品污染以及食品中有害因素的监测数据及相关信息，对食品安全状况进行综合分析和及时通报的活动。制定实施国家食品安全风险监测计划的目的：一是通过风险监测了解我国食品安全整体状况，科学评价食品污染和食源性疾病对健康带来的危害及其造成的经济负担，为有效制定食品安全管理政策提供技术依据。二是通过风险监测，了解掌握国家或地区特定食品及特定污染物的水平，掌握污染物的变化趋势，开展风险评估并适时制定修订食品安全标准，指导食品生产经营企业做好食品安全管理。三是通过风险监测从一个侧面反映一个地区食品安全监管工作的水平，指导确定监督抽检重点领域，评价干预措施效果，为政府食品安全监管提供科学信息。四是通过风险监测指导科学发布食品安全信息，客观评价并发布食品安全客观情况，科学宣传食品安全知识，维护人民群众的知情权，增强国内消费者信心，促进国际食品贸易发展。

由此可见，食品安全风险监测直接关系到政府食品安全管理的水平和效率，是依法监督管理食品安全的重要技术手段。只有通过有效实施风险监测，才能真正建立起以食品安全风险评估为基础的食品安全科

学监管机制，做到从农田到餐桌的全程监测、干预，实现预防为主、先发制人的监管理念。

（三）科学分析食品安全形势，进一步增强紧迫感

改革开放以来，我国食品工业产业迅猛发展，食品产业近10年来保持了20%以上的增速，成为国民经济和人民生活的重要支柱产业之一，同时，我国也成为世界最大的食品市场。虽然近年来食品安全工作取得了长足发展，但也必须看到，由于食品生产经营秩序尚不规范，食品生产经营中的掺杂使假等违法行为时有发生，传统的食品污染物尚未得到有效控制，新的食品安全危害因素又不断产生。种种情况表明，目前我国仍处于食品安全事故风险高发期和矛盾凸显期，食品安全监管任务十分艰巨。因此，在控制食品安全风险方面，我们既要面对传统的常规风险，不断加强对传统食品污染物的监测和控制，又要注重防控在食品中掺杂使假、非法添加非食用物质和滥用食品添加剂的违法犯罪行为，有效应对非常规和非传统的食品安全风险。我们要充分认识食品安全工作的复杂性和艰巨性，以对人民健康高度负责的态度，发挥卫生部门在食品安全风险监测和评估工作中的牵头和协调作用，会同有关部门，认真抓好国家食品安全风险监测计划和本地食品安全风险监测方案的落实工作。

二、明确任务，认真做好2010年国家食品安全风险监测计划实施工作

（一）实施2010年国家食品安全风险监测计划的主要任务

2010年2月4日，卫生部会同工业和信息化部、商务部、国家工商总局、国家质量监督检验检疫总局、国家食品药品监管局等部门，联合印发了《2010年国家食品安全风险监测计划》。6部门组织各方面专家，通过总结以往的监测工作并借鉴国际经验，针对当前我国食品生产经营中的重点污染物、可能存在的有毒有害因素以及食源性疾病谱，确定了今年监测的重点任务。这是卫生部第一次在全国范围内开展的多部门、全过程、经科学设计的风险监测工作，监测任务既包括对产品的常规监测，又有对食品生产经营过程和特定危害因素的专项监测。监测环节涵盖了食品生产加工、流通和餐饮消费各个环节，范围覆盖31个省、自治区、直辖市及新疆生产建设兵团。其中，化学污染物和有害因素安排了29类食品、132个检验项目；食源性疾病致病菌安排了对8大类、13种食品中的8个主要食源性致病菌的监测；食源性疾病监测安排了对全国31个省（自治区、直辖市）及新疆生产建设兵团的312个县有关医疗机构发现的异常病例和异常健康事件的主动监测。与卫生部以往组织开展的食品卫生“两网”监测工作相比，2010年监测计划在选择优先食品和危害因素方面的目的性显著增强，样本量显著增加，对采样的代表性、实施工作的技术性以及数据报送的时效性都做出了进一步明确规定，同时，对计划实施的组织工作及技术机构也提出了更高的要求。

（二）认真总结以往的经验，增强做好工作的信心

新中国成立以来，国家逐步建立了从中央到省、市、县四级疾病预防控制机构，配备了食品检测实验室，形成了覆盖全国的食品卫生检验检测体系。几十年来，各级疾病预防控制机构承担了大量公共卫生和食品卫生检验检测工作。除每年承担数百万份食品抽检、送检样品检验任务外，还承担着对食物中毒、食品污染事故以及其他食源性疾病的卫生学调查、病因学诊断等任务，积累了丰富的经验。

近年来，国家不断加大公共卫生体系建设，食品安全检测能力和设备得到了不断加强，总体检测能力和实验室管理水平不断规范和提高。尤其是从2000年开始，卫生部逐步建立了食品污染物和食源性疾病监测网络，分别在17个省（自治区、直辖市）和22个省（自治区、直辖市）设立食品污染物和食源性疾病致病因素监测点，对消费量较大的60余种食品、常见的79种化学污染物和致病菌进行常规监测。同时还组织开展了4次全国膳食与营养调查，基本掌握了全国居民膳食结构、饮食和疾病谱状况，初步摸清了我国食品中重要污染物的污染水平及动态变化趋势。这些监测数据已经成为制定、修订食品卫生标准、参与国际食品法典工作的主要技术依据，同时也为制定国家食品安全政策和全国监督抽检计划发挥了重要作用。从总体上看，我国在食品安全风险监测能力方面是有一定基础的，全国疾病预防控制机构是开展食品安全风险监测的重要力量。此外，各个相关食品安全监管部门、大专院校和有关科研、技术单位也拥有大量食品安全检测技术资源，卫生行政部门要做好协调，在当地政府的领导下，有效整合资源，充分发挥各部门以及社会检测技术资源在食品安全风险监测中的作用。

（三）对照任务查找不足，进一步提高实施食品安全风险监测的能力与水平

尽管多年来我们在食品污染物监测方面积累了一定经验，但受人力资源、经费支持、技术水平以及信息沟通等方面的限制，无论是污染物还是食源性疾病的监测调查都尚处于起步阶段，主要存在两方面的

问题：

1. 一些地方对食品安全风险监测工作重要性的认识不足 通过前期工作的情况看，一些地区和部门的同志还没有全面把握法律规定的食品安全风险监测制度的要求，对食品安全风险监测的内容、必须承担的法律责任认识不到位，工作不规范，报告不及时，甚至对食品安全隐患不敏感。这些都是我们做好食品安全风险监测工作要努力改进的地方。敏感性和责任意识是做好工作、少犯错误的基础。在此我要特别对广西壮族自治区疾控中心去年及时发现并向卫生厅报告陕西金桥乳粉检出“三聚氰胺”的工作提出表扬，正是因为广西壮族自治区疾控中心的及时报告，“陕西金桥乳粉案件”才浮出了水面，有效防止了被污染的乳粉流入市场。

2. 要正视目前不少疾病预防控制机构的能力与开展法定风险监测的要求不相适应 特别是一些基层疾病预防控制机构，近年来缺乏在食品安全检验检测方面的投入，历史欠账多，距离《食品安全法》要求的风险监测能力存在较大差距，特别是人才队伍建设滞后的问题尤其明显。这些问题不解决，将直接影响到能否履行好法定食品安全风险监测的责任。对此，卫生部已引起高度重视，从2009年以来，我们积极协调、会同有关部门加大这方面的能力建设。

总之，要完成好2010年的风险监测工作任务，一要增强信心，二要有紧迫感，三要努力克服困难，四要边工作、边规范、边建设，把依法履行法定职责放在首位，努力完成好2010年食品安全风险监测计划。

三、加强领导，进一步做好食品安全风险监测基础建设

根据2008年卫生部“三定”方案中有关“加强食品安全风险监测与评估工作”的规定，卫生部党组高度重视，专题研究进一步加强食品安全风险监测和风险评估能力建设的措施。按照陈竺部长提出的建立“先发制人”的食品安全监管机制要求，我们强调要将风险监测信息收集和风险评估工作作为卫生部门能力建设的基础工作，加快食品安全技术支撑能力建设，充分发挥其在食品安全综合协调和综合监督方面的作用。根据法律法规的规定和国务院食品安全整顿方案的要求，在认真完成2010年监测计划的同时，要切实加快中央和地方食品安全风险监测能力建设。

（一）加快全国食品安全风险监测体系建设

国务院《食品安全整顿工作方案》要求，要通过2009—2010年两年的努力，会同相关部门在全国建立起覆盖各省、市、县并逐步延伸到农村地区的食品污染物和食源性疾病监测体系，提高食品中有毒有害物质鉴定排查、风险监测、风险预警、风险评估和技术仲裁的能力，加强食品安全风险监测数据的收集、报送和管理。食品安全风险监测体系建设已经纳入到为期两年的全国食品安全整顿工作之中，国务院还将对此进行考核评估，希望大家一定要高度重视。

2009年，财政部设立了食品安全保障重大专项，对各地尤其是中西部地区的食品安全监测工作提供了一定经费支持，2010年我们将继续争取这项支持。同时，卫生部也在考虑将食品安全纳入医改的重大建设项目，加大支持力度。各省、自治区、直辖市卫生厅（局）都要抓住机遇，主动向政府汇报工作，通过加强领导，完善机制，提高水平，主动出击，确保在2010年底之前完成国务院提出的风险监测体系建设目标。

（二）针对性提高食品安全风险监测能力

实施2010年监测计划，要充分发挥各省（自治区、直辖市）食品安全重点检验室的作用。2009年3月，卫生部印发了《关于进一步加强食品安全监测与评估工作的通知》（卫监督发［2009］19号），对各级卫生部门发展技术能力提出了要求，要求按照边工作边发展的思路，充分利用现有工作基础，不断创造条件，加快建设进度，立足现在，放眼长远，调整思路，搞好规划，统筹考虑人员机构、编制和经费，综合利用不同专业和技术能力的检验机构和社会各方面资源，逐步建立健全与形势和任务相适应的技术支撑队伍。

省级疾病预防控制机构要按照《食品安全法》赋予的职责要求，努力加强自身能力建设，积极创造条件，充实人员和仪器设备，充分调动各方面资源，逐步达到与监测技术相适应的能力与条件。要加强对技术人员的培训和管理，严格按照法律法规的规定以及监测计划实施的技术要求开展工作，不断提高检验工作的质量和能力，做好隐患报告、数据通报和汇总分析工作。国家监测计划是反映国家水平的监测计划，对其样本来源、采样方法、样本数量和检验技术等都有特殊的要求，各地疾病预防控制机构要发挥本地区实施监测计划的技术核心作用，既要做好自身的工作，还要为本地区监测数据质量把好关，做好行政部门的参谋和助手。各级疾病预防控制机构都要高度重视食品安全技术骨干和学科带头人的培养，充实有较高业务素质的专业技术人员，建立起专业队伍，通过加强人员职业道德教育和业务知识、技能培训，不断提高人员技术水平。

（三）加强食品安全信息收集和管理，及时通报食品安全风险信息

一方面，要进一步完善食源性疾病信息报告和主动监测系统，逐步建立与国际接轨的食源性疾病监测、调查、报告、数据分析机制，将食源性疾病信息报告纳入卫生部现有的传染病报告网络，在全国部分医疗机构设立临床监测点，收集分析可疑食源性疾病信息报告，进一步提高各级卫生部门的食源性疾病调查能力和水平。另一方面，要加快食品安全信息网络建设，建立部门间信息沟通平台，实现信息的互联互通，资源共享，提高信息管理水平和综合利用效率。中国疾控中心要加强对省级疾控中心的业务指导，发挥国家食品安全风险监测信息收集分析中心的作用，通过收集、整合食品安全监督管理信息和风险监测信息，公布食品安全监测状况，公布重点控制的污染物“黑名单”。进一步完善食品隐患的预警机制，做到早发现、早调查、早预警、早处理。

（四）加强组织领导，做好部门协调合作

各部门、各系统的食品检测机构是国家食品安全保障的重要资源，必须加强资源利用，充分发挥现有资源的优势和作用。《食品安全法》颁布实施后，卫生部会同工业和信息化部、国家工商总局、国家质量监督检验检疫总局、国家食品药品监管局共同制定了《食品安全风险监测管理规定（试行）》，积极探索建立既分工合作、又相互支持的多部门工作机制。

各省、自治区、直辖市卫生行政部门要统筹规划和加强本地区监测计划的实施工作，加强组织领导，严格检查考核和经费使用管理，要将食品安全风险监测作为一项重要工作，并为承担监测任务的技术机构解决困难和问题，为本地区食品安全风险监测工作负起责任。各地要加强部门协调，分解任务，落实责任，保证国家监测计划的实施质量。要主动开展食品生产、流通和餐饮消费环节对各类食品原料、配料、添加剂的监测，尤其是要将已经公布的“黑名单”物质要作为监测的重点。中国疾控中心要加强对各省、自治区、直辖市工作的技术督导、评估和考核，及时发现工作中出现的问题，实施开展业务交流、培训和质量控制等工作。

食品安全风险监测评估是食品安全的一项重要基础性工作，是卫生系统义不容辞的一项重要任务。2010 年是全面实施国家监测计划和省级监测方案的第一年，许多工作需要从头开始，希望同志们要发扬求真务实的作风，克服困难，积极主动开展工作。要以全新的精神状态，改革创新，不断完善风险监测工作机制，不断提高我们保障人民群众食品安全的工作水平。

（本文为作者于 2010 年 3 月 17 日在实施 2010 年国家食品安全风险监测计划工作会议上的讲话，略有删改）

积极开展肉菜流通追溯体系建设
努力提高质量安全和供应保障水平

商务部部长 陈德铭

党的十七届五中全会，审议通过了《中共中央关于制定国民经济和社会发展第十二个五年规划的建议》，强调要把加快转变经济发展方式贯穿于经济社会发展的全过程和全领域，将坚持扩大内需战略、建立扩大消费需求的长效机制作为今后 5 年的重要任务，并提出坚持发展要更加注重以人为本，更加注重保障和改善民生。“菜篮子”不仅连着经济增长，更是连着民生。党中央、国务院高度重视，国务院常务会议近期专题研究蔬菜供应问题，并下发文件进行部署。各地、各部门做了大量工作，但保供稳价形势仍不容乐观。2010 年以来，我国气候异常，极端天气时有发生，一些地区相继发生了干旱、洪涝等特大灾害，对瓜果、蔬菜等重要农产品生产造成较大影响。10 月份，海南遭遇了 49 年来最大强度降雨天气，灾情之重历史罕见，种植业损失严重。海南是我国重要的蔬菜生产基地，这次洪涝灾害不仅影响到当前市场，可能也会影响到全国冬季蔬菜供应。据监测，10 月 11 日至 17 日，全国主要大中城市蔬菜价格同比上涨 50.4%。因此，我们一定要深刻理解市场形势的复杂性和严峻性，切实提高思想认识，扎扎实实把蔬菜市场供应的有关政策措施和工作要求落到实处。各地要围绕加快建立畅通、高效、安全、有序的蔬菜流通体系，进一步做好加强流通设施建设、加大产销衔接力度、提高应急保供能力、完善市场监测预警、规范市场秩序等工作。特别是要进一步细化“菜篮子”市场保障供应应急预案，加快完善蔬菜、肉类等重要商品储备制度，建立城乡之间、主产区与主销区之间的应急供应协作机制，充分发挥大宗农产品骨干企业在市场调控中的作用，并善于利用国内外两个市场、两种资源，解决好“买难”、“卖难”问题。

为进一步提高我国肉类、蔬菜质量安全和供应保障水平，商务部、财政部决定开展肉菜流通追溯体系建设试点，并于日前联合下发了指导性文件。这次会议的主要任务是，贯彻落实文件精神，部署肉菜流通追溯体系建设试点工作，并开展相关经验交流。刚才，上海、青岛、宁波、大连、杭州几个城市的市长作了很好的经验介绍和发言，听了很受启发，感到振奋和鼓舞。房爱卿同志代表商务部与试点城市签订协议，标志着这项工作正式启动。下面，我代表商务部讲几点意见。

一、充分认识建设肉菜流通追溯体系的必要性和紧迫性

肉菜是与百姓日常生活最为密切的食品。保障“一荤一素”的供应和质量安全，人民群众生活、身体健康和生命安全就有了更大保证，满意度也会显著提升。作为最重要的两类农产品，肉菜流通方式逐步走向现代化，必然带动农产品流通现代化和流通发展方式转变。这两项任务完成好了，商务主管部门才算履行好自己的职责；反过来，如果肉菜质量安全问题频发，流通方式落后，商务主管部门就没有尽到自己的责任。因此，我们会同财政部，依托试点城市和省级商务主管部门，建设肉菜流通追溯体系，促进肉菜流通的安全、高效，是一项以人为本的民心工程，一项转变流通方式的提升工程，具有十分重要的意义。

（一）建设追溯体系，是提高肉菜质量安全水平，保障和改善民生，构建和谐社会的迫切需要

近年来，在党中央、国务院的正确领导和有关方面的共同努力下，我国食品安全工作不断加强，食品安全形势总体向好，但基础依然薄弱，问题时有发生，形势不容乐观。肉菜与人民群众身体健康和生命安全直接相关，质量安全状况更是备受关注。近年来曝光的“毒豇豆”、“瘦肉精”、“发光猪肉”等事件虽属个别情况，但涉及种植、养殖、加工、批发、零售等多个环节，不仅危害人民群众身体健康和生命安全，打击消费信心，而且损害了政府公信力，甚至产生了恶劣的国际影响。如果不从源头和根本上解决这一问题，人民群众不满意，以人为本与社会和谐更是无从谈起。我们必须按照党中央和国务院的部署，依据《食品安全法》的规定，不断探索，着力推动解决。

流通领域肉菜质量安全问题多发，一个重要原因是经营主体责任落实不到位。我国肉菜经营集中度低，包装化、品牌化程度不高。90%～95%的蔬菜经营户是个体，散装和无包装蔬菜占87%以上；75%以上的生猪定点屠宰企业是手工和半机械化操作，白条肉、非包装肉占90%以上，进货查验、索证索票、购销台账等制度难以落实。另外，我国食品质量安全监管涉及多个部门，尚未建立统一的部门间信息共享机制，经营者身份、肉菜来源、流向及质量等信息大部分是纸质的、零散的，标准化、规范化不足，难以实现互联互通、多方共享，让不法分子有隙可乘。

建立肉菜流通追溯体系，不替代任何监管部门的职责。目的是使各流通节点的信息互联互通，形成来源可追溯、去向可查证、责任可追究的质量安全追溯链条，变“点监管”为“链监管”，既充分发挥各监管部门的职能，又加强部门间的执法协作，实现肉菜质量安全的全过程无缝隙监管。这样，出了问题可以很快查到责任主体，避免打击一大片。故意制售有害食品的不法分子将不敢肆意妄为，守法的经营者出于自身利益考虑，也会在食品质量安全上严格把关。追溯体系和信息化管理平台的建设，将大大增强商务主管部门为食品安全监管部门支持和服务的能力，加大执法监管力度；还可以为消费者查询和维权提供帮助，营造安全放心的消费环境。

（二）建设追溯体系，是发挥商务主管部门职能，加强流通行业管理的迫切需要

实行索证索票和台账管理，是《食品安全法》规定的硬性措施。鼓励和支持食品经营者采用先进技术手段，记录食品的来源、流向及相关信息，是《食品安全法》及其《实施条例》规定的重要原则。《食品安全法实施条例》还规定了商务主管部门在食品经营行业管理方面的职责。推动建设肉菜流通追溯体系，是商务主管部门实施行业管理的重要抓手，可以推进产业结构优化，促进食品经营行业健康发展，对整个流通行业发展也十分重要。追溯体系建成后，流通信息的标准化、电子化就会实现，索证索票和台账管理就会更加规范，监管部门的监管效率会显著提高，行业管理与执法监管的协作配合会更加密切，肉菜质量安全就会更有保障，商务主管部门的作用也会更好地发挥。

建设肉菜流通追溯体系，也是商务部支持和保障城市“菜篮子”建设的一项重要措施。随着城市化进

程的不断推进，目前大中城市肉菜供应量平均70%以上来自外埠，本地菜比重持续下降，特别是北方城市本地菜比重更小，保障安全的任务更加艰巨。强化“菜篮子”市长负责制，落实食品安全地方政府责任，在稳定和提高城市自给能力的同时，要坚持全国“一盘棋”，否则每个城市、每个地区都会孤掌难鸣，出了问题也难以追溯源头。建设追溯体系，就是为了顺应全国农产品大流通的趋势，消除“信息孤岛”，逐步实现产、运、批、零全程的链式管理，加强市场监测及运行调控的准确性和及时性，在保障供应和质量安全上为市长们提供服务，当好帮手。

（三）建设追溯体系，是推进农产品流通现代化，转变流通发展方式的迫切需要

近年来我国农产品现代流通迅速发展，但总体上仍较落后，批发市场、集贸市场等传统渠道仍承载着80%以上的生鲜农产品流通量。流通组织化、信息化程度低，设施简陋，方式粗放，98%以上的批发市场仍以现货现金、一对一的对手交易为主；流通链条长、环节多，流通成本高、损耗大、效率低，质量安全难以保障。以人民群众最关心的食品质量安全为主攻方向，以建设肉菜流通追溯体系为突破口，促进农产品流通的现代化，是转变流通发展方式的重要内容。

最新研究表明，信息化已经成为流通现代化的重要标志和流通方式创新的重要载体，发达国家流通业的技术应用程度仅次于金融业。党的十七届五中全会强调，要坚持把科技进步和创新作为转变经济发展方式的重要支撑，为我们转变流通发展方式指明了方向。信息技术的不断创新和互联网的深入发展，“物联网”、“智慧地球”、“未来城市”等概念的提出，为我们提供了新的机遇和强大武器。建设追溯体系，就是要运用现代信息技术，推动流通企业业务流程再造，优化肉菜流通交易和管理方式，促进连锁经营、现代物流和电子商务等现代流通方式发展，提高肉菜流通的组织化程度；创建放心肉菜渠道品牌，扩大品牌化、包装化、标准化肉菜的市场占有率；通过技术手段采集、分析、运用农产品流通信息，稳定以销定产的协作关系，提高质量安全监管水平。总之，从肉菜到农产品，从试点到覆盖全国，以点带面，流通信息化、现代化的步伐就会加快，流通发展方式的转变就会大有希望。

2009年，商务部、财政部在全国10个省、直辖市开展“放心肉”服务体系建设，上海、山东青岛等部分城市探索建立猪肉质量安全信息可追溯系统，取得了积极成效。有的城市还将追溯产品扩大到了蔬菜，进行了积极尝试。特别是上海市，由于肉菜流通基础设施建设、信息化和标准化建设、质量安全追溯体系建设起步较早，基础较牢，效果也比较好，为我们开展试点积累了宝贵经验。这充分说明，开展肉菜流通追溯体系建设试点是有基础的，实践证明也是可行的。希望各位市长和各地商务主管部门的同志高度重视，增强信心，把这项利国利民的大事抓紧抓好。

二、建设肉菜流通追溯体系的基本思路和主要任务

商务部、财政部印发的肉菜流通追溯体系建设指导意见，是在充分调查研究、总结地方先进经验的基础上形成的。基本思路是，深入落实科学发展观，以信息技术为手段，以法律法规标准为依据，以发展现代流通方式为基础，实现索证索票、购销台账的电子化，切实提高肉菜质量安全保障能力，加快流通现代化进程和发展方式转变。

（一）以信息技术为手段，兼顾多样性与统一性

采用先进适用的信息技术是追溯体系建设的核心，没有信息技术支撑，追溯体系的建设就成了无源之水、无本之木。在推进肉菜流通信息化的过程中，应处理好多样性与统一性的关系。多样性是指信息采集手段和载体可以采用多种技术模式。当前，无线射频识别（RFID）、集成电路（IC）卡、条形码以及互联网等技术和方式相对成熟。上海、青岛、南京等地采用比较成熟、成本较低的集成电路技术，成都、无锡等地则采用成本相对较高的无线射频识别技术。每个城市的市场发育程度、流通方式、管理和技术基础、运行成本接受程度都有不同，各试点城市可根据自身实际，选择不同的技术模式，尽快把追溯体系建立和运行起来。

统一性是指采集信息的内容要统一，以满足互联互通要求。具体来说，要做到信息采集指标、编码规则、传输格式、接口规范、追溯规程在全国范围内实现“五统一”。肉菜是典型的全国大市场、大流通，建设追溯体系必须要着眼于实现全国流通信息的互联互通，方案设计既要考虑近期的现实需要，更要考虑未来全国联网的要求。如果各城市之间、各地区之间形成信息孤岛，将来全国联网就会难以实现；如果届时重新改造或另起炉灶，就会造成巨大浪费。我们已经起草了《全国肉类蔬菜流通追溯体系建设规范》，希望大家认真研究，提出宝贵意见。我们还将制定专门的技术标准、管理制度和操作规范，为“五统一”提供支撑。

（二）完善法规标准，严格市场准入

追溯体系是制度设计与技术应用的统一体，需要

完善的法律法规和标准支撑。立法的关键和难点是解决建立追溯体系的直接法律依据问题，在法律尚未对追溯体系信息化做出明确规定的情况下，要坚持多层次立法。商务部将在推进和总结试点工作的基础上，研究制定部门规章，或者修订《流通领域食品安全管理办法》，细化《食品安全法》及其《实施条例》的相关规定。上海、青岛等地的经验表明，结合城市流通管理实际出台地方性法规，是周期短、见效快的好办法。上海市规定生猪及生猪产品产销对接制度，青岛市规定实行“备案登记、查验换证、协议约束、品牌经营、联合监管、全程追溯”为主线的肉品流通监管新模式，为顺利推进猪肉流通追溯体系建设提供了有力保障，值得其他城市学习借鉴。

标准化是农产品现代流通的重要基础和抓手，也是追溯体系建设和运行的基本前提。没有标准，追溯很难实现。我们正抓紧编制流通标准“十二五”规划，力争3～5年内全面完成主要农产品流通标准的制修订工作。一是借鉴发达国家经验，合理确定农产品标准框架体系，加快农产品购销要求、等级、包装、标识、储存、保鲜、追溯等标准的制修订工作。这项工作得到国家标准委的大力支持，2010年底前将有一批标准出台。二是鼓励流通企业符合良好生产规范（GMP）要求，实施危害分析与关键控制点体系（HACCP），申请相关质量安全认证，提高食品安全管理水平。三是完善法规政策，加强宣传引导，加大标准实施力度，督促市场主办者、经营者严格按照标准执行进货查验，强化市场准入管理，逐步做到无法追溯来源的产品不允许上市，上市的都可以追溯。

（三）抓住关键环节，夯实流通基础

追溯体系的建设与流通发展水平密切相关。流通基础设施越完善、现代化程度越高，这项工作就越容易开展。近年来，商务部会同财政部先后开展了“双百市场工程”、“标准化菜市场改造”、“农超对接”、“放心肉服务体系建设”等工作，再加上各城市高度重视，积极推进，城市肉菜流通体系更加完善，为试点工作打下了良好基础。但把追溯体系建设好，还有大量工作要做，尤其要抓好两个关键环节。

从蔬菜来看，要着力抓好批发市场电子化统一结算。目前，80%以上的蔬菜通过批发市场进入城市。管住批发市场，就管住了城市蔬菜流通的主渠道。一方面，应统一政策要求，将全部大型批发市场尤其是一级批发市场全部纳入试点，否则，市场开办者和经营者就会有顾虑，担心因不公平竞争而遭受损失；另一方面，应在批发市场全部推行电子化统一结算，利用技术手段改造交易模式，从流程上强化对经营主体的管理，确保监管信息采集的真实性和有效性，从而满足追溯的需要。据我们了解，一些批发市场和经营户担心电子化结算后税费增加、商业秘密得不到有效保护。这些问题还需进一步研究解决。

从肉类来说，要进一步提高屠宰行业集中度。建好肉类追溯体系，关键在于管住屠宰环节。目前，一些城市定点屠宰企业数量多，条件参差不齐，低水平恶性竞争严重。这个问题不解决，追溯体系很难建立起来，即使建起来也很难真正发挥作用。希望各地结合追溯体系建设需要，按照规划压缩定点屠宰企业数量，把产能进一步向规模化、机械化、规范化的屠宰企业集中。昆明市利用调整城市布局的机会，将当地12家定点屠宰企业缩减为4家，优化了行业布局，淘汰了落后产能，提高了肉品质量安全保障水平，值得学习借鉴。

（四）城市试点先行，逐步全面铺开

总体工作部署上，我们将坚持试点先行、重点突破。选择城市试点主要是考虑：一是城市是肉菜主要销区市场。按年人均消费猪肉40kg、蔬菜120kg计算，一个百万人口城市年均肉菜消费量分别达到4 000万kg和1.2亿kg。全国百万人口以上城市120多个，消费人口聚集，一旦发生问题，危害面和社会影响面都相当广。二是城市批发市场、标准化菜市场、超市等流通基础设施比较完善，建设追溯体系有良好的基础。三是城市具有“菜篮子”市长负责制的体制优势。具体工作安排上，2010年，我们选择上海、大连、青岛等10个有一定基础的城市，从肉菜“一荤一素”入手先行试点。下一步，我们将视情况把其他具备条件的大中城市纳入试点，并逐步扩大到水果、水产品、豆制品等其他农产品。今年未纳入试点的城市，要做一些准备工作或自行开展试点；没有试点城市的省（自治区、直辖市）可以根据自身情况和条件，选择一些城市进行试点；已有试点任务的省（自治区、直辖市）也可以适当扩大范围。

需要特别强调的是，除了在10个城市开展试点外，目前我们还在财政部的大力支持下，开展海南农产品现代流通综合试点，追溯体系建设是其中的一个重要方面。海南农产品辐射全国，追溯体系建设更为复杂，但是要参照试点工作指导意见，研究符合海南特点的追溯体系，尤其要考虑将来与全国的对接问题。

三、关于试点工作的几点要求

建设肉菜流通追溯体系，是一件打基础、利长远的大事，是一项艰巨复杂的系统工程，也是一项需要不断开拓进取的全新任务。大家要高度重视、精心组织，明确任务、突出重点，按照《商务部办公厅 财政部办公厅关于肉类蔬菜流通追溯体系建设试点指导意见的通知》（商秩字［2010］279号）精神和今天签署的协议，把试点工作抓紧、抓实、抓出成效，为下一步向全国推广进而实现追溯体系的网络化和全覆盖打下基础，积累经验。

（一）要作为“一把手”工程全力推进

强化“菜篮子”市长负责制，是国务院的明确要求。与过去相比，现在市长们不仅要让市民的“菜篮子”里面有肉有菜，还要让肉菜质量好、安全有保障。肉菜流通追溯体系建成了，市长们管好“菜篮子”会如虎添翼。因此，希望各试点城市把追溯体系建设纳入“菜篮子”市长负责制总体框架，作为“一把手”工程统筹推动。希望“一把手”亲自挂帅，分管市长直接负责，建立以商务主管部门为枢纽，农业、工商、质监、食品药品监管等相关部门参加的协调机制，形成肉菜流通管理和质量安全监管齐抓共管的局面。

尽管试点的主体是城市，但省级商务主管部门的工作丝毫不能放松。要加大协调力度，为试点城市在资金、人才、制度设计等方面创造条件、提供支持。这项工作要尽可能地争取主动，希望各位厅局长及时向上级领导汇报。

（二）要进一步完善落实试点工作方案

我国地域辽阔，各地情况千差万别，国家出台的任何一项政策措施，都不可能面面俱到。各试点城市要在把握政策实质、遵守法律法规的前提下，认真领会本次会议精神，学习借鉴上海等地的经验做法，进一步完善试点工作方案。要落实责任分工，明确目标进度，细化配套措施，狠抓工作落实，加强监督检查，确保每一项任务落实到位。大家务必要开动脑筋、大胆实践，创造性地开展工作。要及时发现和解决出现的问题，不断总结经验教训，通过健全法律法规、加强制度建设、完善标准体系，为追溯体系建设及运行提供有力保障。

（三）要大力推动现代流通体系建设

追溯体系与现代流通体系建设相辅相成。各地要按照十七届五中全会关于扩大内需、建立扩大消费需求长效机制的要求，抓紧制定商务发展“十二五”规划，并抓住国家推广应用物联网等技术的大好机遇，不断完善流通基础设施，着力推进连锁经营、物流配送和电子商务等现代流通方式，大力提高农产品标准化、品牌化、包装化经营程度，提高流通现代化水平。省级商务主管部门要统筹兼顾，把指导推动追溯体系建设与“双百市场工程”、“标准化菜市场改造”、“农超对接”、“放心肉服务体系建设”结合起来，为试点城市提供支持。试点城市要把发展现代流通纳入本市重点民生工程，切实加以推动。

（四）要加强经费保障，严格资金使用管理

近两年，国家为应对国际金融危机，实行积极的财政政策，中央财政并不宽裕。在这种情况下，2010年中央财政专门安排4亿元资金用于追溯体系建设试点，是很不容易的，充分表明了党中央、国务院对这项工作的高度重视，也充分表明财政部对这项工作的大力支持。但追溯体系的建设和运行需要大量投入，仅靠中央财政资金是不够的，希望各试点城市安排必要的配套资金，确保追溯体系能够建起来、用得上、可持续。

需要强调的是，财政资金都是纳税人的钱，我们决不能浪费挪用，更不能贪污腐败。试点城市商务主管部门要密切配合财政部门，制定完善的资金管理办法，切实用好管好资金，最大限度地发挥资金使用效益，从制度上防范奢侈浪费、贪污腐败等行为。各级商务主管部门、财政部门要加强资金使用情况的监督和检查。

（五）要坚持政府推动，市场化运作

肉菜流通追溯体系建设的过程，也是转变政府职能、调动市场开办者和经营户发挥主体作用、吸引消费者共同参与的过程，要坚持政府推动、市场化运作，综合运用经济、法律、行政手段，不能由政府部门大包大揽。要发挥新闻媒体的力量，宣传树立积极参与追溯体系建设、肉菜质量安全有保障的优秀企业典型，引导消费者主动选购可追溯肉菜。还要充分发挥舆论监督、社会监督作用，促进追溯体系不断完善。

建设全国肉菜流通追溯体系功在当代、利在千秋，人民期盼、任重道远。我们要以党的十七大和十七届三中、四中、五中全会精神为指导，深入落实科学发展观，同心同德，真抓实干，大胆探索，开拓创新，把这项工作认真抓好，为改善民生和促进流通现代化做出新的、更大的贡献。

（本文为作者于2010年10月21日在全国肉类蔬菜流通追溯体系建设试点工作会议上的讲话，略有删改）

加强和改善粮食宏观调控 切实保障国家粮食安全

国家粮食局局长 聂振邦

这次会议的主要任务是，深入学习贯彻党的十七大、十七届三中、四中全会和中央经济工作会议、中央农村工作会议精神，总结2009年粮食流通工作，分析当前面临的新形势，研究部署2010年的工作。

一、求真务实，2009年粮食流通各项工作成效显著

过去的一年，粮食部门深入学习实践科学发展观，认真贯彻落实党中央、国务院关于粮食工作的方针政策，努力克服国际金融危机的冲击和影响，顺利完成年初部署的“抓好收购促增收，充实储备强基础，清仓查库摸家底，加强调控稳市场，深化改革促发展”等重点工作任务，粮食流通各项工作取得新进展，保障了国家粮食安全，为保增长、保民生、保稳定做出了积极贡献。

（一）认真组织开展清仓查库，摸清了粮食库存家底

国务院高度重视全国粮食清仓查库工作，分别召开电视电话会议进行动员部署和总结，中共中央政治局常委、国务院副总理李克强两次到会并作重要讲话，成立了由发展改革委牵头，10个部门和单位共同组成的部际联席会议，办公室设在国家粮食局，具体承担清仓查库的组织协调等工作。地方各级人民政府按照部署和要求，成立相应工作机构，落实职责分工。各级粮食部门科学制订实施方案和检查方法，大规模、多层次培训检查人员。清查中，按照“在地检查”原则，坚持“有仓必到、有粮必查、有账必核、查必彻底”，对发现的问题边查边改，严肃查处涉粮违规违纪案件。据统计，地方各级政府和国家有关部门直接参与检查的人员124 756人，清查储粮库点29 965个，对1 765个重点非国有粮食企业和转化用粮企业粮食库存进行了典型调查，邀请6 375名人大代表和政协委员现场督导清查工作，提高了清查结果的透明度和公信力。

清查结果显示，2009年3月末全国国有粮食企业粮食总库存2254亿kg（原粮，下同），账实相符率99.7%，质量合格率97.1%，宜存率99.1%，全国粮食库存数量真实，质量良好，储存安全，管理比较规范，品种结构趋于合理，区域布局进一步改善。通过清查，达到了国务院领导同志要求的“让政府心中有数、让群众感到放心”的目的，检验和推进了粮食系统各项工作，增进了社会各界对粮食工作的了解，使各级政府落实“米袋子”负责制心中有了底，为加强粮食仓储管理和库存监管积累了丰富经验，为科学实施粮食宏观调控奠定了坚实基础。粮食部门的辛勤工作，得到领导同志的肯定和社会的认可，涌现了一批先进集体和先进个人，在这次会上要进行表彰。

（二）积极抓好粮食收购工作，保护了种粮农民利益

为增加种粮农民收入，2009年国家再次较大幅度提高小麦、稻谷最低收购价格水平，白小麦和红小麦、混合麦分别提高到每千克1.74元和1.66元，提价幅度分别为13%和15%，早籼稻、中晚籼稻和粳稻分别提高到每千克1.80元、1.84元和1.90元，提价幅度分别为17%、16%和16%；加大国家临时存储稻谷、小麦、玉米、大豆和中央储备大豆、菜子油的收储力度；创新托市收购机制，引导加工企业入市收购，对17个省份的中央直属和地方油脂加工企业托市收购油菜子给予补贴，对内蒙古自治区和黑龙江、吉林、辽宁省一定规模以上的大豆压榨企业入市收购大豆给予补贴，对南方16个饲料消费省份的定点企业和中央直属企业到东北三省和内蒙古自治区采购玉米给予补贴；对江苏、安徽、山东、河南、湖北等省部分受灾地区的芽麦实行保护性收购。各级粮食行政管理部门认真落实国家粮食收购政策，切实加强收购工作的组织协调和监督检查，指导和督促国有粮食企业发挥主渠道作用，引导和鼓励多元市场主体积极入市收购。初步统计，2009年全国各类粮食经营企业收购粮食2 876.5亿kg，同比减少25.5亿kg，其中国有粮食企业收购1 632亿kg，同比减少69亿

kg。全年收购托市粮食（含油菜子）919.5 亿 kg，其中小麦 418.5 亿 kg、稻谷 111.5 亿 kg、玉米 275 亿 kg、大豆 46 亿 kg、油菜子 78.5 亿 kg。初步测算，上述政策的实施，拉动市场价格回升，促进农民增收 400 多亿元，为保护农民种粮积极性、扩大农村消费、促进经济平稳较快发展发挥了积极作用。

各地积极采取措施抓收购，主动掌握调控粮源，努力增加农民收入。据黑龙江省反映，农民出售稻谷、玉米、大豆的收入，比 2008 年增加近 70 亿元。新疆维吾尔自治区政府决定，对小麦、稻谷按最低收购价敞开收购，并分别给予每千克 0.2 元和 0.21 元的直接补贴，对油葵实行保护价收购，各项措施使农民增收约 20 亿元。广西、浙江、福建等省、自治区进一步完善储备订单与补贴收购相结合的办法，较大幅度提高了补贴标准。

（三）切实落实各项宏观调控措施，维护了全国粮食市场稳定

1. 加强中央和地方储备粮管理　服从和服务于国家宏观调控、稳定市场粮价的需要，指导中储粮总公司落实中央储备粮轮换计划、油料收购计划和进口转储备计划。会同有关部门下达食用植物油地方储备规模指导性计划。各地按照要求积极充实地方粮食储备规模，健全储备体系，提高储备粮油管理水平。据统计，2009 年末地方粮、油储备分别比上年同期增加 2.8%和 43%，其中河北、山西、陕西、浙江、新疆等省、自治区增加较多。

2. 做好政策性粮食竞价销售、移库和产销衔接工作　根据宏观调控的需要，合理安排政策性粮食竞价销售，2009 年累计成交 655 亿 kg，满足了市场需求。将国家临时存储的 57.5 亿 kg 玉米和 19.5 亿 kg 大豆划转给地方作为临时储备，定向销售给加工企业，促进国产玉米和大豆的加工转化。下达 90.5 亿 kg 临时存储粮和 1.9 万 t 中央储备菜子油跨省移库计划，充实销区库存，优化了库存布局。多次举办粮食产销衔接交易会、贸易洽谈会、精品展销会，签订粮食购销合同 200 亿 kg。认真落实关内销区到东北采购粳稻（大米）运费补贴政策，采购粳稻（大米）62.5 亿 kg，有力促进了产销衔接，搞活了粮食流通。

3. 加强粮食统计、信息和应急体系建设　加强和改进粮食统计工作，认真完成粮食购销存统计、粮油加工业统计和供需平衡调查等基础工作。建立政策性粮食收购 5 日报、大米市场监测旬报、临时收储油菜子和东北地区定向销售月报等制度，调整粮油市场信息监测点布局，健全信息监测系统，加强粮食市场监测预警分析，为粮食宏观调控提供了可靠的决策依据。各地进一步完善本地区粮食应急预案，健全应急保障体系，一些省市积极组织培训和应急演练，不断提高应急保障水平。

4. 加强军粮供应管理工作　牢固树立“以兵为本”服务宗旨，落实“平战结合”工作方针，突出抓紧抓好规范化管理和战备应急保障工作。紧贴部队后勤保障需求，推进军粮供应战备应急机制和应急设施建设，不断提升军粮供应体系的综合保障能力，保证了部队日常供应、重大活动和应急用粮需要。

（四）积极推进粮食流通体制改革，国有粮食企业改革取得新成效

1. 粮食流通体制改革继续深化　积极推进粮食行政管理部门职能转变，把粮食行政管理部门的工作重心转到粮食市场调控、监管和行业指导、服务上来。加强粮食成本利润调查，及时提出政策性收购粮食价格水平建议，研究完善粮食价格形成机制。积极培育和发展多元市场主体，目前具有收购资格的多元市场主体达到 6.7 万个。广东、浙江等省逐级签订粮食安全责任书，制定考核办法并组织实施，促进了粮食行政首长负责制的落实。河南、四川等省加快城镇连锁经营店和农村服务网点建设，初步建成了覆盖全省的新型粮油购销服务网络。

2. 国有粮食企业改革和发展步伐加快　积极协调和配合有关部门制定政策性粮食财务挂账消化、未占用农发行贷款的政策性亏损处理、占用商业银行贷款挂账划转，以及支持企业消化经营性财务挂账等政策，明确中央和地方储备粮承储企业免征营业税、印花税、房产税和城镇土地使用税等政策，为企业改革发展创造良好政策环境。加强对企业产权制度改革的指导，严格规范改革改制行为，保护职工合法权益。截至 2009 年底，全国国有粮食企业总数 18 163 个，其中购销企业 12 567 个，比 1998 年分别减少 65%、59%，企业布局和结构进一步优化，提高了市场竞争力。指导和促进企业加强经营管理，提高经济效益。2009 年全国国有粮食企业统算盈利 52.4 亿元，同比增加 31.1 亿元，为历史最好水平。其中国有粮食购销企业统算盈利 45.2 亿元，同比增盈 26.9 亿元。吉林、黑龙江、河南、云南、陕西、青海等 25 个省份及新疆生产建设兵团实现了盈利，其中北京、上海、山东、湖南和四川等 5 个省（直辖市）已连续 5 年盈利。

3. 粮食产业化经营积极推进　会同农发行出台支持现代粮食流通产业发展的政策，在政策性粮油收储、自主购销和产业化龙头企业发展等方面，加大对企业的信贷支持力度；重新审核重点支持的 1 684 个产业化龙头企业，继续提供贷款支持，促进企业做大做优做强。各地通过信贷支持、财政贴息、退城进郊兴办粮食产业园区等多种方式，积极培育产业化龙头企业，延长产业链条，促进农民增收、企业增效。安徽省出台一揽子促进粮食产业化发展和精深加工的优惠政策，规划和建设产业园区、产业集聚区 98 个，已完成投资 35.6 亿元。湖南省在技改贷款贴息、创建驰名品牌等方面给予政策支持，促进粮食产业化龙头企业发展。

（五）加强粮食流通产业建设，粮食流通现代化水平进一步提高

1. *粮食流通基础设施和物流体系建设迈出新步伐* 落实国务院“建设粮食储备仓容 1 500 万 t、储备油罐 175 万 t”的计划，两年安排中央投资 42.6 亿元用于粮油仓储设施建设。从 2008 年第 4 季度到 2009 年底，已安排中央补助投资 29.5 亿元用于粮油仓储物流和烘干设施专项建设，进一步缓解我国食用油罐容不足和重点粮食产区仓储、烘干能力不足的压力。落实仓房维修改造资金 3 亿元，改善 15 个省份实施政策性粮食收储的设施条件。天津、河北、江苏、福建、广西、甘肃、新疆等地通过直接投资、补助投资或以奖代补等多种形式，加快本地粮食仓储等基础设施建设。

2. *粮食市场体系建设取得新进展* 继续贯彻落实全国粮食市场体系建设规划，22 个省（自治区、直辖市）出台了本地粮食市场建设规划或指导意见。国家粮食交易中心总数达到 22 个，全国统一竞价交易平台联网市场已达 23 个，顺利完成了国家政策性粮食的销售任务。大中城市成品粮油批发市场继续呈现强劲发展势头，浙江省 80%以上的商品口粮通过批发市场中转流通。北京、上海、福建、湖北、广东、江苏、宁夏、浙江、贵州等地出台优惠政策，投入专项资金扶持市场建设。

3. *粮油加工业和科技创新取得新成效* 粮油加工业多元化主体格局初步形成，技术水平不断提升，主要产品产量和企业效益持续增长。以大型龙头企业和粮食物流枢纽为依托，加工产业园区建设明显加快，内蒙古、江苏、山东、湖北、黑龙江等省、自治区在推进精深加工与综合利用等方面亮点突出。组织行业优势资源，申报粮食产后国家工程实验室，国家粮食局科学研究院粮食储藏实验室建设项目正式竣工验收。成功举办以“科学消费植物油”为主题的粮食科技周和科普宣传活动，粮食科技创新体系进一步完善，粮食宏观调控信息保障技术、粮食储藏质量检测等科技研发和推广取得重要成果。

4. *“农户科学储粮专项”工程和“放心粮油”工程取得新成绩* 认真编制农户科学储粮规划，扩大专项实施范围，在辽宁、吉林、江西等 14 个粮食产区，安排中央补助、地方配套和农户自筹资金 6.7 亿元，为 57.2 万个农户建设标准化小型粮仓，改善农户储粮条件，目前辽宁、山东、安徽等省已基本完成建设任务。“放心粮油”工程已经成为深受广大消费者和社会各方面欢迎的“民心工程”。据不完全统计，全国各地放心粮油生产企业已经建立各类销售网点 17 万多个，其中农村网点 6 万多个。山西省和山东济南、陕西西安等地“放心粮油”工程和“主食厨房”工程成效显著。

（六）加强制度建设和市场监管，粮食依法行政能力和服务水平进一步提高

1. *积极推进粮食立法* 以贯彻两部条例为主线，研究制定年度普法依法治理要点，全面总结“五五”普法以来粮食行业法制宣传教育工作，河北、浙江、甘肃省粮食部门的普法工作获得中宣部、司法部、全国普法办表彰。继续做好粮食收购资格和中央储备粮代储资格审核工作，目前全国具有粮食收购资格的经营者 8.55 万个；具有中央储备粮、油代储资格的企业分别为 1 907 户和 208 户，资格仓容、罐容分别达到 10 115 万 t 和 319 万 t，资格企业布局趋于合理。认真贯彻落实党中央、全国人大和国务院关于制定《粮食法》的要求，成立了由 17 个部门有关负责同志组成的领导小组及工作组，认真开展专题调研，积极做好《粮食法（草案）》研究起草工作。

2. *加强监督检查和标准质量工作* 继续巩固和加强监督检查体系、质量监测体系建设成果，全国 31 个省份及新疆生产建设兵团、82%的市地级和 70%的县级粮食部门设立了监督检查机构，纳入国家粮食质量监测体系的质检机构已达 197 个。进一步完善粮食监督检查和质量安全监管制度，加强粮食市场日常监管和政策性粮食购销专项检查，认真督查、查办涉粮案件和粮食质量安全事件。认真贯彻《食品安全法》，继续抓好标准制修订工作，《稻谷》、《玉米》、《大豆》等国家标准相继实施，认真开展粮食质量与原粮卫生的调查、抽查与监测，积极履行国际标准化组织谷物与豆类分技术委员会秘书处职责和成员国义务。

3. *加强粮食仓储规范化管理和安全生产工作* 全面启动仓储规范化管理工作，开展粮食行业安全生产执法、治理和宣传“三项行动”。全面总结近年来粮食行业安全生产工作经验，实地调查分析贵州、吉林等地事故发生的原因，开展粮油仓储设施安全隐患排查工作，强化粮油仓储设施使用管理，进一步加强教育培训，增强安全生产意识，规范操作行为，落实安全责任，严防重特大事故发生。

4. *加强粮食行业服务工作* 发挥粮食行业协会、

粮食贸促会、粮油学会、粮经学会等社团组织作用，成功举办新中国成立60周年成就展、粮油精品展、世界粮食日、爱粮节粮周等活动，充分展示粮食系统改革发展的巨大成就和精神风貌。大力开展“放心粮油”进农村进社区活动。围绕国家粮食安全研究重大问题，积极组织开展课题研究，提出政策建议。继续加强粮食仓储、物流、加工、科技和信息等方面的对外交流与合作，扩大国际合作领域。继续加强新闻宣传和政务信息公开，为粮食流通工作创造良好的舆论环境。

（七）加强党的建设、廉政建设、作风建设和干部职工队伍建设，粮食行业整体素质进一步提高

认真开展深入学习实践科学发展观活动，贯彻落实十七届四中全会精神，加强和改进党的建设，努力把学习实践科学发展观的成果转化为谋划粮食流通科学发展的思路、促进粮食流通科学发展的措施、领导粮食流通科学发展的能力。落实中纪委全会和国务院廉政工作会议部署，以切实保护种粮农民利益、中央扩大内需投资监督检查和全国粮食清仓查库为重点，整体推进粮食系统党风廉政建设。深入开展“讲党性、重品行、作表率”活动，加强机关作风建设，深入实际开展调查研究，扎扎实实为基层群众解难事、做实事、办好事。抓好职工教育培训和技能人才培养，推进职业技能鉴定工作，提高粮食系统干部职工队伍素质。

二、统一认识，正确把握粮食流通工作面临的新形势

2010年是实施“十一五”规划的最后一年，是巩固和发展粮食流通体制改革成果，进一步完善宏观调控政策措施，继续推进现代粮食流通产业发展的关键之年，粮食流通工作面临新的形势和任务，也将迎接新的机遇和挑战。我们要切实把思想和行动统一到中央对国际国内经济形势的判断上来，统一到深入贯彻落实科学发展观的要求上来，统一到中央关于今年经济工作和农村工作的决策部署上来，坚定信心，顽强拼搏，坚决贯彻中央对经济工作和农村工作的总体要求，全面落实“五个更加注重”，紧紧围绕加大统筹城乡发展力度、进一步夯实农业农村发展基础这个主题，紧密结合粮食流通工作实际，深入分析新形势，正确把握工作重点。

（一）根据中央关于经济形势的分析和粮食工作的部署，正确把握粮食流通工作的重点

近些年来，党中央、国务院不断加大强农惠农政策力度，保护和调动地方抓粮、农民种粮积极性，粮食生产连续6年丰收，国家粮食库存充裕，保证粮食安全的物质基础更加坚实，为有效应对国际金融危机和粮食危机、促进国民经济平稳较快发展、维护社会和谐稳定做出了积极贡献。但国际金融危机对我国农业和农村经济的负面影响仍在持续，国际市场主要农产品价格震荡，国内农业和粮食生产基础仍不稳固，种粮比较效益偏低。当前，我国经济形势总体回升向好，但基础还不牢固，资源性税费和资源性产品价格改革都将形成价格上涨压力，粮食生产成本将进一步增加，考虑到通货膨胀预期和国际粮油市场价格等因素，单纯依靠提高粮食价格带动农民增收的空间缩小，促进种粮农民增收和粮食稳产增产的难度加大。要深入贯彻党的十七大和十七届三中、四中全会精神，认真落实中央经济工作会议、中央农村工作会议部署，粮食流通工作的重点是落实各项强农惠农政策，努力促进粮食稳产增产和种粮农民增收；完善宏观调控政策，维护国内粮食市场和价格基本稳定；充分发挥各方面的积极作用，大力推进现代粮食流通产业发展；强化粮食安全的各项基础性工作，切实保障国家粮食安全。

（二）根据国际国内粮食供求和价格形势变化，正确把握粮食宏观调控的重点

近年来，国际国内粮食供需发生深刻变化，粮食宏观调控面临的形势更加复杂，任务更加艰巨。从国际市场看，经过2007—2008年大幅波动后，全球粮食价格回落，呈现震荡整理状态。联合国粮农组织预计2009/2010年度世界谷物产量22.38亿t，消费22.28亿t，库存5.10亿t，库存消费比22.88%，为2003年以来次高水平。但由于经济衰退、气候变化、许多发展中国家粮食生产水平相对较低等原因，世界粮食生产的不确定性增大；受人口增加、生物燃料发展等因素影响，粮食需求将继续呈刚性增长；加上金融投机行为对粮食市场影响加大，粮价大幅度波动的可能性依然存在，世界粮食形势不容乐观。从国内形势看，2009年我国粮食总产量为5 308亿kg，创历史新高，粮食消费保持平稳增长，当年粮食产需基本平衡。分品种看，小麦、玉米产需平衡有余较多，稻谷总量平衡有余但粳稻供求趋紧，大豆产需缺口较大，食用植物油对外依存度高。目前国家掌握的粮食库存充裕，油脂油料库存比去年同期增加一倍多，调控的物质基础比较雄厚，但商品周转库存有所下降，“北粮南运”格局日益突出，畅通粮食流通渠道和加强产销衔接的任务繁重，粮食库存品种结构和区域布局还需进一步优化。从长期趋势看，我国农业资源不足的矛盾将长期存在，促进粮食生产稳定发展的长效机制尚未完全形成，保证粮油市场供应和价格基

本稳定面临较大压力。粮食宏观调控要立足于促进粮食供求总量、品种结构、区域布局基本平衡和市场基本稳定，重点是完善储备体系，充实销区和薄弱地区粮食库存，增强调控市场能力；安排落实好政策性粮食收购和销售，引导粮食生产结构调整，促进粮食生产和流通协调发展；统筹生产、加工、流通、消费和进出口，综合运用储备调节、进出口、产销衔接等措施，稳定粮油产品价格，避免市场大幅波动。

（三）根据粮食流通体制改革进程，正确把握国有粮食企业改革和发展的重点

随着粮食流通体制改革的不断深入，国有粮食企业改革和发展进入了一个崭新阶段，经营管理状况不断好转，连续3年实现盈利。但是，目前企业产权制度改革依然滞后，政策环境需要进一步改善，具有竞争实力企业不多，尤其是部分基层国有粮食购销企业经营机制不活，经营方式粗放，自主经营困难，保持良好发展态势的基础不牢固。国有粮食企业改革和发展要立足于促进现代粮食流通产业发展，服务粮食宏观调控，构建新型粮食购销服务网络体系，发挥主渠道作用，重点是推进基层粮食购销企业战略性兼并重组，优化产权结构，促进企业做大做优做强；积极推进企业转换经营机制，改进经营方式，增强企业活力；指导企业加强经营管理，继续提高经济效益，不断扩大减亏增盈成果。

（四）根据粮食流通产业发展现状，正确把握推进现代粮食流通产业发展的重点

近年来，在各级政府和有关部门的大力支持下，现代粮食流通产业取得长足发展，但与粮食流通工作实际需要和产业结构优化升级的要求相比还有一定差距。主要是：粮油仓储设施的有效仓容和功能不能满足需要，布局不够合理，部分基层网点设施年久失修。据不完全统计，1 000多亿千克仓容亟须维修改造；粮食物流体系和市场体系发展在地区间不平衡，粮油加工产能过剩，科技含量和产品附加值低，推动粮油加工业升级的要求愈显迫切；粮食产业化组织程度低，龙头企业缺少政策和资金支持，对产业发展的带动作用还需要增强；加强行业管理、指导推进产业发展的手段和资源与实际需要差距较大。发展现代粮食流通产业要立足于促进产业结构升级和科学发展，重点是落实好国家扩大内需的政策，切实加强粮食仓储、物流体系和市场体系建设，提高粮食安全储存水平和流通效率；推动粮油加工业升级改造和资源整合，优化产业布局，提高加工产品综合利用率；大力培育和发展粮食产业化龙头企业，延长产业链条，促进农民增收、企业增效和经济发展。

（五）根据全国粮食清仓查库结果，正确把握粮食流通监管工作的重点

在充分肯定粮食仓储管理、库存监管和质量安全监管工作取得明显成效的同时，要高度重视这次清仓查库过程中发现的问题。目前，个别企业政策执行不到位，对库存管理的重要性认识不够，粮食安全储存、安全生产制度落实不到位，存在安全隐患；粮食库存增加，政策性粮食的比重增大，粮食监管机构、队伍建设与新形势下的粮食流通监管任务还不适应；粮食质量安全检验检测手段不完善，原粮卫生监管难度加大，监测预警工作亟待加强。粮食流通监管工作要立足于保障各项粮食流通政策和制度的贯彻落实，保障粮食库存数量真实、质量良好、储存安全，重点是完善监管制度，落实监管责任，健全监管体系，加大监管力度，强化粮食仓储管理、库存和质量监管，加强对粮食流通政策和制度落实情况的监督检查，维护粮食正常流通秩序和质量安全。

三、开拓进取，扎实做好2010年粮食流通各项工作

新的一年，要认真贯彻落实好国务院、国家发展和改革委员会领导同志的重要批示要求，进一步加强和改善宏观调控，保障国家粮食安全，维护粮食市场和价格基本稳定，服务“三农”，促农增收，深化改革，完善储备体系和手段，发展和壮大现代粮食流通产业，切实抓好粮食流通各项工作。2010年粮食流通工作的总体要求是：全面贯彻党的十七大和十七届三中、四中全会精神，高举中国特色社会主义伟大旗帜，以邓小平理论和“三个代表”重要思想为指导，深入贯彻落实科学发展观，认真落实中央经济工作会议、中央农村工作会议的部署和全国发展改革工作会议的要求，按照“发展产业壮实力、加强调控保安全”的基本思路，以加强宏观调控、深化体制改革、发展流通产业、推进依法管粮、加强行业建设为着力点，实现抓好收购、促农增收、保证供应、稳定市场、统筹发展、保障安全的目标，促进粮食流通事业科学发展，为巩固经济回升向好势头、促进国民经济平稳较快发展发挥特有优势，作出新的贡献。

（一）加强和改善粮食宏观调控，维护粮食市场和价格基本稳定

1. 切实抓好粮食收购 2010年白小麦和红小麦、混合麦最低收购价分别提高到每千克1.80元和1.92元，继续提高稻谷最低收购价。各级粮食部门要认真落实小麦、稻谷最低收购价政策，黑龙江、吉林、辽宁、江苏等粳稻主产区要通过储备粮轮换及时充实粳

稻储备，南方销区要利用运费补贴等优惠政策组织企业积极到产区采购。国有粮食企业要积极入市收购，力争多掌握稻谷粮源，以备调控、稳定市场和保证供应的需要。要切实抓好玉米、大豆、油菜子临时收储工作，继续落实和完善对加工企业托市收购的补贴政策。要深入研究分析粮食供求形势和价格走势，加强对粮食收购工作的指导和督促检查，继续发挥国有粮食企业主渠道作用，积极引导多元主体入市收购。各地粮食部门和托市收购主体要提前做好收购准备工作，相互支持，密切配合，共同完成好粮食收购任务，切实把国家粮食收购政策落到实处，防止收购不畅导致“谷贱伤农”。

2. *提高服务水平，方便农民售粮*　各级粮食行政管理部门、中储粮系统、粮食收购企业和其他托市收购政策执行主体要做好政策宣传，接受农民咨询，提供信息服务，增设收购网点，千方百计方便农民售粮。特别是在售粮高峰期间，要尽量缩短农民排队等候时间，努力做到随到随卖，为农民提供热情、周到、细致的服务。要严格执行质价政策，坚持优质优价，不得压级压价损害农民利益，也不得抬级抬价损害国家利益，让农民满意，让党和政府放心。

3. *认真搞好粮油市场调控*　各级粮食部门和调控执行主体要把认识和行动统一到国家粮食宏观调控的政策措施上来，服从和服务于保证供应、稳定市场的大局。继续做好政策性粮食销售，把握竞价销售节奏和力度，满足市场需要，稳定市场价格。做好政策性粮食跨省移库工作，充实薄弱地区库存。各地要高度重视政策性粮食出库等工作，严格执行有关规定，保证销售和出库工作顺利进行。继续按照“做强企业，深度合作，扩大规模，共同发展”的思路，引导和支持沿海、西南、西北地区的粮食销区与主产区建立多形式、深层次、长期稳定的产销合作关系，促进粮食总量、品种结构和区域供求基本平衡。落实好国家农产品进出口调控的要求，防止大豆、油料过度进口冲击国内市场。新春佳节即将到来，各级粮食部门要加强粮油市场调控和监管，精心组织货源，切实保障供给，稳定粮油市场价格，保证粮油产品质量安全，让广大消费者吃上放心粮油。

4. *进一步加强储备粮管理*　切实加强对中央储备粮的行政管理和监督，完善轮换机制，优化区域布局和品种结构，适时增加稻谷特别是粳稻的储备数量，对今年新增的稻谷储备规模，要利用当前收购旺季的有利时机抓紧落实到位。继续推进中央储备粮轮换，通过规范的粮食批发市场公开进行，使轮换与宏观调控要求相适应。完善中央储备粮代储资格认定制度，加强对资格企业的管理，为中央储备粮的存储安全创造条件。配合有关部门开展理顺国债投资建设粮库产权和管理关系的后续工作。各地要进一步加强地方储备粮体系建设和规范管理，充实粮油储备规模和应急成品粮油储备，未完成计划的省份要加大工作力度，按照国家下达的计划抓紧落实到位。

5. *不断完善粮食应急体系和统计、信息体系建设*　进一步完善粮食应急体系，细化和完善粮油储备应急动用方案，健全应急加工和供应网点体系。继续完善军粮供应管理制度，推进应急保障机制和设施建设，提高应急保障能力，保证任何情况下的军粮供应。加强全社会粮食流通和加工业统计工作，组织好社会粮食、食用植物油和油料供需平衡调查，加强粮食市场信息体系建设，做好粮食市场监测预测和信息发布工作。

（二）充分利用清仓查库成果，健全粮食库存管理长效机制

2009 年全国粮食清仓查库在基本原则、组织方式、操作方法等方面有很多创新，发现了各地库存管理中好的做法和经验，也找出了问题和不足。要以这次清仓查库工作为契机，充分利用工作成果，抓紧完善相关制度，用制度管粮、用制度管事、用制度管人，健全粮食库存管理长效机制，加大库存检查力度，推动粮食库存管理工作再上新台阶。完善和落实粮食库存“在地检查”原则，探索建立与粮食事权相适应的库存监管机制。坚持例行检查与专项检查相结合，提前通知与突击暗访相结合，账务检查和实物检查相结合，创新方式方法，规范工作程序，注重检查效果。经常邀请人大代表、政协委员督导监管粮食工作，做好举报和投诉受理工作，及时向社会发布粮食工作信息，增强粮食库存监管工作透明度和公信力。细化仓储管理制度，完善监管机制，督促企业严格内部管理，加强日常管理，逐步实现粮食仓储管理的规范化、精细化。

（三）深化粮食流通体制改革，促进粮食企业健康发展

1. *进一步推进粮食行政管理部门职能转变*　切实落实中央关于粮食工作的方针政策，按照政府职能定位和保障国家粮食安全的要求，加快推进粮食行政管理部门把工作重心转到宏观调控、市场监管、行业指导和做好服务上来。积极推进现代粮食流通产业发展，着力构建新型粮食购销服务网络体系，努力提高全社会粮食流通管理和服务水平，努力保护种粮农民利益，努力保障粮食有效供给，切实维护粮食市场基本稳定。各地要贯彻落实好国务院文件要求，稳定、加强和充实粮食行政管理机构和职能，落实工作经费，确保地方粮食行政管理部门履行好各项行政管理职责。

2. 研究完善粮食价格形成机制　完善粮食价格形成机制是粮食流通体制改革的一项重要任务，摸清各主要粮食品种的生产成本、农民收益等情况，是研究制定粮食价格政策和完善价格形成机制的重要基础。各地要高度重视这项工作，落实调查人员和工作经费，合理选择调查对象，加强分析研究，提出政策措施建议，建立粮食成本利润调查长效机制。

3. 大力推进国有粮食购销企业产权制度改革　加大国有粮食购销企业产权制度改革力度，推进战略性调整，支持企业创新体制机制，完善购销网络，做大做强。支持大型国有粮食经营企业依据有关规定，以资产为纽带，兼并重组基层粮食购销企业，增强购销服务功能和市场竞争力。对规模小、资产质量差、没有区位优势、在粮食流通中不能发挥有效作用，又不能被兼并重组的企业实行租赁或拍卖。积极培育多元市场主体，鼓励和支持多元市场主体参与粮食经营，发挥其发展经济、搞活流通、增加就业的积极作用。

4. 加强对国有粮食企业经营管理工作的指导　指导国有粮食企业提高经营管理水平，增加盈利能力，以及通过贷款重组、呆账核销等有效办法，处理好经营性挂账。建立和完善国有粮食企业联系点制度、经营管理信息通报制度和对重点企业的经营分析制度，促进企业经营管理继续保持良好发展态势。加强对国有资产的监管，盘活资产存量，发挥资产使用效益。协调落实粮食收购资金等有关政策，支持基层粮食购销企业创新经营方式，摆脱经营困境。各地要积极争取地方政府的支持，安排专项资金解决富余职工分流安置中的资金缺口，落实好社会保障和再就业政策，切实维护职工合法权益。

（四）积极推进现代粮食流通产业发展，壮大粮食流通产业实力

1. 加强粮食流通基础设施建设　积极配合有关部门，完成好 1 500 万 t 储备仓容和 175 万 t 储备油罐建设任务，按照有关要求做好项目建设布局，避免低水平重复建设。落实好地方和企业配套资金，加强项目管理，确保如期建成。加快仓房维修改造和技术更新，改善粮食安全储存条件。各地要吸取贵州“10·17”重大安全事故教训，积极争取地方财政支持，加大仓房维修改造力度。加快建设粮食现代物流体系，建设大型物流节点，推广散粮运输，提高粮食流通效率。继续落实粮食市场体系建设规划，完善全国粮食竞价交易系统，规范粮食交易行为，促进粮食市场健康有序发展。各地要积极争取当地政府和有关部门支持，落实配套资金，加快粮食流通基础设施建设进程。

2. 加快发展粮食产业化经营　积极争取各级政府的支持，对粮食产业化龙头企业的固定资产购置、技术引进、技术升级改造和粮食生产基地建设所需资金给予专项补助或贷款贴息，全面提升企业自主创新能力和带动农民增收能力。有条件的地区，要依托粮食产业化发展企业集群，建设粮食物流和产业园区，提升粮食流通产业发展水平。进一步推进“放心粮油”进农村、进社区活动，惠及广大城乡居民。抓好示范企业建设，培育知名品牌，引导和带动全行业共同发展。

3. 推动粮食加工业发展、产业升级和科技创新　落实国家产业调整振兴规划，调整粮食加工业产业结构，防止盲目建设，引导粮油加工业向规模化、集约化方向发展，提高科技含量和附加值。会同有关部门编制完善《粮食加工业发展规划》并组织实施，争取有关部门支持一批粮油加工技术改造升级项目。继续加强粮食行业科技创新体系和科技创新平台建设，推动宏观调控信息、绿色储粮、减少储备损失等国家科技支撑计划项目和高技术产业化重点项目实施，引领行业科技进步。

4. 切实抓好农户科学储粮专项建设　14 个省、自治区务必按照承诺和有关要求，加快实施进度，确保按期完成 2009 年度农户科学储粮专项建设任务。继续加大对农户科学储粮专项的支持力度，积极争取安排中央补助投资。各地要采取有效措施，积极筹措落实资金，强化项目管理，搞好技术指导和服务，使农户科学储粮专项建设达到预期的效果，真正使农民受益。

（五）加强粮食法制建设，积极推进依法管粮

1. 认真完成《粮食法（草案）》研究起草工作　《粮食法（草案）》的研究起草工作是一项系统工程，涉及粮食生产、流通和消费各环节的制度建设，要以确保国家粮食安全为立法宗旨，切实加强调查研究，广泛征求各方面意见，提高立法质量。各地要给予大力支持，积极建言献策，共同完成好这项任务。要继续认真贯彻执行两部条例，进一步做好粮食收购资格审核、粮食行政复议、中央储备粮代储资格认定和对资格企业的检查工作。

2. 加强粮食监督检查和标准质量建设工作　各级粮食行政管理部门要继续加强粮食监督检查体系和质量检验检测体系建设，尤其要重视加强市、县级监督检查机构和队伍建设，完善规章制度，落实工作经费。推进粮食库存监管信息系统建设，建立健全粮食库存管理和监督检查责任制，落实粮食质量安全地方责任。组织开展面向全社会粮食流通的监督检查、中央和地方储备油库存专项检查，加强对最低收购价、临时存储等粮食库存例行检查和政策性粮食购销活动的监督检查，以及收购资格、代储资格、质量安全等专项检查，加大涉粮案件查处力度。继续开展粮食质量安全调查、抽查与监测，加大库存粮食质量安全隐患排查力度，严防不符合质量安全标准的粮食流入口粮市场。

3. 推进粮食仓储管理和安全生产工作　完善粮油仓储制度体系，健全新型粮油仓储管理机制，做好粮油仓储管理办法及其配套制度的宣传和贯彻落实工作。继续深入开展粮油仓储企业规范化管理活动，深刻汲取2009年发生的几起重大安全生产事故教训，强化安全生产意识；深入开展隐患排查治理，规范企业管理行为，落实安全生产领导责任制，加强职工安全知识和技能培训教育，提高自我保护能力，确保粮食安全生产。

（六）总结粮食行业发展经验，认真研究制订“十二五”发展规划

全面总结“十一五”期间粮食行业发展经验，认真分析当前和今后一个时期粮食流通工作面临的新形势、新任务，按照国家关于编制全国“十二五”规划纲要和各地区、各行业专项规划的要求，围绕粮食流通体制改革、宏观调控、产业发展、质量安全等方面，深入研究国家粮食安全战略、流通基础设施建设、现代流通产业发展等重大问题，抓紧编制粮食行业“十二五”发展规划纲要和制修订粮食流通基础设施、市场体系、粮油加工业、科技发展、质量安全体系建设等专项规划，明确主要工作任务和工作重点，研究提出重点政策措施，推进并确保国家粮食安全战略目标的全面实现和现代粮食流通产业的健康发展。当前这项工作已经启动，各地要积极配合，上下联动，加强对建设项目和政策措施的研究论证，积极争取有关方面支持，增强规划编制的科学性、前瞻性和可行性，切实起到指导和推动粮食行业科学发展的积极作用。各地也要结合实际情况，加强部门互动和沟通衔接，及早研究制定本地区发展规划，并认真做好组织实施工作。

（七）深入贯彻落实十七届四中全会精神，着力加强粮食行业自身建设

落实中央部署，牢牢把握服务中心、建设队伍两大任务，以建设一流机关、打造一流队伍、培育一流作风、创造一流业绩为目标，以改革创新精神加强粮食系统党建工作，通过加强新形势下党的建设的新举措、新成效，保障粮食流通事业又好又快发展。进一步加强粮食系统党风廉政建设，加强党员干部廉洁从政教育和领导干部廉洁自律，加大违法违纪案件查办力度。继续加强干部职工队伍建设，推进行业职业资格制度建设，举办第二届全国粮食行业职业技能大赛，开展全国粮食系统先进集体、先进工作者（劳动模范）表彰活动。加强政务信息公开和电子政务建设工作，不断提高粮食工作信息化水平。充分发挥粮食部门政府网和《中国粮食经济》杂志、《粮油市场报》等新闻媒介的作用，积极开展新闻宣传。进一步发挥粮食行业协会、粮食贸促会、粮油学会、粮经学会等社团组织作用，继续加强对外交流与合作，认真开展粮食安全重大战略问题研究，使之服务于粮食流通中心工作。

（本文为作者于2010年1月11日在全国粮食局长会议上的工作报告，略有删改）

深入落实科学发展观 开创食品安全监管和消费维权新局面

国家工商总局副局长　王东峰

这次全国工商行政管理系统食品安全监管暨消费者权益保护工作会议，是继全国工商行政管理工作会议之后总局召开的一次十分重要的专项会议。主要任务是：全面落实科学发展观，深入贯彻党的十七大、十七届三中、四中全会和中央经济工作会议精神，以及全国工商行政管理工作会议的部署，总结2009年的工作，安排部署2010年的工作，交流工作经验，进一步推进流通环节食品安全监管和消费者权益保护工作制度化、规范化、程序化和法治化建设，努力开创流通环节食品安全监管和消费者权益保护工作新局面。总局党组和周伯华局长对召开这次会议非常重视，专门进行了研究，提出了明确要求，特别是周伯华局长在全国工商行政管理工作会议上的重要讲话，不仅充分肯定了流通环节食品安全监管和消费者权益保护工作的成绩，而且部署了新的任务。各级工商行政管理机关和广大干部要深刻学习领会精神实质，认真抓好贯彻落实。各省（自治区、直辖市）工商局分管局长和职能处室的处长及总局各司局主要负责同志积极按时参会，体现了大家对食品安全和消费维权工作的责任感和对会议的重视，相信通过大家的共同努力，会议一定会取得预期成效。下面，我讲几点意见：

一、积极应对国际金融危机，全力维护市场秩序和服务经济平稳较快发展，流通环节食品安全监管和消费者权益保护工作取得显著成效

2009 年是工商行政管理系统应对国际金融危机、服务经济平稳较快发展的重要一年，也是认真贯彻实施《食品安全法》、保障流通环节食品安全、保护消费者合法权益取得新成效的一年。一年来，各级工商机关在当地党委、政府的领导下，全面落实科学发展观，认真贯彻党中央、国务院的部署和中央“保增长、保民生、保稳定”的要求，全面落实全国食品安全整顿工作办公室的部署和全国工商行政管理工作会议的安排，认真开展专项执法检查，强化食品市场监管，加大消费维权工作力度，积极改革创新，各项工作取得了显著成效，保障了食品市场消费安全，有效地保护了消费者合法权益，为应对金融危机、促进经济平稳较快发展、促进和谐社会建设，发挥了重要作用。

（一）认真贯彻实施《食品安全法》，流通环节食品安全和食品添加剂专项整治取得新成效

全国各级工商机关把贯彻落实《食品安全法》和深入开展食品安全专项整治作为强化食品安全监管的重中之重，采取一系列措施，有力地保障了食品市场消费安全。国家工商总局就实施《食品安全法》提出了一个意见，制定了两个规章和八项制度，下发了《关于宣传贯彻实施〈食品安全法〉的通知》，在浙江召开了全国工商系统贯彻《食品安全法》工作会议暨流通环节食品安全监管长效机制建设现场会，推广了浙江、北京、上海、山东、江苏、新疆 6 个单位的典型经验，总局党组书记、局长周伯华同志亲自到会，对贯彻《食品安全法》和落实王岐山副总理的重要批示提出了新的要求。各省（自治区、直辖市）工商局采取有力措施，认真学习宣传贯彻《食品安全法》，切实落实总局有关文件规定，学习宣传贯彻《食品安全法》在全系统取得实实在在成效。

总局和各地工商机关认真贯彻国务院的部署，扎实有效地开展食品安全专项整治。总局下发了《流通环节食品安全整顿工作方案》，及时动员部署。各地突出重点，集中开展重点食品、重点区域以及季节性、节日性食品的专项执法检查、奶制品市场专项执法检查、流通环节打击食品添加剂违法行为专项执法检查、农村食品市场专项执法检查等，有效地解决了流通环节食品安全存在的一些突出问题。总局还在各地自查的基础上，于 2009 年 11 月组织了 15 个督查组进行专项检查，有力推动了食品安全监管和专项整治工作的落实。北京以传承奥运经验、巩固奥运成果为契机，全面提升首都食品流通监管水平，为保障国庆六十周年首都食品市场发挥了重要作用。山东济南、青岛对全运会食品市场全面监控，确保了流通环节食品安全万无一失。上海、浙江、广东、河南、辽宁、河北、山西、江苏在食品专项整治工作中措施有力，特别是专项整治力度大，食品安全示范店建设覆盖面广，效果明显。天津、四川、重庆、陕西、内蒙古、西藏、吉林、黑龙江在流通环节打击食品添加剂违法行为专项执法检查工作中成效明显。同时，各地不断强化食品安全日常巡查和规范化管理，依法核发食品流通许可证，积极推进和落实“两项制度”，有针对性地实施食品分类监管，在规范食品市场经营主体资格、保障食品质量和规范经营行为等方面取得了明显成效，有力地保障了食品市场消费安全。黑龙江、云南、福建、湖北、江西、海南等省食品流通许可证的核发工作部署早、行动快。江苏、广西、贵州、广东、福建等突出重点食品质量监管，强化抽样检验手段，有力促进了流通环节食品质量的提高。湖南、新疆、安徽、宁夏、青海、陕西等地推行“一票通”制度，力度大、效果好。尤其是甘肃省，“一票通”的覆盖率达到了 95%。吉林省全面有序开展全省流通环节食品安全监管规范年建设活动。浙江省宁波市以抓食品准入源头为切入点，推行食品经营者公开评价制度。据统计，2009 年，全系统共检查食品经营户 1 290.2 万户次，检查批发市场、集贸市场等各类市场 25.5 万个次，取缔无照经营食品 8.9 万户，捣毁食品制假售假窝点 3 530 个，查处流通环节食品案件 7.2 万件；检查食品添加剂经营者 48.6 万余户，查处违法案件 1 257 件。共核发食品流通许可证 20.1 万个。

（二）深入开展“质量和安全年”活动，农村商品市场、“家电下乡”市场专项整治工作取得新成果

全国各级工商机关认真贯彻国务院部署的“质量和安全年”活动和温家宝总理、王岐山副总理的重要指示、批示精神，扎实开展农村商品市场和“家电下

乡”市场专项整治，有力地维护了商品市场秩序。总局高度重视，进行专题研究，制订具体方案，及时下发专门通知，做出全面安排部署，并分别于2009年8月和11月先后两次组织专项督查。各地结合当地实际，集中执法力量，突出工作重点，全面开展专项整治工作，取得阶段性成效，有力地维护了“家电下乡”市场秩序，促进了“家电下乡”政策的具体落实。上海、浙江、湖南、江西、内蒙古、安徽等地精心组织，周密部署，查处了一批借“家电下乡”名义制假售假违法案件，社会反响良好。2009年，全系统共查处“家电下乡”市场违法案件2 198件，查处假冒和不合格家电5 316台。各地还全面加强流通领域商品质量监督检查，积极配合相关部门开展建材、室内装饰装修材料等市场专项执法检查，开展“清新居室”行动，依法查处制售假冒伪劣商品违法行为，有效地保护了消费者合法权益。江苏、北京、广东、辽宁等地采取规范商品质量监测、强化不合格商品市场清查等措施，进一步完善了流通领域商品市场准入退出制度。2009年，全系统共查处制售假冒伪劣商品违法案件8.93万件，案值11.01亿元。

（三）大力推进12315行政执法体系“四个平台”建设，消费维权水平得到新的提升

全国各级工商机关将12315行政执法体系“四个平台”建设作为改善民生和维护社会和谐稳定的一项重要工作，深入推进。总局制定下发了《关于加强12315行政执法体系“四个平台”建设的通知》、《关于加强“一会两站”规范化建设的意见》等文件，开发了“全国12315主要数据信息管理系统”，对“四个平台”规范化建设提出明确要求。各地加快12315中心建设和信息化网络升级、系统应用和数据汇总工作步伐，大力推进“一会两站”建设和12315进商场、进超市、进市场、进企业、进学校，消费维权公共服务能力和消费维权社会监督水平进一步提升。截至2009年底，已有11个省级局和328个地市局建立了12315集中受理中心，有22个省级局建立了12315数据分析中心。全国共建立“一会两站”44.2万个，比上年增加1.3万个，城市社区覆盖率达82.9%，农村村镇覆盖率达78.3%。福建、贵州、海南等省将12315行政执法体系“四个平台”建设作为服务民生的重要举措，积极争取地方党委、政府支持，扎实推进；特别是上海市工商局，在总局工作会议后，立即召开有各区县主管区、县长参加的“四个平台”建设工作会议，将部门行为上升为政府行为，有力地提升了“四个平台”建设水平。北京、甘肃、宁夏、广东、湖北通过加快12315系统升级改造步伐、开通12315短信受理平台等措施，12315信息化水平迈上新台阶；浙江、上海、江西、福建、甘肃实现了“一会两站”城乡全覆盖；天津、河北、内蒙古、山东、辽宁采取积极措施，12315“五进”覆盖面不断扩大；济南、厦门结合实际，强化12315申诉举报受理与处理和信息分析利用工作，全力服务全运会、海峡西岸经济区建设和区域经济发展大局，及时受理和处理消费者申诉和举报。2009年，全系统共受理消费者申诉66.05万件，为消费者挽回经济损失6.51亿元。同时，各级工商机关积极会同商务等部门清理损害消费者权益的规定和收费，扎实开展服务领域专项执法检查，进一步规范了服务领域经营行为。上海、天津、浙江、山东突出预付卡领域和美容美发等重点行业，与相关部门、行业协会密切协作，服务领域消费维权工作深入推进。总局下发了《关于开展消费教育和消费引导工作有关问题的通知》，各地会同消费者协会，选择多种多样载体，动员社会各界力量，广泛开展宣传、教育、引导工作，积极营造良好的消费环境，有力地促进了消费需求的不断扩大。宁夏、湖北、四川、浙江结合实际开展丰富多彩的消费教育活动，取得良好效果。

（四）建立健全各项监管制度，流通环节食品安全监管和消费维权长效管理机制建设取得新进展

全国各级工商机关把制度建设作为保障流通环节食品安全和消费者权益保护工作的关键环节，积极有效地推进监管制度建设。国家工商总局结合贯彻《食品安全法》，及时制定颁布了《食品流通许可证管理办法》、《流通环节食品安全监管办法》两个部门规章；下发了《关于食品流通许可证印制发放和管理有关问题的通知》、《食品流通许可证格式》、《食品流通许可证编号编制规则》、《流通环节食品安全示范店规范指导意见》等规范性文件。各地积极推动地方立法立规，建立健全食品流通许可规范化管理和监管工作制度。全系统还集中开展了清理流通环节食品安全行政规章及规范性文件的工作。总局和各地工商机关以制度建设为重点，在长效监管机制上下功夫，建立健全和落实《食品市场主体准入登记管理制度》、《食品市场质量监管制度》、《食品市场巡查监管制度》、《食品抽样检验工作制度》、《食品市场分类监管制度》、《食品安全预警和应急处置制度》、《食品广告监管制度》、《食品安全监管执法协调协作制度》等八项制度，提高了流通环节食品安全监管的制度化、规范化、程序化和法治化水平。按照国家工商总局关于金信工程建设的总体规划，各地工商机关充分运用数字化、信息化、网络化等科技手段，积极构建流通环节食品安全监管业务平台、服务平台和内部管理平台，初步形成了食品安全监管信息化网络体系，提升了流通环节食品安全监管现代化水平。去年国家工商总局启动了《消费者权益保护法》的修订工作，各地广泛参与，认真研究，为进一步完善消费者权益保护法律法规体系提出了许多建设性宝贵意见。同时，各地积极建立健全区域性维权协作制度，加强12315网络平台与其他政府部门公共服务平台的执法协作，完善部门协调配合和与行业协会的情况通报制度，消费维权长效管理机制建设迈上新的台阶。湖南以建立食品抽检等五大机制为重点，提升了食品安全监管的现代化水平。广西建立健全“三个中心、一个平台”食品安全监管机制。北京、海南、新疆、广东、福建、辽宁、黑龙江积极利用信息化手段，大力推进食品安全电子化监管。杭州、西安积极推进小额消费纠纷快速解决、消费纠纷协商和解等制度，消费维权长效机制建设扎实推进。

（五）切实加强培训教育和队伍建设，食品安全监管与消费维权执法能力明显提高

各级工商机关按照建设政治上过硬、业务上过硬、作风上过硬的高素质干部队伍的要求，以贯彻实施《食品安全法》和落实新“三定”为契机，围绕食品安全和消费维权能力建设，加大培训力度，尤其是《食品安全法》出台后，各地分层分类进行全员培训，进一步提高了广大执法人员的监管能力和依法行政的水平。据统计，2009年，全系统共举办《食品安全法》培训班8 945期次，专题讲座3 970场次，培训工商干部115万余人次。同时，各地工商机关按照总局的部署，结合当地实际，严格落实流通环节食品安全监管和消费者权益保护工作责任制度，强化廉政风险点防范管理。各地还以基层食品安全和商品质量监管能力建设为重点，加强基层基础设施建设，努力保障执法装备、设备和经费，食品安全监管与消费维权执法水平明显提高。

总之，一年来，各省（自治区、直辖市）工商局充分发挥垂直管理的体制机制优势，各级工商机关积极努力工作，强化执法，有效维护了食品和商品市场消费安全。国家工商总局各相关司局，尤其是办公厅、法规司、竞争执法局、直销局、消保局、市场司、食品司、企业局、外资局、广告司、个体司、人事司、商标局、纪检组监察局、宣传中心、信息中心、中国消费者报社、中国消费者协会等，形成了上下协调一致的团队力量，发挥了重要职能作用，有力促进了食品安全监管和消费维权工作。经过全国工商系统广大工商干部的共同努力，流通环节食品安全监管和消费者权益保护各项工作取得了显著成绩。这些成绩的取得，是党中央、国务院和各级党委、政府正确领导的结果，是各级工商机关齐心协力共同努力工作的结果，特别是战斗在执法监管第一线的广大干部拼搏奋斗的结果，也是各有关部门积极配合协作的结果。

同时，我们也要清醒地认识到，在新的形势和新的挑战面前，流通环节食品安全监管和消费者权益保护工作还存在差距和不足。主要是按照服务科学发展和促进社会和谐稳定的要求，需要进一步更新思想观念和增强服务意识、发展意识和法制意识；按照有效保障流通环节食品安全和保护消费者合法权益的要求，需要进一步加大专项整治力度和日常监管执法力度；按照构建食品安全和消费维权长效机制的要求，需要进一步建立健全各项监管制度，创新监管机制，强化监管手段，特别是切实抓好制度的实施和落实工作；按照建设“三个过硬”高素质队伍的要求，需要进一步扎实推进食品安全和消费者权益保护工作队伍建设，全面提升监管能力和依法行政水平。对此，全国各级工商机关和广大工商干部必须高度重视，进一步采取有效措施，有针对性地加以改进和提高。

二、进一步认清形势，加大流通环节食品安全监管和保护消费者合法权益工作力度，积极促进经济社会又好又快发展

2010年是实施“十一五”规划的最后一年，也是夺取应对国际金融危机冲击全面胜利、保持经济平稳较快发展势头、为“十二五”规划启动实施奠定良好基础的重要一年。做好今年的食品安全监管和消费者权益保护工作对于促进经济平稳较快发展和构建和谐社会具有十分重要的意义。不久前召开的中央经济工作会议，对当前国内国际形势作了深刻分析和科学判断，对2010年经济工作作了全面部署。全国工商行政管理工作会议上周伯华局长在讲话中结合工商行政管理工作，就认清形势、统一思想和开创各项工作新局面提出了新的要求。各级工商机关要认真学习，深刻领会，认清形势，抓好贯彻落实。根据中央的部署和全国工商行政管理工作会议的安排，2010年流通环节食品安全监管和消费者权益保护工作的总体要求是：高举中国特色社会主义伟大旗帜，以邓小平理论和“三个代表”重要思想为指导，深入落实科学发展观，认真贯彻党的十七大、十七届三中、四中全会和中央经济工作会议精神，紧紧围绕落实中央保持经济平稳较快发展和加快经济发展方式转变的决策部署，根据全国工商行政管理工作会议安排，切实把握“四个只有”，努力做到“四个统一”，以保障流通环节食品安全和有效保护消费者合法权益为目标，在深

化专项整治、强化日常规范监管、完善服务体系、创新机制手段、提升执法效能和服务水平上狠下功夫，深入开展食品安全和“家电下乡”市场专项整顿，全面落实流通环节食品安全监管和消费维权各项制度，切实维护市场秩序和促进经济社会又好又快发展。

（一）深入开展消费教育消费引导和食品安全宣传，切实服务广大消费者、经营者和经济平稳较快发展

1. *加大消费教育和消费引导工作力度，积极服务和促进扩大消费需求及经济平稳较快增长* 各级工商机关要紧紧围绕扩大居民消费需求、改善民生和经济平稳较快增长，创造性地开展消费教育和消费引导工作，按照国家工商总局《关于开展消费教育和消费引导工作有关问题的通知》要求，突出重点，加大力度，选好载体，丰富内容和形式，注重实效，特别是要结合食品安全、商品质量监管和服务领域消费维权等工作，充分利用社会关注度较高、普及性较强的各种载体和形式，通过各类有效途径，动员社会各界力量，继续深入开展对消费者、生产经营者及行业协会的消费宣传教育和引导工作，积极培育消费热点，拓展居民消费领域，增加消费预期，扩大消费需求，充分发挥消费拉动经济增长的重要作用，积极服务经济平稳较快发展大局。国家工商总局将适时召开消费教育和消费引导工作经验交流会，总结和推广工作经验，发挥典型示范引导作用，推进消费教育和消费引导工作向纵深发展。各地要结合当地实际，创造新经验，取得新成果。

2. *加大食品安全和市场消费安全宣传力度，积极服务广大消费者、经营者和食品产业健康发展* 各级工商机关要进一步解放思想，着力破除和消除不适应、不符合科学发展观的思想观念和障碍，强化服务意识、发展意识和法制意识。既要坚持依法监管，切实为经济发展营造良好市场环境，又要加大服务工作力度，促进食品产业健康发展。各级工商机关要认真分析新形势，研究新问题，采取新举措，更好地服务广大消费者，特别是通过实事求是扩大正面宣传和消费知识的宣传，提高消费信心，促进消费者提高自我保护能力，切实解决消费者最关心、最直接、最现实的利益问题。要围绕食品生产经营者的市场准入、结构调整、开拓经营和提高市场竞争能力等各环节，结合工商机关职责，采取有力措施，积极服务企业转变发展方式，帮助企业排忧解难办实事，支持经营者提高产品质量和可持续发展能力，配合有关部门认真贯彻落实食品产业振兴规划。积极开展食品安全监管信息和消费维权信息的综合分析利用工作，既要为政府宏观决策提供参考，又要有针对性地监督、指导经营者提高自律能力和经营管理水平，为食品产业和经济平稳较快发展发挥积极作用。

（二）深入开展流通环节食品安全和食品添加剂专项整顿，切实保障食品市场消费安全

各级工商机关要在去年专项整顿成果的基础上，继续集中执法力量，突出工作重点，强化专项执法检查，加大监管执法力度，着力解决流通环节食品安全的突出问题，圆满完成国务院部署的两年食品安全和食品添加剂专项整顿工作各项任务。

1. *认真开展规范食品经营主体资格专项执法检查* 各级工商机关要对食品经营主体的经营资格进行全面清理、依法规范。要严格执行《食品安全法》及其《实施条例》和国家工商总局下发的《关于食品流通许可证印制发放和管理有关问题的通知》的规定，认真开展规范食品经营主体资格专项执法检查。要按照“谁登记、谁规范、谁负责”的原则，分别由各级食品流通许可、注册登记机构依法实施；按照“谁监管、谁清理、谁负责”的原则，由县级工商局组织，基层工商所采取逐户排查等办法依法实施。对发现存在食品主体准入方面的问题及时依法处理。要在当地政府的统一领导和协调下，按照相关部门的职责分工和工商机关各职能机构的职责分工，依法查处和取缔无照经营食品违法行为。

2. *开展对重点食品和重点区域、重点场所食品经营以及季节性、节日性食品市场专项执法检查* 继续突出消费量大、消费者申诉举报多以及群众日常生活必需的食品，以城乡结合部、社区、车站、码头、旅游景区为重点，加大市场巡查和专项整治力度，严厉打击制售假冒伪劣食品违法行为。要突出抓好对节日性食品以及季节性食品的检查，特别是元旦、春节、“五一”、“十一”、中秋等节日性食品的专项检查，尤其是要强化春节和“两会”期间食品市场监管，针对节日食品市场消费特点，突出重点食品品种和重点区域、场所，加大监管执法力度，重点整治不符合食品安全标准、过度包装、搭售商品、虚假宣传及欺诈消费者等问题，切实保障节日性、季节性食品市场消费安全。同时，要按照总局服务 2010 年上海世博会的总体部署，加强上海世博会期间流通环节食品安全监管工作，完善食品安全预警防范和应急处置机制，切实维护世博会食品市场秩序。

3. *认真开展打击流通环节违法添加非食用物质和滥用食品添加剂专项执法检查* 继续按照全国食品安全整顿工作办公室公布的非食用物质和添加剂的品种名单，对重点食品、重点区域和重点食品经营者，认真开展集中执法检查行动，依法规范食品添加剂经营者主体资格，依照《产品质量法》的规定强化对食品添加剂质量的监管。狠抓大要案件查办工作，依法严厉查处流通环节食品经营者在食品中添加非食用物质和滥用食品添加剂的行为以及违法销售食品添加剂的行为。

4. *认真开展奶制品市场专项执法检查* 要深入贯彻《乳品质量安全监督管理条例》和《奶业整顿和振兴规划纲要》以及国家工商总局的《实施意见》，依法履行《条例》、《纲要》赋予工商机关的职责，严格监督奶制品销售者落实进货查验和进销货台账制度。要加强对奶制品市场的专项执法检查，在检查中发现不符合食品安全标准的，要集中时间和执法力量对城乡市场奶制品经营者开展拉网式逐户清查，对辖区内经营者销售不符合食品安全标准的奶制品要依法监督或责令其全部停止销售、下架退市，不留死角。对已下架退市的奶制品，要在当地政府的领导和协调下，会同相关部门，分工协作，落实监管责任，该由生产企业召回的及时召回，该销毁的坚决依法销毁，严防再次流入市场。各地要按照全国食品安全整顿工作办公室的部署和总局的文件要求，认真负责地做好2008年问题乳粉处理和销毁情况的彻底清查工作，务必高度重视，严格责任制度，确保落到实处。对进口的奶制品，还要重点检查食品合格证、中文标签和中文说明书及相关手续。

5. *认真开展农村食品市场专项执法检查* 要结合农村食品市场特点，突出农民消费者日常生活食品消费的必需品种，加大对农村城镇、集镇、乡村举办的食品交易会、庙会等经营食品的监管力度，严格规范农村食品市场经营秩序。要加大对农村和乡镇各类食品批发市场、集贸市场和食杂店的监管和整治力度，规范连锁配送和送货下乡经营食品行为，依法打击制售假冒伪劣食品违法行为，切实保障农村食品市场消费安全。要认真落实国家工商总局下发的《流通环节食品安全示范店规范指导意见》，按照“两重点、三严格、四统一、五规范”的建设要求，加大工作力度，加快推进农村食品安全示范店建设进程，强化源头治理，充分发挥示范店的示范引导作用，切实维护农村食品市场秩序。

6. *认真开展对食品经营者履行法定责任义务的专项执法检查* 要按照《食品安全法》及其《实施条例》和国家工商总局《流通环节食品安全监督管理办法》的要求，严格依法监督食品经营者履行法定责任和义务。要把经营者严格食品质量市场准入行为、严格建立和执行进货查验与记录制度、严格履行内部食品质量管理等，作为其履行法定责任和义务的重点，列入食品安全专项整治工作，加大监督工作力度，务求实效。要严格监督商场、超市等企业，在巩固索证索票、进货台账“两项制度”成果的基础上，履行好进货查验和查验记录义务，严格落实企业内部食品质量管理责任，规范食品质量市场准入行为，切实把好食品进货关。要加强对食品经营者内部质量管理和质量控制的检查，督促经营者针对食品保质期的不同时间段采取有效的管理措施，引导其采取消费提示和食品有效期管理警示等防范措施，切实对消费者负责。要监督食品经营者建立健全食品安全管理制度，主要是食品质量管理、食品退市、应急处置、消费纠纷解决、从业人员健康管理等制度，切实落实食品安全管理责任。要积极引导食品批发市场、集贸市场、商场、超市与生产加工基地、重点企业建立“场厂挂钩”、“场地挂钩”等协议准入机制，切实从源头上保障食品安全。要积极鼓励有条件的商场、超市等食品经营者依法对查验的许可证件、食品合格的证明文件以及建立的进销货台账，采用信息化网络、扫描、拍照、数据交换、电子表格等科技手段，实行计算机管理；积极引导和督促食品经营者建立健全食品采购、贮存、运输、交易、退市和食品质量管理等环节的电子监控体系，探索和完善流通环节食品安全可追溯机制；积极鼓励和推进有条件的大中型食品企业、商场、超市和批发市场、集贸市场逐步实行计算机网络化管理，并加快与基层工商所信息化网络体系的有效对接，为逐步实现食品安全网上监管创造有利条件。

（三）深入开展食品市场巡查和强化日常规范监管，切实提高贯彻实施《食品安全法》和履行法定职责的能力和水平

要在开展食品安全专项整顿工作的同时，进一步强化食品市场日常规范监管，加大食品市场巡查力度，严格食品市场主体准入管理，严格食品质量监管，严格食品经营者行为的规范，依法查办食品安全大要案件，有效维护食品市场秩序，要进一步创新监管机制和手段，积极构建流通环节食品安全监管保障体系。

1. *严格市场主体准入管理，依法规范证照核发行为* 要严格按照法定条件、程序和有关规定核发《食品流通许可证》；坚持先证后照，对未获得相关许可文件的，一律不予登记注册，切实规范证照核发行为。要继续按照国家工商总局制定下发的《关于对食品经营主体予以特别标注的通知》的规定，对食品经营主体进行特别标注，加大对食品生产经营者的经济户口和信用分类管理力度。建立许可证发放机关与登记注册机关的信息沟通机制，依托工商系统信息化网络体系，实现食品流通许可机构与登记注册机构的互联互通，信息共享，及时依法规范食品经营主体资格。

2. 严格食品质量监管，依法规范食品质量抽样检验行为 要在严格监督食品经营者履行法定责任义务、建立两项制度、严把食品进货关的同时，切实加强对食品质量的监管，强化对食品质量的监督检查，从食品的入市、交易到退市进行全程监管。要加强对食品包装、标识、生产日期、保质期等的监督检查，严格规范食品经营者的经营行为。要严格落实《食品安全法》及其《实施条例》和国家工商总局有关规定和制度，依法开展流通环节食品抽样检验工作，认真执行当地政府有关流通环节食品安全检测计划，严格食品质量抽样检验工作程序和纪律，严格抽样检验信息发布和审核程序，重大情况和重要食品安全信息要及时向当地政府和省级卫生部门报告，各省级工商局要在当地政府领导和协调下研究制定具体办法。同时，要充分发挥食品抽样检验结果的作用，按照有关规定和程序进行消费提示和警示，有针对性地加强食品市场监管执法，并及时将有关情况通报相关职能部门和行业组织，促进食品安全的源头治理和行业自律。要把快速检测作为监管执法现场发现食品质量问题的重要技术手段，不断提升快速检测的科学性、针对性和准确性。快速检测结果不得作为行政执法依据。对快速检测发现有食品质量问题的，务必按照法定程序和经法定的质量检验机构依法检测认定才能作为执法依据。对经法定检验机构依法确认的不合格食品，要依法处理和有针对性地开展市场清查。要加大对不合格食品退市的跟踪监管力度，切实提高食品安全监控水平。要不断健全完善对不合格食品实施行政强制退市和经营者主动退市相结合的管理机制，确保不合格食品及时有效退市，并配合相关部门加强对不符合食品安全标准的食品退市后的跟踪监管，严防再次流入市场。

3. 严格食品市场巡查，依法规范食品市场监督检查和案件查办行为 要按照法律法规的规定和食品市场巡查监管制度的要求，强化市场巡查，将监管重心下移，严格落实基层工商所食品安全日常巡查和属地监管责任制。基层工商所要突出巡查检查重点，通过增加巡查频次、强化巡查措施、完善巡查机制、创新巡查手段，有针对性地开展市场巡查，切实提高巡查效能，着力解决重点市场、重点区域和重点食品经营者的突出问题，建立健全制度规范、责任明晰、执法严格、反应迅速、措施有力的巡查机制。要把监督食品经营者建立和落实各项自律制度作为日常监管的重要任务，及时发现、制止和查处违法行为，并将巡查记录纳入经营者食品安全监管档案和信用分类管理体系，激励守信者，查处违法者。要进一步将食品市场巡查与经济户口管理、食品质量监管、食品分类监管等结合起来，加强对食品经营者食品安全违法行为记录与信用体系建设，完善监管档案，并加强对监管数据的统计和综合分析，切实提高日常巡查的针对性和有效性。

4. 严格落实监管制度和创新监管手段，依法规范行政执法行为 要突出流通环节食品安全监管关键环节、重点部位，结合专项整治工作和日常监管的实际情况，在建立健全监管制度和构建长效监管机制上下功夫，特别要抓好各项监管制度的实施和落实，切实用制度规范行政执法行为。要认真落实国家工商总局制定下发的流通环节食品安全监管八项制度，并在实践中不断细化、完善和创新，切实提高食品安全监管的制度化、规范化、程序化、法治化水平。同时，要加大食品安全监管手段的创新，努力提高监管执法的现代化水平。要认真落实国家工商总局制定下发的《关于积极推进流通环节商品质量和食品安全信息化网络建设工作的意见》，强化网络信息技术在流通环节食品市场主体许可、准入、食品质量监管、市场巡查和执法办案等方面的综合应用。要加快建立流通环节食品经营主体、食品市场质量监管、食品抽样检验、食品安全监管和案件查办数据库，并与工商机关其他方面执法监管信息互联互通，实现数据信息共享。各地要加快推进基层工商所信息化网络体系建设和应用，充分运用无线网络执法平台、移动查询终端等现代科技手段，开展市场巡查和日常监管，有效开展网上预警防范和应急处置工作。要认真落实食品安全预警防范和应急处置各项工作，完善机制，严格责任制度，切实做到超前防范，及时有效处置。

（四）深入开展“家电下乡”等市场专项整顿，切实维护“家电下乡”市场秩序和保护消费者合法权益

要认真贯彻落实中央有关扩大内需，改善和保障民生等一系列决策部署，继续深入开展“家电下乡”等市场专项整顿，进一步强化流通领域商品质量监管和服务领域消费维权工作，大力推进12315行政执法体系“四个平台”建设，切实保护消费者合法权益。

1. 继续加大“家电下乡”等市场专项整顿工作力度，切实维护“家电下乡”市场秩序 中央经济工作会议明确提出，要进一步做好家电、汽车、摩托车下乡工作，继续实施家电和汽车以旧换新政策。各地要紧紧围绕确保中央政策措施深入落实，进一步加大监管执法力度，深入扎实开展“家电下乡”等市场专项整治。要积极配合相关部门加强对中标销售企业及其销售网点的管理，加大家电等商品二手市场监督检查力度，强化家电等商品市场主体准入、交易行为、商品质量的日常监管，严厉打击以“家电下乡”、家

电“以旧换新”名义销售不合格和假冒伪劣商品等违法行为，切实维护“家电下乡”、家电“以旧换新”市场秩序。特别是要积极配合商务、工业主管、质检等部门，督促指导经营者切实规范“家电下乡”、家电“以旧换新”产品售后服务行为；充分发挥12315行政执法体系“四个平台”的作用，及时受理和依法处理消费者有关家电商品的申诉举报，切实保护消费者合法权益。

2. 继续加大商品市场准入退出制度改革工作力度，切实强化流通领域商品质量监督工作　要按照“四化建设”要求，在深入开展专项整治的同时，加快流通领域商品市场准入退出制度改革步伐，强化日常规范监管，进一步健全流通领域商品质量长效监管机制，强化流通领域商品市场监管工作。一是要严格商品市场主体准入。按照法定程序严格商品市场主体准入管理，加强经济户口管理和信用分类监管，按照职责分工依法查处取缔无照经营违法行为，切实规范商品市场主体资格。二是要强化流通领域商品质量监督检查。各地要突出流通领域重点商品强化监管，围绕家用电器、电线电缆、插头插座、节能灯具、汽车配件、装饰装修材料、手机、服装等重点商品，深入开展专项执法检查；严格监督销售者建立并切实执行进货检查验收制度，加强对商品包装、标识以及商品质量的监督检查，加大流通领域商品质量监测力度和不合格商品退市工作力度，依法监督流通领域商品质量。要严格工作程序，按照法定职责和国家有关规定，科学、准确、全面地开展消费提示和警示，对商品质量监督检查的重要信息要及时向当地政府报告，按照规定和程序通报相关部门和相关地工商机关，促进源头治理和区域协作。三是要严厉打击制售假冒伪劣商品违法行为。要强化对违法线索的梳理和分析，加强案件排查和区域执法协作，加大违法案件查办力度，特别是要进一步严格大要案件督查督办制度，依法严厉查处制售假冒伪劣商品违法行为。要继续建立健全重大案件信息库，加强对假冒伪劣案件特点的研究分析，有针对性的加强对重点品种、重点区域违法行为的打击力度，并不断总结经验，切实提高案件查办工作水平和监管效能。同时，要有针对性地会同或者配合相关部门开展联合执法行动，严厉打击制售假冒伪劣商品违法行为，切实维护商品市场秩序。

3. 继续加大服务领域消费维权工作力度，切实保护消费者合法权益　要依法加强服务领域消费维权工作，有效化解服务领域消费纠纷。要与商务等部门和消费者协会、行业协会密切合作，继续深入开展清理损害消费者权益的规定和收费工作。积极会同相关部门、行业协会规范商业零售、家电维修等行业经营行为，并加强与相关部门、行业协会的工作协作和信息通报，针对服务领域存在的一些突出问题和消费者申诉举报热点，共同研究解决的具体措施，完善行业自律制度。要突出美容美发、宾馆饭店、装饰装修等领域服务行为的监管，加大专项执法检查力度。同时，综合运用合同监管和广告监管等执法手段，大力推广合同示范文本，依法制止欺诈消费者等违法行为，依法规范服务领域经营行为。

（五）深入推进12315行政执法体系“四个平台”建设，切实提高消费维权效能和现代化水平

中央经济工作会议提出，要“更加注重改善民生”和“加快解决涉及人民群众切身利益的问题”的要求。各地要按照国家工商总局《关于加强12315行政执法体系“四个平台”建设的通知》等文件部署，进一步完善12315信息化网络，完善功能，规范管理，不断扩大消费维权网络覆盖面，切实提高消费维权效能和现代化水平。

1. 大力推进12315信息化网络体系建设　要继续认真贯彻国家工商总局《关于加强12315行政执法体系“四个平台”建设的通知》的部署和要求，大力推进12315行政执法体系建设，在加大工作力度、完善功能、提升水平和扩大网络覆盖面及规范高效运行上下功夫，充分发挥“四个平台”的作用。要继续建立健全省局和地（市）局相对集中受理12315中心，对还没有落实到位的，要抓好组织实施，确保今年取得新突破。要加强12315数据分析中心和数据库建设，完善12315中心网上受理功能，建立健全12315短消息受理平台，按照国家工商总局统一数据标准加快对12315应用系统的升级改造和数据整合工作。要强化12315数据的综合分析利用，动态分析申诉举报热点和消费市场秩序状况，及时形成12315数据分析报告，切实发挥12315数据在加强市场监管、开展消费警示提示、推动经济结构调整、服务经济发展方面的积极作用。国家工商总局将组织开展对12315行政执法体系“四个平台”建设工作的检查，扎实推进此项工作再上新台阶。

2. 大力推进“一会两站”和12315“五进”规范化建设　要认真落实国家工商总局《关于加强“一会两站”规范化建设的意见》，以健全组织、完善制度、严格程序、规范运行和注重实效为重点，大力推进“一会两站”规范化建设，进一步扩大社会维权网络覆盖面，要努力实现村镇和城市社区“一会两站”全覆盖。充分发挥“一会两站”服务基层群众的作用，方便城乡消费者就近解决消费纠纷，加强对商品和服务的社会监督，及时有效地保护消费者合法权益，为提高消费信心，建设和谐社区、和谐村镇发挥积极作用。同时，要进一步总结经验，加强对商场、超市、市场、企业等方面的督促指导，密切沟通协作，努力扩大12315进商场、进超市、进市场、进企业、进学校覆盖面，畅通消费者申诉举报渠道，并结合实际，积极开展12315进景区、进牧区等工作，切实保护消费者合法权益，积极促进社会和谐稳定。

3. *大力推进消费维权长效管理机制建设* 各地要围绕消费者权益保护工作，大力推进长效管理机制建设，以流通领域商品质量监管、依法规范服务领域经营行为和受理处理消费者咨询、申诉、举报等为重点，建立健全和落实规章制度，建立和完善协作制度。要进一步完善和落实与政府相关部门的协作制度，加强12315网络体系与其他政府部门公共服务平台执法协作。同时，建立健全与消费者协会的合作制度、与行业协会的情况通报制度和与新闻媒体的消费维权互动机制，有效形成消费维权合力，积极营造消费维权的良好氛围。要加强消费者权益保护的地区合作和国际交流，吸收借鉴成功经验，切实推进消费维权长效管理机制建设。同时，各地要积极认真地抓好今年"3·15"活动，突出重点，选择载体，多形式、多途径加大消费维权宣传工作，务求取得新成效。

（六）加强组织领导和法制建设，强化基础和基层基础工作，狠抓检查督查和落实

1. *要进一步加强组织领导* 各地要在地方党委、政府的统一领导下，按照《食品安全法》等法律法规的职能，切实履行法定职责，以保障流通环节食品安全和有效保护消费者合法权益为重点，切实加强组织领导，一把手亲自抓，主管领导具体抓，各内设机构按照职能分工负责，密切协作，切实抓好组织实施和落实工作。要落实各项监管制度，严格责任制度和责任追究制度，积极防范监管的系统性风险和区域性风险。各地要层层研究制定具体的整顿方案和工作方案，明确目标任务和工作责任，精心组织和认真实施流通环节食品安全监管和专项整顿以及消费者权益保护的各项工作。

2. *要进一步加强法制建设和队伍建设* 各级工商机关要加大法制建设力度，积极推进《消费者权益保护法》等法律法规的修订工作，严格监管执法、市场巡查检查和案件查办程序，严格规范行政执法行为，确保具体行政行为合法有效，并能够经得起司法监督，切实完善食品安全监管和消费维权法制体系。各地要按照建设学习型机关和基层的要求，采取学习、培训、岗位练兵、实践锻炼等方式，加大广大执法人员政治理论、业务知识、法规政策、管理技能的学习和培训力度，特别要加强对基层工商所长和基层监管执法人员的培训，努力建设一支政治上、业务上、作风上过硬的干部队伍，为保障流通环节食品安全和保护消费者合法权益提供人才和素质保障。同时，要深入开展对食品经营者进一步学习贯彻《食品安全法》和履行法定责任义务的宣传培训和教育，采取多种形式，突出学习和培训重点，注重实际效果，进一步提高经营者自律和管理水平。

3. *要进一步加强基础建设、基层基础建设和党风廉政建设* 各地要以信息化建设、体制机制制度建设和规范管理建设为重点，大力推进食品安全监管和消费维权工作基础建设，全面提升工作质量、工作效率和工作水平。各地要进一步强化基层，夯实基础，充实基层执法队伍，强化基层执法力量，切实抓好执法装备、设备和经费保障工作，尤其是运用高科技手段监管所需的设施、设备及技术手段，为提高监管执法水平提供坚实的组织保障、人员保障和物质保障，大力推进食品安全和消费维权基层基础建设，不断提升基层监管执法能力和水平。要继续加强作风建设和党风廉政建设，进一步落实党风廉政建设责任制，有效防范流通环节食品安全监管和消费者权益保护工作的廉政风险和监管风险。

4. *要进一步加强协作配合和检查落实工作* 要加强工商机关内设机构之间以及与各有关部门的协作配合，及时通报有关情况，建立健全协调协作机制，切实形成监管合力。要层层加强对食品市场监管和消费维权等工作的指导、督查和考核，采取重点督查、专项督查、交叉检查、明察暗访等多种方式，一级抓一级，层层抓落实，确保组织领导、工作任务、工作措施、工作责任、人员力量和经费保障等落实到位。各级领导干部要深入基层，深入一线了解监管工作的实际情况，尤其要及时发现存在的问题和监管的薄弱环节，有针对性地加强指导，切实研究解决监管执法工作中面临的困难和实际问题，确保各项监管工作落到实处，取得实效。

依法开展流通环节食品安全监管和保护消费者合法权益，任务艰巨，责任重大。各级工商行政管理机关一定要按照落实科学发展观和维护社会和谐稳定的要求，围绕中心，服务大局，加大力度，改革创新，求真务实，开拓进取，努力开创流通环节食品安全监管和消费者权益保护工作的新局面，以饱满的工作热情和优异的工作成绩，为促进经济社会又好又快发展做出新的更大的贡献。

（本文为作者于2010年1月7日在全国工商行政管理系统食品安全监管暨消费者权益保护工作会议上的讲话，略有删改）

大力推进农产品现代流通综合试点 加快完善农产品现代流通体系

商务部部长助理　房爱卿

商务部召开农产品现代流通综合试点座谈会，很有必要，也很重要。近年来，中央农村工作领导小组办公室（简称“中农办”）和财政部对商务工作的支持力度很大。中农办连续5年把农产品流通内容写进中央1号文件，财政部不断加大对农产品流通工作的支持力度。刚才，中农办赵阳局长深刻阐述了搞活农产品流通的重要意义，财政部陈春平处长也强调了试点工作的基本要求，希望大家认真领会，在工作中贯彻执行。下面我谈几点意见。

一、农产品现代流通综合试点的意义

2010年，经过认真研究，财政部和商务部决定在8个省份开展农产品现代流通综合试点。希望试点省份各级商务主管部门充分认识肩负的使命，充分认识试点的重要意义，以高度的责任感，集中精力创造性地做好试点工作，为下一步扩大试点、在全国范围内完善农产品现代流通体系打好基础、积累经验。

（一）开展农产品现代流通综合试点、完善农产品现代流通体系，对解决农产品卖难买难，探索建立农产品产销平衡机制具有重要意义

农产品市场波动不仅在我国，在世界上任何国家和地区都比工业品市场波动大。工业品一旦出现缺口，可以及时组织生产，但农产品有生产周期，自然和市场的双重约束对农产品的供求平衡影响非常大。除个别品种外，我国大部分农产品市场波动比美国、日本和欧盟成员国要大很多。这与我们千家万户生产、千家万户批发和零售，现代化水平低，以及信息不对称有直接关系。一些地方既存在农产品卖难现象，又有买难问题。主要原因是我国各个地区农产品流通模式差别很大，有的农产品是局部生产、局部消费，有的是全国生产、全国消费。但无论哪种模式，流通平衡都容易受到各方面因素的影响。比如受韩国泡菜事件和日本大白菜短缺影响，吉林、辽宁、黑龙江的大白菜出口增加，需要其他地区的白菜向东北流通。2010年小宗农产品价格出现剧烈波动，被老百姓戏称为“豆你玩”、“蒜你狠”、“辣翻天”、“姜你军”和“糖高宗”等。解决这些问题应当依靠不断完善农产品现代流通体系，形成大市场、大流通和大贸易，建立起解决买难、卖难的长效机制和符合中国特色的农产品现代流通模式，这是农产品现代流通综合试点需要解决的重要课题。

（二）开展农产品现代流通综合试点、完善农产品现代流通体系，对保障食品安全、改善民生具有重要意义

随着生活水平提高，以前简单的白菜、萝卜、土豆几个品种已经不能满足广大群众多样化的消费需求。同时，随着人口流动性提高，个性化需求增大。尽管我国农产品质量已有很大改善，但农产品质量安全问题还是经常困扰着广大群众，影响正常生活。这些问题都需要通过建立农产品现代流通体系来解决。绝大部分农产品通过市场销售，把好市场关对保障农产品质量安全非常重要，对改善民生、落实执政为民宗旨意义重大。

（三）开展农产品现代流通综合试点、完善农产品现代流通体系，对解决“三农”问题、促进农民增收、转变农业发展方式具有重要意义

农产品从田间到餐桌，价格有很大差距，不仅消费者负担加大，农民收益也并未增加，流通企业也未获得更大利益，主要原因是流通成本过高。如果建立起现代流通体系，就会减少流通环节，提高流通效率，降低农产品损耗，农民就能增加收入，消费者也能多受益，流通企业也能获得更好的经济效益。因此，加快建设农产品现代流通体系对实现现代农业、促进农业发展方式转变具有不可或缺的作用。试点省份商务主管部门主要负责同志对此应有充分的认识，要高度重视这项工作，决不能将试点搞成简单的项目建设，要与财政等部门互相配合，共同把工作做好。

二、农产品现代流通综合试点的思路和重点

农产品现代流通综合试点工作既是以往“双百市场工程”、“农超对接”等工作的发展和深化，又是一项全新的工作。商务部与财政部已联合下发指导意见，对试点工作提出了明确要求。试点省份在开展综合试点工作时，要加强研究，实现四个转变，把握好四个重点。

（一）工作思路要实现四个转变

一要实现从单纯流通节点建设向流通链条和流通网络建设转变。以往我们开展的农产品批发市场、农贸市场升级改造，大型流通企业建设，只是节点的建设。这次试点不能仅体现在点上，要体现在线上和面上，体现流通链条怎么建立以及市场和企业如何布局。要综合考虑各方的因素设计试点方案，要统筹规划、统筹布局，不能简单停留在单一的项目建设上。二要实现由改造提升流通设施向推进现代流通模式转变。应当从以往重点关注农产品批发市场和农贸市场硬件升级改造，转向推广现代流通模式。要改变以往农产品流通盲目性大的状况，推行订单农业，建立稳定的供求关系。不仅要改造流通设施，采用冷链物流等现代流通手段，更要减少流通环节，继续推广农超对接、产销衔接等现代流通模式。三要实现由分步设计、分步实施向总体设计、分步实施转变。以往升级改造农贸市场只涉及农贸市场，缺少通盘和总体框架的考虑。此次综合试点不同，试点县、市和省份都要有总体规划和方案设计，在此基础上分步实施。四要实现由完全的市场化运作向政府引导和市场化相结合转变。以往开展农超对接和批发市场改造，企业或市场建成项目，政府只负责拨付补贴资金，项目运行完全是市场化运作。此次试点要充分发挥商务、财政等部门的作用，引导和推动农产品批发市场和连锁企业等试点承办单位推进现代流通模式，既要实现农产品流通公益功能，又要坚持市场规律，保持项目生命力。

（二）把握好四个工作重点

一是统筹制定和实施规划，构建布局合理的农产品现代流通网络。没有规划和蓝图，现代流通网络就难以形成。做好规划的前提条件，是充分了解当地的现状。试点地区要从农产品生产、加工、流通和消费的实际出发，树立大市场、大流通的观念，着力做好试点城市的农产品流通网络建设改造，科学规划，稳步实施。列入试点的市县要制订试点方案和农产品流通体系发展规划，试点省份应在市县方案和规划的基础上，结合专家指导意见，完善省级试点方案和农产品流通体系建设规划。二是加快农产品流通基础设施建设，打造现代化流通节点。流通节点有三种：第一种是收购节点，包括农产品集配中心、农业合作社和农产品经纪人等。目前农产品经纪人是主要形式，然而经纪人收购关系较为脆弱，要采取措施向合作社、集配中心、大企业建基地发展。第二种是批发节点，包括产地批发市场、销地批发市场、集散地批发市场。有的批发市场兼具产地、销地和集散地特征。批发市场既要加强加工配送、冷藏仓储、预选、分级、包装、配送等设施建设，也要改进交易模式，引入会员制、拍卖模式。究竟该选取哪种模式，试点省份应组织批发市场认真研究。第三种是零售节点。目前标准化菜市场和连锁超市在城市社区有所发展，但农贸市场依然是农产品零售主要形式。试点省份应结合当地特点和社会发展需要，研究探索建设改造农产品零售网点。在节点建设过程中，既要加强冷藏保鲜和物流建设，也要充分发挥电子信息平台作用，为复杂的多式联运找到好的解决方案。三是建立稳定的产销关系，形成完整的农产品供应链。农产品具有特殊性，供应链建设是一个难点。引导大型连锁超市、农产品批发市场、农业产业化龙头企业在农产品产地建设采购基地、加工中心、配送中心、冷藏仓储设施，推进“订单农业”；在农产品重要集散地或消费地开设农产品专卖店或销售专柜，与学校、餐饮、酒店、食堂建立直接供货关系；通过提供市场信息、销售渠道或生产服务等多种方式来引导农民专业合作社发展，带动农民加入合作社或由大企业统一组织生产，扩大生产规模。综合试点应该采取多种模式减少流通环节，由原来的随机卖，变成一种长期稳定的供销关系。政府应该引导各方通过经济关系和利益协调机制形成供应链，产地投资建设销地专卖店，销地投资建设产地集配中心。出现卖难的时候，销地优先销售产地投资方的蔬菜；出现买难的时候，产地优先将蔬菜供给销地投资方。农超对接项目原则上应同时包含大型连锁超市承建的子项目和农民专业合作社、农业产业化龙头企业承建的子项目。试点区域内如无符合资质条件的大型连锁超市，应在全国范围内选择，如无合适的农民专业合作社，应在周边地区选择。四是加快制订实施标准，促进农产品流通的标准化、品牌化和包装化。目前我国大部分农产品都没有包装、没有品牌，直接影响食品安全。实现农产品标准化、包装化、品牌化，建立追溯体系，对农产品质量安全是一个强有力保障。陈德铭部长十分重视农产品流通标准化建设工作，商务部正在组织制订洋葱、土豆、青椒、黄瓜、西红柿、豇豆和冬瓜等7个农产品流通标准，将对这些产品的分级、包装、标签、贮运和购销等作出

规范性要求。农产品流通标准化是试点工作的重要内容。试点省份选择项目承办单位时应优先选择积极贯彻标准的单位。要采取多种方式引导试点项目承办单位，参与农产品流通标准制修订工作，并认真实施已出台或即将出台的有关标准。推动农产品流通主体将管理流程标准化，提高管理水平和农产品流通效率。

三、农产品现代流通综合试点的工作要求

（一）抓紧工作进度，细化实施方案

各试点省份要按照本次会议的要求，结合当地实际，进一步细化完善试点工作方案，确保切实可行。方案既要反映总体要求，又要发挥大家的创造性；既符合标准化、规范化的总体工作要求，又能充分反映地方特色。只有这样的方案在实施时才能达到预期目的。

（二）明确目标责任，加强动态监管

此次农产品流通综合试点的第一责任人是试点省份商务主管部门的主要负责同志，具体责任人是分管负责同志。相关处室要有专人负责，全程跟踪。对项目实施状况进行动态监管，保证项目工程进度。制定详细的项目验收标准及操作办法，组织相关领域专家和专业审计人员组成验收组，确保项目质量。严格信息报送制度，要求试点承办企业及时准确填报工程进度和市场经营信息，把信息填报情况作为项目验收的重要参考。

（三）严肃财经纪律，加强资金管理

试点工作责任重大，要保障实施效果和资金安全。要加强项目资金管理和审计工作，拨付和使用补贴资金严格遵守国家规定，将补助资金切实用在农产品现代流通综合试点上。任何单位不得骗取、挪用或者截留财政专项资金，对于违反规定，弄虚作假，存在严重问题的单位，商务部、财政部不仅要全额收回资金，而且将取消其以后年度申请资格，触犯法律的，将依法追究有关单位和个人的责任。

（四）加强组织领导，争取地方配套政策

加大协调力度，积极争取试点省、市、县各级人民政府和有关部门在规划、用地、用水、用电、资金等方面出台配套优惠政策，按工业用地政策落实农产品批发市场用地，引导金融机构加大信贷支持力度，采取措施吸引社会资金投入农产品流通基础设施建设。中央财政支持力度虽然比历年都大，但与实际需要相比仍然有很大缺口，希望地方财政也相应加大配套支持力度，引导试点单位加大投入，形成中央、省、市、县和企业共同加大投入的局面，为试点提供强大的资金和政策支持。

（五）深入调研，及时总结和推广先进经验

试点工作是一项新工作，大家一定要重视调研，在调研的基础上完善方案，在实施的过程中总结经验。商务部将对 8 个省份的试点进度和质量进行比较，宣传好的经验，整改出现的问题，逐步探索出一套适合中国国情的农产品现代流通体系并在全国范围推广。

农产品现代流通综合试点工作是一项惠农、利民的重要工作。中央财政拿出 6.8 亿元支持 8 个省份建设农产品现代流通体系，力度之大，前所未有。希望各试点省份高度重视，切实负起责任把工作做好，为改善民生、转变农产品流通发展方式、促进我国经济发展作出贡献。

（本文为作者于 2010 年 10 月 26 日在农产品现代流通综合试点座谈会上的讲话，略有删改）

抓住机遇　迎接挑战　推动我国农产品加工业持续健康发展

农业部农产品加工业局局长　张天佐

一、我国农产品加工业发展情况

20 世纪末，我国农业生产进入产需基本平衡、丰年有余的新阶段后，开始大规模进行农业结构调整、延伸产业链条，由此推动我国农产品加工业的全面发展。特别是进入 21 世纪以来，随着我国居民消费水平和消费结构的快速变化，我国农产品加工业得到迅速发展，取得了显著成效。

1. 总量持续增长，贡献显著增加　2000 年以来，

我国农产品加工业一直保持比较快的增长态势。有3组数字可以直观地反映21世纪以来我国农产品加工业的巨大变化：全国规模以上农产品加工企业总数由2000年底约5.5万个，发展到2009年底的13.6万个，增长了2.5倍；全国规模以上农产品加工业总产值由2000年的1.7万亿元，发展到2009年底的9.5万亿元，增长了4.6倍；全国规模以上农产品加工业从业人员由2000年的1 500万人，增加到2009年的2 525万人，增长了67%；2009年上缴税金达3 190亿元，比2000年的772亿元翻了两番。

2. 结构不断优化，品牌、质量不断提升　近年来，为适应消费升级的要求，我国农产品加工业不断调整产业和产品结构，形成了以食品工业为主体的农产品加工业，食品工业产值占农产品加工业产值的比例由2005年的40%，增加到2009年的47%，产品结构呈现多样化趋势，方便食品、快餐食品、休闲食品、营养保健食品等发展迅速。与此同时，农产品加工企业品牌建设意识增强，无公害农产品、绿色食品和有机农产品、地理标志农产品数量不断增加，“三品一标”认证产品总数达到7万多个，占全国农产品商品量的30%。

3. 自主创新步伐加快，核心竞争力不断增强　“十一五”期间，为了提高农产品加工业的科技创新能力，农业部启动实施了全国农产品加工研发体系建设，依托科研院所、大专院校和科技型龙头企业，分领域、分品种重点支持建设了200多个农产品加工技术研发中心，围绕农产品加工中的共性关键技术、高新技术装备、重大产品开发、产品质量安全、物流配送等重大产业问题，开发出了一批拥有自主知识产权、专利技术的新装备，制定了一批国家或行业标准，缩短了我国农产品精深加工技术装备与国际先进水平的差距，提升了我国农产品加工业的自主创新能力，增强了产业核心竞争力。

4. 产业加速集聚，加工产业带粗具雏形　“十一五”期间，农业部在全国认定了350个农产品加工业示范基地，命名了580多个农产品加工示范企业，积极推动农产品加工企业以区域优势农产品资源为依托，加快调整和扩张，主动承接产业转移，实现了向优势产区集聚发展。目前，以农业部16种优势农产品58个优势区域和大城市郊区为依托，逐步形成了特色农产品加工产业带和加工区。黄淮海地区优质专用小麦加工产业带、东北及内蒙古东部玉米和大豆加工产业带、长江流域优质油菜加工产业带、中原地区牛羊肉加工产业带、东北及华北西北地区奶业加工产业带、环渤海湾地区和西北黄土高原苹果加工产业带、中南和西南地区柑橘加工产业带、沿海及重点江河湖泊流域优质水产品加工产业带等加工产业带粗具雏形。

5. 产业布局日趋合理，东部、中部、西部协调发展　我国农产品加工业的区域梯次发展格局正在形成，东部发达地区和大城市郊区积极吸引外资，加强自主创新，培育了一大批外向型、规模骨干型的农产品加工业，促进了我国农产品加工业国际竞争力的提升；中部地区充分利用农业资源优势，积极发展粮食、畜产品等加工业，农产品加工业已逐步成为中部地区解决农民就业、增加农民收入的有效途径，成为促进中部地区崛起的重要产业支撑；西部欠发达地区依托特色农业优势，积极发展特色农产品加工业，初步形成了一批特色鲜明的农产品加工优势产业集群，带动了小城镇的发展，成为当地县域经济发展的增长点，在带动西部大开发和脱贫致富中发挥了积极作用。

6. 带动能力进一步增强，农民就业、增收的效果明显　农产品加工业的发展促进了农业的发展和增值增效，推动了农产品结构调整，延长了农业产业链条，带动了农业产业化经营，推动了农民就业和增收。据统计，2009年全国各类农业产业化经营组织达到22.4万个，参与农业产业化的农户超过1亿户，实现每年每户平均增收1 900多元。目前，全国规模以上农产品加工业从业人员2 500多万人，其中60%以上为吸纳农民就业，提供的劳动者报酬约4 700多亿元，其中农民从中获得的报酬达到近60%，为农民就业及增收作出了重要贡献。

我国农产品加工业发展成就斐然，最根本的一条就是得益于各级党委政府的高度重视和良好的发展环境。近年来，党中央国务院高度重视农产品加工业发展。十七届三中全会决定提出：“引导加工、流通、储运设施建设向优势产区聚集”，“发展产业化经营，促进农产品加工业结构升级”。2005年以来连续6年发布的6个中央1号文件和《国务院办公厅关于促进农产品加工业发展的意见》（国办发〔2002〕62号）等政策性文件均对农产品加工业的发展提出了明确要求。各级农产品加工业主管部门积极落实中央要求，因地制宜，加大了农产品加工业的推进力度，工作效果明显，对我国农产品加工业的发展起到了积极促进作用。

二、我国农产品加工业发展面临的机遇和挑战

当前，全球经济加速融合，2008年国际金融危机以来，随着全球经济的回暖和我国经济启稳向好，

我国农产品加工业发展迎来总体有利的环境。总体来说，共有4个有利方面：一是消费拉动。从国际经验看，工业化、城镇化快速发展的阶段，往往是食品消费结构加快变化和加工食品需求迅速上升的阶段。目前我国处于工业化、城镇化发展的重要时期，而人均GDP预计2010年也将到达4 000美元，城乡居民对加工食品的消费需求将进入高速增长期，这为我国农产品加工业持续增长提供了强大的发展动力。二是政策推动。中央制定了一系列应对金融危机、保持经济平稳较快发展的强农惠农政策和刺激经济发展的一揽子计划，实施了重点产业调整和振兴规划，为农产品加工业发展创造了良好的宏观环境。三是现代农业带动。农业生产规模化、标准化、组织化程度不断提高，农产品优势区域布局逐步形成，农产品加工企业和农户的利益联结日益紧密，为农产品加工业奠定了坚实基础。四是新科技驱动。科技发展日新月异，发酵工程、酶工程、膜技术、超临界萃取技术、微电子技术等现代技术与装备及一些新材料的研究不断取得新突破，这些新技术为提升农产品加工技术装备水平提供了重要的条件。

但是，我们要保持清醒的头脑，有两类问题必须引起高度关注：

第一类问题：从产业内部看，我国农产品加工业起点低、发展慢，与发达国家相比存在着较大差距，需要引起我们的高度关注。一是大而不强。目前发达国家农产品加工业产值与农业产值的比值大约为2～4∶1，而我国仅为1.6∶1；技术装备水平不高，总体上约80%以上的农产品加工技术装备处于20世纪末的世界平均水平；农产品加工标准体系不健全，部分标准陈旧，有些领域仍无标准；企业管理落后，生产管理不严。二是生产集中度不高。企业大群体和小规模并存，目前我国农产品加工企业年均营业收入多在1 000万～2 500万元之间，绝大多数是中小企业，规模以下企业约占76%，企业年均营业收入不足300万元；产业集中度不高，最大的农产品加工企业年销售收入也仅100多亿元。三是产业链不健全。产业上游环节，适合加工的专用品种少，加工专用原料生产滞后，专用原料的缺口大。以橙汁为例，约95%需要依赖进口，在初加工环节，产地初加工设施简陋、方法原始，造成产后损失大、利益流失多、安全隐患突出等问题；产业下游市场发育不良，物流设施建设滞后，流通业态落后。四是资源利用不充分。以植物纤维资源利用为例，我国每年有7亿t左右的秸秆、1 000万t的玉米芯、1 000万t的米糠、1 000万t的麦麸和700万t的蔗渣等亟待深度开发利用。

第二类问题：从外部发展环境看，首先是生产要素制约的影响日益突出，在发展过程中面临包括信贷、土地、技术、人才、原材料等各方面生产要素的制约，融资难、用地难、技术瓶颈、人才不足、专用原料缺乏等问题普遍存在；其次是生产成本快速增加，人民币升值、原料、能源和劳动用工价格的持续上涨、通胀预期等因素，使得企业盈利空间大幅压缩；三是节能减排压力大，在我国农产品加工物耗、能耗、水耗高以及转变经济发展方式的背景下，产业和环保政策门槛将提高，技术改造、升级面临成本大幅上升；四是国际竞争加剧，跨国企业正伺机进入我国粮食、棉花、肉类、饲料加工等行业，挤压着我国农产品加工企业的发展空间。如国内大豆行业实际加工总量的80%以上已由外商独资或参股的企业所控制。此外，发达国家农产品贸易技术壁垒日趋体系化，我国农产品出口面临很大制约。

当前，随着科技进步日新月异，高新技术产业化进程加快，全球范围内农产品加工业发展迅速，呈现出了明显的趋势性特征。一是农产品加工跨国企业的全球重组十分活跃，通过独资、合资、并购等方式，实现企业发展规模化、全球化；二是加工企业积极采用新技术、新工艺、新材料，技术装备水平和加工转化精深程度大幅度提高，农产品加工技术逐步实现高新化；三是随着全球能源资源供需矛盾的日益突出，各国生物能源开发热情高涨，促进了农产品加工业在能源领域发展的超常化；四是为提高加工效益，实现低碳减排，大力推进资源的高效精深加工和副产物的有效开发，发展方式逐步实现可持续化；五是为提高质量安全水平，发达国家的农产品加工企业普遍建立了科学完整的产品标准体系和全程质量控制体系，实行农产品产前、产中、产后各环节严格的标准化管理，质量控制推行标准化。

今后一个时期是我国全面建设小康社会的关键时期，也是城镇化、工业化、农业现代化同步推进的重要时期，加快农产品加工业发展具有重大战略意义。我们必须认清形势，明确重点，抓住机遇，迎接挑战，加快学习、借鉴和消化吸收各国的先进技术和经验，加快提高我国农产品加工业发展水平。

三、进一步推进我国农产品加工业发展的工作思路和重点

推进农产品加工业发展必须坚持以转变发展方式为主题，以推进结构调整为主线，以优势、特色农业产业带为依托，以发展产地初加工和精深加工为重点，加快技术创新，强化引导推动，争取政策扶持，努力实现我国农产品加工业持续、稳定、健康发展。

目前，农业部正在积极谋划“十二五”期间农产品加工业的发展，初步预测“十二五”期间我国农产品加工业总体可以保持年均13%增长速度，2015年规模以上农产品加工业总产值要在现在的基础上实现翻一番，农产品加工业与农业产值比超过2∶1。具体工作重点有以下四个方面：

（一）大力推动农产品加工业的科技进步

1. 加快提升农产品加工科技应用水平　随着食品化学、生物技术、工艺技术、装备技术、营养学及其他相关学科的发展，我国农产品加工业广泛应用现代技术展现了良好的前景。我们要加强学科建设和基础性研究，组织联合攻关，广泛应用新技术，尽快提高行业的科技水平。

2. 加快提高农产品加工装备水平　工艺是灵魂，设备是关键。没有先进的农产品加工技术装备，就没有现代化的农产品加工业。长期以来，我国农产品加工技术装备没有得到应有的重视，技术研发滞后，产品结构简单、能耗高，单机多、成套设备少、生产率低，稳定性和可靠性差，缺乏整体竞争力，大规模企业的高端设备大量依赖进口，这与我国装备制造业大国地位极不相称。因此，必须加强农产品加工机械装备的研究，广泛应用新材料、新技术、新工艺，推进加工设备的集成化、智能化，切实提高我国的加工装备水平，满足农产品加工业快速发展的需要。

3. 加快提高农产品加工综合利用率　农产品大多含有碳水化合物、淀粉、木质素、纤维素、半纤维素、油脂、蛋白质等多种成分，借助于现代技术可以生产各种附加值高的产品。而我国目前农产品加工产业链短，精深加工少，综合利用率低，不仅浪费了资源，还在一定程度上污染了环境。因此，必须加强农产品资源综合利用的研究，鼓励应用先进的技术和装备，通过大力发展农产品精深加工，延长加工产业链，吃干榨尽各种可利用资源。

4. 加快完善农产品加工质量安全体系　农产品加工是通过机械工程手段采用物理、化学、生物等方法对农产品进行加工处理的过程。由于环节多、过程长，加工过程中造成二次污染的几率较大。因此，必须加强农产品加工标准体系建设，大力推行GMP、CAP、HACCP等质量安全管理规范，开展安全检验检测技术和设备的研发以及农产品加工安全风险评估，确保质量安全。

（二）启动农产品加工提升工程

1. 启动农产品产地初加工惠民工程　通过国家扶持引导，帮助广大农户、农民专业合作组织开展产地储藏、烘干、保鲜等初加工设施建设。近期的重点为玉米烘干和储藏环节、马铃薯窖藏环节、苹果预冷保鲜贮藏环节、果蔬烘干环节，建设一批产地初加工储藏、烘干、保鲜设施。

2. 扶持一批农产品加工领军企业加快技术装备的改造升级　重点支持农产品加工领军企业进行技术装备改造升级，以农产品精深加工、综合利用和节能减排为重点，引导企业加快更新改造，以此带动加工各行业的产业升级和技术进步。

3. 支持农产品加工技术研发体系建设　分领域、分品种、分区域选择有一定影响力和带动作用的科研院所或领军企业，扶持建设农产品加工研发中心，进一步加强研发仪器设备和小试、中试设施建设，尽快提高我国农产品加工业创新和研发能力。

（三）大力提升农产品加工公共服务能力

1. 搭建技术对接平台，加强农产品加工技术筛选与推广　以农产品精深加工、综合利用和节能减排为重点，组织相关技术及装备的筛选、引进、推广，加强高效、节能、安全和质优的新型技术与装备的推广应用。以适合广大中小农产品加工企业使用的技术和装备为重点，广泛开展技术对接和推广活动，普及先进适用技术。

2. 搭建经贸合作平台，促进区域间的经济贸易合作　大力推动“东西合作”，支持举办全国性或区域性的农产品加工经贸促销活动，促进农产品加工市场体系的发育。积极支持农产品加工企业，参加国内外大型展览展销，促进市场开拓。

3. 搭建信息服务平台，强化对农产品加工业的行业引导和服务　以服务政府决策和企业发展为中心，加强分品种、分行业的跟踪研究和监测分析。加强农产品加工国际标准的跟踪，及时收集、掌握和整理国际性标准组织以及美国、日本、韩国、欧盟等主要贸易国农产品进出口的标准及政策动态，及时发布有关信息，引导行业健康发展。

（四）推进农产品加工业规范发展

1. 引导企业规范管理行为　以农产品加工质量安全为重点，加强对企业的引导和监督，健全农产品加工标准和质量安全控制体系，指导企业推行GMP、HACCP和ISO9000族系质量管理与控制体系。

2. 加强加工专用原料生产　结合新一轮的《优势农产品区域布局规划》的实施，按照农产品加工的特性要求，选育加工专用品种，推进农产品加工原料生产的规模化、专业化、标准化和产业化，在全国培育一批具有区域特色、示范带动作用大的全国农产品加工专用原料生产示范基地。

3. 推进农产品加工产业集聚区发展　在农产品优势产区和农产品产业带，依托产地优势农产品资源，推进农产品加工产业集聚区发展，整合带动农产品加工骨干企业发展产地精深加工，引导农产品加工产业梯度转移，促进农产品加工业向优势产区聚集。在全国具有区位特色和产业优势的县（市、区）建立培育一批全国农产品加工产业集聚示范区。

今后一个时期是我国全面建设小康社会的关键时期，也是城镇化、工业化、农业现代化加快推进的重要时期，加快发展农产品加工业具有重大战略意义。可以相信，在各级政府大力支持和广大农产品加工科研人员以及企业的共同努力下，我国农产品加工业必将会持续、健康、稳定地发展。

强化措施　保质保量 完成食品安全风险监测任务

卫生部监督局局长　苏　志

这次会议的主要任务，是检查各地工作进展、总结工作经验、梳理问题、探讨解决问题的办法，全力推进食品安全风险监测工作，确保顺利完成2010年任务。下面我针对会议主题先做个发言，供大家参考：

一、进一步增强责任意识，高度重视食品安全风险监测工作

“三聚氰胺事件”后，我国政府为了有效防控食品安全问题，努力改善我国的食品安全状况，在新颁布的《食品安全法》中特别规定“国家建立食品安全风险监测制度，对食源性疾病、食品污染以及食品中的有害因素进行监测。”《食品安全法实施条例》进一步明确要求，食品安全风险监测应满足食品安全风险评估、食品安全标准制定与修订、食品安全监督管理等的需要。国务院2009年食品安全整顿工作方案提出要在两年时间内建立覆盖各省（自治区、直辖市）、市、县并逐步延伸到农村地区的食品污染物和食源性疾病监测体系，加强食品安全风险监测数据的收集、报送和管理。为了保证食品安全风险监测工作的顺利进行，《食品安全法》和《实施条例》对食品安全风险监测的主要任务及其承担部门做出了明确规定，要求国务院卫生行政部门会同国务院有关部门制定、实施国家食品安全风险监测计划。省、自治区、直辖市人民政府卫生行政部门根据国家食品安全风险监测计划，结合本行政区域的具体情况，组织制定、实施本行政区域的食品安全风险监测方案。《实施条例》进一步规定，食品安全风险监测工作由省级以上人民政府卫生行政部门会同同级质量监督、工商行政管理、食品药品监督管理等部门确定的技术机构承担。承担食品安全风险监测工作的技术机构应当根据食品安全风险监测计划和监测方案开展监测工作，保证监测数据真实、准确，并按照食品安全风险监测计划和监测方案的要求，将监测数据和分析结果报送省级以上人民政府卫生行政部门和下达监测任务的部门。食品安全风险监测分析结果表明可能存在食品安全隐患的，省、自治区、直辖市人民政府卫生行政部门应当及时将相关信息通报本行政区域的市级和县级人民政府及其卫生行政部门。

《食品安全法》针对卫生部门的专业特点和工作能力以及食品安全风险监测与卫生部门承担的食品安全风险评估、食品安全标准制定等职能的关系，把组织实施食品安全风险监测的牵头工作交给了卫生部门，既体现了国家和人民对卫生部门的高度信任，更要求卫生部门严格依法履职，全面承担起组织开展风险监测的相关法律责任。2010年4月，国务院副总理、国务院食品安全委员会主任李克强同志在全国食品安全工作电视电话会议上作重要讲话，特别强调要依法加强食品安全整顿工作，强化措施，落实责任。食品安全风险监测工作是全国食品安全整顿工作的重要内容之一，我们一定要认真贯彻全国食品安全工作电视电话会议和李克强副总理重要讲话精神，采取有力措施，狠抓工作落实。啸宏副部长在2010年3月卫生部实施2010年国家食品安全风险监测计划工作会议上提出明确要求，各地要扎实做好今年的食品安全风险监测工作。一要认真学法，二要明确任务，三要加强领导。认真学法，就是要解决认识问题，切实提高履职意识；明确任务就是要狠抓各项工作的落实；加强领导，就是要落实责任制，加强督促指导，并及时研究解决食品安全风险监测工作中的问题。

当前我们的主要任务就是要认真落实卫生部会同

5部门联合下达的《2010年国家食品安全风险监测计划》。各地要按照法律规定尽快制定和实施本地区的食品安全风险监测方案。按照2010年度国家食品安全风险监测计划，要求在全国31个省（自治区、直辖市）和新疆建设兵团全面展开化学污染物及有害因素、食源性致病菌和食源性疾病的监测，至少覆盖30%的人口。按照计划要求，各地应在每个季度最后1个月的20日之前向卫生部报送监测数据和分析结果。

2010年是我们在全国范围内依法全面展开食品安全风险监测的第一年，对不少地区来讲是一项全新工作，即使一些参加过两网监测的地区也感到有一定压力。我们这次会议的目的就是要对前一阶段的工作进行总结，对各地工作中发现的问题及其原因进行深入分析，并在此基础上群策群力，充分发挥我们全行业的智慧和创造性商讨解决问题的办法，有力地推动今年的工作。

二、积极开拓，努力解决工作中的突出问题

为了认真贯彻实施《食品安全法》关于食品安全风险监测的规定，卫生部在充分会商有关部门的基础上联合发布了《食品安全风险监测工作管理规定（试行）》和《2010年国家食品安全风险监测计划》，成立了国家食品安全风险评估委员会，3月17日召开了全国食品安全风险监测计划实施工作会议，全面启动了2010年风险监测计划的实施工作。目前，各地工作进展总体是好的。不少地方已会同有关部门制定并上报了地方食品安全风险监测方案，并开始进入具体的实施阶段。特别是一些西部省份在各方面条件都十分困难的情况下，积极、主动、创造性地开展工作，很快打开了食品安全风险监测的工作局面。如青海省，3月17日北京会议后行动迅速，很快提出了《青海省2010年食品安全风险监测方案》，并与商务、经委、质监、工商、食品药品监管、出入境检验检疫等六厅局进行了很好的沟通和协调。玉树地震发生后，在积极参与抗震救灾工作的同时，开展了食品中违法添加物质、粮食和水产品等监测工作，完成了食源性疾病监测试点医院的部署工作。宁夏回族自治区也已完成对蔬菜类、蘑菇类、炒货等158份样品的检测工作。北京、吉林、浙江、福建、广东、贵州、陕西等地已完成了第一季度的监测任务。一些省、直辖市如北京、河北、浙江、江西、河南、湖南、广东、四川等，在国家计划的基础上结合本地食品安全状况增加了监测项目或采样量，北京市在完成致病性微生物定性监测的同时，率先开展了致病性微生物的定量监测。

但是，我们也发现，各地工作进展情况严重不平衡，有些地方的工作还有很大差距。表现在监测方案至今尚未制定下发；部门协调不力，监测方案迟迟没有会签；工作经费不落实，甚至卫生部2009年下拨的风险监测补助经费还没有划拨给承担任务的单位。分析存在上述问题的原因，我们认为，首先是有的地方对食品安全风险监测工作重视不够，没有认真抓落实；二是有的同志工作中存在畏难情绪，有等、靠思想；三是角色转变不到位，习惯于传统、熟悉的工作，还没有把工作重心真正转移到新的法定职责上来。这次会议我们要交流一些地方的经验和好的做法，促进相互学习、相互启发，有针对性地解决上述问题，这样才能确保今年食品安全风险监测任务的完成。在各地经验和做法的启发下，我想就如何面对工作中的困难谈几点想法。

（一）切实加强领导，落实责任

食品安全风险监测工作是一项系统工程，具有实施周期长、工作环节多、技术难度高等特点，所以，必须要切实加强领导，强化组织管理。切实加强领导，首先是卫生行政部门的领导要把食品安全风险监测法定职责的履行提上重要议事日程，加强组织协调，督促指导工作落实。各级疾控中心特别是省级疾控中心是承担风险监测的业务骨干和主要责任单位，中心领导务必加强对食品安全风险监测等相关技术工作的领导。要做到组织落实、人员落实和责任落实。3月北京会议后各地都在切实加强领导、落实责任方面做了不少尝试，浙江、重庆等地出台了专门文件，天津、云南等地成立了由分管厅（局）长负责的食品安全风险监测领导小组形成相对固定的组织管理体制，福建省卫生厅还成立了跨部门的省食品安全风险监测和评估工作小组，参与单位包括卫生、农业、海洋渔业、质监、工商、食药监、粮食、出入境检验检疫等部门。这些地方的做法对大家应该有所启发。

（二）争取政府强有力的领导和支持

针对当前执行食品安全风险监测计划中存在的部门协调不力和地方配套经费不落实等问题，我们要充分依靠地方政府的统一领导和组织协调机制。各级卫生行政部门要积极给政府当好参谋，向政府汇报风险监测工作的重要性以及与当地食品安全监督管理的关系，争取政府强有力的领导和支持。湖南省卫生厅在这方面有一些很好的做法，值得大家借鉴。3月北京会议后，湖南省卫生厅及时向政府进行了汇报，提出了建立和完善食品安全风险监测体系的总体设想，并

提出要把食品安全风险监测体系纳入到卫生监督体系等公共卫生体系建设，纳入深化医药卫生体制改革的总体框架和政府考核目标。在卫生厅的努力下，湖南省政府第52次常务会议做出决定，在省疾病预防控制中心的基础上建立省食品安全风险评估监测中心，并同意适当安排2010年所需食品安全监管经费。因此我们建议：一是制定食品安全风险监测方案的内容要与各级政府重视、人民群众关注、有关部门列为重点监督内容的食品安全问题紧密结合起来，切实让食品安全风险监测工作在各级政府的食品安全监管工作中发挥应有的作用；二是我们要定期向政府领导汇报风险监测工作情况、发现的食品安全风险隐患以及工作的成效；三是一旦发现食品安全问题，应当依法及时向政府报告和有关监管部门通报情况，提出工作建议。只有这样才能引起地方政府领导的高度重视，充分体现卫生部门在食品安全综合监管方面的职能作用。从各地上报的阶段性工作总结来看，不少省份都有这方面的体会和做法，如天津、河北、江西、贵州等地都在争取地方政府重视和地方财政支持方面做了很有成效的工作。

（三）加强协调沟通，联合相关部门共同做好风险监测工作

根据《食品安全法》和《食品安全法实施条例》以及有关规定，国务院卫生行政部门和省级卫生行政部门分别牵头制定、组织实施国家和地区食品安全风险监测计划或监测方案，但风险监测工作不是卫生部门一家可以独立承担和完成的工作。在食品安全分段监管的模式下，如果相关职能部门不参与进来，我们的很多工作不可能做到位，不仅在确定监测项目、样品采集和检验等技术环节不能满足监测工作的需要，更主要的是无法实现法律关于食品安全风险监测应满足政府食品安全监管需要的目的。因此，我们建议如果通过积极做工作仍然不能达成部门间共识的，卫生行政部门要及时向政府报告，请求政府帮助协调。

三、强化措施，狠抓2010年食品安全风险监测工作的落实

（一）严格按照2010年国家食品安全风险监测计划要求，保质保量完成任务

2010年是依法实施国家食品安全风险监测计划的第一年，卫生部会同5个部门联合下发计划，中央财政专门投入近8千万元风险监测补助经费，我们一定要打好这一攻坚战。凡是不能按照进度上报数据，请省级卫生厅（局）向卫生部做出书面说明，以便我们掌握情况。另外，没有完成会签的要尽快完成会签，会签中遇到的问题要和相关部门很好地沟通，沟通有困难的要及时向省级人民政府汇报。

（二）加强食品安全风险监测质量控制

各地的食品安全风险监测一定要按照统一要求加强质量控制。可以说，离开统一的质量控制就没有国家或地方的食品安全风险监测。我们已委托中国疾控中心营养与食品安全所起草《国家食品安全风险监测质量控制手册》等一系列质控文件，将尽快出台。

（三）注重风险监测结果的运用

充分发挥食品安全风险监测在国家和地方食品安全监管中的重要作用。风险监测中一旦发现问题，一定要及时报告、通报，原则上由省卫生厅（局）在上报卫生部的同时，及时上报省政府。同时加强风险信息管理，依法公布食品安全风险监测信息。为此，卫生部监督局正在依据《食品安全法》和《食品安全法实施条例》以及卫生部等5部门发布的《食品安全风险监测管理规定（试行）》，起草食品安全风险监测发现问题或隐患的数据快速通报程序。

（四）加强督导检查

为了推动2010年风险监测工作，下一步我们还要对2010年国家食品安全风险监测计划实施情况进行督导。督导组将由有关行政人员和技术专家组成，通过督导，更深入地了解各地工作情况、总结经验、发现问题，更加扎实开展食品安全风险监测工作。督导检查结果将向全国通报。我们要求各省（自治区、直辖市）卫生行政部门在卫生部督导检查前先期开展有针对性的自查工作，找准工作薄弱环节，狠抓落实。

（五）及早组织制定2011年食品安全风险监测计划

在认真总结2010年工作的基础上，及时启动研究制定2011年国家食品安全风险监测计划。在此，我对2011年计划的制定提几点建议：一是计划要满足食品安全监管的三大需要，国家食品安全标准审评委员会、国家食品安全风险评估专家委员会、国务院负责食品安全监管的职能部门分别根据各自需要提出建议。二是国家计划要充分满足地方食品安全监管工作的需要，为国务院和地方食品安全监管政策的制修订提供科学数据。三是要努力提高食品安全风险监测的效率，要尽可能发现问题和隐患，尽可能发现规律。所以，监测计划一定要有重点、要有针对性。建议组成一个由多部门、多领域、多层面的相关专家与行政人员组成的起草专家小组。2011年的计划研制工作应抓紧，按照要求在2010年9月印发，以便各

地及早安排明年的工作。

四、着力加强风险监测制度和能力建设

食品安全风险监测是一项基础性工作，也是一项长期任务。我们目前的工作基础和水平与《食品安全法》的要求、与国际水平还存在较大的差距。从国内各地区看，风险监测工作水平也是参差不齐。我们要有强烈的紧迫感和使命感。一是要继续加快制度建设，进一步完善风险监测各项工作机制，规范风险监测工作。卫生部正在组织起草《食品安全风险监测技术机构能力条件与工作规范》以及与质量控制、技术培训等相关的各项技术规范。二是下大力气加强能力建设。卫生部正在向国家发展和改革委员会提出加强全国卫生系统食品安全风险监测能力建设的专项规划和“十二五”规划。三是中央和地方都要大力加强人员培训力度，所谓“提高能力”首先强调的是人的能力。卫生部还将利用我们各地各级卫生行政部门和疾控机构的优势资源组成技术协作团队专项研究食品安全风险监测、评估和预警工作相关的政策与技术问题。

我们要积极创造条件，克服一切困难，把2010年的工作做好；同时，我们要抓住国务院食品安全两年整顿工作的契机，通过不懈努力，大力提高我国食品安全风险监测工作水平，在不太长的时间内力争把覆盖全国并延伸到农村的食品安全风险监测体系建设起来。

（本文为作者于2010年6月18日在2010年国家食品安全风险监测工作研讨会上的讲话，略有删改）

落实生猪屠宰规划纲要　促进生猪屠宰行业健康发展

商务部市场秩序司司长　向　欣

这次会议主要是全面部署2010年商务系统食品安全和生猪屠宰管理工作，研究贯彻落实《全国生猪屠宰行业发展规划纲要（2010—2015）》的工作措施。下面，我代表商务部畜禽屠宰管理办公室就全国生猪屠宰行业管理工作报告如下：

一、2009年全国生猪屠宰管理工作取得新进展

2009年《食品安全法》颁布实施，生猪屠宰管理工作转交市场秩序司负责。一年来，在商务部党组的正确领导下，在有关部委和各地方部门的支持配合下，各级商务主管部门的同志们紧密围绕保障肉品卫生和质量安全重点工作，认真贯彻落实《食品安全法》、《生猪屠宰管理条例》（以下简称《条例》），加强生猪屠宰行业监管，取得了积极的成绩。

（一）政策法规标准体系充实完善

2009年，商务部按照《条例》的要求出台了《全国生猪屠宰行业发展规划纲要（2010—2015）》（以下简称《纲要》）。这部《纲要》对今后屠宰行业结构调整具有重要指导意义；同时，起草了《生猪定点屠宰厂（场）分级管理办法》，修订了《生猪定点屠宰厂（场）资质等级要求》，正在抓紧推动出台。另外，我们已经推动出台了《猪屠宰与分割车间设计规范》等一系列国家或行业标准，对促进行业标准化经营发挥了重要作用。地方法规制度不断完善，截至2009年底，全国共有10个省出台了条例，26个省制定了地方政府规章，推动全国畜禽屠宰管理工作进入法制化轨道。其中，陕西省出台《牲畜屠宰管理条例》，为小型生猪屠宰场点的审批和管理提供了法规依据；黑龙江省《畜禽屠宰管理条例》明确了屠宰监管经费来源等问题。截至2009年8月，共有16个省（自治区、直辖市）印发了生猪定点屠宰厂（场）定点设置规划，为调整行业布局和结构提供了重要依据。

（二）行业监管成效显著

各级商务主管部门加强监管能力建设，狠抓日常监管，肉品质量安全状况进一步改善。一是执法能力不断加强，截至2009年底，全国已有80%的市、县成立了专（兼）职屠宰执法队伍。商务部在全国242个市、县开展商务综合行政执法和12312市场监管公共服务平台建设试点，有效强化了生猪屠宰监管力

量，丰富了执法手段，提升了监管效能。二是监管制度不断完善。大连、宁波等地着力构建猪肉质量安全长效管理机制，建立了完善的信息报送、台账管理、不合格肉品召回、无害化处理等制度；北京、青岛、厦门等地建立了生猪定点屠宰厂瘦肉精自检和定期报告制度；河北、陕西等地实行驻厂监督、远程监控等监管方式，有效规范了企业经营行为；河北、新疆兵团等地积极探索联合执法、区域协作执法等机制，有效加强了部门和地区间的配合。三是专项整治成效明显。2009 年，各地商务主管部门按照国务院《食品安全整顿总体工作方案》要求和商务部统一部署，先后开展了打击私屠滥宰、制售注水肉、打击滥用添加剂和非食用物质等一系列专项行动。全国累计出动屠宰执法人员 80 余万人次，取缔私屠滥宰窝点和不合格定点屠宰场点 2 500 余个，没收私宰肉、注水肉和病害肉 163 万 kg，有效净化了肉品市场秩序。四是积极开展宣传培训。商务部组织开展了《条例》的实施一周年宣传活动，印制了“肉品科学消费”宣传画；配合《食品安全法》和《条例》的宣传，全国累计印发宣传册 200 余万份，媒体宣传报道近 1 800 次，举办不同层次的培训班 95 期，近 8 000 名行业管理人员、企业负责人、技术人员及检验人员接受了培训，《食品安全法》、《条例》广为人知、深入人心。

（三）屠宰行业取得较快发展

2009 年，全国生猪定点屠宰企业屠宰量达到 3.16 亿头，比上年增加 12.8%，其中规模以上屠宰企业屠宰量达 2.1 亿头，较上年增加 11%，规模化程度提升明显。各地商务主管部门通过支持企业升级改造、兼并整合等方式，有效推动了生猪屠宰行业整体水平的提高。陕西、广东、广西等地分别投入 2 000万、5 000 万、645 万元财政资金对企业技术改造进行支持，有效提升了企业技术水平；安徽省积极推动生猪定点屠宰企业换证工作，通过换证关闭了 269 家未达标企业，淘汰率达到 17%。

（四）“放心肉”服务体系建设积极推进

2009 年商务部、财政部在北京、上海、山东、广东等 10 个省、直辖市开展了“放心肉”服务体系建设试点，安排 3 亿元资金用于试点地区屠宰监管技术系统、肉品质量安全信息可追溯系统和大型企业冷链建设，取得了阶段性的成效。一是提升了企业冷链管理水平，30 余个冷链建设项目承担企业累计投资近 14 亿元，新增冷库面积 10 万 m^2，购置冷藏运输车 1 000 余台，新设品牌肉专卖店（柜）5 000 余个，试点地区冷鲜肉市场份额提升明显。二是提升了屠宰监管能力。上海、青岛等地通过远程监管和可追溯系统的使用，及时发现企业存在的违法违规行为，出现肉品质量安全事故后迅速查明原因，追究责任，此举受到老百姓的好评。未列入试点的地区也积极参与“放心肉”服务体系建设，广西壮族自治区实施“八桂千乡放心肉”工程，宁波、秦皇岛等市积极建设猪肉质量安全可追溯系统，“放心肉”服务体系影响日益扩大。

二、屠宰行业管理工作面临新形势

2009 年生猪屠宰行业管理工作取得了一定成绩，但是仍面临不少问题。一是行业的整体水平仍然比较低，生猪屠宰企业多、小、乱、差的局面依旧没有根本改观，恶性竞争严重。据调查，全国 2.1 万个生猪定点屠宰企业中，小型屠宰场点 9 154 个，占 44%；从机械化程度来看，完全实现机械化屠宰的企业仅占 10%，相当一部分企业仍沿用手工屠宰模式，给肉品卫生和质量安全造成较大隐患。同时由于把关不严、流通秩序不规范、产品同质化严重等原因，屠宰行业“小挤大”问题十分突出，严重阻碍了屠宰行业现代化转型。二是管理基础仍然薄弱，大部分地区执法队伍编制、机构和经费问题仍未得到解决。全国屠宰执法人员中具有行政编制的仅占 20.6%，事业编制和临时聘用人员分别占执法人员总数的 41.2% 和 38.2%，执法主体资格不合法的问题仍然制约着监管工作的开展；由于监管手段缺乏，监管职责得不到有效落实，制售注水肉、病死病害肉等违法事件时有发生，甚至一些大型企业也出现违法经营的问题。但是，我国生猪养殖方式、交通运输方式、居民消费习惯都已经发生了深刻变化，资源节约和环境保护的压力也相应增大，使得加快屠宰行业结构调整和现代化转型任务越来越迫切，越来越重要。

我们还应当看到，生猪屠宰管理工作面临着一系列新的目标和要求。胡锦涛总书记关于加快经济发展方式转变、推进产业结构调整的重要讲话，为加快推进生猪屠宰行业结构调整和布局优化指明了方向。中央经济工作会议关于调结构、保民生、促消费的方针为我们抓好生猪屠宰管理工作提出了新的要求。2009 年底国家成立了食品安全委员会，食品安全工作被摆在了更加重要的位置。按照食品安全委员会的要求，商务部成立了部食品安全领导小组，上午姜部长就商务领域食品安全工作任务做出指示和要求。在新形势下，我们从事屠宰管理的同志们要认真学习、深刻领会中央领导的讲话精神，对食品安全和“放心肉”工作要有更加清醒的认识，以高度负责的态度把食品安全和“放心肉”工作抓紧抓好。

三、贯彻落实《纲要》是做好生猪屠宰行业管理工作的核心

针对上述问题和面临的形势，经过各方面的努力，我们推动出台了《纲要》。这部《纲要》在指导地方制定生猪定点屠宰厂（场）设置规划，优化行业布局，促进行业健康发展方面具有重要作用。在此，我着重谈谈《纲要》的几项重点内容。

（一）关于《纲要》的指导思想和发展目标

在指导思想上，强调以人为本，推动屠宰行业布局调整和结构优化，提高产业集中度，提升定点屠宰企业的技术装备和管理水平，提升猪肉产品卫生和质量安全保障能力，提升对规模化养殖的带动能力，更好满足人民群众对安全优质猪肉产品的消费需求。

总体目标是通过实施规划纲要，全国逐步形成以跨区域流通的现代化屠宰加工企业为主体，区域性肉品加工企业发挥重要配送功能，以供应本地市场的定点屠宰企业为补充，梯次配置、布局合理、有序流通的产业布局，确保消费者吃上“放心肉”。

（二）强调调整优化行业布局，大力淘汰落后产能

《纲要》对调整优化行业布局、淘汰落后产能加以重点关注：

1. 对各地生猪定点屠宰厂（场）设置规划的制（修）订提出了要求　一是在定点企业的数量规划上，综合考虑生猪养殖规模、屠宰加工能力、市场消费能力、交通状况等现实因素，采取行政区划和人口数量相结合的办法，对生猪定点屠宰厂（场）的数量进行了原则规定。原则上，直辖市和常住人口在500万以上的城市城区要少于4个，其他地级以上城市城区要少于2个，县（市）全境设1个，有条件的地方可不设屠宰厂（场）。西部地区和其他欠发达地区市、县可根据实际情况适当放宽。全国生猪定点屠宰厂（场）数量控制在3 000个左右。二是为加强环境保护，在定点屠宰企业的设置区域上做了明确规定，在污染源、供水水源地、自来水取水口和密集居住区等环境敏感地区，易产生有害气体、烟雾、粉尘等污染源的工业企业所在地区或场所不得设置屠宰企业。对新建项目必须执行环境影响评估和项目竣工环境保护验收，严格落实环保标准。三是在产区销区布局上，鼓励在生猪主产区设立大型现代化屠宰加工企业；鼓励在主销区发展具有分割、配送功能的肉品加工配送企业。按照《纲要》要求，到2015年，在全国生猪主产区（包括生猪养殖基地县、调出大县，下同）培育一批年屠宰量在100万头以上的大型定点屠宰厂（场），其屠宰量占全国的比重逐步提升。

2. 严格执行法规标准，淘汰落后产能　为实现《纲要》所提的设置目标，《纲要》要求各地商务主管部门严格执行标准，关闭不达标企业，大力淘汰落后产能。按照《纲要》的要求，到2013年，全国手工和半机械化等落后的生猪屠宰产能淘汰30%，到2015年淘汰50%，其中大城市和发达地区力争淘汰80%左右。这个目标充分考虑了东部和中西部地区的差异，手工和半机械化屠宰产能主要分布在中西部地区，受制于经济发展水平、交通和消费习惯等多方面差异，中西部地区在淘汰落后产能上困难更大，因此在淘汰比例上对东部和中西部设定了不同的目标。同时，在步骤上采取分阶段推进，对不达标企业设定了整改过渡期，对整改期结束仍不达标的，要坚决取消其定点资格。《纲要》还充分考虑了城乡差异，对农村边远和交通不便农村地区在政策上有所区别。

（三）实施分类管理，注重规范流通秩序

对边远和交通不便农村地区允许设置小型屠宰场点，一并与生猪定点屠宰厂（场）实行分类管理是《条例》中规定的原则，可以有效地解决因城乡差异造成的定点企业数量过多，监管手段不足的问题。为保证分类管理制度的有效执行，《纲要》强调要对流通秩序进行规范，一是打破地方封锁，要求各地不得限制卫生和质量合格的猪肉产品进入本地市场，逐步形成大流通格局。二是监督跨区域销售的定点屠宰厂（场）按照要求配备符合猪肉质量安全要求的冷链运输设施。到2015年，跨区域销售的定点屠宰厂（场）全部配置与流通范围相适应的冷链设施、运输车辆。三是加强对边远和交通不便的农村地区的小型屠宰场点流通范围的监管。四是严厉打击私屠滥宰。通过上述措施，保证行业公平竞争和肉品安全供应。

（四）推行分级管理制度，促进大型屠宰企业发展，发展冷链流通

促进大中型屠宰企业发展，适度提高屠宰行业集中度是保障肉品质量安全的重要措施。《纲要》提出要尽快推行分级管理制度，依据《食品安全法》和《生猪屠宰管理条例》等法律法规，制定《生猪定点屠宰厂（场）分级管理办法》和《生猪屠宰企业资质等级要求》，将定点屠宰厂（场）划分为若干等级进行相应管理，从而鼓励、引导生猪定点屠宰厂（场）改进生产和技术条件，加强质量安全管理，提高高等级屠宰厂（场）的肉品市场占有率，通过市场化手段将技术落后的屠宰厂（场）淘汰出局，从而实现行业的规模化、标准化、品牌化经营。同时，《纲要》还提出要从促进企业兼并重组，支持企业延伸产业链条，培育自主品牌，发展清洁生产，调整产品结构等

方面支持大型企业发展。

《纲要》还强调要创新流通方式，发展冷链流通。冷链流通是保证肉品质量安全的重要手段，也是提升企业竞争力的重要措施。《纲要》提出要引导大型定点屠宰厂（场）、肉类配送企业发展肉品分割配送中心，配置冷链设施，创建鲜肉品牌，扩大冷鲜肉和分割肉生产规模，扩张品牌肉连锁销售网络。到2015年，要培育一批以大中城市为重点销售范围的区域性肉品加工配送企业；使定点屠宰厂（场）通过连锁店、专卖店等渠道销售的猪肉产品比例明显提升(10%左右)；一批猪肉产品批发市场的低温仓储设施得到改造和提升。另一方面，积极引导冷鲜肉消费。倡导食用冷鲜肉和小包装分割肉，引导群众逐步改变喜食热鲜肉和白条肉消费习惯，从而带动企业冷链管理水平的提高。

为保证上述重点任务得到有效落实，《纲要》提出要加强法规标准建设，完善有关资金支持政策，促进行业协会发展，加大宣传培训力度，特别是要按照商务部、财政部、环保部、卫生部等九部门《关于加强猪肉质量安全监管工作的意见》要求，切实建立部门监管联动机制，共同抓好监管执法工作。

四、2010年主要工作任务

2010年是《全国生猪屠宰行业发展规划纲要(2010—2015)》实施的第一年，生猪屠宰管理工作要以保障肉品卫生和质量安全为核心，紧紧围绕《纲要》的落实，着力抓好以下五项重点工作：

（一）以生猪定点屠宰企业审核换证为契机推动压点工作

我国对生猪实行定点屠宰制度，《条例》对生猪定点屠宰企业的设立规定了严格的条件。但从目前情况来看，一些地方在定点屠宰厂的设置上把关不严，达不到《条例》规定条件和有关标准的企业大量存在，给肉品卫生和质量安全造成极大隐患，也催生了严重的恶性竞争。因此，《纲要》将调整优化行业布局，大力淘汰落后产能作为首要任务加以强调。近期我部下发了《商务部办公厅关于严格执行标准 做好生猪定点屠宰企业审核换证工作的通知》，对这项工作进行了具体部署。开展生猪定点屠宰企业审核换证是当前落实《纲要》压点任务和要求的一个重要契机，各地一定要牢牢把握，要统一思想认识，加强组织领导，尽快拿出具体工作方案，按照《通知》规定的审核标准和程序抓紧组织实施，按期完成压点工作任务，使不达标的企业得到彻底的清理，确保审核换证后的企业完全符合《条例》及有关标准的规定。需要强调的是，生猪定点屠宰企业进行审核换证是维护《条例》严肃性和权威性，确保肉品卫生和质量安全的一项重要工作，其政治性非常强。各地一定要制定完善的应急预案，妥善应对和解决换证工作中可能出现的各类矛盾和问题，同时做好舆论引导，防止出现群体性事件，保证工作有序进行。

（二）切实加强行业监管，建立行业信用分类监管制度

加强行业监管，是确保屠宰环节肉品安全的“要害”。近年来，我们在强化监管方面下了很大功夫，但部分地方注水肉、病害肉、私屠滥宰等问题还非常严重，甚至可能引发行业系统性风险。国务院2010年食品安全整顿计划中，将畜禽屠宰整顿列为一项重要任务。我们正在制定整顿工作方案。各地要结合开展整顿工作，采取有效措施，切实加强行业监管，促进肉品安全形势根本好转。一是要尽快开展专项检查，督促屠宰企业建立并严格执行生猪入厂（场）检查验收、宰前停食静养、屠宰操作、肉品品质检验、无害化处理、不合格肉品召回、索证索票及购销台账等制度。相关制度没落实的，要责令限期整改；整改仍达不到要求的，取消定点资格。二是要落实监管责任，严防死守。建立并严格执行监管责任制，对定点屠宰企业要包干到人、责任到人，加强日常监管；对反映比较集中的私宰窝点、注水窝点及其他顽固窝点，要安排专人进行重点盯防。因监管不到位导致严重违法违规的，严肃追究相关人员责任。三是要强化监管能力。食品安全责任主要在地方政府。李克强副总理最近批示，要加强基层特别是县一级的监管能力建设。各地要积极争取政府支持，充实监管力量，配备必要的检验检测和调查取证等装备。没有专门执法队伍的，要抓紧建立。四是要加强部门协作，发挥社会公众作用。要建立完善的部门联合执法机制和信息通报制度，加强与相关部门协作配合，共同打击私屠滥宰、注水肉等违法行为；切实发挥12312热线等电话作用，调动社会力量参与，及时发现并查处违法违规行为。五是要做好应急处置工作。要建立专门的突发事件应急预案，细化程序、时限及相关工作要求，有效防范、妥善处置猪肉安全事件。

2010年，我们也将在创新监管机制上出台一些措施，其中一个就是信用分类监管制度。主要想法是建立专门的屠宰企业信用档案，全面归集屠宰企业资质、落实规章制度及被举报投诉、违法违规等信用信息，并根据信用状况将屠宰企业划分为A、B、C、D四类，分别代表守信、基本守信、失信、严重失信四个等级。对于不同信用等级的企业，采取有针对性的分类监管措施。对A级守信企业，减少检查次数，优先给予政策支持；对B级基本守信企业，增加检查次数，加强守法经营教育；对C级失信企业，列入“黑名单”予以重点监管并向社会公示；对D级严重失信企业，依法取消定点屠宰资格。屠宰企业信用状况发生变化的，还将对信用等级进行动态调整。多次违法违规或者性质严重的，降低信用等级并强化监管；在较长时间内守法纪录良好的，提高信用等级。目前，我们正在制订方案，近期就将正式下发实施。

（三）加快推进分级管理

按照《纲要》要求，2010年将全面推行生猪定点屠宰厂（场）分级管理。目前《生猪定点屠宰厂（场）分级管理办法》和《生猪定点屠宰厂（场）资质等级要求》已起草、修订完毕，并广泛征求意见，预计将于上半年陆续出台。《办法》草案及修订后的《资质等级要求》规定从低到高分为A、AA、AAA、AAAA。同时，为鼓励和引导高级别屠宰企业国际化、品牌化经营，特设AAAAA级。商务部负责组织AAAAA和AAAA级认定工作，省级商务主管部门负责组织AAA和AA级认定，市级商务主管部门负责组织A级认定。为保证分级工作的权威性和公正性，具体评审和现场核查均规定由专家委员会按程序执行。

实施分级管理是行业管理的通行做法，对于推动行业发展、规范行业秩序有多重好处。一是形成对屠宰行业的客观划分，有利于实施分类监督管理。对高级别企业，要通过各种政策给予支持，鼓励其规模化生产和连锁经营、配送，进行兼并重组，优化行业布局；对不同级别企业或级别以外企业监管频次、方法要有所区别，确保企业合法经营。二是通过规定企业的肉品运输、存储条件和相关处罚手段，用技术和市场化手段做到分级管理与流通范围“挂钩”，有助于扩大品牌肉市场份额。三是形成市场自动甄别机制，有助于消费者多样化选择。级别越高，表明企业设施越完备、管理越先进、质量保障能力更强、产品结构更丰富。同时，通过分级管理可以发现屠宰企业存在的突出问题，为淘汰落后产能工作提供有力支撑。这项工作正在紧锣密鼓的筹备中，除《办法》、《标准》外，专家库筹建、评审细则、指南制订也有了很好的基础。各地要对本地生猪屠宰企业状况作全面了解，做到心中有数；要积极向商务部推荐专家，以备届时评审工作需要；要积极争取财政部门支持，早作汇报，确保落实评审工作费用；要广泛征求企业、专家意见，预见评审过程中可能遇到的困难和问题，做好相应准备工作。

（四）继续做好“放心肉”服务体系建设

2009年我们在10个省、市开展的“放心肉”服务体系建设试点工作取得了一定成效，地方对这项政策的反应不错。但是，作为加强屠宰管理工作的重要举措，这项工作需要进一步总结改进。2009年试点地区商务主管部门要加快工作进度，确保按期完成试点工作任务。2010年“放心肉”服务体系建设政策正在研究，主要有三方面内容：一是继续加强行业监管执法能力，建设屠宰企业监管系统，形成中央、省、市、县四级监管网络。二是在部分基础较好的大中城市开展肉品质量安全信息可追溯系统建设，形成从生猪入厂到肉品销售的完整信息链，确保责任可追溯。三是支持边远地区和少数民族地区生猪定点屠宰企业进行标准化示范改造，达到《条例》及有关标准规定的基本要求，保障肉品安全供应。各地要认真调查研究本地区屠宰企业和市场情况，学习试点地区以及广西、浙江宁波、河北秦皇岛等地的经验，探索符合本地区实际的“放心肉”服务体系建设模式。商务部将支持具备一定条件、有一定工作基础的地区开展“放心肉”服务体系建设。

（五）抓好行业培训等基础性工作

当前，我们行业管理的基础性工作还比较薄弱，各地要加以重视，重点做好三个方面的工作：

1. *加强对从业人员的资质等级管理*　据初步统计，全国20余万屠宰行业从业人员（包括生猪屠宰技术人员、肉品品质检验人员和企业管理人员）中，相当一部分人员缺乏必要的专业技能，未经培训考核便上岗操作，给肉品卫生和质量安全带来了较大隐患，亟待加强管理。推行从业人员资质等级管理制度，就是要联合有关部门，建立屠宰行业从业人员资格准入及备案管理、持证上岗、等级评定以及违规退出和公示等一整套制度，对从业人员进行全方位规范。具体而言，对于肉品品质检验人员，《条例》规定必须经考核合格方能上岗，要抓紧制定《肉品品质检验人员管理规定》并完善相关标准，对资格准入和考核发证等作出规定。各地要加大对屠宰企业肉品品质检验人员配备情况的检查，一旦发现未按照规定配备必要的人员，要按照《条例》进行处罚，情节严重的，要取消定点资格。对于其他专业屠宰技术人员，要探索建立技能水平评价制度，对其专业技能水平进行考核评价，将评价结果与个人绩效挂钩，将企业配备具备专业技能人员的比例与分级管理挂钩，与引导扶持政策挂钩，充分调动屠宰企业和职工的积极性，参加职业技能培训和考核。对于屠宰企业管理人员，要加强培训，引导其树立食品安全第一责任人的意识，规范经营行为。对取消定点屠宰资格的企业的主要管理人员，要按照《食品安全法》等法律的规定，5年内禁止从事相关生产经营管理工作。违法聘用此类人员的企业，也要取消定点资格。为做好这项工作，我们将联合有关部门，出台有关屠宰行业从业人员培训和资质管理规定，用3年左右的时间，在全国范围内分级分批对屠宰行业从业人员分类进行培训、考试并发放相应的资质证书。明天的培训班上我们还要进行专门介绍。各地要按照商务部要求，做好本地区从业人员的分类统计和组织动员，确保此项工作顺利开展。

2. 建立信息统计报送制度　信息统计报送各地一直都在做，但是主动、定期、规范的信息统计和报送制度尚未建立起来，信息掌握不全面、不及时给工作造成了一定影响。去年商务部已经运行了新的屠宰行业管理信息系统，希望各地能够尽快熟悉，按照系统要求做好审核换证、企业经营动态、监管执法、行业培训等信息报送工作。

3. 加强宣传　各地要重视宣传工作，制定详细的宣传计划，主动加强与媒体的联系，结合重点工作进行专项宣传，扩大工作影响力；在重大纪念日如《食品安全法》、《条例》实施周年日，要开展形式多样的宣传活动，为法律实施营造良好舆论氛围。

（本文为作者于2010年4月1日在全国商务系统食品安全暨屠宰行业管理工作会议上的讲话，略有删改）

加大结构调整力度 推进茧丝绸产业升级

商务部市场运行司司长　王炳南

本次会议回顾了近年来国家茧丝绸行业开展的主要工作及成效，总结了“东桑西移”工程的成果和经验，分析了行业面临的国内外形势，部署了下一阶段的重点工作。下面，我就做好茧丝绸行业“调结构、创品牌、促升级”工作，结合大家关心的一些问题，讲四点意见：

一、2009年以来国家茧丝办主要工作

2009年以来，国家茧丝办认真贯彻党中央、国务院“保增长、扩内需、调结构”部署，在各地茧丝绸主管部门的共同努力下，在行业协会的积极协助下，扎实推进了以下几个方面工作：

（一）落实扶持政策，巩固提高“东桑西移”工程效果

2009年，按照《茧丝绸行业“十一五”发展纲要》和“东桑西移”工程总体部署，积极落实“东桑西移”工程蚕茧基地深化巩固提高、灾后恢复重建以及配套技术攻关等建设项目，下达中央财政资金4 940万元，共扶持项目72个。召集全国17个省（自治区、直辖市）茧丝绸主管部门和企业的代表，在广东和四川召开了两次座谈会，对“东桑西移”工程进行了阶段性总结评估。2010年上半年，继续加强“东桑西移”工程后续跟踪管理工作，并组织所有实施“东桑西移”工程的地区，严格按照相关规定，对财政扶持资金使用情况开展了自查自纠，保证了“东桑西移”工程的实施效果。

（二）举办展会搭建平台，积极扩大丝绸消费

先后组织举办了2009年、2010年“中国丝绸交易会”、“2009年中国国际丝绸博览会”、“茧丝绸行业应对危机扩大消费研讨会”等主要会议，成功举办“2009年海峡两岸纺织丝绸合作研讨暨资本对接会”，搭建了国内外及海峡两岸纺织丝绸业界在资金、技术、人才、品牌、营销网络等方面的合作平台。为贯彻落实《关于搞活流通扩大消费的意见》（国办发[2008] 134号）文件精神，在中央财政支持中小商贸企业发展专项资金中，落实资金1 000万元，安排32个项目，重点支持丝绸企业开拓国内市场，创新丝绸营销模式，推动江苏、浙江、山东、广东、辽宁试点省建立以现代流通业为基础的丝绸营销网络，为促进丝绸消费发挥了积极作用。

（三）深化储备管理制度改革，不断提高市场调控能力

为支持丝绸行业应对金融危机，国家茧丝办积极会商国家发展和改革委员会、财政部、工业和信息化部出台了《厂丝收购贷款中央财政贴息资金管理办法》、《丝绸骨干企业增加厂丝收购实施细则》等政策措施，2009年分两批，落实37个企业收购厂丝8 000t，探索了国家厂丝储备与商业储备、地方储备

相结合的新机制，对稳定蚕桑和工业生产、促进行业经济效益的企稳回升起到了积极作用。

2010 年以来，联合财政部共同调研，结合茧丝绸行业出现的新形势、新变化、新特点修订《国家厂丝储备管理实施办法》，不断完善国家厂丝储备制度和投放程序，增强储备调控能力。上半年，受消费回暖、农产品价格普涨以及旱涝等异常天气影响，茧丝供应整体偏紧。为稳定市场供应，国家茧丝办于 1 月、2 月和 4 月分 4 次投放国家储备厂丝 1 300 多 t，适时缓解了供需矛盾。储备投放期间，茧、丝价格运行相对平稳。

（四）加强桑蚕茧丝生产指导，确保蚕桑生产规模稳定

2009 年以来，国家茧丝办组织召开了市场形势分析会、收烘工作会、综合利用研讨会等，研究蚕茧生产形势，加强茧丝绸市场监测，发布行业运行情况分析，还举办了蚕桑技术骨干培训会，培训了技术人员 200 多人。会同农业部门下发桑蚕茧丝生产指导性计划，指导蚕茧生产，确保了蚕茧生产规模，促进了蚕农增收。同时，进一步强化收购管理工作，会同工商部门下发多个工作文件，指导各地加大对蚕茧收购秩序的巡查力度，做好收购管理工作。据各地反映，2010 年春茧收购秩序总体较好，基本做到了有序收购、按质论价、不打“白条”。

（五）着手制定生丝电子检测国际标准，增强我国在世界丝绸业的话语权

2010 年 4 月份，《生丝电子检测分级规定和试验方法》标准提案获 ISO 纺织品国际标准化组织立项。该标准的制定将由我国主导，日本、韩国、印度、意大利、瑞士、法国、德国、肯尼亚等 8 国派专家参加，这标志着我国丝绸行业乃至纺织工业第一项国际性标准正式启动制定。2010 年 7 月份，国家茧丝办支持召开了标准项目组的第一次会议，瑞士、意大利、日本、印度派员参会，各国专家在会上充分讨论协商，达成了一系列共识，为早日完成标准草案的制定打下了基础。

我在这里向各位同志汇报国家茧丝办去年以来所做的主要工作，希望同志们能够了解，并多参与监督，共同推动行业发展。国家茧丝办的主要职能是对全行业加强指导、协调，应该说责任很重，而手段和政策并不多，但我们正通过自身努力，争取获得更多的政策支持。

二、我国茧丝绸行业面临的形势

茧丝绸行业是集贸工农于一体的产业，是中国未来软实力文化的代表。茧丝绸行业在改革开放以前，为国家创汇立下了汗马功劳。但由于多方面的原因，目前行业发展遇到了一些困难，需要我们对这个行业倾入感情和热情来工作。茧丝绸行业链条长，环节多，一头连着农业，一头连着国际市场，哪个环节出了问题，都会对行业发展产生影响，全行业应该同舟共济，克服困难，协调发展。2010 年以来，茧丝绸行业面临较为严峻的市场形势。

（一）桑园面积总体下降，呈现东减西增局面

桑园面积东部逐步缩小，西部逐步增加，这是产业转移的必然，是推进“东桑西移”顺应时代发展的结果。2010 年春，桑园面积已连续 3 年下降，但降幅比 2009 年减少 8 个百分点。其中东部地区浙江、山东、江苏桑园面积分别下降 0.8 万 hm^2、0.67 万 hm^2、0.53 万 hm^2，合计 2 万 hm^2，占全国总减量的 63.1%。中西部地区经过“东桑西移”，桑园面积总体有所增加，特别是广西增加了 1.93 万 hm^2，进行了适度的替代，填补了东部的缺口。

（二）春茧产量同比增加，但收购价格趋高

受农业生产成本上升、蚕茧产量连续两年下降、国内缫丝产能过大、旱涝冰冻异常天气等因素影响，2010 年春蚕茧收购时间推迟、价格高位运行。江苏、浙江、山东等优质茧产地每 50kg（担）达 1 600～1 800元，广东、安徽、广西、云南等地每 50kg 达 1 400～1 550 元，四川、重庆、湖北、湖南等地每担达 1 150～1 350 元，均为历史最高水平。春茧产量约为 25 万 t，同比增长 9%。这将刺激秋季蚕农种桑养蚕的积极性，预计下半年蚕茧产量将高于 2009 年同期。

（三）丝绸出口有所回升，但复苏形势仍不明朗

我国丝绸产品出口比重较高，国际市场变化是我国茧丝绸行业发展的主要晴雨表。人民币 2010 年以来升值较快，对长期依赖出口市场的丝绸行业影响较为明显。2009 年，丝绸产品出口额同比下降 17.5%。2010 年前 6 个月，丝绸产品出口扭转了连续 4 年下降的局面，比去年同期增长 8.3%，但仍比 2008 年同期低 11.5%，出口的回升既有去年同期基数偏低，也有出口价格大幅提高的因素。在欧美国家经济复苏动力不足、贸易摩擦加剧、茧丝价格居高不下的背景下，扩大丝绸产品出口仍面临较大困难。

总体看，2010 年我国茧丝绸市场面临形势较为严峻，不确定因素较多，但也存在诸多有利因素。国民经济的平稳较快发展，为丝绸行业稳定运行提供了重要基础，国内消费市场需求不断扩大，为丝绸业提供了巨大市场空间，特别是国家搞活流通、扩大消费政策措施，为丝绸业健康发展提供了动力。因此，我们要趋利避害，增强信心，努力创新，实现茧丝绸行业持续健康发展。

三、“调结构、创品牌、促升级”工作总体安排

2010年茧丝绸工作总体思路是，以“调结构、创品牌、促升级”为主线，以改善农业生产、提升工业水平、优化贸易结构为主要内容，以平台搭建、政策引导、储备调控为手段，大力推进科技创新、品牌建设和产业升级，全面增强产业竞争力，促进茧丝绸行业稳步发展。未来5～10年，是我国茧丝绸行业整体发展的关键时期，也是由丝绸大国向丝绸强国转变的关键时期。这就要求我们充分发挥政府的导向作用和行业组织的协调作用，出台政策措施，但更重要的是调动企业的主观能动性和蚕农的积极性，大力促进结构调整和产业升级。

在“调结构、创品牌、促升级”工作中要坚持三项原则：一是要坚持市场化走向，发挥企业主体作用。按照市场经济规律办事，就是要体现企业是市场经济的主体。在茧丝绸行业，众多的企业，尤其是有实力的茧丝绸企业，是行业的脊梁。二是要坚持品牌化战略。品牌代表着企业在国内外市场上的发言权和定价权。企业要着力于在研发和营销两个方面下功夫。目前，浙江、江苏等地许多企业正在由加工型向设计营销型转变。在品牌营销方面，这几年商务部重点宣传了“中国制造”、“中国劳务”，下一步将宣传“中国丝绸”。从企业来讲，丝绸品牌营销除了建立专卖店，也可以进行有形店和无形店的结合，通过网购来实现跨越式发展。三是要发挥政府搭台引导、协会沟通协调作用。茧丝绸行业是一个市场化比较强的行业，也是一个特殊的传统行业。虽然茧丝绸行业主要靠企业创新发展，但是政府可以加大投入、搭建平台、做好服务、增强信心，协会也可以做好沟通协调、发挥桥梁作用，共同推动行业的健康发展。2010年下半年，我们将从以下四个方面加大工作力度：

（一）调整产业结构，推动优化升级

2010年以来，我们先后会同财政部企业司到广西、浙江调研茧丝绸业转型升级情况，积极争取财政资金支持。经多次协商，初步同意在今后3～5年内，中央财政支持加强科技创新，推动产业升级，重点解决行业发展瓶颈问题，促进茧丝绸产业水平整体提升。一是科技创新建设。为解决茧丝绸行业面临的共性科研难题，将选择一批制约茧丝绸行业发展，但有一定研究基础的瓶颈问题，先易后难，予以重点突破。主要包括：优良桑、蚕新品种研发；桑、蚕病害的防治技术和药品开发；高效设施化蚕业生产装备研发；蚕桑资源综合利用产品研制；茧丝绸加工、染整、混纺交织关键技术研发；丝绸清洁生产、节能减排技术和装备研发；茧丝绸生产信息化应用技术等。研发这些技术要充分发挥科研机构、大专院校、研发中心，以及大型企业的作用，共同攻关，合力推进。二是产业升级建设。为促进先进科研成果的及时转化，体现集群发展的方向，下一步将依托科技创新，重点支持茧丝绸产业综合示范基地、产业科技园区和产业区域集群等。采取前期考察、跟踪服务、专家论证、成熟一批组织一批等方式，以补贴、以奖代补、贴息等形式，促进产业升级。

（二）开展丝绸品牌推广试点，继续办好丝绸展会

在2009年安排1 000万元中央财政支持的基础上，2010年继续安排了3 000万元用于丝绸营销网络及品牌建设，按照集中支持的方式，在全国重点支持20个品牌。参照各地2008年、2009年出口、生产的总量、产值，兼顾东中西部，确定了6个省。商务部、财政部的文件已经印发，大家可以到网上查看。希望有关省在选择企业支持时，扶优扶强、突出重点、集中使用，按上限安排扶持资金。此外，2010年已成功举办2010中国丝绸交易会，还要举办2010中国国际丝绸博览会，这两个展会都是列入中央财政支持的展会。主办单位要下大力气办好2010中国国际丝绸博览会，务使展会达到宣传丝绸产品和品牌、扩大丝绸贸易的实效。

（三）扩大厂丝储备规模，提升市场调控能力

1. *改革储备调控办法* 研究修订了《国家厂丝储备管理办法》。下一步，我们要本着公平、公正、公开的原则，探索有效的方式，完善对厂丝储备调控的改革。国家厂丝储备收储投放方式的变化是公开交易信息、公开交易价格的有益尝试。希望大家积极支持，提出宝贵意见和建议，不断完善调控方式、方法。

2. *扩大厂丝储备规模* 我们与财政部门协商提出，逐步建立起国家储备与地方储备相结合的储备体系，探索建立政府储备与商业储备相结合的新型储备模式。合理确定厂丝储备规模，力争达到厂丝年产量的10%。下一步要开展试点，以中央财政贴息方式支持建立重点企业参与、与国家储备联动的地方储备。各地要根据实际，积极探索新措施、新办法，进一步提高市场调控能力。

（四）加强行业管理，保障平稳运行

以规划、标准和法律法规为基础，做好行业管理工作。要充分调研、科学论证，编制好茧丝绸行业

“十二五”规划，引导行业健康平稳发展。要加强茧丝绸行业各项标准的制定和宣贯，特别是要全力做好生丝电子检测国际标准的制定工作，在限定的3年期内完成。目前茧丝绸行业涉及行政许可规定的有《全国缫丝绢纺企业生产经营资格核准》和《鲜茧收购资格认定》，其审批执行都已下放到地方，各地要结合实际制定实施细则，依法对上述两项行政许可予以核准。各地要建立健全茧丝绸行业管理机构，加强与相关部门的协调，指导茧丝合理生产，规范蚕茧收购秩序，不断提升茧丝绸行业管理工作的质量和水平。

四、对下一步工作的几点要求

2010年全行业“调结构、创品牌、促升级”，就是要推动产业增长方式发生质的转变，对已延续多年的贴牌代工等产业增长方式进行创新。这是一项艰巨、长期的工作。在这里，就做好下一阶段工作提出四点要求：

（一）高度重视，加强领导，认真做好行业管理工作

茧丝绸业作为传承中国几千年文化的古老特色产业，至今还在为农民增收、工人就业和生态环保发挥积极的作用。各级茧丝绸主管部门要以高度的责任感重新审视茧丝绸产业，使这一古老产业在现代经济大潮中得到振兴和发展。在发挥政府对产业引导作用的同时，注重充分发挥企业的主体作用，切忌代企业决策。

（二）整合资源，创建环境，加快推进结构调整

结构调整是一项全局工程、系统工程。相比大部分制造行业，茧丝绸产业既有外向型明显、劳动密集等普遍性，又有链条较长、源于农产品等特殊性，结构调整任务重。各地要结合宏观经济形势，整合现有政策资源，从财税、金融、工业、贸易等各个方面为结构调整创造良好环境。有条件的地区可以出台配套政策，扶优、强中、汰劣，推动茧丝绸业产品、产能、市场、人才等各层次结构调整。

（三）创新思路，深化改革，全面提高茧丝绸行业竞争力

茧丝绸主管部门要在深入调研的基础上，认真总结行业新特点、新变化；要抓住生命科学、电子技术、材料科学等快速发展的机遇，提高茧丝绸生产销售的标准化、信息化、科学化水平；要在蚕茧流通、储备调控等重点领域，继续深化改革，创建公平竞争环境；要更加积极地承担国际茧丝绸业的责任，鼓励企业在国际上发出更多的声音。

（四）扎实工作，强化监督，用好用足各项扶持政策

茧丝绸业经济总量较小，是我国传统产业、文化产业、民生产业，得到党和国家领导人的高度重视和各级政府的大力扶持。近几年，商务部实施了“东桑西移”工程，重点强化了蚕桑生产；国际金融危机爆发后，出台了支持骨干企业收储厂丝和加强营销网络建设等各项支持政策，稳固了产业基础。下一步，还将从“调结构、创品牌、促升级”的角度出发，出台若干扶持政策。各级茧丝绸主管部门要继续保持在“东桑西移”工程实施过程中体现出来的优良作风，协调有关部门，扎实工作，强化监督，用好用足各项扶持政策，确保各项政策发挥实效。

（本文为作者于2010年8月14日在全国茧丝绸工作现场会上的讲话，略有删改）

依靠科技进步 推进纺织工业健康发展

中国纺织工业协会会长 杜钰洲

召开这次纺织工业科技大会，学习贯彻党中央十七届五中全会精神，发布《纺织工业“十二五”科技进步纲要》，同时举行对第“十一五”规划最后一个年度科技成果及优秀教育和学生的奖励，是落实党中央“关于制定国民经济和社会发展第十二个五年规划的建议”的实际行动。

“十二五”时期是我国全面建设小康社会的关键时期，是深化改革，加快转变经济发展方式的攻坚时期。中央在“建议”中确立的“十二五”规划的指导思想是：制定“十二五”规划，必须高举中国特色社会主义伟大旗帜，以邓小平理论和“三个代表”重要思想为指导，深入贯彻落实科学发展观，适应国内外形势新变化，顺应各族人民过上更好生活新期待，以科学发展为主题，以加快转变经济发展方式为主线，深化改革开放，保障和改善民生，巩固和扩大应对国际金融危机冲击成果，促进经济长期平稳较快发展和社会和谐稳定，为全面建成小康社会打下具有决定性意义的基础。

纺织工业作为我国国民经济的传统支柱产业、重要的民生产业和国际竞争优势明显的产业，是我国“十二五”时期促进制造业由大变强的重点产业之一。根据“建议”的要求，纺织工业要坚持走中国特色新型工业化道路，必须适应市场需求变化，根据科技进步新趋势，发挥我国产业在全球经济中的比较优势，发展建立结构优化、技术先进、清洁安全、附加值高、吸纳就业能力强的现代产业体系。这里已经鲜明的概括了纺织工业在“十二五”期间依靠科技进步和创新作为加快转变发展方式的重要支撑的五大主要作用点，使纺织工业达到持续发挥在全球经济中的比较优势这样的市场地位。而加强这一支撑作用的主要参照系，是市场需求变化和科技进步新趋势。这一重要支撑的核心内涵恰恰是科技第一生产力和人才第一资源。纺织工业协会依据“建议”的这一重要精神，结合在“十一五”期间学习贯彻中央有关科技发展的理论和应对国际国内新趋势，新世纪以来纺织工业科学发展，推进产业调整振兴，落实纺织工业“十一五”科技发展纲要实践总结，集中行业智慧首先编制成《纺织工业“十二五”科技进步纲要》，并以此带动和促进全行业和纺织产业重点地区，尽早落实《建议》的精神。纺织工业协会将在科技进步纲要的基础上陆续扩展和深化，编制“纺织工业品牌培育纲要”、“纺织工业可持续发展纲要”、“纺织工业人才强国纲要”，并尽早作出“十二五”行业完整的规划意见。下面我再讲三点内容。

一、充分认识纺织工业“十一五”时期产业提升和转变发展方式取得的成就

“十一五”时期是我国发展史上极不平凡的5年，应对国内外环境的复杂变化和重大风险挑战，在中央大政方针的指引下，全行业艰苦努力，抓住机遇，化解矛盾，战胜困难，取得了发展、提升和转变发展方式的明显进步。纺织工业协会应对2005年开始的后配额时期，释放比较优势机遇和贸易保护主义的挑战，引导行业既要防止借机重新走“大干快上”粗放发展的老路，又要积极应对挑战加快产业提升。早在“十一五”前一年，即2004年就提前公布了“十一五”纺织工业科技发展纲要，明确提出28项关键技术攻关项目和10项关键成套装备攻关目标，在“十一五”期间，又对“28+10”项目进行两次细化和调整。这一纲要很快为国家各综合部门重视和采纳，从而得到了国家政策的有力支持。现在这些项目大部分已经进入了产业化推广，成为“十二五”推广项目的骨干。

在这一纲要的指引下，通过行业内外的创新发展，使纺织工业科技含量和创新能力、质量效益、环境友好、劳动生产率均大幅提高，自主研发、集成创新、引进消化吸收再创新硕果累累。大量成果产业化，成为行业在新时期转变发展方式的重要支撑。纺织工业在“十一五”期间全要素生产率（产值），从2005年的62.52%上升到75.78%，提高了13.27个百分点，比2000年提高了31.81个百分点。“十一五”期间，新型纤维材料攻关实现了一系列重要突破，涤纶、粘胶等化学纤维走上以自主研发技术为主体的高起点、大规模、低成本的国产化道路，差异化水平不断提高，对天然纤维和纤维素纤维应用开发不断有新的进步。新型纺纱技术、新型织造技术和非织造技术、清洁染整技术、产业链系列产品开发创新技术、新型产业纺织品和生态健康纺织品技术、新型装备制造业技术、计算机与信息化技术以及数字化、智能化、纳米技术、生物技术等精细化工技术在纺织工业应用领域有较大扩展，与纺织前沿攻关相关的应用数学、应用物理、应用化学等自然科学领域和交叉学科前沿技术等的应用基础研究取得一系列成果。自主品牌建设使大批本土产品在品质质量、创新活力、快速反应能力和社会责任的整体素质提升，不仅得到国内市场广泛认同，而且已经具备逐步走上国际市场的条件。这些进步成为推动中国纺织工业从承接全球纺织服装制造环节向承接全球纺织服装创造力和供应链控制力高端转移以及推进在国内东中西结构梯度转移的重要基础条件。下面一组数据能够清晰地展现纺织行业转变发展方式的重大变化：

——2008年，中国纤维加工量比2000年增长158%，同期全球生产纤维增长31.78%，扣除中国使用量后世界纤维加工量下降10%；而“十一五”前四年中国纤维加工量增长36.58%，扣除中国增加量后世界纤维加工量下降了16.75%，反映出中国在国际市场的比较优势仍在提升。

——2008年中国化纤产量2 415万t，占世界总产量的比重超过52%，是当年中国棉花产量的3.2倍，比2000年增长247%。同期世界化纤产量增长了35%，扣除中国的增产部分后世界化纤产量下降了19%。现在中国化纤使用量已经占全部纤维的

65%以上，这次棉花危机必定进一步引发中国化纤产业加速从数量向品种质量差异化发展转变，必将加速中国化纤产业超仿真技术的迅速发展。正如本纲要特别规划的，在"十二五"期间达到超仿真棉年产800万t左右。

——纺织工业的发展进一步转向内需拉动。内需持续高增长和消费结构提升成为中国纺织工业发展的第一拉动力。规模以上企业在过去的4年从3.65万户增加到2009年的5.37万户，同期，从业人数增长了12.81%，创造产值增长了83.65%，人均产值按可比价增长56.82%，其中内销比重从71%上升到81%。

——"十一五"前4年纺织工业万元产值减排24.44%，节能38.69%，聚酯循环再生纤维产能达700万t，年产量已经达到400万t。

——从2001年到2010年9月，纺织品服装贸易顺差累计10 856亿美元，占全国贸易顺差的85.98%，在2006年以后，虽然机电产品和新兴产业出口增长迅速，但纺织顺差累计6 404亿美元，仍占全国的60.87%。今年1～9月，纺织贸易顺差是全国其他出口产品贸易顺差的1.15倍。

——服装和面料出口的增长结构发生根本性转变。"十五"期间，主要体现了加入WTO后比较优势的释放效应，服装出口额增长98.65%，其中数量增长的贡献率占89.93%，价值增长贡献率10.07%；而"十一五"的前4年，服装出口额增长51.41%，其中数量增长的贡献率从98.65%下降到35.49%，价值增长贡献率从10.07%提高到64.51%。同样，各种纺织面料织物出口在"十五"期间出口额增长128%，其中数量增长贡献率为74.25%，价值增长贡献率为25.75%；而在"十一五"的前4年出口增长35.36%，其中数量增长贡献率从74.25%下降到27.47%，价值提升贡献率从25.75%上升到72.53%。这是对我国纺织工业产业提升的有力验证。

——在市场配置资源的基础作用和中西部大开发的宏观战略以及3年调整振兴规划影响下，2010年1～9月，我国纺织固定资产投资持续快速增长，但东部完成固定资产投资占全国的比重从2005年的77.32%下降到53.93%，中部比重从2005年的16%上升到34.71%，西部从2005年的6.7%上升到8.36%。东部率先发展正在从数量向质量效益提升，已经有众多国内著名品牌企业在新疆落地，以往劳动力输出大省河南、安徽、江西、湖北、湖南、四川等省已经成为积极承接产业转移的重点地区，有大批纺织工业园区正在兴建，大批新的纺织产业集群在中西部兴起。

然而，正如"十二五"规划建议指出的，纺织工业发展形势中还存在许多粗放的、不协调、不可持续的因素，特别是经过金融危机冲击后，全行业更加清醒的感到已经实现的发展方式的转变和提升是远远不够的。更增强了加快落实"十二五"规划"建议"精神，既要抓住难得的历史机遇，又要面对诸多可以预见和难以预见的风险挑战。这就要求发布的"十二五"科技纲要中应融入新的思想、新的认识和措施。

二、提高产业核心竞争力，发挥科技进步和创新的重要支撑作用

2000年，纺织工业在总结"九五"期间完成大规模结构调整和国有企业战略性调整任务的时候，就在全行业宣布了抓住新世纪的历史机遇，要在2020年建成现代化纺织强国的目标。经过"十五"时期和"十一五"时期的调整振兴、转变发展方式为主线的大发展，纺织工业在中央近期一系列方针政策的指导下，集中思考如何利用全面建设小康社会的第二个十年，加速调整升级，转变发展方式，实现纺织强国的奋斗目标。根据对国内外形势的判断和总结"十五"、"十一五"规划的实践成果，初步拟定纺织强国的四大奋斗目标，即在2020年基本建成纺织科技强国、纺织品牌强国、纺织可持续发展强国和纺织人才强国。这四大战略目标的实践过程贯穿着优化产业结构、生产力结构、企业组织结构和区域协调发展战略布局结构持续进行一系列战略性调整。

科技强国是纺织强国的重要基石，品牌强国是纺织强国核心竞争力，承载市场高附加价值的集中表现，可持续发展强国是纺织强国的重要着力点，也是贯彻节约资源和保护环境这一基本国策的客观需要。以上四大战略目标成为纺织工业"十二五"科技进步纲要确立的（50＋110）重点攻关和推广项目的战略性基础。

——开拓新型纤维资源是中国纺织工业发展现代产业体系的第一个战略课题。突破高功能化学纤维核心技术，事关我国战略性新型产业和综合国力的自主发展；突破对占世界产量60%左右的常规化纤的高技术差异化瓶颈，尤其是超仿棉高性能、高技术、高环保、高生态安全纤维大规模产业化，是事关中国纺织工业可持续发展和产业安全具有全局性的战略课题；开发可再生纤维素纤维具有同样的战略意义。当前的棉花危机凸现了这一战略的现实意义。

——发展纺织先进装备制造业是中国纺织工业从自主做大到自主做强的重大战略选择。以自主研发、集成创新为主，引进消化吸收自主创新为主，发展中

国自己的先进装备制造业，这是中国纺织工业从艰苦创业年代，到建设世界纺织大国新时期，再到由大变强的冲刺阶段的战略选择。纺织工业使用什么样的装备手段，是中国特色纺织工业现代性竞争力的最根本标志。装备的信息化、数字联动自动化、智能化，需要多学科、多产业、国内外的创新要素和多种人才的创造力集成。

——以纤维材料资源和技术装备为基础，从事新型纺纱、织造与非织造、染整，直到服装、家用纺织品和产业用纺织品的工艺创新攻关，新产品开发和品牌创造是纺织工业的软实力与硬实力有机结合。自然科学与社会科学，科学发展与技术发明，科技攻关与工程转化，物质创造与文化创意等集成创新，拥有无比的复杂，需要无比的活力。值得一提的是，首次把新产品开发能力和品牌创造能力列入制造业由大变强这一战略高度来强调。表明了从科技攻关到成果产业化再到向品牌价值转化这一市场配置创新资源的完整要求。把品牌创造能力作为产业整体素质来要求，在此基础上要求发展拥有国际知名品牌和核心竞争力的大中型企业。

——信息化技术融入纺织工业的研发、设计、生产、营销、供应链管理与决策，国内外资源配置，在电子商务，物流网条件下竞争与合作，纵向与横向产业链整合全过程，是一项无所不在的具有时代标志性的战略课题。

——应用基础研究是产业技术进步和创新的源头。在“十二五”纺织科技纲要中特别列出具有全面战略性的重点目标。比如影响产业国际竞争力具有普遍意义的战略性课题，影响产业可持续发展的战略性课题，可能出现纺织产业革命性突破的课题，学科综合交叉前沿性课题等等。希望能给重点研究机构和大专院校以提示和引导，也能促进有关行政部门和大型企业、金融和风险投资机构给予应有的重视和资金投入。

中国纺织工业协会之所以尽早发布纺织工业“十二五”科技进步纲要，还有一个思考，就是中央在科学制定“十二五”规划建议，对纺织行业来说最重要的是抓住时机，在实践中落实，在落实中加深对建议的领会。如果等到各方面规划出台再研究纺织行业的纲要，担心会贻误时机。

三、构建科技创新体系，实现“十二五”纺织工业科技进步纲要目标

在我们充分肯定中国纺织工业科技进步加快，创新能力提升的同时，我们也应清醒地看到，纺织科技工作总体上仍以跟踪模仿为主，原创科学成就和自主创造的关键核心技术还不多。走出一条有中国特色的自主创新道路，任务紧迫，责任重大。

在中央关于“十二五”规划的建议中，专门在第28条中阐述了“完善科技创新体制机制”，这是有关国家层面倡导的方向，对纺织行业都适用。全行业必须认真结合行业技术进步和提升创新能力的实际需要，认真贯彻。

深化科技体制改革是解放创新活力，提升行业创新能力最重要的动力。参照“建议”中一系列构建创新体系的措施，需要行业高度重视，纺织工业协会将因地、因时组织实施。

——加强科学研究与高等教育有机结合，建设国际行业创新体系，强化基础性、前沿性技术和共性技术研究平台建设，加强军民科技资源和共性技术研究平台建设，加强军民科技资源集成融合，“十一五”已经有许多融合，取得重要成果，许多“十二五”课题仍在融合中推进攻关，推进各具特色的区域创新体系建设，产业集群、基地市的创新、公共技术服务平台和行业性产品开发中心、检测中心等，鼓励发展科技中介服务，深化科研经费管理制度改革，争取行业重点攻关项目和产业创新同盟的政策支持，完善科技成果评价奖励制度。要更好地吸引行业的有识企业，继续支持、捐助纺织之光科教基金，还要争取更多企业的支持，争取能对一些基础研究项目给予特别奖励，同时要发挥好香港桑麻基金等社会资源对科技进步和人才培养的大力支持。

——重点引导和支持创新要素向企业集聚，加快建立以企业为主体、以市场为导向，产学研相结合的技术创新体系。这是现阶段纺织行业科技研发、攻关最重要的组织形式，效果也很突出，需要进一步总结经验，推广引导。

——增强科研院所和高校创新动力，鼓励大型企业加大研发投入。纲要提出要大于3.5%，目前有的企业达到10%，激发中小企业创新活力。目前，要扩大协会和地方政府合作共建公共服务平台，发挥五大服务体系的作用，发挥企业家和科技领军人才在科技创新中的主要作用。

——在政府层面，有关创新体系的政策措施，将不断完善，我们要充分争取政策支持，比如支持企业创新和科研成果产业化的财政金融政策，加大政府对基础的投入，推进重大科技基础设施建设和开放共享。我国纺织类大学和研究院所、有关重点实验室、工程中心等也可以吸收企业投资，建成公共服务平台。协会检测中心与地方政府或企业合作的模式运

作，已经取得很好的效果。

促进科技和金融结合，培育和发展创业风险投资。目前，国内还没有出现纺织行业风险投资，美国的风险投资对国内企业的投资已经出现。

实施知识产权战略，完善知识产权法律制度，加强知识产权创造、运用、保护、管理。这已经成为协会与国外组织合作的重要内容，对内部如何依法保护和依法加强知识产权的运用、保护、管理已经提上日程。

——抓住国家教育改革时机，全面提高高等教育质量，加快发展继续教育，支持民族教育，建设学习型企业。要尊重知识，尊重学校自主办学，尊重教师、学生主体地位，更新教育思想和方法，改革课程设置，引导探索、思考行业难题。引导和支持大学做好培养人才这一中心工作，同时积极开展基础前沿研究和社会服务。通过教育改革，把创新教育作为素质教育的重要内涵，贯穿教育全过程，在创新实践中培养造就宏大的具有全球竞争力的创新人才队伍，营造诚信和谐的创新环境，形成让"科技工作者更加自由地讨论、更加专心地研究、更加自主地探索、更加自觉地合作"的社会氛围。

——构建创新体系的核心思想是坚持以人为本，促进合作。科学管理思想对构建创新体系非常重要。我们已经知道，协作和分工产生生产力，不费资本分文，这是社会劳动的自然力。一定的生产方式或一定的工业阶段始终与一定的共同活动方式或一定的社会阶段相联系着，而这种共同的活动方式本身就是生产力。我认为在创新体系构架中，科学管理同样是创新能力的自然力。

——坚持开放，有效利用全球创新资源。以开放的态度对待人类创造的一切知识技术，防止自我封闭，不断拓展全球视野和战略眼光，加强国际交流合作，提升我国科技原创能力和创新能力及引进消化吸收再创新能力，转变跟踪发展模式，大幅降低对外技术的依赖程度，赢得竞争优势和主动权。

（本文为作者于2010年11月19日在第二次纺织科技大会上的讲话，略有删改）

齐心协力 扎实工作 推动绿色食品和有机食品持续健康发展

中国绿色食品发展中心主任 王运浩

这次"三品一标"工作会议是在新形势下召开的一次十分重要的会议，对推动当前和今后一个时期"三品一标"工作具有重要的指导意义。根据会议安排，我向大家简要报告2009年绿色食品、有机食品工作开展的情况，及对2010年绿色食品和有机食品工作进行具体安排。

一、2009年绿色食品、有机食品工作取得的进展和成效

2009年，绿色食品、有机食品发展面临的机遇与挑战并存。发展绿色食品、有机食品写入党的十七届三中全会《决定》；中央1号文件对绿色食品和有机食品基地建设提出了明确要求；农业部党组对绿色食品、有机食品工作作出了一系列决策和部署，都为发展绿色食品、有机食品创造了难得的政策环境和条件。与此同时，我们也充分估计到金融危机以及农产品质量安全形势给绿色食品、有机食品发展带来的压力。在机遇与挑战面前，在农业部党组的正确领导下，在部农产品质量安全监管局的指导下，在各地农业部门的大力支持下，中心班子认真谋划，整个工作系统共同努力，绿色食品和有机食品保持了平稳健康发展的态势。

2009年，我们共认证绿色食品企业2 297个，产品5 865个。全国有效使用绿色食品标志的企业达到6 003个，比去年同期增长2.3%，产品达到15 707个，比去年同期减少1.7%。绿色食品粮油、蔬菜、水果、茶叶、肉类、水产品等主要产品产量占全国同类产品总量的比重进一步提高。绿色食品年销售额达到3 162亿元，比2008年增长21.8%，出口额达到21.6亿美元，占全国农产品出口总额的5.6%。绿色食品种植业面积达到0.13亿 hm^2，约占全国主要农作物种植面积的8%。通过绿色食品认证的国家级和省级农业产业化龙头企业分别达到263个、1 090个，分别占30%和20%。绿色食品产品质量年度抽检合格率达到98.8%，比2008年提高0.4个百分点。

2009年，中绿华夏有机食品认证中心认证有机食品企业345个，比2008年增加15%。有机食品认证企业总数达到1 003个，产品总数达到4 955个，分别比2008年增长21.1%和21.4%。在国家认监委和中心分别组织的产品质量抽检中，中绿华夏有机食品产品合格率达到100%。在国内同行业中，目前中绿华夏认证的有机食品发展规模和品牌影响力继续保持领先地位。一年来，我们重点抓了以下五个方面的工作：

1. *积极稳妥地组织产品认证* 2009年，以防范质量安全风险为前提，我们在产品认证上继续强化从严从紧的指导思想，虽然导致发展速度有所减缓，但夯实了绿色食品持续健康发展的基础。为了提高认证工作的规范性和有效性，我们进一步规范和完善了认证标准体系；通过严格审核申请认证企业主体的资格和类型，依据相关办法，提高了部分高风险产品生产企业的进入门槛；加强了对各地认证检查质量的核查，并强化了工作监督机制。

在此基础上，各地充分发挥自身优势和特色，积极争取政策和资金支持，有力地推动了本地区绿色食品的发展。黑龙江省级财政继续安排3 000万元资金支持全省绿色食品发展；北京、江苏、浙江等地通过实施奖励政策，有效地调动了企业发展绿色食品的积极性；江苏、浙江、湖南、云南等省将“三品一标”工作列入各级农业部门绩效考核的重点，并加强认证工作的督查，有力地促进了全省绿色食品加快发展。四川省支持绿色食品发展的财政专项资金由2008年的40万元增加到2009年的250万元，全省新认证绿色食品企业和产品同期分别增长了108%和42%。

2. *继续稳步推进标准化基地建设* 截至2009年底，全国共有25个省、自治区、直辖市的307个单位（1个地市州、262个县、44个农场）建成绿色食品大型原料标准化生产基地432个，面积达到0.07亿 hm^2，产量5 717.6万t，涵盖69种优势农产品和地方特色产品。基地对接龙头企业1 138个，带动1 296.5万个农户，直接增加农民收入6.5亿元以上。经过5年的努力，绿色食品基地建设已走出了一条以品牌化带动农业标准化和产业化的新路子，成为绿色食品事业发展的新“亮点”。黑龙江省绿色食品原料标准化生产基地面积已达306.7多万 hm^2，占全国总面积的45%。江西省创建的53.3万 hm^2 绿色食品原料标准化生产基地，促进基地农户户均增收500元以上。山东、安徽、湖北、四川、宁夏、青海、新疆等省、自治区在农业主管部门的支持下，不断加大投入力度，基地建设也取得了明显成效。

3. *切实抓好证后监管工作* 2009年，我们认真落实农业部“农产品质量安全整治暨执法年活动”的各项工作部署，围绕“三品”专项整治，强化各项绿色食品监管制度。企业年检，各地绿色食品发展中心结合本地实际，制定具体实施方法和工作方案，进一步提高了覆盖率和实效性。产品抽检，中国绿色食品发展中心和地方绿色食品发展中心共组织4 509个产品的抽检，抽检比例达到25%，比2008年提高了5个百分点，共检出不合格产品39个。黑龙江、吉林、湖南、四川等15个绿色食品发展中心积极争取支持，主动筹措专项经费，自行安排了1 636个产品抽检。市场监察，累计在全国101个城市、316个各类市场抽取5 908个产品，发现不规范用标产品106个，查处假冒产品33个。北京、上海、天津、广州、宁波等绿色食品发展中心重点加强市场监察工作，在消费相对集中城市较好地维护了绿色食品品牌形象。产品公告，强化了淘汰退出机制，通过有关媒体对抽检不合格产品、用标不规范企业及时予以了公告。辽宁省绿色食品发展中心认真落实属地管理职责，自筹经费，在全省范围坚持开展产品公告。此外，为了方便企业规范用标，加强证后监管，我们改革了绿色食品编号制度。从目前来看，新制度运行平稳，基本达到了预期效果。

4. *进一步强化技术支撑能力建设* 2009年，中心加大了标准建设力度，制定了标准建设3年规划，完成了由农业部立项的《绿色食品 畜禽饲养防疫准则》等9项标准制修订工作；安排自有资金，启动了《绿色食品 米酒》等4项产品标准的制订；发布了《华北地区绿色食品苹果生产操作规程》等21项生产操作规程。目前，通过农业部发布的绿色食品标准已达到152项，绿色食品标准体系进一步完善。安徽省绿色食品发展中心组织专家分类制定全省绿色食品原料标准化基地管理规则，并以地方标准发布实施，为基地建设提供了有效的技术支撑。云南省绿色食品发展中心利用“三品一标”认证，推广各类农业标准8 400多项次，有力地促进了全省农业标准化生产水平的提高。

为了有效防范绿色食品认证风险，我们全面加大了质量安全预警工作步伐。按照简便实用的原则，建立了绿色食品质量安全预警工作机制，出台了预警管理规范、预警信息上报与分析评估程序等制度，建立了以信息收集、评估和处置为核心的工作方式。按照这套系统，开展了对转基因木瓜等5项安全信息的分析处置工作，效果已初步显现。下一步，我们将在蔬菜、茶叶和肉类等3个产品类别上开展试点，总结经验后全面推行。有机食品也根据行业特点，出台了《风险预警及应急处理办法》，以增强风险控制能力。

5. *积极开展品牌宣传和市场服务* 中心重点抓

了3项工作：在甘肃兰州召开了全国绿色食品宣传工作会议，提出了进一步加强宣传工作的意见，明确了宣传工作的指导思想、目标任务和重点工作。按照“循序渐进、不炒作”的原则，制定了宣传工作3年规划，启动了主题年宣传活动。创新工作模式和机制，在山东烟台成功召开了第十届中国绿色食品博览会。此次绿博会不仅取得了66.8亿元的贸易成果，而且首次组织256个绿色食品标准化基地参展，进一步扩大了绿色食品事业的影响。绿博会期间，我们还成功举办了“绿色食品基地建设研讨会”、“亚太地区绿色食品和有机食品与现代农业发展国际研讨会”，赢得了方方面面的一致好评。在农业部农产品促销项目的支持下，我们还在上海成功举办了第三届中国国际有机食品博览会，组织国内绿色食品和有机食品企业参加了日本、德国、美国3个境外专业展会。

各地绿色食品发展中心在积极配合中国绿色食品发展中心落实各项重点工作和重大活动的同时，采取多种形式和手段，主动开展品牌宣传和市场服务工作，取得了很好的效果。浙江省绿色食品发展中心将经常性宣传与集中性宣传相结合，促进管理部门、新闻媒体、生产企业、消费者互动，宣传工作有声有色。甘肃省绿色食品发展中心创新和丰富宣传形式，开展了绿色食品宣传歌曲征集活动。广东省绿色食品发展中心精心策划创办《绿色食品》杂志，建立起了行业交流和宣传平台。黑龙江、吉林、内蒙古、湖南、江西、新疆等省、自治区绿色食品发展中心创造条件，先后组织举办了具有区域特色的绿色食品专业展会。北京、福建等省、直辖市绿色食品发展中心积极引导和指导企业开展绿色食品专业营销渠道和网络建设，培育市场，促进消费，提升绿色食品品牌价值。

2009年绿色食品、有机食品工作取得的成效来之不易，这是农业部党组高度重视和正确领导的结果，是地方各级政府和农业部门积极支持和大力推动的结果，是整个工作系统共同努力、开拓进取的结果。在此，我代表中国绿色食品发展中心向长期以来关心、支持绿色食品事业发展的各级领导，向整个工作系统的同志们表示衷心的感谢!

在看到成绩的同时，我们还应该清醒认识到绿色食品事业发展仍然面临一些挑战，一些课题尚需努力加以破解。一是区域发展不平衡。部分地区由于政策支持不足、工作力度不够，发展绿色食品的环境条件、资源优势和市场潜力还没有充分发挥出来，少数地区仍然长期徘徊不前。目前，江苏、山东、浙江、黑龙江、湖北、安徽、辽宁、福建、江西、广东、湖南、四川12个省份的绿色食品企业总数和产品总数已分别占全国总数的74.5%和76.2%。黑龙江、安徽、江西、江苏、内蒙古、四川、新疆、湖南8个省份的绿色食品标准化基地面积已占全国总面积的83.6%。二是品牌的公信度和影响力有待进一步提升。一方面，由于个别产品存在质量安全问题，少数企业用标不规范，假冒现象时有发生，一定程度上影响了绿色食品的品牌形象，要求我们必须始终严格证后监管。另一方面，许多消费者对绿色食品仍然缺乏科学、准确的理解，品牌形象还没有真正深入人心，部分企业还没有真正增强绿色食品品牌的意识，需要我们加强深度宣传，进一步扩大绿色食品品牌的社会影响力，增强市场拉动力。三是体系队伍能力建设有待进一步加强。当前，绿色食品事业发展面临的形势和任务对整个工作体系队伍的能力建设提出了更高的要求，需要通过扩大队伍规模，提高人员素质，强化职能职责，创新体制机制，以适应推动产品认证、基地建设不断发展的需要，适应强化认证审核、证后监管核心业务工作的需要，适应做好品牌宣传、市场服务等基础工作的需要。此外，我们还需要关注有机食品市场过度炒作，部分地方盲目发展的问题，始终坚持“因地制宜、实事求是、严把标准、规范运作”的原则，切实维护“中绿华夏”有机食品的品牌形象。

二、扎实推进2010年绿色食品、有机食品工作

2010年，绿色食品、有机食品工作的总体要求是，认真贯彻中央农村工作会议、全国农业工作会议精神，紧紧围绕农业部党组确立的“两个千方百计”、“两个努力确保”的中心任务，按照农产品质量安全工作的总体部署，继续规范产品认证，强化证后监管，加强质量安全预警，加快市场体系建设，积极推进制度机制创新，努力提升品牌的认知度和公信度、提升品牌的影响力和竞争力，促进绿色食品、有机食品持续健康发展，进一步发挥其在推动农业标准化生产、提高农产品质量安全水平、促进农业增效和农民增收中的示范带动作用。

按照这个工作思路，今年绿色食品工作系统要重点抓好以下6项工作：

1. 继续规范产品认证 继续坚持“从严从紧、积极稳妥”的工作方针，既要积极组织产品认证，防止大起大落，又要切实防范认证风险，保持绿色食品平稳健康发展。争取全年新认证绿色食品企业2 000个，产品5 000个，有效使用绿色食品标志企业总数达到6 200个，产品总数达到16 000个。具体采取3项措施：一是继续重点组织各级农业产业化龙头企业、大型食品加工骨干企业、国内知名品牌企业和出

口企业发展绿色食品，提高产业发展质量和效益。同时，积极引导农民专业合作社发展绿色食品，提高农民专业合作社标准化生产、规范化管理、品牌化经营的水平，促进农超对接，实现农业增效和农民增收。中国绿色食品发展中心将与农业部经管总站合作，在调研工作的基础上，提出专门的指导性意见，共同推进此项工作。二是进一步完善续展认证制度，创新工作机制，将续展工作与证后监管更加紧密地结合，降低成本，提高企业续展率。三是修订认证程序，完善认证技术规范，强化认证现场检查、监督抽查，逐步推行“先培训、后申报”的工作制度和企业内检员制度，改进专家评审工作，防范履责风险和产品认证风险，进一步提高认证工作的规范性和有效性。

2. *切实加强证后监管*　2010 年监管工作要紧紧围绕“保证产品质量、规范企业用标”两大中心任务，完善各项监管制度，充分调动各方面力量，全面落实企业年检、产品抽检、市场监察、质量安全预警等监管措施，尽最大努力保证绿色食品少出问题和不出大问题。一是加强企业年检督导检查。根据质量安全预警和历年产品抽检情况，选择部分省地，重点对蔬菜、茶叶、肉类、水产品、葡萄酒等 7 大类产品生产企业进行年检工作有效性督查。二是提高产品质量抽检的有效性。结合部监管局的安排，2010 年中心将组织抽检产品 3 150 个，约占 2009 年用标产品总数的 20%，加上各地绿色食品发展中心自行安排的抽检，全年产品抽检总数力争超过 4 500 个，抽检覆盖率达到 28%。改革抽检计划下达方式，提高高风险产品的抽检比例，并适度向续展产品倾斜。根据不同季节，分批分类下达敏感产品抽检计划。三是扩大标志市场监察范围。逐步从省会城市向地市级城市延伸，并适当引入市场机制，扩大市场监察成效。进一步加强与工商部门合作，及时沟通信息，加大打击假冒产品和纠正不规范用标的力度。四是提高质量安全预警和突发事件处置能力。在 2009 年试运行的基础上，将质量安全预警产品由原来的 3 大类扩大到 5 大类，增加水产品等类别。五是启动绿色食品企业内检员制度，力争年底实现在 50%的绿色食品企业设立内检员，强化企业责任，从源头加强监管工作。

3. *稳步推进标准化基地建设*　继续以优势农产品产业带、特色农产品规划区和农业大县为重点，按照“严格管理、规范程序、成熟一个、发展一个”的思路，稳步推进绿色食品原料标准化生产基地建设。2010 年基地建设要在 3 个方面下功夫：一是提高基地建设质量。建立标准化基地专家评审制度，发挥专家技术支撑作用。组织开展基地年度监督检查工作，探讨建立和推行基地产品抽检制度。加强标志监管，对未经认证的基地产品，明确不得使用绿色食品标志。二是争取政策和资金支持。按照融入现有各类农业标准化基地建设项目的思路，积极争取各级农业部门的支持，加大对绿色食品标准化基地建设的资金投入力度。三是做好基地服务工作。2010 年，中心进一步完善了绿色食品生产资料有关管理制度，强化了质量安全监管措施。各地要加大绿色生资工作的力度，将绿色生资发展及推广服务工作与标准化基地建设更加紧密地结合起来。同时，进一步研究相关对策和措施，促进标准化生产基地原料与绿色食品加工企业的有效对接。

4. *加大宣传、市场和信息工作力度*　2010 年的宣传工作要以纪念绿色食品事业发展 20 周年为契机，以贯彻《关于进一步加强绿色食品宣传工作的意见》为重点，开展以下工作：一是采取“润物无声”的方式，继续围绕主题宣传年开展活动。包括组织网上绿色食品知识讲座、开展绿色食品知识竞赛等。二是组织好绿色食品 20 周年系列纪念活动。中心已制定了具体工作方案，目前正抓紧筹备。各地绿色食品发展中心可结合本地实际，开展形式多样的宣传活动。三是继续办好中国绿色食品 2010 上海博览会和第四届有机食品国际博览会。今年的绿博会将上升到由农业部主办，成为农业部主办的 4 个重点展会之一。我们要精心策划，抓紧筹备，力争在品牌宣传、贸易成果上取得新的突破。市场建设，要在调研工作的基础上，研究推进绿色食品市场体系建设的意见，指导各地开展国内外展销活动，支持建立专业营销渠道，探索绿色食品市场建设有效途径。信息服务，要利用“金农工程”创造的条件，加快绿色食品和有机食品信息网络建设，完善网上认证和监管信息系统，进一步增强服务功能。

5. *努力夯实事业发展的基础*　一是积极创造法规和政策条件。加强与农业部相关部门的沟通和汇报，争取支持，尽快修订和出台《绿色食品标志管理办法》。2010 年是实施“十一五”规划的最后一年，各地绿色食品发展中心要着眼“十二五”规划，积极争取将绿色食品工作纳入当地农业农村经济发展的整体规划，以获得持续的政策支持。二是进一步完善标准体系。中国绿色食品发展中心将按照《三年规划》，继续推进绿色食品标准体系建设。在争取农业部支持的同时，中心继续自筹资金，开展《绿色食品 渔业饲料及饲料添加剂使用准则》等 13 项标准制修订工作；结合优势农产品区域规划和试点基地，制定畜牧、水产部分产品的养殖生产操作规程范本，以指导各地制定区域性生产操作规程。三是加强对监测机构的管理和服务。探索建立对绿色食品监测机构的激励机制、退出机制和动态管理机制，完善监测机构能力验证工作，充分发挥监测机构在质量把关、质量监督、质量安全预警上的技术支撑作用。四是加强体系队伍建设。各地绿色食品发展中心要在抓好自身建设的同时，工作机构、职能职责要向下延伸，以发挥体系整体优势，增强工作合力。要进一步加强认证检查员和标志监管员“两员”队伍建设，启动企业内检员队伍建设，不断提高素质，发挥核心业务骨干作用。

6. 扎实推动有机食品规范健康发展　一是继续稳步推进产品认证工作，力争今年新认证有机食品企业360个，产品2 000个，保持认证率达到85%以上，认证企业总数达到1 150个，产品总数达到5 000个。同时，根据市场需求，适当拓展业务范围。二是严格规范认证，切实加强证后监管。认证环节，要严把材料审核关、现场检查关、产品质量关，确保认证工作的有效性。证后监管，要综合采取企业自查、非例行检查、交流检查、同行评估、市场用标规范性检查、产品抽检等手段，突出蔬菜、水果、畜产品、蜂产品等重点产品。三是推进有机农业基地建设。按照农业部今年为农民办实事的要求，选择8个国家级重点扶贫县开展有机农业基地建设试点工作，探索基地建设与产品认证对接的方式和途径。四是实施品牌战略计划，进一步提升中绿华夏有机食品品牌形象。加快“中绿华夏”证明商标注册，继续推进IFOAM认可和ISO65国际认可，加强国际互认合作和境外认证工作。

2010年是绿色食品事业发展20周年，我们要以此为新的起点，在农业部的领导下，在地方各级政府和农业部门的支持下，按照陈晓华副部长重要讲话所提出的要求，立足“三农”工作大局，增强责任感和使命感，振奋精神，扎实工作，努力开创绿色食品事业发展的新局面，为加快我国现代农业建设、提高城乡人民生活质量作出更大的贡献。

（本文为作者于2010年3月18日在全国“三品一标”工作会议上的讲话，略有删改）

明确目标　强化措施
推进无公害农产品及地理标志科学发展

农业部农产品质量安全中心主任　陈生斗

根据会议安排，下面我就认真做好无公害农产品和农产品地理标志工作讲几点意见：

一、2009年工作取得明显成效

2009年，无公害农产品和农产品地理标志工作系统认真贯彻落实全国农产品质量安全监管工作会议精神，在各级政府和农业行政主管部门的正确领导下，紧紧围绕农业农村经济发展大局，把实现科学发展作为核心目标，以提升农产品质量安全水平和发挥机构职能作用为重点，深化改革、创新机制，推动无公害农产品和农产品地理标志事业持续稳定发展，各项工作取得了明显成效。

1. 认证认定稳步推进　根据农业部农产品质量安全中心工作部署，各地按照农产品主产区和优势农产品产业带建设要求，全面加快“米袋子”、“菜篮子”产品认证进程，加强分类指导，充分挖掘认证潜力，促进地区、行业和产业间协调发展。全年新认定产地6 800个，新认证产品9 507个，分别完成全年目标任务的136%和159%。同时，统筹谋划和推动复查换证工作，通过督促指导，全年共完成到期复查换证产品5 243个，复查换证率保持在75%以上，较好地稳定了产品认证的数量和规模，提升了无公害农产品的品牌公信力。

2. 认证风险有效控制　根据农产品质量安全形势的要求，坚持从严从紧的原则，进一步规范了相关认证程序，并对无公害农产品认证申报要求进行了适当的调整和完善。一是将拥有培训合格的内检员作为申请认证的资质条件之一；二是停止受理乡镇人民政府等非生产性主体的认证申请；三是严格按照农业部公布的《实施无公害农产品认证的产品目录》受理产品认证申请；四是从严把握便捷式复查换证申请和考核条件，明确要求现场检查比例不得低于年度到期复查换证产品总数的5%；五是强化产地认定过程中的环境检测和评价工作；六是全面推进产地认定和产品认证一体化运行。为确保获证无公害农产品质量安全，研究制定了《无公害农产品风险预警管理规范》，进一步明确无公害农产品申请人和证书持有人是获证产品质量安全第一责任人，要求各级工作机构要有固定渠道搜集整理无公害农产品质量安全信息，并及时进行筛选、分析、评估，采取相应的风险预警管理措施。通过这些措施，进一步降低了认证风险，提高了产品质量安全水平。2009年无公害农产品抽检合格率为历年最高。

3. *证后监管全面加强* 在加快发展、扩大总量规模的同时，证后监督管理进一步加强。根据农产品质量安全整治暨执法年活动的统一部署，会同中国绿色食品发展中心组织开展了“三品”专项整治。在各地全面开展自查自纠的基础上，派出5个督查组对10个省份的整治工作进行了重点督导，对专项整治活动中发现的问题依法作了处理，撤销4个获证单位35个产品的无公害农产品证书，责令18个获证单位限期整改，并提请省级农业行政主管部门对20个冒用无公害农产品标志的违法行为进行了依法查处。在各地申报的基础上，将23个省级工作机构列入2009年全国无公害农产品标志推广与监管试点范围，将63个县（市、区）纳入标志推广与监管示范县创建计划，并对前几年开展创建活动、符合验收条件的26个示范县进行了验收。同时，分两次对16个省份的1 487个获证产品进行了监督抽检，抽检合格率分别为99.1%和99.2%，并对跟踪监测过程中发现的问题依照规定进行了处理。

4. *地理标志登记保护积极推进* 全年共受理农产品地理标志登记申请398件，评审通过并完成公示产品209个，产品登记步伐明显快于2008年。新委托产品品质鉴定检测机构20个，与省级工作机构联合举办核查员培训班11期，培训人员1 200人。成功举办首届全国农产品地理标志产品品质鉴定检测机构培训研讨班和农产品地理标志核查员师资培训班，培训师资119人。在充分调研和广泛研讨的基础上，制定了《农产品地理标志产品名称审查规范》和《农产品地理标志公共标识设计使用规范》。启动了农产品地理标志获证产品跟踪抽检工作，对9个省份28个获证产品、190个样品的品质指标和安全性指标进行了抽检，获证产品安全性指标全部合格。同时，在工作推进过程中强化了与有关部委的沟通协调和交流，积极参与WTO对华贸易政策审议和中欧、中瑞农产品地理标志贸易谈判等重要文件的起草工作，派人参加了第二次中欧经贸高层对话会议、亚洲地区农村发展及地理标志农产品和食品质量研讨会等国际会议，组织实施了中欧农产品地理标志合作研究项目。

5. *支撑体系建设不断强化* 进一步优化无公害农产品定点检测机构布局，新委托检测机构8个，重新委托合同到期检测机构44个，终止委托检测机构3个。认真落实检测信息月报制度，及时掌握检测机构的抽样、检测、收费及抽检农产品的风险因子等情况。根据《农产品质量安全法》和《食品安全法》有关规定，对照新颁布的无公害食品行业标准，全面修订了认证产品目录。组织专家对21项无公害食品行业标准进行了审定。全年组织举办各类无公害农产品培训班104期，培训人员17 632人。为探索建立有效的激励机制，充分调动体系队伍的工作积极性，启动了无公害农产品优秀检查员推荐和评选工作，首次在全国工作系统表彰无公害农产品优秀检查员635名。

无公害农产品和农产品地理标志事业之所以得到快速发展，得益于部党组的正确领导，得益于各级地方人民政府和农业行政主管部门的大力支持，得益于整个工作系统的扎实工作。

二、牢牢把握事业发展的有利时机

无公害农产品和农产品地理标志经过多年的推动和发展，已经具有一定的总量规模和品牌影响力，当前无公害农产品和农产品地理标志发展具备不少有利条件，迎来了良好的发展机遇。

1. *政策环境好* 党中央、国务院和部党组高度重视农产品质量安全监管和“三品一标”工作。2010年中央1号文件明确提出要积极发展无公害农产品、绿色食品和有机食品，要充分运用农产品地理标志促进特色农业发展。2009年12月份召开的全国农业工作会议提出了“两个千方百计”和“两个努力确保”的目标任务。在2010年1月召开的全国农产品质量安全监管工作会议上，陈晓华副部长强调要大力发展“三品一标”，不断提高“三品一标”的公信力和品牌形象，积极推动获证企业依法规范包装标识，鼓励有条件的企业加快可追溯平台建设，实现“生产有记录、流向可追踪、信息可查询、质量可追溯”，要大力扶持和引导农民专业合作社开展“三品一标”认证，通过认证不断提高内部管理水平，促进“农超对接”，实现农业增效和农民增收。这次“三品一标”工作会议，陈晓华副部长亲自到会并做了重要讲话，为无公害农产品和农产品地理标志工作指明了方向，确定了重点，提出了要求。我们一定要认真落实党中央、国务院和部党组的部署，按照陈晓华副部长的要求，增强责任感、使命感和紧迫感，全力推进事业又好又快发展。

2. *发展空间大* 无公害农产品发展最主要的任

务是解决农产品的生产标准化和消费安全问题。随着城乡居民收入的增长和生活水平的提高，无公害农产品消费需求日益增长。目前我国通过认定的无公害农产品产地面积仅占全国耕地总面积的35%左右，认证产品总量还不到全国食用农产品商品量的30%。按照部里要求，要通过8～10年的努力，力争使我国食用农产品无公害生产面积扩大到70%，产品总量占食用农产品商品量的比例增加到60%。据调查，我国独具特色的地域品牌农产品种类多、品质好、消费市场大，在全国15 600件有规模、有特色、有市场的地域品牌农产品中，仍有90%的产品未纳入依法登记保护和特色农产品产业发展规划。从数量规模上看，无公害农产品和农产品地理标志发展空间都相当大。另外，按照农产品质量安全监管工作的发展需要，无公害农产品在保障生产和消费安全的基础上，还要发挥标准化生产示范带动、便捷市场准入和质量追溯功能，农产品地理标志将承载促进特色农业和优势农产品发展的重任。从功能作用上看，无公害农产品和农产品地理标志发展潜力巨大，需要加大力度，继续推进。

3. 推进基础实　十七届三中全会《中共中央关于推进农村改革发展若干重大问题的决定》强调，要加强农业标准化和农产品质量安全工作，严格产地环境、投入品使用、生产过程、产品质量全程监控，切实落实农产品生产、收购、储运、加工、销售各环节的质量安全监管责任，杜绝不合格产品进入市场。实质上就是强调，上市销售的农产品都应当符合无公害农产品要求。《农产品质量安全法》规定，质量安全方面存在问题的五种农产品不得上市销售，其实也就是规定：达不到无公害农产品市场准入条件的农产品不得上市销售。目前各地在推进农产品标准化生产、优势农产品生产基地建设和大中城市农产品市场准入制度实施过程中，都明确把通过无公害农产品产地认定和产品认证作为基本条件，这无疑是对无公害农产品发展的极大推动。从各地陆续出台的推进措施看，越来越多的地方政府把发展无公害农产品和加快农产品地理标志培育保护纳入到当地农业农村经济发展规划和年度目标责任考核范围，并加大了财政资金方面的投入。无公害农产品和农产品地理标志已成为各级农业行政主管部门依法实施农产品质量安全监管、科学推动特色农产品产业升级和培育地域特色优势区域经济发展的重要抓手，推进无公害农产品和农产品地理标志发展的基础越来越实。

但是我们也应当清醒地看到，无公害农产品和农产品地理标志在地区、行业和产业间发展还不平衡，与当前农业农村经济的发展要求相比，与人民群众对安全优质品牌农产品的需求相比，还有大量的工作要做。近年发生的农产品质量安全事件告诫我们，确保我国农产品质量安全的任务仍然艰巨，无公害农产品应在“保障消费安全，满足公众需求”方面发挥更大的作用。我们要立足当前，把握时机，优化环境，增强信心，乘势而上，争取在一个较高平台上创造新的成效；更要着眼长远，充分调动各种资源，发挥各方面积极性，坚持不懈地扎实推进事业发展。

三、努力做好2010年各项工作

2010年是完成“十一五”规划任务、谋划“十二五”发展的关键一年，扎实推进无公害农产品和农产品地理标志工作，对实现部党组提出的“两个千方百计”和“两个努力确保”的目标，巩固和发展当前农业农村经济大好形势意义重大。我们要全面贯彻落实部党组的部署，努力做好2010年的各项工作。

2010年无公害农产品和农产品地理标志工作的总体思路是：以科学发展观为指导，深入贯彻全国农业工作会议精神，按照全国农产品质量安全监管工作的总体部署，积极扩大总量规模，着力强化监督管理，全面提升品牌公信力，进一步创新工作机制，改进工作方法，扎实推进无公害农产品和农产品地理标志事业持续健康发展，为推进农业标准化生产、促进现代农业建设作出新的贡献。

2010年工作的总体目标是：力争全年新认证无公害农产品6 000个，其中种植业产品3 000个，畜牧业产品1 500个，渔业产品1 500个；新认定无公害农产品产地5 000个，其中种植业产地3 000个，畜牧业产地1 000个，渔业产地1 000个；积极做好到期无公害农产品产地和产品复查换证工作；力争新登记农产品地理标志200个；确保获证无公害农产品和地理标志农产品不发生重大质量安全事件，跟踪监测合格率保持在98%以上。

围绕全年工作目标，我们要在巩固已有工作成绩的基础上，努力适应新形势和新任务要求，在以下五个方面狠下功夫：

（一）加快认定认证，不断扩大总量规模

坚持全面加快发展，迅速扩大总量规模，仍然是无公害农产品当前和今后一个时期的主要任务。要加大产地认定和产品认证推动力度，实施整体推进和规模发展。在工作重点上，要围绕大规模开展的“菜篮子”产品生产标准化创建活动，突出抓好重点产业、规模基地的整体认定和认证。在推进方式上，要和农业标准化生产示范基地、优势农产品产业带、“一村一品”、农业产业化等项目紧密结合起来。在工作布

局上，要积极实施区域发展总体战略，充分发挥比较优势，相互促进，协调发展。西部地区，要着力促进重点县域和重点行业发展，努力提高政府重视力度，增强自身发展能力；华北、华中和东北地区，要充分挖掘地域优势、资源优势和行政推动优势，加强基地建设，加快规模发展；东部及华南地区，要率先增强无公害农产品市场竞争力和可持续发展能力，注重发挥技术经济优势，打造名优品牌，稳定数量规模发展。

另外，2010 年到期复查换证产品首次超过 1 万个，要切实抓好复查换证工作，确保无公害农产品良性发展。各级工作机构要高度重视，及早谋划，加强督导，及时跟进。在工作推进中，要突出三个重点：一是数量，要确保换证率，巩固已有的工作成果；二是质量，要加强生产过程控制，切实把好现场检查质量关，要进一步规范产地环境检测工作，强化质量考评，充分发挥检测机构在产地环境检测过程中的把关作用；三是效率，要提高整个工作系统的审查时效性，确保产品认证的有效衔接，实现顺畅的市场准入和市场销售。同时，各地要结合工作推进情况，继续加强研究，进一步完善本地区、本行业详细的便捷式复查换证条件和操作规范，从严把关便捷式复查换证工作。

（二）强化证后监管，着力提升品牌公信力

产品质量安全是无公害农产品监管的重中之重，要全面提高监管的有效性，确保无公害农产品质量稳定可靠，切实提升安全优质农产品品牌公信力。一是强化全程质量安全控制。加强产地动态监管，及时掌握生产基地环境变化动态及规律，突出关键控制点，前移质量保障关口；认真开展产品质量抽检，建立健全无公害农产品监测信息共享机制；大力推进生产全程监控，对无公害农产品认证和生产经营实施全面监管。2010 年计划在组织整个系统开展无公害农产品逐级综合检查的基础上，探索建立交叉互查制度。二是依法实施标志监管。针对当前无公害农产品标志使用率偏低且包装标识不够规范的现状，要在总结近年来标志推广与监管工作经验的基础上，全面规范无公害农产品包装标识管理。对 3 年来纳入标志推广与监管示范县创建范围的区县，组织全面验收，总结提升示范县创建过程中探索出的包装标识监管模式，并加以推广；进一步加大标志推广力度，以提高标志使用率为着力点，全面推进和规范无公害农产品包装与标识；按照《农产品包装和标识管理办法》规定，指导获证单位建立包装标识管理制度，开展包装标识市场专项检查，依法查处违法违规包装标识行为。三是不断提升监管能力。探索建立和完善无公害农产品监测预警和应急处置机制，加强重大活动期间应急处置能力和风险防范能力建设，切实保障世博会、亚运会期间农产品质量安全。积极构建无公害农产品监督检查与执法联动工作机制，依法查处违法行为。要深入实施无公害农产品内检员制度，落实好生产经营企业的第一责任，健全无公害农产品生产过程质量控制长效机制。

同时，要充分利用农交会、特色农产品展示展销活动和农业网络信息平台，通过举办论坛、新闻发布会等方式，扎实做好无公害农产品和农产品地理标志品牌宣传活动，不断扩大品牌影响力。加强与各类公共媒体合作，围绕重要工作部署和重大工作进展，加大宣传力度，不断扩大事业影响力。

（三）加大登记保护力度，积极推动特色农业发展

目前，农产品地理标志管理工作呈现快速推进的良好势头，已步入制度化、规范化和常态化管理轨道。今年着重抓好四个方面工作：一是大力推进登记。积极开展农产品地理标志资源调查，进一步摸清农产品地理标志资源状况。有计划、有重点地做好农产品地理标志登记的组织申报和审查评审工作。围绕“一村一品”富民工程和特色农业发展等农业项目建设，大力推进农产品地理标志登记保护，优先将知名度高、产业发展潜力大、有相应农民专业合作组织指导经营的传统地域特色优势农产品予以登记保护。二是加强证后跟进服务。积极规范用标，引导证书持有人建立标志使用数据库，落实标志使用协议制度，做好标志使用管理工作，探索完善标志加贴和印刷相结合的使用模式；加大证后监督抽检工作力度，切实保障产品质量。三是不断完善制度规范。进一步完善审查评审程序，探索建立农产品地理标志产品质量控制技术规范专家预审和产品特色品质申报前检测评价制度，积极做好申报指导和把关服务，不断提高登记申报质量和工作效率。制定农产品地理标志产地环境和产品质量符合性评价规范、国外农产品地理标志登记规范、农产品地理标志专家评审（复审）程序、农产品地理标志产品标识标注规范等配套技术规范，着手农产品地理标志登记保护立法调研。四是强化合作交流。加强与农产品地理标志登记保护发达国家、地区及有关国际组织的合作交流，积极参与中欧、中瑞等涉农知识产权和国际贸易谈判研究，组织实施农产品地理标志国际合作交流项目。

（四）加强体系队伍建设，增强事业发展活力

目前各地正在加紧落实十七届三中全会提出的农产品质量安全监管体系建设要求，各级工作机构要充分利用有利时机，完善体系队伍，强化职能，理顺关系，充实人员，争取更加有利的工作条件和手段。一是积极推动工作机构向地、县延伸，不断充实贴近生产一线的技术人员，切实将整个工作系统打造成为农产品质量安全依法监管的重要力量和业务支撑体系。二是全面加强无公害农产品和农产品地理标志业务培训，进一步规范无公害农产品检查员和内检员管理。无公害农产品要重点加强内检员培训，确保培训工作适应认证申报工作进度需要，积极落实好2010年农业部为农民办26件实事中“开展无公害农产品内检员培训”要求，在西藏和新疆举办培训班，为当地无公害农产品生产单位定向培训一批内检员。农产品地理标志培训要重点加强审核员培训，尽快壮大队伍、提高能力。三是进一步优化无公害农产品和农产品地理标志检测机构区域和产品布局，建立检测考核激励机制，不断提高检测工作水平。同时，要加强无公害农产品和农产品地理标志政策研究，为事业持续、健康发展提供理论支撑。

（五）强化改革创新，扎实推进工作机制完善

改革创新是事业持续健康发展的根本动力，当前要重点抓好三个方面的工作：一是改革完善无公害农产品标准体系。以全程质量控制为主线，以制定认证类标准、引用检测类标准、细化生产类标准为重点。对产品标准，明确每个（类）产品的检测项目（参数）、检测限量值和检测方法；对产地环境标准，按产品类别分类制定，技术内容以引用为主；对生产技术类标准，由各地农业部门根据当地实际情况，制定实用的生产技术规程和操作手册。二是探索无公害农产品和农产品地理标志可追溯管理。要结合各地农产品产地准出、市场准入制度的实施，积极开展无公害农产品和农产品地理标志质量追溯试点。2010年农业部农产品质量安全中心计划重点选择条件较好的100个无公害农产品获证单位和5～8个获证地理标志农产品探索建立质量安全追溯管理平台，以包装标识为载体，通过规范生产记录和严格落实标准化生产，实现从农田到市场全程可追溯控制。三是创新无公害农产品和农产品地理标志发展机制。结合农业标准化示范县（场）项目的实施，总结无公害农产品标准化生产示范模式；结合“菜篮子”产品生产标准化创建活动，积极探索以县为基础的农产品地理标志登记保护示范区建设，在主体培育、技术规范、监管追溯、人文历史及品牌打造等方面进行试点、示范；结合“金农工程”项目实施，开展认证登记评审方式改革调研，积极探索无公害农产品认证和农产品地理标志登记网上申报试点。

加快发展无公害农产品和积极做好农产品地理标志登记保护工作，是建设现代农业的重要内容，是实现千方百计保持农民增收和努力确保不发生重大农产品质量安全事件工作目标的重要举措，是时代赋予我们的重要任务。各级工作机构一定要按照本次会议的统一部署，扎实推进各项工作，以实际行动保障世博会、亚运会农产品质量安全，为不断提升我国农产品质量安全水平、大力推进现代农业建设做出积极贡献。

（本文为作者于2010年3月18日在全国“三品一标”工作会议上的讲话，略有删改）

实践科学发展观　推动食品工业持续稳定发展

中国食品工业协会会长　王文哲

受中国食品工业协会第五届理事会的委托，向第六次会员代表大会作工作报告：

一、我国食品工业发展状况

中国食品工业协会第五届理事会期间，正是我国国民经济和社会发展第十一个五年计划实施时期。全国食品工业在国民经济持续向好的背景下，经过全行业的共同努力，克服诸多不利因素的影响，取得了较好的成绩和较快的发展。《全国食品工业“十一五”发展纲要》所规划的各项主要经济指标超额完成。

（一）食品工业主要经济指标完成情况

2010年是我国《食品工业“十一五”发展纲要》实施的最后一年，食品工业战线认真贯彻落实中央经济工作会议精神，坚持科学发展观，克服困难，以扎实工作、锐意进取的科学态度和实干精神，在我国食品工业战胜2009年世界金融危机影响、经济持续好转的基础上，一定能继续保持平稳较快发展，超额完成“十一五”发展纲要规定的目标。

2010年上半年全国食品工业完成销售值27 942.18亿元，同比增长26.03%；利税总额4 352亿元，同比增长25.5%。其中利润1 767亿元，同比增长20.4%。

2009年，全国食品工业总产值（规模以上企业，下同）49 678亿元，比2005年的20 473亿元增长了143%，平均年递增约25%。《全国食品工业“十一五”发展纲要》（以下简称《纲要》）中规划的“食品工业总产值2010年达到40 900亿元，年均增长15%”，已提前实现。

（二）2006—2009年全国食品工业发展特点

1. 充分满足市场需求，是食品工业持续稳定发展的基础。

2. 产品结构不断丰富，安全、质量不断提高，更好地适应了消费需求。

3. 企业组织结构得到调整。

4. 市场化资源配置方式，为食品工业的持续稳定发展提供了保障。

5. 近些年兴起的“订单农业”，实际上就是农业优质资源的配置与食品工业发展的有机结合。

（三）存在的主要问题

1. 食品工业企业规模小，产业集中度较低。

2. 食品工业工业化程度低。

3. 食品工业科技自主创新能力低。

4. 食品安全隐患仍然突出。

二、中国食品工业协会第五届理事会工作回顾

中国食品工业协会第五届理事会成立以来，认真贯彻执行党的十七大方针政策，本着“立足企业，做好服务；产业发展，责无旁贷；政府委托，积极尽力”的原则，坚持为企业和行业服务，为政府部门和社会服务，为促进食品工业持续较快发展，作出了新的贡献。

（一）为食品安全立法建言献策，着力推进食品安全法律法规的贯彻实施

为完善我国食品安全法律体系，遏制影响恶劣的食品安全事件，提高食品安全总体水平，从2005年起，国家开始启动《食品安全法》立法工作。中国食品工业协会努力配合国家有关部门做好立法工作，及时反映食品行业和企业诉求，积极为立法工作建言献策。中国食品工业协会在《食品安全法》立法和贯彻落实法律法规过程中，开展了大量工作，取得了显著成绩。

（二）维护企业权益，加强行业自律

在五届理事会领导下，中国食品工业协会始终把维护企业合法权益，加强行业自律工作放在重要位置，积极为企业排忧解难，优化行业发展环境，并采取具体有效的措施和方法，开展行业自律，提高行业运行质量。

（三）深化“三个服务”，促进行业发展

五届理事会以来，中国食品工业协会依照《关于加快培育和发展工商领域协会的若干意见》要求和《中国食品工业协会章程》，更加自觉主动地做好为政府服务、为行业和企业服务，服务于促进食品工业持续繁荣与发展的大局。

1. *努力为政府服务*　2009年，根据工业和信息化部的部署，中国食品工业协会完成了《全国食品工业“十一五”发展纲要》中期评估报告。2009年，根据卫生部监督局《商请协助开展食品基础标准清理相关准备工作的函》，中国食品工业协会组织成立了3个专家组，汇总撰写了《食品基础标准清理相关准备工作总结报告》。2010年4月，工业和信息化部部署了“食品工业质量安全‘十二五’发展纲要”的编写工作。中国食品工业协会编写出“食品工业质量安全‘十二五’发展纲要（讨论稿）”。2009年，中国食品工业协会积极组织进出口业务经验丰富的食品骨干企业，配合卫生部门开展“无国家标准的进口普通食品及普通食品原料”处理工作，提出了《关于管理进口无食品安全国家标准食品办法的建议》呈报卫生部监督局。

2009年1月，温家宝总理等国务院领导在国务院发展研究中心呈报的一份农民卖马铃薯难问题的情况反映上作出重要批示，中国食品工业协会，及时全面地提出了解决马铃薯卖难问题的措施和建议，得到国家发展和改革委员会与工信部的高度认可。2008年和2009年应商务部要求，中国食品工业协会还就汇源果汁与可口可乐、卡夫与吉百利、帝亚吉欧与水井坊、香港中信与冠生园等并购或股权转让案，提出了咨询报告。

2. *积极为行业和企业服务*　五届理事会期间，中国食品工业协会充分发挥信息统计职能，为行业和企业发展服务。2006年以来，中国食品工业协会在国家统计局的指导帮助下，修订了《全国食品工业统计报表制度》，新增了《规模以上食品工业科技工作情况》、《食品按品牌分类市场销售情况》、《食品生产中能源消耗及成本核算情况》、《食品原辅料价格采购情况》等辅助报表。五届理事会期间，中国食品工业协会进一步加大力度推动龙头食品企业发展和食品强县建设，把农业种植（养殖）基地与农业产业化结合

起来，推进工、农业一体化，总结推广龙头食品企业的发展经验，撰写了《关于食品工业发展新模式新机制的调研报告》，编印了《国家各部门对龙头食品企业政策扶持汇编》。经过多年精心培育，龙头食品企业和食品强县已经形成了一定规模，对促进和带动区域经济的发展，做出了突出贡献。继续做好《中国食品质量报》等的编辑、出版、发行工作。

（四）加强自身建设，夯实服务基础

五届理事会以来，中国食品工业协会按照社会主义市场经济体制对中介组织定位的要求，深入开展学习实践科学发展观活动，强化自身建设，工作思路有创新、工作内容有深化、工作方法有发展、工作面貌有改进、工作质量有提高，在开创工作新局面方面，迈出了扎扎实实的步子。

完善规章制度，用制度管人、管事、管行动；积极激励和完善专业委员会，以专业机构做好专业服务，创出为企业服务的新路子；改善办公条件，筹建信息化办公系统。

三、对新一届理事会及今后主要工作的建议

（一）服务企业，协会之本

中国食品工业协会从一个国家事业单位，转制为社会团体，从食品工业管理部门，改革为中介服务组织。从转制改革的实践中，我们体会到协会的工作，必须从企业、行业需要出发，为企业、行业排忧解难办实事，要让企业深切感受到协会对优化企业、行业发展环境发挥重要作用，协会工作的业绩应体现在推动企业、行业的发展进程中。

（二）做好食品工业综合平衡发展，当好政府参谋

中国食品工业协会在社会主义计划经济体制时期，是政府管理食品工业的一个“抓总部门”，担负食品工业的“统筹、规划、协调”任务。社会主义市场经济体制时期，中国食品工业协会应发挥自己的优势，当好政府的参谋，做好我国食品工业“十二五”发展规划建议的编制工作。

（三）推动龙头食品企业发展战略的实施，走食品工业农工一体化道路

以市场为导向，以新型工业化为先导，以农业为基础，三者结合发展龙头食品企业，促进食品工业与农业产业化协调发展，是我国食品工业与农业持续发展的战略举措。加快龙头食品企业的发展与壮大，推动行业进一步完善与优化工农结合模式。

（四）进一步做好全国食品行业科技进步奖励表彰工作

建立以企业为主体的技术创新体系，完善产学研结合机制，提高食品行业科技水平和自主创新能力，培育创新型（试点）企业，积极组织科技成果推广和产业化实践，提高新产品的比重，为食品工业又快又好发展提供科技支撑。

（五）进一步做好国际交流与合作

加强与国际同行间的联系，密切往来，增进友谊，组织国际间的经济技术交流、展览和考察活动，利用好国外的食物资源，创造有利条件为组织国内企业到国外建厂、拓展国际市场、参与国际竞争提供服务。

（六）发挥专业委员会的作用，提高为企业服务的质量

中国食品工业协会要坚定不移地巩固和发展这一为企业服务的有效模式，进一步提高服务质量与水平，创新服务内容、扩大服务范围，从行业发展需要出发，创造条件，建设新的专业委员会，全方位为企业提供高质量的服务。

（七）加强自身建设，不断提高服务质量和水平

中国食品工业协会要在履行职能的过程中，与时俱进，不断加强自身建设，培育高素质的优秀团队，改进服务方式，扩大服务领域。

（本文为作者于 2010 年 9 月 28 日在中国食品工业协会第六次全国会员代表大会上的讲话，略有删改）

转变发展模式 提升行业整体素质

中国乳制品工业协会理事长 宋昆冈

本次年会是三鹿奶粉事件将满两年时召开的。两年来，在政府各级领导、行业同仁和社会各界的共同努力下，乳制品行业的整改工作取得了很大成效，生产和市场也逐步得到了恢复，乳制品行业正朝着好的

方向发展。但是我们必须看到，乳制品行业仍然面临着一些深层次的矛盾，要用科学发展观统领行业的发展，转变发展模式，提升发展质量，引导行业走上持续、健康、稳定的发展之路。

进入21世纪以来，我国奶牛养殖业、乳制品加工业快速发展，实现了由贫奶大国到乳业大国的历史性跨越，奶类总产量居世界第三位，乳制品工业已发展成为品种结构比较齐全、技术装备先进、粗具规模的现代化食品行业。快速发展的乳制品工业，对于改善城乡居民膳食结构、提高国民身体素质、丰富城乡市场、提高人民生活水平，以及优化农村产业结构、增加农民收入、促进社会主义新农村建设发挥了巨大推动作用，对于带动畜牧业和食品机械、包装、现代物流等相关产业发展也具有重要意义。

我国乳业经过连续多年的高速度发展后，一些深层次的问题和矛盾逐渐显现出来，已经影响到了我国乳业的持续健康发展。如产业布局不合理，重复建设严重，加工能力过剩；奶畜养殖规模小、水平低，原料乳成本高，收购秩序混乱，奶源大战，生鲜乳质量不稳定，安全隐患多；市场有效需求不足，产品结构性过剩等矛盾日益突出；产品质量安全保证体系不健全，质量安全事故时有发生等。特别是，2008年发生的三鹿奶粉事件，是这些矛盾长期得不到有效解决的集中表现。

三鹿奶粉事件发生以来，国务院及政府有关部门迅速采取有效措施，完善法规政策，对乳制品行业进行整顿改造。这些法规政策的实施，对规范行业秩序，维护行业健康发展，保障产品质量安全，都将发挥重要的作用。但从企业和行业的角度来看，必须以科学发展观调整发展思路，转变发展模式，实施行业升级改造，全面提升行业素质，才能够使乳制品行业走上健康、持续、良性的发展道路。我认为，乳制品行业的升级改造主要应从以下几方面做起：

一、树立行业道德准则、升华企业文化、培育良好行风、重塑行业形象

这些年来，乳制品行业是一个迅速扩张的行业，注重发展、崇尚竞争，散、乱、无序成为行业的突出特点。不断发生的质量安全事件，虽说仅是个别现象，但已经使行业“恶名”远扬。本质上讲，这是一个行业道德问题，是一个行业风气问题。乳制品行业要重塑行业形象，获得广大消费者的信任，必须从树立行业道德准则、升华企业文化、改变行业风气做起。

（一）树立行业道德准则

每一个行业都应有自己的行为道德准则。乳制品行业的道德准则是：产品质量安全第一、消费者利益至上、诚信经营、以和为贵。乳制品行业的所有从业者都要以行业道德准则，指导企业的生产经营活动，处理好与消费者的关系，处理好同行之间的关系，处理好与相关合作方的关系，处理好与员工之间的关系，处理好经济效益与社会责任的关系，培育良好行风。

（二）升华企业文化

企业文化是企业的灵魂，体现了企业的价值观，决定了企业的经营理念、处事风格、职工队伍的修养和精神面貌。在市场竞争的大潮中，一些企业成功了，一些企业艰难前行，一些企业翻船覆舟失败了，虽然原因是多方面的，但无不与企业文化有关。比如，有的企业崇尚和谐，造就企业与企业之间的和谐、企业与消费者的和谐、企业与奶农的和谐、企业内部的和谐，和谐的环境为企业提供了良好的发展机遇；有的企业崇尚竞争，在“竞争”中求发展，在充满各种矛盾的环境中生存；有的企业是“利己主义”，在价值观上想到的仅是自己，所以，在社会责任与企业利益发生矛盾时、在本企业与相关合作方的经济利益上，则是损人利己，结果失去了“诚信”，路越走越窄。在乳制品行业遭受信用危机的当今，发掘和建设良好的企业文化，培育崇高的行业道德，树立良好的行业风气，对企业健康稳定发展、造就“百年老号”，越发显得必要。本次年会专门设立“企业文化论坛”，请一些成功企业介绍他们多年来形成的优秀企业文化、经营理念、治企之道、管理方略，广大会员要从中汲取营养，丰富自己企业文化内涵，升华自我，改观面貌，共同树立行业新形象。

（三）树立科学发展观

企业的发展要遵循行业发展的规律，要有一个适度的发展速度。这是因为乳制品行业的基础——奶牛养殖业的发展不可能超越自然规律。高指标、超常规，以速度求发展，是造成行业发展畸形的一大原因。所有企业都要审视自己的发展轨迹，树立科学发展观，用科学的理念指导自己的发展。转变高速度、高指标、高风险的发展思路，树立以质量、效益为中心的发展理念。

（四）改变市场竞争模式，树立“共同发展型”的竞争观念

竞争是市场经济的特点之一，但竞争并不是绝对的、无限的。过度竞争对乳制品行业的健康发展是不利的，其结果是社会资源的浪费，企业经济效益的损失。乳制品行业的竞争必须是在有关政策的约束下的

竞争，遵守行业职业道德，反对以挤垮对手为“目标”的恶性竞争，摒弃只讲竞争不讲合作的竞争模式，树立“共同发展型”的竞争观念。

二、改变原料基地建设模式

原料乳是一种特殊的食品原料。因为乳容易腐败变质，极易受到污染，而且污染物很难在加工过程中被去除，最终被消费者食用。所以，原料乳的质量是产品质量安全的关键，这一点乳制品行业的每一位从业者都是十分清楚的。

我国奶源基地建设在不同的时期有着不同的模式。在改革开放前，乳制品是短缺商品，全国的牛奶产量尚不足100万t，乳制品企业都是国有企业，在城市，是牛奶公司，原料基地清一色的国有牧场和集体奶牛场，没有市场经济的成分。乳制品工业基本上是一个一条龙式的封闭的运营模式，加工厂和奶牛场是一个十分稳定的关系。改革开放以后，为了满足市场对乳制品的需求，快速发展乳制品生产，政府鼓励农民发展个体奶牛饲养，如以奶换料政策、饲料地政策等。国有牧场将自养的奶牛下放给农民饲养，乳品厂到农村建立奶站，收购奶农的牛奶生产乳制品。这样，原料生产与乳制品加工开始处于不稳定的“买卖关系”。到了20世纪90年代，这种关系进一步发展，提倡“奶牛下乡，牛奶进城”公司加农户的做法，一些加工厂将自办牧场奶牛分散到农民家庭饲养，一些企业基本上没有了自控奶源，全部靠收购分散的奶源。在80年代和90年代，奶站基本都是属于企业的，由企业经营管理。进入2000年以后，奶站开始由私人经营，奶农和加工厂之间多了一道中间环节“奶贩子”。这就是我们现在的乳制品工业的生产加工模式。这种“买卖关系”的生产加工模式，在当时的情况下是行之有效的，对于促进牛奶产量的快速提升，改善乳制品市场供应，推动我国乳业的快速发展发挥了重要作用。

但时至今天，我国已是世界第三牛奶生产国，乳制品市场已发生根本变化，并且已经出现结构性产品过剩的情况，乳和乳制品已经成为居民膳食构成的一部分。特别是，广大消费者对食品质量安全日益关注，这种“买卖”式的生产加工模式已经不能适应。这种模式是造成乳制品行业一系列矛盾的根源。原料质量不稳定，掺杂使假现象时有发生，安全隐患多；奶价随着供求关系的变化而忽高忽低，压级压价、损害奶农利益；奶源大战与倒奶现象交替进行；乱建厂、重复建厂等。

三鹿奶粉事件发生后，国家对奶站进行了清理整顿，实施收奶许可证管理制度，关掉一批达不到技术要求的奶站。但在许多地方，一些奶站并没有改变其“中间商”的身份，原料乳质量安全仍然存在隐患。所以，改变原料基地发展模式，发展自有奶源是乳制品行业升级改造的重要内容。一是加大自有奶源的发展力度，提升对原料乳的掌控能力，保障原料乳的质量安全。争取用3年的时间，企业生产所用原料乳，自有奶源（自办牧场、控股牧场、合作牧场）所占比例达到50%以上，彻底消除“自由奶源”。二是将奶站作为企业的第一车间来管理，用2年的时间将奶站收归企业所有，或由企业直接经营，彻底消除收奶的中间环节。三是改变目前按数量计价的收奶办法，实施以乳固体、质量综合计价的新办法。

三、培育和造就一支高素质、高技术水平的职工队伍

乳业由于其产品的特点，不仅对生产企业技术装备水平、管理能力要求较高，而且对职工队伍的素质、技术水平也有较高的要求。包括高级管理层和职工队伍。而目前，许多企业在这方面差距较大，重营销人员的培养使用，轻技术队伍的培养和建设。一些企业的总经理、高管层是外行，对乳制品或食品加工没有专业知识基础，一线的技术工人多数没有相应专业基础或经过专业培训，有些只是受过短期培训的农民工，职工队伍不稳定。这样的职工队伍，已经不能适应现代化乳制品工业的要求，必须加速培育和造就一支高素质、高技术水平职工队伍。争取用3年的时间基本达到：一是高层管理人员从事乳制品或食品行业工作经历5年以上者占60%以上；二是中层以上管理人员（生产、品控、采购、奶源）具有食品工程、食品卫生（营养）、动物科学专业大专以上学历者占80%以上；三是工段长、车间主任获得国家职业技能鉴定高级技工及以上等级证书的人数占80%以上；四是车间主要工段的操作工人，如：杀菌、浓缩、制粉、发酵等工段，获得国家职业技能鉴定技工证书的人数占60%以上；五是从事质量检验与感官评鉴的人员，持有国家职业技能鉴定机构颁发的化验员、评鉴员资格证书者占80%以上。

四、企业管理实现规范化

近几年来，一些企业特别是大中型企业在企业管理上，普遍推行ISO、GMP、HACCP等先进的管理方式，并通过了资质认证。但是，有的企业把这种先进的管理方式当成一种“摆设”，仅是“写在纸上、

挂在墙上”，在实际的管理中并未得到严格执行。他们并未认识到实施这些先进管理方式的作用和意义。实施GMP、HACCP管理方式是《乳品质量安全监督管理条例》所要求的，各乳制品企业必须做到，在实际的管理工作中必须认真执行。要求各企业：一是用1年的时间，婴幼儿食品生产企业全部实施危害分析与关键控制点管理体系（HACCP）；乳制品企业全部实施良好生产规范（GMP）；二是用1年的时间，所有乳制品生产企业建立并实施乳制品企业诚信管理体系，并获得A级以上等级。升级改造是乳制品行业走上健康发展的必由之路，行业的所有企业都要抓住时机，积极开展工作，争取用最短的时间完成行业的升级改造。我相信，经过三聚氰胺事件洗礼过的乳制品工业必将迎来更加辉煌的明天。

（本文为作者于2010年8月21日在中国乳制品工业协会第十六次年会上的讲话，略有删改）

着力转变发展方式
完善绿色生态饲料工业体系

中国饲料工业协会会长　白美清

中国饲料工业协会召开这次理事会，主要议题是贯彻中央经济工作会议和农村工作会议精神，落实科学发展观，研讨促进全国饲料行业在后金融危机时期实现可持续发展的问题，明确全行业前进的方向和战略目标，并充实加强协会的领导机构，以便在新时期充分发挥协会的积极作用，更好地为实现饲料强国的战略任务服务。

一、充分认识新时期新特点，为建设绿色生态饲料工业体系而努力

2009年是进入21世纪以后最困难的一年，也是我们取得震惊世界成就的一年。我国国民经济最重大的成就就是战胜了国际金融危机和经济衰退的冲击，保持了国民经济增长8.7%的速度，从而使我国的综合国力又上升到一个新水平，使全世界对中国的崛起不得不刮目相看。中国人民比任何时候都更加扬眉吐气，中国国力比任何时候都更加壮大，中国在国际事务中的影响力比任何时期都更加突出。作为国民经济的重要部门之一的中国饲料工业，同其他部门一样，在党和政府的正确领导下，继续保持了增长好势头，全年饲料工业总产值达到4 500亿元，同比上升5.7%；商品饲料总产量1.4亿t，同比增长2.4%。其特点是：大型企业增长加快，企业整合的速度加快，科技进步的步伐加快。因而在国内国际市场的竞争力空前增强。

当前，我国正面临新的时期、新的转折。我们必须看到：一方面我们正处于后金融危机时期，世界经济正在缓慢地复苏，不稳定、不平衡的因素依然存在；另一方面我们又处于新的科技革命的前夜，呈现出极为良好的战略机遇期。充分认识当前形势的这两大特点，对于我们领会中央经济工作会议精神，领会中央关于加快经济发展方式转变的战略决策至关重要。正如胡锦涛同志所指出的：“国际金融危机表面上是对我国经济增长速度的冲击，实质上是对经济发展方式的冲击”。他还深刻指出：“目前，世界经济发展模式确实不可持续。发达国家过度消费模式难以为继，世界经济增长模式调整势在必行”。这次国际金融危机、经济衰退以及全球性的气候变暖、环境变化，促使我们思考：传统的高消耗、高污染、高GDP、高消费的工业化旧模式，是难以持续下去的。《世界自然资源保护大纲》中说：“地球不是从我们父辈那里继承来的，而是我们从自己后代那里借来的。我们要为子孙后代留下一个赖以生存和发展的地球家园”。用湖南人民的评论，我们现在的发展模式是“吃了祖宗饭，断了子孙路”。这是多么深刻啊！值得三思。因此，中央强调的转变发展方式，有着深刻内涵和丰富的内容，有着战略性、长远性、前瞻性的意义。温家宝总理最近指出：“我们要依靠科学技术实现中国的可持续发展，依靠科学技术形成少投入、多产出和少排放、多利用的消费模式，走出一条生产发展、生活富裕、生态良好的新型工业化、城镇化的道路。必须建设低投入、高产出、低消耗、少排放、能循环、可持续的国民经济体系，转变现有发展模式与消费方式”。这就是我国国民经济面临的新任务，也

是新机遇、新挑战和新考验。我们要以科学发展观为指导，以创新驱动为动力，在建设中国特色社会主义的实践中走出一条新的发展模式、新的发展途径。危机孕育科技革命，时代催生科技革命。这场新的科技革命的特征就是绿色、生态、可持续、得实惠，其内容包括生物工程、海洋工程、宇宙航天工程、新能源、新材料等。我们的任务就是要迎接这场新的科技革命，把握新的机遇，寻求新的增长，占领新的科技制高点，使我们整个国民经济转到可持续发展的轨道上来。这不仅有益于当代，而且有益于子孙后代，有益于整个地球和谐发展。

从我国饲料工业的发展看，30 年来每年平均以 9%左右的速度增长，用较短的时间走完了资本主义工业国上百年走过的路，取得了举世瞩目的成就，中国已经成为世界上第二个饲料大国。但是，我们也要看到，在发展过程中，也难免不沾染上旧工业化道路带来那些弊端，比如看重眼前而不注重长远，重经济效益而不注重社会效益，重量的扩张而不重质的提升，重生产而不注重环保等，我们很少在治污染上下工夫，更少在生态建设上做文章，这些表现在饲料配方、养殖模式、运营方式等方方面面。比如对耕地和水资源的污染日益恶化，对原料的污染，对环境的破坏，有很多方面已达到了惊人的程度。现在江河湖泊、内海近海、赤潮、蓝藻的屡次泛滥，这与我们饲料滥用药物、较为普遍地采用死鱼烂虾原始的喂养方式等是分不开的。至于动物粪便的污染、药物的残留更是始终没有解决的严重问题，而且有加剧之势。我们不仅要看到污染的大厂、大户、大源头，也要看到那些星罗棋布、散布甚广的小厂、小户、小源头，它们聚少成多，积重难返，其危害程度绝不可低估。这一关不突破，中国就不能由饲料大国走向饲料强国。出路何在呢？就是要根据党中央、国务院提出的着重发展方式的转型，走绿色生态饲料业、养殖业的发展道路。我们的奋斗目标应该在全国建设安全、营养、高效、低耗、绿色、生态的饲料工业体系，走上真正的可持续、得实惠的新路子。这是振兴畜牧饲料业的根本出路，是形成科学、系统的饲料工业体系的必然要求。谁早认识到这一点，谁就会掌握先机，攻占科技制高点，取得市场上的主动权。

最近，我们在山东、广东、海南、北京等地对一些骨干企业进行了调查。我们看到各地的骨干企业正在迅速成长壮大，特别是六和这批第一团队的企业正在跨越式发展，同时像海大、旺大、溢多利等后起之秀也迅速跟进。在这些地方我们都看到了发展绿色生态饲料的好做法、好苗头。比如山东六和集团采取发酵板技术解决鸡鸭粪便的污染问题，他们又在延伸产业链，通过建立担保公司进行综合性的服务，帮助养殖大户解决了资金、技术、营销等难题，受到了广大养殖户的欢迎。在海南罗牛山农牧科技公司，他们采用液态饲料养殖的新方法，避免了鼠耗等损失，母猪也很爱吃，既省料又促进了猪的健康生长，降低了成本。在饲料物流方式上也进行改革，从饲料厂直接用散装汽车散运，取代传统的袋装袋运的落后方法，实现了物流无缝对接，提高效率，节约成本。广东海大集团，他们以新的服务方式推广新的养殖模式，按销售区域配备技术人员，进行全方位服务。努力用好上市募集的资金，兴办新厂，改造老厂，取得了可观的效益。广州金银卡公司，他们生产推广“三无”饲料（无抗体、无激素、无化学药物），使饲料安全上了新水平，让百姓放心，消除了消费者的疑虑，开拓了市场空间。广东溢多利科技股份有限公司，他们运用现代生物技术和先进的植物提萃技术，生产了具有知识产权的绿色酶制剂、动保药品等高科技产品。从这些经验中，我们看到了方向和希望，看到了绿色生态饲料的广大前景和拓展空间。只要循着这个方向走下去，就一定能使我国实现饲料强国的目标，找到一条积极可靠、可持续发展的新路子。

当前，正面临国民经济发展的一个极好的战略机遇期，今后四五年是很关键的时间。2010 年，“十二五”规划即将制定，并在 2011 年启动。我们一定要抓住时机，赶上这班车，在新的科技革命到来之际，努力奋斗，不断创新，精益求精，使我们绿色生态饲料业发展到一个新境界、新水平。为此，我们认为需要做好以下工作：

1. *广泛进行思想动员，使全行业充分认识转变发展方式，向绿色生态饲料转型的重大意义* 这是新时代的要求，人民的愿望，大势所趋，潮流所向。也是饲料企业成长的锁匙，行业发展的关键。特别是饲料企业的领导者一定要把这件大事提到日程，抓在手里，千方百计增加这方面的投入，确保发展，不要掉队。错过良机，就有被淘汰的危险；抓住机遇，就可能开辟新天地。

2. *要制订规划，抓住重点* 要结合各地、各企业的实际，选准重点，组织力量攻关突破。比如改进饲料配方，推广“三无”饲料等绿色生态产品；抓好天然添加剂的开发；着力减少对空气、水、土和环境的污染，实行低碳经济，循环经济；改善畜禽、水产饲养方法，有步骤地淘汰落后的、掠夺式的原始喂养方式，切实做到科学养殖，等等。要结合制定“十二五”规划，作好安排，组织力量落实。中国饲料工业协会将在今年召开全国饲料添加剂大会，研究推广新型饲料添加剂，推进行业科技进步等问题。

3. *要实行更加紧密的产、学、研相结合，大力开展自主创新* 大型企业和公司，一定要有自己的知识产权，要有自己的专利，要有自己的名牌产品。要总结经验，采取新的措施吸引科技人员参加新产品的研发上来，千方百计调动他们的积极性。有作为的企业一定要广纳人才，集聚智力，人才兴才能企业旺。

4. *各级协会要围绕建设绿色生态饲料这个主题，发挥桥梁和纽带作用* 深入企业调查研究，发现新经验；帮助组织攻关，排难解纷，为企业搞好咨询服务。同时，要积极向政府反映行业的困难和问题，争取政府的政策支持。

二、加强饲料协会的建设，更好地为饲料行业可持续发展服务

中国饲料工业协会是改革开放的产物，是在市场经济中诞生的，是在邓小平理论的正确指导下成长、壮大的。在新时期，我们要转变发展方式与模式，建设绿色生态饲料业同样需要各级饲料协会的配合与合作，发挥其中介组织的积极作用，团结全行业的各个方面，为共同实现饲料强国的战略目标而奋斗。我认为，首先需要在实践中加深对行业协会地位、作用、运行机制的再认识。在计划经济中，政府直接指挥企业；而在市场经济的条件下发生了根本的变化，成为政府、协会、企业的三元化组织结构。党中央、国务院多次指出，协会是“中介组织”，是作为宏观管理与调控的政府部门，同作为市场经济主体的企业之间的桥梁，是不可缺少的中介。随着改革的不断深化和市场经济的发展，协会等中介组织的职能越来越为社会所认识，发挥的作用越来越明显。

由于协会具有民间性、自律性、国际性的特点，在经济全球化、市场国际化、行业产业化的新形势下，行业协会作为新生的中介组织，具有广阔的发展空间和发展前景。协会的路子会越走越宽，方式会越来越灵活，功能会越来越大。但是，我们也必须看到，协会的作用，取决于四个方面：一是取决于政府机构改革、转变职能、简政放权的进度；二是取决于市场经济发展的程度；三是取决于本行业企业组织化的程度；四是取决于协会等中介组织自身建设的进度，特别是人才聚集的程度。从总体上看，协会等中介组织，正处于过渡的阶段，工作具有逐步过渡的特点。因此，组织上在向“企业家办会”的目标逐步过渡。在工作方针上具有逐步推进的特点。从实际出发，协会提出的“量力而行，尽力而为，拾遗补缺，逐步前进”是正确的，协会工作既不能“急”，也不能“等”，关键在于要有人才，要发挥主观能动性。实践证明，有为才能有位，有活动才有生命力。各地协会之间工作有差距，差距就在发挥人才的主观能动性上。

在面临新时期、新任务的情况下，迫切需要加强各级协会的建设，使之能担当起新时期的各项工作，构建起以服务为主线的饲料协会工作网络。

1. *要充实健全总会，巩固提高地方协会* 协会要增加权威性、代表性，增强辐射力和凝聚力。一要扩大组织基础，充实领导力量，要广泛吸收饲料行业的各方面代表人物和著名企业家参与领导。这次理事会就要决定增补一些新鲜血液进入总会领导班子。二要吸收先进的市、县协会参加总会工作。三要指导帮助地方协会搞好，推动个别未建立协会的省份，创造条件把组织建立起来。协会可采取多种模式，如四川、湖南、上海、河北的模式等都可试行，不断改进提高。总之，要有个能办实事的工作机构。要为地方协会创造开展工作的条件，争取各地党政领导部门的支持。四要抓紧协会中、青年干部的培养，逐步轮训协会干部，选拔德才兼备、热心于饲料事业的中青优秀人才，充实班子。同时，对离开工作岗位、德才兼备、身体健康、威信高、经验多、思想好的老干部，协会要注意把他们吸收到协会工作中来，充分发挥他们的积极作用。

2. *建立协会工作的智库* 中国饲料工业协会已建立专家委员会，2010 年要起步开展工作。要广泛吸纳各方面的专家学者和有实践经验的人才，担任起行业各方面的咨询工作，逐步形成行业的“智库”。要使协会成为“人才荟萃”之所，更有力地服务企业，服务政府，为行业的发展献言献策，当好参谋。地方协会可根据实际情况，因地制宜抓紧做好这方面的工作。

3. *要切实加强协会的思想建设* 各级行业协会是在党领导下的饲料企业和行业的民间社团，协会是自律、自治的群众组织，它具有群众性、公共性的特点。协会以服务为宗旨。中国饲料工业协会成立以来，不少同志实际上是“义工”、“半义工”，是以“志愿者”的身份献身于行业工作的。协会的崇高使命，就是为国分忧，为民服务，为国家的饲料安全、为解决 13 亿人的吃肉问题贡献力量。对于协会工作，我看有两句话：“升官发财，请走别路；怕苦怕累，莫入此门”。在行业中一定要大力倡导职业道德、企业文化、个人修养。全行业中要形成“以创新求创利，以创利谋创业”的新品格、新风貌。对于行业中存在的不正之风、腐败的“潜规则”，要旗帜鲜明地加以反对。要继承饲料行业的优良传统，并与时代精神结合起来，更好地为新时期、新任务贡献力量，做

好工作。

4. *必须改进运行方式*　协会要不断改善运行方式，提高工作质量。这次在广东同省协会的同志座谈，关于今后工作方式如何改进，集中大家的意见，我认为要重点抓好“联系企业、抓好典型、搞好协调、聚集人才”。概括成四句话：“从企业中吸取营养，从典型中总结升华，从协商中形成合力，从聚才中形成智库”。这样工作就会有活力，有生气，有成效。

5. *要加强协会的经常性工作*　每个协会，都要本着从实际出发，量力而行，尽力而为的精神，每年制订计划，抓几件实事，深入调查研究，密切联系企业，为他们解决几个实际问题。这样积之以时日，就会出效果、出人才，以工作实绩争取应有的地位，以良好的信誉得到应有的支持。协会就会迈出新步伐，开拓新局面，做出新成就。

（本文为作者于2010年2月2日在中国饲料工业协会第五届理事会第三次会议上的讲话，略有删改）

中国肉类工业发展概况

中国肉类协会

资料显示，2009年全国肉类总产量7 642万t，比上年增长5%，为肉类的总供量提供了保障，为肉类加工业发展提供了物质基础。但在品种结构上，牛、羊肉生产量仍显不足，其价格一直处于坚挺。2009年我国肉类工业面临的突出问题仍是畜禽产品价格的极不稳定性。以主导品种生猪为例，在国家政策倾斜、支持鼓励发展中，是年生猪饲养、母猪存栏、仔猪繁育都超出预设量。与此同时，也受动物疫情及甲型H1N1流感传播的直接威胁，随之引起的生猪价、仔猪价逐月下滑，猪粮比价从3月的1∶7.64下跌到6月的1∶5.66，虽然短期内亦有回升，但仍徘徊在黄色警区边缘。致屠宰毛白差率一直摆动在36%走势中。为此，国家启动保护性应急收储政策。禽肉及禽蛋增产，对市场起到积极地调剂性作用，但价格也一直处在应时性波动中。肉类工业处于畜禽产品向肉类产品转化的地位，其连接着城市与农村、养殖与消费，上游的波动必然通过工业环节反映到市场振荡，同时，全球经济危机也给肉类工业带来一定影响，除企业发展资金瓶颈外，内外需求总体疲软，肉类进出口贸易量出现收窄。我国肉类工业在积极应对诸多严峻挑战的形势下，随着工业现代化、集约化、规模化的提升，产品结构的调整，服务质量的改善，仍取得了平稳发展。

一、肉类工业企业集约化、规模化水平进一步提高

（一）规模企业明显增加，是历年来年度增加最多

资料显示，2009年全国规模以上肉类屠宰及肉制品加工企业达3 696个，其中畜禽屠宰加工为2 076个、肉制品加工为1 620个，两种企业结构比为56∶44。另外，有肉类罐头制造企业91个。畜禽屠宰及肉制品加工规模以上企业总数比2008年增加600个，其中屠宰增加277个，制品加工增加323个；肉类罐头制造企业增加3个。充分体现了企业实现产能的规模在日益提升。

（二）规模企业投资明显增长

2009年全国规模以上畜禽屠宰及肉制品加工企业工业资产总额达到2 256亿元，比上年增加442.4亿元，增长24.4%。其中畜禽屠宰加工形成资产额为1 154.4亿元，增加193.5亿元，增长20.1%；肉制品加工资产额为1 101.6亿元，增加248.8亿元，增长29.2%。在投资量增长中，畜禽屠宰和肉制品加工投资比重出现新变化，屠宰由2008年的53%降为51%，肉制品加工由47%上升为49%。另外，肉类罐头制造资产额为51.76亿元，增加12.77亿元，增长32.8%。数据表明，畜禽屠宰及肉制品加工对社会投资仍保持着较强的吸引力，尤其是肉制品加工及肉类罐头制造，其投资增长呈现出较大发展的态势。随着规模企业尤其是集团化企业的扩张和发展，一些无优势的、生产能力落后的企业在挑战中将逐步被淘汰。

（三）规模企业销售收入显著增升

2009年全国规模以上畜禽屠宰及肉制品加工业销售总收入达到5 167.4亿元，比上年增加925.1亿元，增长21.8%。其中畜禽屠宰加工销售为2 924.2亿元，增加500.8亿元，增长20.7%；肉制品加工销售为2 243.2亿元，增加424.3亿元，增长

23.3%。销售总收入中，畜禽屠宰与肉制品加工的销售额比重与2008年基本持平，维持在57∶43水平。另外，肉类罐头制造销售为94.7亿元，增加39亿元，增长70%。

综上分析，2009年其资产总额（投入）与销售总额（收入）之比比较稳定，在一定意义上体现了企业产能状况，往期投入已见成效，成熟度在提高。畜禽屠宰及肉制品加工综合投入与产出比为1∶2.29，比2008年降低0.05个百分点。其中，畜禽屠宰加工投入与产出比为1∶2.5，比2008年降低0.02个百分点；肉制品加工投入与产出比为1∶2.0，比2008年降低0.1个百分点。另外，肉类罐头制造投入与产出比为1∶1.83，比2008年提高0.4个百分点。

（四）企业经济效益逐渐改善

2009年全国畜禽屠宰及肉制品加工业规模以上企业实现利润总额205.9亿元，比2008年增加52.2亿元，增长33.9%。其中畜禽屠宰加工实现利润为103.7亿元，增加23.3亿元，增长29%；肉制品加工实现利润为102.2亿元，增加28.9亿元，增长39.4%。另外，肉类罐头制造实现利润为4.2亿元，增加2.1亿元，增长100%。在畜禽屠宰及肉制品加工实现总利润中，畜禽屠宰加工实现利润比肉制品加工利润的绝对增量增加1.5亿元，但其增长幅度明显低了10多个百分点。

肉类工业企业投入在增加，技术装备在提升，经营状况在改善，效益积累在上升，但仍是低利行业，主要由于其在产业链上所处之位置和职能之作用（如价格干预）决定了效益的体现在某种程度上还有"靠天吃饭"之因素。2009年畜禽屠宰及肉制品加工综合销售利润率仅为3.99%，比上年3.64%略升0.35个百分点。其中畜禽屠宰加工销售利润率为3.53%，比上年3.32%，略升0.21个百分点；肉制品加工销售利润率为4.55%，比上年4.03%略升0.52个百分点。另外，肉类罐头制造销售利润率为4.44%，比上年3.77%略升0.67个百分点。

2009年全国畜禽屠宰及肉制品加工企业中，亏损企业仍有412个，占规模以上企业11.2%，较上年下降了2.5个百分点；亏损金额达到12.8亿元，较上年增加0.7亿元。其中，畜禽屠宰亏损企业为225个，占全国屠宰及肉制品加工规模企业的6.1%，下降了1.3个百分点；占屠宰企业10.84%，下降了1.95个百分点；其亏损金额为8.26亿元，增加了0.97亿元，占行业全部亏损额的64.4%。肉制品加工亏损企业为187个，占全国屠宰及肉制品加工规模企业5.06%，下降了1.21个百分点；占肉制品加工企业11.55%，下降了3.64个百分点；其亏损金额为4.56亿元，减少了0.46亿元，占行业全部亏损额的35.6%，下降了5.8个百分点。另外，肉类罐头制造亏损企业为11个，减少了5个；占肉类罐头制造企业的12.1%，下降了6.1个百分点；其亏损金额为0.1亿元，较2008年减亏0.03亿元。

上述数据表明，在畜禽产品入市极不稳定、价格涨跌低迷中，屠宰及肉制品加工企业艰难地把握经济运行，行业的经营亏损较2008年略有增加，2009年所达到的亏损额仍为近年来行业亏损最高。

二、企业经济结构进一步得到调整

（一）规模结构

2009年畜禽屠宰及肉制品加工企业的规模结构中，大、中型仅占9%，但其在行业资产中占有60%，销售及创利占一半以上。大型企业为26个，占规模企业总量的0.7%，其资产总额为612.4亿元，占27.2%；销售收入1 111.3亿元，占21.5%；创利50.5亿元，占24.5%。中型企业为307个，占规模企业总量8.3%，其资产总额754.3亿元，占33.4%；销售收入1 509.8亿元，占29.2%；创利53.9亿元，占26.2%。小型企业为3 369个，占91%，其资产总额889.4亿元，占39.4%；销售收入2 546.3亿元，占49.3%；创利101.4亿元，占49.3%。下面分述屠宰加工企业及肉制品加工企业的规模状况：

1. *屠宰加工企业规模结构* 2009年畜禽屠宰加工中的大型企业为14个，其资产额为244亿元，销售收入341.7亿元，实现利润13.1亿元，分别占屠宰加工业的0.68%、21.1%、11.7%和12.6%；中型企业为176个，资产额为404.2亿元，销售收入929.9亿元，实现利润27.5亿元，分别占屠宰加工业的8.5%、35%、31.8%和26.5%；小型企业为1 886个，资产额为506.2亿元，销售收入1 652.6亿元，实现利润63.1亿元，分别占屠宰加工业的90.9%、43.9%、56.5%和60.9%。在屠宰加工业中，大中型企业与小型企业的产销量正处在抗衡中。

2. *肉制品加工企业规模结构* 2009年肉制品加工企业中的大型企业为12个，占肉制品加工企业的0.7%；其资产额为368.36亿元，占肉制品加工业总额的33.4%；销售收入为769.5亿元，占34.3%；创利为37.4亿元，占36.6%。中型企业为131个，占8.1%，其资产额为350亿元，占31.8%；销售收入579.96亿元，占25.9%；创利26.45亿元，占25.9%。小型企业1 477个，占91.2%，其资产额383.17亿元，占34.8%；销售收入为893.68亿元，占39.8%；创利38.33亿元，占37.5%。上述结构表明，企业规模群体正在形成，大型企业虽占不到1%数量，但其资产、销售及效益已占行业的1/3以上比重，预期将会继续增升。

肉禽罐头制造业没有大型企业，仅有中小企业两类，但是中型企业在资产、销售和创利方面已占有1/2以上。其中，中型企业为13个，仅占14.3%，其资产达到34.7亿元，占67%；销售收入56.7亿元，占59.9%；创利2.16亿元，占51.4%。小型企业为78个，占85.7%，其资产为17.1亿元，占33%；销售收入37.9亿元，占40.1%；创利2.07亿元，占48.6%。

（二）经济结构

企业经济结构随着投资主体加快的多元化，企业性质发生了急剧变化。目前，国有及集体企业数量已不及7%，其资产量及销售收入不足4%，创利仅为3%；私营及其他企业已占据4/5，外商及港台投资企业显著增升，投资及效能占到1/4。肉类屠宰加工及肉制品加工企业中，国有及集体企业249个，占行业规模企业的6.74%。其资产为75.36亿元，占3.34%；销售收入194.24亿元，占3.76%；创利5.59亿元，占2.71%。股份制企业144个，占3.9%，其资产190.2亿元，占8.43%；销售收入256.5亿元，占6.9%；创利9.58亿元，占4.65%。私营和其他企业为3 042个，占82.3%，其资产为1 368.79亿元，占60.67%；销售收入3 403.67亿元，占65.87%；创利139.75亿元，占67.87%。外商及港台投资企业为261个，占7.1%，其资产额621.69亿元，占27.56%；销售收入1 213亿元，占23.47%；创利50.98亿元，占24.76%。下面分述屠宰加工企业及肉制品加工企业经济成分结构变化：

1. 屠宰加工经济结构 2009年畜禽屠宰规模企业中，国有及集体企业189个，占屠宰加工企业9.1%；其资产为42.6亿元，占3.69%；销售收入151.3亿元，占5.18%；创利4.5亿元，占4.3%。股份制企业79个，占3.8%；其资产为136.8亿元，占11.85%；销售收入269.2亿元，占9.2%；创利6.9亿元，占6.7%。私营及其他企业为1 799个，占84%，其资产为871.2亿元，占75.5%；销售收入2 318亿元，占79.3%；创利91.8亿元，占88.5%。外商及港台投资企业为64个，占3.1%，其资产额103.9亿元，占9%；销售收入185.7亿元，占6.3%；创利0.38亿元，占0.4%。纵观屠宰加工企业，民营企业投资及其产能占4/5。

2. 肉制品加工企业经济成分结构 2009年肉制品加工规模企业中，国有及集体企业60个，占3.7%，其资产额为32.7亿元，占2.9%；销售收入为42.9亿元，占1.9%；实现利润0.99亿元，占1%。股份制企业65个，占4%，其资产额53.4亿元，占4.9%；销售收入87.2亿元，占3.9%；实现利润2.63亿元，占2.5%。私营企业989个，占61.1%，其资产额301.7亿元，占27.4%；销售收入706.3亿元，占31.5%；创利为31.59亿元，占31%。外商及港台投资企业197个，占12.1%，其资产额为517.8亿元，占47%；销售收入1 027.3亿元，占45.8%；实现利润50.6亿元，占49.5%。其他企业为309个，占19.1%，其资产额195.9亿元，占17.8%；销售收入379.4亿元，占16.9%；创利16.3亿元，占16%。

2009年肉禽罐头制造企业中，国有企业包括产能已失去权重，民营企业已控制主导。国有及股份制企业4个，占肉禽类罐头制造规模企业仅4.4%，其资产额为7.9亿元，占15.2%；销售收入为5.3亿元，占5.7%；创利仅0.03亿元，占0.6%。私营企业58个，占63.7%，其资产额24.7亿元，占47.7%；销售收入61.1亿元，占64.6%；创利2.8亿元，占66.5%。外商及港台投资企业为12个，占13.2%，其资产额为9.3亿元，占18%；销售收入13.1亿元，占13.8%；创利0.8亿元，占19%。其他企业为17个，占18.7%，其资产额为9.8亿元，占18.9%；销售收入15.1亿元，占15.9%；创利0.6亿元，占14%。

三、肉类工业经济形成区域梯度

据以下数据显示：一是资产投入总量，以鲁、豫、川、辽、吉、苏、皖、蒙、黑、冀10位为第一梯度，2009年形成资产量为1 741亿元，占全国规模以上企业总量的77%；以闽、京、鄂、湘、粤、浙、沪、晋、渝、津为二梯度，资产量为412.3亿元，占资产总量的18%；以赣、陕、桂、云、新、甘、贵、青、宁、藏、琼为三梯度，资产量为102.7亿元，占资产总量的5%。二是产品销售收入额。以鲁、豫、川、辽、蒙、吉、苏、冀、京、黑10位为第一梯度，2009年销售额为4 275.5亿元，占全国规模以上企业总销售额的83%；以皖、湘、鄂、粤、渝、闽、浙、赣、沪、陕为二梯度，销售额为753.5亿元，占总销售额的14%；以晋、津、桂、云、贵、新、甘、青、宁、藏、琼为三梯度，销售额为138.4亿元，占总销售额3%。三是规模企业利润额。以豫、鲁、川、苏、辽、蒙、皖、冀、黑、桂10位为第一梯度，2009年实现利润174.7亿元，占全国规模以上企业利润总额 85%；以鄂、湘、陕、粤、闽、赣、浙、吉、渝、沪为二梯度，实现利润 28.4 亿元，占全国规模以上企业利润总额 14%；以晋、京、新、贵、甘、云、琼、青、藏、宁、津为三梯度，实现利润 2.81 亿元。由于 2009 年津、宁负创利，使区域利润结构发生变化。

四、肉类产品结构略有调整

据资料显示，2009 年全国肉类总产量达到 7 642 万 t，比上年增长 5%。其中猪肉为 4 889 万 t，增长 5.8%；牛肉为 636 万 t，增长 3.6%；羊肉 389 万 t，增长 2.4%；禽肉 1 595 万 t，增长 4.1%。禽蛋产量 2 741 万 t，增长 1.4%。在肉类产品中，牛、羊肉处于供需紧张平衡，价格一直坚挺，牛、羊屠宰加工缺乏整合，市场秩序不良，大多数企业经营吃紧，开工不足。

据有关信息显示，2009 年全国定点生猪屠宰企业屠宰量达 3.16 亿头，占出栏量 49%。其中规模以上企业屠宰量达 2.1 亿头，占定点屠宰量的 66.5%。

与产量的变化相适应，2009 年全国人均肉类占有量达到 57.3kg，比 2008 年增加 2.5kg。其中猪肉人均占有量为 36.7kg，比 2008 年增加 1.9kg；牛肉人均占有量为 4.8kg，比 2008 年增加 0.1kg；羊肉人均占有量为 3.0kg，比 2008 年增加 0.13kg；禽肉人均占有量为 12.0kg，比 2008 年增加 0.4kg；禽蛋人均占有量为 20.6kg，比 2008 年增加 0.3kg。

2009 年我国猪肉、禽肉、牛肉、羊肉、杂畜肉的结构比重依次为 64：21：8.3：5.1：1.6。与 2008 年相比，猪肉上升 1 个百分点；禽肉维持原比重；牛、羊肉各下降 0.1 个百分点；杂畜肉下降 0.8 个百分点。继续坚持以猪肉业稳定发展，禽业积极发展，牛、羊业加快发展的总原则，既保障了市场肉类总量需求的平衡，又保障了肉类结构在调整中的替代，总体上既符合我国居民消费习惯、民族特点和动物生物体生长周期以及市场的变化。但相比世界肉类品种总体结构的变化趋势（世界肉类品种总结构比重中，猪肉、禽肉、牛肉、羊肉、杂畜肉分别为 40：30：24：5：1），近年来我国肉类结构的调整，虽战略思路符合科学发展和市场需要，而实践调整的进度显示是缓慢的，甚至牛、羊肉比重还在下降。其原因有人们认识所致，如投入与风险问题，也有政策倾斜力度不够。

肉类制品结构随着市场需求的变化得到进一步调整。据测算，2009 年肉类制品加工占肉类总产量的比重为 14.7%，比上年下降了 0.4 个百分点；其产量预计达到 1 120 万 t，比上年增加 50 万 t，增长 4.7%。其中，中西式制品结构约为 45：55。西式技术制作的制品中，高温制品约占 40%，低温制品约占 60%；中式肉制品数量在技术改进中有了新的提升。

五、品牌成为强势企业增强市场竞争力的重要战略

在市场竞争日趋激烈，在食品质量与安全凸显的今天，品牌作为技术、素质和信誉的综合表现的附着物呈现给社会和公众，代表了物质和精神文明。品牌战略昭示了企业技术水平、素质水平和诚信水平的不断提升，是企业持续发展和科学发展结合的体现，对推动地方经济和引导规范市场行为起到了积极的作用。2009 年止，肉类行业历年来获得中国名牌产品数共 49 个，涉及企业 40 个；获中国驰名商标品牌 37 个；上市企业达 13 个。

肉类制品产业正处在发展中，加工企业正处在发展整合中，所以不可否认，其产品质量的不稳定时有发生，尤其是在新开发产品中，这种现象更有之。多数企业的技术力量不足，缺乏与发展相适应的技术性储备，缺乏产品机理研究，因而，产品更新（调整）缓慢。一些企业仍维持在一线品牌二线市场中。同时，在市场机制不健全的状态中，企业的创制问世新产品必然受到社会跟风的冲击威胁，所以大型企业和优势企业一定要坚持在强化技术和管理的基础上，稳步推进做好市场工作和服务工作。

全国水产品进出口贸易情况

农业部农业贸易促进中心

2009 年我国水产品进出口总量为 667.9 万 t，进出口总额为 159.6 亿美元，同比分别下降 2.4%和

0.13%。其中出口量为294.2万t，同比下降0.6%；出口额为107亿美元，同比增长1%。进口量为373.7万t，进口额为52.6亿美元，同比分别下降3.8%和2.6%。贸易顺差54.4亿美元，比2008年同期增加2.3亿美元。水产品出口额继续位居大宗农产品出口首位，占农产品出口总额的27%，较2008年提高0.8个百分点。

一、贸易方式

2009年国际水产品原料价格波动较大，部分国家以防止资源外流为由限制其原料水产品出口，同时我国来进料加工水产品主要出口市场受金融危机的影响，经济低迷，消费需求下降。在上述种种压力下，我国水产品来进料加工出口困难重重，出口量、出口额同比分别下降8.6%和4.0%，占出口总额的比例较2007年下降了3.6个百分点。

一般贸易出口形势总体好于2008年，对虾、贝类、罗非鱼、鳗鱼、淡水小龙虾、大黄鱼和斑点叉尾鮰等名优养殖水产品仍是主要出口品种。鳗鱼、淡水小龙虾和大黄鱼出口形势较2008年略有好转。贝类、罗非鱼和斑点叉尾鮰出口形势严峻，罗非鱼出口单价持续大幅下降，已经严重威胁到产业发展。海洋捕捞头足类产品、虾蟹类和冻鱼出口大幅增长，成为一般贸易出口的亮点。贸易方式和一般贸易主要出口品种分别见表1、表2。

表1 贸易方式

（单位：万t、亿美元）

贸易方式	2009年		2008年		同比增减（%）		占出口总额（%）	同比（%）
	数量	金额	数量	金额	数量	金额		
一般贸易	195.9	69.2	188.8	66.6	3.9	4.1	64.7	1.9
来进料加工贸易	98.3	37.8	107.7	39.5	−8.6	−4.0	35.3	−1.9

表2 一般贸易主要出口品种

（单位：万t、亿美元）

出口品种	占一般贸易出口额比例（%）	2009年		2008年		同比增减（%）	
		数量	金额	数量	金额	数量	金额
对虾	17.8	18.8	12.3	19.4	11.9	−3.5	3.5
贝类	12.0	22.0	8.3	26.5	9.7	−17.1	−14.9
罗非鱼	10.3	25.9	7.1	22.4	7.3	15.4	−3.2
鳗鱼	7.7	4.3	5.3	4.3	5.4	持平	−2.4
淡水小龙虾	2.3	2.3	1.6	2.4	1.5	−2.2	6.1
大黄鱼	2.1	4.8	1.5	4.4	1.4	10.4	2.7
斑点叉尾鮰	1.0	1.7	0.7	1.9	0.7	−11.5	持平
合计	53.0	79.8	36.7	81.3	37.9	−1.8	−3.2

二、出口大类

按照海关进出口税则大类统计，各出口大类变动较大。主要是由于2009年国家调整了出口退税政策，初级加工水产品退税率由征13%、退5%调整为征13%、退13%；深加工产品由征17%、退13%调整为征17%、退15%，仍有两个百分点的税收。企业多采取了调整产品报关种类的办法，因此2009年数据与往年数据可比性不强，难以反映加工方式的实际变化情况。出口大类对比见表3。

表3 出口大类对比

（单位：万t、亿美元）

出口大类	数量	同比增减（%）	占出口总量（%）	金额	同比增减（%）	占出口总额（%）
制作或保藏的产品	73.9	−32.3	25.1	34.3	−30.4	32.1
初级冻鱼及鱼片	135.3	12.3	46.0	39.4	21.1	36.8
初级软体类	30.4	21.9	10.3	10.0	54.6	9.3
初级甲壳类	18.9	117.5	6.4	10.4	174.2	9.7
活鱼	12.9	−7.1	4.4	3.9	−19.6	3.6
干熏及盐渍鱼	5.6	−4.6	1.9	2.9	1.9	2.7
海藻及其制品	3.0	−21.9	1.0	1.2	−14.9	1.1
冰鲜鱼	4.3	−6.6	1.5	1.5	14.2	1.4

三、出口市场

主要出口市场基本格局没有发生大的变化，日、美、欧、韩依然是我国最重要的出口市场（表4），占我国水产品出口总额的比例为69.8%，比2008年下降2.5个百分点，其中日本和韩国市场降幅最为明显。东盟市场和我国台湾市场表现抢眼，出口量和出口额均大幅增加。水产品市场集中度进一步降低，市场多元化步伐加快。

表4 主要出口市场

（单位：万t、亿美元）

出口市场	数量	同比增减（%）	金额	同比增减（%）	占出口总额比重（%）	同比增减（%）
日本	56.4	−12.8	26.7	−3.6	25.0	−1.1
美国	49.9	2.5	20.3	0.6	19.0	0.0

（续）

出口市场	数量	同比增减（%）	金额	同比增减（%）	占出口总额比重（%）	同比增减（%）
欧盟	49.1	−0.9	17.5	−0.7	16.4	−0.4
韩国	42.0	−4.9	10.1	−7.9	9.4	−1.0
东盟	35.3	31.1	7.6	20.8	7.1	1.1
中国香港	12.6	1.8	7.3	13.8	6.8	0.7
中国台湾	7.6	10.2	3.8	89.6	3.6	1.7
俄罗斯	7.5	−24.0	2.9	−22.8	2.7	−0.8

四、出口省份

山东、广东、辽宁、福建、浙江、海南等沿海省份仍是我国水产品主要出口省份（表5），出口额之和占全国出口总额的91.7%。其中，福建凭借对台贸易的快速增长，出口额同比增长31.3%，超过浙江成为第4大出口省份。江西和湖北作为最重要的内陆出口省份，出口额同比分别增长43.7%和32.2%。

表5　主要出口省份

（单位：万t、亿美元）

省份		数量	同比增减（%）	占出口总量（%）	金额	同比增减（%）	占出口总额（%）
沿海前6位	山东	92.2	−8.1	31.3	33.7	−3.5	31.5
	广东	39.6	4.1	13.5	16.9	4.4	15.8
	辽宁	49.9	−7.5	17.0	15.7	−2.4	14.7
	福建	39.9	36.1	13.6	15.3	31.3	14.3
	浙江	41.9	−5.9	14.2	12.8	−10.6	12.0
	海南	11.2	2.2	3.8	3.6	−11.9	3.4
内陆前3位	湖北	2.3	19.4	0.8	1.3	32.2	1.2
	江西	1.1	4.5	0.4	1.3	43.7	1.2
	吉林	1.0	−11.7	0.3	0.5	−13.7	0.5

五、进口情况

2009年供国内食用水产品进口量为114万t，进口额为17.3亿美元，同比分别增长1%和1.8%，主要品种有鱿鱼、鳕鱼、鲑鱼、带鱼、鳙鲽鱼类以及其他未列明冻鱼等，继续为满足国内不同消费需求，丰富国内水产品市场发挥着重要作用。来进料加工原料进口量为128.9万t，进口额为22.3亿美元，同比分别下降8.4%和3.5%。俄罗斯、美国、东盟、挪威、日本、欧盟等是我国可食用水产品和来进料加工原料主要进口市场（表6），其中从俄罗斯、东盟、欧盟和加拿大进口均出现不同程度下降，从挪威进口大幅增加，从美国和日本进口有一定增长。鱼粉进口继2008年大幅增加后，2009年小幅下降，进口量为130.8万t，进口额为13亿美元，同比分别下降3%和6.9%。秘鲁和智利依然是我国最重要的鱼粉进口国，其中从智利进口增加，从秘鲁进口减少。

表6　主要进口国家和地区

（单位：万t、亿美元）

国家或地区	占进口总额比例（%）	2009年		2008年		同比增减（%）	
		数量	金额	数量	金额	数量	金额
俄罗斯	23.6	75.9	12.4	78.0	13.0	−2.6	−4.2
秘鲁	14.9	85.7	7.9	99.9	9.9	−14.2	−20.5
美国	12.7	38.5	6.7	33.5	6.4	14.8	4.9
智利	9.9	41.0	5.2	29.7	4.1	37.6	27.4
东盟	7.2	28.1	3.8	33.8	3.9	−16.7	−1.6
挪威	5.3	14.8	2.8	8.8	1.9	69.7	47.8
日本	4.2	12.0	2.2	11.5	1.9	4.9	13.9
欧盟	3.8	13.3	2.0	20.4	3.2	−34.6	−36.3
加拿大	3.0	6.1	1.6	7.1	1.9	−13.9	−12.6

六、进出口额趋势分析

水产品出口的每次增长或下降无不和重大国际国内事件有着密切联系。2007年6月FDA宣布对我国产4种水产品实施“自动扣留”措施，随即，水产品出口额连续3个月下降。2008年初，我国南方部分地区遭受历史罕见的低温雨雪冰冻灾害，渔业生产受到严重影响，一些重要出口品种大量冻死，同时国际能源价格大幅上涨，我国劳动力成本大幅提高，水产品出口连续两个月处于较低水平，之后随着生产的逐渐恢复和加工出口企业克服生产成本增加的能力不断增强，水产品出口逐步恢复，全年水产品出口额首次突破100亿美元大关。2009年国际金融危机席卷全球，国际贸易遭遇前所未有的困难，水产品出口也不例外，春节过后水产品出口订单锐减，据调研了解2月份山东和广东地区企业开工率不足50%，2月全国水产品出口额仅4.2亿美元，同比下降24.7%，出口额之少和降幅之大均为历史罕见。之后通过多方努力，年初以来水产品出口大幅下降的势头得到有效控制，水产品出口在波动中出现积极变化，3月份开始企稳反弹，降幅有所收窄，9月份、11月份和12月份水产品单月出口额分别达到10.45亿美元、10.5亿美元和12.4亿美元，连续3次刷新月度出口额新高。在前11个月水产品累计出口额负增长的情况下，最终实现全年水产品出口额正增长。

我国造纸工业发展现状

中国造纸协会

一、全国纸及纸板生产及消费情况

(一) 主要产品情况

新闻纸生产量480万t，占纸及纸板总产量的5.56%，同比增长4.35%；消费量461万t，占纸及纸板总消费量的5.38%，同比增长8.22%。未涂布印刷书写纸生产量1 510万t，占纸及纸板总产量的17.48%，同比增长7.86%；消费量1 497万t，占纸及纸板总消费量的17.47%，同比增长8.09%。涂布印刷纸生产量590万t，占纸及纸板总产量的6.83%，同比增长7.27%；消费量463万t，占纸及纸板总消费量的5.40%，同比减少0.86%。其中，铜版纸生产量500万t，占纸及纸板总产量的5.79%，同比增长8.70%；消费量399万t，占纸及纸板总消费量的4.66%，同比减少0.50%。生活用纸生产量580万t，占纸及纸板总产量的6.71%，同比增长5.45%；消费量529万t，占纸及纸板总消费量的6.17%，同比增长5.17%。包装用纸生产量575万t，占纸及纸板总产量的6.66%，同比增长2.68%；消费量587万t，占纸及纸板总消费量的6.85%，同比增长3.16%。白纸板生产量1 150万t，占纸及纸板总产量的13.31%，同比增长2.68%；消费量1 160万t占纸及纸板总消费量的13.54%，同比增长2.56%。其中，涂布白纸板生产量1 100万t，占纸及纸板总产量的12.73%，同比增长2.80%；消费量1 110万t，占纸及纸板总消费量的12.95%，同比增长2.68%。箱纸板生产量1 730万t，占纸及纸板总产量的20.02%，同比增长13.07%；消费量1 809万t，占纸及纸板总消费量的21.11%，同比增长12.71%。瓦楞原纸生产量1 715万t，占纸及纸板总产量的19.85%，同比增长12.83%；消费量1 758万t，占纸及纸板总消费量的20.52%，同比增长13.27%。特种纸及纸板生产量150万t，占纸及纸板总产量的1.74%，同比增长7.14%；消费量144万t，占纸及纸板总消费量1.68%，同比持平。

从2009年的生产和消费形势分析来看，全年生产和消费均呈平稳增长态势，增速分别比上年回落0.30个百分点和0.86个百分点。生产量增幅10%以上的品种有箱纸板和瓦楞原纸，消费量增幅10%以上的品种有瓦楞原纸、箱纸板。

(二) 主要产品2000—2009年生产及消费情况

1. 新闻纸　2009年新闻纸生产量480万t，较上年增长4.35%，增幅增加2.13个百分点；消费量461万t，较上年增长8.22%，增幅回落0.18个百分点。2000—2009年生产量年均增长率为14.23%，消费量年均增长率为12.09%。

2. 未涂布印刷书写纸　2009年未涂布印刷书写纸生产量1 510万t，较上年增长7.86%，增幅增加3.38个百分点；消费量1 497万t，较上年增长8.09%，增幅增加4.11个百分点。2000—2009年生产量年均增长率为9.63%，消费量年均增长率为9.71%。

3. 涂布印刷纸　2009年涂布印刷纸生产量590万t，较上年增长7.27%，增幅回落0.57个百分点；消费量463万t，较上年减少0.86%，增幅回落10.48个百分点。2000—2009年生产量年均增长率为20.52%，消费量年均增长率为9.30%。其中，2009年铜版纸生产量500万t，较上年增长8.70%，增幅回落0.82个百分点；消费量399万t，较上年减少0.50%，增幅回落9.76个百分点。2000—2009年生产量年均增长率为21.29%，消费量年均增长率为8.85%。

4. 生活用纸　2009年生活用纸生产量580万t，较上年增长5.45%，增幅回落0.32个百分点；消费量529万t，较上年增长5.17%，增幅回落0.50个百分点。2000—2009年生产量年均增长率为9.80%，消费量年均增长率为8.98%。

5. 包装用纸　2009年包装用纸生产量575万t，较上年增长2.68%，增幅回落2.98个百分点；消费量587万t，较上年增长3.16%，增幅回落2.80个百分点。2000—2009年生产量年均增长率为4.11%，消费量年均增长率为2.48%。

6. 白纸板　2009年白纸板生产量1 150万t，较上年增长2.68%，增幅回落3.99个百分点；消费量

1 160万 t，较上年增长 2.56%，增幅回落 3.94 个百分点。2000—2009 年生产量年均增长率为 17.00%，消费量年均增长率为 13.07%。其中，2009 年涂布白纸板生产量 1 100 万 t，较上年增长 2.80%，增幅回落 4.20 个百分点；消费量 1 110 万 t，较上年增长 2.68%，增幅回落 4.14 个百分点。2000—2009 年生产量年均增长率为 20.85%，消费量年均增长率为 16.26%。

7. 箱纸板　2009 年箱纸板生产量 1 730 万 t，较上年增长 13.07%，增幅增加 0.57 个百分点；消费量 1 809 万 t，较上年增长 12.71%，增幅增加 1.10 个百分点。2000—2009 年生产量年均增长率为 17.67%，消费量年均增长率为 15.08%。

8. 瓦楞原纸　2009 年瓦楞原纸生产量 1 715 万 t，较上年增长 12.83%，增幅回落 0.60 个百分点；消费量 1 758 万 t，较上年增长 13.27%，增幅回落 1.35 个百分点。2000—2009 年生产量年均增长率为 13.02%，消费量年均增长率为 11.33%。

9. 特种纸及纸板　2009 年特种纸及纸板生产量 150 万 t，较上年增长 7.14%，增幅回落 9.53 个百分点；消费量 144 万 t，与上年持平，增幅回落 5.88 个百分点。2000—2009 年生产量年均增长率 10.72%，消费量年均增长率 6.75%。

二、主要生产经济指标完成情况

据国家统计局统计，2009 年 1～11 月规模以上造纸生产企业 3 686 个，从业人员 71.10 万人；工业总产值（当年价）为 4 162 亿元，较上年同期4 190亿元下降 0.67%；工业销售产值（当年价）为 4 077 亿元，较上年4 049亿元增长 0.69%；主营业务收入 3 998亿元，较上年同期 3 970 亿元增长 0.71%；产销率 98.00%，较上年同期 96.64%增长 1.36 个百分点；产成品存货 235.8 亿元，较上年同期 297.7 亿元下降 20.79%；利税总额 341.3 亿元，较上年同期 364.1 亿元下降 6.26%。其中，利润总额 210.0 亿元，较上年同期 228.2 亿元下降 7.98%；资产总计 5 016亿元，较上年同期 4 697 亿元增长 6.79%；资产负债率 58.69%，较上年同期 59.74%降低 1.05 个百分点；负债总额 2 944 亿元，较上年同期 2 806 亿元增长 4.92%；在统计的 3 686 个造纸生产企业中，亏损企业有 714 个，占 19.37%，同比降低 0.09 个百分点。

2009 年 1～12 月造纸生产企业工业总产值（当年价）4 660 亿元，较上年 4 571 亿元增长 1.95%；产销率 98.20%，较上年 97.09%增长 1.11 个百分点；工业销售产值（当年价）4 578 亿元，较上年 4 439亿元增长 3.13%。

根据上述相关资料分析，2009 年造纸生产企业主营业务收入约 4 500 亿元，比上年增长 4%左右；利税总额约 382 亿元，比上年下降 2%左右。其中，利润总额约 220 亿元，比上年增长 5%左右，但吨产品利润较上年降低约 3.3%。综观全年主要生产经济指标，完成情况比较理想，总体经济效益较好。

三、纸浆生产和消耗情况

据中国造纸协会调查资料，2009 年全国纸浆生产总量 6 674 万 t，较上年 6415 万 t 增长 4.03%，增幅较上年减少 4.06 个百分点。

2009 年全国纸浆消耗总量 7 980 万 t，较上年 7 360万 t，增长 8.42%。其中，木浆 1 866 万 t，较上年增长 14.90%，比例占 23%，较上年增加 1 个百分点；非木浆 1 175 万 t，较上年下降 9.41%，比例占 15%，较上年下降 3 个百分点；废纸浆 4 939 万 t，较上年增长 11.26%，比例占 62%，较上年增加 2 个百分点。木浆中，进口木浆比例上升 3 个百分点；废纸浆中，进口废纸浆比例上升 2 个百分点，国产废纸浆比例与上年持平；非木浆中，稻麦草浆比例比上年下降 2.5 个百分点，下降幅度较大，竹浆、苇（荻）浆、蔗渣浆比例与上年基本持平，竹浆和蔗渣浆消耗量均比上年有所增加。2009 年纸浆总消耗量比 2000 年增长 186%，其中国产纸浆消耗量 2009 年比 2000 年增长 171%。以上数字表明，全国纸浆消费总量随着纸及纸板的增长呈增加趋势。纸浆结构中，非木浆比例继续呈明显下降趋势，废纸浆增幅加大，支撑着纸浆结构的调整。由于进口木浆和进口废纸浆分别增长 38%和 14%，进口纤维原料量（包括废纸）占纸浆总消耗量为 44%，比上年增长 5 个百分点，表明我国造纸原料对国外依存度加大。

四、纸及纸板、纸浆、废纸及纸制品进出口情况

（一）主要产品进出口情况

2009 年纸及纸板进口 334 万 t，比上年 358 万 t 降低 6.70%；出口 405 万 t，比上年 403 万 t 增长 0.50%。出口量较上年略有增加，但仍未达到 2007 年 461 万 t 历史最高出口量，出口量比进口量多 71 万 t。纸浆进口 1 367 万 t，比 2008 年 952 万 t 增长 43.59%；出口 8.70 万 t，比 2008 年 7.23 万 t 增长 20.33%。废纸进口 2 750 万 t，比 2008 年 2 421 万 t

增长 13.59%；出口 0.003 万 t，比 2008 年 0.002 万 t 增长 50.00%。纸制品进口 16 万 t，比 2008 年 18 万 t 降低 11.11%；出口 195 万 t，比 2008 年 211 万 t 降低 7.58%。

2009 年进口纸及纸板、纸浆、废纸、纸制品合计 4 467 万 t，较上年 3 749 万 t 增长 19.15%；用汇 145.17 亿美元，较上年 166.27 亿美元降低 12.69%。2009 年进口纸及纸板平均价格为 965.25 美元/t，比 2008 年 1 018.35 美元/t 平均下降 5.21%；进口纸浆平均价格为 500.20 美元/t，比上年 704.25 美元/t 平均下降 28.97%；进口废纸平均价格为 137.99 美元/t，比上年 229.60 美元/t 平均下降 39.90%。

2009 年出口纸及纸板、纸浆、废纸、纸制品合计 608.70 万 t，较上年 621.23 万 t，降低 2.02%；创汇 77 亿美元，较上年 78 亿美元降低 1.28%。2009 年出口纸及纸板平均价格为 962.06 美元/t，比 2008 年 991.87 美元/t 平均下降 3.00%；出口纸浆平均价格为 1 045.48 美元/t，比上年 1 359.91 美元/t 平均下降 23.12%；出口废纸平均价格为 218.78 美元/t，比上年 203.03 美元/t 平均上涨 7.76%。

2009 年纸及纸板进出口总量中，进口量较大的品种有箱纸板、涂布白纸板、瓦楞原纸和未涂布印刷书写纸，合计进口量 241 万 t，约占纸及纸板总进口量的 72%。进口幅度同比普遍降低，降幅较大的品种有涂布印刷纸（下降 33.33%）、特种纸及纸板（下降 28.95%）、其他纸及纸板（下降 27.27%）。出口量较大的品种有涂布印刷纸、涂布白纸板、生活用纸、未涂布印刷书写纸、特种纸及纸板，合计 364 万 t，约占纸及纸板总出口量的 90%。出口保持增幅的品种有铜版纸（上升 36.08%）、涂布白纸板（上升 15.09%）、生活用纸（上升 7.69%）等。

2009 年我国纸浆、废纸、纸及纸板进出口贸易总体特点是作为造纸原料的纸浆和废纸进口量均呈增加趋势，其中纸浆增幅较大，进口量较上年增长 43.59%，废纸进口量较上年增长 13.59%，而纸及纸板进口量继续下降，出口量较上年略有增加且大于进口量。

（二）主要产品 2000—2009 年进出口情况

2009 年纸及纸板进口量大于出口量的主要品种有包装用纸、箱纸板、白纸板、瓦楞原纸、其他纸及纸板；出口量大于进口量的主要品种有新闻纸、未涂布印刷书写纸、涂布印刷纸、生活用纸、特种纸及纸板。

1. 新闻纸　2009 年出口量大于进口量，净出口量 19 万 t。

2. 未涂布印刷书写纸　2009 年出口量大于进口量，净出口量 13 万 t。

3. 涂布印刷纸　2009 年出口量大于进口量，净出口量 127 万 t。其中，铜版纸 2009 年出口量大于进口量，净出口量 101 万 t。

4. 生活用纸　2009 年出口量大于进口量，净出口量 51 万 t。

5. 包装用纸　2009 年进口量大于出口量，净进口量 12 万 t。

6. 白纸板　2009 年进口量大于出口量，净进口量 10 万 t。其中，涂布白纸板 2009 年进口量大于出口量，净进口量 10 万 t。

7. 箱纸板　2009 年进口量大于出口量，净进口量 79 万 t。

8. 瓦楞原纸　2009 年进口量大于出口量，净进口量 43 万 t。

9. 特种纸及纸板　2009 年出口量大于进口量，净出口量 6 万 t。

五、生产布局与集中度

根据中国造纸协会调查资料分析，2009 年纸及纸板生产量有所下降的省（自治区、直辖市）有河北、广西、上海、辽宁、吉林、山西、甘肃共 7 个，其余省份都有不同程度增长，其中广东省纸及纸板产量增加超过 100 万 t，增产 162 万 t。

2009 年我国东部地区 12 个省（自治区、直辖市），纸及纸板产量占全国纸及纸板产量比例为 71.3%，比上年降低 0.7 个百分点；中部地区 9 个省（自治区）比例占 21.4%，比上年降低 0.2 个百分点；西部地区 10 个省（自治区、直辖市）比例占 7.3%，比上年提高 0.9 个百分点。

2009 年纸及纸板产量超过 100 万 t 的省份有山东、浙江、广东、江苏、河南、河北、福建、湖南、四川、安徽、重庆、湖北、广西和江西 14 个省（自治区、直辖市），产量合计已达 8 010 万 t，占全国纸及纸板总产量的 92.71%，比上年增长 0.57 个百分点，比上年增产 657 万 t。

2009 年纸及纸板年产量超过 100 万 t 的造纸生产企业有玖龙纸业（控股）有限公司年产 652 万 t，理文造纸有限公司年产 355 万 t，山东晨鸣纸业集团股份有限公司年产 299 万 t，金东纸业（江苏）有限公司年产 228 万 t，山东太阳纸业股份有限公司年产 220 万 t，华泰集团有限公司年产 155 万 t，宁波中华纸业有限公司（含宁波亚洲浆纸业有限公司）年产 148 万 t，中冶纸业集团有限公司年产 101 万 t。以上 8 个造纸生产企业 2009 年比上年增产 326 万 t，约占全国纸及纸板增产量的 49%。纸浆年产量超过 100 万 t 的企业为海南金海浆纸业有限公司，年产 112 万 t。上述相关数据表明，2009 年全国造纸生产布局略有变化，东部地区仍然是我国造纸工业的主要生产区域，重点省（自治区、直辖市）和重点造纸企业生产集中度有所提高。

六、造纸企业经济类型结构与规模结构

根据国家统计局提供的 2009 年 1～11 月规模以上造纸生产企业的相关数据分析，2009 年国有及国有控股企业有 80 个，占 2.17%，较上年 2.89%减少 0.72 个百分点；“三资”企业有 418 个，占 11.34%，较上年 11.71%减少 0.37 个百分点；集体及其他企业有 3 188个，占 86.49%，较上年 85.40%增加 1.09 个百分点。在造纸企业主营业务收入总额中，国有及国有控股企业占 12.43%，较上年 17.34%减少 4.91 个百分点；“三资”企业占 29.38%，较上年 32.97%减少 3.59 个百分点；集体及其他企业占 58.19%，较上年 49.69%增加 8.50 个百分点。在利税总额中，国有及国有控股企业占 9.55%，较上年 18.79%减少 9.24 个百分点；“三资”企业占 29.64%，较上年 30.78%减少 1.14 个百分点；集体及其他企业占 60.81%，较上年 50.43%增加 10.38 个百分点。其中，利润总额中，国有及国有控股企业占 5.17%，较上年 18.44%减少 13.27 个百分点；“三资”企业占 31.97%，较上年 34.03%减少 2.06 个百分点；集体及其他企业占 62.86%，较上年 47.53%增加 15.33 个百分点。

2009 年国内造纸生产企业经济类型结构仍在调整变化，与 2008 年相比规模以上造纸生产企业数量由3 494个上升至 3 686 个，增加了 192 个。其中，集体及其他企业增加 204 个，而国有及国有控股企业数量却减少 21 个，“三资”企业增加 9 个。2009 年亏损企业数 714 个。其中，国有及国有控股企业占 3.92%，“三资”企业占 15.69%，集体及其他企业占 80.39%。

按照我国大、中、小型企业划分标准，2009 年在 3 686 个规模以上造纸生产企业中，大中型造纸企业 425 个，占 11.53%；小型企业 3 261 个，占 88.47%。在纸及纸板产品主营业务收入中，大中型企业占 60.30%，小型企业占 39.70%。在利税总额中，大中型企业占 64.22%，小型企业占 35.78%；在利润总额中，大中型企业占 65.81%，小型企业占 34.19%。

2009 年主要产品新增产量中，重点骨干企业增量已占总增量的 72%。目前已有一批优秀企业率先由传统造纸业向现代造纸业转变，对产业结构调整和产业优化升级起着重要支撑和推动作用。

七、环境保护

根据环境保护部统计，2008 年制浆造纸及纸制品产业（统计企业 5 759 个，比上年减少 59 个）用水总量为 108.96 亿 t，其中新鲜水量为 48.84 亿 t，占工业总耗新鲜水量 549.63 亿 t 的 8.89%。重复用水量为 60.12 亿 t，水重复利用率为 55.18%，比 2007 年提高 3.78 个百分点。万元工业产值（现价）新鲜水用量为 94.0t，比 2007 年减少 30.1t，降低 24.3%。

造纸工业 2008 年废水排放量为 40.77 亿 t，占全国工业废水总排放量 217.38 亿 t 的 18.76%，比 2007 年降低 0.49 个百分点。造纸工业废水排放达标量为 37.51 亿 t，占造纸工业废水排放总量的 92.00%，比 2007 年提高 2 个百分点。排放废水中化学需氧量（COD）为 128.8 万 t，比 2007 年 157.4 万 t 减少 28.6 万 t，占全国工业 COD 总排放量 404.8 万 t 的 31.82%，比 2007 年减少 2.92 个百分点。万元工业产值（现价）化学需氧量（COD）排放强度为 25kg，比 2007 年降低 37.50%。造纸工业废水处理设施年运行费用为 46.2 亿元，比 2007 年增加 2.8 亿元，增长 6.45%。

2 第二部分

相关行业发展概况

粮油食品加工业

一、基本情况

（一）大米加工业

2009 年，全国入统大米加工企业 7 687 个，比上年增加 376 个。其中，日加工能力 100t 以下的企业 5 011个，占大米加工企业总数的 65.19%，比上年减少 285 个；日加工能力 100～200t 的企业 1 941 个，占 25.25%，比上年增加 443 个；日加工能力 200～400t 的企业 165 个，占 7.42%，比上年增加 165 个；日加工能力 400～1 000t 的企业 115 个，占 1.5%，比上年增加 27 个；日加工能力 1 000t 以上的企业 38 个，占 0.49%，比上年增加 14 个。加工企业数量排名前 10 位的依次是江西 1 273 个，黑龙江 1 167 个，湖北 948 个，安徽 493 个，辽宁 419 个，江苏 398 个，湖南 352 个，广东 333 个，四川 325 个，吉林 314 个。大米加工企业主要分布在稻谷主产区，是属于原粮依赖程度较高的行业。2009 年我国大米企业稻谷年处理能力为 19 423.7 万 t，较 2008 年增加 3 377.2万 t，增幅为 21%。产能排名前 10 位的依次是黑龙江 4 122.4 万 t，湖北 2 368.1 万 t，江西 2 352.3万 t，安徽 1 868.6 万 t，江苏 1 306.9 万 t，吉林 1 061.4 万 t，湖南 999.6 万 t，辽宁 993.2 万 t，四川 637.5 万 t，福建 578.2 万 t。2009 年我国大米产量 5 723.8 万 t，较 2008 年增加 940.8 万 t，增幅为 19.7%。其中，特等米 1 606.5 万 t，标准一等米 3 565.4 万 t，标准二等米 370.6 万 t，糙米 76 万 t，其他 105.3 万 t。由于竞争激烈及人民消费质量日益提升，大米加工企业设备质量也逐年提高。大米产量排在前 10 位的依次是黑龙江 870.3 万 t，湖北 772.3 万 t，安徽 697.2 万 t，江西 637.9 万 t，江苏 532.1 万 t，湖南 371.4 万 t，辽宁 205.8 万 t，四川 201.4 万 t，福建 196.1 万 t。2009 年我国大米加工企业的产能利用率为 44.4%，较 2008 年下降 2.9%，产能明显过剩。产能利用率排名前 10 位的依次是天津 73.5%，上海 61.6%，江苏 61.4%，广东 57.6%，安徽 56.3%，河南 56.1%，湖南 56%，内蒙古 52.3%，福建 51.2%，湖北 49.2%。2009 年入统大米企业工业总产值 1 535.4 亿元，产品销售收入 1 533.7亿元，出口交货值 15.3 亿元，利润总额 25.3 亿元，资产总计 782.8 亿元，年末从业人数 17.2 万人，分别比 2008 年增长 22.1%、21.3%、－10%、3.3%、23.1%和 8.2%。

（二）小麦粉加工业

我国小麦粉加工业自市场化以来，由于民营、外资、合资、股份制等多种经济成分的进入，以及国有小麦粉加工企业的改制，依靠企业自身的力量在愈来愈激烈的市场竞争中逐步发展壮大并完善起来，目前行业已进入快速发展时期。但行业集团化和规模化水平仍然很低，行业利润低下。2009 年全国小麦加工能力已达 3.5 亿 t/年，而全国平均小麦消费量仅在 1.15 亿 t/年左右，小麦粉加工行业设备平均开工率仅为 32%，行业平均利润率为 1.18%。当前我国面粉系统调整所有制结构、国有企业改制已取得阶段性成果。多元化、多渠道的新格局业已形成，全行业的兼并、重组、联合正在加快步伐。但从总体看，“小、散、低”的状况并未从根本上改变。就以企业规模来说，除了入统的企业以外，2009 年正式注册的小麦加工厂达 4 万个（处理小麦 50t/d 以下的），企业“大而不强，小而不精”的状况仍普遍存在，产品品种单调，科技含量低，附加值不高，深度加工不够，综合利用少，环境保护差，因而缺乏经济实力和竞争能力。这种状况亟待改善。当务之急是小麦粉加工业要着力转变发展方式，企业及其领导人对此要有紧迫感、使命感。当前，我国正处于后危机时期，处于新的科技革命的前夜，又面临粮食紧平衡的新阶段，不论国内市场、国际市场，对面粉制品的需求越来越旺，要求越来越高，安全标准越来越严。过去那种高消耗、高污染、追求高 GDP 的路子已不可能持续发展。企业要发展，要兴旺，就一定要探索绿色、生态、可持续、得实惠的新路子。小麦粉加工业及相关联的面食业，一定要根据中央的精神，把重点放在转变发展方式上。改变原有的、落后的发展方式，向安全、优质、高效、低耗、绿色、生态的面粉工业体系的方向前进。谁先认识并掌握先机，先抢占科技的制高点，谁就会赢得主动权，在竞争中发展壮大，立于不败之地。但是转变发展方式涉及一系列根本问题，是个系统工程，是长期的战斗任务。要从行业和企业的实际出发，搞好规划，抓住重点，逐一突破，稳步推进。从小麦粉加工行业的发展情况看，应当抓住以下几个问题：

（1）要和优化产品结构、实施名牌工程结合起来，特别是要根据“安全、营养、风味、快捷”的原则，注意开发安全性能好、营养成分高、具有独特风味的产品，使面粉食品向多元化、大众化的方向发展，创造名牌、开拓市场，以更佳的产品、更佳的服务，取得更佳的市场效益和经济效益。

（2）抓好传统的“面食三宝”的开发，引导走上现代化、产业化的轨道，使之发扬光大、占领市场。现在方便面、挂面已经形成规模，但其他产品还未打开局面，有待我们去开拓，比如馒头，就大有潜力，要推广天津、济南、西安等地的经验。

（3）要十分关注面粉和面食添加剂的使用。粮油食品工业“成也在添加剂，败也在添加剂”。要下决心整顿添加剂的使用，如对人体有害的要坚决禁止使用。比如面粉增白剂，许多骨干企业都倡议要停用，这个提议很好，一定要下决心，否则后患无穷。有害东西要用天然的、安全的添加剂来代替。为此要加强对添加剂的科研与开发。

（4）要抓深度加工、综合利用。要使小麦的每个部分都得到充分利用，不使浪费。要结合实际发展循环经济、低碳技术、节能减排，降低能耗，减少污染。这方面许多地方都有一些搞得好的经验，应下决心推广。

（5）有条件的骨干企业要向产业链、流通链延伸，建立从生产、加工、物流到消费，从田间到餐桌的全过程产业链、流通链，并相应建立从源头到消费终端的全程食品安全监督体系。实践证明，这也是大型企业健康持续发展的必由之路。

（三）食用植物油加工业

2009年我国入统食用植物油加工企业1 321个（日油料加工能力30t以上的食用植物油加工企业）。其中，日加工能力100t以下的企业523个，占食用植物油加工企业总数的39.6%；日加工能力100～200t的企业251个，占19.0%；日加工能力200～400t的企业278个，占21.0%；日加工能力400～1 000t的企业146个，占11.1%；日加工能力1 000t以上的企业123个，占9.3%。2009年，食用植物油年油料加工能力为10 946.3万t，年油脂精炼能力为3 389.9万t，分别比上年增加3 080万t和661.3万t，增长39.2%和24.2%；食用植物油统计产量为2 780.9万t，实际产量为2 288万t（从食用植物油产量2 780.9万t扣除外购原油精练量402.2万t和外购国内成品油分装量90.7万t）分别比上年增加487.3万t和360.2万t，增幅为21.2%和18.7%；实际年油料加工能力7 364.8万t。按企业经济类型划分，年油料加工能力、年精炼能力和食用植物油产量，外商及港澳台商投资企业分别为2 819.6万t、1 241.9万t和1 255.8万t，分别占总数的25.9%、36.8%和45.4%；民营企业分别为7 098.8万t、1 785.9万t和1 271.1万t，分别占总数的65.0%、53.0%和45.9%；国有及国有控股企业分别为981.3万t、1 342.8万t和240.4万t，分别占总数的9.1%、10.2%和8.7%。2009年食用植物油加工能力排名前3位的省份是江苏1 473.3万t、黑龙江1 463.9万t和山东1 421.6万t；精炼能力排名前3位的是江苏577.2万t、广东370.1万t和山东321.8万t；食用植物油产量前10位的省份是江苏511.0万t、山东367.5万t、广东273.5万t、天津184.5万t、湖北182.6万t、福建122.3万t、上海121.1万t、河北120.8万t、黑龙江100.5万t和广西96.9万t。从产品结构看，精炼油的产量为2 070.4万t。其中，一级油为1 250.8万t，二级油为83.7万t，三级油1 71.5万t，四级油为564.4万t。另外，食用调和油的产量为118.7万t。年食用植物油产量10万t以上的企业71个，比2008年增加14个，总产量达1 631.8万t，占入统食用植物油企业总产量的58.7%。产量位居前3位的企业是益海嘉里（中国）658.0万t、中粮集团有限公司183.5万t和九三粮油工业有限公司83.6万t。2009年食用植物油产量以大豆油、菜子油、棕榈油和花生油为主，4个品种的统计产量达2 419.1万t，占食用植物油总产量的87.0%。其中，大豆油产量为1 405.6万t，占总产量的50.6%；菜子油产量为556.2万t，占总产量的20.0%；棕榈油产量为312.5万t，占总产量的11.2%；花生油产量为144.8万t，占总产量的5.2%。其他油品的产量和所占比重是：玉米油87.7万t，占3.2%；棉籽油83.1万t，占3.0%；葵花籽油39.6万t，占1.4%；米糠油13.2万t，占0.5%；芝麻油11.7万t，占0.4%；油茶籽油6.9万t，占0.2%；橄榄油6.7万t，占0.2%；其他油脂112.8万t，占4.1%。2009年，入统食用植物油企业工业总产值3 690.8亿元，产品销售收入3 622.0亿元，出口交货值46.3亿元，利税总额115.8亿元，利润总额81.6亿元（产值利润率为2.2%，较2008年的1.3%提高了0.9个百分点），资产总计2 531.7亿元，负债合计1 479.6亿元，年末从业人数15.4万人，分别比上年增长7.4%、5.6%、－0.5%、4.9%、82.4%、73.0%、57.6%（资产负债率为58.4%，较2008年的64.1%下降了5.7个百分点）和18.7%。

二、值得关注的几个问题

食物是人类生存的基础，也是国家稳定和社会发展的永恒主题。粮油及其制品是食物的最重要组成部分，是人类生存繁衍的基础。米、面、油及其产品与人们生活息息相关，一直是人们和媒体所关心议论的热点问题。为适应时代发展的新要求，一些问题应引起我们粮食工业企业的高度重视，通过研讨，达成共识，以利粮油加工业的健康发展。

（一）关于粮油产品的质量与安全问题

《中华人民共和国食品安全法》已于2009年6月1日起实施，这是一部保障我国食品安全，保护人民身体健康和社会和谐稳定的大法。为有利于食品安全法的贯彻执行，国家成立了“国务院食品安全委员会”，从立法和成立权威机构来保障食品安全，可见食品安全的重要性。作为食品生产企业和相关企业，都应把食品的质量与安全放在第一位。为确保粮油产品的质量与安全，对粮油加工企业来说，除了把好粮油原料的采购、储存关，严格按国家质量标准组织生产外，还要研究和避免在生产过程中的潜在危害。例如，在使用植物油加工中高温蒸炒、高温压榨和高温脱臭等工艺可能会对产品安全带来的负面影响；由于食用植物油加工中使用的助剂较多，诸如溶剂、石蜡、磷酸、盐、碱以及各类助滤剂、脱色剂等，为了食用油的更加安全，就需要研究和采用对油脂及其产品更加安全的助剂。最近国家公布了GB 16629—2008《植物油抽提溶剂》新标准，规定自2010年6月1日起强制实施，此标准代替原GB 16629—1996《6号抽提溶剂油》。修改后的6号溶剂油除馏程由60～90℃缩短到62～76℃外，还降低了苯、溴、硫的含量，从而使食用植物油的质量与安全更有保证。食用植物油加工企业应积极执行新标准，采用新的溶剂。在没有其他更好的新助剂替代之前，必须按要求严格采用食品级的和食品行业所允许使用的助剂。不得随意使用低级别的和劣质助剂，要特别重视将成品食用油脂及其制品中的过氧化值、反式脂肪酸和黄曲霉素等微量有害物质的含量控制在允许范围之内。

要抓紧研究解决地沟油等非食用油脂混入市场以及散装油容器污染等问题。在使用添加剂时，腐竹企业要按规定严格控制添加范围和添加剂量，严禁超范围使用和超量添加，在其他粮油产品加工中，严禁添加非食用物质和滥用食品添加剂，对在加工过程中或在产品中可加可不加的食品添加剂一律不准使用等。前段时间，国务院食品安全委员会办公室印发了《关于落实国务院领导同志对〈警惕食品加工行业潜规则的危害〉一文批示精神的情况报告》，报告中列举了形形色色的“潜规则”，如使用荧光增白物质将金针菇、白灵菇增白；腐竹、粉丝中使用吊白块；面条中使用硼酸与硼砂增加口感；腐竹、米线中使用乌洛托品等。报告中提出，要加强风险监测和监督检查，要将大米、面粉的检查范围扩展至全行业和各环节，组织专家研究分析可能的安全隐患。我们一定要认真贯彻国务院领导同志的批示精神，清理粮油及其制品在加工中的潜在危害，以确保粮油及其产品的绝对安全。

（二）关于粮油产品的“适度加工”与标准的修订问题

为了消费者的营养与健康，近两年来业内对粮油加工过程中出现的片面追求成品粮油的过精、过细、过白和过度精炼，造成大量营养成分流失、出品率降低和能耗大幅度提高等现象进行了认真反思。大家认为，在粮油加工中应该提倡“提高纯度、控制精度、适度加工”对纠正大米过精、面粉过白、油色过浅的“过度加工”有了共识。为了将‘过度加工’提倡“适度加工”落到实处，我们认为现有米、面、油产品的国家质量标准应该考虑修订。例如，在油脂方面，建议将现国家标准中的一级油作为凉拌专用油，将现国家标准中的二级油、三级油和四级油上升为新国家标准中的一级油、二级油和三级油，不再设四级油，达到以标准引领消费的目的。又如，在面粉中添加过氧化苯甲酰等化学增白剂会带来许多副作用和食品安全隐患，必须修改现行的国家标准。

（三）关于产能过剩问题

在我国粮油加工业，个别地区和品种的产能过剩较为严重是不争的事实。通过对产能过剩进行客观分析，我们认为粮油加工业的产能过剩具有两重性，既有消极的一面，也有积极的一面。对在低水平上的重复建设，造成国家财力物力大量浪费的落后产能，必须严格禁止。但过剩也有其积极的一面，那就是有过剩才有竞争，有竞争才能促使粮油加工业不断采用新技术、新工艺、新设备，形成先进产能。目前，我国粮油加工业的现状是设备陈旧、工艺落后、产品质量不稳定、产出率低、能耗高、污染严重和经济效益差的低水平落后产能过剩，而高水平的先进产能不足。为此，我们要促使落后产能企业通过重组、改造和提升，转变为先进产能。与此同时，要鼓励有实力的大型企业通过兼并，改造落后产能，适度发展先进产能；要提倡通过竞争，通过发展先进产能淘汰落后产能。根据国务院常务会议精神，粮油加工行业要加快淘汰落后产能的步伐，促进行业健康、持续发展。

（四）关于节能减排问题

举世瞩目的哥本哈根气候会议尽管没有取得最圆满的结局，但为了挽救地球，改善已被恶化了的人类生存环境，世界各国对从现在起实施“低碳经济”，进行“低碳生活”，实现“低碳增长”有了共识。我国政府向世界宣布的“低碳承诺”是不会改变的。承诺宣布：到2020年，我国单位GDP碳排放量比2005年下降40%～50%；到2020年非石化能源占一次性能源消费的比重达到15%左右。通过植树造林和加强森林管理，森林面积比2005年增加4 000万hm^2，森林蓄积量比2005年增加13亿m^3。也就是说，我们一方面要减碳，另一方面要增氧。由此可见，实现这一承诺，任务十分艰巨，并将全面影响我国经济社会的发展。实现这一承诺，要靠全社会的共同努力。对粮油加工行业来说，今后节能减排工作必将放到更加重要的位置，要研究改进工艺，改进设备，严格管理，纠正“大马拉小车”，杜绝发生“跑、冒、滴、漏”的现象，提高余热、余气和循环水的利用率，做到节约一度电、一滴水和一粒煤；要杜绝噪音、污水、粉尘和烟尘等污染环境。鉴于粮油加工企业的生产原料及其产品都是国家的重要特殊商品，因此节约一粒粮、一滴油，千方百计提高出品率仍是必须长期坚持的，要对“过度加工”造成的能耗提高、营养下降、出品率降低的做法进行认真反思，并加以纠正。要采取措施，严禁再上高消耗、高污染的建设项目，让节能减排、保护环境、“低碳经济”、“低碳生活”、“低碳增长”的意识牢牢扎根于企业之中和企业的员工之中。

（五）关于转基因食品的安全问题

2010年“两会”期间，不少代表就转基因食品安全问题发表了两种截然不同的看法，至今人们对其安全性仍有许多疑虑。我们认为这是出于对食品安全的疑虑，是对消费者负责的表现。为此，有这样那样的疑虑，甚至担心是可以理解的。了解转基因食品是否安全，对我们粮油加工企业来说是至关重要的，因为今后我们生产的米、面、油产品的原料是否采用转基因技术，决定着市场供应的食品是否属于转基因食品、决定着其是否安全。为此，粮油加工企业都要关心转基因食品安全性的讨论和最终结果。2010年5月17日中国科协在北京举办了“2010中国科协学术报告会——科学家的社会责任”，就当前社会上关心、讨论较多的热点问题，邀请了中国农业科学院生物技术研究所所长、博士生导师林敏研究员作了题为“转基因生物技术研究与应用”的报告，他向与会者介绍了全球转基因农作物商业化种植情况、我国政府的态度以及转基因食品的安全性。通过转基因技术的应用，能培育出多抗、优质、高产、高效的农作物新品种，大大提高了品种的改良效率，并可降低农药、化肥的投入，在缓解资源约束、保障粮食安全、保护生态环境、拓展农业功能等方面潜力巨大。自1996年首例转基因农作物产业化应用以来，产业化应用规模迅速扩大，截至2009年底，全球已有25个国家批准24种转基因作物的商业化应用。以转基因大豆、棉花、玉米、油菜为代表的转基因作物种植面积由1996年的170万hm^2发展到2009年的13 333.3万hm^2，14年间增长了79倍。其中，2009年美国的种植面积为6 400万hm^2，巴西2 140万hm^2，阿根廷2 130万hm^2，印度840万hm^2，加拿大876万hm^2，中国370万hm^2，巴拉圭220万hm^2，南非210万hm^2。值得一提的是，2000年以来，美国先后批准了6个抗除草剂和药用转基因水稻，伊朗批准了1个转基因抗虫水稻商业化种植，加拿大、墨西哥、澳大利亚、哥伦比亚4国批准了转基因水稻进口，允许食用。有些国家虽然种植转基因产品，其目的是出口，不是自己食用。

随着转基因农作物的产业化，生态和经济效益十分显著。为此，发达国家纷纷把发展转基因技术作为抢占未来科技制高点和增强农业国际竞争力的战略重点。与此同时，国际上对转基因食品的安全性问题一直争论至今未有定论。发达国家中的英国、法国、德国、意大利、日本、俄罗斯等大多数国家和欠发达国家还没有认可。由于此事涉及人类生存的大事，现在的科学技术水平还无法验证使用了转基因食品几十年或上百年后，对人类的生理特征将会产生何等影响，因此不能不引起世界各国人民的疑虑。我国是一个人口大国，解决13亿人口吃饭问题始终是头等大事。突破耕地、水资源约束，减少环境污染，保障国家粮食安全和农产品有效供给，归根结底要靠科技创新与应用。经过多年的努力，我国在重要基因发掘、转基因新品种培育及产业化应用等方面都取得了重大成果。党中央、国务院高度重视转基因技术研究与应用，2006年将转基因生物新品种培育重大专项列入《国家中长期科学和技术发展规划纲要（2006—2020年）》；2008年7月，国务院批准启动了转基因生物新品种培育重大专项；2009年6月，国务院发布了《促进生物产业加快发展的若干政策》，提出“加快把生物产业培育成为高技术领域的支柱产业和国家的战略性新兴产业”；2010年中央1号文件提出，“继续实施转基因生物新品种培育科技重大专项，抓紧开发具有重要应用价值和自主知识产权的功能基因和生物新品种，在科学评估、依法管理基础上，推进转基因新品种产业化”。遵照党中央和国务院的总体部署，按照“加快研究、推进应用、规范管理、科学发展”的指导方针，我国转基因生物技术正在积极健康地向前推进。

（本文由中国粮油学会、中国粮食行业协会提供相关资料，由本编辑部汇总整理）

油料加工业

一、基本情况

（一）企业规模和处理能力

2009年，我国油料加工业克服了原材料涨价、国内外油脂市场异常波动等诸多不利影响，科学决策、谨慎运作，仍然取得了较快的发展速度和较好的经济效益。全国入统食用植物油加工企业1 321个。其中，日加工能力100t以下的企业523个，占食用植物油加工企业总数的39.6%；日加工能力100～200t的企业251个，占19.0%；日加工能力200～400t的企业278个，占21.0%；日加工能力400～1 000t的企业146个，占11.1%；日加工能力1 000t以上的企业123个，占9.3%。2009年，食用植物油加工业年处理油料能力为10 946.3万t，油脂精炼能力为3 389.9万t，分别比2008年增加3 080.6万t和661.3万t，同比增长39.2%和24.2%。食用植物油统计产量为2 780.9万t，实际产量2 288万t，分别比2008年增加487.3万t和360.2万t，增幅为21.2%和18.7%；实际年处理油料7 364.8万t。

1. 年油料处理能力、精炼能力和食用植物油产量按企业不同规模划分　日加工能力100t以下的企业分别为384.2万t、503万t和111.1万t，分别占总数的3.5%、14.8%和4.0%；日加工能力100～200t的企业分别为752.9万、459.0万t和187.7万t，分别占总数的6.9%、13.5%和6.8%；日加工能力200～400t的企业分别为1 680.1万t、564.1万t和336.7万t，分别占总数的15.3%、16.7%和12.1%；日加工能力400～1 000t的企业分别为1 784.3万t、838.9万t和565.3万t，分别占总数的16.3%、24.8%和20.3%；日加工能力1 000t以上的企业分别为6 344.8万t、1 025.0万t和1 580.0万t，分别占总数的58%、30.2%和56.8%。2009年食用植物油加工业油料处理能力排名前3位的是江苏（1 473.3万t）、黑龙江（1 463.9万t）和山东（1 421.6万t）；精炼能力排名前3位的是江苏（577.2万t）、广东（370.1万t）和山东（321.8万t）。

2. 年油料处理能力、精炼能力和食用植物油产量按企业经济类型划分　外商及港澳台商投资企业分别为2 819.6万t、1 241.9万t和1 255.8万t，分别占总数的25.9%、36.8%和45.4%；民营企业分别为7 098.8万t、1 785.9万t和1 271.1万t，分别占总数的65%、53.0%和45.9%；国有及国有控股企业分别为981.3万t、1 342.8万t和240.4万t，分别占总数的9.1%、10.2%和8.7%。

（二）产量与经济状况

食用植物油产量前10位的是江苏（511.0万t）、山东（367.5万t）、广东（273.5万t）、天津（184.5万t）、湖北（182.6万t）、福建（122.3万t）、上海（121.1万t）、河北（120.8万t）、黑龙江（100.5万t）和广西（96.9万t）。从产品结构看，我国精炼油产量为2 070.4万t。其中，一级油产量为1 250.8万t，二级油为83.7万t，三级油为171.5万t，四级油为564.4万t。另外，食用调和油产量为118.7万t。其中，年产量10万t以上的企业71个，比上年增加14个，总产量达1 631.8万t，占入统食用植物油企业总产量的58.7%。产量位居前3位的企业分别是益海嘉里（中国）（658.0万t）、中粮集团有限公司（183.5万t）和九三粮油工业集团有限公司（83.6万t）。

食用植物油产量以大豆油、菜子油、棕榈油和花生油为主，四个品种的统计产量达2 419.1万t，占食用植物油总产量的87%。其中，大豆油产量为1 405.6万t，占总产量的50.6%；菜子油产量为556.2万t，占总产量的20%；棕榈油产量为312.5万t，占总产量的11.2%；花生油产量为144.8万t，占总产量的5.2%。其他油品的产量和所占比重为：玉米油87.7t，占3.2%；棉籽油83.1万t，占3.0%；葵花籽油39.6万t，占1.4%；米糠油13.2万t，占0.5%；芝麻油11.7万t，占0.4%；油茶籽油6.9万t，占0.2%；橄榄油6.7万t，占0.2%；其他油脂112.8万t，占4.1%。

2009年，入统食用植物油企业工业总产值

3 690.8 亿元，产品销售收入 3 622.0 亿元，出口交货值 46.3 亿元，利税总额 115.8 亿元，利润总额 81.6 亿元（产值利润率为 2.2%，较 2008 年的 1.3% 提高了 0.9 个百分点），资产总计 2 531.7 亿元，负债合计 1 479.6 亿元，年末从业人数 15.4 万人，分别比上年增长 7.4%、5.6%、－0.5%、4.9%、82.4%、73%、57.6%（资产负债率为 58.4%，较 2008 年的 64.1%下降了 5.7 个百分点）和 18.7%。

二、科研、新产品与新技术

（1）2009 年度粮食行业获得 3 项国家科技进步二等奖。由北京中粮科学研究院等单位完成的“蛋白质饲料资源技术开发及产业化”、河南工业大学等单位完成的“国家粮仓基本理论及关键技术研究与推广应用”、武汉工业学院等单位完成的“粮食保质干燥与储运减损增效技术开发”3 项成果荣获 2009 年度国家科技进步二等奖。

（2）2010 年 2 月，河南工业大学与郑州四维粮油工程技术有限公司合作研究开发的“10 000t/年醇洗大豆浓缩蛋白工业化生产技术研究”，通过河南科技厅组织的鉴定。该项目在对国内外最新技术研究的基础上，完成了年产 10 000t 醇洗大豆浓缩蛋白工艺设备设计、专用设备制作、成套设备安装和调试。经过对该项目主要工艺技术指标和产品质量考核和检验，该技术达到国内领先水平，接近国际先进水平，具有良好的应用前景。

（3）2010 年 3 月，江苏省丹阳正大油脂有限公司被农业部认定为江苏省唯一的国家农产品粮油加工技术研发专业分中心。国家农产品加工技术研发专业分中心的认定，是农业部依据《农产品加工业“十一五”发展规划》和《国家农产品加工技术研发中心及分中心管理办法》的有关要求，通过单位自主申报、地方主管部门审查推荐、专家评审及网上公示等程序，构建以企业为主体、以科研院所和大专院校为依托、产学研相结合的农产品加工科技创新平台，以此推动我国农产品加工业的技术进步和产业升级。

（4）2010 年 4 月，经过 10 多年的努力，甘肃省农业科学院作物研究所培育成功两个胡麻杂交种——陇亚杂 1 号和陇亚杂 2 号。近日这两个新品种已通过甘肃省品种审定委员会的审定。据介绍，胡麻杂交种增产效果非常突出，陇亚杂 1 号区域试验平均单产达 1 956kg/hm^2，较对照品种陇亚 8 号增产 10.27%，每公顷产量最高可达 3 900kg。陇亚杂 2 号区域试验平均单产 1 896.6 kg/hm^2。这两个品种含油率均在 40%以上，且抗病、抗倒伏，综合性状等表现优越。

（5）2010 年 5 月，武汉市科技局在武汉组织召开了由湖北百信食品有限公司、武汉工业学院完成的“系列多肽产品加工技术研究与应用”成果鉴定会。本项目研究了玉米肽、花生肽、大豆肽、酪蛋白肽、胶原蛋白肽、核桃肽、油茶籽肽、米糠肽、棉籽肽和菜籽肽等 10 种动植物肽的制备方法和分离纯化工艺，开展了理化特性分析和生理活性评价。项目整体技术居国内领先水平。

（6）2010 年 4 月，由湖南省粮食行业协会、湖南省粮食经济科技学会主办，湖南盈成油脂工业有限公司承办的“湖南油脂产业发展研讨会”在长沙举行。中国粮油学会、湖南省粮食局等有关单位的领导和湖南农业大学、江南大学、武汉工业学院、国家粮食局武汉科学研究设计院等院校的专家、教授分别就油脂行业宏观形式、产业政策、油脂营养与安全、油脂加工新工艺等方面作了专题报告，剖析了油脂企业当前所面临的挑战和机遇。

（7）2010 年 7 月 23 日，“第二批国家能源研发（实验）中心”命名大会在人民大会堂召开，中粮集团申报的“国家能源生物液体燃料研发（实验）中心”获国家能源局正式授牌命名。国家发展和改革委员会副主任、国家能源局局长张国宝为中心授牌，集团党组成员万早田和中粮科学研究院院长李建作为集团代表参加了命名授牌仪式。“国家能源生物液体燃料研发（实验）中心”旨在建设创新型国家，促进能源结构优化升级和能源科技进步，推进产学研联合，开展生物液体燃料领域的技术攻关，促进产业科技进步和生物质能源产业可持续发展。

（8）2010 年 8 月，烟台莱阳齐花特香纯正花生油有限公司申报的发明成果——齐花牌“坚果营养保健调和油”荣获国家发明专利。据介绍，该油品采用高山丘陵地带产核桃、花生、油茶籽、葵花籽、红花籽、芝麻、玉米胚芽 7 种油料，经纯物理压榨精制调配而成，对冠心病、高血压等有预防和辅助治疗的作用，对儿童和老年人的身体、记忆力具有重要的保健作用。产品于 2006 年 12 月申报国家发明专利，于 2010 获得国家知识产权局授予的专利证书。

（9）2010 年 8 月，国家农产品加工技术油脂（芝麻）研发中心在河南省农科院成立。该中心是依托河南省农科院农副产品加工研究所建立的全国农产品加工技术研发体系的组成部分。中心在芝麻加工领域，如芝麻香油的标准化生产、芝麻素等芝麻木脂素类活性物质制备、芝麻制品质量安全控制及快速检测、芝麻综合利用等方面具有独特优势。中心将在芝麻等油料加工技术创新及质量安全控制技术研究、行业发展战略及相关政策研究、科技人才培训、国际合作与交流、科技成果转化、示范与推广等方面开展工作。

(10) 2010 年 9 月，“首届中国食品产业商机交易大会暨中国食品产业发展高峰论坛”上，中粮福临门 DHA 谷物多食用调和油在粮油行业组中独占鳌头，获得“最具营养价值的食用油”和“最具创新价值的食用油品牌食品”两项组委会大奖。这次组委会奖项评选秉持公开公正的原则，邀请了众多食品行业权威专家担任评委，并综合大量的消费者调查得出最终结论，具有很高的公信力。中国食品产业商机交易大会由中国商业联合会、中华全国商业信息中心联合主办。

(11) 2010 年 12 月，由山东省科技厅副厅长孙伟主持，鲁花集团、江南大学承担的国家科技成果鉴定会在鲁花集团培训中心举行。会议鉴定了两项内容：一是“花生油葵花籽油新工艺及标准化安全生产”；二是“生物技术在高温花生粕领域的应用”。两个课题的任务来源分别是“十一五”国家科技支撑计划和山东省重大专项。鉴定会上，与会专家认真审查了由鲁花科技中心提供的各种技术报告、检测报告，并到鲁花生产基地进行了现场考察，通过对比国内外科技进展状况，鉴定委员会专家一致认为：“花生油葵花籽油新工艺及标准化安全生产”项目的花生油、葵花籽油总体加工技术达到国际领先水平。对于“生物技术在高温花生粕领域的应用”项目，鉴定委员会认为“该项目总体达到国际先进水平，其中在生物技术去除花生粕中黄曲霉毒素的研究方面达到国际领先水平”。

三、工程项目

(1) 2010 年 1 月，湖北华饴木本油脂有限公司近日在长阳县举行年产 2 万 t 木本油料投产庆典仪式。该项目 2009 年 6 月开始建设，2009 年 11 月一期加工厂房及生产线建成，达到 6 000t 木本油料的年生产能力，2010 年元月投产，同期第一批木本食用油面市；2010 年 5 月二期工程开始动工，12 月投产，将达到年产 2 万 t 木本油料的生产能力。项目以油茶籽为原料，采用双螺旋冷榨技术、连续精炼技术、全密闭自动灌装技术，并在木本油料加工行业率先引入医药行业 GMP 标准。

(2) 2010 年 2 月，中粮集团与湖北荆州市人民政府、公安县人民政府就油料蛋白加工项目签署战略合作协议。这是迄今为止中粮集团在湖北省品种最全、规模最大的一笔投资。本次中粮集团油料蛋白项目共投资 5 亿元，将在公安县建成年加工 25 万 t 油菜子、6 万 t 棉籽，年产值达 13 亿元的现代化工厂。中粮集团也在安徽省巢湖市居巢区民营经济园内建设日产 1 000t 油菜子加工生产线及相关配套设施。项目占地 43.3hm^2，总投资约 5.2 亿元，该项目是巢湖市与央企成功对接的第一个项目，也是第一个世界 500 强企业落户居巢区的项目。项目建成后，可年加工油料 30 万 t，实现产值 15 亿元，利税 1. 5 亿元，对巢湖市粮油行业的健康发展具有较强促进作用。

(3) 2010 年 3 月，四川西中油橄榄有限责任公司投资 2.4 亿元，在四川金堂建设集油橄榄科研、种植、销售、观光、旅游休闲为一体的万亩油橄榄科技产业园项目。项目将建设中国最大规模的油橄榄生产、深加工基地，同时打造油橄榄景观田、西班牙风情度假酒店等。总投资 5 000 万元，建油橄榄核心示范园，橄榄油加工厂、西班牙火腿加工厂各一座，并配套建设遗传育种中心。

(4) 2010 年 3 月，秦皇岛金海工业公司大豆分离蛋白项目开工建设，建成后可年产分离蛋白 7 000t。据了解，项目总投资 1 390 万美元，预计年均新增产值 9 750 万元。项目以原有生产线的低温豆粕为原料生产组织蛋白和分离蛋白。项目将与日本专业公司合作，引进国际先进水平的工艺和管理经验，投产后一方面可以缓解国内对高档分离蛋白的需求，另一方面则可提高我国分离蛋白档次和质量，提高在国际市场的竞争力。

(5) 2010 年 6 月，伟成油脂有限责任公司年处理百万吨棕榈油项目开工建设。伟成油脂有限责任公司是马来西亚伟成集团投资设立的外资企业，项目总投资约 6 亿元人民币，主要生产多种棕榈油精炼产品。项目分三期建设，一期建日处理能力 1 000t 精炼、分提生产线一条，建设工期一年半；二期建日处理能力 1 000t 精炼、分提生产线一条；三期再建日处理能力 1 000t 精炼、分提生产线一条，最后达到日处理 3 000t 的生产能力。

(6) 2010 年 6 月，宁夏亨源粮油有限公司 2 万 t 胡麻油生产线在海原新区正式落成投产，这是目前宁夏最大的胡麻油生产线。宁夏亨源粮油有限公司成立于 2009 年 5 月，目前，该公司拥有压榨、精炼、浸出三条生产线，“亨源香”牌胡麻油已远销上海、福建、内蒙古、山西、河南等地。2 万 t 胡麻油生产线落户海原，有助于带动当地及周边油料产业的发展壮大，进一步延长农产品产业链，对调整产业结构、增加农民收入发挥重要作用。

(7) 2010 年 6 月，湖北宜城市经济开发区白庙工业园的楚谷香粮油加工项目正式动工建设。该项目由湖北楚谷香粮油集团有限公司投资 2 亿元兴建，项目建成后可年产10万t一级菜子油、20万t精米、1.5万t米糠油和1万t脂肪酸，年产值达20多亿元，可实现利税5 000多万元。项目预计2011年5月建成投产，届时将有效促进湖北宜城市农民增收，同时推动该市农产品加工产业做大做强。

（8）2010年7月，总投资5.95亿元的益海集团金海食品公司低温豆粕项目开工建设。该项目由益海集团金海食品公司增资建设，采用低温豆粕作为加工原料，经过醇洗法工艺生产高质量大豆浓缩蛋白，并生产组织蛋白和功能性蛋白。项目建成后可年产低温豆粕10万t、浓缩蛋白3.5万t、分离蛋白1.5万t、组织蛋白7 000t，预计可实现年销售收入35.5亿元。

（9）2010年7月，中纺粮油工业有限公司在广东湛江项目开工，项目为日加工大豆3 000t，年产值约50亿元人民币。中纺粮油公司是中纺集团设立的专门从事油脂油料加工、经营和管理的专业化公司，目前油脂加工能力达到2.2万t/d，位居国内粮油加工行业前3位，其中在珠三角地区已形成日加工大豆8 000t，年加工大豆230万t的产能。

（10）2010年8月，湖北省云梦县30万t油菜子及棉籽加工项目近日奠基。该项目是湖北省20个农产品加工园建设项目之一，总投资4.65亿元，年加工30万t双低油菜子、生产10万t菜子油/棉籽油（含5万t甘油二酯）。项目由湖北佳富实业有限公司建设，采用预榨浸出工艺加工。

（11）2010年8月，总投资2.2亿元的河北康恩菲尔德油脂加工项目在容城县奠基。该项目由美国嘉吉公司与保定惠农饲料有限公司合资建设，计划占地8hm²，分两期建设。一期投资1.2亿元，主要新建150t/d玉米胚芽预榨及120t/d浸出生产线各一条。建成后预计产值4亿元，利税2 500万元。二期工程投资1亿元，计划建设100t/d精炼车间、400t/d精炼油车间和油脂小包装车间，建成后，年加工玉米原油5万t。产值5亿元，利税4 000万元。

（12）2010年11月，由鲁花集团投资亿元建设的一座年产10万t的浓香花生油生产工厂在辽宁阜新正式开业。该工厂5月份开工建设，11月份建成投产，实现了当年立项、当年建厂、当年投产，再现了神奇的“鲁花速度”。鲁花此次布局东北，在辽宁阜新建厂，不仅能进一步增强鲁花产品的覆盖能力，也将进一步提升鲁花造福三农的能力。阜新是东北地区主要的花生产区，花生种植规模居辽宁省第一位。该市优质花生种植总面积达9.6万hm²，年产量28万t。通过该工厂的生产拉动，可以使阜新及周边地区发展花生配套基地6.67万hm²，带动100万农民增收致富。

（13）2010年11月12日，中粮黄海粮油工业（山东）有限公司120万t粮油加工项目竣工。该项目总投资10.2亿元，建设内容包括大豆压榨、精炼等加工以及配套仓储物流设施。至此，中粮黄海年加工能力达到180万t，年产值100亿元左右，成为山东地区最大的油脂加工企业。该项目竣工，进一步提高了中粮集团粮油加工能力，有利于促进区域油脂市场的繁荣，增强了国家宏观调控能力。中粮黄海120万t粮油加工项目是在中粮集团“打造全产业链粮油食品企业”战略指引下，实施“扩大规模、完善布局”战略的重大成果。

（14）2010年12月，山东鲁花集团在广东麻涌建设6万t/年浓香花生油及调和油项目。项目位于新沙工业园，占地面积约3.33hm²，计划总投资5 000万元。项目建成后，中国3大植物油品牌中粮福临门、益海金龙鱼、鲁花全部在麻涌扎根发展，对该镇打造华南地区粮油食品综合生产基地具有重要意义。

（15）2010年12月，中储粮镇江粮油加工及仓储物流项目，是中国储备粮管理总公司投资13亿元在江苏省镇江市建设的重点项目，也是国家2008年拉动内需新增1 000亿元国债投资项目之一。项目2009年2月正式开工，2010年年内全部建成投产，可形成从粮食到物流、仓储、加工的完整产业链，可储备油脂油料60万t，年加工油料100万t，年加工油脂50万t。

四、油脂标准

（1）2010年3月，“《油茶子油》国家标准修订方案研讨会”在江西南昌召开。此次研讨会由全国粮油标准化技术委员会油料及油脂技术工作组主办，江西绿海油脂有限公司承办。现行《油茶子油》国家标准（GB 11765—2003）已经实施近7年，随着生产方式不断发展，现有标准已无法适应市场的变化。研讨会的目的是为促进我国油茶籽加工行业健康有序发展，保护消费者权益，更好地规范和推动全国油茶产业的发展。《油茶子油》国家标准项目组负责人汇报了标准制修订情况，参会的粮油行业科研院校、协会和企业代表分别作了大会发言。

（2）2010年6月1日起，《植物油抽提溶剂》（GB 16629—2008）新标准强制实施，此标准代替原GB 16629—1996《6号抽提溶剂油》。《植物油抽提溶剂》所属产品主要适用于食用油脂抽提。规定了由石油直馏馏分、重整抽余油或凝析油馏分经精制而成的植物油抽提溶剂的要求和试验方法、检验规则、标志、包装、运输、贮存及交货验收。其对比旧标准最大的改变，是修改后6号溶剂油除馏程由60～90℃缩短到61～76℃外，还降低了苯、溴、硫的含量。6号溶剂油作为粮食用主要浸出用溶剂被广泛使用。但因其馏程较宽，且含有对人体有害的芳烃等物质，与社会对食品安全日益增长的要求不相符。

(3) 2010年11月19日，“全国粮油标准化技术委员会油料及油脂技术工作组2010年第四次工作会议——《食品安全国家标准 食用大豆粕》制修订启动暨第一次专家研讨会”在无锡召开，卫生部国家食品安全标准处、全国粮油标准化技术委员会、中国粮油学会油脂专业分会、武汉工业学院和全国粮油标准化技术委员会油料及油脂技术工作组、北京疾控中心、吉林卫生监督局等代表出席了会议。本次会议由国家粮食储备局无锡科学研究设计院、武汉工业学院和全国粮油标准化技术委员会油料及油脂技术工作组联合主办。全国粮油标准化技术委员会秘书长龙玲莉对标准制修订提出了要求。

五、油脂会议

(1) 2010年4月，中国粮油学会油脂分会在浙江省衢州市召开了“2010年第一次会长办公扩大会议”。会议由浙江老树根油茶开发有限公司承办，王瑞元会长主持会议。参加本次会长办公扩大会议的会长、名誉会长、秘书长、专家组组长及部分常务理事共计60多人。会议期间，王瑞元会长做了“浅析我国粮油市场的价格走势”主题报告，会议期间王瑞元会长就社会各界关心的“地沟油”问题也发表了讲话，他指出：防止“地沟油”返回餐桌，是粮油行业有良知科技人员的共同呼声；“地沟油”是一种资源，可以作为工业用油，回收处理“地沟油”是政府为老百姓办好事的一项具体措施；对“地沟油”应加强监管，加强道德教育、良知教育和科普教育。

(2) 2010年4月24～25日，由中粮食品营销有限公司、中国粮油学会油脂分会等单位共同发起的“2010中国食用油发展趋势研讨会”在杭州隆重举行。大会形成了以“天然优质、营养健康、引领创新、决胜未来”为发展方向的《2010中国食用油发展趋势杭州宣言》。中国粮油学会油脂分会王瑞元会长提出了未来食用油行业发展的七大发展趋势。其中油脂产品必须按照“安全、优质、营养”的要求方向发展，食用植物油加工企业的品牌意识将进一步增强，低碳经济、节能减排和环境保护意识在产业中将不断增强等趋势得到了与会者的认同。

(3) 2010年7月，“中国粮油学会第六届学术年会”在北京召开。中国科协和国家粮食局有关领导出席会议并讲话。大会以科技创新、全面服务国家粮油食品安全、提升公众营养与健康、推动企业节能减排、促进社会低碳经济为主题，特邀中国工程院院士盖钧镒和国家粮食局流通与发展司司长何毅分别就“中国大豆产业和转基因食物安全”、“粮油科技‘十一五’执行情况与‘十二五’规划制定的思路”作了报告。大会表彰了获得中国粮油学会2009年度科技进步奖、第六届优秀论文奖、第二届全国粮油科技工作者奖、第二届优秀团体会员奖、首届全国粮油优秀科技创新型企业奖的团体和个人。

(4) 2010年9月6日，“中国粮油学会油脂分会第十九届学术年会暨换届大会“在黑龙江鹤岗市九州大酒店召开。来自全国油脂界的专家、学者、企业家、业内人士等代表参加了盛会。市委常委、副市长徐祝新到会致辞。大会由中国粮油学会油脂分会主办，由黑龙江万源粮油食品有限公司协办。徐祝新在致辞中代表市委、市政府，对中国粮油学会油脂分会第十九届学术年会暨换届大会在我市召开表示祝贺。大会进行了换届选举。

(5) 2010年11月6日，由大连商品交易所联合大马交易所共同主办的“第五届国际油脂油料大会”在广州举行。论坛的主题是“在全球宏观经济进入恢复期的背景和国内收储政策的支撑下，我国油脂油料企业如何提升产业水平和行业竞争力”，来自国家粮食局粮油信息中心、农业部、中粮及马来西亚植物油总署、巴西大豆种植协会等政府部门和机构的嘉宾就国内外油脂工业发展及大豆、棕榈油等油脂油料供求形势、全球植物油价格展望等主题进行了演讲，并召开了油脂油料市场风险管理专题论坛。

（武汉工业学院食品学院 何东平）

大豆加工业

一、基本情况

（一）资源概况

1. 世界大豆生产情况　2009年世界大豆总产量为23 095万t，较2008年增长9.6%。世界大豆主产国有美国、巴西、阿根廷、中国、印度和加拿大等（表1）。表1中6个国家的大豆总产量，约占世界大豆总产量的92.7%，基本构成了世界大豆产量的主要市场份额。

表1　2009年世界大豆主产国生产情况

国　别	收获面积（khm^2）	单产（kg/hm^2）	总产量（万t）	同比增长（%）	占世界比例（%）
美　国	30 207	2 666	8 054	10.5	34.9
巴　西	20 565	2 817	5 992	3.6	26.0
阿根廷	16 380	2 822	4 623	−2.6	20.0
中　国	9 190	1 630	1 498	−3.6	6.5
印　度	9 600	942	905	−17.5	3.9
加拿大	1 195	2 790	334	23.7	1.4

注：表中数据来自于《2010年中国农村统计年鉴》。

2. 我国大豆生产情况　根据中国农业统计资料显示，2009年，我国大豆播种面积为9 190khm^2，较2008年增长0.7%；单位面积产量为1 630kg/hm^2，同比增长−4.3%；总产量为1 498万t，同比增长−3.6%。产量较大的省、自治区为黑龙江、安徽、内蒙古、吉林、河南、江苏、四川等，约占全国总产量的74.1%（表2）。

表2　2009年我国大豆主产区生产情况

主产省区	播种面积（khm^2）	单产（kg/hm^2）	总产量（万t）	同比增长（%）	占全国比例（%）
黑龙江	4 008	1 477	591.9	−4.6	39.5
安　徽	970	1 285	124.7	−2.4	8.3
内蒙古	840	1 362	114.4	1.0	7.6
河　南	467	1 842	86.0	−3.0	5.7
吉　林	437	1 875	82.0	−9.4	5.5
江　苏	233	2 613	60.9	1.2	4.1
四　川	221	2 278	50.4	−0.4	3.3

注：表中数据来自于农业部《2009年中国农业统计资料》。

（二）加工业概况

1. 世界大豆加工概况　根据美国农业部2009年公布的世界大豆供需平衡和豆油、豆粕主产国产量报告显示，2009/2010年度世界大豆压榨量为20 340万t，同比增长5.9%；世界豆油总产量为3 788万t，同比增长6.3%；世界豆粕总产量为16 039万t，同比增长6.3%。其中，世界各主要大豆加工国2009/2010年度大豆压榨量、豆油和豆粕产量见表3。

表3　2009/2010年度世界豆油、豆粕主要生产国加工情况

主要生产国	压榨量		豆　油		豆　粕	
	产量（万t）	同比增长（%）	产量（万t）	同比增长（%）	产量（万t）	同比增长（%）
美　国	4 613	2.0	874	2.5	3 767	5.9
巴　西	3 184	1.4	614	2.0	2 450	0.7
阿根廷	3 500	10.3	690	13.3	2 643	6.5
中　国	4 410	7.5	753	3.0	3 469	6.8

2. 我国大豆加工概况　国家粮油信息中心资料，2009/2010年度我国大豆压榨量将达到4 410万t，较2008/2009年度增加300万t。2007—2009年我国大豆压榨能力继续保持增加态势。据不完全统计，3年之内至少有16个大型大豆压榨油厂建成投产，合计日压榨大豆能力接近4.5万t左右，年平均新增大豆压榨能力近1.5万t。其中，日压榨能力超过1 000t的分别有九三集团防城港公司，日压榨大豆能力为5 000t；广西钦州华港油厂，日压榨大豆能力为2 000t；广西钦州汇海粮油公司，日压榨大豆能力为3 000t；福建元成豆业公司，日压榨大豆能力为3 000t；天津邦基公司，日压榨大豆能力为4 000t；辽宁金海源公司，日压榨大豆能力为3 000t；浙江舟山中海公司新厂，日压榨大豆能力为3 000t；江苏益海泰兴公司，日压榨大豆能力为6 000t；江苏民康油脂公司，日压榨大豆能力为1 200t；山东青岛渤海公司，日压榨大豆能力为6 000t；山东得利斯集团大豆压榨项目，日压榨大豆能力为1 500t；辽宁天丰公司，日压榨大豆能力为1 500t；黑龙江孙吴联凯公司，日压榨大豆能力为1 500t；黑龙江庆安阳达公司，日压榨大豆能力为1 500t；黑龙江吉庆公司，日

压榨大豆能力 1 200t；黑龙江鸿源公司，日压榨大豆能力为 1 000t。2009 年我国大豆加工企业中，变化最为突出的就是国有企业大举收购民营企业，尤其以中纺集团为代表，国有企业在大豆压榨领域中的比重大幅提升。2009 年，3 大国有企业扩张战略各有特色。一是九三集团沿海油厂产能利用率大幅提高。2007、2008 年九三集团进口大豆量占全国进口总量的 4%，而 2009 年已提升至 8%。绝对数量也是如此，2008 年九三集团进口大豆量约 139 万 t，而 2009 年增至 335 万 t 左右。九三集团在沿海地区有 3 家油厂，日加工产能累计约 15 000t，一年按 300 天正常生产计算，年加工量为 450 万 t，产能利用率达 74%，远远高于全国平均产能利用率。二是中粮集团发展全产业链，进口量保持稳定。2007—2009 年，中粮集团大豆进口量每年都保持在 420～440 万 t，但是此间中粮集团所占比重从 14%降至 10%。三是中纺集团大举收购民营企业。2009 年收购了沈阳金石、大连连王、福建金石、四川金石、湛江华农、湛江富虹，新收购的油厂与原有的在华东、广东的油厂，日产能已累计达到 2 万 t。故中纺集团由大豆代理进口型成功蜕变成加工型，这也是国有企业比重大幅提高的原因所在。

我国大豆压榨产业正在形成外资企业占 40%、国有企业占 23%、民营企业占 37%的格局，大豆加工企业的弱势局面一定程度上得到了遏制，并且随着民营企业的发展壮大，三足鼎立的局面日趋形成。2009 年，产能过剩仍是行业特征。经过 2008 年的集中改扩建过程，我国大豆加工企业的整体规模水平已大幅提高，3 000t/日以上的油厂已占 54%。我国虽然完成了技术换代，加工能力各方面水平显著提高，但产能过剩也成了行业不可避免的事实。据统计，我国规模以上油厂大豆压榨总产能达 279 250t/日，其中黑龙江地区 5 320t/日，沿海地区 226 000t/日。若年压榨时间按 300 天计算，沿海地区就可压榨大豆 6 780 万 t，这些大豆全部交由沿海地区油厂压榨，沿海油厂的产能利用率也仅 61.9%。产能过剩问题，已得到国家上层的注意，并且出台了相关限制政策。大豆压榨产能的过剩，也意味着企业在压榨行业中的布局结束。企业都想提升自身竞争力，集团式的优势不言而喻，但在搏击市场的时候，应该站在我国整个油脂油料的大舞台来布局。我国的大豆压榨产业已基本成熟，市场空间变小，而油菜籽、棉籽、葵花籽压榨领域还需要进一步技术升级、资源整合，市场空间较大。2009 年，压榨国产大豆油企困惑重重。2008 年国家的收储政策，使压榨国产大豆的油厂范围大大缩小，压榨国产大豆的油厂只剩下黑龙江、内蒙古及吉林部分地区。2009 年虽然国家出台了一系列支持东北油厂补贴收购大豆的政策，但相对进口大豆的低廉价格仍优势不足，因此国产大豆的压榨仍集中在黑龙江、吉林。2009 年秋，国家政策不仅继续保护农民的利益，还考虑了国产大豆压榨厂的利益，给予补贴收购加工。尽管现在原料充足了，但部分企业为争夺产品的市场份额，仍在大打价格战。

黑龙江省是我国最大的非转基因大豆主产区，聚集了大量的大豆加工企业，非转基因大豆加工业已成为全省优势明显、特色鲜明的农产品加工重要产业。根据黑龙江省大豆协会统计，2009 年全省拥有大豆油脂加工企业 150 余个，年处理量达到 700 万 t，占全国加工能力的 1/10。由于受进口大豆冲击，目前全省大豆加工企业季节性开工特别明显，部分企业停产，复产的企业也均属阶段性开工，利润行情好就开工，行情不好就停工。到 2009 年末，黑龙江省补贴压榨的企业 81 个，合计产能近 4 000 万 t，远超过全省的大豆产量，存在着明显的产能过剩。其中，多数是中小型加工企业，这些企业大都建在原料产地，产品同质性问题突出，缺乏市场竞争力。由于国内植物油及调和油一直缺乏统一标准，大豆压榨业的市场准入门槛很低（仅有 QS 标准），竞争无序，相互倾轧，这也是我国大豆压榨业产能过剩的根本原因之一。2009 年全省省级大豆压榨重点龙头企业 25 个，年加工能力 910 万 t。其中，九三油脂工业集团在国内大豆加工企业中加工能力位居第二；阳霖油脂集团年处理大豆 180 万 t，跻身全国民营油脂企业前列；我国最大的大豆工业园区——大庆日月星大豆高新工业园，依托黑龙江省非转基因大豆主产区优势，生产非转基因的绿色、有机、无公害的大豆产品；农垦垦区大豆年加工能力达到 200 万 t，实现了以大豆加工企业为龙头，带动生产基地和承包职工的产加销、贸工农一体化的经营格局，初步形成了大豆产业化体系。目前黑龙江大豆加工业主要有豆油、豆粕、分离蛋白、浓缩蛋白、组织蛋白、大豆胚芽、异黄酮、卵磷脂、蛋白饮料、多糖、木糖醇等产品。

二、科研、新产品、新技术

（1）由国家大豆工程技术研究中心、东北农业大学、中科院东北地理与农业生态研究所等单位，经过 3 年艰苦攻关完成的“大豆超高产技术试验示范与配套技术研究”省级科技攻关课题，于 2009 年 2 月 18 日在哈尔滨通过了由黑龙江省科技厅组织的科技成果鉴定。“大豆超高产技术试验示范与配套技术研究”课题是黑龙江省重点科技攻关项目之一。研究人员针对黑龙江省季节性的气候特点，在采取原有“三良五精”技术基础上，提出配合滴灌技术和化控技术——采取先进的灌溉方式缓解干旱天气对大豆的影响，并利用化控技术调节植株的生长发育，保花促荚，提高产量。不仅超出了国家大豆超高产品种的产量潜力标准，而且创下了我国东北大豆单产最高水平。有关专家表示，该项目的成功完成，将对如何采取有效栽培方法提高我国大豆品种产量潜力起到积极的推动作用，并将为黑龙江省粮食工程和国家粮食安全战略的顺利实施提供强有力的技术支撑。

（2）“大豆优质蛋白与高纯磷脂开发与产业化示范”是“十一五”期间科学技术部为全面提升我国食品加工产业科技创新能力，而组织实施的国家科技支撑计划“食品加工关键技术研究与产业化开发”重大项目中的重大新产品开发与产业化示范课题之一。2009 年 2 月 20 日，该项目在广州通过了由科学技术部组织的科技成果验收。该项目由大庆日月植物蛋白（集团）有限公司、国家大豆工程技术研究中心主持，联合山东谷神生物科技有限责任公司、江南大学、黑龙江双河松嫩大豆生物制品有限责任公司、中国食品发酵研究院等 11 个单位共同承担。验收专家委员会一致认为，课题组经过 3 年攻关，153 人的潜心研究，围绕大豆浓缩蛋白与组织蛋白改性技术研究及系列产品开发，高品质大豆磷脂生产技术的产业化研究与产业化示范，攻克了大豆浓缩蛋白的连续式酒精浸出技术、非膨化挤压大豆蛋白生产技术、无机膜法高品质浓缩大豆磷脂生产技术、CO_2超临界氢化大豆磷脂生产技术等关键技术，研究成果填补了国内空白，达到国际先进水平，显著提升了我国大豆加工产业发展的整体科技水平；课题组研发了 7 项具有国际先进水平的大豆深加工生产新工艺，开发新产品 9 种，新设备 5 台（套），建成示范生产线 6 条、中式示范线 2 条、生产示范基地 3 个；申请和获得国家发明专利 25 项，制定技术标准 8 项，发表论文 54 篇，获省部级奖励 2 项，完成了任务书规定的考核指标。

（3）国家“863”重大项目“强优势大豆杂交种配置与运用”现场交流会于 2009 年 8 月 28 日在太原召开。中国工程院院士盖钧镒、吉林省农业科学院孙寰研究员及该项目课题主持人赵丽梅研究员、中国农业科学院常汝镇研究员、国家大豆产业体系首席专家韩天富研究员和黑龙江省农业科学院刘忠堂研究员等 20 余位国内大豆研究权威到会，并深入晋中市榆次区、祁县等 6 个实验点观摩指导。我国大豆杂优研究开始最早，一直处于世界领先水平。1985 年，山西省农业科学院品种资源研究所卫保国研究员首先发现了大豆光敏不育材料。此后，卫保国开始尝试拓展“三系”选育，有创造性地进行“两系”选育。2009 年 5 月，国家“863”重大项目“强优势大豆杂交种配置与运用”课题得到国家的进一步支持，山西省农科院品种资源研究所成为全国 8 个项目研究承担单位之一，卫保国承担了更为重要的研究课题。在座谈交流和现场观摩中，与会专家认为，山西省农业科学院品种资源研究所实验田的制种效果十分喜人，显示出我国杂交大豆研究正在走出试验阶段，走向应用阶段。

（4）“全国农产品（大豆）加工预警数据采集工作站工作人员培训班”于 2009 年 9 月 28 日在哈尔滨举办。来自全省 5 个工作站的负责人和具体工作人员、省大豆协会以及当地主管部门参加了培训班。根据《农业部办公厅关于下达 2009 年农产品加工预警服务项目任务的通知》（农办企［2009］8 号）精神，黑龙江省工信委开展了数据采集站的申报认定工作。省工信委于 8 月 17 日下发了《关于开展全国农产品（大豆）加工预警系统首批数据采集工作站申报工作的通知》，9 月份下发了《关于认定全国农产品（大豆）加工预警数据采集工作站的通知》，认定集贤县福厚油脂有限公司、黑龙江省祥源油脂有限责任公司、黑龙江省友谊盛源油脂有限公司、海伦市东源制油厂、黑龙江海伦大豆批发市场有限公司等 5 个企业为全国农产品（大豆）加工预警数据采集工作站。大豆预警承办单位——黑龙江省中小企业技术创新服务中心举办了这次“全国农产品（大豆）加工预警数据采集工作站工作人员培训班”，聘请专家讲解了大豆加工预警工作的意义、预警指标的含义，并与预警协办单位黑龙江省大豆协会及在场企业家研究探讨了指标的科学性及实用性。培训班上，黑龙江省中小企业技术创新服务中心领导部署了下一步预警工作任务，为各工作站颁发了牌匾。本次培训班的成功举办，是黑龙江省大豆加工预警工作一个新的进展，预示着黑龙江省大豆加工试预警工作已经开始。

三、国内外市场概况

（一）国内市场

1. 大豆供需平衡分析　据国家粮油信息中心资料显示，2009/2010 年度我国大豆总供给量为 5 348 万 t，同比增长 3.8%；总需求量为 5 345 万 t，同比增长 10.0%（表 4）。由于 2009/2010 年度我国大豆供需有 3 万 t 的剩余，所以该年度供需环境相对平衡。

表 4　2009/2010 年度我国大豆市场供需平衡情况

（单位：万 t）

名　称	2008/2009 年度	2009/2010 年度	同比增长（%）
产量	1 554	1 498	−3.6
进口量	3 600	3 850	6.9
总供给量	5 154	5 348	3.8
压榨量	3 900	4 400	12.8
食品与其他用量	915	900	−1.6
出口量	45	45	0.0
总需求量	4 860	5 345	10.0

2. 豆油供需平衡分析　根据国家粮油信息中心统计数据分析，2009/2010 年度我国豆油总供给量为 1 013 万 t，同比增长 3.2%；总需求量为 1 004 万 t，同比增长 5.7%；总需求量小于总供给量 9 万 t，则该年度供需环境相对宽松（表 5）。

表 5　2009/2010 年度我国豆油市场供需平衡情况

（单位：万 t）

名　称	2008/2009 年度	2009/2010 年度	同比增长（%）
产量	712	753	5.8
进口量	270	260	−3.7
年度供给量	982	1 013	3.2
食用消费量	845	920	8.9
年度国内消费量	938	989	5.4
出口量	12	15	25.0
年度需求量	950	1 004	5.7

3. 豆粕供需平衡分析　根据国家粮油信息中心统计数据分析，2009/2010 年度我国豆粕总供给量为 3 494 万 t，同比增长 6.9%；总需求量为 3 435 万 t，同比增长 5.0%；总需求量小于总供给量 59 万 t，则该年度供需环境相对宽松（表 6）。

表 6　2009/2010 年度我国豆粕市场供需平衡情况

（单位：万 t）

名　称	2008/2009 年度	2009/2010 年度	同比增长（%）
生产量	3 248	3 469	6.8
进口量	20	25	25.0
年度供给量	3 268	3 494	6.9
饲用消费量	2 900	3 250	12.1
年度国内消费量	3 169	3 345	5.6
出口量	101	90	−10.9
年度需求量	3 270	3 435	5.0

（二）国际市场

1. 世界大豆供需平衡分析　据美国农业部公布的供需报告显示，2009/2010 年度世界大豆总供应量（包括产量和进口量）为 30 986 万 t，同比增长 8.4%；总需求量（包括国内消费量和出口量）为 31 536万 t，同比 6.3%；总需求量大于总供给量 550 万 t，则该年度供需环境相对紧张（表 7）。主要出口国有美国、阿根廷、巴西等；主要进口国有中国、欧盟等。

表 7　2009/2010 年度世界大豆供需平衡情况

（单位：万 t）

名　称	2008/2009 年度	2009/2010 年度	同比增长（%）
产量	21 064	23 095	9.6
进口量	7 524	7 891	4.9
总供给量	28 588	30 986	8.4
压榨量	19 198	20 340	5.9
国内消费量	21 980	23 475	6.8
出口量	7 693	8 061	4.8
总需求量	29 673	31 536	6.3

2. 世界豆油供需平衡分析　据美国农业部公布的供需报告显示，2009/2010 年度世界豆油总供应量（包括产量和进口量）为 4 684 万 t，同比增长 5.1%；总需求量（包括国内需求量和出口量）为 4 702 万 t，同比增长 4.7%；总需求量大于总供给量 18 万 t，则该年度供需环境相对紧张（表 8）。主要出口国有美国、阿根廷、巴西、欧盟 27 国等；主要进口国有中国、印度、巴基斯坦等。

表 8　2009/2010 年度世界豆油供需平衡情况

（单位：万 t）

名　称	2008/2009 年度	2009/2010 年度	同比增长（%）
产量	3 563	3 788	6.3
进口量	893	896	0.3
总供给量	4 456	4 684	5.1
国内需求量	3 578	3 751	4.8
出口量	912	951	4.3
总需求量	4 490	4 702	4.7

3. 世界豆粕供需平衡分析　据美国农业部公布的供需报告显示，2009/2019 年度世界豆粕总供应量（包括产量和进口量）为 21 422 万 t，同比增长 5.8%；总需求量（包括国内需求量和出口量）为 21 402万 t，同比增长 4.8%；总需求量小于总供给量 20 万 t，则该年度供需环境相对宽松（表 9）。主要出口国有美国、阿根廷、巴西、印度等；主要进口国有中国、欧盟等。

表 9　2009/2010 年度世界豆粕供需平衡情况

（单位：万 t）

名　称	2008/2009 年度	2009/2010 年度	同比增长（%）
产量	15 094	16 039	6.3
进口量	5 163	5 383	4.3
总供给量	20 257	21 422	5.8
国内需求量	15 187	15 879	4.6
出口量	5 237	5 523	5.5
总需求量	20 424	21 402	4.8

四、质量管理与标准化工作

（一）质量管理

1. *豆制品产品质量国家监督抽查*　国家质量监督检验检疫总局组织对 2009 年豆制品产品质量进行了国家监督抽查，抽查了北京、辽宁、吉林、黑龙江、上海、江苏、浙江、安徽、福建、江西、山东、河南、湖南、广东、广西、重庆、四川 17 个省、自治区、直辖市 179 个企业生产的 200 种豆制品产品。本次抽查依据强制性国家标准 GB 2711—2003《非发酵性豆制品及面筋卫生标准》、GB 2712—2003《发酵性豆制品卫生标准》、GB 2760—2007《食品添加剂使用卫生标准》等标准的规定，对豆制品产品的标签、铅、总砷、苯甲酸、山梨酸、糖精钠、甜蜜素、安赛蜜、脱氢乙酸、菌落总数、大肠菌群、沙门氏菌、致贺氏菌、金黄色葡萄球菌、苏丹红Ⅰ～Ⅳ号、吊白块、黄曲霉毒素 B_1 等 17 个项目进行了检验。抽查中发现有 18 种产品不合格，存在的主要质量问题：一是本次抽查中有 10 种产品菌落总数和 4 种产品大肠菌群不合格。其中重庆市南岸区亚松森食品厂生产的川妹子卤香豆干菌落总数为 52 000cfu/g，超过标准限量近 70 倍。二是本次抽查中有 1 种产品苯甲酸、3 种产品脱氢乙酸、1 种产品甜蜜素、2 种产品安赛蜜、1 种产品山梨酸含量超标。强制性国家标准 GB 2760—2007《食品添加剂使用卫生标准要求》规定，豆干再制品中山梨酸的最大使用量为 1.0g/kg，发酵豆制品中才允许使用脱氢乙酸，豆干再制品和发酵豆制品中均不允许使用苯甲酸、甜蜜素、安赛蜜。三是本次抽查中有 1 种产品总砷含量为 0.7mg/kg，超过国家标准（≤0.5mg/kg）规定的要求。

2. *酱油产品质量国家监督抽查*　国家质量监督检验检疫总局组织对 2009 年酱油产品质量进行了国家监督抽查，抽查了北京、天津、河北、上海、江苏、浙江、安徽、湖北、山东、湖南、广东、河南 12 个省、直辖市 79 个企业生产的 100 种产品（不涉及出口产品），产品实物质量抽样合格率为 89%。此次抽查依据强制性国家标准 GB 18186—2000《酿造酱油》、GB 2717—2003《酱油卫生标准》、GB 2760—2007《食品添加剂使用卫生标准》以及强制性部颁标准 SB 10336—2000《配制酱油》等标准的规定，对酱油产品中的感官、氨基酸态氮、总酸、全氮、铵盐、可溶性无盐固形物、总砷、铅、黄曲霉毒素 B_1、苯甲酸、山梨酸、菌落总数、大肠菌群、沙门氏菌、志贺氏菌、金黄色葡萄球菌以及标签等 17 个项目进行了检验。经检验，涉及人身健康的主要安全项目黄曲霉毒素 B_1、重金属含量等指标全部符合国家标准规定的要求。抽查中发现的主要质量问题：一是个别产品菌落总数超标。菌落总数反映食品被污染的程度。强制性国家标准 GB 2717—2003《酱油卫生标准》规定，可直接用于佐餐的餐桌酱油中菌落总数应≤30 000cfu/mL。抽查中有个别产品菌落总数超过国家标准规定的要求。二是个别产品防腐剂苯甲酸超标。强制性国家标准 GB 2760—2007《食品添加剂使用卫生标准》规定，酱油的苯甲酸使用量应≤1.0g/kg，抽查中有个别产品防腐剂苯甲酸超过国家标准规定的限量。三是个别产品氨基酸态氮、全氮、可溶性无盐固形物等酱油产品特征指标不合格。酱油的鲜味来自于其中所含有的氨基酸形式存在的氮元素，氨基酸态氮、全氮、可溶性无盐固形物是衡量酱油质量优劣的重要特征指标之一，在产品标准中，酱油的质量等级主要是依据酱油中氨基酸态氮、全氮含量不同来区分。抽查中有个别产品氨基酸态氮指标、全氮、可溶性无盐固形物指标低于标准规定的要求。

（二）标准化工作

（1）由商务部批准、中国食品工业协会豆制品专业委员会组织起草的《臭豆腐（臭干）》和《纳豆》行业标准，于 2009 年 1 月 14 日在北京通过评审组审定。《臭豆腐（臭干）》行业标准和《纳豆》行业标准均为首次制定。这两项标准的制定有利于规范臭豆腐的生产和市场销售，促进生产企业提高产品质量和技术水平，从而保护消费者的利益，对加强产品的质量安全监督具有重要意义。

（2）国家质量监督检验检疫总局、国家标准化管理委员会于 2009 年 3 月 28 日批准发布了《大豆》（GB 1352—2009）新的国家标准，并于 2009 年 9 月 1 日起正式实施。新修订的《大豆》国家标准为强制性国家标准，修订后的标准与世界发达国家的标准处于一个标准水平。大豆标准修订的主要内容：一是增加了高油大豆和高蛋白大豆的质量要求；二是调整了普通大豆定等级指标；三是调整了大豆分类；四是增加了不同等级的损伤粒率要求；五是增加了标签标识要求。

(3) 国家质量监督检验检疫总局、国家标准化管理委员会于2009年4月27日批准发布了《豆腐干》(GB/T 23494—2009)国家标准。本标准适用于豆腐干产品的生产、销售和检验；非大豆的其他豆类加工的产品可参照执行。本标准不适用于未经制浆工艺制成的豆腐干。

(4) 国家质量监督检验检疫总局、国家标准化管理委员会于2009年6月26日批准发布了《方便豆腐花(脑)》(GB/T 23782—2009)国家标准。本标准规定了方便豆腐花(脑)的术语和定义、产品分类、要求、试验方法、检验规则和标志、包装、运输及贮存；本标准适用于方便豆腐花(脑)的生产、检验和销售。

(5) 国家质量监督检验检疫总局、国家标准化管理委员会于2009年9月30日批准发布了《黄豆酱》(GB/T 24399—2009)国家标准。本标准规定了黄豆酱的技术要求、试验方法、检验规则及标签、包装、运输、贮存的要求；本标准适用于以黄豆为主要原料，经微生物发酵酿制的酱类。

五、行业管理

(1)"大豆产业联盟筹备工作会议"于2009年4月13日在哈尔滨召开，来自国内大豆产业的企业、大学、科研机构等17个单位参加了会议。科学技术部政策体制改革司副司长李新男、黑龙江省教育厅厅长张永洲、黑龙江省科技厅厅长赵敏、哈尔滨市科技局副局长孔宪一以及来自17个联盟会员单位的负责人出席了会议，李新男副司长发表了重要讲话。他指出，构建大豆产业技术创新战略联盟，是有效解决我国产学研合作主要问题的一项重要措施。希望"大豆产业联盟"要紧密围绕国家产业发展布局和战略发展，紧密合作，自觉维护联盟的利益，实行开放式建设，不断吸收创新资源。在国家产业发展政策指导下，选择联盟的技术发展目标，体现国家特别是产业发展的战略要求，高效运行，充分发挥联盟内技术优势、产业优势，以企业为主体，市场为导向，切实发挥产学研各方优势，建立共同投入、利益共享机制，以突破行业发展技术瓶颈，解决产业的共性、特性关键技术问题，全面提升我国大豆产业的自主创新能力。

(2)"中国大豆产业发展机制创新试点工作会议"于2009年5月11日在大庆召开，来自农业部、商务部、中国大豆产业协会负责人及全国大豆龙头加工企业、大豆合作社的60余名代表参会。会议分析了当前国产大豆在洋大豆低价冲击下面临的严峻形势，同时确定在黑龙江省大庆市林甸县、齐齐哈尔市克东县、内蒙古自治区扎兰屯市、黑龙江农垦总局红星农场四个地区进行大豆产业发展机制创新试点，通过规模化、标准化种植，探索建立企业与农户间的利益联结机制，形成产业合力，从而拯救危机中的中国大豆产业。按照计划设想，该项试点将由大庆日月星有限公司、九三集团等多个国内大型大豆加工企业"承诺价格，合作社承诺质量，双方约定数量，地方政府监督协调"，按照有机大豆的加工标准组织生产，打造中国的有机大豆品牌，使有机大豆制品附加值比常规大豆制品提高20%，从而形成企业与农户间利益共享、风险共担的运行机制，提高国产大豆产业的整体竞争力。此次会议为期2天，与会者将主要围绕"健全和完善大豆产业体系"，"构建科学、高效、互利的大豆产业服务机制"，"建立大豆产品质量安全的全程保障体系"，"形成农户和加工企业共创品牌，共享收益的质量价格机制"等四个方面进行研讨。

(3) 由中国食品工业协会豆制品专业委员会主办的"第二期全国豆制品生产工艺技术研讨培训班"于2009年8月3～7日在北京举行。本次培训班学员来自全国各地的豆制品生产企业，平均工作年限为5年以上；培训老师由长期在豆制品企业从事技术和管理工作的专家组成。根据学员结构和特点，本期培训班主要围绕豆制品生产中制浆工艺控制、油炸豆腐的加工制作、各类豆腐凝固成型生产操作过程、卤制豆腐干/素鸡/千张/百叶的生产、素制品制作工艺、豆制品生产过程中的危害因素及关键点控制、豆制品企业的厂房设计工艺布局及豆制品生产的技术原理与标准化等八大方面的内容进行面授、详解和答疑。在理论学习的同时，培训班还安排学员到河北高碑店"豆豆"集团进行了现场参观。培训期间，对参加培训的学员进行了考核，并对考试合格者颁发了结业证书。

(4)"第八届世界大豆研究大会"于2009年8月11～15日在北京召开，来自38个国家和地区的2 176名代表参加了大会。农业部副部长张桃林到会致辞。本次大会以"描绘全球大豆生产蓝图，确保大豆安全、可持续供给"为主题，通过会议交流和科技展览，为各国参会代表提供良好的借鉴和启示，对推动世界大豆科研水平提升和产业可持续发展具有十分重要的意义。与会代表们围绕大豆产业的关键环节和瓶颈问题，加强技术交流，协同科技攻关，共享科研成果，为推动世界大豆产业的可持续发展、保障世界食物安全、构建和谐世界做出应有贡献。本次大会分学术报告、大豆产业论坛和中国国际大豆产业展览会三大板块，为大豆科研和产业界人士提供了交流平台，使世界大豆同行共同分享大豆科研和产业方面所取得的最新成果。在为期5天的会议期间，来自世界40多个国家和地区的1 000多名代表针对大豆种质资源、遗传育种、分子生物学与生物技术、栽培生理与生产管理、植物保护、大豆储藏与加工、大豆产品与应用、供求与贸易政策等议题开展了交流和研讨。

（5）“国家大豆产业技术体系2009年度工作会议”于2009年12月7～8日在南京召开，来自农业部、中国农业科学院、中国农业大学、南京农业大学等多所高校及科研院所单位的领导、产业技术体系岗位专家、综合试验站站长及其团队成员共计100多人参加会议。会议期间，与会人员听取了各功能研究室主任、岗位专家和综合试验站站长的2009年度工作汇报，对照任务书中规定的考核指标进行量化打分，提出改进意见和建议。并充分肯定了大豆产业技术体系建设工作取得的显著成效，肯定了实施整体联动的九大措施。主要包括：一是继续强化岗位专家与综合试验站建立对接关系，解决综合试验站的技术来源和岗位专家联系生产实际的问题；二是进一步密切综合试验站间的互助合作关系，使不同试验站取长补短，共同进步；三是推动综合试验站与科技示范县的合作，加快体系研究成果的转化；四是充分发挥区域专家组作用，通过多学科协作解决区域性产业发展关键问题；五是以功能研究室为单位组建技术研发协作网，攻克全局性、长期性关键技术难题；六是通过设立顾问专家组，发挥老专家的传帮带作用；七是促进产业技术体系建设与其他项目的整合，提高资源利用效率；八是加强体系内外科技队伍的联系，发挥体系的核心和引领作用；九是要求岗位专家与国外同领域权威专家建立稳定合作关系，扩宽技术和信息来源，扩大体系的国际影响。

（中国包装和食品机械总公司行业办公室　王国扣）

淀粉加工业

2009年是继续应对国际金融危机、加快转变发展方式的关键年，是“十一五”规划的收官年，也是“十二五”规划的谋划年。

一、基本情况

（一）资源概况

根据有关资料报道，2009年全国玉米总产量16 397.5万t，比2008年减少1.17%（表1）。2009年我国玉米消费情况为：饲用60.3%，工业用27.4%。2009年世界玉米产量78 749.7万t，其中美国为30 738.6万t，占世界总产量的39.03%；中国为16 397.5万t，占世界总产量的20.82%。

表1　2009年全国玉米主产区产量

（单位：万t）

省、自治区	2009年产量	2008年产量	同比增长（%）
河北	1 465.3	1 442.1	1.61
山西	654.3	682.8	−4.17
内蒙古	1 341.3	1 410.8	−4.93
辽宁	963.1	1 189.0	−18.99
吉林	1 810.0	2 082.9	−13.10
黑龙江	1 920.2	1 822.1	5.38
山东	1 921.5	1 887.5	1.80
河南	1 634.0	1 615.0	1.18
陕西	526.1	483.6	8.79
其他	4 161.7	3 975.8	4.68
总计	**16 397.5**	**16 591.6**	**−1.17**

（二）加工业概况

根据中国淀粉工业协会不完全统计，2009年我国淀粉总产量1 802.70万t，与2008年基本持平。其中玉米淀粉1 725.52万t，与2008年持平；木薯淀粉47.43万t，同比下降47%；马铃薯淀粉16.72万t，同比下降48%；甘薯淀粉9万t，同比增长25%；小麦淀粉4.03万t，同比下降5.18%。

表2　2009年我国淀粉产量和品种情况

品　种	产　量（万t）	占总淀粉（%）	同比增长（%）
玉米淀粉	1 725.52	95.72	2.39
木薯淀粉	47.43	2.63	−47.03
马铃薯淀粉	16.72	0.93	−47.99
甘薯淀粉	9.00	0.50	25.00
小麦淀粉等	4.03	0.22	−5.18
合计	**1 802.70**	**100.00**	**−0.86**

1. 我国淀粉及深加工品产量和品种情况　由于受多种因素的影响，2009年我国淀粉总产量是近10年来第一次没有明显增长的一年，但深加工品种的产

量却都有较大幅度的增长（表 2、表 3）。

表 3 2009 年我国淀粉深加工品产量与品种情况

主要品种	产 量（万 t）	占总产量（%）	同比增长（%）
变性淀粉	112.93	10.99	32.42
结晶葡萄糖	238.78	23.24	13.52
液体淀粉糖	588.88	57.33	13.57
糖醇	86.67	8.44	7.00
合 计	**1 027.26**	**100.00**	**14.76**

2. *淀粉产量分布及生产规模情况* 从我国地区生产情况统计，山东省不但连续多年占据着我国玉米淀粉总产量的首位，而且在全国所占的比例也在增加（2008 年为 41.51%，2009 年为 45.07%）；其次是吉林和河北省，分别占全国玉米淀粉总产量的 19.88% 和 14.45%。该 3 省玉米淀粉产量之和，占全国玉米淀粉总产量的 79.39%。全国玉米淀粉产量 10 万 t 以上的企业 33 个，玉米淀粉总产量为 1 536.90 万 t，占玉米淀粉总产量的 85.25%（表 4）。

表 4 2009 年我国淀粉产量分布及生产规模情况

地 区	淀粉产量（万 t）	占总产量（%）	企业数（10 万 t/年）	企业最大产量（万 t/年）
山东	812.40	45.07	11	213.66
吉林	358.35	19.88	6	159.61
河北	260.50	14.45	8	56.37
河南	105.86	5.87	5	28.00
陕西	77.20	4.28	2	62.84
广西	41.00	2.27		
其他 15 个省区	147.40	8.18	1	63.50
合计	**1 802.71**	**100.00**	**33**	

注：其他 15 个省、自治区为山西、内蒙古、辽宁、黑龙江、江苏、浙江、湖北、四川、云南、甘肃、宁夏、青海、新疆、广东、海南。

二、市场及进出口情况

2009 年我国淀粉及其深加工品市场仍然继续经受着金融危机的影响，由于原料价格居高不下，企业生产步履维艰，利润甚微。

2009 年我国玉米淀粉等 9 种产品的进出口情况，从总量看，2009 年进口总量为 1 034 399 t，高于 2008 年的 646 817t，同比增长了 59.92%；出口总量少于 2008 年的 771 697t，同比下降了 37%。从单品种进口情况看，山梨醇由于国内产量继续增加，且到岸价上涨了 26%，因而进口量大幅度减少。玉米淀粉本来就因为原料价格居高不下，成本偏高，再加上到岸价上涨了 50%，故进口量是近 10 年来最低的水平。木薯淀粉由于国内冰雪灾害的影响而减产，且到岸价比 2008 年下降了 25%，因此进口量创历史最高水平。马铃薯淀粉进口量是 2008 年的近 2 倍，其原因：一是受灾害的影响，马铃薯减产，国内马铃薯淀粉供不应求；二是到岸价大幅下降至已接近 2006 年反倾销时的价格。从单品种的出口情况看，淀粉类产品中除木薯淀粉外，出口量均同比下降，下降幅度在 14%～51%不等。产品离岸价除糊精及变性淀粉外同比也均有下降，下降幅度大的是马铃薯淀粉为 16%。糖醇类产品中，甘露醇出口量同比持平，离岸价同比下降 25%。山梨醇出口量同比下降 21%，但由于离岸价维持在较高水平，所以还是创汇产品。

表 5 2009 年我国淀粉及部分深加工品进出口情况

商品名	进口（t）	与 2008 年相比（%）	出口（t）	与 2008 年相比（%）
玉米淀粉	965	−72	289 787	−35
木薯淀粉	831 987	80	464	51
马铃薯淀粉	35 004	182	8 712	−56
小麦淀粉	1 243	−29	11 978	−41
山梨醇	1 877	大幅度减少	50 078	−21
甘露醇	505	−39	4 444	持平
肌醇	11	−21	2 647	9
糊精及变性淀粉	160 872	12	117 522	−46
化学纯果糖	1 935	−56	1 010	大幅度增长
合计	**1 034 399**	**60**	**486 642**	**−37**

三、我国淀粉加工业生产技术发展情况

（一）生产规模

我国淀粉加工业发展至今，凸显出两大特点：一是行业集中度明显增强，形成了以大企业、大集团为主导地位的格局（表 6、表 7）。玉米淀粉出现了年产 200 万 t 以上的企业 1 个，年产 40 万 t 以上的企业共 13 个，年产量占全国总产量的 2/3；变性淀粉出现了 2 个年产 10 万 t 以上的企业，年产 5 万 t 以上的企业 8 个，产量占全国总产量的 60%；结晶葡萄糖企业最大年产量 93 万 t，占全国总产量的 2/5；液体淀粉糖年产量 100 万 t 以上的企业 2 个，产量占全国总产量的 40%。二是产业集群发展，形成了以原料主产区为主的区域布局。2009 年，山东、吉林、河北 3 省玉米主产区淀粉加工消耗玉米量和黑龙江、内蒙古、云南、甘肃 4 省、自治区马铃薯主产区淀粉加工消耗马铃薯量均占全国淀粉加工消耗玉米和马铃薯量的 80%以上。

表6 2009年我国玉米淀粉生产规模

项　目	2009年	2008年	同比增长（%）	项　目	2009年	2008年	同比增长（%）
年产100万t以上企业（个）	5	5	0	年产30万t以上企业（个）	2	4	－50.00
年产100万t以上企业总产量（万t）	718.54	694.92	3.40	年产30万t以上企业总产量（万t）	66.10	123.33	－46.40
占全国玉米淀粉总产量（%）	41.64	41.24	0.97	占全国玉米淀粉总产量（%）	3.83	7.32	－47.68
年产40万t以上企业（个）	8	9	－11.11	年产10万t以上企业（个）	18	12	50.00
年产40万t以上企业总产量（万t）	439.44	504.22	－12.85	年产10万t以上企业总产量（万t）	312.82	362.76	－13.77
占全国玉米淀粉总产量（%）	25.47	29.92	－14.87	占全国玉米淀粉总产量（%）	18.13	21.52	－15.75

表7 2009年我国部分淀粉深加工品生产规模

项　目		2009年	2008年	同比增长（%）
变性淀粉	年产5万t以上企业（个）	8	6	33.33
	年产5万t以上企业总产量（万t）	67.74	48.49	39.70
	占全国总产量（%）	59.98	56.86	5.49
	年产3万t以上企业（个）	3	5	－40.00
	年产3万t以上企业总产量（万t）	11.83	20.03	－40.94
	占全国总产量（%）	10.48	23.49	－55.39
	年产1万t以上企业（个）	15	7	114.29
	年产1万t以上企业总产量（万t）	28.08	12.2	130.16
	占全国总产量（%）	24.86	14.31	73.72
结晶葡萄糖	年产20万t以上企业（个）	3	2	50.00
	年产20万t以上企业总产量（万t）	140.23	107.66	30.25
	占全国总产量（%）	58.73	51.18	14.75
	年产10万t以上企业（个）	5	4	25.00
	年产10万t以上企业总产量（万t）	66.57	58.86	13.10
	占全国总产量（%）	66.57	27.98	137.92
	年产5万t以上企业（个）	3	5	－40.00
	年产5万t以上企业总产量（万t）	21.15	35.57	－40.54
	占全国总产量（%）	8.86	16.91	－47.60
	年产2万t以上企业（个）	3	1	200.00
	年产2万t以上企业总产量（万t）	10.82	3.05	254.75
	占全国总产量（%）	4.53	1.45	212.41
液体淀粉糖	年产100万t以上企业（个）	2	2	0.00
	年产100万t以上企业总产量（万t）	240.3	255.62	－5.99
	占全国总产量（%）	40.81	49.3	－17.22
	年产10万t以上企业（个）	12	8	50.00
	年产10万t以上企业总产量（万t）	244.46	116.43	109.96
	占全国总产量（%）	41.51	22.45	84.90
	年产5万t以上企业（个）	8	9	－11.11
	年产5万t以上企业总产量（万t）	53.21	103.92	－48.80
	占全国总产量（%）	9.04	20.04	－54.89

（二）新工艺、新产品、新技术与综合利用

在国家产业政策的引导下，淀粉加工企业越来越认识到必须加大技术创新力度，延长产业链，加快经济增长方式的转变，改增量发展为增效发展。据不完全统计，目前，淀粉加工业内已有国家级研发中心7个，省级研发中心18个，市级研发中心15个，研发成果显著。新产品方面，如玉米绵白糖，是西王集团以自产的玉米果糖和无水葡萄糖为主要原料复配而成

的一种产品，该产品晶莹透彻、质地绵软，为食用糖家族增添了新品种，市场前景广阔。稀有糖品阿拉伯糖，是唐传生物科技公司采用生物法制取得的一种功能性糖，不但已形成规模化生产，而且是全球出口第一例。高纯度低聚果糖，是由江南大学和江苏梁丰食品集团有限公司共同研制完成的，该产品采用生物发酵法，与其他方法相比，具有产品纯度高、回收率高、成本低、资源浪费小、环境污染低等优点。目前95%低聚果糖干粉已上市，质量达到相关国际标准，价格相比日本同类产品有较大的优势。新工艺方面，如催化三步法生产羧甲基淀粉钠，该新工艺克服了现有的溶剂法和干法存在的缺点，具有配方合理、工艺简单、可连续化操作等优点，且生产成本低廉、产品质量优良。陕西科技大学生命科学与工程学院完成的L-苹果酸一步发酵法较之两步发酵法有很多优势。新技术方面，如一种不用玉米，只用玉米芯就能生产柠檬酸并联产木糖醇的独创工艺由安徽丰原发酵技术工程研究有限公司开发成功，实现了柠檬酸原料的“非粮”替代，可大大提高柠檬酸产品的市场竞争力。综合利用方面，如山东龙力生物科技有限公司利用生产功能糖的下脚料糖渣生产燃料乙醇。北大荒马铃薯产业有限公司与黑龙江巴斯德生物饲料有限公司合作，用生产马铃薯淀粉后的薯渣生产生物饲料。西王集团以葡萄糖母液为原料生产低聚异麦芽糖，为葡萄糖母液的开发利用开辟了一条新途径。

四、我国淀粉加工业发展中存在的问题

（一）产品结构不合理

目前淀粉加工业产品以玉米淀粉、结晶葡萄糖、高纯葡萄糖浆、麦芽糖浆、氧化淀粉、山梨醇等为主，淀粉糖绝大多数为液态产品，结构不合理，既不能适应市场变化的需要，又造成市场竞争激烈。

（二）原料利用率低

玉米淀粉加工业是工业用粮大户，年用玉米2 600万 t 左右，比较先进的企业原料利用率只有97.5%，且高低差距较大。加工过程中近千万吨的副产品，其中绝大部分未深加工而作为下脚料廉价出售。实际上，副产品中含有的成分均比淀粉价值高，有待进一步开发。

（三）创新能力不足

在玉米淀粉加工业浸泡等一些共性技术、工艺上自主创新能力不足。20年过去了，国内玉米的浸泡时间几乎没有多大改变仍为48～50h，而国外的浸泡时间多为24～36h。与国外相比我国玉米浸泡的时间平均高出近20h，如果能把浸泡时间缩短，就能使玉米淀粉加工业在节能降耗方面向前迈进一大步。

（中国淀粉工业协会 董延丰）

制 糖 工 业

一、制糖期基本情况

2009年我国产糖省、自治区由原来的18个减少至15个，主要沿边境地区分布，主产糖区集中在北部、西北部和西南部。甘蔗糖产区主要分布在广西、云南、广东、海南及邻近省、自治区；甜菜糖主要分布在新疆、黑龙江、内蒙古及邻近省、自治区。与糖料种植相关的人员近4 000万人。2009/2010年度制糖期全国食糖总产量中，甘蔗糖占94.4%，甜菜糖占5.6%。我国的食糖生产销售年度为10月1日至翌年的9月30日，开榨时间由北向南各不相同。甜菜糖厂一般在9月底或10月初开机生产；甘蔗糖厂中湖南省10月底或11月初开榨，广西、广东、海南等省、自治区11月中旬或12月初开榨，云南省12月底或次年1月初开榨。

2009/2010年度制糖期制糖生产已顺利结束。自2009年10月4日新疆伊力特糖业有限责任公司开机生产标志着本制糖期开始，至2010年5月31日云南镇康南华南伞糖业有限公司最后一个停机。2009/2010年度制糖期历时240天，比上制糖期减少31天。截止到2010年9月，全国共有制糖生产企业（集团）49个，开工糖厂276个。其中，甜菜糖生产企业（集团）5个，糖厂36个；甘蔗糖生产企业（集团）44个，糖厂240个；另有炼糖企业10个。2009/2010年度制糖期，全国共生产食糖1 073.83万t。其中，优级、一级白砂糖988.39万t，绵白糖32.02万t，精制糖18.72万t，赤砂糖和红糖28.45万t，原糖及其他6.25万t。本制糖期，全国糖料种植面积1 608.5khm^2，同比减少9.48%。其中，甘蔗

种植 1 468.1khm²，同比减少 5.68%；甜菜种植 140.4khm²，同比减少 36.3%。全国糖料入榨量 10 112.51万 t，其中甘蔗入榨量 9 374.55 万 t，甜菜入榨量 737.96 万 t。2009/2010 年度制糖期食糖产量、播种面积、开工糖厂数见表 1。

表 1 2009/2010 年度制糖期全国糖料播种面积、食糖产量基本情况

企业名称	糖料播种面积（khm²）	实际入榨糖料量（万 t）	产糖量（万 t）	开工糖厂数（个）
全国累计	**1 608.51**	**8 591.99**	**1 073.83**	**276**
甘蔗糖合计	**1 468.15**	**8 100.83**	**1 013.83**	**240**
广东	126.00	834.00	85.77	32
其中湛江	108.00	733.94	73.03	22
广西	963.33	5 560.00	710.20	102
云南	305.17	1 364.87	177.15	77
海南	62.67	262.00	31.81	20
福建	3.61	32.24	3.48	2
其他	7.37	47.72	5.42	7
甜菜糖合计	**140.36**	**491.16**	**60.00**	**36**
黑龙江	44.18	83.20	9.89	9
新疆	64.67	321.00	38.44	14
内蒙古	24.40	53.50	7.01	5
其他	13.78	33.46	4.66	8

2009/2010 年度制糖期糖价持续走高，甘蔗收购价格较去年有较大幅度增长，平均收购价格 344 元/t,平均每吨上涨 81 元。其中广西甘蔗平均收购价格 357.92 元/t；甜菜收购价格较去年略有降低，平均收购价格 305 元/t。2009/2010 年度制糖期全国制糖行业主要技术指标：甘蔗平均单产 57.0t/hm²，甜菜平均单产 41.7t/hm²。甘蔗平均含糖分 14.38%，甜菜平均含糖分 15.5%。甘蔗糖产糖率 12.54%，甜菜糖产糖率 12.1%。

二、市场概况

（一）国内食糖市场

2009/2010 年度制糖期，食糖生产继续呈现周期性下滑趋势，全国食糖产量 1 073.83 万 t，较上制糖期减少 169.29 万 t，减幅为 13.62%；甘蔗糖产量下降至 1 013.83 万 t；甜菜糖产量下降至 60 万 t（接近近 10 个制糖期的最低水平），占总产量的比重已不足 6%。食糖消费量 1 379 万 t，比上制糖期减少 11 万 t，同比下降 0.79%，年人均食糖消费量为 10.6kg。食糖消费格局与前几年相比没有太大变化，食糖消费总量中民用消费为 36%（餐饮消费与零售业终端销售商品糖比例为 1∶4），工业消费比例为 64%。2009/2010 年制糖期，全国食糖综合平均价格 5 161 元/t，工业累计销售平均价格为 5 006 元/t。全国制糖行业销售收入 576.64 亿元（其中综合利用产品销售收入 39 亿元），同比增加 104.94 亿元；实现利税总额 122.82 亿元，同比增加 81.72 亿元。农民种植糖料收入同比增加 50.16 亿元。2009/2010 年度制糖期，我国制糖行业运行特征：

（1）随着食糖生产企业进一步兼并重组，企业结构得到优化，以大型企业集团为主导的食糖生产格局初步形成。产量超过 30 万 t 的企业集团已经发展到 12 个，占全国产糖量的 68%。

（2）2009/2010 年度制糖期是国家对食糖市场宏观调控力度比较大的制糖期，经国务院批准，动销国家储备糖满足市场供应，保持了食糖市场价格适度平稳运行。全行业经济效益明显改善，农民种植糖料收入稳步增加，扭转了上制糖期大部分企业亏损的局面。

（3）主产糖省、自治区糖料种植规模化、机械化程度进展缓慢，糖料生产劳动力成本增加明显，劳动力供求压力进一步加大；糖料推广工作进展缓慢和储备品种不足，新品种培育与繁育工作任务依然艰巨。

（二）国际食糖市场综述

2009/2010 年度制糖期国际食糖走出了由高到低和再走高的过程。纽约期货价格在 2010 年 1 月底创下了 30 年的新高 30.40 美分/磅（注：磅为非法定计量单位，1 磅等于 0.453 6kg）。这主要是由于印度出现了干旱，导致甘蔗和食糖生产大幅减产，印度食糖产量 1 470 万 t，下降了 1 230 万 t。全球在 2008/2009 年度制糖期的食糖缺口为 900 万 t。受国际高糖价格的影响，在 2009/2010 年度制糖期，主要产糖国家普遍增加甘蔗种植面积。印度食糖产量大幅增加到 1 850 万 t，期初巴西食糖产量将达到 3 500 万 t，增加 18%。根据国际主要咨询机构的预测，2009/2010 年度制糖期，全球食糖缺口下降到 500 万 t。纽约原糖价格从 2 月直线下跌至 5 月初的 13 美分/磅。一年多的食糖高价位运行，致使很多进口国家尽量消费库存，当国际糖价下跌后，食糖贸易活跃；巴西出现的干旱和亚洲的巴基斯坦等国家出现的暴雨洪涝，导致甘蔗受损，食糖减产；墨西哥、泰国、菲律宾等传统的出口国，也不同程度地进口食糖。以上诸多因素成为推动国际糖价止跌回升的重要原因。加之外汇市场美元从 5 月份的暂时坚挺后恢复跌势，致使以美元计价的大宗商品价格普遍上涨，国际基金大举炒作商品期货，致使国际糖价在 9 月底又上升至 27 美分/磅。国际糖价走出了 V 字形，结束了 2009/2010 年度制糖期。2009/2010年度制糖期，国际食糖市场具有以下特征：

（1）全球食糖产量低于预期，食糖消费继续保持稳步增长。

（2）全球气候异常对农作物生产不利，虽然种植面积普遍增加，但是食糖产量增加滞后。

（3）全球食糖库存普遍处于低位，进口需求增加。而食糖的相对刚性需求没有由于食糖高价受到太大冲击。

（4）全球制糖能力没有明显增加，出口国家港口能力没有增加。

（5）土地、肥料、水利、电力、人工成本都在提高，致使全球制糖成本普遍提高，因而影响食糖价格。

（6）美元汇率长期没有改善的迹象，投资投机以美元计价的大宗商品期货，成为国际基金的避险渠道。

（7）全球长期的低利率的货币政策和大量提供现金挽救经济危机，使货币供应量增加，造成全球的通货膨胀。

（8）全球房地产处于高价，而股票市场处于低迷，商品期货市场或成为投资和投机渠道的补充。

以上这些微观和宏观因素，将继续成为影响2010/2011年度制糖期国际食糖价格的基本因素，虽然预测2010/2011年度制糖期全球食糖供求可能过剩300万t，但是，国际糖价仍可能继续维持在高价位运行。

（三）食糖进出口贸易

2009/2010年度制糖期，食糖进口比上制糖期略有增加。我国食糖进出口贸易情况分别见表2、表3。

表2　2000—2010年全国食糖进口与贸易方式统计表

（单位：万t）

年度	合计	一般贸易	来料加工	进料加工	保税仓库进出境货物	边贸	其他
2000	**64.07**	16.01	0.82	46.61		0.28	0.35
2001	**119.87**	85.07	3.52	30.86		0.11	0.31
2002	**118.31**	80.77	1.12	35.24			1.18
2003	**77.51**	61.74	1.30	14.17			0.30
2004	**121.43**	99.26	1.19	18.63			2.35
2005	**138.97**	85.04	5.67	41.29			6.97
2006	**136.54**	99.30	3.50	20.72			12.93
2007	**119.34**	99.18	1.59	13.28	5.22		
2008	**77.99**	61.91	1.97	8.89	3.67		1.55
2009	**106.45**	83.02	0.17	9.93	12.77		0.56
2010	**101.29**	95.43	0.61	4.99			0.26

注：2010年统计数字截止到8月底。

表3　2000—2010年全国食糖出口与贸易方式统计表

（单位：万t）

年度	合计	一般贸易	来料加工	进料加工	保税仓库进出境货物	边贸	其他
2000	**41.48**	3.74	0.80	36.80		0.11	0.03
2001	**19.56**	1.25	2.96	15.31			0.04
2002	**32.58**	1.77	0.87	29.82			0.12
2003	**10.32**	2.15	0.88	5.71		1.29	0.29
2004	**8.52**	1.92	0.87	5.26			0.48
2005	**35.83**	2.21	4.16	29.11			0.35
2006	**15.45**	2.49	3.06	9.61			0.29
2007	**11.05**	2.24	2.80	5.98			0.03
2008	**5.84**	1.76	2.15	1.51			0.42
2009	**6.39**	2.21	0.90	3.15			0.13
2010	**6.68**	4.96	0.58	0.76		0.22	0.16

注：2010年统计数字截止到8月底。

三、行业工作

（1）2009年11月1～2日，中国糖业协会在河南省郑州市召开了《2009/2010年度制糖期全国食糖产销工作会议暨全国食糖、糖蜜酒精订货会》。会议通过相互交流、分组讨论，分析了2009/2010年度制糖期糖料生产、食糖产销形势和存在的问题，提出了解决问题的意见和建议。

（2）2009年11月29日，由环保部总量司组织、中国糖业协会承担的“制糖行业污染物排放分析报告和总量控制方案”课题验收会在北京召开。控制方案在深入分析制糖行业污染物排放现状的基础上，提出了“十二五”及中长期糖业污染物排放控制目标和治理方案以及产业结构调整建议。

（3）2009年12月23日，《“十二五”我国糖业产业结构调整指导意见》编制小组召开第一次工作会议。中国糖业协会向国家发改委、工信部汇报了编制进展情况，与会领导就指导意见的编制工作进行了深入讨论。同时，听取了中国糖业协会关于《中国糖业信息统计预警系统建设方案》的工作汇报。

（4）2010年1月22日，由农业部组织的“全国糖料工作会议”在广西南宁召开。各省、自治区分别介绍了本省糖业发展情况，分析存在的制约因素以及采取的对策措施，与会专家也从品种、市场等方面分析并提出推进糖业发展的建议。

（5）2010年2月23日，为进一步做好2009/2010年度制糖期食糖产销平衡工作，确保国内食糖市场平稳运行，中国糖业协会在北京组织召开了“大型食品企业座谈会”。各用糖企业汇报了2009年的用糖情况、淀粉糖等替代品的使用情况，并针对当前糖价运行给企业带来的影响和国家储备糖拍卖过程中出现的问题进行了反映和交流。国家有关部委领导认真听取了各企业的汇报，同时介绍了国家对食糖行业宏观调控的原则和思路，并对用糖企业代表关心的问题进行了解答。

(6) 2010年3月2日，中国糖业协会和广西糖业协会在广西南宁联合召开了“2010年广西食糖交易会暨中国糖业协会商业流通会员会议”。本次会议上，国家有关部委领导就国家制糖行业相关政策等方面内容做了介绍。广西、云南、广东等食糖主产区糖业协会的负责同志通报了2009/2010年度制糖期产销情况和产量预测，并对国家宏观调控提出了意见和建议。

(7) 2010年3月5日，国家工信部消费品司在贵州省贵阳市召开了“全国糖精行业2010年计划工作会议”。会议总结了全国2009年糖精产、销情况；分析国际、国内糖精市场发展趋势，听取2010年糖精生产计划安排建议；研讨糖精行业发展和行业清洁生产有关问题；修改《关于开展糖精生产经营秩序整顿工作的通知》(征求意见稿)，并提出修改意见。

(8) 2010年3月29～31日，中国糖业协会理事长贾志忍任组长、中国轻工业联合会综合业务部副主任查长全同志为副组长等9人组成的“中国糖都”考核专家组，就广西崇左市申报“中国糖都”进行了为期3天的考核。通过考核，专家组成员一致认为：崇左市是中国第一产糖市，基本具备授予“中国糖都”称号的条件。2010年4月27日，中国轻工业联合会、中国糖业协会联合发文，授予广西壮族自治区崇左市“中国糖都”称号。

(9) 2010年6月2日，工信部会同环保部、国家工商总局、质监总局在北京召开整顿糖精生产经营秩序工作座谈会。经过与会代表认真讨论研究做出如下工作安排：由各省区工信部门牵头，环保、工商、质检等部门密切配合，按照《通知》的要求，制定详尽的工作方案，立即对重点地区和重点企业进行调查，对非定点企业坚决予以取缔，9月底前各地工信部门要总结整顿工作的成效，并书面上报工信部。

(10) 2010年6月14～16日，中国糖业协会第四届会员代表大会在北京召开。会上，代表们认真听取并审议了三届理事会的各项工作报告，充分肯定了第三届理事会卓有成效的工作。会议表决通过了《关于中国糖业协会三届理事会工作报告的决议》、《关于中国糖业协会三届理事会财务工作报告的决议》、《关于修改中国糖业协会章程的决议》、《关于修改中国糖业协会会费收缴（标准）办法的决议》。大会选举产生了中国糖业协会第四届理事会。选举陆宝明同志为理事长，闫卫民同志为秘书长。与会领导为获得制糖行业“十强”企业授牌，为中国糖业第二届专家组专家颁发了聘书。

(11) 2010年6月16～18日，由世界糖业研究组织主办、中国糖业协会承办、英国糖业集团协办的“世界糖业研究组织2010年年会及研讨会”在北京召开。此次研讨会以“发展中的世界糖业”为主题，邀请了来自国际糖业组织、联合国粮农组织等机构的专家和学者，围绕糖业对经济发展所作出的贡献、食糖在食品安全方面所作出的贡献等议题发表演讲。

(12) 2010年7月14日至16日，中国糖业协会贾志忍一行赴印度尼西亚参加“第十六届亚洲国际糖业会议”。贾志忍在会上作了关于《中国糖业的现状及发展趋势》的报告，并回答了代表的提问。会议期间，贾志忍还分别会见了国际糖业组织总干事以及印度尼西亚、泰国、菲律宾、印度等国糖业机构负责人。

(13) 2010年7月20日，中国糖业协会在宁夏银川组织召开信息员工作会议。本次会议在充分肯定信息员工作的基础上提出了进一步完善信息体系建设的建议和要求。并就如何做好信息工作以及如何加强对会员单位的服务进行了充分讨论，提出了意见与建议。

（中国糖业协会　胡志江）

蔬菜加工业

一、基本情况

(一) 资源情况

从20世纪80年代实施“菜篮子”工程以来，我国的蔬菜产业得到了长足发展，蔬菜产量大幅增长，品种日益丰富，质量不断提高，市场体系逐步完善。目前已是种植业中仅次于粮食的第二大农作物，成为我国农业和农村经济发展的支柱产业。据农业部统计，2009年我国蔬菜播种面积18 414.3khm^2，同比增加了538.4khm^2；总产量61 823.8万t，同比增加2 583.5万t；2009年我国蔬菜播种面积和产量分别占世界的43%和49%，均居世界第一，我国人均占有蔬菜量为460多kg，超出世界平均水平200多kg。各项数据显示我国已经成为世界上最大的蔬菜生产国。目前我国已基本形成了华南冬春蔬菜、长江上中游冬春蔬菜、黄土高原夏秋蔬菜、云贵高原夏秋蔬菜、黄淮海与环渤海设施蔬菜、东南沿海出口蔬菜、西北内陆出口蔬菜以及东北沿边出口蔬菜八大蔬菜重点生产区域。蔬菜产业的健康发展带来了较高的经济效益。据农业部种植业司统计，2009年全国蔬菜（含西、甜瓜）总产值约8 800亿元。在满足自身供应的同时，我国生产的蔬菜还大量出口，2009年在我国农产品贸易逆差达到129.6亿美元的情况下，蔬菜出口却创造了66.7亿美元的顺差。

2009年山东省依然是全国蔬菜种植面积最大的省，山东蔬菜（含瓜类）播种面积1 756.0khm^2，总产量为8 937.2万t，分别占全国的9.54%和14.46%；总产值1 527.4亿元，占山东省农业产值的47.38%；出口创汇20.1亿美元，占全国的31.2%；设施蔬菜面积达到866.7khm^2，占全国的20%以上，蔬菜产业已成为山东省农民增收的支柱产业。山东省寿光市一地就达到80亿kg，占全国总产量的1.29 %。2009年蔬菜产品质量稳定。农业部组织实施“无公害食品行动计划”以来，蔬菜质量安全工作得到全面加强，质量安全水平有了明显提高。农业部2009年农产品质量安全例行监测结果显示，蔬菜检测合格率达到96.4%，保持了比较高的质量水平。

（二）加工业概况

2009年我国蔬菜加工业在农产品贸易中占据了重要地位。随着蔬菜安全质量稳步提高，蔬菜加工业的不断发展，国内蔬菜加工水平和商品品质不断提升，产品品种、产后处理和产品安全性等方面与发达国家的差距不断缩小。蔬菜加工业在强化特色蔬菜产后处理，积极发展深加工，延长产业链，提高附加值；加快特色蔬菜质量标准体系建设、规范行业标准、提升产品市场竞争力、培育名牌产品等方面取得了快速发展，蔬菜已成为增加农民收入的支柱产业。

1. *生产及加工技术* 近年来，我国蔬菜加工技术装备与工艺水平进一步提高，如高温短时杀菌技术、无菌包装技术、冻干技术等在生产中得到进一步应用。在脱水蔬菜领域，我国研制的真空冻干技术设备取得了可喜进步，一些国内知名冻干设备厂家的技术水平已达到国际先进水平。我国能打入国际市场的高档脱水蔬菜，基本上采用了国产的真空冻干技术生产。另外，微波干燥和远红外干燥技术也在少数企业中得到应用。在速冻设备方面，我国已开发出螺旋式速冻机、流态化速冻机等设备，满足了国内速冻行业的部分需求。国家大宗蔬菜产业技术体系在2009年正式启动。蔬菜产业技术体系将按照从生产中来、到生产中去、与国家科研计划项目上下密切衔接的运行机制，整合国内优势研究力量，围绕我国蔬菜产业中品种、栽培、病虫防控、设施设备、采后处理与加工、产业经济等各个环节的技术需求进行综合攻关研究。这一体系的建立对于提高我国蔬菜生产水平、提高产品质量、增强国际竞争力、保障我国蔬菜产业的可持续发展具有重要意义。

2. *蔬菜加工业的发展* 2009年我国蔬菜加工业取得进一步的发展，国际竞争力得到了更进一步提高，外向型蔬菜加工产业布局已基本形成。蔬菜生产不仅满足了国内消费，而且扩大了出口，蔬菜出口量已居世界第一位。2009年我国各地继续加大投入力度，积极扶持发展设施蔬菜生产。山东是蔬菜种植大省，蔬菜面积、产量、产值、出口创汇等指标一直位居全国前列。2009年山东出台多项措施，进一步发展蔬菜产业，计划到2015年，建设1 000个蔬菜标准化生产基地，培育100个蔬菜集约化育苗中心，全省蔬菜播种面积稳定在2 000khm^{2}左右，其中设施蔬菜面积力争扩大到1 000khm^2。通过未来5年发展，山东蔬菜总产量将达到1.1亿t，总产值达到1 800亿元以上，将鲁北地区建设成以京津为主要市场的优质特色蔬菜生产基地，鲁南地区建设成为面向江浙沪的优质、高端特色蔬菜生产基地和大型蔬菜仓储物流中心。国内市场占有率稳定在20%左右，蔬菜产品抽样检测合格率达到98%以上，“三品一标”产品认证数量增加30%以上，产品商品化处理和精（深）加工率达到65%以上。

2009年2月24日，江苏省兴化市脱水蔬菜协会与中国检验认证集团江苏分公司举行了江苏省农产品出口基地（GAP）的签约仪式，并确定将在该市建立全省第一个出口蔬菜安全示范区。至此，兴化市获得了脱水蔬菜出口的“绿色通行证”。兴化市年产蔬菜100多万t，其中香葱种植面积13.3khm^2，经国家质量监督检验检疫总局批准，成为“原产地保护产品”，其生产标准成为江苏省“省标”。120多个脱水蔬菜加工企业，年生产脱水蔬菜7万多t。产品出口20多个国家和地区，成为亚洲最大的蔬菜加工出口基地。

2009年3月，国内最大规模和水平最高的辣椒碱提纯生产基地，在天津市津南区国家级农业科技园建成。该基地建筑面积1.3万m^2，总投资8 000万元，建成了一条日加工干红辣椒 60t 的自动化生产线，可年产高纯度的辣椒碱 4t，填补了该领域的国内产业市场空白。新建成的辣椒碱提纯生产基地还可年产 250t 红色素、200t 辣精、500t 辣椒油，年总产值 2 亿元，使本市成为全国最大的辣椒深加工产业基地，使辣椒这一红色产业逐步成为本市的区位优势和特色产业。该产业还可带动本市 400 多户辣椒种植，种植面积达到 $10khm^2$。

2009 年 7 月，北京中环易达设施园艺科技有限公司与沈阳靓马集团有限公司签署合作协议。沈阳靓马集团有限公司将投资 2 亿元建设小韩村蔬菜工厂，北京中环易达设施园艺科技有限公司将在 10 年的战略合作期内持续提供最新的研发成果。小韩村蔬菜工厂是以工厂化方式进行绿色与有机蔬菜立体化、多层次生产的大型蔬菜工厂，建筑面积达 40 000m^2，分为科技展示区、生产示范区和配套设施区，并配有 10 000m^2 的冷藏车间。该蔬菜工厂通过计算机系统对温度、湿度、光照、二氧化碳和营养液要素进行精确控制，实现蔬菜周年连续高效生产，同时采用立体化、多层次栽培模式，大幅度提高空间利用率，产量是常规生产的 5～10 倍。该蔬菜工厂建成后，每年可供应绿色蔬菜、有机蔬菜及保健蔬菜 83 万 kg。

2009 年 8 月，由四川省农业厅等部门牵头，以“四川泡菜与健康”为主题的“首届中国四川泡菜国际论坛”在眉山举行，四川省着力打造区域特色鲜明的泡菜加工区，已初步形成了以成都市新都区为中心的泡菜加工区，以眉山市东坡区为中心的调味泡菜集群，以南充、宜宾、内江为代表的传统名腌菜加工区，以成都市郫县、资阳市雁江区为代表的川菜调味品泡菜加工区。“四川泡菜”将千年加工工艺与现代食品生物技术和食品工程技术相结合，实现了由传统的作坊式生产向机械化、规模化、多元化、标准化发展的转变。2009 年 6 月，四川省政府出台《关于加快现代农业产业基地建设的意见》，明确提出，一要在四川着力建设包括攀西早市蔬菜区、川西加工外销蔬菜区、川南早春蔬菜区、川东北特色蔬菜区、川西北高地秋淡蔬菜区等 5 个市场竞争力更强、区域和产品特色更加突出的商品蔬菜优势区；全省蔬菜面积、产量和产值至 2012 年均进入全国前 3 位。二要强化精深加工，构建基地农产品生产、保鲜、初加工、精深加工配套的协作体系。做到有特色产业就有大龙头带动，形成大龙头带大产业、大产业支撑大龙头的产业化格局。到 2012 年和 2015 年，农产品加工率将分别实现 50%和 60%以上，年销售收入过亿元的龙头企业分别达到 150 个和 200 个。

2009 年 10 月 30 日，农业部在宁夏银川市举行全国蔬菜标准园创建活动启动仪式，决定今明两年在全国蔬菜发展重点区域创建蔬菜标准园 400 个，通过集成技术、集约项目、集中力量，稳定提高蔬菜质量安全水平，提升产业发展质量效益，增强产业竞争力。

3. 蔬菜加工业的布局 目前，我国蔬菜加工产业逐步向布局集中、产业集聚的方向发展。我国蔬菜加工产业已形成了西北番茄酱加工基地、东部及东南沿海干制、罐头、速冻和腌制蔬菜加工基地。山东、福建、浙江、新疆、江苏、广东是我国蔬菜出口的主要省、自治区。我国脱水蔬菜加工也形成了东南沿海省份及宁夏、甘肃、内蒙古等西北地区产业带。

我国蔬菜产品的出口基地大都集中在东部沿海地区，近年来产业正向中西部扩展。我国的脱水蔬菜加工主要分布在东南沿海省份及宁夏、甘肃、内蒙古等西北地区，例如青椒、红椒主要集中在内蒙古及宁夏、甘肃一带加工；我国干辣椒出口量已占世界干辣椒出口量的 20%以上，其中贵州是我国的著名辣椒产区。而蔬菜罐头、速冻蔬菜加工主要分布在东部及东南沿海地区，在福建、山东、云南、陕西等省份集中了蘑菇、芦笋等罐头生产，其中福建出口的蘑菇罐头占全国蘑菇出口额的 70%左右；竹笋罐头以浙江、福建、江西为主产区。在浓缩汁、浓缩浆加工方面，我国的番茄酱的加工占有非常明显的优势，形成非常明显的浓缩蔬菜加工带，以西北地区（新疆、宁夏和内蒙古）为主的番茄酱加工基地。而直饮型蔬菜及其饮料加工则形成了以北京、上海、浙江、天津和广东等省、直辖市为主的加工基地。在我国腌制蔬菜产业中，榨菜产业主要集中在重庆、浙江、贵州，酱菜产业主要集中在大城市如北京等，山野菜如蕨菜加工主要集中在东北等省，泡菜主要集中在山东的青岛、东北的沈阳、四川的成都等地。2009 年 6 月，农业部发布了《全国蔬菜重点区域发展规划（2009—2015 年）》。根据规划，到 2015 年全国将初步建成具有较强市场竞争力和特色的 8 个蔬菜重点区域。针对蔬菜生产季节性强、蔬菜产品新鲜易腐、贮运困难一的特点，根据气候、区位优势以及产业基础，农业部规划将全国蔬菜产区划分为 4 大功能区 8 大重点区域，包括华南冬春蔬菜重点区域、长江上中游冬春蔬菜重点区域、黄土高原夏秋蔬菜重点区域、云贵高原夏秋蔬菜重点区域、黄淮海与环渤海设施蔬菜重点区域、东南沿海出口蔬菜重点区域、西北内陆出口蔬菜重点区域、东北沿边出口蔬菜重点区域。按照规划，到 2015 年，重点区域基地县蔬菜播种面积占全国的

42%，蔬菜产量占全国的48%，出口量和出口额占全国的90%以上，蔬菜生产对农民人均纯收入的贡献额超过1 200元，产品安全质量达到无公害食品要求，产品商品化处理和精（深）加工率达到65%以上。

二、国内外市场概况

（一）国内市场

近年来，北方设施蔬菜发展较快，南方冬春蔬菜稳定发展，对均衡全年蔬菜供应发挥了重要作用。2009年北方设施蔬菜种植面积超过666.7khm²，较上年同期增加约133.3khm²；南方10省秋冬种植蔬菜面积2 563.1khm²，同比增加46.9khm²。生产稳定发展为保市场供应奠定了坚实的基础。

2009年入冬以来，河北、北京、山西、湖北、湖南等地都先后提早地遭遇突如其来的暴雪及冰冻雨灾害，尤其是河北、山西等地的蔬菜生产大棚设施均遭受重创。全国许多地方蔬菜生产、运输、市场供应受到较大影响，菜价不同程度走高；同时近段时间汽油价格、燃气价格上调，运输成本增加，也是拉动蔬菜价格上涨的原因。据农业部批发市场价格信息网监测，随着低温雨雪天气逐渐过去，跨区流通与市场交易趋向正常，受灾地区蔬菜价格开始回落。太原市和石家庄市蔬菜平均批发价格从11月14日后连续回落，目前已分别比11月13日回落约20%和30%。从全国看，10月份“菜篮子”产品批发价格指数为148.5，比去年10月份下降2.7个点，比今年1月份下降8.6个点。11月份前两周，“菜篮子”产品批发价格指数保持在146左右，和近几年同期相比差别不大，说明蔬菜市场总体运行平稳。

2009年大蒜价格涨幅较大，上涨主要原因为受前两年微利的影响，种植面积减少加上部分地区干旱导致大蒜产量减少，2009年比去年大蒜种植面积至少减少了200多khm²。同时受甲型H1N1型流感影响引起的收购商抢购囤货，大蒜价格从1元/kg涨到10～12元/kg。

（二）国际市场

2009年，受国际金融危机影响，我国农产品贸易发展遇到严峻挑战，进出口贸易总额及进口和出口额均出现加入WTO后的首次下降，进出口总额为921.4亿美元，比上年下降7.1%。其中出口额为395.9亿美元，同比下降2.3%。蔬菜出口相对平稳，2009年1～12月出口量为802.7万t，同比下降2.0%；出口额为67.7亿美元，同比增长5.2%，呈量减额增态势。进口量为8.8万t，同比下降15.3%；进口额为1.0亿美元，同比下降10.9%。贸易顺差为66.7亿美元，同比扩大5.5%。

三、行业工作

（1）“第十届中国（寿光）国际蔬菜科技博览会”于2009年4月20日至5月20日在山东省寿光市举行。以“绿色、科技、创新、发展”为主题的此届蔬菜科技博览会，由农业部、商务部、科技部、中国国际贸易促进委员会、环境保护部、国家质量监督检验检疫总局、中华全国供销合作总社、国家外国专家局、中国农业科学院、国家旅游局、国家标准化管理委员会、中国科学技术协会、中国农业大学和山东省人民政府主办，30多个驻华大使馆、外国商协会、国际组织参与协办，山东省省直有关部门、潍坊市人民政府、寿光市人民政府承办。与往届菜博会相比，第十届菜博会将在3个方面实现新突破，一是在合理展览布局、强化展览效果上实现新突破，共展示蔬菜、果品、花卉2 000多个品种，300多项新技术新成果；二是在展示蔬菜文化艺术景观、带动旅游发展上实现新突破，设计制作200多个融合蔬菜文化、中国传统文化和现代农业科技的蔬菜艺术景点；三是在丰富展会内容、提高理论研讨水平上实现新突破，展会取得了丰硕的成果。

（2）“第七届中国果菜产业发展论坛”于2009年11月8～11日在海南省三亚市召开，本届论坛以“绿色果菜——寻求金融危机下的发展机遇”为主题。其宗旨在于为各级政府、专家学者、企业家和基层组织提供扩大交流、促进贸易、加强合作、共赢发展的最佳平台。从而实现果菜产业健康、和谐发展，促进农业发展、农民增收，做大做强中国果菜产业，让安全健康的中国果菜走向世界。

（3）“2009中国国际果蔬、加工技术及物流展览会”于2009年11月13～15日在广州召开，本次展会由中国果品流通协会、中国出入境检验检疫协会联合主办。本届展会主题为“健康果蔬，合作共赢”。

（4）“2009年长江流域蔬菜经济技术协作交流会”，于2009年11月25～28日在浙江省丽水市召开，本次会议由中国园艺学会长江蔬菜协会主办，浙江省农业科学院蔬菜所和丽水市农科院承办。会议围绕促进蔬菜产业化的主题，讨论了蔬菜安全生产、新技术、新品种、新生产资料及蔬菜经济和技术发展的新概念、新思维和新路径，并对开展省际和城市间蔬菜产业经济技术的协作进行了交流。

（山东省农机研究所　孙众沛　褚幼辉　刘方全）

茶叶加工业

一、中国茶叶在世界上的地位

据FAO-IGG统计，2009年世界和中国（大陆，下同）茶叶产量、出口量、进口量和消费量等见表1。其中，部分数字与中国农业统计数字稍有差异，表内所列数字和后面的分析均根据FAO-IGG统计。

表1 2009年世界和中国茶叶产量、出口量、进口量和消费量

项 目		产量（万t）	出口量（万t）	进口量（万t）	消费量（万t）	价格（美元/kg）
世界	2008年	392.61	161.43	170.05	378.38	2.39
	2009年	392.84	153.53	162.30	381.25	2.69
	同比增长（%）	0.95	-5.15	-4.76	0.76	12.56
中国	2008年	125.76	29.69	0.90	96.97	
	2009年	131.00	30.30	1.00	101.71	
	占世界（%）	33.35	19.74	0.62	26.68	
	同比增长（%）	4.17	2.05	11.11	4.89	

2009年，全球茶叶产量达到392.84万t，比上年增加不到1%。其中，绿茶产量增加了3%，红茶由于主要生产国斯里兰卡、肯尼亚、印度尼西亚等严重干旱减产2%。世界茶叶产量的增长，主要是中国绿茶产量的持续增长抵消了其他几个主要产茶国茶叶产量的下降。近10年来中国茶叶产量持续增长，2009年已达到131万t，占世界茶叶产量的33.35%，牢固确立了世界最大产茶国的地位。中国茶叶产量的增长，得益于中国政府贯彻实施农村致富和提高家庭收入等发展政策。FAO-IGG秘书处通过分析竞争型农业企业的销售毛利，证实了企业经营茶叶可能获得最大回报。同时主张不要通过扩大生产面积来增加茶叶产量，而要采用高产茶树品种和无性系来替换低产及已过经济寿命的茶树。2009年世界茶叶出口量为153.53万t，较上年减少5%以上，主要原因为红茶的供应量紧缺，降幅达到6%，为120万t，但中国茶叶出口总量达到30.30万t，增加了2%，特别是绿茶出口量的增加，保证了世界绿茶出口增加1%，达到27.82万t。2009年世界茶叶的消费量增长了不到1%，为381.25万t，这种增长是在2008年已经显著增长4%的基础上取得的。该增长主要是由于家庭收入水平的迅速提高，消费增长最明显的是中国和印度。中国茶叶消费量在2008年增长8%的基础上，2009年进一步增长近5%，是世界上最大的茶叶消费国。

二、中国茶叶基本情况

2009年1月中下旬和3月中旬，中国华南和长江上中游局部茶区遭受了"倒春寒"的气候影响，但由于各级有关部门及时组织抗灾，避免了冻害发生，不仅使茶叶开采期比上年提前了7～10天，而且茶叶产量也显著增加，保证了春茶购销两旺和全年茶叶的增产增值。

（一）茶园面积

根据中国农业部发布的信息，2009年全国茶园面积188.6万hm^2，比上年增长12.1万hm^2，增幅为6.9%。在茶园发展和建设中，茶树良种和技术推广进一步加快，全国无性系良种茶园面积为77.13万hm^2，比上年增长13.3%，在全国茶园总面积中所占比例由上年的38.9%上升到41.3%，提高了2.4%，其中福建、浙江、广东3省已超过或接近世界平均水平。由于政府对茶叶清洁化生产的重视，2009年全国无公害和有机茶园面积持续增加。其中无公害茶园面积由上年的105万hm^2，2009年增加到117.5万hm^2，增长11.9%；2009年有机茶园面积达到9.1万hm^2，比上年增长15.1%。

（二）茶叶生产和出口

2009年全国茶叶总产量在上年增产7.9%的基础上，2009年达到134万t（略高于FAO-IGG统计数字），比去年增长7%。全国茶叶总产值413亿元，比上年增长16.9%。同时在茶叶总产量中，名优茶比例继续明显增加，2009年全国名优茶总产量53万t，比上年增长9%；名优茶总产值308亿元，增长19.3%。名优茶产量和产值分别占全国茶叶总产量和总产值的39.6%和74.6%。2009年我国茶叶出口30.3万t，均价基本持平微增，出口金额7.05亿美元，上升3.3%。2009年除河南、广东、海南3省茶叶略有减产外，其他产茶省、自治区、直辖市都是增产，增产较多的产茶省是江西、福建、贵州，分别增加1.66万t、1.30万t和1.08万t。增收最多的是浙江，2009年比上年增收11.6亿元，增长17.6%，其次是贵州，增收7.5亿元，湖北增收6.9亿元，福建增收5.8亿元，湖南增收5.5亿元。

近年来，茶叶深加工产品在国内市场深受欢迎，2009年销售量已达到800万t，产值接近400亿元，茶多酚和速溶茶等深加工产品产值超过100亿元，茶叶深加工产品利用的茶叶资源约占全国茶叶总产量的15%，茶叶深加工产品产值与传统茶的农业产值已基本相当甚至超过。低咖啡因茶、超微茶粉、γ-氨基丁酸茶、功能茶和花香型绿茶、花香型红茶等新型茶也相继进入市场。

（三）茶叶机械化

由于茶产业的快速发展，促进了茶叶机械行业的发展，根据浙江、福建等产茶省的统计资料估算，目前全国约有较成规模的茶叶机械生产企业300余个，年生产茶叶机械加工设备25万余台（套），茶叶机械保有量超过150万台，大宗茶加工基本实现机械化，名优茶加工机械化水平也已超过80%。同样由于政府对茶叶清洁化生产的重视，各产茶省、自治区、直辖市积极进行茶叶加工厂的优化改造，淘汰了一批落后的茶叶加工厂，茶叶加工机械化、清洁化水平有较大改善，加工规模化、标准化水平也有所提高。例如浙江省，通过资源整合和布局调整，全省茶叶初制厂1999年为8 339个，经过优化改造，淘汰了2 963个布局欠合理且改造无望的茶叶初制厂，2009年茶叶初制厂已优化至5 876个。

（四）发展特点和存在问题

我国茶叶生产多年持续增产增收，主要依赖于面积的增加，2008年全国约有前几年发展的40万hm^2新茶园未开采，2009年又新建茶园12.1万hm^2，并且目前部分产茶省新茶园发展欲望仍较高。当前的茶叶市场产、销现状是基本平衡，若茶园面积继续扩大，将可能带来供过于求、茶贱伤农的忧患。

近年来我国茶树无性系良种，取得了2009年无性系良种茶园占全国茶园总面积41.3%的好成绩，但与世界平均水平相比，尚有差距。中国目前的传统茶经济，实际上是一种名优茶经济，2009年名优茶产量和产值分别占全国茶叶总产量的39.6%和74.6%。名优茶采摘用工量大，但茶区的采茶工雇用越来越困难，不少茶区反映，2009年每天80元工资还很难请到采茶工，这对浙江、江苏等经济发达茶产区名优茶及时采摘影响较大。我国是世界茶叶产、销大国，年产、销量占世界的三分之一强，但反映在茶叶品牌打造上难度较大，中国目前不仅没有世界茶叶品牌，国家品牌也寥寥无几，究其原因主要是社会上茶叶评比太多太乱，缺乏权威性和公正性，不利于品牌的培育和发展。近年来，中国的茶叶外销量增加不明显，基本稳定在世界茶叶出口量的五分之一水平上。内销量虽然有所增长，但市场也不稳定。

三、行业动态

（1）2009年5月20～21日，联合国粮农组织（FAO）政府间茶叶工作组在意大利罗马粮农组织总部召开专业会议，专门讨论茶叶贸易与质量、“茶汤”最大农药残留量（MRLS）及茶叶地理标志三个议题。来自中国、印度、斯里兰卡、肯尼亚、印度尼西亚、孟加拉国、美国、德国等国的茶叶代表团和世界知识产权保护组织（WIPO）、世界卫生组织农业残留联席会议（JMPR）及国际食品法典农药残留委员会（CCPR）等国际组织代表参加了会议。我国农业部调研员封槐松、中国农业科学院茶叶研究所研究员、中国工程院院士陈宗懋和浙江省农业厅研究员罗列万出席会议。会议先后由斯里兰卡、印度代表和我国代表陈宗懋主持。中国茶叶代表团代表分别在会上作了“关于茶叶贸易与质量”、“‘茶汤’最大农药残留量（MRLS）检测方法与数据采集”及“茶叶地理标志在中国”等专题发言。会议通过讨论就有关议题达成共识。

（2）2009年2月19～20日，中国工程院农业学部、中国茶叶学会和国家茶产业工程技术研究中心在杭州联合召开“技术创新与茶产业可持续发展研讨会”，中国工程院5位院士和来自中国农业科学院茶叶研究所、浙江、广东、安徽、湖南、福建等省科研院校及企业的茶学专家80余人参加会议。与会专家在茶产业发展策略和未来规划达成共识，建议我国未来茶园面积要根据市场需求稳步发展，将提高茶叶产品质量和产业效益放在首位；名优茶的发展今后要立足于一芽一、二叶优质茶的生产；要提高茶业机械化水平，推进茶叶连续化、清洁化加工；要继续重视茶叶质量安全，提高茶叶产品卫生质量水平；重视茶叶功能成分的开发利用，开辟茶叶新用途，重视功能成分终端产品的开发，拉长产业链，促进茶产业持续发展。

（3）中国是绿茶主产国，目前围绕绿茶生产，浙江、湖北、贵州等产茶省分别在打造“浙江绿茶”、“湖北绿茶”和“贵州绿茶”等品牌。2009年3月11日浙江省质量技术监督局还发布了DB 33—2009《浙江绿茶》省级标准。

四、茶产业发展展望

由于自然灾害影响，2010年春天冻害严重，造成春茶产量下降，但由于中、后期天气状况良好，预计多数产茶省份茶叶产量仍将保持稳定，部分还出现增长势头，加上新增茶园的投产，全年茶叶产量仍基本会保持稳定。由于受种植成本、供应量、采茶工等多重因素制约，2010 年名优茶的总体价格将会比 2009 年明显上升，但大宗茶的价格仍会保持稳定或略有增加。同样是受气候影响，2010 年名优茶生产前期影响较大，故 2010 年全年的名优茶产品质量，总体会有所下降，但是由于消费容量仍在扩大，带来的后果将是价格上升和上年库存的减少，销售压力不大。2010 年茶叶出口量会保持稳定状态。针对国内外市场行情和一些茶区盲目扩大茶园面积的状况，农业部明确提出，我国茶产业的发展，必须坚持稳定面积和提高品质、单产、效益的指导方针，但预计近一、两年盲目扩大茶园面积的状况还很难完全制止，故预计 2010 年全国茶园面积还会继续扩大，但增幅将会逐步回落。

（中国农业科学院茶叶研究所　权启爱）

蜂产品加工业

一、基本概况

蜂产品加工业是食品工业的重要组成部分。据统计，中国蜜蜂存养量约 840 万群，占世界蜂群数的 1/8，居世界首位。现全国年均加工蜂蜜约 40 万 t，蜂王浆约 3 500t，蜂花粉约 5 000t，蜂胶约 350t，还有数量不定的蜂蜡、蜂毒、蜂蛹、蜜蜂幼虫等产品，均位居世界第一。其中蜂王浆年加工量占世界总量的 9 成以上；蜂蜜、蜂花粉、蜂胶及其制品年出口量约占总产量的一半；蜜蜂饲养量、蜂产品总产量、蜂产品出口量均居世界第一。近年来，国内消费者对蜂产品保健作用的认识在提升，关注度也在增加，内销市场处于逐渐扩大状态。加上现今人们对提高生活质量、延年益寿的愿望增强，对天然食品、绿色食品、营养保健品消费量需求看涨，也促使了蜂产品消费的增长。现在的蜂产品中，特别是蜂蜜的销售势头很好，国内销售量已占总销售量的 2/3，不再单一依赖出口，而其余蜂产品的销售也处于稳定增长之中。

二、2009 年蜂产品出口情况

（一）蜂蜜

国际金融危机从 2008 年下半年开始已逐渐影响到我国蜂蜜的出口，导致蜂蜜出口数量减少，出口价格下跌，出口企业蜂蜜积压严重。据初步统计，2009 年初，湖北、浙江、安徽、江苏等省份蜂蜜出口企业的蜂蜜库存量在 1.5 万 t 以上，造成资金周转严重困难。为了摆脱困境，出口企业不得不压低蜂蜜收购价。为此，上述四省的一些出口大企业于 2009 年 3 月下旬在合肥经协商一致，出台了 2009 年春季油菜蜜收购的最高限价，与 2008 年同期相比，降幅达 40%，其他企业也纷纷响应。

据海关统计，2009 年我国蜂蜜出口总量为 7.19 万 t，比 2008 年下降了 15.19%；出口金额 1.26 亿美元，比 2008 年下降了 14.4%；平均单价 1.75 美元/kg，比 2008 年上升了 0.93%。出口前 20 位的国家是日本、比利时、英国、马来西亚、西班牙、葡萄牙、德国、荷兰、波兰、澳大利亚、南非、法国、摩洛哥、新加坡、印度、沙特阿拉伯、越南、俄罗斯、泰国和也门（表 1）。2009 年 1 月，美国政府对中国出口的蜂蜜最高征收 2.85 美元/kg 的反倾销关税。为此，美国几乎没有直接从中国进口蜂蜜。为了规避反倾销，许多中国蜂蜜开始通过其他国家进入美国，引起了美国各方面的强烈抵制。2009 年湖北省连续 10 年领跑蜂蜜出口，主要出口省份出口情况见表 2。

（二）蜂王浆

2009 年，全国蜂王浆的总产量为 3 500t 左右。其中，国内市场销量处于相对平稳状态，基本与 2008 年持平，总量达 2 000t 左右；国际市场销售量大幅下滑，总量达 1 300t 左右，下降幅度超过 20%。根据中国海关统计，2009 年 1～12 月，我国出口鲜蜂王浆 541.67t，同比下降 39%；出口金额 1 201 万美元，同比下降 36%。蜂王浆冻干粉出口 248.83t，同比增长 8%；出口金额 1 546 万美元，同比增长 4%。蜂王浆制剂出口 643.56t，同比下降 11%；出口金额 802 万美元，同比下降 18%（来自《2009 年 1～12 月蜂王浆产品出口统计数据》，食品商务网）。这是自 2003 年以来出口蜂王浆首次下滑，主要原因是受国际金融危机影响。鲜蜂王浆的主要出口市场是传统的日本市场，占中国出口鲜蜂王浆的 61%，日方对蜂王浆产品抗生素类药物残留的要求越来越严格，合格原料减少而使得价格上升，加之日方的检测项目较多，加大了企业的成本和出口周期。2009 年，鲜蜂王浆出口日本的数量为 319t，下降了 53%；出口价格为 23 美元/kg，同比上升 10.5%；出口金额为 737 万美元，同比下降 48%。2009 年欧盟国家从我国进口的鲜蜂王浆数量和价格也有下降，进口量为 113t，下降了 5.86%；进口额为 260 万美元，下降了 11%。而拉丁美洲进口我国蜂王浆 18t，同比增加 165.89%；进口额 42.52 万美元，增幅达 166.32%。

表 1　2009 年我国海关统计蜂蜜出口（前 20 位）

序号	出口国别（地区）	2009 年			同比增长（%）		
		数量（kg）	金额（美元）	单价（美元/kg）	数量	金额	单价
1	日本	25 192 232	47 601 269	1.89	−24.92	−23.21	2.28
2	比利时	12 536 410	21 862 435	1.74	−0.08	−3.63	−3.55
3	英国	8 896 467	15 320 227	1.72	141.9	122.17	−8.16
4	马来西亚	2 873 111	4 765 383	1.66	83.27	72.35	−5.96
5	西班牙	2 112 650	3 451 985	1.63	57.02	61.08	2.58
6	葡萄牙	2 068 280	3 425 111	1.66	0	0	0
7	德国	1 943 460	3 278 535	1.69	−0.82	−7.43	−6.67
8	荷兰	1 932 255	3 246 004	1.68	−37.82	−41.88	−6.53
9	波兰	1 410 560	2 286 774	1.62	−30.39	−33.42	−4.34
10	澳大利亚	1 337 820	2 147 677	1.61	64.76	77.28	7.60
11	南非	1 138 370	1 854 978	1.63	74.98	64.00	−6.28
12	法国	1 091 850	1 746 596	1.60	−36.43	−37.95	−2.40
13	摩洛哥	1 002 656	1 337 240	1.33	8.03	4.90	−2.90
14	新加坡	925 305	1 823 528	1.97	−49.85	−46.14	7.39
15	印度	910 035	1 107 409	1.22	−70.77	−73.47	−9.23
16	沙特阿拉伯	666 382	1 089 095	1.63	192.22	169.12	−7.90
17	越南	638 664	805 776	1.26	−55.02	−73.03	−40.03
18	俄罗斯	558 830	576 365	1.03	627.64	369.00	−35.54
19	泰国	469 120	708 319	1.51	1 204.56	3 839.48	201.98
20	也门	466 326	833 682	1.79	56.79	58.96	1.38
	其他	3 802 761	6 651 473	1.75	−72.75	−66.76	21.97
总　计		**71 973 544**	**125 919 861**	**1.75**	**−15.19**	**−14.40**	**0.93**

表 2　2009 年蜂蜜主要出口省份出口情况

出口省份	出口量（t）	金额（万美元）	单价（美元/kg）	数量增减（%）	金额增减（%）	单价增减（%）
湖　北	21 311	3 701	1.74	23	17	
安　徽	11 000	1 843	1.66	−13	−12	1
山　东	7 931	1 609	2.03	23	26	3
浙　江	7 226	1 206	1.67	−2	−2	0
江　苏	5 833	1 000	1.71	−72	−69	8
河　南	5 693	984	1.73	3	6	3
辽　宁	4 323	741	1.72	11	10	0
四　川	2 392	389	1.62	−24	−25	−1
湖　南	1 594	282	1.77	35	17	−14
天　津	1 278	226	1.77	31	31	0
吉　林	594	164	2.76	−1	−5	−5
陕　西	761	163	2.14	−53	−54	−1
北　京	887	156	1.75	50	74	16
上　海	768	136	1.77	−33	−32	1

（续）

出口省份	出口量（t）	金额（万美元）	单价（美元/kg）	数量增减（%）	金额增减（%）	单价增减（%）
广　东	716	87	1.22	208	127	－26
新　疆	390	77	1.99	113	131	9
宁　夏	414	60	1.45	36	18	－14
河　北	345	51	1.47	－48	－52	－8
内蒙古	159	24	1.54	78	93	9
福　建	136	21	1.54	453	454	－4
江　西	40	14	3.41	－42	2	77
广　西	98	14	1.41	9	15	6

随着国外对食品安全的要求不断提高，特别是欧盟各国农药残留监控标准不一，加大了出口企业的风险，影响了企业对国际市场的销售与开发。2009年蜂王浆冻干粉出口248.83t，同比增长8.12%；出口额154.62万美元，同比增长4.28%。其中日本进口132.33t，增幅达42%；进口额886.95万美元，同比增38.1%。荷兰进口8.74t，增幅达337%；进口额51.64万美元，同比增加268.88%。意大利进口4.2t，同比减少40%；进口额24.43万美元，同比减少36.18%。美国进口25.94t，同比减少34%；进口额134.01万美元，同比减少43%。

三、标准化工作

标准化工作是国家相关部门持续支持领域，2009年颁布并实施了“蜂蜡”和“蜂胶”两项产品国家标准、“蜂胶中铅的测定”和“花粉中总汞的测定方法”两项重金属含量测定国家标准以及“蜂蜡中石蜡的测定”一项检测国家标准；实施了“蜂王浆中土霉素、四环素、金霉素、强力霉素残留量的测定”等19项蜂产品中农兽药残留检测国家标准（其中2008年颁布12项，2009年颁布7项）、“蜂胶中阿魏酸含量的测定方法”等4项品质评价国家标准（2008年颁布）。农业系统支持开展了蜂产品中葡萄糖、果糖、蔗糖和麦芽糖的测定方法，及蜂产品理化检验方法、蜂花粉中黄曲霉毒素的测定方法、蜂产品感官评定方法制定、蜂蜜溯源编码规则等标准的制定工作。

受卫生部食品安全综合协调与卫生监督局委托，2009年12月17日，福建省疾病预防控制中心在福州举行蜂蜜安全标准制修订研讨会。据标准主要起草单位介绍，该标准的名称是中华人民共和国食品安全国家标准《蜂蜜》，属于全文强制性标准。该标准规定了蜂蜜的要求、生产加工过程的卫生要求、包装、标识、运输、贮存和试验方法，适用于所有蜂蜜，包括各种直接食用的蜂蜜产品。会议提供的标准稿对蜂蜜的强制性要求包括：原料要求（不得含有来源于雷公藤、南烛、博落回等蜜源植物的有毒物质）、感官要求（规定了色泽、滋味、气味和物理性状）、理化要求（规定了水分、果糖和葡萄糖、蔗糖的含量要求）、污染物（规定了铅和锌的限量）、兽药残留（规定了四环素族抗生素、氯霉素、硝基呋喃、链霉素和8种磺胺的残留限量）、农药残留（规定了氟氯苯氰菊酯、双甲脒、氟胺氰菊酯、溴螨酯的残留限量）和微生物指标（包括菌落总数、大肠菌群计数、霉菌计数、嗜渗酵母、沙门氏菌、志贺氏菌和金黄色葡萄球菌要求），以及加工过程卫生要求和包装、标识、贮存、运输要求。2009年，我国共发布11项蜂产品国家推荐性标准（表3）。

表3　2009年我国共发布11项蜂产品国家推荐性标准

标准号	标准名称
GB/T 23405—2009	蜂产品中环己烷氨基磺酸钠的测定　液相色谱—质谱/质谱法
GB/T 23407—2009	蜂王浆中硝基咪唑类药物及其代谢物残留量的测定　液相色谱—质谱/质谱法
GB/T 23408—2009	蜂蜜中大环内酯类药物残留量测定　液相色谱—质谱/质谱法
GB/T 23409—2009	蜂王浆中土霉素、四环素、金霉素、强力霉素残留量的测定　液相色谱—质谱/质谱法
GB/T 23410—2009	蜂蜜中硝基咪唑类药物及其代谢物残留量的测定　液相色谱—质谱/质谱法
GB/T 23411—2009	蜂王浆中17种喹诺酮类药物残留量的测定　液相色谱—质谱/质谱法
GB/T 23412—2009	蜂蜜中19种喹诺酮类药物残留量的测定方法　液相色谱—质谱/质谱法
GB/T 23870—2009	蜂胶中铅的测定　微波消解—石墨炉原子吸收分光光度法
GB/T 24283—2009	蜂胶
GB/T 24313—2009	蜂蜡中石蜡的测定　气相色谱—质谱法
GB/T 24314—2009	蜂蜡

四、质量管理工作

（一）主要问题

近年来，经过全国上下各方面的共同努力，我国蜂产品的安全质量状况和市场秩序都有了显著的改观。但依然存在着诸多问题，有些问题还相当严重。主要表现在以下3个方面：

1. *蜂蜜掺假方式不断翻新，掺假现象有加剧的趋势* 目前假蜂蜜有如下5种类型：一是用饴糖、果葡糖浆直接冒充蜂蜜，成本只有蜂蜜的1/10；二是白糖加水和硫酸进行熬制，硫酸裂解白糖，使双糖成分变为单糖，从而冒充蜂蜜，熬得时间越长颜色越深；三是少用糖，多用水，采取添加增稠剂的方式来增加假蜂蜜的浓度；四是用糖稀增加稠剂；五是用甜蜜素和色素直接勾兑。由于蜂蜜中富含果糖，加上高果糖淀粉糖浆具有成本低、感官上不易与蜂蜜区分等特点，添加高果糖淀粉糖浆一直是蜂蜜掺假的主要方式。由于碳-4植物糖检测方法仅能检出光合作用为碳-4途径来源的碳-4植物（玉米或甘蔗）糖含量的测定，而对碳-3途径来源的植物（如大米）糖浆未能检出。一些蜜蜂生产企业和中间商钻了现行国家蜂蜜标准的漏洞，大量利用碳-3途径来源的植物糖浆（如大米糖浆）。另外，有一些专业的糖业公司以赢利为目的，专门生产能通过国内外蜂蜜标准各项指标检测的各种糖浆，并向蜂产品加工企业推销。缺乏标准的有效约束使企业对往蜂蜜中掺加糖浆趋之若鹜，对纯蜂蜜的依赖程度严重下降，造成纯蜂蜜的需求量下降、价格下跌，严重打击专业养蜂者的积极性。近年来，国内蜂蜜造假已向规模化、专业化发展。据保守估计，假蜂蜜约占国内蜂蜜市场份额的40%以上。假蜂蜜外观比真蜂蜜还清亮诱人，透明无杂质，一般消费者往往会被吸引，加上这种“蜂蜜”价格非常便宜，故卖得很火。

2. *兽药残留超标现象仍较为严重* 蜂蜜及蜂王浆中兽药残留是一个老生常谈的问题，近年来虽有好转，但由于我国的蜂场普遍规模小，生产方式落后，技术水平低，蜂病防治措施力度不够，缺乏控制药物残留的意识。有些蜂农对蜂病用药缺乏基本常识和专业防治技术，错误认为抗生素药物是治疗蜂病的万能药，甚至还有许多蜂农不知道国家已颁布禁用氯霉素等药物的规定，蜂群常年不断用药，从而使蜂产品抗生素残留超标。加上生产和流通领域中有部分蜂药中可能含有过量抗生素或违禁药物；生产、加工用具（包括蜜蜂巢脾、蜂箱）受到抗生素污染和蓄积，使蜂蜜中兽药残留现象仍较为严重。

3. *蜂蜜制品泛滥* 由于现行蜂蜜标准中关于蜂蜜产品名称和产品标识的规定不完善，使大量的“蜜膏”、“蜜汁”等蜂蜜制品在市场上出现。所谓“蜜膏”、“蜜汁”，实际上是企业在蜂蜜中掺入大量的糖浆等物质，利用消费者认识不足和现有标准的空子，以合法的方式销售掺入了其他物质的蜂蜜制品。销售这些蜂蜜制品，企业不但能获得高额利润，而且由于不受标准限制，经营风险很低。可以说，“蜜膏”、“蜜汁”等蜂蜜制品已经达到泛滥的程度，大部分经营蜂蜜产品的企业同时销售蜂蜜制品，也就是将一些不合格的蜂蜜贴上“蜜膏”等标签加以销售；一些企业甚至根本不经营蜂蜜，而只销售这种没有标准限制的蜂蜜制品。这表面上是蜂蜜及其产品的销售问题，但实际上将会对未来的养蜂业造成毁灭性的打击，已经到了非治不可的程度。

（二）针对以上问题开展的主要工作

1. *实施蜂产品全过程质量控制和溯源管理* 一是生产过程质量控制。包括产地管理，蜂种选育和利用，蜂病诊断和蜂场用药的规范，严格休药期管理，生产用具管理和以优质优价鼓励蜂农生产优质产品，建立原料基地等。二是加工过程质量控制。加强原料、半成品和成品的质量检验，防止加工设备和辅料造成二次污染，按照标准程序生产、加工和包装产品等。三是流通环节质量控制。注意包装的完好性和保质期，严格保存条件等。蜂产品可溯源研究在国内已经开始，目前可追溯体系建立受到国家社会公益和农业部产业技术体系资助的团队正在加紧进行相关技术的研发，已同时设置了多个模拟实验点，开展了可溯源意识和工作的培训；国标委下达的由安徽省标准化研究院制定的《农产品追溯要求 蜂蜜》国家标准已推出征求意见稿，说明国家对可溯源工作已非常重视。

2. *积极推广成熟蜜的生产方式* 我国目前普遍采用的非成熟蜜生产方式始于20世纪50年代后期，在当时的政治、经济形势下，蜂农为扩大蜂蜜产量，采取“一天一甩”的生产方式，造成原蜜成熟度差，须经加热、浓缩以脱掉水分等加工过程，使得蜂蜜所含的天然营养成分减少，质量下降。这样的蜂蜜生产方式，其产品已无法适应国内外市场对蜂蜜品质的要求。在世界主要蜂蜜生产国中，仅我国生产和出口加工蜜，这与世界养蜂业的发展趋势很不适应。因此，我们应积极推广成熟蜜生产，坚持优质优价，促进蜂蜜生产的结构性调整，让消费者真正享受高品质的天然成熟蜂蜜。养蜂学会及蜂产品协会都做了大量的推广培训工作。

3. *加大蜂业的组织化程度* 积极倡导产供销联合，推行“小规模、大群体”思路，大力发展以蜂产品加工企业为龙头，以养蜂合作社和养蜂大户等为主体的蜂业联合体，发展订单蜂业，走“公司＋蜂农”或“公司＋合作社＋蜂农”的产业化经营模式，减少生产的盲目性，提高产品质量安全，增加经济效益。龙头企业应肩负起蜂产品质量安全的责任，应该为蜂农服务。组织蜂农培训、蜂用兽药的统一采购和应用、养蜂基地建设、残留监控检测和溯源体系建立等，逐步实现从田头到餐桌的蜂产品质量安全的全程管理。应充分发挥行业协会和学会组织的作用，采用各种形式，大力宣贯与蜂产品质量相关的有关法律法规和标准等，进一步提高行业诚信自律意识和标准化水平。

4. *加大生产和流通领域监管力度* 完善各级蜂业管理机构及其职能，在蜂蜜生产的各个环节加大对检测的投入力度，从原料到成品每个环节层层严格把关，可避免大量的有质量安全问题的蜂产品流入市场。在流通领域，由政府相关部门和检测机构配合，加大监控和处罚力度。同时，加强蜂产品质量认证宣传和推行无公害、绿色和有机认证和应用管理工作。

5. *开展完善蜂蜜国家标准的前期研究和针对性检测方法研究，及时修订标准* 由于现行的蜂蜜国家标准对掺假的检测方法和仲裁方法均为碳-4植物糖检测，而这种方法在检测碳3-途径的植物的糖浆方面仍然有缺陷，未能完全检出。正是因为这种缺陷，目前已有国外进口商要求蜂蜜必须双符合：同时满足高果糖淀粉糖浆检测阴性和碳-4植物糖符合要求。现行国家标准在对蜂蜜掺假的制约方面存在一定的缺陷，有必要进行完善。农业部、质检系统都在开展针对蜂产品品质、安全和加工的检测方法研究，包括化学残留、生物毒素和品质检测方法。随着国家对食品检测的仪器投入力度加大，GC/MS/MS、LC/MS/MS、同位素质谱、生物检测技术等高新检测技术研究越来越多。

6. *开展蜂药的专项调查* 蜂蜜中抗生素残留肯定与蜂群用药相关，但现在几乎所有的蜂药生产者都标称自己的蜂药是高效低残留的。蜂蜜中诸如氯霉素这一类不易降解的、不许或限制使用的抗生素残留的来源是否与蜂药有关，受到农业部产业技术体系资助的团队开展了探索蜂产品中污染物残留途径和代谢情况的研究，同时针对养蜂生产环节蜂机具污染状况进行分析和评估。

五、行业诚信建设

2009年是蜂产品行业诚信建设硕果累累的一年，中国蜂产品协会在2008年6月启动了行业信用评价试点工作，目前已经取得初步成效。首批18家蜂产品生产经营企业通过了信用评价，荣获了A级以上信用等级。按照商务部、国资委2009年深入开展行业信用评价工作的部署，进一步推动行业信用体系的建设，提高行业信用水平和企业信用风险防范能力，2009年第二批蜂产品行业信用评价工作进展顺利。同时在第二次全国蜂胶工作会议上，形成了规范蜂胶市场的行业自律公约。这些都为我国蜂产品行业健康、快速发展奠定了诚信基础。2009年11月，2009“全国蜂产品行业诚信商店”名单公布。至此，全国已有200多个蜂产品专卖店成为“全国蜂产品行业诚信商店”，覆盖了全国近20多个省（自治区、直辖市），在诚信经营、规范蜂产品市场起到了很好的示范带头作用。为更好地引导行业规范发展，保证“诚信商店”的服务质量，从2009年起，被授予“诚信商店”称号的单位均须签订“诚信商店承诺书”。各“诚信商店”将承诺书和监督电话悬挂在商店内，接受消费者和行业协会的监督。专业合作社是促进互助合作、提高组织能力、加强规范生产的有效方式，同时，也在技术推广和提高产品质量的过程中发挥了积极作用。为进一步从源头上抓好质量安全管理，推动专业合作社的持续健康发展，2009年中国蜂产品协会还公布并表彰了第二批39个“全国蜂农专业合作社示范社”。其中，北京2个，上海1个，山西1个，内蒙古1个，江苏1个，浙江6个，安徽8个，江西9个，山东1个，河南3个，湖北2个，湖南3个，四川1个。

（中国农业科学院蜜蜂研究所　闫继红）

食用菌加工业

在严峻的国内外经济环境中，2009年是我国食用菌行业继续保持健康发展的一年。这说明我国食用菌产业近年来在政府、协会以及企业的共同努力下，发展稳定并具备了一定的抗风险能力，各地方政府发展食用菌的积极性提高。最令行业欣喜的是，食用菌产业在新农村建设中所作的贡献得到高度评价。胡锦涛总书记对我们食用菌产业的关心和关注，使得全行业从业者大受鼓舞，并使得我们更加有信心带领农民走上种菇致富的道路。

一、基本情况

（一）总产量

改革开放以来，食用菌快速发展成为我国的新兴特色产业，各省、市、县把发展食用菌作为当地“菜篮子工程”、特色农业、创汇农业、农村脱贫致富、循环农业等重要项目来抓，全国食用菌产量迅速提高。根据统计资料，2001年我国食用菌产量为781.9万t，2003年为1 038.7万t，2006年为1 474万t，2009年为2 020.6万t。由此可见，2001年至2009年9年间增长了1.6倍，平均每年增长10.5%。我国食用菌栽培种类很多，目前形成商品的有50多种。据中国食用菌协会统计，2009年产量排在前10位的品种分别为平菇、香菇、黑木耳、双孢菇、金针菇、毛木耳、鸡腿菇、姬菇、茶树菇、草菇。其中黑木耳的产量增加最为明显，与去年相比增加了41.9%。排在前6位的6个品种总产量占2009年全国总产量的77.7%，与去年相比增加了约1个百分点，这6个品种依旧为我国食用菌产品的主要品种。2009年香菇、平菇、双孢菇总产量为1 054.5万t，占总产量的52.2%。由此说明，随着我国食用菌产业其他种类食用菌产量增加，特别是近年来推出的白灵菇、杏鲍菇、茶树菇、真姬菇等受到了市场的青睐和各地菇农的广泛欢迎，增强了食用菌市场竞争力，成为我国食用菌产业新的增长点。

（二）单位产量

食用菌与绿色植物栽培上最大的不同在于可以立体栽培，因此单位产量不能以面积来计算。食用菌的单产是以产菇鲜重占培养料干重的百分数来计算，称为生物学效率，如1kg干培养料产鲜菇0.9kg，即为生物学效率为90%。我国食用菌种类多，栽培模式多样，不同种类、不同栽培方式，单位产量不同。如果按照占地面积计算，工厂化栽培除外，那么密度大的立体栽培种类单产高。我国现在单位面积产量最高的是平菇，采用日光温室大棚墙式栽培每亩每季产量可达15 000kg以上。一年至少30 000kg以上。我国食用菌总产量虽然很高，但单位产量仍然较低。以双孢蘑菇为例，目前我国每平方米产量一般在9kg左右，最高也有报道达到25kg，但只是个别生产场、基地或实验地能达到这一水平。然而，发达国家，如法国、荷兰、美国等双孢蘑菇平均产量为25～30kg/m^2，最高产量可达到40kg/m^2以上。而且金针菇的工厂化生产水平也与日本、韩国等国家有一定的差距。我国单产水平低，提高单产的潜力很大。对一个产业，高产、优质、高效还加上生态、安全，是发展的最基本要求。

（三）主产地区

从全国食用菌产量分布情况看，2009年排在前8位的省份分别是河南、山东、福建、河北、黑龙江、江苏、浙江和四川。这8个省产量合计为1 330.6万t，占全国总产量的65.9%。从全国食用菌产值分布情况看，2009年产值超过50亿元的有山东、河南、河北、福建、广东、黑龙江、江苏、浙江、吉林9个省，比2008年增加了3个省。

河南省食用菌栽培种类从以前的黑木耳和银耳发展到当前平菇、香菇、金针菇、双孢蘑菇、白灵菇等数10种，逐渐形成了以西峡和泌阳香菇为主，伏牛山脉山区的黑木耳、毛木耳和香菇的木腐菌两大产区，近年又形成了以夏邑双孢蘑菇为主的草腐菌产区。河南省食用菌产业可以说是飞速发展，1993年全省产量只有8.5万t，而2007—2009年基本维持在225万～226万t之间。快速发展的原因为地处中原，气候跨南北；交通发达，高速公路、铁路四通八达；河南也是人口大省，农村富余劳动力多。

福建省是我国食用菌产业发展最早、栽培种类最多、食用菌生产总体技术水平最高的省。可以说很多种类的商业栽培和新的栽培技术均起源于福建。双孢蘑菇生产处于国内领先，产量占全国40%～50%；出口量占70%～80%。福建食用菌生产已经逐步向集约化、工厂化、规模化栽培发展，初步形成了生产、加工和市场的区域化和专业化格局。双孢蘑菇的栽培主要集中在漳州、莆田、福鼎，寿宁、政和、屏南主要是香菇的生产和销售，长汀和屏南为夏季地栽香菇的生产与销售；白背毛木耳的集约化生产与加工销售也主要集中在漳州；古田则主要以香菇、银耳的专业化生产为主；此外还有仙游和顺昌的姬松茸、罗源的秀珍菇、竹荪等规范化栽培和加工基地；金针菇和杏鲍菇的小型工厂化周年生产等各具特色。

山东省的食用菌栽培，由过去平菇为主的单一格局已发展为当前的平菇、双孢蘑菇、香菇、金针菇、草菇、木耳等6大种类。鲁北香菇主产区、鲁西双孢蘑菇主产区、鲁中金针菇和珍稀菇类主产区、鲁南黑木耳和香菇产区、鲁南平菇主产区。其中，平菇稳健发展，产量一直在该省占首位。2009年该省平菇产量71.54万t，占全省食用菌总产量的34.7%，较2000年增长了347.1%，双孢蘑菇2000年的产量只有9万t，2007年达到39.60万t，增长了208.4%。但由于近两年全球金融危机，作为主要的出口品种，

2009年产量下降到24.47万t。同时，鸡腿菇、白灵菇、杏鲍菇等珍稀菇类发展迅速，取得了良好的经济效益。

食用菌是浙江省的特色优势产业，尤其是香菇生产历史悠久，香菇也是浙江食用菌中种植数量最多、分布区域最广、产量产值最高的第一大菇种。庆元—龙泉—景宁是世界香菇的发祥地，“庆元香菇”获得了国家原产地域保护和证明商标。同时食用菌生产区域布局十分明显，主要集中在浙中南一些山区县，其中产值超过5 000万元的有庆元、磐安、龙泉、江山等24个县，产值约占全省总产值的85%。经过近几十年的发展，该省食用菌已经初步形成丽水市、金华的香菇，嘉善、平湖、苍南的双孢蘑菇，开化、江山的金针菇，开化、云和的黑木耳，龙泉的灵芝，常山的猴头菇等6大基地，这些基地鲜菇生产量占全省95%以上。浙江省食用菌产业已经逐步从数量型经济增长向质量型经济增长转变。

河北省食用菌栽培种类多样，省财政设专门项目，每年出资400万元支持食用菌产业技术研发和推广，所以发展速度很快。栽培量较大的是平菇（含姬菇）、金针菇、双孢菇等。冀州的姬菇、平泉滑子菇和夏季香菇、灵寿金针菇、馆陶双孢蘑菇等一大批在国内外市场具有较高的知名度。河北省食用菌2009年产量为190.77万t，仅次于福建省，排第4位。

二、市场分析

平菇主要分布在河南、河北、江苏、山东、辽宁、广东、四川，产量占全国的70%以上。平菇是食用菌中栽培数量最大、从业人数最多、食用人群最广的品种之一，价格便宜，国内消费市场大。由于平菇的生理抗性较强、适应性较广，一年四季均可栽培，而且其生物学效率是食用菌中最高的品种，故而得到了广大菇农的欢迎。尤其初学食用菌技术者，几乎无一例外的把平菇作为技术练兵的对象，可以说相当一部分农民朋友因种平菇而脱贫致富。平菇多以市场鲜销为主，兼以部分盐渍品加工，干品数量很少，平菇价格最高时段是5～12月份，即反季节平菇价格最高，均价为5.8元/kg；价格最低时段是在春节后3、4月份均价为2元/kg。2007—2009年平菇价格走势较稳，并有逐渐上升的趋势。

香菇是我国产量居第二位的食用菌，主产栽培在浙江、福建、河南、河北、湖北、辽宁、陕西等省，占总产量的80%左右。在参与全球贸易的众多农产品中，我国香菇占有市场的绝对优势。由于栽培技术熟练，食用文化丰富，预计今后20年甚至更长时期，全球香菇市场也将为我国主宰。主要是因为香菇生产65%～80%为手工劳动，因此工资水平较我国高出10～20倍的国家和地区自然竞争不过我们。周边国家如越南、印度尼西亚、巴基斯坦、俄罗斯等，工资成本虽不高，但因为缺少栽培和食文化底蕴，无法与我国竞争。我国独创的花菇挑蕾选优、木屑包大田层架栽培、半地下室栽培等，处于世界领先水平。据调查，2008—2009年香菇价格不断走高，主要是因为反季节鲜菇数量减少，栽培量减少导致价格上扬。

双孢蘑菇是我国产量居第三位的食用菌，主要栽培区域在福建、浙江、四川、河南、湖北、山东、河北等省。双孢菇是世界上生产数量最大、消费人群最广尤其受发达国家消费者青睐的主要品种之一，也是我国出口食用菌的主要品种。泰国、马来西亚、新加坡、印度尼西亚、菲律宾等南亚国家是我国传统的双孢蘑菇产品出口地。对大多数欧美国家的双孢菇出口的数量则是按照各国的配额制度进行的。美国和加拿大是我国双孢蘑菇产品出口的另一个重要市场，也是极具潜力的市场。各类蘑菇罐头、干、鲜菇是我对北美地区的主销产品。在我国双孢菇的产销有明显特点，就是“产地不销，销地不产”，其中原因主要是双孢菇的出口数量大、价值高，产品大多被订购或收购，仅有少量规格、质量较差的产品供应市场，国人消费量少，还未形成消费双孢菇的习惯。正因为双孢菇主要是供应出口市场，所以受国际经济局势影响较大，2008年受全球金融危机的影响，双孢蘑菇收购价格一度跌至每千克1元以下，销售价格比成本低了一半，菇农叫苦不迭，与2007年市场差价达到3.6元。2009年春节过后，全国各产地双孢菇价格逐渐走高，上海等地达到每千克16元，其他主产地也逐渐恢复到每公斤6～7元，而且销售渠道十分顺畅。

黑木耳是黑龙江、湖北、河南、四川、吉林的主要栽培品种。据统计，2009年我国大部分黑木耳主产区的产量较2008年都有所增加，尤其是黑龙江省产量增加比较明显，2009年该省黑木耳产量为124.25万t，较2008年增长了44%。目前，北京农产品批发市场上黑木耳干品的价格为50～76元/kg，福建主产地市场的批发价格40～48元/kg，湖北农产品批发市场价格46～60元/kg，黑龙江东宁绥阳黑木耳大市场批发价格约34～74元/kg。

毛木耳主要生产于福建、四川和山东。毛木耳的口感和营养不如黑木耳好，所以价格也比较低廉，一级干品售价为25元/kg左右。消费市场主要是一些小餐馆和饭店。毛木耳因为口感等没有黑木耳好，近几年消费量和产量都逐步下降，所以希望广大菇农朋友要控制和适量生产，全国2008年产98万t，2009

年下降为88.9万t。

金针菇的生产相对分散，农业栽培和工厂化生产并存，农业方式生产规模较大的有河北、四川等地，工厂化生产主要集中在上海、北京、广东、山东、福建、浙江等省有较多分布。金针菇适宜于工厂化生产，利用冷库、冷气进行周年生产，并且市场需求也越来越大，所以近几年金针菇工厂化生产发展较快，仅在山东省内已经建建成和在建的金针菇工厂化生产企业就有32个，目前全国还在陆续有金针菇工厂化生产车间建成。2008年至2009年金针菇的平均价格有下降趋势。在金针菇大量上市的时期，特别是顺季金针菇上市时，价格普遍走低，造成个别中小型金针菇工厂化生产企业倒闭。价格低的原因是：2009年韩国金针菇大量出口到我国，1～7月向我国出口3 600多t，金额近200万美元。只要有韩国金针菇销售的市场，金针菇价格一般比其他地区低30%左右，原因是韩国金针菇产业受到政府大力的补贴支持。

在各种新兴人工栽培食用菌中，茶树菇、秀珍菇、白灵菇、杏鲍菇和鸡腿菇的发展引人注目，茶树菇和秀珍菇在福建、浙江、江苏已成为栽培广泛的主要种类；白灵菇成为北京、新疆、河南的主要栽培种类；杏鲍菇在广东、河南、山东、黑龙江、江苏、上海、天津等地均已成为主要栽培菌种。2009年茶树菇干品的平均市场价格为每千克49.8元。白灵菇属于珍稀品种，还没有真正走上老百姓的餐桌，主要是供应大型宾馆和高级饭店，而且价格也是不断上升，白灵菇属于低温菇，转化率低，所以白灵菇工厂化生产成本较高，而且消费市场大，深受消费者的青睐。杏鲍菇市场价格较稳定，但是与往年相比价格仍有上涨，主要是因为原材料价格不断上涨，劳动力成本加大，市场需求进一步扩大，价格也会逐渐升高。

三、行业工作

（一）积极推进小蘑菇新农村建设工作

2009年，中国食用菌协会在山东聊城市举办了“全国小蘑菇新农村建设表彰会”。会上对“小蘑菇新农村行动计划”实施3年来作出突出贡献的30个优秀团体、100名突出贡献者、100个“百强村”、10个“十强县”进行了表彰。协会开展“小蘑菇新农村行动计划”3年来，得到了全国各地协会、主管部门和广大会员的响应。截至2008年底，已有278个村（镇、县）成为了“全国小蘑菇新农村建设行动村”，经协会审定200个行动村为示范村。这些行动村、示范村食用菌总产量达到48万t，产值12.2亿元。每个村食用菌产量基本达到2 000t，产值600万元，食用菌产值占村农业产值的50%以上，村人均收入4 000多元，50%以上的行动村成为县级以上精神文明村。这些行动村，已成为通过发展食用菌产业建设社会主义新农村一支重要力量和不可多得的亮点。

（二）搭建服务平台，促进交流与合作

通过节、会活动搭建服务平台，加强和促进会员、行业的交流与合作，是协会服务会员的一项重要工作内容。2009年协会与各地方政府共举办行业大型会议6场，这些会议都具有规模大、规格高等特点。不仅会议代表自身受益，也促进了地方经济发展。协会举办节、会活动在一定程度上满足了会员和产业发展的需要，会员对此予以肯定，反响很好。

（三）做好宣传，培育市场

市场在商品经济中是至关重要的，是经济发展的龙头。随着食用菌产业的不断发展，解决好市场问题是根本。尤其在当前发生国际金融危机期间如何拉动消费，扩大内需，进一步拓展国内市场成为当务之急。为此，协会除通过媒体广为宣传外，重点作了两件事：

1. 举办“小蘑菇大产业健康万里行”活动 由中国食用菌协会主办，江苏安惠生物科技有限公司承办的全国“小蘑菇大产业”健康万里行分别在石家庄、沈阳、杭州等地共举行了15场报告会。健康万里行活动旨在邀请专家学者，通过报告会的形式，传播食用菌饮食文化和健康理念，介绍食用菌产业的状况和前景，探讨食用菌产品开发与利用，对进一步提高全社会的食用菌认识水平有着非常重要的意义。通过“小蘑菇大产业健康万里行”活动，食用菌知识和食用菌健康饮食理念将更加普及，食用菌生产加工技术及其产品将备受关注，拓展了消费市场。

2. 举办“第五届中国国际食用菌烹饪大赛”活动 2009年中国食用菌协会举办了“第五届中国国际食用菌烹饪大赛遵化杯邀请赛”。这次国际食用菌烹饪大赛活动是第四届，近500名团体和个人选手参加了赛事活动，其中境外国家和地区参赛人员50多名，共推出食用菌菜品500多道，在国内国际食用菌行业和餐饮业引起广泛反响，特别是为拉动国内食用菌产品社会需求，促进食用菌的烹饪应用和市场开发，让世界更多地了解中国食用菌产品及安全营养健康和丰富多样的食用菌菜肴起到积极的推动作用。在此次烹饪大赛期间，还组织召开了“全国食用菌主产基地及企业学习《食品安全法》论坛”活动。

（四）国际交流与合作

1. 参加国际会议，进行友好访问 2009年，应

新西兰蘑菇生产者联盟秘书丹尼尔·克瑞斯坦尼洛先生的邀请，协会会长、国际蘑菇学会副主席李树萍率代表团对新西兰食用菌企业进行了友好访问，双方进行了友好会谈。代表团受邀访问了 Cresta Mushrooms 有限公司，之后出席了国际蘑菇学会执委会在澳大利亚召开的执委会会议。协会充分利用国际蘑菇学会副主席的身份，积极加强对外交往与合作，加强与各国食用菌行业组织的联系和沟通，当好中国企业与国际同行交流的桥梁和纽带，为中国食用菌企业走出国门，开拓市场铺路架桥，提供服务和便利。

2. 承办了援外培训班　受商务部的委托，2009 年在北京承办了为期 14 天的“发展中国家食用菌推广与应用官员研修班”，来自缅甸、格鲁吉亚、蒙古等 11 个国家，23 名学员参加了此次研修培训活动。此次培训展示了中国食用菌产业发展现状，食用菌领域先进的成果，以及中国取得的成就。协会承办援外培训班的意义不仅在于推进国际食用菌领域的交流与合作，而且增加了中国与世界各国的友谊。

（五）援建什邡菌种场竣工

2009 年 6 月，中国食用菌协会在四川省什邡市举行援建菌种场竣工，为提高菇农素质和生产技术水平，中国食用菌协会将用两年左右的时间，在什邡市举办多种免费食用菌专题培训班。协会援建的菌种场，年产 50 万瓶，是一个标准化和现代化程度较高的菌种场。此举不仅可以解决菇农的菌种问题，还可以起到示范带头的作用，促进当地食用菌产业健康发展。

（六）召开了“首届海峡两岸食用菌技术与产业发展研讨会”

“首届海峡两岸食用菌技术与产业发展研讨会”于 2009 年 10 月 18 日在江西庐山举办。研讨会为海峡两岸的技术部门、科研院所、生产企业提供了交流平台，并为海峡两岸的技术协作、信息交流提供了极好的机会。会议期间，海峡两岸 25 名专家、学者就“食用菌发展状况与政策”、“食用菌技术与产业发展”、“食用菌标准、产品、市场、营销与文化”、“食用菌与旅游、休闲产业开发”等四个主题进行了广泛而深入的研讨。

（中国食用菌协会　李　静）

乳制品制造业

一、基本情况

（一）牛奶生产

2009 年全国奶牛存栏为 1 260.3 万头，同比增长 2.2%。其中前 5 位省、自治区为内蒙古 227.3 万头，同比增长－7.5%，占全国的 18.0%；黑龙江 197.0 万头，同比增长 40.6%，占全国的 15.6%；新疆 170.4 万头，同比增长－16.9%，占全国的 13.5%；河北 167.4 万头，同比增长 16.9%，占全国的 13.3%；山东 83.8 万头，同比增长 3.2%，占全国的 6.7%。2009 年全国奶类产量为 3 732.6 万 t，同比增长－1.3%。其中，牛奶产量为 3 518.8 万 t，同比增长－1.0%。牛奶产量前 5 位省、自治区分别为内蒙古 903.1 万 t，同比增长－1.0%，占全国的 25.7%；黑龙江 528.7 万 t，同比增长 4.0%，占全国的 15.0%；河北 451.5 万 t，同比增长－10.5%，占全国的 12.8%；河南 281.9 万 t，同比增长 1.0%，占全国的 8.0%；山东 236.3 万 t，同比增长 2.5%，占全国的 6.7%（表 1、表 2、表 3）。

表 1　2009 年全国奶牛存栏前 5 位省份情况

地　区	存栏数（万头）	比 2008 年增长（%）	占全国比例（%）
全国总计	**1 260.3**	**2.2**	**100.0**
内蒙古	227.3	－7.5	18.0
黑龙江	197.0	40.6	15.6
新　疆	170.4	－16.9	13.5
河　北	167.4	16.9	13.3
山　东	83.8	3.2	6.7

表 2　2009 年全国奶类总产量前 5 位省份情况

地区	产量（万 t）	比 2008 年增长（%）	占全国比例（%）
全国总计	**3 732.6**	**－1.3**	**100.0**
内蒙古	934.0	1.4	25.0
黑龙江	534.7	4.3	14.3
河　北	461.0	－10.5	12.4
河　南	301.3	0.9	8.1
山　东	258.1	1.3	6.9

表3 2009年全国牛奶产量前5位省份情况

地区	产量（万t）	比2008年增长（%）	占全国比例（%）
全国总计	**3 518.8**	**−1.0**	**100.0**
内蒙古	903.1	−1.0	25.7
黑龙江	528.7	4.0	15.0
河　北	451.5	−10.5	12.8
河　南	281.9	1.0	8.0
山　东	236.3	2.5	6.7

（二）经济运行状况

2009年，全国有规模以上乳制品制造企业（即全部国有和年主营业务收入500万元及以上非国有工业企业）803个，比2008年减少12个，同比增长−1.5%。其中内资企业692个，比2008年减少6个，增长−0.9%，占企业总数的86.2%；港澳台商投资企业20个，比2008年减少2个，增长−9.1%，占企业总数的2.5%；外商投资企业91个，比2008年减少4个，增长−4.2%，占企业总数的11.3%。2009年全国规模以上乳制品制造企业共完成工业总产值1 668.1亿元，同2008年相比增长了11.9%。其中内资企业完成987.8亿元，同比增长14.3%，占全行业的59.2%；港澳台商投资企业完成55.0亿元，同比增长9.7%，占全行业的3.3%；外商投资企业完成625.4亿元，同比增长8.5%，占全行业的37.5%。2009年全国规模以上乳制品制造企业实现工业销售产值1 599.7亿元，同比增长13.3%。其中内资企业956.5亿元，同比增长15.7%，占销售总值的59.8%；港澳台商投资企业54.2亿元，同比增长8.5%，占销售总值的3.4%；外商投资企业589.0亿元，同比增长10.1%，占销售总值的36.8%。

2009年全行业流动资产合计556.3亿元，同比增长26.9%；固定资产合计395.9亿元，同比增长11.3%。其中不同类型企业固定资产合计分别为：内资企业239.1亿元，同比增长13.1%，占全行业的60.4%；港澳台商投资企业10.6亿元，同比增长0.2%，占全行业的2.7%；外商投资企业146.2亿元，同比增长9.4%，占全行业的36.9%。全行业资产总计1 154.0亿元，同比增长22.4%。其中内资企业674.3亿元，同比增长25.7%，占58.4%；港澳台商投资企业57.2亿元，同比增长2.3%，占全行业的5.0%；外商投资企业422.6亿元，同比增长20.6%，占全行业的36.6%。2009年全国乳制品制造企业负债合计619.2亿元，同比增长16.2%，资产负债率53.7%，比2008年降低2.9个百分点。其中内资企业负债389.6亿元，同比增长23.4%，负债率57.8%，同比降低1.1个百分点；港澳台商投资企业负债27.7亿元，同比增长4.3%，负债率48.4%，同比提高0.9个百分点；外商投资企业负债202.0亿元，同比增长5.9%，负债率47.8%，同比降低6.6个百分点。

全行业工业产品销售率为95.9%，比2008年同期提高1.2个百分点。其中内资企业为96.8%，比2008年提高1.2个百分点；港澳台商投资企业为98.6%，比2008年降低1.1个百分点，外商投资企业为94.2%，比2008年提高1.3个百分点。2009年全行业利税总额为177.2亿元，同比增长70.5%。其中利润104.6亿元，同比增长159.4%；税金72.7亿元，同比增长14.2%。利润占利税的比重为59.0%。内资企业利税总额为97.4亿元，同比增长94.5%。其中利润56.8亿元，同比增长211.1%；税金40.6亿元，同比增长27.6%。利润占利税总额的比重为58.3%。港澳台商投资企业利税总额为9.5亿元，同比增长46.4%。其中利润5.1亿元，同比增长36.9%；税金4.4亿元，同比增长58.9%。利润占利税总额的比重为53.3%。外商投资企业利税总额为70.2亿元，同比增长48.5%。其中利润42.6亿元，同比增长132.7%；税金27.6亿元，同比增长−4.7%。利润占利税总额的比重为60.7%。

全行业人均完成利税79 517元/(人·年)，其中内资企业62 680元/(人·年)，港澳台商投资企业157 037元/(人·年)，外商投资企业114 518元/(人·年)。全行业人均利润46 916元/(人·年)，其中内资企业36 558元/(人·年)，港澳台商投资企业83 762元/(人·年)，外商投资企业69 520元/(人·年)。全行业成本费用利润率为6.86%，其中内资企业6.26%，港澳台商投资企业6.85%，外商投资企业7.87%。全行业亏损企业数160个，同比增长−28.3%，亏损企业数占规模以上企业的19.9%，这比2008年降低了7.4个百分点。其中内资企业136个，占内资企业总数的19.7%，比2008年降低了7.1个百分点；港澳台商投资企业4个，占港澳台商投资企业总数的20.0%，比2008年降低了2.7个百分点；外商投资企业20个，占外商投资企业总数的22.0%，比2008年降低了10.7个百分点。全行业亏损企业亏损总额12.1亿元，同比增长−56.7%。其中内资企业7.1亿元，同比增长−48.9%，占全行业的58.6%；港澳台商投资企业0.3亿元，同比增长−2.8%，占全行业2.6%；外商投资企业4.7亿元，同比增长−65.9%，占全行业的38.8%。

2009年全国规模以上乳制品制造企业共生产乳制品1 935.1万t，同比增长12.9%，产量前5位省份分别为内蒙古379.5万t，同比增长5.9%，占全国的

19.6%；山东202.9万t，同比增长38.1%，占全国的10.5%；河北196.6万t，同比增长3.8%，占全国的10.2%；黑龙江176.8万t，同比增长4.7%，占全国的9.1%；陕西117.2万t，同比增长5.1%，占全国的6.1%（表4）。其中液体乳1 641.6万t，同比增长13.5%。产量前5位省份分别为内蒙古348.5万t，同比增长5.5%，占全国的21.2%；山东189.2万t，同比增长44.8%，占全国的11.5%；河北179.8万t，同比增长2.8%，占全国的11.0%；黑龙江111.5万t，同比增长－0.1%，占全国的6.8%；江苏93.6万t，同比增长16.7%，占全国的5.7%（表5）。乳粉产量为111.7万t，同比增长11.1%。乳粉生产主要分布于黑龙江和内蒙古及西部地区，其中产量前5位的省份为黑龙江41.7万t，同比增长13.5%，占总产量的37.4%；内蒙古24.6万t，同比增长15.7%，占总产量的22.0%；陕西8.1万t，同比增长29.2%，占总产量的7.3%；新疆4.9万t，同比增长－8.4%，占总产量的4.4%；湖南4.6万t，同比增长41.1%，占总产量的4.1%（表6）。

表4　2009年全国乳制品产量前5位省份情况

地区	产量（万t）	比2008年增长（%）	占全国比例（%）
全国总计	**1 935.1**	**12.9**	**100.0**
内蒙古	379.5	5.9	19.6
山　东	202.9	38.1	10.5
河　北	196.6	3.8	10.2
黑龙江	176.8	4.7	9.1
陕　西	117.2	5.1	6.1

表5　2009年全国液体乳产量前5位省份情况

地区	产量（万t）	比2008年增长（%）	占全国比例（%）
全国总计	**1 641.6**	**13.5**	**100.0**
内蒙古	348.5	5.5	21.2
山　东	189.2	44.8	11.5
河　北	179.8	2.8	11.0
黑龙江	111.5	－0.1	6.8
江　苏	93.6	16.7	5.7

表6　2009年全国乳粉产量前5位省份情况

地区	产量（万t）	比2008年增长（%）	占全国比例（%）
全国总计	**111.7**	**11.1**	**100.0**
黑龙江	41.7	13.5	37.4
内蒙古	24.6	15.7	22.0
陕　西	8.1	29.2	7.3
新　疆	4.9	－8.4	4.4
湖　南	4.6	41.1	4.1

2009年全国完成乳制品工业产值最多的5个省份分别为内蒙古322.8亿元，同比增长10.8%，占全国的19.4%；黑龙江283.0亿元，同比增长25.2%，占全国的17.0%；山东157.7亿元，同比增长11.0%，占全国的9.5%；河北118.7亿元，同比增长－0.8%，占全国的7.1%；广东96.2亿元，同比增长12.3%，占全国的5.8%（表7）。2008年全国乳制品规模以上企业年平均人数为22.3万人，应付工资89.2亿元，付福利费用5.9亿元（表8）。2009年我国私营企业继续得到发展，至2009年底共有企业350个，比2008年增加2个；实现工业总产值287.4亿元，同比增长18.1%，占全行业的17.2%；利税总额25.9亿元，同比增长31.8%，占全行业的14.6%；利润总额14.3亿元，同比增长42.9%，占全行业13.6%。

表7　2009年全国规模以上乳制品产值前5位省份情况

地区	产值（亿元）	比2008年增长（%）	占全国比例（%）
全国总计	**1 668.1**	**11.9**	**100.0**
内蒙古	322.8	10.8	19.4
黑龙江	283.0	25.2	17.0
山　东	157.7	11.0	9.5
河　北	118.7	－0.8	7.1
广　东	96.2	12.3	5.8

表8　2008年全国乳制品行业企业性质分布情况

类别	年平均人数（人）	应付工资总额（亿元）	应付福利总额（亿元）
全国总计	**222 878**	**89.2**	**5.9**
其中：内资企业	155 464	54.0	3.8
港澳台商投资企业	6 070	3.8	0.1
外商投资企业	61 344	32.5	2.0

（三）产品结构

2009年，全行业乳粉产量约112万t。据中国乳制品工业协会对103个会员单位（工业总产值占全行业的89.2%）的统计，在乳粉类产品中，全脂乳粉占24%，全脂加糖乳粉占4%，脱脂乳粉占2%，婴幼儿乳粉占52%，中老年乳粉占7%，调味乳粉占7%，其他乳粉占4%。2009年，全国奶油产量约3.5万t；干酪产量约1.5万t，其中原干酪约占9.3%，加工干酪约占90.7%；炼乳产量约16万t，其中甜炼乳约占97%，无糖炼乳约占3%。2009年，全国液体乳产量为1 641.6万t，其中巴氏杀菌乳约占13%，灭菌乳约占68%，酸乳约占19%。

（四）大型骨干企业

2009年，完成工业总产值前10位的企业工业总产值达1 022.8亿元，占全国规模以上企业工业总产值的61.3%（表9）；销售收入前10位的企业销售收入达1 011.2亿元，占全国规模以上企业总销售收入的62.3%（表10）；利税总额前10位的企业完成利税总额153.8亿元，占全国规模以上企业利税总额的86.8%（表11）；乳粉产量前10位企业总产量59.9万t，占全行业的53.6%（表12）；液体乳产量前10位的企业总产量达743.5万t，占全国规模以上企业液体乳总产量的45.3%（表13）。

表9　2009年乳制品生产企业工业总产值位居前列的企业

单位名称	工业总产值（万元）	单位名称	工业总产值（万元）
内蒙古蒙牛乳业（集团）股份有限公司	2 615 388	黑龙江摇篮乳业股份有限公司	277 911
内蒙古伊利实业集团股份有限公司	2 510 000	西安银桥生物科技有限责任公司	274 606
杭州娃哈哈集团有限公司	1 875 116	圣元营养食品有限公司	245 318
维维集团	927 100	北京三元食品股份有限公司	237 764
光明乳业股份有限公司	549 164	济南佳宝乳业有限公司	231 815
多美滋婴幼儿食品有限公司	385 812	福州明一乳业有限公司	210 238
黑龙江乳业集团	357 771	广东雅士利集团股份有限公司	195 613
美赞臣营养品（中国）有限公司	355 039	沈阳乳业有限责任公司	175 670
黑龙江省完达山乳业股份有限公司	352 172	新希望乳业控股有限公司	171 315
黑龙江飞鹤乳业有限公司	299 985	哈尔滨太子乳品工业有限公司	138 521

资料来源：中国乳制品工业协会。

表10　2009年乳制品生产企业销售收入位居前列的企业

单位名称	销售收入（万元）	单位名称	销售收入（万元）
内蒙古蒙牛乳业（集团）股份有限公司	2 549 821	黑龙江摇篮乳业股份有限公司	255 677
内蒙古伊利实业集团股份有限公司	2 378 206	圣元营养食品有限公司	243 441
杭州娃哈哈集团有限公司	1 886 389	北京三元食品股份有限公司	237 959
维维集团	899 200	西安银桥生物科技有限责任公司	237 591
光明乳业股份有限公司	794 316	福州明一乳业有限公司	208 213
多美滋婴幼儿食品有限公司	364 759	济南佳宝乳业有限公司	190 855
黑龙江省完达山乳业股份有限公司	335 742	沈阳乳业有限责任公司	175 670
黑龙江乳业集团	308 423	新希望乳业控股有限公司	169 441
黑龙江飞鹤乳业有限公司	300 000	广东雅士利集团股份有限公司	164 613
美赞臣营养品（中国）有限公司	295 425	山西古城乳业集团有限公司	149 554

资料来源：中国乳制品工业协会。

表11　2009年利税总额位居前列的企业

单位名称	利税总额（万元）	单位名称	利税总额（万元）
杭州娃哈哈集团有限公司	669 164	西安银桥生物科技有限责任公司	22 714
内蒙古蒙牛乳业（集团）股份有限公司	266 880	广东雅士利集团股份有限公司	21 916
内蒙古伊利实业集团股份有限公司	224 187	福州明一乳业有限公司	21 432
美赞臣营养品（中国）有限公司	97 782	济南佳宝乳业有限公司	18 780
维维集团	81 116	山西古城乳业集团有限公司	15 702
光明乳业股份有限公司	76 807	沈阳乳业有限责任公司	15 074
黑龙江飞鹤乳业有限公司	39 000	黑龙江兴安岭乳业有限公司	12 465
澳优乳品（湖南）有限公司	30 610	哈尔滨太子乳品工业有限公司	11 081
黑龙江乳业集团	27 937	黑龙江摇篮乳业股份有限公司	10 324
黑龙江省完达山乳业股份有限公司	24 093	江西美庐乳业有限公司	8 635

资料来源：中国乳制品工业协会。

表12　2009年乳粉产量位居前列的企业

单位名称	产量（t）	单位名称	产量（t）
黑龙江飞鹤乳业有限公司	116 478	圣元营养食品有限公司	28 230
内蒙古伊利实业集团股份有限公司	89 345	美赞臣营养品（中国）有限公司	27 072
黑龙江摇篮乳业股份有限公司	87 523	多美滋婴幼儿食品有限公司	24 149
黑龙江省完达山乳业股份有限公司	87 292	江西美庐乳业有限公司	23 310
黑龙江乳业集团	65 128	广东雅士利集团股份有限公司	22 931
西安银桥生物科技有限责任公司	38 215	黑龙江兴安岭乳业有限公司	22 622
福州明一乳业有限公司	35 535	黑龙江省农垦龙王食品有限责任公司	21 635

（续）

单位名称	产量（t）	单位名称	产量（t）
哈尔滨太子乳品工业有限公司	17 534	杭州娃哈哈集团有限公司	15 434
北京三元食品股份有限公司	17 180	山东德正乳业有限公司	13 215
光明乳业股份有限公司	16 471	山西古城乳业集团有限公司	11 860

资料来源：中国乳制品工业协会。

表 13　2009 年液体乳产量位居前列的企业

单位名称	产量（t）	单位名称	产量（t）
内蒙古蒙牛乳业（集团）股份有限公司	2 686 015	新希望乳业控股有限公司	243 298
内蒙古伊利实业集团股份有限公司	1 754 300	石家庄君乐宝乳业有限公司	197 081
光明乳业股份有限公司	700 477	南京卫岗乳业有限公司	173 132
维维集团	473 360	山东亚奥特乳业有限公司	171 890
北京三元食品股份有限公司	344 712	山东得益乳业有限公司	159 035
西安银桥生物科技有限责任公司	332 510	山西古城乳业集团有限公司	143 850
黑龙江乳业集团	307 474	徐州绿健乳业有限责任公司	113 022
黑龙江省完达山乳业股份有限公司	293 453	浙江李子园牛奶食品有限公司	99 543
济南佳宝乳业有限公司	292 560	浙江金华市佳乐乳业有限公司	82 793
沈阳乳业有限责任公司	250 500	宁夏夏进乳业集团股份有限公司	81 427

资料来源：中国乳制品工业协会。

二、市场状况

（一）乳制品消费

中国乳制品制造业经过一年多的调整恢复，正在逐步从 2008 年的危机中走出，但是人们对乳制品的消费仍然比较谨慎，只要有一点儿负面消息，消费者都会非常紧张，由于 2009 年国内乳制品行业“事件”不断，因此这一年国内乳制品消费状况也是在反复中前行。根据国家统计局资料，2009 年全国城镇人均购买鲜奶 14.91kg，奶粉 0.48kg，酸奶 3.88kg，与 2008 年大体相当；农村乳制品消费量得到增长，由 2008 年的 3.43kg 增长到 3.60kg，增长主要来自原本消费较低的中部地区，人均消费由 2008 年的 1.87kg 增长到 2.54kg，可谓增长迅速。

（二）原料乳收购价格

2009 年，全国原料乳收购的平均价格略低于 2008 年。受三聚氰胺事件影响，企业使用国产乳粉量减少，乳粉进口量激增，出口量锐减，乳粉的产区如内蒙古、黑龙江等地，企业乳粉积压严重，部分企业被迫减产或停产，收奶量减少，导致原料乳收购价格下滑；而南方和西部的部分地区却是奶源紧缺，收奶价格有所增加。从地区平均价格来看，东北、华北与 2008 年比有所降低，而华东、华南、中南和西北则比 2008 年有所增加（表 14）。

表 14　2009 年全国部分企业原料乳收购价格　（单位：元/kg）

单位名称	2008 年平均	2009 年平均	单位名称	2008 年平均	2009 年平均
北京三元食品股份有限公司	3.00	2.75	沈阳乳业有限责任公司	2.20	2.70
多加多乳业（天津）有限公司	3.10	3.15	吉林省乳业集团广泽有限公司	2.66	2.29
天津海河乳业有限公司	2.29	2.84	哈尔滨惠佳贝食品有限公司	2.68	2.86
天津津河乳业有限公司	2.89	3.37	哈尔滨乳多宝乳业有限责任公司	2.95	2.70
天津中芬乳业有限公司	2.86	2.60	哈尔滨太子乳品工业有限公司	2.73	2.63
河北乖乖嘉年华食品有限公司	2.12	2.25	黑龙江澳佳乳业有限公司	3.00	3.20
石家庄君乐宝乳业有限公司	2.50	2.31	黑龙江辰鹰乳业有限公司	2.14	2.52
山西古城乳业集团有限公司	2.78	3.26	黑龙江飞鹤乳业有限公司	2.65	2.59
山西田仁乳业有限责任公司	2.19	2.57	黑龙江乳业集团	2.90	2.80
呼伦贝尔海乳乳业有限责任公司	2.38	1.63	黑龙江省富裕明星食品有限公司	2.66	2.41
内蒙古红城乳业有限公司	2.34	1.78	黑龙江省格球山乳品有限责任公司	2.30	2.60
内蒙古蒙牛乳业（集团）股份有限公司	3.15	3.06	黑龙江省农垦华威乳业有限公司	2.95	2.10
内蒙古伊利实业集团股份有限公司	3.05	3.04	黑龙江省农垦龙王食品有限责任公司	2.20	2.30
本溪木兰花乳业有限公司	2.82	2.83	黑龙江省完达山乳业股份有限公司	2.76	2.41

（续）

单位名称	2008年平均	2009年平均	单位名称	2008年平均	2009年平均
黑龙江兴安岭乳业有限公司	2.54	2.40	圣元营养食品有限公司	2.76	2.49
黑龙江摇篮乳业股份有限公司	3.40	2.30	威海金宝乳业有限公司	2.30	2.60
光明乳业股份有限公司	3.86	3.66	河南花花牛乳业有限公司	3.05	2.40
上海晨冠乳业有限公司	3.12	3.76	河南三剑客奶业有限责任公司	2.70	2.90
南京卫岗乳业有限公司	3.09	3.13	河南三色鸽乳业有限公司	2.80	2.60
维维集团	2.10	2.90	焦作市博农乳业有限责任公司	2.20	2.80
徐州绿健乳业有限责任公司	2.80	2.80	洛阳巨尔乳业有限公司	2.60	2.65
杭州娃哈哈集团有限公司	2.62	2.29	湖南南山食品有限公司	2.78	2.88
杭州味全食品有限公司	4.40	3.80	湖南亚华乳业有限公司	2.85	2.97
宁波市牛奶集团有限公司	3.62	3.50	湖南阳光乳业股份有限公司	2.80	3.00
瑞安市百好乳业有限公司	2.50	3.40	广东东泰乳业有限公司	3.45	3.57
浙江金华市佳乐乳业有限公司	2.64	2.93	广东燕塘乳业有限公司	3.34	3.78
浙江李子园牛奶食品有限公司	2.90	3.24	深圳市晨光乳业有限公司	4.43	4.24
浙江熊猫乳品有限公司	2.45	2.26	广西皇氏甲天下乳业股份有限公司	3.16	3.82
安徽益益乳业有限公司	2.90	2.90	广西灵山百强水牛奶乳业有限公司	5.80	6.80
滁州市奶业有限责任公司	2.65	2.56	四川菊乐食品有限公司	3.15	3.35
福建长富乳品有限公司	3.00	3.18	新希望乳业控股有限公司	2.42	2.85
江西美庐乳业有限公司	2.86	2.95	贵阳三联乳业有限公司	2.60	3.08
江西牛牛乳业有限责任公司	3.20	3.20	贵州好一多乳业股份有限公司	3.44	3.45
江西维雀乳业有限公司	2.80	3.00	大理来思尔乳业有限责任公司	2.10	2.06
济南佳宝乳业有限公司	2.79	2.66	大理银河乳业有限责任公司	2.50	2.80
临沂盛能乳业有限责任公司	2.75	2.80	陕西关山乳业有限责任公司	2.20	2.35
山东百慧乳业有限公司	2.60	2.60	陕西和氏乳品有限公司	2.31	3.60
山东得益乳业有限公司	2.81	2.61	陕西红星乳业有限公司	2.60	2.60
山东德正乳业有限公司	1.96	2.60	西安银桥生物科技有限责任公司	2.75	2.98
山东凤祥乳业有限公司	2.91	2.33	兰州庄园乳业有限责任公司	2.20	2.60
山东鹏程食品股份有限公司	2.00	2.40	宁夏红果乳业有限公司	2.41	2.10
山东亚奥特乳业有限公司	3.18	3.20	宁夏夏进乳业集团股份有限公司	2.58	2.21
山东银香大地乳业有限公司	2.60	2.70	新疆明旺乳业有限公司	2.74	2.13

资料来源：中国乳制品工业协会。

（三）进出口

1. 进口　2009年，三鹿奶粉事件影响依然，加之国际乳制品价格较2008年度有所降低，致使我国乳制品进口量大增，尤其是乳粉类产品更是增长1倍以上。2009年1～12月份，我国乳制品累计进口量达59.7万t，货值10.3亿美元，同比分别增长70.2%和19.3%。其他乳制品（乳糖、零售包装婴幼儿乳粉、干酪素、乳清蛋白粉等）累计进口量14.1万t，货值7.4亿美元，同比分别增长30.6%和38.7%。其中，乳粉进口量为24.7万t，货值5.8亿美元，同比分别增长144.3%和45.8%；乳清粉进口28.9万t，货值2.8亿美元，同比分别增长35.5%和-8.9%；奶油进口2.8万t，货值0.66亿美元，同比分别增长109.9%和11.2%；干酪进口1.7万t，货值0.70亿美元，同比分别增长22.1%和-5.6%（表15）。

表15　2009年乳制品进口情况

产品名称		数量（t）	比2008年增长（%）	金额（万美元）	比2008年增长（%）
液体乳		12 779	71.9	1 970	57.3
乳粉	脱脂乳粉	70 443	28.2	15 601	-27.4
	全脂乳粉	174 969	298.2	41 953	140.0
	调味乳粉	1 375	-35.2	486	-41.5
	合计	246 787	144.3	58 041	45.8
炼乳		1 732	103.2	398	27.0
酸乳		1 526	94.4	436	51.9
乳清粉		288 754	35.5	28 422	-8.9
奶油		28 444	109.9	6 566	11.2
干酪		16 977	22.1	6 966	-5.6
乳品合计		**596 999**	**70.2**	**102 799**	**19.3**

数据来源：中国海关。

2009年进口的其他乳制品中，乳糖类产品5.96万t，同比增长7.1%，货值3 441万美元，同比增长−21.4%；零售包装婴幼儿乳粉进口量为6.2万t，同比增长47.9%，货值6.05亿美元，同比增长52.6%(表16)；

表16　2009年其他乳制品进口情况

产品名称	数量（t）	比2008年增长（%）	金额（万美元）	比2008年增长（%）
乳糖类	59 592	7.1	3 441	−21.4
零售包装婴幼儿乳粉	62 442	47.9	60 452	52.6
酪蛋白类	6 253	39.8	4 299	−22.8
白蛋白类	12 365	130.7	5 854	53.1
合　计	**140 653**	**30.6**	**74 046**	**38.7**

数据来源：中国海关。

2. **出口**　与进口大幅增长形成鲜明对比的是，2009年我国乳制品出口持续低迷。2009年1～12月份，共出口乳制品3.68万t，同比增长−69.5%，还不到“三鹿事件”前每年出口量的1/3；出口金额0.57亿美元，同比增长−81.1%。其他乳制品累计出口量1 664t，同比增长−69.0%；货值863万美元，同比增长−74.3%。其中，液体乳出口2.0万t，同比增长−47.9%；货值1 334万美元，同比增长−54.9%。乳粉出口0.97万t，同比增长−84.7%；货值0.31亿美元，同比增长−87.0%。炼乳出口3 692t，同比增长−54.2%；货值571万美元，同比增长−51.2%。其他乳制品中酪蛋白类出口1 362t，同比增长−70.5%；货值730万美元，同比增长−77.5%（表17、表18）。

表17　2009年乳制品出口情况

产品名称		数量（t）	比2008年增长（%）	金额（万美元）	比2008年增长（%）
液体乳		20 030	−47.9	1 334	−54.9
乳粉	脱脂乳粉	0	−99.9	0	−99.9
	全脂乳粉	8 051	−86.4	2 561	−88.4
	调味乳粉	1 687	−45.4	525	−48.9
	合计	9 738	−84.7	3 086	−87.0
炼　乳		3 692	−54.2	571	−51.2
酸　乳		844	−23.6	115	−33.3
乳清粉		316	−92.7	34	−93.0
奶　油		2 046	−58.8	501	−70.8
干　酪		115		48	
乳品合计		**36 780**	**−69.5**	**5 689**	**−81.1**

数据来源：中国海关。

表18　2009年其他乳制品出口情况

产品名称	数量（t）	比2008年增长（%）	金额（万美元）	比2008年增长（%）
乳糖类	102	−82.7	22	−47.7
零售包装婴幼儿乳粉	152	31.5	88	77.4
酪蛋白类	1362	−70.5	730	−77.5
白蛋白类	48	47.9	23	19.4
合　计	**1664**	**−69.0**	**863**	**−74.3**

数据来源：中国海关。

2009年1～12月份，全国进出口乳制品数量逆差56.0万t，进出口货值逆差9.7亿美元，分别比2008年度增长143.5%和73.2%。

三、政策法规及重要活动

（一）政策法规

（1）2009年卫生部组织对乳制品标准进行清理，并开始了质量安全国家标准的制定工作。本次乳品质量安全标准清理制定工作完成后，最终有66项乳品质量安全标准通过国家食品安全审评委员会的审核，包括产品标准15项、生产规范2项、检测方法标准49项，并已于2010年3月26日发布。

（2）为帮助乳品企业度过行业危机下的艰难时光，2009年初财政部将原定的贴息政策实施期限延长3个月至2009年3月底。此后，财政部于7月底再次宣布将原料奶收购贷款中央财政贴息政策的实施期限延续至2009年12月底，至此原料乳收购贷款中央财政贴息政策的实施期限已由原来的3个月延长至15个月。

（3）2009年初农业部制定了《2009年生鲜乳专项整治行动实施方案》和《全国奶牛优势区域布局规划（2008—2015年）》。

（4）2009年2月28日，《中华人民共和国食品安全法》（第9号主席令）公布，包括总则、食品安全风险监测和评估、食品安全标准、食品生产经营、食品检验、食品进出口、食品安全事故处置、监督管理、法律责任和附则等内容。该法将生产企业作为食品安全的第一责任人，要求食品生产经营者应当依照法律、法规和食品安全标准从事生产经营活动，对社会和公众负责，保证食品安全，接受社会监督，承担社会责任。对原料使用、生产、销售、进出口等内容进行规定，明确了部门的监管职责，并要求建立食品召回制度、统一食品国家安全标准和取消食品“免检制度”等。该法自2009年6月1日起实施。

（5）2009年7月20日，《中华人民共和国食品安全法实施条例》（第557号国务院令）公布实施，《实施条例》各章与《食品安全法》相对应，主要是为了进一步落实企业作为食品安全第一责任人的责任，强化事先预防和生产经营过程控制，以及食品发生安全事故后的可追溯，进一步强化各部门在食品安全监管方面的职责，完善监管部门在分工负责与统一协调相结合体制中的相互协调、衔接与配合，并将食品安全法一些较为原则的规定具体化，增强制度的可操作性。

（6）2009年3月23日，农业部发布了《生鲜乳收购站标准化管理技术规范》，对生鲜乳收购站的基础设施、机械设备、质量检验、人员要求、操作规范、管理制度、卫生条件做出具体规定。

(7) 2009 年 4 月 22 日，卫生部等 6 部门发布《关于加强生鲜乳品抗生素残留量管理的公告》(2009 年第 6 号)，禁止企业进行“无抗奶”的宣传，规范市场秩序。

(8) 2009 年 6 月 5 日，卫生部等 7 部委下发了《关于贯彻实施〈食品安全法〉有关问题的通知》，要求各地部门要依法履行监管责任，加强食品安全各环节的监管，做好工作衔接。做好企业食品标准备案工作，自 2009 年 6 月 1 日起，卫生部门负责食品企业标准备案工作，质检部门不再负责食品企业标准备案工作，之前已经备案的企业标准继续有效。各有关部门督促企业进行自查清理，企业生产的食品没有食品安全国家标准或者地方标准的，应当制定企业标准，作为组织生产的依据。各省级卫生行政部门要按照企业标准备案工作的要求，开展食品企业标准备案工作，加强企业标准备案管理工作。要规范食品相关产品企业生产行为，各生产单位要在 2010 年 6 月 1 日前完成自查清理工作，并依照相关规定和程序对未列入食品安全国家标准的食品相关产品及新品种向卫生部申请批准。另外通知还要求，要扎实推进食品安全整顿工作，认真贯彻执行食品安全标准、加强风险监测和评估体系建设。

(9) 2009 年 6 月 26 日，国家工业和信息化部、国家发展和改革委员会联合发布了《乳制品工业产业政策（2009 年修订）》(工联产业 [2009] 第 48 号)，该政策是根据《乳品质量安全监督管理条例》、《中华人民共和国食品安全法》及相关法律法规规定，结合乳制品工业发展的实际情况，对原《乳制品工业产业政策》、《乳制品加工行业准入条件》进行了整合修订而成的。该版产业政策在原 2008 版产业政策的基础上加入了乳制品流通和监督管理的内容，具体为：政策目标、产业布局、行业准入、奶源供应、技术与装备、投资融资、产品结构、质量安全、组织结构、资源节约与环境保护、消费和流通、监督管理、其他及名词解释等。产业政策提出了稳定可控的奶源基地产生鲜乳数量的概念，并且对新建加工项目（企业）选址、生鲜乳收购、检测、原辅料做了具体要求。乳制品加工企业要加强市场销售跟踪服务，建立和完善重大事项应急处置制度和机制。发现其生产的乳制品不符合乳制品质量安全标准、存在危害人体健康和生命安全危险或者可能危害婴幼儿身体健康或者生长发育的，应立即停止生产，报告有关主管部门，告知经销商、消费者，召回已经出厂、上市销售的乳制品，并记录召回情况。乳制品加工企业对召回的乳制品应当采取销毁、无害化处理等措施，防止其再次流入市场。各级地方工业主管部门会同相关部门负责对本地乳制品生产企业执行本产业政策的情况进行监督检查。各省、自治区、直辖市工业主管部门负责依法淘汰落后乳制品加工生产能力，对属地符合准入条件的乳制品生产企业实行社会公告，接受社会舆论监督。

(10) 2009 年 7 月 17 日，工业和信息化部、财政部及商务部正式下发奶粉收储相关文件，正式启动 5 万 t 奶粉收储计划，收购以贴息的形式进行。

(11) 2009 年 9 月 27 日，国家质量监督检验检疫总局印发《乳制品生产企业落实质量安全主体责任监督检查规定》的通知，包括总则、生产企业质量安全主体责任、监督检查程序、监督检查结果处理、监督检查工作要求、附则等内容。《规定》2009 年 10 月 1 日起施行。

(12) 2009 年 12 月 30 日，工业和信息化部、国家发展和改革委员会、监察部、农业部、商务部、卫生部、中国人民银行、国家工商总局、国家质量监督检验检疫总局和国家食品药品监管局 10 部委在人民大会堂举办《食品工业企业诚信体系建设工作指导意见》发布暨试点启动仪式。宣布在黑龙江省乳制品行业、河南省肉类加工行业启动企业试点工作。此次启动仪式标志着全面推进食品工业企业诚信体系建设工作正式启动。

(二) 三鹿牌婴幼儿乳粉事件后续处理工作

2009 年 1 月 21 日，石家庄市中级人民法院作出刑事判决，认定被告人张玉军犯以危险方法危害公共安全罪，判处死刑，剥夺政治权利终身；认定被告人耿金平犯生产、销售有毒食品罪，判处死刑，剥夺政治权利终身，并处没收个人全部财产。三鹿集团股份有限公司等 22 个责任企业愿意向患儿主动赔偿，对近 30 万名确诊患儿给予一次性现金赔偿，并共同出资建立了医疗赔偿基金，患儿今后一旦出现相关后遗症，发生的医疗费由该基金给予报销。人保部、卫生部、保监会于 2009 年 1 月 8 日下发了《关于做好婴幼儿奶粉事件患儿相关疾病医疗费用支付工作的通知》，强调为保障因食用含三聚氰胺婴幼儿配方奶粉而患病婴幼儿的权益，由对此次事件负有责任的企业出资建立患儿医疗赔偿基金，并委托中国人寿保险股份有限公司代管，对患儿急性治疗终结后到 18 周岁以前可能发生的与此相关的疾病给予免费治疗。

(三) 并购及新扩建

(1) 2009 年 2 月，新希望乳业以 6 450 万元受让昆明雪兰 42.9%国有股权和“雪兰”商标。

(2) 2009 年 2 月 20 日，蒙牛马鞍山现代牧业有限公司项目在肥东县白龙镇长王村开工建设。项目总投资6.5亿元人民币，建设规模为2万头，项目分两期建设，计划在两年内完成。2009年8月底前从国外引进不少于3 000头优质高产的纯种荷斯坦奶牛，2009年年底前引进6 000头；2010年底前达到16 000头，至2011年底达到20 000头的奶牛存量。同时，征用6.67hm^2永久性农业建设用地，用于乳制品加工。

(3) 2009年3月，雅培公司耗资约合2亿元人民币打造的雅培，在华首家营养品工厂在广州开发区竣工并投产。广州工厂的产品将专供中国市场，工厂将全部采用来自新西兰的奶源。

(4) 2009年3月4日，三元集团与三元食品的全资子公司河北三元组成的“联合竞拍体”最终以6.17亿元成功拍得三鹿资产，包括三鹿集团的土地使用权、房屋建筑物、机器设备等可持续经营的有效资产和三鹿集团所持有的新乡市林鹤乳业有限公司98.80%的投资权益。

(5) 2009年3月6日，光明乳业股份有限公司以1元价格出售江西英雄51%股份，同时将1亿多元的债权余额整体作价2 000万元一并转让予华恒实业。江西英雄不再被许可使用“光明”乳制品商标。

(6) 2009年6月，完达山并购河北贝兰德乳业51%的股权，成立了河北完达山贝兰德乳业有限公司。9月8日，完达山乳业收购宝泉岭圣元乳业资产。

(7) 2009年7月6日，中粮集团与厚朴投资共同组建一家新的公司(中粮集团持股70%)，投入61亿港币分别向蒙牛认购新股，以及向老股东购买现有股份，新公司在分别完成相关收购后将持有蒙牛扩大后股本的20%，成为“中国蒙牛”第一大股东。

(8) 2009年7月10日，伊利天津奶粉项目的签约仪式在天津市滨海新区举行。此次伊利投资兴建的天津奶粉项目，投产后年销售收入预计可达20亿元左右，将是华北地区规模最大的奶粉项目。

(9) 2009年7月28日，光明食品(集团)有限公司接盘上海实业控股有限公司手中30.18%的股权，共计3.14亿股，收购价为15.5亿元，转让后，光明食品将直接和间接持有光明乳业65.45%的股份。

(10) 2009年9月中旬，光明乳业德州有限公司二期工程正式投产，此次扩建总投资达到1.2亿元。

(11) 2009年9月20日，凯雷投资集团、上海复星高科技(集团)有限公司向雅士利注资，分别占有雅士利17.3%和6%股份，成为其战略股东。

(12) 2009年9月28日，柳州三元搬迁新建乳品加工厂项目开工，该项目占地1.33 hm^2，厂房建筑面积5 000 m^2，总投资约2 500万元，建设周期一年，投产后的生产能力约为3万t。

(13) 2009年11月初，三元母公司首都农业集团与河北国信资产运营有限公司签署协议，购买后者所持唐山三鹿、恒天然三鹿牧场等资产。根据协议，首农集团将购买国信资产。5月5日、5月8日通过公开竞拍方式取得的石家庄三鹿集团股份有限公司原持有的唐山三鹿70%的股权，唐山康圣乳业70%的股权以及唐山恒天然三鹿牧场15%的股权。

(四) 行业重大活动

(1) 2009年6月1日是第9个世界牛奶日，6月6～10日是第12个全国乳品营养周，2009年宣传的主题是“安全、诚信、和谐”。中国乳制品工业协会从2009年4月份就开始了牛奶质量安全的宣传活动，在央视、《经济日报》等媒体做了报道；接受了央视《新闻会客厅》、《面对面》等栏目和慧聪网、中国经济网的专访。在协会的号召下，全国各地方协会和骨干企业在当地开展了形式多样的乳品营养宣传活动。天津、上海、陕西、河南、湖南和宁夏等省、自治区、直辖市的地方协会和乳制品骨干企业均在当地举行了行之有效的宣传活动，促进了乳品消费信心的恢复和营养知识的普及。6月9日，由中国乳制品工业协会主办的“2009年世界牛奶日”和“全国乳品营养周”(以下称乳品营养周)宣传活动在北京举行。乳品营养周的宣传主题是：“国产牛奶放心喝”。伊利、蒙牛、三元和君乐宝等4个国产品牌乳制品企业向北京市属社会福利院捐赠了5 000箱牛奶。北京市接受救灾捐赠事务管理中心向4个企业颁发了证书和证明。活动期间，还召开了乳制品质量安全报告会。国家工业与信息化部消费品工业司、国家发展和改革委员会、国家质量监督检验检疫总局食品司市场准入处、北京市社会福利事务管理中心、北京市接受救灾捐赠事务管理中心、市属福利院代表以及中国农业大学乳品专家和企业代表等出席了活动并讲话或作报告。中国乳制品工业协会理事长宋昆冈做了《国产牛奶放心喝，中国乳业从危机到信心》的报告，常务副理事长牟静君出席活动并讲话。

(2) 2009年8月21～23日，“中国乳制品工业协会第十五次年会暨第九次乳品技术精品展示会”在南京召开。来自全国乳制品行业及相关行业的代表共千余人出席会议。会议围绕“实践科学发展观，建设和谐乳业”的主题，深刻反思“三聚氰胺事件”发生的根源，认真汲取经验教训，提出了建设和谐乳业、推动乳制品行业健康、持续发展的思路。会议总结了三聚氰胺事件发生以来国务院及有关部门为推动行业健康发展所采取的政策措施以及行业贯彻执行情况、行业整改工作所取得的成效；分析了目前行业所面临的形势和存在的主要问题，提出了解决问题的建议。国家工业和信化部消费品工业司、南京市政府的领导出席开幕式并发表重要讲话。中国乳制品工业协会理事长宋昆冈作了题为《实践科学发展观，建设和谐乳业》的主题报告，报告中全面分析了导致三聚氰胺事件发生的五个方面的原因，指出了目前行业发展中所存在的问题，提出了建设和谐乳业的构想：建设和谐的原料乳收购秩序；建立和谐的市场秩序；建立和谐的企业关系；建立与消费者的和谐关系，树立正确的成本、价格观，消除低成本低价格的“唯价格论”的经营理念，树立科学的新产品开发和产品差异化观念。年会期间，分别举行了“自律、和谐、科学发展企业家辩论会”、“国际乳业市场及新科技发展趋势”、“市场经济‘立交桥’”和“质量安全宣贯大讲堂”四个专场论坛，各论坛分别围绕不同的主题，邀请数十位国内外知名企业家、专家等作了精彩的发言。年会同期举办第九次乳品技术精品展示会，展出面积1万多m^2，展位400余个，包括来自美国、法国、德国、丹麦、荷兰、俄罗斯等国和国内近200个知名机械设备、包装材料、印刷、乳制品生产配料及添加剂等企业参加展出。

（中国乳制品工业协会　岳增君）

烟 草 加 工 业

2009年是新世纪以来我国经济发展最为困难的一年，也是烟草行业坚决贯彻中央决策部署，坚定信心，主动应对，扎实工作，各方面工作取得明显成效的一年。烟草行业面对市场环境重大变化和卷烟税收政策重大调整，在党中央、国务院和工业和信息化部的领导下，以邓小平理论和“三个代表”重要思想为指导，深入贯彻落实科学发展观，围绕年初确定的“烟叶防过热，卷烟上水平，税利保增长”目标任务，全面抓好各项工作的推进和落实，在全行业干部职工艰苦努力下，继续保持了良好发展态势。

一、基本情况

2009年，全年实现工商税利5 131.13亿元，同比增加559.26亿元，增长12.23%。其中，实现税费（含国有资本收益）4 163.4亿元，同比增加864.6亿元，增长26.21%。这一年，我国烟叶生产面临复杂多变形势，存在明显偏热苗头。针对烟叶生产出现的新情况新问题，国家烟草专卖局冷静分析，果断决策，明确提出把“烟叶防过热”作为行业工作的中心任务，要求通过扎实开展现代烟草农业建设，全面加强烟叶工作管理，努力提高烟叶工作水平，保持烟叶生产稳定发展。各烟叶产区按照国家局要求，以高度负责态度，认真抓好各项措施落实，烟叶生产总体保持了良好发展。全年卷烟出口357万件，同比增长21%。其中，境外生产卷烟171万件，同比增长12.9%。烟草进出口总值27.32亿美元，同比增长28.41%。其中，出口总值8.74亿美元，同比增长18.26%。

二、科研、新产品、新技术

2009年，行业以增强企业核心竞争力为目标，高度重视自主创新，建立健全行业科研创新体系，将工业企业技术中心建设摆在更加突出的位置，完善标准化和质量监督体系，实施重大项目带动战略、知识产权战略和标准化战略，努力在关键技术上取得重大突破，为增强行业总体竞争实力、实现企业由大变强和行业的可持续发展提供强有力的技术支撑，推动了烟草科技工作的深入开展，为建设“严格规范、富有效率、充满活力”的中国烟草作出了新的贡献。完善了烟草基因组计划重大专项方案并提交国家局办公会审议，着手筹备组建国家烟草基因研究中心。成立了减害技术重大专项专家委员会，审议确定了卷烟减害技术重大专项2009年度立项项目计划和经费安排。会同烟叶公司完成了特色优质烟叶开发重大专项方案的编制工作并正式启动，确定了特色优质烟叶开发重大专项2009年度立项项目和经费安排。成立了卷烟增香保润重大专项专家委员会，会同运行司共同审议确定卷烟增香保润重大专项——减害降焦课题。印发了《国家烟草专卖局关于大力推进卷烟减害降焦努力提升技术创新水平的意见》，确定了今后一段时期行业减害降焦工作的目标和主攻任务。完成了2008年度国产卷烟7种有害成分释放量分析检测工作，确定了国产卷烟7种有害成分释放水平。深入开展了卷烟危害性指标体系的验证和深化研究、卷烟辅助材料、卷烟配方设计参数对主流烟气霍夫曼分析物的影响研究、卷烟减害应用技术研究。

在重大专项中，一是烟草育种课题完成了16个烟草新品种的审定工作，推进中国烟草种质资源平台建设，正式启用中国烟草种质资源库实物库和网络系统，研究确定了2009年度中国烟草种质资源库的供种计划，进行了中国烟草种质资源平台建设2009年度中期检查工作，起草了中国烟草育种工作协作平台方案，完成了中国烟草种植区划研究成果的汇编和发布工作。二是卷烟调香课题完成行业首期卷烟高级调香师、调香师班学员国内教学、论文答辩和国外培训任务，完成2007年度卷烟调香方向工程硕士研究生班教学工作，进行了行业今后3年卷烟调香人才培养需求情况调研。三是特色工艺课题启动了低强度松散回潮技术与设备研究开发、分段式低温滚筒叶丝干燥技术与设备研究开发研究项目，组织开展卷烟品牌多点加工均质化研究、面向分组加工及订单生产的柔性制造系统研究。继续开展烟梗膨胀制粒、隧道式多喷嘴加料（香）机等关键主机设备的研制；研究确定了国产造纸法再造烟叶发展思路，提出了国产造纸法再造烟叶今后发展方向和攻关任务。

三、国内外市场概况

（一）国内市场概况

1. 现代烟草农业建设取得实质性进展。按照“一基四化”总体要求，全国共安排现代烟草农业试点单位143个，其中整县推进3个，整乡推进41个。进一步加强烟叶生产基础设施建设。全年共安排专项资金99.7亿元，同比增加18.3亿元，增长22.45%；新建密集式烤房16.59万座，新修机耕路9 097.12 km、沟渠 9 669.21km。全国商品化供苗面积达94%，同比提高12.7个百分点；机械化整地比例57.7%，同比提高8.7个百分点；密集式烤房烘烤比例66.8%，同比提高20个百分点。通过采取以上措施，促进了烟农增产增收。据统计分析，2009年烟叶平均单产达到2280kg/hm^2，同比增加13.5kg；均价每千克 14.4 元，同比增加 0.28 元；种烟农户150.61万户，户均收入达2.44万元。

2. 全行业始终坚持“控制总量、稍紧平衡”方针，切实抓好“保牌、稳价、规范、增效”各项措施落实，把“保增长”建立在尊重市场规律、优化资源配置、规范经营秩序、保持价格稳定、切实加强管理“五个基础”之上，确保了税利增长目标顺利实现。一是精心组织卷烟消费税政策调整工作。经过努力，按静态算账，全年增加消费税594亿元，圆满完成中央财政增收任务。二是努力保持卷烟产销协调发展。卷烟产销保持稳定增长。全国现有持证卷烟零售客户495.3万户，卷烟零售毛利率达到8.9%。三是重点骨干品牌保持持续增长。在严峻复杂的经济形势面前，重点骨干品牌良好发展趋势没有改变，集中度进一步提高，这是2009年经济运行一大亮点，也是实现税利增长的关键所在。四是开拓国际市场取得新的进展。加快推进烟叶进口境外实体化运作，继续推动与跨国烟草公司合作，积极支持卷烟工业境外办厂。全年卷烟出口357万件，同比增长21%。其中，境外生产卷烟171万件，同比增长12.9%；烟草进出口总值27.32亿美元，同比增长28.41%。其中，出口总值8.74亿美元，同比增长18.26%。

（二）国外市场概况

世界烟草产业是全球化程度和市场集中度最高的产业之一，目前在中国以外的国际烟草市场上，菲莫国际公司、英美烟草公司、日本烟草公司和帝国烟草公司这4家跨国烟草公司，基本都是在120～180个国家和地区开展业务，2009年上述4家跨国烟草公司卷烟销量占中国以外国际卷烟市场的比重达64%。

1. 菲莫国际公司是世界第一大跨国烟草公司

2009年，菲莫国际公司继续推进并购重组，投资4.52亿美元收购哥伦比亚第二大烟草公司Protabaco（预计2010年上半年完成最终收购）。投资2.56亿美元收购瑞典火柴公司在南非的鼻烟和烟丝业务；在挪威、法国等收购了一些烟丝商标。同时，针对不同的目标市场，菲莫国际公司强化产品创新，丰富“万宝路”红色、金色、黑色和淡蓝系列产品，对“百乐门”和“蓝星”品牌进行升级改造，对高、中、低档品牌进行优化组合。为应对金融危机的影响，菲莫国际公司实施效率提升和成本节约计划，通过优化生产布局、改进原料供应和加强现金流管理等，较为有效地减少了成本费用支出。总体来看，凭借强大的品牌优势，立足于宽广的市场领域，菲莫国际公司2009年卷烟销量基本稳定。其中“万宝路”销量为3 020亿支，比上年下降2.8%；“蓝星”销量为908亿支，比上年下降1.7%。从地区市场来看，2009年菲莫国际公司在亚洲市场销售卷烟2 262亿支，比上年增长1.1%，其中“万宝路”销量比上年增长4.3%。在欧盟市场销售卷烟2 353亿支，比上年下降3.3%；在东欧、中东和非洲市场销售卷烟2 987亿支，比上年下降1.5%；在拉美和加拿大市场销售卷烟1 038亿支，比上年增长4.4%。在卷烟销量出现下降的同时，2009年菲莫国际公司非卷烟类烟草制品销量比上年增长了33.2%。受卷烟销量下降和美元升值的影响，2009年菲莫国际公司主要财务指标—销售收入、税收、利润等出现了不同程度的下降。

2. 英美烟草公司是世界第二大跨国烟草公司 2009年，英美烟草公司原董事会主席杜立石宣布辞职并出任全球矿业巨头力拓集团的董事长，63岁的前爱尔兰银行行长理查德?巴罗斯成为英美烟草公司新任董事会主席。高层变动没有改变英美烟草公司的既定战略，2009年英美烟草公司继续推进并购重组，投资4.94亿美元收购了印度尼西亚第4大卷烟制造商本图公司85%的股份；以培育4大"全球驱动品牌"为核心，积极推进品牌扩张；通过重组生产点和加强供应链管理，不断提高生产效率和节约成本费用。总体来看，2009年英美烟草公司实现了较为强劲的增长，离1995年确立的"世界第一跨国烟草公司"的目标也越来越近。全年共销售卷烟7 240亿支(包括合资企业在内为9 070亿支)，比上年增长1%。其中"健牌"销量为610亿支，比上年下降4%；"登喜路"销量为410亿支，"好彩"销量为260亿支，"波迈"销量为680亿支，分别比上年增长9%、4%和10%。从地区市场来看，2009年英美烟草公司卷烟销量在亚太市场增长了3%、在美洲市场下降了6%、在西欧市场增长了6%、在东欧市场下降了4%、在非洲和中东市场增长了11%。在卷烟销量增长、价格提高和成本费用得到有效控制的共同作用下，2009年英美烟草公司实现销售收入比上年增长20.1%，已经超过了菲莫国际公司，税收、利润等指标也实现同步增长。

3. 日本烟草公司是世界第三大跨国烟草公司 2009年日本烟草公司继续推进并购扩张战略，并把并购重点向烟叶生产环节延伸，先后收购了英国一家烟叶供应商和巴西一家烟叶供应商，在美国合资组建了一家烟叶公司。日本烟草公司继续把经营重点放在培育"云丝顿"、"骆驼"、"柔和七星"等8个"全球旗舰品牌"上。为应对金融危机和国内烟草市场持续萎缩的影响，日本烟草公司不断加大对国际烟草市场的拓展步伐，在意大利、法国、英国、波兰、俄罗斯、土耳其、韩国等市场上取得了较好业绩。全年共销售卷烟5 884亿支，比上年下降3.2%。其中，在国内市场销售卷烟1 535亿支，比上年下降5.1%；占国内市场的份额为65.1%，比上年提高0.2个百分点；在国际市场销售卷烟4 349亿支，比上年下降2.5%。日本烟草公司8个"全球旗舰品牌"在国际市场销量为2 434亿支，比上年下降0.9%。其中"云丝顿"销量为1 214亿支，比上年下降4.1%；"骆驼"销量为418亿支，比上年下降1.8%；"柔和七星"销量为182亿支（含国内销量为976亿支），比上年下降3.0%；"乐迪"销量为343亿支，比上年增长18.2%。除烟草业务外，日本烟草公司目前还经营食品、药品等非烟草业务，2009年非烟草业务销售收入占总销售收入的比重为7.4%。

4. 帝国烟草公司是世界第四大跨国烟草公司 其烟草业务目前覆盖卷烟、雪茄烟、鼻烟、烟丝、卷烟纸等，烟草产品组合非常全面。帝国烟草公司以烟草制品配送为主的物流业务已发展成为欧洲最大的物流系统之一。2009年帝国烟草公司有效整合上一年度收购的阿塔迪斯公司烟草业务，并把重点放在促进销售增长、优化生产布局和加强现金流管理等方面，全年（财政年度）销售卷烟3 222亿支，比上年增长9.5%。其中"大卫·杜夫"品牌销量增长12%，"JPS"品牌销量增长11%，"威斯"品牌销量下降8%；销售烟丝25 950t，比上年增长3.2%。帝国烟草公司目前共有33个卷烟厂、20个非卷烟类烟草制造厂和3个卷烟纸厂，其产品销往160多个国家和地区。从卷烟市场布局看，2009年在英国销售208亿支，在德国销售239亿支，在西班牙销售303亿支，在欧盟其他国家销售593亿支，在美洲销售138亿支，在世界其他国家和地区销售1 741亿支。

除中国烟草总公司和四大跨国烟草公司外，世界烟草市场上还有众多中小型烟草公司。2009年，这些中小型烟草公司合计卷烟销量约为14 500亿支。奥驰亚集团曾经是全球第一大跨国烟草公司。但自2008年集团所属的菲莫国际公司分离出去以后，其烟草业务规模大为下降，目前奥驰亚集团从事烟草业务的有菲莫美国公司、美国无烟烟草公司和约翰·米德尔顿雪茄烟公司3个全资子公司。2009年，奥驰亚集团共销售"万宝路"1 265亿支，比上年下降10.6%；"万宝路"在美国市场上的占有率为41.8%，比上年下降0.1个百分点。销售无烟烟草6.45亿听（或盒），比上年下降2.4%；销售雪茄烟12.6亿支，比上年下降3.6%。韩国烟草人参公社在韩国具有市场垄断地位。2009年在韩国市场销售卷烟591亿支，比上年下降5.8%；占韩国市场的比重为62.3%，比上年下降4.3个百分点。卷烟出口到30多个国家和地区，俄罗斯、中国是其主要的目标市场，2009年共出口卷烟368亿支，比上年下降5.4%。雷诺美国公司是美国第二大烟草公司，英美烟草公司拥有其42%的股份，目前下属有雷诺烟草公司、美国鼻烟公司、圣达菲天然烟草公司和NiconovumAB尼古丁替代品公司。2009年，雷诺美国公司共销售"骆驼"品牌212亿支，比上年下降9.2%；销售"波迈"品牌146亿支，比上年增长70.9%。销售湿润鼻烟3.56亿听，比上年增长6.4%。

四、质量管理与标准化工作

（一）质量管理

2009年，为了全面加强烟草质检机构建设，国家烟草专卖局印发了《关于全面加强烟草质检机构建设的意见》，推进质量安全制度和体系建设不断完善，质量监督有效性不断提高。根据全年抽查显示，2009年卷烟产品质量合格率为100%，卷烟产品有关质量安全指标的合格率为100%，烟用添加剂和卷烟材料相关指标得到有效控制。烟叶工商交接等级质量合格率稳步提高，预计2009年合格率在63%左右，比2008年提高约3个百分点。按照国家局关于调整卷烟盒标焦油最高限量的要求，全面落实了国家局关于从2009年1月1日起生产的卷烟盒标焦油最高限量不得超过13mg/支的规定，2009年全国卷烟焦油量加权平均值为12.2mg/支，较2008年下降0.6 mg / 支。骨干品牌在焦油量明显下降的同时，继续保持较高的质量水平和风格特征，且彰显较强的个性，一些新品牌（规格）在降焦增香保持风味的技术创新方面迈出可喜步伐，履约工作迈出实质性步伐。从2009年1月1日起，全面执行《中华人民共和国境内卷烟包装标识的规定》，卷烟包装标识全面改版，标志着我国烟草行业履约工作已迈出实质性步伐。

（二）标准化工作

2009年，组织开展了卷烟、农业、烟机和烟用材料标准与国际、国内相关标准的"对标"工作。完成了"卷烟出口目的国（地区）重要信息资源共享平台"信息系统建设并正式投入运行，初步建立了对国外技术性贸易措施的预警机制。编制了2009年度标准制修订项目计划，已报批国家标准8项，发布行业标准71项，行业现行有效的标准已达425项，正在制修订的标准有164项。发布了《烟草农业标准体系》、《烟草机械标准体系》（修订）。稳步推进"卷烟贮存期间质量变化研究"等多项重点标准研制工作；确定了《卷烟》系列国标修订工作的基本思路。进行了卷烟工业、商业、烟机制造、醋纤等企业自主制定、现行有效的企业标准统计分析，调研了河南中烟等5个企业开展标准化工作情况。起草了《烟草添加剂安全性评价及管理规程（试行）》，组建了烟草添加剂安全性评估委员会。评审出行业标准创新贡献奖获奖项目5项（二等奖3项、三等奖2项）。推荐《烟草及烟草制品　转基因的测定》标准参评国标委组织的"中国标准创新贡献奖"（评为三等奖）。参加了ISO/TC 126第28次会议，答复了《烟草及烟草制品　箱内片烟密度偏差率的无损检测　电离辐射法》国际标准项目（ISO/DIS 12030）有关质询。2009年8月，ISO/DIS 12030获得国际标准化组织投票通过，这是我国烟草行业在继2009年实现国际标准提案"零"的突破后取得的又一重大进展。

五、行业管理

1. *坚决贯彻卷烟产品消费税调整政策，圆满完成财政增收任务*　2009年，面对卷烟消费税政策的重大调整，国家局制定了"价税财"联动的调整方案。全行业顾全大局、思想统一，坚决贯彻国家局的部署安排，落实卷烟消费税调整各项工作，自行消化调整部分的卷烟消费税，保持市场和价格稳定。经过全行业共同努力，2009年新增消费税600亿元，圆满完成财政增收任务，用实际行动践行了"两个至上"行业共同价值观。

2. *卷烟新老包装标识替换工作顺利完成*　2009年1月1日，根据《中华人民共和国境内卷烟包装标识的规定》，我国境内生产的所有非出口卷烟和国外进口卷烟条、盒包装增加了30%的警示语区域。行业工商企业大力做好卷烟新老包装标识的替换工作，保证卷烟市场平稳过渡，认真履行了对《烟草控制框架公约》的承诺。

3. *高度重视技术创新，自主创新能力进一步提升*　2009年，国家局在湖北等地召开自主创新高层论坛，对实施"烟草育种、卷烟调香、特色工艺、减害降焦"4大战略课题进行了深入研讨，自主创新思路、方法、手段和经验等得到了总结和交流，企业技术中心建设明显加强，卷烟增香保润、卷烟减害技术、特质烟叶开发、中式卷烟制丝生产线等重大专项实施取得积极进展。加强卷烟产品质量监督，全年全国卷烟抽查焦油含量实测平均值为12.2mg/支，同比下降0.6mg/支。

4. *省级工业公司董事会建设进一步完善*　2009年，国家局、总公司出台了《关于加强董事会建设的意见》，明确和细化了董事会在公司发展战略、投资管理、预算管理、薪酬管理、制度建设等方面的职权。在第一批董事会建设取得成效的基础上，江西、陕西、江苏等几个省级工业公司董事会相继建立并开始运作。

5. *大力加强行业队伍建设，努力提高干部职工素质*　全国烟草行业政治工作会议强调，全面加强行业领导班子建设，优化领导班子年龄、知识和专业结构，配齐配强省、市局（公司）主要负责人，有计划地安排机关干部到基层一线任职、挂职。2009年，国家局机关选派8名年轻干部赴地震灾区基层单位接受锻炼。全行业深入开展“两个至上”在岗位主题实践活动，企业文化服务品牌建设深入开展，教育培训工作取得新进展，建立了教育培训体系，开展多种技术比武竞赛活动。2009年“五一”前夕，“第五届全国烟草行业先进集体、劳动模范表彰大会”在北京隆重举行，对58个全国烟草行业先进集体、117名全国烟草行业劳动模范进行了表彰。

（郑州烟草研究院 王英元）

酿酒工业

一、基本情况

（一）行业总体情况

我国饮料酒制造业自2004年以来，经过5年的产业结构调整，到2009年白酒产量稳中有增，低度白酒有了较大的市场空间，品质稳定的优良白酒越来越受到消费者的青睐；啤酒产量稳步上升，连续8年居世界第一，风味向低浓度、低色泽、不同口味多品种方向发展；葡萄酒产量多年来保持两位数的快速增长，全汁葡萄酒已成为主流，干型、半干型占到总产量的一半以上；黄酒克服地区界限，开始向北方扩张。经过改革、改制，企业结构日趋现代化，以国营为主的第一所有制形式发生了很大变化，形成了外国独资、中外合资、国有、集体、私营等多种所有制并存的经济格局。经过并购、重组，强强联合，企业集团化正在形成，这些酿酒企业集团的形成，引领和规范了行业的发展，成为行业的榜样和中坚。

由于不断完善标准体系，强化食品安全意识，健全食品安全检测检验体系，健全事故预防和应急处置机制，加快食品安全诚信体系建设，积极构建科学的食品安全体系，酒类产品的安全得到了充分保障。随着科学发展观的深入人心和企业技术改造力度的加强，全行业循环经济、清洁生产、节能减排的环保意识有了很大的加强。随着社会的进步和经济的发展，社会责任已经成为企业在市场竞争中获得优势的战略行为，努力履行企业社会责任是企业保证可持续发展和增强核心竞争力的有效途径；全行业的社会责任意识得到了提升。

（二）行业经济运行情况

1. 行业总体运行情况　2009年全国饮料酒总产量为5 188.6万kL，同比增长−5.74%。其中发酵酒精产量为731.7万kL，同比增长7.40%；白酒产量为706.93万kL，同比增长23.82%，增幅比上年同期上升了8.03个百分点；啤酒产量为4 236.38万kL，同比增长7.09%，增幅比上年同期上升了1.63个百分点；葡萄酒产量为96.00万kL，同比增长27.63%，增幅比上年同期上升了3.80个百分点；黄酒产量为100万kL，同比增长14.0%。

2009年1～11月，白酒累计产量前5个省是四川、山东、河南、辽宁、湖北，累计产量分别为137.18万kL、77.41万kL、62.44万kL、43.42万kL、38.48万kL，其累计产量合计占全国白酒总产量的57.50%。啤酒累计产量前5个省是山东、河南、广东、浙江、湖北，累计产量分别为471.12万kL、353.99万kL、327.65万kL、240.01万kL、235.35万kL，其累计产量合计占全国啤酒总产量的40.12%。葡萄酒累计产量前5个省、市是山东、吉林、河北、河南、天津，累计产量分别为30.38万kL、18.45万kL、9.62万kL、9.35万kL、4.15万kL，其累计产量合计占全国葡萄酒总产量的88.59%。

2009年我国饮料酒制造业完成工业总产值超过3 700亿元，同比增长20.4%。其中，1～11月，实现主营业务收入、利税总额分别为3 390亿元和764亿元，同比增长21.7%和22.1%；利润总额为349亿元，同比增长26.1%。1～11月，我国饮料酒制造业，累计实现产品销售收入前5个省是四川、山东、河南、江苏、湖北，累计实现产品销售收入分别为802.57亿元、556.33亿元、215.10亿元、193.52亿元、180.72亿元，其累计实现产品销售收入合计占全国的比重为57.48%。2009年，在国内刺激经济政策与经济振兴方案的共同作用下，我国白酒、啤酒、黄酒、葡萄酒等子行业规模以上企业的经济效益指标逐步好转，呈现出主营业务收入稳步回升、利润总额逐步好转、销售利润率同比上升、亏损收窄及亏损面降低、从业人数逐步增加的良好局面。基于国内巨大的消费市场，国际资本开始大量介入中国酒业，并购与重组不断，而部分骨干企业也开始在布局全球市场方面，迈出实质性的步伐。2009年饮料酒制造业继续秉承以市场需求为导向，以满足消费为目标，在注重社会效益的同时，赢得了良好的经济效益。在产业规模、技术改造、节能减排、产品质量、食品安全、人才建设、社会责任等诸多方面都取得了较好的成绩。总体来看，行业内各项经济指标均有不同程度的增长，增速稳中有升，符合产业政策总的发展方向。

2. 分行业运行情况

（1）白酒　2009年工业总产值超过2 000亿元，同比增长27.5%，高于饮料酒制造业20.4%的同比增长，所占比重达到55.5%。白酒行业产品销售率为95.3%，行业销售形势稳中有升。2009年1～11月，白酒行业实现主营业务收入1 858亿元，利税总额457亿元，分别同比增长30.5%和24.8%，比饮料酒制造业同比增幅分别高8.8和2.8个百分点。利润总额235亿元，同比增长25.7%，虽然略低于饮料酒制造业26.1%的总体利润增幅，但其占比仍高达67.3%。新税制的实施对白酒行业并未带来太大影响，加上白酒行业本身具备的利润优势，借助白酒企业近年来利润较高增长的强劲势头，全行业因此得以持续盈利。同时，白酒行业企业亏损率只有9.3%，在饮料酒几个主要行业中保持最低。在市场方面，传统名优企业继续扩张在全国市场的份额，老牌二线名酒也纷纷发力，借助传统品牌优势与产品结构升级拓展市场。

（2）啤酒　2009年全年工业总产值同比增长9.3%，产品销售率略低于上年水平，但仍达到了产销平衡。1～11月，啤酒行业实现主营业务收入1 143亿元，利税总额232亿元，分别同比增长10.4%和18.4%，低于饮料酒制造业的增长幅度。从2008年起，为应对原材料价格上涨等因素，啤酒行业采取了全线提价的策略，使长期困扰该行业的高投入低产出矛盾得到了一定缓解。目前，作为市场主体的常规产品已基本提价到位，啤酒行业的总体价格基本保持稳定，全行业产值的增长速度开始回归平稳。啤酒的行业亏损率在饮料酒各行业中仍是最高，同时，啤酒行业两极分化态势加剧，大型骨干企业对行业经济效益贡献巨大。骨干企业新产品开发力度不断加强，高端产品、高附加值产品不断投放市场，加上各自雄厚的市场营销能力、品牌号召力等，加快了行业集中的步伐。

（3）葡萄酒　2009年实现工业总产值超过200亿元，同比增长20.4%。近两年，随着葡萄酒市场趋于理性，葡萄酒的价格也逐渐回归理性。同时，葡萄酒新兴省份产量的迅猛增长，使葡萄酒行业进一步维系产量高增长的局面。1～11月，葡萄酒行业实现主营业务收入222亿元，利税总额48亿元，分别同比增长19.1%和16.8%，利润总额28亿元，同比增长19.9%。目前，葡萄酒行业的整体利益空间仍然巨大，百亿元产值实现利润继续保持饮料酒各行业的最高水平。近几年来，原装进口葡萄酒市场急速升温，但在冲击国内葡萄酒市场的同时，也将先进的葡萄酒文化传播进来，这有助于我国国内葡萄酒消费走向成熟。

（4）黄酒　2009年增速有所提升。全年完成工业总产值接近100亿元，同比增长15.2%。1～11月份，黄酒行业实现主营业务收入75亿元，同比增长3.1%，实现利税总额12亿元，同比降低0.9%。近几年，黄酒行业区域覆盖面迅速加大，传统区域格局正在被打破，一些新兴省份的崛起，成为黄酒行业产量增长的主要动力。黄酒行业产品结构调整开始提速，逐步摆脱黄酒产品传统的低档次困扰，并由此带动了黄酒产品整体附加值的提高。

3. 进出口情况　从进出口情况看，2009年我国进出口酒类产品达1 417百万美元，其中进口酒类产品为1 047百万美元，比2004年的246百万美元提高了4.26倍；而出口酒类产品仅为370百万美元，虽然为2004年出口额的1.88倍，但不容忽视的是我国酒类产品出口数量占国内产量的比重很低，而且产品出口价格偏低，出口国家和地区单一，主要以周边亚洲国家和地区为主，欧美主流市场仍未进入。也就是说，我们酿酒行业的产品还没有完全打开国际市场，这是我国饮料酒制造业值得思考和迫切关注的问题。

从上述经济运行情况可以看出，近年来由于行业中，骨干酒类生产企业依靠自己强大的经济实力和科研实力，深入开展科学技术研究，通过产品结构的调整，满足了广大消费者的需求，增强了企业的竞争能力，也提高了企业的经济效益，全行业更加注重投入产出效率、资源利用和环境保护的关系。

二、行业工作

（一）关注特色区域建设

中国酿酒工业协会为了提升重点产区的知名度，规范荣誉称号的命名，增强其权威性及透明度，组织制订了《关于授予中国酿酒行业特色区域荣誉称号的行为规范》。2009年7月，中国轻工业联合会委托中国酿酒工业协会牵头组成考察组到宜宾实地考察3个月后，根据相关标准和程序，经严格评估，由协会与中国轻工业联合会联合授予宜宾“中国白酒之都”荣誉称号。同年经严格评估后，又授予青岛市红酒坊特色街区“中国（青岛）国际葡萄酒街”荣誉称号。

（二）推动行业原料基地和市场建设

为了推动酿酒行业原料基地和市场建设，中国酿酒工业协会组织召开了“中国酿酒工业协会啤酒原料专业委员会成立大会暨产业发展论坛”；“中国酿酒工业协会市场专业委员会成立大会暨首届 CIADE 酒业市场论坛”；“中国国际葡萄酒峰会暨首届中国国际葡萄酒技术贸易与投资年会”等多次专题活动。通过活动加强了行业交流，讨论了事关行业市场和原料基地的建设现状及发展前景问题，增强了全行业原料基地和市场建设的意识，有力地促进了行业内原料基地和市场建设工作，推动了酿酒行业健康有序的发展。

（三）夯实基础，加速行业信息化建设

中国酿酒工业协会于 2009 年 4 月 17 日在山东泰安顺利召开了“首届全国酿酒行业信息工作会”，发布了《中国酿酒工业协会关于推进行业信息化工作的指导意见》和《中国酿酒工业协会信息员工作细则》，在全行业推动了信息化建设工作。中国酿酒工业协会自 2006 年开始创办中国酿酒工业协会官方网站以来，目前网站设有栏目 28 个。2009 年协会网站又新开两个栏目，一个是“永不落幕的酒业网博会”，另一个是“中国酿酒工业协会信息中心”。网站及时了解全国酿酒行业生产运行态势，为会员企业日常经济决策提供依据。在办好网站的同时，协会充分利用纸质媒体资源，继续办好《会员通讯》、《酒精》、《中国黄酒》、《中国酿酒工业行业信息》等内部交流资料，并在办好《啤酒科技》等行业公开发行刊物的基础上，积极申请创办《酒》杂志等行业科技类期刊，为行业提供广泛的信息服务，深受企业欢迎。

（四）积极推进行业转变经济发展模式

长期以来，中国酿酒工业协会围绕推动中国酒业向绿色经济、低碳经济转型开展了一系列科研、专题报告、经验交流等活动。2009 年 9 月由工业和信息化部、中国轻工业联合会主办、中国酿酒工业协会承办的“酿酒行业推行清洁生产现场交流会”在广州珠江啤酒集团公司召开。会议通过树立清洁生产典型企业、总结清洁生产经验、加强企业交流，推动酿酒行业清洁生产工作迈向新台阶。

同时，中国酿酒工业协会积极参与编写了《我国玉米加工业发展现状与展望》、《酿酒行业“十一五”科技发展需求》、《推动酒精行业节能减排、转变经济增长方式的综合性政策研究》、《酒精行业清洁生产专项》等技术报告，指导行业企业清洁生产和节能减排工作。中国酿酒工业协会积极参加了国家环保总局组织的《国家先进污染防治示范技术名录》和《国家鼓励发展的环境保护技术目录》的编制工作，将啤酒行业的 10 项内容列入目录，以引起有关部门的关注和企业的重视。

为了将行业内清洁生产和节能减排工作深入开展下去，中国酿酒工业协会与北京工商大学等单位，组织相关技术人员 50 多人，在行业中开展了调查工作，先后完成了白酒、啤酒、黄酒、果露酒和酒精行业的产排污染系数制订工作。为我国第一次全国污染源普查，提供了产排污系数，能够及时、准确地测算相应行业的污染物产生量和排放量，为推动企业清洁生产和节能减排、污染治理工作提供了科学依据。

（本文由编辑部根据中国酿酒工业协会提供的相关资料汇总整理）

蚕丝加工业

一、基本情况

（一）蚕桑生产

1. 产量　2009 年全国桑园面积 79.8 万 hm^2，与 2008 年同比下降 8.52%；蚕茧发种量 1 457.15 万张，同比下降 19.10%；蚕茧产量 57.41 万 t，同比下降 17.76%；蚕茧收购量 49.33 万 t，同比下降 13.60%；蚕茧收购均价 1 081.76 元/50kg，同比增长 30.15%；蚕农收入 124.21 亿元，同比增长 11.22%。全国桑园面积共减少 7.46 万 hm^2，其中上半年减少 7.2 万 hm^2，下半年部分地区桑园面积有所增加，合计减少 0.26 万 hm^2。其中，江苏、浙江、山东和广东等东部地区桑园面积减少 3.49 万 hm^2；中西部地区除四川、陕西、云南等地桑园面积较 2008 年基本持平或略有增加外，重庆、广西、江西和湖南等地减少 4.38 万 hm^2。江苏、重庆、山东、广西等地共计减少 5.83 万 hm^2，占全国比重的 78.13%。全国蚕茧产量共下降 12.40 万 t，其中春茧下降 8.63 万 t，降幅达 27.63%；夏秋茧下降 3.77 万 t，降幅约 5.5%。其中，江苏、浙江、山东和广东等东部地区减少 6.91 万 t；中西部地区除广西增产 1.17%外，其他地区共减少 5.49 万 t。山东、浙江、安徽、云南、广东、江苏和重庆地区蚕茧产量分别下降30.70%、29.10%、25.70%、25.08%、24.57%、23.40%和23.20%。由于2009年蚕茧产量大幅下降，茧丝价格稳步回升，加之经济形势下半年转好，丝绸企业对原料需求大幅增加，蚕茧收购价格呈现快速回升态势。其中，春茧收购价格每50kg 974.55元，同比增长2.16%；夏茧收购价格每50kg 968.79元，同比增长约18.15%；秋茧收购价格每50kg 1 104.16元，同比增长约57.71%。广东、广西、浙江、江苏、安徽和四川等主产区收购价格回升幅度超过30%，山东、云南和重庆等地升幅在25%～30%。全国每公顷桑园平均收益15 390元，效益大幅提高；每50kg蚕茧净利润至少在80元以上，同比提高约25%。部分地区通过蚕桑综合利用开发，每公顷桑园平均收益19 500元，同比提高约25%，蚕农增收12.53亿元以上。重庆市率先推出蚕桑综合利用示范园资助建设，试点桑园175.3hm^2，综合利用收入达1 386万元，公顷桑效益79110元，是传统养蚕效益的214%。

2. 资源分布　我国蚕茧产地分布广，但主产地较集中。2009年蚕茧产量在6万t以上的省、自治区有5个，分别是广西、江苏、浙江、四川、广东，产量之和占我国蚕茧总产量的65%左右。其中广西蚕茧产量继续领先全国，占全国产量的1/4多。蚕茧产量在1万～6万t之间的有山东、安徽、云南、陕西、重庆、湖北、河南7省、直辖市，产量之和占总产量的25%左右。蚕茧产量在1万t以下的有江西、山西、湖南、贵州4省，产量之和占总产量的3%左右。除此之外，我国还有一些零星蚕区，但产量很少。

（二）加工量、产值、利税、固定资本投资

2009年全国生丝产量15.5万t，与2008年同比增长11.98%；绢丝3.86万t，同比增长19.05%；蚕丝及交织物7.05亿m，同比增长5.45%。丝绸工业总产值1 523.93亿元，同比增长8.24%；主营业务收入1 470.94亿元，同比增长9.44%，较2008年增加4.9个百分点；利润43.92亿元，同比增长22.28%，较2008年增加14.63个百分点，但仍低于全国纺织工业25.39%的平均增长水平。其中，缫丝加工实现利润8.47亿元，比2008年同期增长46.37%；绢纺和丝织加工实现利润21.25亿元，同比增长16.71%；丝印染精加工实现利润1.77亿元，同比增长66.03%；丝制品制造实现利润5.26亿元，同比增长8.77%；丝针织制造实现利润7.17亿元，同比增长19.07%。由于2008年秋茧和生丝价格处于近年最低位置，随着2009年生丝价格大幅回升，再加上2008年本身基数较低，使得缫丝、丝织及丝制品加工利润同比增幅较大。

随着国家应对国际金融危机一系列政策措施和国务院关于《纺织工业调整和振兴规划》的出台，在“加大蚕丝收购”政策的实施以及国内市场走强等利好因素刺激下，加上2009年茧丝原料供应偏紧的影响，茧丝价格从2009年一季度开始企稳并逐步回升。截止到12月底国内干茧和生丝（3A级）每吨平均价格较年初分别上涨67.1%和54.7%，较2008年10月茧丝最低时分别上涨126.3%和85.8%。

2009年丝绸行业计划投资总额为67.75亿元，同比增加8.34%；实际完成投资额55.78亿元，同比增加26.15%，占计划投资额的82.3%；当年以来到目前为止施工项目总数为135个，同比增加13.76%；其中新开工项目数91个，同比增加4.41%。截至12月底，已实现竣工项目数64个，同比增加45.95%，占施工项目总数的47.4%，表明该行业投资项目进展情况正常。

二、新技术、新成果

（一）西南大学研究获得重大突破，蚕丝粗细颜色均将可控

2009年西南大学家蚕基因组研究团队再次取得重大突破，成功绘制出世界首张家蚕基因组DNA甲基化图谱，为今后家蚕丝腺器官吐丝的粗细、颜色等经济性状的研究奠定了坚实基础。西南大学家蚕基因组研究团队利用新一代测序技术，构建了世界上第一张昆虫甲基化图谱——家蚕丝腺甲基化图谱，通过对家蚕中95%全基因组的信息研究，发现约有0.11%的基因组被甲基化修饰，且与家蚕丝腺器官中的基因密切相关。这也就意味着DNA甲基化图谱的绘制，将有助于日后科学家“自由掌控”家蚕吐丝的粗细、颜色等各种性状，进而影响家蚕产丝性能，提高家蚕研究培育的经济价值。作为世界首张昆虫甲基化图谱，家蚕甲基化图谱的完成，不但为理解昆虫表观遗传学调控提供了重要的参考资料，也为进一步发掘家蚕人工驯化过程中的遗传研究奠定了坚实的基础。

（二）用蚕宝宝研制治疗肿瘤新药获得成功

这一成果为沪、浙两地学者联合攻关的结果，中国科学院上海生命科学院、浙江大学和浙江理工大学的十多位专家历经20余年研究，创造性将蚕蛹作为生物反应器，来表达细胞因子等活性蛋白，用于生产肿瘤生物治疗新药。目前，该成果已获国家新药临床批准，全面进入临床试用，先后被列入国家“九五”重点科技攻关项目、国家“十五”重大科技专项“863”计划，并已获得“国家技术发明奖”和多项国家发明专利。

(三) 用丝绸材料制成隐身斗篷取得成功

最近科学家利用丝绸制成一种隐身斗篷，虽然目前这件隐身斗篷只能在可见光以外的无线电波和红外线之间的光谱范围内起作用，但是通过改进，可能会让它在更短的光波范围内起作用，甚至其中包括可见光。这种材料既具有医学应用价值，又能使人类或物体隐形成为可能，它是用覆盖了一层金属物质的丝绸制成，每个微小的螺旋线就是一个“开口环谐振器”，开口环谐振器对光具有独特的影响作用，它们可以吸收或者反射特定波长范围内的光，或者弯曲光线，使它们从物体表面绕过，每平方厘米丝质超材料上拥有1万个开口环谐振器。通常情况下太赫兹波可以顺利通过丝绸，不会对其产生任何影响。但是当太赫兹波接触到这种新型金属丝绸时，后者会产生共振。因为丝绸具有生物相容性，在植入人体后不会引起免疫排斥，因此这种金属丝绸可以广泛应用到医学领域。利用这种材料制作隐身斗篷只是其中一个方面，把它应用到医学领域才能发挥它的最大价值。放射线研究者可以用这种材料覆盖器官，以便更好地查看到器官被挡住的部分。糖尿病患者还可以把它当做一个血糖传感器：当血糖水平发生变化时，这种超材料也会发生相应变化。这种变化可以通过无线电波的形式发射出去，而且利用手机可以发现它。

(四) 蚕宝宝可以“定向培育”

蚕宝宝是胖是瘦，斑纹是否漂亮，结出的蚕茧颜色是白色还是彩色？这些都能被研究者“自由掌控”。西南大学家蚕基因研究团队对外宣布，我国家蚕突变基因研究取得重大进展，在世界上率先发现60多个家蚕中新的突变基因，揭示了基因遗传规律，并将其准确定位在染色体上，一些突变基因已经被克隆鉴定。作为鳞翅目类昆虫的代表性物种，家蚕是5000年前由中国野桑蚕驯化而来的，其基因上的特定遗传变异与特定遗传性状之间，到底有着怎样的变化和联系，在学术界被列为急需攻克的课题。通过16年的潜心研究，家蚕研究团队通过大量的实验，发现了60多个家蚕中新的突变基因，每一个突变基因都代表一种家蚕的遗传性状，能帮助研究者“自由掌控”蚕宝宝的胖瘦、吐丝的颜色、斑纹有多少等，为遗传学研究提供了大量新材料和研究模型。在庞大的家蚕家族中，有许多长相、血型、体色、体型等各不相同的蚕类，它们具有的研究应用价值也不尽相同，比如蚕茧质量好的则具有良好经济价值，斑纹漂亮的观赏性就高。

(五) 蚕丝深加工自动化控制技术被攻破

广西柳州市自动化科学研究所抓住行业急需解决的关键技术问题，研发出蚕丝深加工自动化控制技术。技术人员通过集成创新，运用自动化控制技术和信息化技术对缫丝厂的触蒸、煮茧、缫丝理绪、复摇翻丝、纤度检验、产量统计、后整等传统的缫丝加工工艺和生产设备进行研究和技术改造，对各主要生产工艺参数、生产信息进行自动检测和采集管理，并与信息化管理系统联网，实现集中监控，实现了生产关键工序的自动化控制和信息化管理。项目科技集成创新性强，成果成熟性好，解决了茧丝加工增值关键、共性技术难题，填补了国内空白，达到了国内同类技术领先水平。

三、国内外市场概况

(一) 国内市场

随着国家“扩大内需”政策的实施，人们生活品位的不断提高，加上丝绸产品结构的调整，大量适销对路丝绸新品种逐步投放市场，丝绸商品内销比例得到稳定增长。丝绸产品已经重点转向内衣、家纺及装饰品等消费领域，长丝针织T恤、真丝涂层面料服装等已进入高端品牌消费，尤其是丝绸家纺、装饰用品、丝毛混纺、丝针织内衣等耗丝量较大的丝绸新产品问世，对有效拉动丝绸内销市场稳步增长发挥了积极作用，也给茧丝绸业发展带来了新的机遇。全国蚕丝被年产量已达700万条以上，年增长幅度在20%以上，年消耗蚕丝1.5万t左右。目前，内销市场消化茧丝量已达到30%左右，并呈逐年增长趋势，已成为我国茧丝绸行业新的经济增长点。

(二) 国外市场

2009年真丝绸商品出口26.69亿美元，与2008年同比下降18.8%。在连续3年小幅下跌的情况下，2009年出现了较大幅度的下跌，已是连续4年负增长，但10月、11月出口数据已经连续两月出现降幅收窄。蚕丝类出口数量20 445.1t，比2008年同期减少16%；出口金额46 845.21万美元，比2008年同期减少20.9%；单价22.91美元/kg，比2008年同期减少5.88%。蚕丝机织物出口24 013.35万m，与2008年同比增长1.46%；出口金额70 302.99万美元，同比减少7.78%；单价2.93美元/m，同比减少9.03%。其中，坯绸出口数量18 950.23万m，比2008年同期增长2.45%；出口金额48 236.56万美元，比2008年同期减少9.31%；单价2.55美元/m，比2008年同期减少11.5%。印染绸出口数量4 702万m，比2008年同期增长6.84%；出口金额20 363.52万美元，比2008年同期减少2.13%；单价4.33美元/m，比2008年同期减少8.46%。

真丝绸商品主要出口市场依次为美国、印度、意大利、日本、香港特别行政区、巴基斯坦、英国、德国、韩国、法国，美国占22.41%的市场份额。主要市场中，印度和巴基斯坦成为寒冬中的亮点，分别增长10.45%和52.48%，新兴市场巴基斯坦的排名由2008年的第11位跃升至第6位；对其他市场出口均有较大降幅，对香港特别行政区降幅最大，达34.74%，对美国的出口降幅也高达26.76%。

进口方面，我国2009年丝制品及服装进口总额2.54亿美元，同比增加20.26%，占纺织品及服装进口总额186.46亿美元的0.98%。其中丝制品进口总额1.16亿美元，同比增加11.16%，占纺织品进口总额163.71亿美元的0.71%。2009年丝制服装进口总额0.68亿美元，同比增加47.41%，占服装进口总额22.75亿美元的2.98%。显示我国丝制纺织品和服装外贸形势良好。

四、质量管理与标准化工作

(一)《热带亚热带桑树高产种植技术规范》国标通过专家初审

2009年12月底，国家蚕业标准化技术委员会在成都召开国家标准审定会，由广东省罗定市质监局负责牵头编写的《热带亚热带桑树高产种植技术规范》国家标准在会上通过了专家的初审。专家们对该标准稿给予了较高的评价，认为一个县级质监部门能承担国家级标准的制订实在少见，能编写出如此较高水平的标准更是难能可贵。根据有关专家提出的意见和建议，该标准经进一步修改完善后由国家标准化管理委员会颁布实施。

(二)《蚕丝被》国家标准出台

《蚕丝被》国家标准已由国家标准化管理委员会以2009年第9号公告批准发布，标准代号为GB/T 24252—2009，实施日期为2010年2月1日。《蚕丝被》国家标准的发布实施，有望改变目前蚕丝被质量鱼龙混杂的状况。新发布的GB/T 24252—2009《蚕丝被》国家标准，是在原《蚕丝被》行业标准基础上，对原行业标准的部分内容修改后上升为国家标准的。新发布的国家标准在蚕丝被的定义、包装标注规定、等级、内在质量、外观质量、工艺质量等方面对蚕丝被进行了新的规定。另外，标准明确了以蚕丝为主要填充物的被类才可称为蚕丝被，分为纯蚕丝被和混合蚕丝被两类。其中蚕丝含量为100%的称为纯蚕丝被，蚕丝含量达到50%及以上的为混合蚕丝被。

(三)《纺织品丝绸术语》、《桑蚕绢丝》等国家、行业标准审定会召开

《纺织品 丝绸术语》、《桑蚕绢丝》等国家、行业标准审定会于2009年9月在厦门召开。全国丝绸标准化委员会主任、中国丝绸协会秘书长、中国丝绸工业总公司副总经理钱有清到会发表重要讲话，全国丝绸标准化委员会秘书长周颖主持会议。全国丝绸标准化委员会委员及标准起草单位的代表34人参加了会议。会议认为，全面整理和编写《丝绸术语》国家标准，规范丝绸专业术语和名词的含义与范围，提高丝绸术语的准确表达，直接关系到行业的教学、科研、生产、贸易、管理乃至市场消费各个环节，不仅对整个行业具有广泛的指导意义，而且对弘扬我国传统丝绸文化，促进国际交流，增强国际影响，加快实现丝绸强国战略具有更加深远的意义。

五、行业管理

(一) 2009年蚕茧收购质量监督检查工作

自2009年5月28日开始，浙江、河南、四川、重庆、江苏、云南、山东、陕西、江西等蚕茧主产地区的各级纤检机构，根据当地鲜茧上市交易的时间陆续开展了蚕茧质量监督检查工作。截止到6月20日，纤检机构共出动900人次，检查茧站550余个，检查茧量2 500多t。现场处理处罚收购行为不规范的茧站33个，立案查处严重质量违法案件12起。重点检查蚕茧收购加工企业执行国家相关标准及地方标准，采用客观、科学的检测方法评定收购蚕茧质量的情况，检查收购中是否存在收购毛脚茧、过潮茧、统茧、虫害茧（非病源性虫害）等严重质量问题，检查收购中是否存在压级压价、损害茧农利益的行为，检查收购、加工后的蚕茧是否采取有效的安全保障措施予以分类置放、贮存等，坚决打击收购毛脚茧、过潮茧及收购中压级压价、损害蚕农利益等严重违法行为。

通过几年来纤检机构坚持不懈地开展蚕茧收购质量监督工作，2009年多数产区的蚕茧收购加工行为得以规范，收购秩序比较稳定，质量监管效果明显。其中占江西全省蚕茧产量1/3的桑蚕产地——修水县收购秩序井然，茧站全部采用电脑评茧仪仪评收茧，按质结算，实现了优质优价，劣质低价。同时，茧农质量意识普遍增强，大多数茧农都做到了筐装售茧，下茧分拣另售，基本上消除了丙纶包装袋和售统茧的现象。重庆市建立了纤检机构、区县质监部门和茧丝绸主管部门之间的信息沟通平台，及时沟通有关信息，齐抓共管，保证了收购秩序的稳定。山东省泰安市针对检查中发现的无资质收购鲜茧的违法者，以书面材料形式向行业行政主管部门及时通报情况，联合

查处收购鲜茧违法活动，维护了企业的合法利益。

（二）提升标准水平，推动丝绸标准国际化工作

标准化工作是支撑行业实现结构调整和优化升级的技术保障。一是积极争取《生丝电子检测分级规定和试验方法》申报 ISO 国际标准项目获得通过以及项目的组织实施工作。二是不断加强标委会队伍建设和技术人才的培训，努力适应标准国际化的需求。三是完成国家标准化委员会下达的《合成纤维丝织物（坯绸）》、《桑蚕丝色织领带绸》等两项国家标准制定任务；完成 2009 年工业和信息化部下达的《柞蚕绢丝》、《柞蚕绢丝织物》、《桑蚕丝/氨纶弹力丝织物》、《生丝电子检测试验方法》、《桑蚕丝针织服装》等 9 项行业标准的送审。四是开展标准化基本知识培训工作，提高企业标准化生产水平和标准化人员的素质。

（三）继续做好高档丝绸标志推广使用工作

2009 年继续做好企业申报认证、监督管理、标志使用和消费者咨询投诉等日常管理工作，进一步加大宣传力度，选择有影响力的媒体，采取广告及新闻报道等形式继续宣传标志及使用企业；进一步完善高档丝绸标志质量标准，根据新颁布的《蚕丝被》等国家标准及使用实践情况，对现有《质量手册》进行修订完善；探索高档丝绸标志营销体系建设；进一步扩大国际宣传，加强高档丝绸标志的国际交流，逐步使高档丝绸标志产品的品质认证得到国际认可。

（四）国家桑蚕干茧公证检验实验室陕西检验室成立

随着国家对桑蚕产业的战略调整及“东桑西移”工程实施，陕西作为国家重要的优质原料茧生产和生丝加工基地，该省的蚕桑产业将会得到迅速发展，成为带动农民增收的一项重要产业。为了促进桑蚕产业发展，有效指导茧丝工农业生产，规范茧丝交易行为，提高公证检验工作对桑蚕干茧质量的引导和控制，服务地方经济发展，2007 年陕西省纤维检验局提出建立陕西省桑蚕干茧国家公证检验实验室的申请。建成后的实验室年检测能力可以达到 5 000t。2009 年实验室相继通过计量认证/授权扩项评审、“三合一”扩项复评审和实验室验收，目前该实验室已正式运行。运行后，在提供科学公正的检验数据的同时，该实验室还将充分发挥技术机构对产业发展的指导作用，为地方政府提供产业质量分析报告，为产业的健康发展提供技术支撑。

（五）“东台蚕茧”被国家工商行政管理总局批准注册为中国地理标志证明商标

2009 年，“东台蚕茧”被国家工商行政管理总局批准注册为中国地理标志证明商标，这是我国蚕桑产业上第一个、也是唯一的一个商标，是东台茧丝绸史上一件大喜事，充分体现了该市深远的丝绸文化底蕴和特定的蚕茧品质，是茧丝绸产业发展史上的一个新的里程碑。

（中国农业科学院蚕丝业研究所　梁培生）

饲料加工业

2009 年，在国际金融危机冲击全球经济的背景下，我国饲料行业克服了主要畜产品价格波动、原料价格高位运行等不利因素影响，积极应对、妥善处置突发畜产品质量安全事件，着力推进技术创新、管理变革、产业升级，在全行业的共同努力下，饲料产品供应稳定，质量稳步提升，为保障畜产品有效供给创造了条件，为促进畜牧业平稳较快发展作出了重要贡献。

一、主要特点

纵观 2009 年，我国饲料生产呈现出先抑后扬的走势，第 1、第 2 季度全国饲料产量连续两个季度出现下滑，上半年同比降幅达到 5.4%。但在国家一系列稳定奶业生产、调控生猪价格、遏制生产下滑政策措施的作用下，畜牧业生产逐步向好，饲料生产自第 3 季度开始出现恢复性增长，第 4 季度出现放量增长，走出了一个漂亮的“V”型反转，一举扭转了上半年产量下滑的势头，实现了总产值、总产量的持续增长。总的来看，我国饲料行业 2009 年的运行特点主要表现在以下几个方面：

1. *总量增加但增速放缓*　全年饲料行业总产值达 4 500 亿元，同比上升 5.7%，商品饲料总产量 1.4 亿 t，同比上升 2.4%。商品饲料产量尽管保持了持续增长的势头，但增幅出现明显下降，较 2007 年的 11.5%、2008 年的 10.8%的增幅分别低了 9.1 个百分点和 8.4 个百分点，是自 2001 年以来增幅最低的一年。

2. *产品结构变化出现新趋势* 全年配合饲料产量为10 696万t，同比增长1.0%；配合饲料占总产量的76.4%，同比下降0.5个百分点，自2005年以来首次出现下降。浓缩饲料产量为2 708万t，同比增长7.0%；浓缩饲料产量占总产量的比重为19.3%，同比提高0.8个百分点，自2005年以来首次提高。添加剂预混合饲料产量为595万t，同比增长9.0%，占总产量的4.3%，同比提高0.3个百分点，结束了连续两年比重下滑的趋势。所以出现浓缩饲料和添加剂预混合饲料快速增长这种结构性变化，这是因为：一是由于畜禽产品价格下滑，养殖利润下降，一些中小规模的养殖户为降低成本更多地采用自购玉米等大宗原料，外购浓缩饲料和添加剂预混合饲料增多、配合饲料减少；二是由于规模化养殖发展迅速，规模化养殖场对饲料产品提出了更高要求，一些添加剂预混合饲料企业看准"商机"，加强个性化服务，为规模化养殖场量身订制预混料产品，在相当程度上扩展了添加剂预混合饲料产品的市场。两种因素叠加，导致配合饲料、浓缩饲料、添加剂预混合饲料市场需求发生一稳、两增的变化。

3. *猪饲料大幅增长，禽饲料下滑* 在国家稳定生猪价格、促进标准化规模养殖政策的积极作用下，2009年生猪存、出栏稳定增长，猪饲料消费量增加，猪饲料产量达到5 103万t，同比增长11.5%，连续两年保持10%以上的增幅。占商品饲料产量半壁江山的禽饲料由于存栏下降，在连续5年快速增长后首次出现下降，蛋禽饲料产量达2 433万t，同比下降8.7%；肉禽饲料产量达4 173万t，同比下降0.9%。水产、反刍饲料继续保持快速增长势头，增幅均在10个百分点以上。

4. *饲料生产区域集中度进一步提高* 我国中部6省饲料产量可达3 220万t，同比增长5.1%；东部10省饲料产量6 430万t，同比增长2.6%；中东地区产量合计占全国总产量的68.9%，比重同比上升0.6个百分点。西部12省、自治区、直辖市饲料产量2 500万t，同比增长0.8%；东北3省饲料产量1 850万t，同比基本持平。

5. *产业集中度进一步提高* 大型饲料企业仍是2009年增产的主力，在较高生产基数上，山东六和集团产量增长14.2%，全年饲料总产量有望达到900万t；江西正邦集团、陕西石羊（集团）、贵港瑞康饲料有限公司等企业产量增幅均超过20%。在大企业产量提升的同时，中小企业产量仍在下滑，农业部对重点跟踪的116个中小型饲料企业调查结果显示，平均产量同比下降了8.3个百分点。

6. *饲料与畜禽养殖环节质量安全总体稳定提升，局部问题反弹* 2009年农业部抽检饲料样品6 937批次，总体合格率达到90.93%，同比提高了2.3个百分点；在抽检的3 062批次饲料样品中，没有发现瘦肉精、莱克多巴胺、沙丁胺醇等违禁药物检出，仅有1批次样品中检出地西泮；检测蛋白饲料原料、奶牛饲料及其他饲料产品4 230批次，三聚氰胺检出率为0.66%，比2008年下降了3.33个百分点。在饲料质量安全总体水平稳中有升的同时，生猪养殖环节瘦肉精问题出现了反弹且有向肉牛养殖环节扩散的苗头，饲料中高铜、高锌问题在个别地区仍很严重，畜产品质量安全形势依然十分严峻。

二、发展机遇

近年来，我国饲料行业经历了严峻考验，虽有波折但仍保持了较好的发展势头，取得了一定成绩。但是，我们也应该看到，国际金融和经济环境正在发生深刻变革，我国农业农村经济社会正在发生深刻变革，畜牧业发展正在发生深刻变革，饲料行业发展的环境正在发生深刻变革。面对复杂的环境，我们应该认清当前饲料发展的有利条件和制约因素，抓住发展机遇，增强信心，努力促进我国饲料行业继续健康发展。分析形势，当前我国饲料发展面临着难得的发展机遇，我们高兴地看到：

1. *我国动物性食品需求的增长，为饲料行业发展提供了广阔的市场* 人口的增长、城乡居民生活水平的不断提高和城镇化进程的加快，决定了我国畜产品和水产品需求仍将在较长时间内保持刚性增长。为了保障养殖产品有效供给，我们建设现代畜牧业、发展水产养殖业，而产业规模的不断扩大和规模化养殖程度的不断提高，必须依靠现代饲料工业作为基础保障，不断发展的养殖业在对饲料工业支撑能力提出更高的要求的同时，也为饲料工业的发展提供了强大的动力。

2. *健全完善的法规和管理体系，为饲料行业发展创造了良好的法制和市场环境* 目前，我国已制定了以《饲料和饲料添加剂管理条例》为核心、6个配套管理办法和一系列配套规章为补充的比较完备的饲料法规体系，建立了省、市、县三级饲料管理队伍，形成了覆盖全国的饲料质检体系。多年来，各级饲料管理部门"以法治饲"，通过严格行政许可、强化饲料质量安全监管工作，逐步淘汰散乱差企业，严厉打击假冒伪劣产品、违禁药物和违禁添加物，在消费者、企业和政府之间建立形成了一个良好的饲料质量安全运行机制，为饲料企业构建了良好的发展环境。

3. *饲料企业中已经形成了引领饲料行业发展的*

主导力量 经过多年的发展，饲料行业中一大批企业在大浪淘沙的市场竞争中脱颖而出，成为行业发展的领军者。2008年全国饲料产量超过30万t的生产企业集团已经达到37个，总产量为5 716万t，占全国产量的41.8%。而其中的新希望、东方新希望、唐人神、广东温氏、大成等五大饲料企业集团2008年饲料产量都在290万t以上，并已进入世界饲料企业30强之中。这些大型企业在市场中成长，具有很强的抗风险能力，他们依托资金、技术和管理优势，不断探索发展模式，扩展发展空间，已经成为我国饲料行业的中流砥柱，成为未来行业发展的引领者，因此我国饲料行业发展具有强劲的发展动力。

4. 完备的配套产业体系，为饲料行业的发展提供了坚实的支撑保障 饲料是以粮食及其副产品为原料的加工产品，是动物科技成果的重要载体，饲料行业的发展离不开科技、教育、机械、化工、医药等领域的基础支持。目前，我国饲料机械制造技术和能力已达到国际水平，除满足国内饲料生产需要外，成套机组产品已打入国际市场；国内饲料添加剂工业迅速崛起，主要维生素、氨基酸产品全部实现自给，部分产品在国际市场已占据较大份额；企业与科研机构合作日益紧密，技术研发能力进一步加强，各大农业院校源源不断地为行业培养输送了大批专业人才；基础条件的改善，支撑能力的提高，为饲料工业的发提供了强有力的支持和保障。

（全国饲料工作办公室 李大鹏）

水产品加工业

一、基本情况

2009年面对国际金融危机带来的不利影响，农业部和各级渔业主管部门积极采取措施，在中央保增长、扩内需、调结构政策带动下，全国渔业生产和渔业经济运行平稳。

（一）生产情况

1. 产量 据《中国渔业统计年鉴》显示，2009年我国水产品总产量为5 116.40万t，比上年增长4.51%，占世界水产品总产量的35%左右。其中，海水产品产量2 681.55万t，占总产量的52%，同比增长3.20%；淡水产品产量2 434.85万t，占总产量的48%，同比增长5.99%。在国内渔业生产中，鱼类产量2 990.72万t，其中甲壳类产量532.42万t，贝类产量1 171.98万t，藻类产量149.12万t，头足类产量64.33万t，其他产量110.12万t。总产量中，养殖产量3 621.68万t，占我国水产品总产量的70.79%，占全球养殖水产品总量的67%；捕捞产量1 494.72万t，占捕捞水产品总产量的29.21%，占全球总量的16%。

2. 水生生物资源养护 2009年水生生物资源养护行动再掀高潮，农业部与北京、江苏、福建、辽宁、浙江、重庆、四川、广东、新疆、天津、内蒙古、山东、河北13个省（自治区、直辖市）级人民政府联合举办全国水生生物增殖放流活动，全年累计增殖放流各类水产苗种245亿尾。2009年6月6日，农业部与部分省、自治区、直辖市同步开展了形式多样的水生生物资源增殖放流活动，当天全国共举行大小活动上百场，累计投放各种重要水生生物苗种30亿尾，创单日增殖放流之最。海洋伏季休渔制度作出调整。2009年2月27日，农业部发出《关于调整海洋伏季休渔制度的通告》，对伏休制度进行了调整完善：三个海区的休渔时间统一向前延长半个月；定置作业休渔时间由不少于两个月调整为不少于两个半月；休渔作业类型统一调整为除单层刺网和钓具外的所有作业类型；取消了闽粤交界海域的特别休渔管理区域。

（二）水产品加工

1. 生产规模 2009年我国水产品加工企业9 635个，比2008年减少336个，同比下降3.37%。年加工能力为2 209.17万t，同比增长0.53%。水产品加工业冷库7 548座，同比增长1.47%。其中，冻结能力为49.97万t/d，同比增长15.98%；冷藏能力为360.36万t/次，同比增长7.35%；制冰能力为21.27万t/d，同比下降8.43%。

2. 加工产量与产值 2009年我国水产品加工总量为1 477.33万t，同比增长8.01%。淡水加工产品为227.93万t，同比增长13.50%。海水加工产品1 249.40万t，同比增长7.07%。冷冻水产品941.12万t，同比增长10.59%，其中冷冻品489.68万t，同比增长14.88%；冷冻加工品451.44万t，同比增长6.29%。鱼糜制品及干腌制品产量为223.54万t，同比增长15.53%，其中鱼糜制品84.79万t，同比增长3.52%；干腌制品为138.75万t，同比增长24.34%。藻类加工制品为90.46万t，同比增长10.74%。罐制品为22.08万t，同比增长0.28%。鱼粉产量为136.5万t，同比下降7.79%。鱼油制品产量为2.47万t，同比下降73.23%。2009年我国水产品加工总产值2 026.6亿元，同比增长33.69%。

二、科研、新产品、新技术

1. *罗非鱼产业良种化、规模化、加工现代化的关键技术创新及应用* 由中国水产科学研究院淡水渔业研究中心、上海海洋大学等单位完成的“罗非鱼产业良种化、规模化、加工现代化的关键技术创新及应用”项目，在罗非鱼引进、消化、吸收基础上，创新性地通过系统选育和生物技术集成，培育出4个国家审定良种（奥尼鱼、吉富品系尼罗罗非鱼、“新吉富”罗非鱼、“夏奥1号”奥利亚罗非鱼），覆盖我国罗非鱼产业80%以上；通过良种早繁、大规格鱼种培育、配合饲料应用、池塘改造和水质调控等技术组装集成，建立了罗非鱼规模化健康养殖技术体系，促进了罗非鱼养殖大面积高产和产品质量的提高，为国内外市场提供了安全的水产蛋白源；研究开发了罗非鱼从原料到加工的质量安全控制技术，推进了加工“零废弃”，提高了资源利用率，减少了环境污染。该项目促进了罗非鱼种源、养殖及加工三大产业的形成，保证了我国罗非鱼养殖产量、加工出口和产业链规模全球第一的地位，创造了显著的经济和社会效益。该成果获国家科技进步二等奖。

2. *液熏贝类产品生产工艺研究* 项目成果由荣成泰祥集团和中国水产科学研究院黄海所共同完成，项目成功开发出太平洋牡蛎和紫贻贝的液熏罐头的配方和生产工艺，所采用液熏技术与传统的烟熏技术相比：生产操作方便；生产过程中无污染气体排放；产品中苯并芘含量明显小于传统烟熏产品，食用更安全。

3. *东方海洋胶原蛋白生产线建成投产* 由山东东方海洋科技股份有限公司（以下简称东方海洋）投资1 000万元与中国海洋大学合作建设的胶原蛋白生产线在东方海洋建成投产，预计每年从鱼类加工下脚料里提取胶原蛋白200t，产值5 000万元，增值30多倍。

三、国内外市场运行情况

（一）国内贸易

2009年上半年，在金融危机和国际市场消费持续萎缩等负面因素影响下，我国水产品批发市场月度价格普遍低于上年同期；但是下半年随着国内一揽子经济刺激政策逐渐发挥作用，我国经济企稳回升，消费市场回暖，水产品批发市场月度价格普遍高于上年同期水平。总的看来，2009年市场运行较为平稳，交易数额稳步增加，价格波动幅度明显低于上年。据对全国50个水产品定点批发市场情况统计，2009年水产品批发市场综合平均价格15.05元/kg，同比微涨0.03%。其中，海水产品综合平均价格26.21元/kg,同比上涨3.29%；淡水产品综合平均价格11.07元/kg，同比下降4.11%。另据对全国35个批发市场成交情况统计，2009年市场成交量、成交额分别为538.34万t和834.78亿元，同比分别增加6.33%和12.1%。

（二）进出口贸易

2009年我国水产品进出口总量667.9万t，总额159.6亿美元，同比分别下降2.4%和0.13%。其中，出口量294.2万t，同比下降0.6%；出口额107亿美元，同比增长1%。进口量373.7万t，进口额52.6亿美元，同比分别下降3.8%和2.6%。贸易顺差54.4亿美元，比2008年同期增加2.3亿美元。水产品出口额继续位居大宗农产品出口首位，占农产品出口总额（395.9亿美元）的27%，较2008年提高0.8个百分点。

1. *贸易方式* 2009年国际水产品原料价格波动较大，部分国家以防止资源外流为由限制其原料水产品出口。同时，我来进料加工水产品主要出口市场受金融危机影响，经济低迷、消费需求下降。在此压力下，我水产品来进料加工出口困难重重，出口量、出口额同比分别下降8.6%和4.0%，占出口总额的比例较2008年下降了3.6个百分点。

2. *出口品种* 对虾、贝类、罗非鱼、鳗鱼、淡水小龙虾、大黄鱼和斑点叉尾鮰等名优养殖水产品仍是主要出口品种。鳗鱼、淡水小龙虾和大黄鱼出口形势较上年略有好转。贝类、罗非鱼和斑点叉尾鮰出口形势严峻，罗非鱼出口单价持续大幅下降，已经严重威胁到产业发展。海洋捕捞头足类产品、虾蟹类和冻鱼出口大幅增长，成为一般贸易出口的亮点。

3. *出口市场* 主要出口市场基本格局没有发生大的变化，日、美、欧、韩依然是我国最重要的出口市场，占我国水产品出口总额的69.8%，比2008年下降2.5个百分点，其中日本和韩国市场降幅最为明显。东盟和我国台湾市场表现抢眼，出口量和出口额均大幅增加。水产品市场集中度进一步降低，市场多元化步伐加快。

4. *出口省份* 山东、广东、辽宁、福建、浙江、海南等沿海省份仍是我水产品主要出口省份，出口额之和占全国出口总额的91.7%。其中福建凭借对台贸易的快速增长，出口额同比增长31.3%，超过浙江成为第四大出口省份。江西和湖北作为最重要的内陆出口省份，水产品出口额同比分别增长43.7%和32.2%。

5. 进口情况　2009年供国内食用水产品进口量114万t，进口额17.3亿美元，同比分别增加1%和1.8%，主要品种有鱿鱼、鳕鱼、鲑鱼、带鱼、鳙鲽鱼类以及其他未列明冻鱼等，继续为满足国内不同消费需求，丰富国内水产品市场发挥着重要作用。来进料加工原料进口量128.9万t，进口额22.3亿美元，同比分别下降8.4%和3.5%。俄罗斯、美国、东盟、挪威、日本、欧盟等是我国可食用水产品和来进料加工原料主要进口市场，其中从俄罗斯、东盟、欧盟和加拿大进口均出现不同程度下降，从挪威进口大幅增加，从美国和日本进口有一定增长。鱼粉进口继2008年大幅增加后，2009年小幅下降，进口量130.8万t，进口额13亿美元，同比分别下降3%和6.9%，秘鲁和智利依然是我国最重要的鱼粉进口国，其中从智利进口增加，从秘鲁进口减少。

（三）市场需求分析及预测

2010年水产品市场仍将继续保持平稳运行的局面。一是随着中央对惠农政策的不断落实，渔业生产将继续保持稳定的发展格局，水产品产量将保持稳步增长，市场供给将充足稳定。二是随着CPI的走高，粮食、肉、蛋、蔬菜等农产品价格会有不小的涨幅，水产品市场价格低廉的优势更加突显出来，有利于刺激国内水产品消费的增长，市场交易额、交易量将会持续增加。三是2010年经济工作要着力提高宏观调控水平，保持经济平稳较快发展。把扩大内需作为保增长的根本途径，把加快发展方式转变和结构调整作为保增长的主攻方向。中央扩大内需的举措将会有力地拉动包括水产品在内的市场消费，促进水产品市场健康稳定的发展。

2010年，国际金融危机对世界各国实体经济的影响将逐步减弱，国际消费市场的需求逐渐转暖。我国拥有世界上规模最大的水产养殖业和较为先进的水产品加工贸易体系，水产品贸易所具有的价格和生产成本的国际竞争力优势的基本格局没有改变，而且政府也积极通过调整出口退税率、为加工出口企业提供金融支持等政策来促进企业的发展。预计我国水产品出口贸易将会出现出口量、出口额双升态势；进口量、进口额的增幅将呈现“前低后高”的态势。预计2010年下半年受来料加工生产规模加大的影响，增幅将有较大的弹升。

四、质量管理与标准化工作

1. 继续把质量安全放在突出首位　2009年农业部重点加强基础性工作，制订了《产地水产品质量安全监督抽查工作暂行规定》，建立了产地水产品质量安全监督抽查数据库，改革产地水产品质量安全监督抽查组织方式，实行异地检测、抽查结果公开制度。以主要出口品种和国内市场消费的大宗品种为重点，以硝基呋喃类代谢物、孔雀石绿、氯霉素等禁用药物为主要监测指标，加强产地水产品质量安全监督抽查工作。首次随机抽取被检单位，并公开发布抽检结果，发挥社会和市场监督作用，取得比较好的效果。水产品质量安全水平稳步提高，全年综合产地和市场检测合格率达97%以上，同比增长1.5个百分点。

2. 水产品质量安全问题研讨会召开　2009年6月12日，农业部农产品质量安全监管局召开了“水产品质量安全问题研讨会”。本次会议议题主要是梳理和分析水产品存在的主要质量安全问题；对问题的危害程度、产生原因和关键环节进行讨论分析，力求探讨解决方案。

3. 农业部开展“三品”专项整治行动督查工作　2009年8月4日农业部发布《关于开展无公害农产品、绿色食品、有机农产品专项整治行动督查工作》通知，在全国开展“三品”专项整治督查工作。通知规定，各省级农业部门2009年8月30日前完成本地区、本行业“三品”工作的督查。8月31日～9月6日，农业部将选择10个省份进行重点督查，每个省份督查时间3天左右。

4.《干海参》、《干紫菜》国家标准颁布　《干海参》国家标准（SC/T 3206—2009）于2009年10月1日正式实施。新发布的《干海参》标准在原有感官、水分、盐分指标的基础上，增加了蛋白质、水溶性还原糖、复水后干重率、含砂量等指标，其质量评价指标有助于界定劣质、掺假的干海参产品。《干紫菜》国家标准从2009年12月1日起正式实施，对干紫菜的定义、分类、技术要求、检验方法、检验规则、标签和标志、包装、运输及贮存等方面作了规定，还对各类干紫菜设定了相应的卫生指标及微生物指标等，如干紫菜铅含量每千克不得高于1mg，无机砷不得高于1.5mg等。

5.《冷冻鱼糜加工技术规范》、《带壳虾干》广东省渔业地方标准通过专家审定　《冷冻鱼糜加工技术规范》标准由中国水产科学研究院南海所主持制订，标准对冷冻鱼糜加工企业的基本要求、加工技术操作要点、产品质量及生产纪录等要求进行了合理的限定和详细的描述，使标准更具实用性，可操作性强。标准的制订和实施，对规范冷冻鱼糜加工企业生产行为，提高企业标准化意识，提高产品质量，确保冷冻鱼糜产品的食用安全性，保障人民身体健康都具有重要作用。《带壳虾干》由中国水产科学研究院南海所主持制定，规定了带壳虾干的要求、检验方法、检验规则、标签、标志、包装、运输及贮存，使标准更具实用性，可操作性强。标准的制订和实施，对监控带壳虾干产品质量、规范产品市场，确保广大消费者安全、放心的食用带壳虾干产品都具有重要作用。

五、行业管理

（一）服务行业，引导产业良性发展

1. *构建流通平台，推动水产品内销* 为积极落实中央提出的“扩内需、保增长、惠民生”重大举措，中国水产流通与加工协会紧密围绕行业发展需求，立足于行业服务，在促进国际贸易健康发展的同时，积极开拓国内市场，为扎实推动水产品内销稳定发展做了大量的工作。2009 年分别在北京、上海、重庆、广东、福建等地举办了鳗鱼、海参、罗非鱼、脆肉鲩、鱼糜制品等系列推介活动。

2. *协助水产企业开拓国际市场* 中国水产流通与加工协会根据国际市场需求情况，有重点地组织企业参加了欧洲国际海产品展览会、迪拜水产展、台北食品展、韩国水产展、澳洲食品展等活动，取得了良好收效。

（二）举办专业研讨会、交流会研讨产业热点问题

1. *湛江对虾论坛召开* 4 月 15～17 日，由中国水产流通与加工协会主办，湛江市饲料行业协会、湛江市水产进出口企业协会承办的 2009 中国对虾产业发展论坛在湛江成功召开，论坛围绕对虾贸易现状与发展前景、对虾饲料与营养及对虾加工贸易、对虾养殖及产品质量安全等专题展开了深入探讨，为应对金融危机对对养虾业的冲击出谋划策。

2. *鳕鱼来进料加工产业座谈会召开* 6 月 17 日，应鳕鱼来进料加工企业的要求，中国水产流通与加工协会在青岛召开了鳕鱼来进料加工产业座谈会。会议探讨了我国鳕鱼来进料加工业的现状，以及当前面临的主要问题，在鳕鱼原料合理价格方面达成共识，拟组建来进料加工工作委员会，围绕鳕鱼、鱿鱼及鲆鲽鱼类等来进料原料开展工作。

3. *罗非鱼危机与产业整合研讨会召开* 7 月 19 日，南方报业集团在广州召开了“罗非鱼危机与产业整合”研讨会，会上云集了业内最具代表性的人物，一起为罗非鱼产业诊断把脉、出谋划策、探寻出路，在构建高度自治、责权统一、强有力的行业协会及管理规范行业秩序方面达成共识。

4. *第六届罗非鱼产业发展论坛在南宁召开* 11 月 9～10 日，由中国水产流通与加工协会与中国水产科学研究院淡水渔业研究中心、广西壮族自治区水产畜牧兽医局共同举办的“第六届罗非鱼产业发展论坛”在南宁召开。本届论坛旨在探讨金融危机大环境下，我国罗非鱼产业如何渡过危机，有效规避贸易保护主义对策，保持产业的健康、有序发展。与会代表就苗种场规范、养殖过程中抗生素的使用、无序竞争、冰衣等问题进行深入探讨与广泛交流，分析了 2009 年罗非鱼出口价格低迷的成因及美国罗非鱼消费市场的变化情况。

（三）中国水产流通与加工协会海参分会在京成立

2009 年 11 月 17 日，中国水产流通与加工协会海参分会成立大会在北京隆重举办。会上，我国著名水产加工专家管华诗院士当选为海参分会会长，全体海参分会会员企业向社会公开发表了《海参产品质量承诺书》。海参分会全体会员企业向全社会郑重承诺：牢固树立海参产品质量，加强在海参育苗、养殖、加工、流通等各环节的自律，严格遵守《农产品质量安全法》、《食品安全法》等法律法规，依法生产经营，自愿接受社会各界的监督。

（四）重大事件

1. *欧盟考察我国出口水产品卫生管理体系* 经中国与欧盟双方协商，5 月份欧盟食品兽医办公室 4 位官员分两组，对我辽宁、浙江、福建、广东 4 省出口水产品卫生管理情况进行了考察。欧盟官员此次共考察了 2 个水产养殖场、5 艘捕捞渔船和 13 个水产加工厂，检查内容包括：养殖场的日常水质监测、苗种收购、养殖管理；捕捞渔船的硬件设施、卫生条件、生产过程管理；加工企业出口卫生注册相关材料，以及原料养殖、原料收购、生产加工、储存、运输、监测、出口等各环节自检自控体系，检查相关记录和档案材料、相关实验室内部控制体系和运行机制。

2. *新增水产品出口退税上调目录* 6 月 3 日，财政部和国家税务总局联合发布《关于进一步提高部分商品出口退税率的通知》（财税［2009］88 号），提高部分商品的出口退税率。此次出口退税率上调的水产品主要涉及冷冻、制作保藏的鱼类，经过初、深加工的贝类、海参、藻类等，其出口退税率分别提高到了 13％或 15％。该通知自 2009 年 6 月 1 日起执行。

3. 积极应对欧盟“非法、未管制、未报告”捕鱼活动（IUU）新规 为切实做好输欧水产品合法性认证工作，根据农业部渔业局安排，中国水产流通与加工协会会同中国渔业协会远洋渔业分会于2009年10月12～13日在大连召开“中欧水产品贸易问题座谈会”，介绍欧盟IUU条例及有关要求，讨论输欧水产品认证工作相关事宜，帮助各输欧水产品企业提前做好准备，确保我国出口欧盟水产品贸易在欧盟实施IUU管理条例初期能平稳过渡，避免由于欧盟政策调整可能导致的我国水产品出口欧盟临时中断等问题。

4. 对虾反倾销日落复审工作正式启动 中国水产流通与加工协会经过半年的国内调研与积极推动，于11月20日向主要对虾生产贸易企业发布了《关于应对2010年度输美对虾反倾销“日落复审”的紧急通知》，12月3日在海口召开了“对虾日落复审应对协商会”，国内近50余家大型对虾贸易企业积极响应并参与应诉筹备工作，标志着2010年度输美对虾反倾销“日落复审”工作的正式启动。

5. 全国水产品加工产业现状调查启动 12月4日，中国水产流通与加工协会在海南省海口市召开了“全国水产品加工产业现状调查工作启动会议”，会议研究并初步确定了全国水产品产业现状调查提纲，确定了相关的调查内容及调查方法与方案。

6. 农业部公布2010年水产品加工专业分中心名单 依据《农产品加工业“十一五”发展规划》和《国家农产品加工技术研发中心及分中心管理办法》的有关要求，按照公平、公正、公开的原则，通过单位自主申报、地方主管部门审查推荐、专家评审及网上公示等程序，2009年底，农业部认定山东省农业科学院农产品研究所等76个单位为国家农产品加工技术研发专业分中心。其中中国水产科学研究院南海水产研究所（水产品国家中心）、中国海洋大学、华中农业大学、海南泉溢食品有限公司、广西南宁百洋饲料集团有限公司、福建长乐聚泉食品有限公司、湖南益阳益华水产品有限公司、大连工业大学、中国水产科学研究院东海水产研究所、大连水产学院、江苏南通海达水产食品有限公司、浙江工商大学、山东东方海洋科技股份有限公司、广东湛江国联水产开发股份有限公司等，被认定为水产品加工专业分中心。

（中国水产流通与加工协会 陈丽纯）

林产品加工业

一、经济林、竹及花卉产业

2009年，我国新造经济林面积100.26万hm^2，比2008年增长17.84%。各类经济林产品总产量达到1.27亿t。水果产量为11 182万t，比2008年增长13.94%，其中苹果、柑橘和梨分别为3 268万t、2 364万t和1 473万t；干果产量为673万t，比2008年增长26.11%；林产饮料产品的产量为143万t，比2008年增长7.51%；林产调料产品的产量为47万t，比2008年增长8.70%；林产工业原料产量156万t，比2008年增长16.83%；木本油料产量为122万t，比2008年增长16.03%；竹笋干、食用菌等森林食品产量为263万t；木本药材的产量为153万t。

2009年我国竹材产量为13.56亿根，比2008年增长7.47%。其中毛竹8.76亿根，篙竹4.80亿根，分别占全部竹材产量的64.61%和35.39%。村及村以下各级组织和农民生产竹材11.27亿根，占全部竹材产量的83.11%。2009年我国油茶籽产量为117万t，占木本油料产量的96.05%，比2008年增长8.13%。油茶产业产值达82亿元。2009年我国花卉种植面积63.26万hm^2，切花切叶124亿支，盆栽植物近20亿盆，观赏苗木50亿株，草坪2.32亿m^2。具有一定规模的花卉市场4 300多个，花卉企业3.45万个。其中大中型花卉企业6 700多个，花卉从业人员387万人，花农110万户，控温温室面积和日光温室面积分别为2 709万m^2和11 463万m^2。

二、木材生产及林产工业

1. 木材产量正常回落 我国由于受雨雪冰冻灾害和地震灾害影响，清理受损林木和灾后重建，2008年木材产量大幅增加，2009年木材产量正常回落，为7 068.29万m^3，比2008年减少12.83%。从木材产品结构看，原木产量6 476.27万m^3，比2008年减少11.98%；薪材产量592.02万m^3，比2008年减少21.17%。从木材生产单位看，林业系统内生产的木材为 2 604.78 万 m^3，比 2008 年下降 9.04%，占全部木材产量的 36.85%。其中，系统内国有林场、事业单位生产木材 1 294.60 万 m^3。系统外企、事业单位采伐自营林地的木材 222.98 万 m^3，同比下降 12.61%，占全部木材产量的 3.15%。乡（镇）集体企业及单位生产木材产量 368.32 万 m^3，同比下降 16.48%，占全部木材产量的 5.21%。村及村以下各级组织和农民个人生产的木材 3 872.22 万 m^3，同比下降 14.87%，占全部木材产量的 54.78%。

2. 锯材产量持续增长　2009 年，我国全部锯材产量为 3 229.77 万 m^3，比 2008 年增长 13.69%，其中热带锯材产量 147.44 万 m^3，占全部锯材产量的 4.56%。

3. 人造板产量快速增长　2009 年，我国人造板产量首次突破 1 亿 m^3，达到 11 546.65 万 m^3，比 2008 年增长 22.71%。其中，热带材人造板产量 595.46 万 m^3，仅占全部人造板产量的 5.16%。在全部人造板产量中，胶合板 4 451.24 万 m^3，比 2008 年增长 25.71%，占全部人造板产量的 38.55%；纤维板 3 488.56 万 m^3，比 2008 年增长 20.02%，占全部人造板产量的 30.21%。其中，中密度纤维板产量为 3 131.64 万 m^3；刨花板产量 1 431.00 万 m^3，分别比 2008 年增长 14.27%和 25.28%，分别占全部人造板产量的 27.12%和 12.39%；其他人造板 2 175.85 万 m^3（细木工板占 67.96%），比 2008 年增长 19.53%，占全部人造板产量的 18.84%。另外，2009 年人造板表面装饰板产量为 2.53 亿 m^2，单板产量为 2 714 万 m^3。从分省情况看，人造板生产依然主要集中在东部地区，江苏、河南、山东、河北、广西、福建、安徽、广东 8 省（自治区）产量均超过 500 万 m^3，8 省（自治区）人造板产量共计 8 694.49 万 m^3，占全国人造板总产量的 75.30%。其中，江苏、河南、山东和河北 4 省的人造板产量，均已突破 1 000 万 m^3。

4. 木地板产量保持稳定增长　2009 年，我国全部木地板产量达到 3.78 亿 m^2，比 2008 年增长 0.17%。在木地板产量中，实木地板 8 139 万 m^2，占全部木地板产量的 21.56%；实木复合地板 11 771 万 m^2，占全部木地板的 31.18%；强化木地板 12 716 万 m^2，占全部木地板产量的 33.68%；竹木复合地板 2 011 万 m^2，占全部木地板产量的 5.33%。木地板产量最大的省份是浙江省，产量达到 7 224 万 m^2。

5. 木制家具产量继续增长　2009 年，我国木制家具产量为 20 501.01 万件，比 2008 年增长 8.20%。

6. 木浆产量下降　2009 年，我国纸和纸板总产量 8 640 万 t，比 2008 年增长 8.27%；纸浆产量 6 674万 t，比 2008 年增长 4.04%，其中木浆产量 551 万 t，比 2008 年下降 18.01%。

7. 林化产品产量恢复增长　2009 年，我国松香类产品产量 111.70 万 t，比 2008 年增长 4.66%，其中松香产量为 100.16 万 t，同比增长 5.92%；松节油产量 11.23 万 t，同比增长 37.17%；栲胶 11 000t，同比增长 17.81%；紫胶产量 1 992t，同比下降 31.10%。

三、木材产品市场供给与消费

（一）木材供给

我国木材产品市场供给由国内供给和进口两部分构成。国内供给包括商品材、农民自用材和农民烧柴、木质纤维板和刨花板；进口包括进口原木、锯材、单板、人造板、家具、木浆、木片、纸和纸制品、废纸及其他木质林产品。2009 年我国木材产品市场总供给为 42 234.49 万 m^3，比 2008 年增长 13.74%。

1. 商品材　2009 年，我国商品材产量为 7 068.29万 m^3，比 2008 年减少 12.83%。其中，原木产量 6 476.27 万 m^3，薪材（不符合原木标准的木材）592.02 万 m^3，分别比 2008 年减少 11.98% 和 21.17%。

2. 农民自用材和烧柴　根据“十一五”采伐限额推算，我国农民自用材和烧柴折合木材供给量为 4 604.17万 m^3。其中，农民自用材为 1 560.38 万 m^3，农民烧柴为 3 043.79 万 m^3。

3. 木质纤维板和刨花板　2009 年，我国木质纤维板产量为 3 430.43 万 m^3，刨花板（普通刨花板和定向刨花板）产量为 1 426.3 万 m^3，分别比 2008 年增长 18.23%和 25.31%；木质纤维板和刨花板折合木材供给 8 314.22 万 m^3，扣除与薪材产量的重复计算部分，木质纤维板和刨花板相当于净增加木材供给 8 225.42 万 m^3。

4. 进口　2009 年，我国木质林产品进口折合木材 18 436.62 万 m^3。其中，原木 2 805.93 万 m^3，锯材（含特形材）1 293.33 万 m^3，单板和人造板 211.39 万 m^3，纸浆及纸类（木浆、纸和纸板、废纸和废纸浆、印刷品）13 492.83 万 m^3，木片 497.88 万 m^3，家具、木制品及木炭 135.26 万 m^3。

5. 其他　2009 年，我国超限额采伐、上年库存等形式形成的木材供给约为 3 800 万 m^3。

（二）木材消费

我国木材产品市场消费由国内消费和出口两部分构成。国内消费包括工业与建筑用材消费、农民自用材和烧柴消费；出口包括出口原木、锯材、单板、人造板、家具、木浆、木片、纸和纸制品、废纸及其他木质林产品。2009年木材产品市场总消费为42 189.48万m^3，比2008年增长13.58%。

1. 工业与建筑用材消费　据国家统计局和有关部门统计，按相关产品木材消耗系数推算，2009年我国建筑业与工业用材折合木材消耗量为32 516.47万m^3，比2008年增长17.64%。其中，建筑业用材（包括装修与装饰）11 664.15万m^3，比2008年增长40.74%；家具用材（指家具的国内消费部分，出口家具耗材包括在出口项目中）5 009.42万m^3，比2008年增长11.87%；造纸业用材13 884.55万m^3，比2008年增长6.68%；煤炭业用材945.24万m^3，比2008年减少9.30%；车船制造、铁路、化纤等其他部门用材1 013.11万m^3，比2008年增长23.88%。

2. 农民自用材和烧柴　根据产量测算，农民自用材消耗量为1 560.38万m^3，农民烧柴消耗量为3 043.79万m^3。由于农民自用材消耗中有很大一部分用于农民建房，约合1 404.34万m^3，扣除这部分与建筑用材消耗的重复计算后，农民自用材和烧柴消耗量为3 199.83万m^3。

3. 出口　2009年，我国木质林产品出口折合木材6 473.18万m^3。其中，原木1.27万m^3，锯材128.29万m^3，单板和人造板1 821.63万m^3，纸浆及纸类（木浆、纸和纸板、废纸和废纸浆、印刷品）1 570.06万m^3，家具2 722.17万m^3，木片、木制品和木炭229.76万m^3。

（三）木材产品市场供需的特点

2009年，我国木材产品市场供需的主要特点：一是供给方面。国内实际供给、进口总量增加，木材产品供给总规模扩大。二是需求方面。国内需求回升，但区域分化明显，出口小幅回落，木材产品总需求扩大。三是价格方面。木材产品总体价格水平年内波动中回升，但总体价格水平比2008年小幅下降。

1. 国内实际供给与需求扩大　从国内供给看，虽然2009年我国商品材产量比2008年有较大幅度减少，但若考虑超限额采伐、库存调整等因素，国内木材产品实际供给仍然有较大幅度增加；同时，尽管原木进口量减少，但锯材等木材加工产品进口量增加，木材产品进口总量增加，木材产品市场供给总规模扩大。从国内需求看，虽然受国际金融危机的影响，我国宏观经济增长趋缓，但仍然保持较高的经济增长率。为应对国际金融危机，国家实施积极的财政政策和适度宽松的货币政策，增加固定资产投资，刺激内需市场扩大。宏观经济增长与固定资产投资的豁达，有效拉动了基本建设用材和生产用材的国内市场需求。由于国家采取了包括提高家具等木材产品的出口退税率在内的一系列出口促进措施，2009年木材产品出口在外需萎缩的环境下只有小幅度的下降。从总体上看，木材产品的总需求仍有较大幅度的回升。

2. 区域市场差异明显　从各区域木材市场看，东北市场由于国产木材的减少，而且木材产品结构中针叶材多、阔叶材少，一般材多、优质材少，小径材多、大径材少，加上俄罗斯进口木材的价格和径级优势，国产木材市场受到进口材较大冲击。西北市场由于本地木材资源供给相对短缺，加上西部大开发战略实施，木材销售市场表现活跃。在西南地区，边贸木材市场一度相当活跃，但由于木材价格下降，库存积压等原因，市场总体表现较为平淡。东部及沿海地区是国内木材消费的主要市场，木材销售形势较好，特别是福建、广东等地区大径级松木、杉木的市场表现活跃。

3. 木材产品总体价格水平年内在波动中回升，但全年价格水平仍然小幅下降　2009年木材产品市场价格在波动中小幅下降，但总体价格水平仍然低于2008年水平。主要原因：一是由于美元币值反弹和国际石油价格的大幅回落，木材产品进口成本和运费下降，导致木材产品进口价格的大幅下降，进而拉低了国内木材产品市场的总体价格水平；二是随着国内经济的复苏，对木材产品需求的扩大，木材产品价格从第三季度开始回升，但由于第一、二季度价格降幅较大，故全年的平均价格水平仍然小幅回落。

四、主要林产品价格

据国家统计局资料显示，2009年我国木材产品价格指数为95.58%。其中，一季度为95.84%，二季度为93.77%，三季度为94.53%，四季度为98.18%。林产品价格指数为94.05%。其中，一季度为88.81%，二季度为86.73%，三季度为96.52%，四季度为104.14%。

1. 原木　根据国家统计局调查的月度数据，2009年除云南松和红松外，各种原木的购进价格基本平稳。红松原木的购进价格从年初的1 104.6元/m^3小幅攀升至4月的1 267.9元/m^3，然后开始缓慢回落，降至8月份的1 121.1元/m^3后开始上扬，9月份达到1 230.7元/m^3，之后缓慢回落到年末的1 200.9元/m^3；落叶松原木的价格相对稳定，1～5月份稳定在900.3～910.3元/m^3之间，6～11月份在924.1～939.34元/m^3之间波动，12月份回落至905.9元/m^3；马尾松原木的价格水平保持稳定，一直在600～610元/m^3范围，直到10月份开始小幅上涨，到

12月份达到了632.9元/m^3；杉木原木的价格小幅波动，从年初的774.4元/m^3，其间小幅波动，12月份达到了776.3元/m^3；云南松原木的价格波动起伏较大，在1月份的价格为1 026.6元/m^3，到4月达到1 367.8元/m^3的高位，然后迅速下降到1 182.3元/m^3的水平，8月份价格上扬到另一个高位1 377元/m^3，然后又迅速回落到9月份的1 150.5元/m^3，之后价格开始攀升，11月份的价格为1 364.4元/m^3，年末价格回落到1 350.9元/m^3。

2. *锯材* 2009年，普通锯材的全年平均购进价格为2 228.2元/m^3，比2008年下降了6.54%。其中，落叶松厚板波动较大，从1月份的1 133.2元/m^3上升到2月份的1 178.6元/m^3，然后开始回落，一直下降到7月份的最低点1 061.8元/m^3，8月份开始回升，一直上涨到年末的1 257.3元/m^3的水平；杉木厚板价格起伏波动也比较大，从年初1 055.1元/m^3的水平开始波动，4月份达到了价格最低点991.3元/m^3，6月份迅速上扬到1 099元/m^3，然后开始缓慢回落，12月份下降到1 042.1元/m^3；马尾松厚板的价格总体趋势攀升，1月份是全年价格的最低点，为1 128.4元/m^3，之后价格开始上升，4月份价格增幅最大，上升到1 349.1元/m^3，5月份上升到最高点1 364.4元/m^3，之后价格开始小幅回落，7月份到达一个低位1 241.5元/m^3，然后开始攀升到11月份的最高点1 388.6元/m^3，但12月份下降到1 293.6元/m^3。

3. *人造板* 2009年，胶合板和刨花板平均出厂价格分别为1 222元/m^3和723.5元/m^3，比2008年分别降低了3.49%和4.54%；纤维板的平均出厂价格为826元/m^3，比2008年上涨了1.43%。从各月出厂价格走势看，胶合板价格基本平稳，从年初的1 180.2元/m^3，小幅上升后基本维持1 200元/m^3的水平，6月份价格上扬到1 353.1元/m^3，7月份回落到1 241.8元/m^3，然后基本保持平稳，年末价格为1 229.9元/m^3；纤维板价格持续小幅上升，从年初的800.6元/m^3，增长到年末的897.2元/m^3；刨花板在前半年价格波动较大，1月份是全年价格的最低点632.2元/m^3，2月份上升到802.6元/m^3，之后小幅波动，到5月份达到了最高点814.2元/m^3，6月份回落到678.3元/m^3，之后价格微幅上涨，年末达到688.7元/m^3。

4. *木浆* 2009年，机械木浆和化学木浆的平均出厂价格分别为3 357.4元/t和3 885元/t，比2008年分别下降20.43%和11.96%。从各月的出厂价格走势看，木浆价格都呈现缓慢的上升趋势。机械木浆的价格上升幅度较小，从年初的3 285.1元/t开始缓慢下降，到4月份达到最低点3 217.8元/t，6月份价格上扬到3 336.6元/t，7月份回落到3 317.9元/t，然后逐步上升到年末的3 597.8元/t的水平；而化学木浆上升幅度较大，年初在3 700元/t的水平，小幅下滑后，5月份上升到4 020元/t左右，6月份价格下降到3 806.5元/t的低点，之后价格稳步攀升，12月份价格达到4 311.6元/t的高位。从购进价格来看，机械木浆和化学木浆的年均价格分别为4 313.6元/t和4 201.6元/t。机械木浆和化学木浆的购进价格都是先下降后上升，机械木浆从年初的4 465.8元/t持续下降到5月份的4 170.5元/t，然后开始稳步上升，年末达到了4 537.6元/t。化学木浆从1月份的4 308元/t，下降到5月份的最低点3 922.6元/t，然后开始回升，到12月份上涨至4 616.9元/t。

五、主要林产品进出口

（一）基本态势

2009年我国林产品进出口贸易大幅减少，但出口减幅小于进口减幅，出现了贸易顺差；在全国商品进出口贸易中，林产品出口所占比重提高，进口所占比重略有下降。2009年，林产品进出口贸易总额为702.18亿美元，与2008年同比减少8.16%。其中，林产品出口363.16亿美元，与2008年同比下降4.47%，但低于全国商品出口15.87%的下降速度，占全国商品出口额的3.02%，与2008年同比提高了0.36个百分点；林产品进口339.02亿美元，比2008年减少11.80%，略高于全国商品进口11.20%的下降速度，占全国商品进口额的3.37%，比2008年降低了0.02个百分点。2009年林产品贸易顺差为24.14亿美元。

（二）林产品进出口贸易特点

2009年，我国林产品进出口贸易以木质林产品为主，且木质林产品的份额略有提高。在林产品进出口贸易总额中，木质林产品和非木质林产品分别占69.74%和30.26%，与2008年同比，木质林产品的份额提高了1.41个百分点；在林产品出口额中，木质林产品占73.94%，与2008年同比提高了2.38个百分点；在林产品进口额中，木质林产品占65.24%，与2008年同比提高了0.12个百分点。

（三）林产品主要进出口市场

2009年我国林产品出口主要集中于美、日市场，进口则以美、俄和东南亚市场为主，进出口的市场集中度有所下降。2009年，林产品出口总额中各洲所占份额分别为：亚洲42.17%、北美洲27.51%、欧洲21.50%、非洲3.58%、大洋洲3.20%、拉丁美洲2.06%，与2008年同比，亚洲提高了5.84个百分点，北美洲和欧洲分别下降了2.80、3.51个百分点；林产品进口总额中各洲所占份额分别为：亚洲43.63%、欧洲20.84%、北美洲18.09%、拉丁美洲9.47%、大洋洲5.00%、非洲2.97%，与2008年同比，亚洲、欧洲和非洲分别下降了2.06、1.15和0.18个百分点，拉丁美洲和大洋洲分别提高了2.58和0.66个百分点。

从主要贸易伙伴看，前5位出口贸易伙伴依次是美国、日本、中国香港、英国和德国。前5位出口贸易伙伴集中了49.25%的林产品出口市场份额，比2008年减少0.97个百分点。其中，美国减少了2.47个百分点，中国香港增加了1.45个百分点。前5位进口贸易伙伴分别为美国、印度尼西亚、马来西亚、泰国和俄罗斯。前5位进口贸易伙伴集中了51.24%的林产品进口市场份额，比2008年下降了4.57个百分点，其中马来西亚、俄罗斯和印度尼西亚分别下降了2.57、1.30和0.82个百分点，泰国提高了0.74个百分点。

（国家林业局发展规划与资金管理司 刘建杰 于百川）

农作物秸秆加工业

一、基本情况

2009年，我国粮食总产量达到53 082万t，比2008年增加211万t，创历史最好记录。作为粮食生产附属产物的秸秆，产量也达到历史新高。有效利用秸秆，避免焚烧秸秆，实现秸秆利用的经济效益、社会效益和生态效益，成为农作物秸秆加工业的关键问题。在国家有关部门和各地政府积极推动和支持下，2009年我国秸秆综合利用取得了显著成果，各地投资建设了一批秸秆人造板、秸秆直燃发电、秸秆沼气、秸秆气化、秸秆成型燃料等综合利用项目。同时，多种形式的秸秆还田、保护性耕作、秸秆快速腐熟还田、过腹还田、栽培食用菌等技术的推广应用，在一定程度上减少了秸秆焚烧现象。

（一）主要成就

1. *秸秆粉碎还田和秸秆养畜成效显著* 2009年，全国秸秆粉碎还田机保有量达48.52万台，机械化秸秆还田面积达24 927.23khm²，比2008年增加了2161.75khm²。秸秆养畜是推动种养殖业有机结合、发展农业循环经济的关键环节，是保障动物性食品供给、降低粮食安全压力的必然选择，是治理秸秆焚烧的长效手段，是促进农民增收、加快建设社会主义新农村的现实途径。2009年，秸秆捡拾打捆机全国保有量0.77万台，青饲料收获机保有量2.15万台，秸秆捡拾打捆面积699.82khm²，机械化青贮秸秆7 258.21万t，比2008年增加563.06万t，增幅达到8.4%。

2. *秸秆生物反应堆技术发展迅速* 秸秆生物反应堆技术作为设施农业发展的一项增产、增效实用技术，各级政府加快了推广秸秆反应堆技术的力度。2009年2月在白银市成功召开了全国秸秆生物反应堆现场会后，天津、山东、甘肃、陕西、辽宁、河北、江苏、河南等省市也举行了现场会，把该项技术作为重点推广的实用技术。

3. *秸秆能源化利用技术发展势头喜人* 秸秆等农林废弃物已经被称作“生物质能资源”，许多发达国家已经把它当成仅次于煤炭、石油、天然气的第4大能源，也是我国秸秆利用发展趋势。目前，我国秸秆的能源化利用主要有秸秆发电、秸秆沼气、秸秆气化、秸秆压块、秸秆制乙醇等技术。秸秆发电是秸秆能源化最有效的途径。2009年，山东潍坊昌邑、辽宁昌图、湖北当阳、江苏高邮首镇等秸秆发电厂先后点火运行，内蒙古自治区巴彦淖尔、重庆垫江、河北泰达、江苏高邮朝阳和南通海安、山西应县等秸秆发电开工建设，增添了当地秸秆利用途径，提高了秸秆利用率。秸秆沼气、秸秆气化、秸秆压块等适用于一家一户的技术，在我国农村也一步一步发展起来。

（二）成效显著的地区

在各级政府的指导下，全国各地加大了秸秆综合利用工作的力度，秸秆利用普遍取得了良好的效果，江苏、山东、甘肃、陕西等省农作物秸秆综合利用效果较为突出。

1. *江苏省* 2009年，江苏省围绕省人大常委会《关于促进农作物秸秆综合利用的决定》和全省农作物秸秆综合利用推进会上提出的工作目标，以10个秸秆机械化还田示范县、5个试点县和30个示范乡镇建设为抓手，全力推进稻麦秸秆机械化还田利用，取得明显成效。夏秋两季，各示范试点县和示范乡镇共投入大中型拖拉机 2.26 万台，秸秆还田机 6.38 万台，完成稻麦秸秆机械化全量还田作业面积 539khm²。其中，夏季完成麦秸秆机械化全量还田作业面积 269.8khm²，比计划目标超额完成 72khm²；秋季完成稻秸秆机械化全量还田作业面积 269.2khm²，比计划目标超额完成 53khm²。示范试点区域麦秸秆机械化还田率平均达 57.6%，稻秸秆机械化还田率平均达 53.7%。其中，10 个示范县的麦秸秆和稻秸秆平均还田率分别达 69%、62.2%，张家港市、高邮市、扬州邗江区稻麦秸秆机械化还田率都在 70%以上。

2. 山东省　为了进一步提高农作物秸秆综合利用率和利用效益，减少农业资源浪费和环境污染，避免秸秆焚烧给第十一届全运会召开带来的影响，2009 年山东省安排了 2 000 万元用于济南、淄博、潍坊、滨州、德州、泰安、济宁、东营、临沂 9 个市的秸秆利用项目的补助，规定了秸秆生物反应堆和秸秆栽培食用菌、秸秆青贮（微贮）池建设、秸秆热解气化站建设、秸秆收贮站建设、户用沼气秸秆产气、秸秆综合利用企业奖励补助标准。济南市采取直接还田、秸秆收储、打捆外运等综合利用方式，综合利用率超过 95%，比 2008 年提高 5 个百分点，重点区域内超过 98%，比 2008 年提高 4%。

3. 甘肃省　2009 年，甘肃省把秸秆饲料化技术作为转变草食畜牧业发展方式、提升牛羊产业发展水平和促进农民增收的重要抓手，要求各市州、县（市、区）和省直有关部门要切实把秸秆资源转化利用摆上重要议事日程。为了鼓励秸秆循环利用助推甘肃畜牧业发展，除了将青贮机械、压块、包装等相关机具纳入农机购置补贴范围，信贷金融机构还要对秸秆综合利用企业和农机服务组织购置秸秆处理机械给予信贷支持。2009 年，甘肃省青贮饲料 95.45 万 t，建成青贮氨化池 4 万多个，建设秸秆养畜示范户 1.5 万户，加快了秸秆饲料化步伐。

4. 陕西省　秸秆焚烧的治理作为陕西省各级政府关心的一个热点问题，2009 年投入 2 000 万元用于秸秆机械化综合利用工作。陕西省积极鼓励秸秆利用企业、畜牧企业、专业合作社和机械购置大户，补贴标准从 2008 年的每台 3 万元增加到 4.5 万元，秸秆综合利用机械保有量达到 15 万多台。农机部门积极推行以机具保面积，以机械化促利用，疏堵结合，以疏为先的秸秆利用工作模式，使 2009 年夏秸秆利用和禁烧实现新突破，“三夏”期间机械化综合利用水平达到 53%。作为省会的西安市，为了治理秸秆焚烧工作，制定了禁烧工作的实施方案以及奖惩细则，还划拨专款用于奖励秸秆禁烧工作成绩突出的乡镇。“三夏”期间，秸秆综合利用率达到 95.4%，创历史最高水平。

（三）发展不平衡

2009 年我国在秸秆粉碎还田、秸秆养畜、秸秆生物反应堆技术、秸秆能源化利用技术等方面取得了一定的成就，但是由于政策、资金、技术及认识等方面的差距，致使我国秸秆利用仍然存在严重的问题。其中，突出表现在焚烧秸秆现象屡禁不止。秸秆综合利用还存在利用率低、产业链短和产业布局不合理等问题。存在这些问题的主要原因：一是对秸秆综合利用认识不足。一些地区没有把秸秆真正作为资源来看待，缺乏统筹规划，综合利用推进不力。二是秸秆资源与利用现状不清。长期以来，由于对秸秆利用的重视程度不够等原因，尽管有关部门和专家开展了一些调查和分析工作，但仍存在着秸秆资源不清、利用现状不明等问题。三是市场化机制不完善，缺乏政策激励。目前，各地还没有建立有效的市场机制和储运体系，秸秆商品化水平低，缺乏鼓励秸秆综合利用的具体政策措施，秸秆产业发展滞后。四是缺乏农民经济实用的配套技术设备。在农作物轮作茬口紧的多熟农区，秸秆便捷处理设施不配套，农民收集处理秸秆的难度大，随意遗弃和露天焚烧现象严重；秸秆综合利用新技术应用规模较小，尤其是适宜农户分散经营的小型化、实用化技术缺乏，各项技术之间集成组合不够。据环境保护部环境监察局发布的《2009 年 6 月 12 日全国秸秆焚烧分布遥感监测秸秆情况》所知，仅 12 日一天，利用卫星监测到安徽、河北、河南、湖北、江苏、山东、陕西、四川、天津、云南等省（直辖市）的秸秆焚烧火点达 372 个（不包括云覆盖下的火点信息）。其中云南有火点 1 个，涉及 1 个地市的 1 个县（市）；天津有火点 1 个，涉及 1 个地市的 1 个县（市）；四川有火点 10 个，涉及 3 个地市的 5 个县（市）；陕西有火点 3 个，涉及 1 个地市的 3 个县（市）；山东有火点 79 个，涉及 11 个地市的 27 个县（市）；江苏有火点 65 个，涉及 2 个地市的 7 个县（市）；湖北有火点 1 个，涉及 1 个地市的 1 个县（市）；河南有火点 65 个，涉及 8 个地市的 17 个县（市）；河北有火点 10 个，涉及 5 个地市的 7 个县（市）；安徽有火点 137 个，涉及 6 个地市的 10 个县（市）。由此可见，在全国范围内秸秆焚烧还十分严重，有关领导和业内人士应给予关注。

二、新产品和新技术

2009 年，我国农作物秸秆的科研、新产品、新技术的研究开发取得新进展，在秸秆综合利用技术、秸秆青贮、秸秆发电锅炉的研发等方面取得了突出成就，有力地推进了农作物秸秆的综合利用，大大提高了农作物秸秆的经济价值、社会价值。

（1）山东省济宁市梁上县科泰生物工程技术研发中心研发的“农作物秸秆综合加工利用技术”，于2009年2月取得成功，并完成产业化设计。该项技术以各种作物秸秆为原料，以“逆流萃取”、“木质素溶脱剂添加”为核心技术，依次反应依次分离提取生产纤维素、木质素、复合肥等系列产品，高倍增值，且其加工生产过程无废水、废气、废渣等“三废”，产品无氯、硫、钠“三害”残留。

（2）据2009年2月10日报道，山东省科学院生物研究所专家在研究中发现，木霉在天然培养基上可产生大量的烃类物质及其衍生物，所产生的烃类物质的C链长度一般在C9～C35之间。木霉还能够产生酮、酸、醇、烯、酯等。木霉能够在自然条件下迅速分解秸秆、木材等木质纤维素，产生许多直链烃类和芳香烃类化合物及其衍生物，也就是柴油的主要部分，为秸秆转化生物柴油提供了一种新的可能性。

（3）由国家发展和改革委员会、国家能源局组织国内多个科研院所进行原始创新研发的“固定床生物质气化装置”，于2009年2月20日在江苏省高邮市界首镇点火，标志着由我国自主研发的固定床生物质气化装置获得成功。该技术年消耗秸秆3万t，将对我国生物质能转化为多种能源起到示范和推广作用，能使秸秆转换成液化气、电等商业用品，同时该设备具有投资规模小、适应我国原料收集、产出能源品种多、易推广等特点。

（4）由江苏省句容市戴庄有机农业合作社和南京林业大学经过两年攻关，联合研制出利用农作物秸秆、稻壳生产生物醋和有机肥料项目，于2009年4月在句容市秸秆碳素厂正式投产。该技术的主要生产工艺是采取秸秆粉碎、干燥，在缺氧的条件下，加热至700～800℃的高温，产生的气体经冷却得到干馏液，再分离得到醋液，可作为有机农业生产的病虫害防治剂。剩余物降温后，成为有机农业生产的良好肥料。

（5）南通普吉实业有限公司与南京林业大学合作，于2009年5月研制开发了“以草代木”秸秆板材专利技术制成的木轮，成功替代原有木制轮，既节约了大量木材又降低了生产成本。南通普吉实业有限公司利用该技术，建立了年产3万m^3复合包装轮项目，将秸秆、小径木、枝桠材、刨花以及木材加工剩余等材料，经干燥、铺装成型热压、切割等工段而成，制成的包装轮用于钢丝绳的配套包装，填补了国内钢丝包装行业的空白。该项目投产后每年将节约木材6万m^3，每天可消耗当地麦秸、稻草2.4t，使有限的资源再生利用，减少秸秆焚烧和木材加工废弃物排放，每年可为国家节约3万m^3成材。

（6）由农业部规划设计研究院主持研发的“玉米秸秆高效生态循环利用工程技术”项目，于2009年5月13日通过了农业部科技成果鉴定。农业部科教司组织的科技成果鉴定委员会认为，这项技术具有新颖性和创造性，填补了国内空白，达到国际先进水平。该项目是农业部规划设计研究院研发3年的成果，以玉米秸秆制取生物质能源为核心，包括玉米秸秆制取酒精初级产品、农村沼气工程等生物质能源利用技术，以发展畜禽产业为主，生产乙醇燃料为辅，并将酒糟饲养畜禽、发酵粪便养殖蚯蚓、蚯蚓饲喂禽鱼等多项技术集成，形成生态农业循环经济产业链，节省产业链的运营成本和秸秆运输物流成本。项目消除了玉米秸秆对环境的负面影响，是实现零排放的循环经济产业工程，对改善生态环境，实现农业可持续发展都将起到积极的作用，有利于促进资源节约型、环境友好型社会和新农村建设。创建的循环经济产业化模式，为生产绿色食品、企业增效、农民增收创造了条件，为东北、西北地区农民找到了一条投资少、简易可行的致富之路。

（7）由江苏省经贸委、环保厅联合组织，对万达锅炉公司自主研发的国内首台流化床锅炉，于2009年5月20日进行了新产品鉴定。该锅炉在中节能宿迁生物质能发电公司2年试用，成功解决了我国秸秆等生物质发电结渣、腐蚀、空气污染等难题，可以投入批量生产。据测算，锅炉设计成本为国外炉排式锅炉的一半，烟气排放物达到国家火电厂标准，具有重大推广价值。根据宿迁公司负责人胡越介绍，2台万达75t/h流化床锅炉，不仅能烧秸秆，还能大量“吃进”稻秸、树根等35种生物质，均匀燃烧不结渣，热效率达90%以上，年消化秸秆等生物质17万～20万t，节约标准煤9.8万t。尤其令人欣喜的是，从2007年2月投产至2009年5月，企业外供电力2亿多千瓦时，实现销售收入1.8亿元、利润1 000多万元，在我国生物质发电企业率先赢利。

（8）由东北农业大学张永根教授主持的黑龙江省科技厅项目“水稻秸秆机械化青贮技术”应用现场会，于2009年9月30日在尚志市一面坡镇长营村召开。项目组经过潜心研究，解决了水稻秸秆青贮专用添加剂、水稻适宜收获期和收贮方式以及配套的裹包青贮设备等机械化水稻秸秆青贮技术难题，使稻秸青贮的品质、营养价值和饲喂效果都优于微贮和氨化等常规秸秆处理方法。饲养试验结果表明：在奶牛日粮中使用水稻秸青贮可取代50%玉米青贮而不影响奶牛生产性能，每头牛每年可节省饲料成本500元左右。利用该项科研成果可以实现在田间进行机械化水稻包裹青贮，容易形成产业化，此项技术既可缓解青贮饲料来源不足的矛盾，又可减轻水稻秸利用不当造成的环境污染。应用、普及和推广这项实用技术具有非常显著的经济效益、社会效益和生态效益。

（9）由江苏洛基木业有限公司与南京林业大学共同承担的“稻麦秸秆人造板制造技术与产业化”项目，获2009年国家科技进步二等奖。该项目是江苏洛基木业有限公司投入近千万元研发费用，研制出利用稻草和麦秆做成零甲醛地板，填补了国内空白，获得多项国家专利。该地板比普通地板的强度更高。普通地板密度是880kg/m^3，秸秆地板是960kg/m^3。

三、政策促进与行业管理

秸秆综合利用的提高不仅需要国家各级政府大力支持，还需要社会各种力量的鼎力支持。国家在政策制定，各地政府、组织在举办召开的各种活动中都倾注了相当的关注，在产业政策支持、科研开发支持等方面都采取了重大举措，保障了秸秆产业的良好发展。

（一）政策促进

（1）2009年2月1日，中共中央国务院颁布了2009年中央一号文件，提出大力开展保护性耕作，开展鼓励农民秸秆还田奖补试点，扩大秸秆固化气化试点示范工作。

（2）2009年2月9日，为贯彻落实国务院办公厅关于抓紧编制秸秆资源综合利用中长期发展规划的意见，加快推进秸秆综合利用，实现秸秆的资源化、商品化，促进资源节约、环境保护和农民增收，国家发展和改革委员会、农业部发布了《关于编制秸秆综合利用规划的指导意见》，提出各省、自治区、直辖市等应根据各地实际情况编制当地的规划，并提出了编制规划的指导思想、基本原则及主要任务和进度要求。规划目标提出，2010年在东部发达地区、中心城市周边、机场和高速公路沿线地区基本实现禁烧。力争到2015年，在全国建立较完善的秸秆还田、收集、储运体系，基本形成布局合理、多元利用的秸秆还田和产业化综合利用格局，秸秆综合利用率超过80%。在区域发展中要求各地区尤其是农业主产区，应因地制宜重点选择当地优势产业带，以小麦—水稻和小麦—玉米为主，在秸秆剩余量大、茬口紧、焚烧严重的地区开展秸秆综合利用。近期对于交通干道、机场、城市周边等重点地区，要重点规划，尽快解决秸秆的季节性和结构性过剩问题。在品种上，重点解决量大面广的玉米、小麦、水稻、棉花秸秆及各地农业优势产业的秸秆。

（3）2009年5月20日，江苏省第十一届人民代表大会常务委员会第九次会议通过了《江苏省人民代表大会常务委员会关于促进农作物秸秆综合利用的决定》并以法律许可的最快速度于6月1日正式实施，是我国省级首部禁止农作物秸秆焚烧和促进综合利用的地方性法律法规。该法规规定了地方各级人民政府是推进秸秆综合利用和秸秆焚烧工作的责任主体，制定、落实有利于秸秆综合利用的财政、投资、税费、价格等政策，加快推进秸秆综合利用。法规还提出任何单位和个人不得在禁烧区域内露天焚烧秸秆，不得将秸秆弃置于河道、湖泊、水库、沟渠等水体内，并且要求逐步扩大禁止焚烧的区域范围，到2012年底实行全行政区域禁烧。

（二）主要行业活动

（1）2009年2月19日，由民革中央倡导，民革中央社会服务部、民革甘肃省委、白银市人民政府共同举办的“全国秸秆生物反应堆技术”示范推广现场会在白银市召开。全国人大副委员长、民革中央主席周铁农，国家林业局副局长李育材，中央统战部、国家林业局、水利部、农业部、中国扶贫发展中心、科技部、环保部、国家质量监督检验检疫总局等部委有关领导、专家和省直有关部门负责同志出席会议。秸秆生物反应堆技术已在白银试验示范获得成功，对于农业生产具有明显的经济效益和生态效益，市场前景广阔。据介绍，每亩温室可消化3～6t玉米秸秆，产量明显提高，减少农药使用量35%以上，农产品质量明显改善，食用安全性大幅度提高。

（2）2009年3月5～6日，“全国农作物秸秆能源化利用现场经验交流会”在山东召开，农业部科技教育司司长白金明出席会议并讲话，各省、自治区、直辖市及计划单列市农村能源办公室主任及相关企业负责人参加了会议。会议交流了秸秆沼气和热解气化示范推广经验，部署启动了2009年秸秆沼气集中供气示范工程。白金明要求，各地要高度重视农作物秸秆能源化利用工作，在巩固已有成果的基础上，着力推广一批大型沼气工程建设；要按照“三废变三料”的要求，不断拓宽工作领域，推动产业转化升级，促进农作物秸秆能源化利用工作又好又快发展。

（3）2009年11月9～10日，国家发展和改革委员会、农业部在安徽省合肥市联合召开了“全国农作物秸秆综合利用现场经验交流会”。会议的主要议题是以科学发展观为指导，认真贯彻落实《国务院办公厅关于加快推进农作物秸秆综合利用的意见》，交流各地开展秸秆综合利用工作的经验，研究部署下一步工作。国家发展和改革委员会副主任解振华、农业部副部长陈晓华出席会议并讲话。会议还邀请石元春、张齐生两位院士等有关专家作了专题报告。有关省市、企业代表分别围绕秸秆人造板、秸秆造纸、秸秆发电、秸秆堆肥、秸秆压块等农作物秸秆综合利用产业化取得的成绩和经验进行了交流。

(4) 2009 年 11 月 9 日，农业部农机推广总站与国能生物发电集团有限公司就农作物秸秆发电项目签署战略合作协议。通过战略合作，农业部农业机械化推广总站与国能生物发电集团有限公司将整合各自优势，积极探索“能源、环保、农业增效、农民增收”的生物质能利用新途径和新方法。共同开展生物质能发电上游产业链的建设和研究，开发适合中国国情的农作物秸秆收、加、储、运各环节的专用设备，探索生物质能综合利用和生物质原料产业链市场化运作模式，并分类指导农作物秸秆资源的利用途径和利用规模，充分发挥农作物秸秆资源的社会效益、经济效益和环境效益。

(5) 2009 年 12 月 21～24 日，全国农作物秸秆和农村沼气“三沼”综合利用研讨会在泰安市召开。来自全国各地的 30 余名生态能源领导、专家学者齐聚泰山脚下，就今后农作物秸秆综合利用，“三沼”综合利用工作的总体目标、重点工作、相关配套政策措施、2010 年全国秸秆能源化利用实施方案和农村“三沼”综合利用试点项目实施方案等问题展开研讨。

（天津市农业机械与农业工程学会
辛永波　宋　樱　胡　伟）

食品与包装机械制造业

一、经济运行情况

据统计 2009 年我国食品与包装机械工业总产值较 2008 年同比增长 17.65%，销售产值增长 17.84%。2009 年全行业销售总产值达到 1 484 亿元。其中食品机械 756.8 亿元，包装机械 727.2 亿元。食品与包装机械全年出口额 12.53 亿美元，较 2008 年下降 17.02%；进口额 22.45 亿美元，较 2008 年下降 22.64%。2009 年我国机械工业全行业出口交货值，较 2008 年下降 21.86%，而食品和包装机械却增长了 5.55%，增幅虽然不大，但在 2009 年的国际经济形势下已很不容易。因此，行业总体发展趋势看好，略高于整个机械行业的整体水平。但 2009 年也出现了一个不大正常的现象，自 6 月份开始，全行业新产品产值与 2008 年同期相比一直在下滑，虽然 12 月本月新产品产值与 2008 年同期相比增长 19.11%，但全年累计新产品销售产值与 2008 年相比下降了 8.37%。这说明 2009 年行业新产品开发步子大大放缓了，全年仍呈负增长。新产品跟不上说明行业技术进步不快，这将影响到 2010 年及以后的销售市场，没有技术进步的新产品支撑，国内的高端用户就有可能把设备采购的对象转向国外先进的机型，这对国内行业的长远发展非常不利。而国际发达国家往往在经历一个销售低迷期以后，会推出一系列技术进步的产品，他们把销售相对不畅的产品加以改造或创新，以新的技术、新的机型参与下一轮的市场竞争，一旦市场转暖，新机型的竞争力就非常强，在经历过一段萧条以后他们反而增强了竞争力。我们没有经历过这样的萧条，但一定要增加设备的科技含量，使本身的产品具有更高的性价比，以便在市场转暖以后，以全新的优质高效的设备去抢占市场先机，这一点应引起全行业的极大关注。

二、加强行业产学研合作，积极争取国家项目

为了提高本行业的科技创新能力，以应对国内外市场竞争形势，2009 年乘“中国食品和包装机械工业协会成立 20 周年”、“中国机械工程学会包装和食品机械分会成立 20 周年”、“开办中国国际食品加工和包装机械展览会 20 周年”、“第十一届北京中国国际食品加工和包装机械展览会开幕”共同举办庆典之机，中国食品和包装机械总公司牵头组建了中国食品和包装机械产业技术创新战略联盟（以下简称战略联盟），共有 40 余个行业骨干企业、科研单位和知名院校参加。该战略联盟是由行业内一批优秀企事业单位组成的，基本上涵盖了行业的各个领域。战略联盟是我国本行业先进生产力、先进创新团队和研发能力的代表，是本行业在国际市场竞争中强有力的技术支撑，也是推动本行业科技进步的生力军。

为了提高本行业的科技水平，中国食品和包装机械工业协会协助企事业单位积极争取国家项目，于

2009年向工业和信息化部上报了14项科技与技改项目，其中获批5项，即："高效节能制冰设备研究开发"与"马铃薯储藏技术与装备"（以上两项为中国包装和食品机械总公司承担）、"环保型多功能烟熏炉"（嘉兴市瑞邦机械工程有限公司承担）、"肉类加工机械技术改造项目"（石家庄晓进机械制造科技有限公司承担）、"浓酱类灌装封口自动化一体机研制"（广州南联实业有限公司承担）。协会同时向中国机械工业联合会上报了技术改造项目16项，即：广州达意隆包装机械设备有限公司的"高速节能PET瓶吹瓶关键技术研发及产业化"；石家庄晓进机械制造科技有限公司的"产品升级改造"；合肥中辰轻工机械有限公司的"年产15台套高精度定量灌装伺服旋盖生产线"；江苏新美星包装机械有限公司的"PET瓶含果粒乳饮料洁净包装技术及装备产业化"；廊坊百冠包装机械有限公司的"连续式无菌热包装工艺"；广州南联实业有限公司的"产品升级与标准修订"；中天昊宇科技股份有限公司的"摇摆式杀菌釜形成生产能力"；江苏华宇飞凌包装机械有限公司的"高黏度高产能旋转定量灌装生产线"；哈尔滨金美乐商业机械有限公司的"质量升级、扩大产能改造"；汕头粤东机械实业有限公司的"高效节能产品升级改造"；桂林桂北机械有限责任公司的"包装机械产品升级"；柳州市精业机器有限公司的"全自动塑料双工位注吹中空成型机的研发"；广西梧州市正一机械厂的"产品按欧盟标准升级改造"；中国包装和食品机械总公司的"高效节能制冰设备研究开发"和"智能化节能型挂面加工关键设备研究开发"；广西机械工业研究院的"白糖全自动包装设备研发"等，这些项目的实施，将进一步推进行业的科技进步。

三、主要行业活动

（1）中国食品和包装机械工业协会第四届第四次理事会，于2009年5月14～16日在浙江省温州市召开。此次会议得到了中天昊宇和华联机械总公司的大力支持，会议取得圆满成功。本次会议除了总结2008年的协会工作外，还举行了应对国际金融危机、力求行业发展的高峰论坛。论坛发言踊跃，各抒己见，达到了交流观点、启迪思路、共谋发展的目的，取得了可喜成绩。会议代表参观了中天昊宇温州工厂和华联机械总公司的温州工厂，会议代表对这两个企业的经营思路及所取得的成就表示赞赏，认为这两家企业为行业树立了榜样，更加增强了做大做强企业、做精做细产品的信心，同时也激发了行业同仁为行业作贡献的热情，与会代表对行业发展增强了信心。会议还通过了成立中国食品和包装机械工业协会薯类加工机械分会的提案，分会的办公地点设在中国农业机械化科学研究院。

（2）由中国食品和包装机械工业协会和中国包装和食品机械总公司联合举办的"第十届中国国际上海食品加工和包装机械展览会"，于2009年6月在上海举办，展出面积12 000m^2。同年10月在北京举办了"第十届北京国际包装和食品机械展览会"，展地面积20 000多m^2，该两项展会吸引了不少国外采购商，参展企业反映良好。在北京的展会期间，结合中国食品和包装机械工业协会成立20周年、中国机械工程学会包装和食品机械分会成立20周年，举办了一系列的庆祝活动，如高峰论坛、组建了产业技术创新战略联盟，表彰了为行业创建、发展作出重大贡献的先驱者、科学技术带头人、优秀企业及优秀青年等。

（3）2009年组织行业企业赴国外参加国际食品加工和包装机械展览会。出展的国家有美国、西班牙、南非、印度和日本，企业对参展的效果反映良好。在印度展会后期，上海普丽盛轻工设备有限公司几乎走访了印度所有乳品企业，取得了良好效果。美国展会已确定只认中国两个单位可以组展，其中一个就是中国食品和包装机械工业协会。这是因为：一是因为对方要求有规范展会的管理，二是该协会在历届展会的组展中工作规范，规模较大，从而得到认可。肉类加工机械分会组织企业赴法兰克福参展也得到大会主办方的认可。

（4）2009年组织参加了南宁博览会。南宁博览会是我国与东盟10国共同举办的博览会，我国与东盟10国（简称"10＋1"）正在逐步走向零关税（正在实施），我国与东盟10国的关系占有十分重要的地位，东盟10国在我国南宁均设有商务联络处，我国十分看重与东盟的关系，每届博览会都有贸易签约，博览会的规模越来越大，签约越来越多。我协会在南宁博览会上展出一个整馆，东盟各国对此展会都十分重视，都有专业展团，成交量越来越大。这个博览会在东盟各国颇具影响，是一个与东盟贸易的重要窗口，我国食品和包装机械在东盟已形成影响力，一些企业与东盟诸国建立了商务往来关系。

（5）由中国食品和包装机械工业协会主办的"中国食品和包装机械行业'十二五'发展规划"专家座谈会，于11月23日在京召开。来自全国各地的骨干企业、大专院校和科研院所30余名代表出席了会议。会议在协会秘书长楚玉峰的主持下，专家们围绕食品和包装机械行业国内外发展现状、行业中存在的主要问题、行业发展环境、发展思路、发展重点、发展目标等进行了研讨。中国食品和包装机械协会李树君理事长发言时指出，讨论“十二五”发展规划要以科学发展观为指导，围绕转变发展方式、创新发展模式的总体要求，从实际出发，真实反映行业在“十二五”时期的重点、难点，着力解决关键性问题，提出我国食品和包装行业“十二五”发展规划的思路，努力提高规划的战略性、前瞻性、指导性和可行性。从目前行业发展来看，我国食品和包装机械技术进步比较慢，自动化、智能化成套设备研发速度跟不上欧美等发达国家，直接影响了我国食品的安全性和技术进步，在一定程度上成为我国食品工业发展的制约因素。与会专家们就我国食品和包装机械的绿色化、智能化、高速化、精密化、标准化等问题，提出了很多宝贵意见和建议。大家就“十二五”期间我国包装和食品机械应优先发展肉及肉制品加工成套设备、饮料罐装成套设备、乳品加工成套设备、果蔬加工成套设备、智能化包装设备等5类产品达成共识。

（中国食品和包装机械工业协会　何南至）

棉花加工机械制造业

一、生产情况

据不完全统计，截止到2009年底，我国获得棉花加工生产许可证的锯齿轧花机生产企业有28个，其中有15个企业倒闭或停转产，正常生产企业13个；参与此次调查的企业有4个，占正常生产企业的31%。同时，获得生产许可证的打包机生产企业有24个，其中12个企业倒闭或停转产，还有12个企业正常生产；参与此次调查的企业有4个，占正常生产企业的33%。按照工业总产值计算，行业内排名前7位的棉花加工机械制造企业总人数为2 298人，其中工程技术人员320人；固定资产净值10 366.16万元，完成工业总产值48 005.78万元，利税总额4 764.68万元。2009年，共有8个棉花加工机械企业生产轧花机883台，打包机435台（其中400型打包机408台），皮棉清理机1 412台，籽棉清理机283台，锯齿剥绒机976台。其基本情况见表1。

表1　2009年棉花加工机械企业基本情况

单位名称	工业总产值（万元）	销售额（万元）	利税总额（万元）	固定资产净值（万元）	职工总人数（名）	轧花机（台）	打包机（台）
南通棉花机械有限公司	19 609	17 281	2 259	1 646	427	0	307
邯郸金狮棉机有限公司	8 563	12 460	646	5 473	984	243	0
大丰市供销机械厂有限公司	5 179	5 463	285	636	301	290	0
启东市供销机械有限公司	4 019	3 077	380	1 328	206	0	25
山东华棉棉花机械有限公司	4 700	3 900	560	343	118	175	0
荆州市白云棉花机械有限公司	3 936	3 977	255	562	136	0	73
高密圣达机械有限公司	2 000	1 800	380	378	126	175	30
合　计	48 006	47 958	4 765	10 366	2 298	883	435

二、生产许可证工作

1. *棉花加工机械产品生产许可证审查部职责*　全国工业产品生产许可证办公室棉花加工机械产品生产许可证审查部，是根据国家质量监督检验检疫总局国质检监函［2002］39号“关于对部分棉花加工机械产品实行生产许可证制度的通知”文件精神设立的。审查部设在中华全国供销合作总社郑州棉麻加工机械质量监督检验测试中心，中华全国供销合作总社棉麻局派员参加审查工作。审查部受全国工业产品生产许可证办公室的委托，承担棉花加工机械产品生产许可证发（换）证工作的有关事宜。

2. *棉花加工机械产品生产许可证审查部工作*　根据《中华人民共和国工业产品生产许可证管理条例》、《中华人民共和国工业产品生产许可证管理条例实施办法》的精神，结合我国棉花加工机械产品生产、销售与使用等各个环节产品质量与安全管理工作形势的需要，积极组织筹备棉花加工机械产品生产许可证期满换证工作及相关会议。

3. 棉花加工机械产品生产许可证审查情况　截止到2009年12月31日，已取得棉花加工机械产品生产许可证的企业数量为49个。其中，生产400型棉花打包机的企业有15个，生产200型棉花打包机的企业有24个，生产锯齿轧花机的企业有28个，生产皮棉清理机的企业有14个，生产籽棉清理机的企业有12个。2009年审查生产许可证的企业数量11个，对15个棉花加工机械制造企业进行了棉花加工机械产品生产许可证换证工作。基本情况见表2。

表2　棉花加工机械产品生产许可证换证情况

企业名称	明细	说明
山东天鹅棉业机械股份有限公司	锯齿轧花机：MY126 - 19.4、MY109 - 19.4、MY171 - 17、MY139 - 14.8、MY121B - 17、MY96 - 17、MY80C - 17；液压棉花打包机：MDY - 400、MDY - 400A、MDY - 400B	换证
邯郸金狮棉机有限公司	锯齿轧花机：6MY168 - 17、MY112 - 19.4、6MY98 - 17、6MY88 - 17、6MY80B - 19.4、MY80 - 19.4；液压棉花打包机：6MDY - 400	换证
山东桓台福鑫机械厂	锯齿轧花机：MY - 98	换证
大丰市供销机械厂有限公司	锯齿轧花机：MYJ - 80A、MYJM - 90D、MYJM - 108D、MY98、MYJ - 90A、MYJ - 100B、MY100 - 16A、MYJM80D	换证
大丰市长江机械制造有限公司	锯齿轧花机：MYJ - 80E、MYJ - 80D、MYJ - 90E、MYJ - 98、MYJ -108D	换证
荆州市楚凌机械有限公司	锯齿轧花机：6MY80A - 19.4、6MY90A - 18、MY - 96	换证
山东华棉棉花机械有限公司	锯齿轧花机（组装型）：MYJ - 98、MYJ - 98C、MYJ - 118、MYJ - 151	换证
山东新联金棉麻机械有限公司	锯齿轧花机：MYJ - 98、MYJ - 98C、MYJ - 118、MYJ - 151（组装型）；籽棉清理机：MQZT - 6、MQZXH - 6（组装型）；皮棉清理机：MQP - 400×1500、MQP - 400×1800、MQP - 400×2000、MQP - 400×1250（组装型）	换证
盐城银都机械制造有限公司	锯齿轧花机：MYJ - 80、MYJ - 90、MYJ - 108	换证
衡水棉机有限责任公司	液压棉花打包机：：MDYS - 400	换证
邯郸纺织机械有限公司	液压棉花打包机：MDY - 400、MDY - 200	换证
汤阴机械制造有限责任公司	液压棉花打包机：MDY - 400、MDY - 200	换证
南通棉花机械有限公司	液压棉花打包机：MDY - 400	换证
南通越江棉花机械有限公司	液压棉花打包机：MDY - 400、MDY - 200	换证
山东欣弘发机械有限公司	液压棉花打包机：MDYA - 400	换证

三、标准化工作

1. 中华全国供销合作总社棉花加工工业标准化技术委员会职责　根据国家有关的方针、政策，向中华全国供销合作总社提出棉花加工机械标准化工作的任务、措施和建议；负责组织制定和修订棉花加工机械标准化体系表，提出制、修订棉花加工机械国家标准和行业标准的规划和年度计划的建议；根据国家有关部门批准的计划，组织棉花加工行业对相关的国家标准和行业标准的制定、修订和复审工作；组织审查棉花加工机械国家标准和行业标准送审稿的审查工作，并提出审查结论意见，提出强制性标准或推荐性标准的建议；受有关部门委托，负责棉花加工机械国家标准和行业标准的宣讲、解释工作；监督和调查已颁布标准的执行情况，收集对标准的反馈意见，担负棉花加工机械标准化工作的技术咨询，并提出成果奖项目的建议；依法接受委托，承担棉花加工机械地方标准、企业标准的起草、制定、审查和咨询等服务工作；接受有关部门的委托，办理与棉花加工机械标准化工作有关的事宜；承担本行业标准化范围内产品质量及标准化水平评价工作；承担本行业引进项目的标准化审查工作，并向项目有关部门提出标准化水平分析报告。

2. 标准的制修订工作　为了使棉花行业标准更合理、更适用，标准的制、修订应从如下几个方面考虑：制定出的标准必须首先解决标龄老化和标准滞后的问题，标准的研究、制定要与科研同步，标准制定要与产业化同步，要以企业为主体，以自主创新为核心，实现标准的国际突破，以科技创新推动标准化战略的实施，实现棉花行业标准总体水平的跨越式提升，棉花行业的标准应该充分体现出技术先进、充分利用资源、环境保护、安全生产。截止2009年12月底，共向中华全国供销合作总社科技部申报了“棉籽多肽粉”、“棉籽精粉”、“籽棉干燥机”、“开模喂料机”、“运模车”、“打模机”、“锯片”、“清绒机”、“轧花企业粉尘检测方法”、“棉花包装　聚乙烯薄膜套袋”、“棉包IC卡数据采集器”、“棉花加工术语”标准12项。其中，需制定的标准8项，需修订的标准4项。

四、棉花质量检验体制改革与新产品

截至2009年12月31日，列入棉花质量检验体制改革更新改造计划的棉花加工企业已有1 962个，完成设备更新改造并开始送检的企业已有1 384个，占计划改造企业总数的70.5%。2009年度全国大包棉花送检量255万t，比2008年全年送检量下降40.1%；送检量占全国加工总量的40%，比2008年同期下降17%。2009年，由中华全国供销合作总社郑州棉麻工程技术设计研究所承担的新产品开发项目共5项，包括MGZ-7C可调式脉冲-搁板增热籽棉干燥机、MJZT-15A塔式籽棉加湿机、MJPT-5A塔式皮棉加湿机、MJHZ-A型籽棉回潮率在线检测装置、MJH-400B皮棉回潮率在线检测装置。

（中国棉花协会棉花加工分会　尹青云　王思楠）

第三部分

政策法规及重要文件

全国生猪屠宰行业发展规划纲要
（2010—2015年）

（商务部 2009年12月31日）

猪肉是我国绝大多数居民的主要肉品来源，生猪屠宰是我国实行严格市场准入的行业之一，承担着服务“三农”、满足居民猪肉消费需求、保障肉品卫生和质量安全的产业功能和社会责任。为引导生猪屠宰行业科学、有序、健康发展，促进行业结构调整和技术进步，提高肉品质量安全水平，根据《中华人民共和国食品安全法》、《生猪屠宰管理条例》、《生猪屠宰管理条例实施办法》的有关精神和要求，制定本规划纲要，规划期为2010－2015年。

一、我国生猪屠宰行业发展现状

1998年《生猪屠宰管理条例》的实施标志着我国生猪屠宰行业已进入依法管理的新阶段。10余年来，生猪屠宰行业发生了以下积极变化：

（一）猪肉卫生和质量安全水平有较大提高

随着生猪定点屠宰制度的落实，县级以上城市猪肉供应已基本上来自生猪定点屠宰企业（包括生猪定点屠宰厂（场）和小型屠宰场点，下同），乡镇进点屠宰率近95%，私屠滥宰现象得到有效遏制，食用猪肉引起的食品安全事件明显减少。

（二）行业技术水平升级加快

全国机械化屠宰厂（场）已达到3 000余家，较实行定点屠宰制度前增加了10倍，部分定点屠宰企业的生产装备、工艺技术达到或接近世界先进水平。

（三）企业规模化、品牌化效应开始显现

2008年，全国规模以上定点屠宰企业2 205家，约占全国定点屠宰企业总数的10%，年屠宰量已占全部定点屠宰量的68%；一些屠宰加工企业开始实行品牌化经营，全国已有肉类注册商标500多个。

（四）管理有序的开放式流通格局基本形成

破除地区市场封锁取得进展，一些大型屠宰加工企业已在全国或较广区域内配置生产资源，依托自身质量、品牌和规模优势，运用先进流通方式拓展销售市场，品牌肉连锁店、专卖店、冷链运输快速发展，优质猪肉产品已部分实现跨区域流通。

（五）屠宰管理法规和标准体系逐步完善

2008年新修订的《生猪屠宰管理条例》及配套办法已颁布实施；屠宰相关标准进一步健全，对定点屠宰企业规范化、标准化生产起到规制和引导作用。

（六）屠宰执法体系初步形成

大部分省、区（市）、县成立了生猪定点屠宰管理机构，全国已有2 000多支专（兼）职生猪屠宰执法队伍，生猪屠宰监管力量得到加强。

当前我国生猪屠宰行业仍存在一些突出问题：产能总量严重过剩，落后产能比重过大；行业布局和结构不合理，产业集中度偏低；相当一部分定点屠宰企业设备设施简陋，未达到相关标准，屠宰操作规范和检验检疫制度尚未落实；约75%的定点屠宰企业实行代宰制，产品形态同质化、忽视品牌建设的现象仍很普遍，恶性竞争严重；屠宰行业从业人员特别是屠宰技术人员和肉品品质检验人员专业技能有待进一步提高；生猪屠宰执法在人员、经费、装备和检测能力等方面仍严重不足。这些问题不仅对猪肉质量安全构成了潜在威胁，也对生猪屠宰行业的现代化转型和持续健康发展产生了不利影响。

我国经济社会发展进入了新的阶段，生猪养殖方式、居民消费结构发生了积极变化，交通运输状况得到极大改观，同时资源节约、环境保护的压力越来越大，全社会对猪肉卫生和质量安全的关切也越来越高，《食品安全法》也对食品安全工作提出了更高的要求。面对新形势，迫切需要加强对生猪屠宰行业发展的规划指导，优化行业布局，提升管理水平，促进资源合理配置，切实保障肉品质量安全。

二、指导思想、基本原则和发展目标

（一）指导思想

以科学发展观为指导，坚持以人为本，以优化布局、减控总量、升级改造、规范经营为着力点，推动屠宰行业布局调整和结构优化，提高产业集中度，提升定点屠宰企业的技术装备和管理水平，提升猪肉产品卫生和质量安全保障能力，提升对规模化养殖的带动能力，更好满足人民群众对安全优质猪肉产品的消费需求。

（二）基本原则

1. *严格标准，保障猪肉卫生和质量安全* 严格执行《生猪屠宰管理条例》及其实施办法规定的定点屠宰厂（场）的设置条件和标准，淘汰落后产能，推动行业技术进步，推行机械化屠宰、标准化管理、规模化和品牌化经营，强化定点屠宰企业履行出厂肉品质量安全第一责任人的责任，提高肉品质量安全保障水平。

2. *大力减控总量，优化行业布局* 结合城市规划，综合考虑当地和周边地区生猪养殖规模、屠宰加工能力、市场消费能力、交通状况以及资源环境承载力，压缩过剩屠宰产能，推动兼并重组，促进城乡、产区销区和东中西部的合理布局，遏制重复建设和过度竞争。

3. *实施分级管理，提高产业集中度* 根据定点屠宰厂（场）的设备设施、卫生安全条件、工艺流程、管理水平和屠宰规模等标准，对定点屠宰厂（场）实行分级管理，鼓励等级高的定点屠宰厂（场）实施品牌化战略，开展跨区域经营，提高冷链配送能力，扩大市场占有率。

4. *净化市场环境，促进公平竞争* 完善法规标准，加强执法队伍建设，严厉打击私屠滥宰，依法规范生猪定点屠宰企业经营行为，严格禁止小型生猪屠宰场点的肉品跨区域流通，清理并废止阻碍生猪定点屠宰厂（场）跨区域经营的有关政策措施。

（三）发展目标

通过实施规划纲要，全国逐步形成以跨区域流通的现代化屠宰加工企业为主体，区域性肉品加工企业发挥重要功能作用，以供应本地市场的定点屠宰企业为补充，梯次配置、布局合理、有序流通的产业布局，确保消费者吃上“放心肉”。具体目标如下：

1. *行业集中度进一步提升，规模化、品牌化经营发展壮大* 到2015年，在全国生猪主产区（包括生猪养殖基地县、调出大县，下同）培育一批年屠宰量在100万头以上的大型定点屠宰厂（场），其屠宰量占全国的比重逐步提升；实行品牌化经营的生猪定点屠宰厂（场）数量适度增长。

2. *行业技术管理水平显著提升，机械化屠宰、标准化管理再上新台阶* 依据《生猪屠宰管理条例》，到2015年，定点屠宰厂（场）的待宰间、急宰间、厂房、屠宰设备、预冷间以及工艺流程等全部达到相关标准；建立并使用与屠宰规模相适应的污水处理设施，实现达标排放；建立严格的肉品品质检验制度，配备资质合格的检验人员和必要的检验设备；建立产品质量管理体系以及生猪进厂（场）检查登记、无害化处理、质量追溯、缺陷产品召回、运输工具使用、信息报送等相关制度。定点屠宰企业从业人员（包括屠宰技术人员、肉品品质检验人员和经营管理人员，下同）均经过专业培训，肉品品质检验人员均取得执业资格证书。

3. *猪肉产品结构得到优化，综合利用率有所提高* 初步改变我国猪肉产品白条肉多、分割肉少；热鲜肉多、冷鲜肉少；高温制品多、低温制品少以及综合利用率低的现状。到2013年，争取县城以上城区猪肉小包装销售比例由目前的10%提升至15%，冷鲜肉市场份额由目前的10%提升至20%，到2015年上述比例分别达到20%和30%左右。

4. *采用现代经营方式的企业明显增加，冷链流通得到广泛应用* 到2015年，培育一批以大中城市为重点销售范围的区域性肉品加工配送企业；定点屠宰厂（场）通过连锁店、专卖店等渠道销售的猪肉产品比例明显提升；一批猪肉产品批发市场的低温仓储设施得到改造和提升；跨区域销售的定点屠宰厂（场）全部配置与流通范围相适应的冷链设施、运输车辆。

5. *淘汰落后产能取得重大进展，市场秩序明显好转* 到2013年，全国手工和半机械化等落后的生猪屠宰产能淘汰30%，到2015年淘汰50%，其中大城市和发达地区力争淘汰80%左右。边远和交通不便的农村地区设置的小型屠宰场点符合《生猪屠宰管理条例》的有关规定，技术装备和管理水平符合猪肉卫生和质量安全生产的基本要求。私屠滥宰现象明显减少，形成公平有序的竞争环境。

三、生猪屠宰行业发展的主要任务

（一）完善设置规划，优化行业布局

各地要以保障猪肉卫生和质量安全为宗旨，抓紧制（修）订生猪定点屠宰企业设置规划，并报商务部备案。新规划要把握好以下重点：

1. *严格控制定点屠宰厂（场）数量* 原则上，直辖市和常住人口在500万以上的城市城区要少于4家，其他地级以上城市城区要少于2家。县（市）全境设1家，有条件的地方可不设屠宰厂（场）。西部地区和其他欠发达地区市、县可根据实际情况适当放宽。小型生猪屠宰场点的设置数量也要按照《生猪屠宰管理条例》的要求严格把握。

2. *下列地区不得设置定点屠宰企业* 污染源、供水水源地、自来水取水口和密集居住区等环境敏感地区，易产生有害气体、烟雾、粉尘等污染源的工业企业所在地区或场所。其他有关法规和标准有规定的从其规定。

3. 鼓励在生猪主产区设立大型现代化屠宰加工企业　鼓励在主销区发展具有分割、配送功能的肉品加工配送企业；鼓励在确保产能减量大于增量的前提下，关闭中小型屠宰厂（场）及小型屠宰场点，设置大型生猪定点屠宰企业。

（二）严格执行标准，实施分类管理

各地商务主管部门要在当地政府的领导下，按照《关于加强猪肉质量安全监管工作的意见》（商秩发[2009] 437号）要求，会同有关部门，做好生猪定点屠宰企业审核换证工作。要根据《生猪屠宰管理条例》第八条和《生猪屠宰管理实施办法》第七条规定的条件及相关标准，逐一审核本地定点屠宰企业，对符合设置规划，达到条件和标准的，确定为生猪定点屠宰厂（场）；对供应城区的未达到定点标准的定点屠宰企业，在确保卫生和质量安全前提下，应限期整改，整改期原则上不超过12个月。整改期结束仍无法达到定点标准的，报请设区的市级人民政府坚决取消其定点资格。被关闭企业职工安置问题及其他善后工作由各地政府采取多种形式和渠道妥善处理。对边远和交通不便的农村地区的小型屠宰场点，各地要根据实际制订管理办法，在严格监管，严把基本卫生和质量安全生产条件、检疫条件的前提下予以审批，其生产的猪肉产品只能在当地供应。

（三）加快行业升级改造，提升技术和管理水平

对符合定点屠宰设置规划，达到定点条件和标准的定点屠宰厂（场），要推动其在屠宰加工、肉品品质检验、冷链设施、综合利用、无害化处理和污水处理等方面进行升级改造，严格执行屠宰操作和同步检验等制度；要督促其建立肉品质量安全管理体系和可追溯体系，鼓励其采用能满足卫生和质量安全要求的先进工艺，通过ISO9000管理体系等认证。

（四）促进企业兼并重组，优化资源配置

鼓励支持先进的屠宰加工企业以多种方式兼并重组，实现规模化、低成本扩张。要重点加大城市及其周边定点屠宰企业的整合力度，通过多种方式，促进集中合并。积极支持、引导撤并的定点屠宰厂（场）和小型屠宰场点融入大型屠宰企业的生产、加工、配送和销售等供应链管理体系，转为其购销网点和分割配送点，妥善解决当地农民散养猪的收购和肉品供应问题。

（五）支持企业延伸产业链条，培育自主品牌

支持先进的屠宰加工企业开展屠宰、加工、配送、销售一体化经营。鼓励生猪定点屠宰厂（场）采用“厂场挂钩”、订单生产以及建设生猪养殖基地等方式，扩大协议养殖或自养生猪规模；支持屠宰加工、肉类配送企业发展肉品分割配送中心，配置冷链设施，创建鲜肉品牌，扩张品牌肉连锁销售网络。加强对代宰企业的监督管理，规范代宰行为，引导代宰企业向自营和品牌化经营方向发展。

（六）加强环境保护，发展清洁生产

加强对现有生猪定点屠宰企业的环境治理，依法关闭或迁出位于饮用水源地、密集居住区等环境敏感地带的企业；对新建项目必须执行环境影响评估和项目竣工环境保护验收，严格落实环保标准；要求并支持生猪定点屠宰厂（场）建立排污设施，确保污染物达标排放；倡导清洁生产、节能减排和资源综合利用的屠宰生产方式，推广生猪定点屠宰厂（场）沼气工程，发展循环经济。

（七）提倡科学消费，积极调整产品结构

倡导食用冷鲜肉和小包装分割肉，引导群众逐步改变喜食热鲜肉和白条肉消费习惯。支持定点屠宰厂（场）建立冷却间和分割车间，配备冷链物流设施，扩大冷鲜肉和分割肉生产规模。要针对市场需求的变化，在猪肉加工及副产品处理上积极落实“变大为小、变粗为精、变生为熟、变废为宝、变害为利”的方针，支持定点屠宰企业大力发展肉品深加工和副产品综合利用，逐步解决肉类产品同质化、经营粗放和低水平恶性竞争等问题。

（八）建设诚信体系，推动屠宰企业诚信守法经营

督促屠宰加工企业加强自律，发动企业踊跃参与诚信经营创建活动。推动部门间信息沟通，形成生猪产业链上完整的信用信息记录，实现信用信息的共享。推动屠宰企业内部信用管理制度建设，增强风险防范能力。推行信用分类管理，建立全国定点屠宰企业违法违规信息的收集、信用评价和发布制度以及违规退出机制。

（九）加强国际合作，提高企业国际竞争力

广泛开展国际交流与合作，积极引进先进的管理经验和技术，借鉴成熟的国际标准和动物福利新理念，为我国屠宰加工企业参与国际竞争提供条件。鼓励先进的屠宰加工企业到国外建厂，以及通过控股、兼并等多种形式开展跨国经营。逐步消除各种贸易壁垒，鼓励、支持先进屠宰加工企业，获取肉品出口资格，发展出口业务，提升我国肉类产品的国际竞争力。

四、保障措施

（一）加强标准和制度建设

抓紧出台《畜禽屠宰检验规程》等标准，修订完善已有标准，将部分涉及肉品质量安全的推荐性国家标准升级为强制性国家标准。加快推行生猪定点屠宰厂（场）分级管理制度。依据《食品安全法》和《生猪屠宰管理条例》等法律法规，制订《生猪定点屠宰厂（场）分级管理办法》和《生猪屠宰企业资质等级要求》，将定点屠宰厂（场）划分为若干等级，等级越高标志着企业技术、管理和产品质量水平越高，肉品可能的流通范围也越大，实现促进先进企业发展，逐步淘汰落后企业的目标。

（二）加大资金支持力度

运用中央和地方财政资金，引导企业加大投入，开展“放心肉”服务体系创建工作。组织开展试点，使用中央财政专项资金，支持建设屠宰行业监管技术系统和肉品质量安全信息可追溯系统；支持大型定点屠宰厂（场）发展冷链和跨区域销售网络；支持少数民族和边远落后地区的定点屠宰企业标准化改造。地方商务主管部门要根据《生猪屠宰管理条例》精神和国务院建设“放心肉”服务体系要求，向政府财政申请专项配套资金，在落实好中央财政支持项目的同时，结合各自实际，支持生猪定点屠宰厂（场）进行升级改造，加强检验检疫能力建设，新建或改造污水处理和无害化处理设施，对因优化布局关闭的屠宰企业予以适当补偿。

（三）维护行业公平竞争

坚持营造开放、公平、竞争、有序的肉品流通环境。各地不得限制外地经检疫和检验合格的猪肉产品进入本地市场；对跨区域销售的生猪定点屠宰厂（场），应要求其配备与销售范围相适应、符合肉品保鲜卫生所需温度条件的储存、运输和装卸容器、工具和设备。严格禁止小型屠宰场点跨行政区域销售猪肉产品的行为。依法清理阻碍企业跨地区兼并重组的各种限制性和歧视性规定，促进机械化生猪屠宰资源在全国范围内的优化重组。

（四）建立健全屠宰监管体系

建立健全生猪屠宰管理机构和执法队伍，整合、充实、加强商务系统的执法力量，落实执法人员编制、装备和工作经费。支持和鼓励有条件的地方运用现代信息和网络技术，建立监管技术平台，加强对定点屠宰厂的监管，实时发现并及时处理违法违规行为；建立肉品质量信息可追溯系统，形成对有问题肉品从零售、批发、屠宰到养殖层层追根溯源的能力。加强对定点屠宰企业的监管，监督其依法生产、诚信经营。开展对屠宰管理和执法人员的培训，提高业务素质和执法水平。规范执法程序，统一执法文书，建立执法责任制，落实失、渎职责任追究和执法评议考核制度，加强执法档案管理。严格把握一般违法行为和犯罪行为的界限，做好涉嫌犯罪案件向司法部门的移送工作。

（五）强化地方政府职责和部门、地区间的协调配合

各地政府要切实承担起猪肉卫生和质量安全监管工作的责任，统筹协调有关部门，妥善处理本规划纲要实施中的相关问题，提高屠宰行业整体水平，促进行业健康发展。各地商务主管部门要加强与发展改革、工业、财政、环境保护、农业、卫生、税务、工商、质检、食品药品监管、物价等部门的沟通，研究制订进一步促进屠宰行业健康发展的政策措施，建立生猪养殖、屠宰加工、猪肉流通、消费全过程监管的协同机制。加强与农业部门的合作，在养殖基地建立生猪质量安全监测及预警系统，及时掌握养殖环境、疫病防控、兽药和饲料添加剂使用、病死猪处理等方面的信息，延伸猪肉产品质量安全信息可追溯链条。建立地区间、部门间的执法协作机制，开展联合执法，严厉打击私屠滥宰及制售注水肉、病害肉等违法违规行为。

（六）广泛开展宣传和培训

积极向广大消费者宣传肉品科学消费常识，增强其食品卫生和质量安全意识和品牌消费意识；大力向生猪定点屠宰企业和肉品经营者开展《食品安全法》和《生猪屠宰管理条例》等法律法规的宣传，提升其守法经营意识；广泛开展“放心肉”服务体系建设的宣传活动，形成全社会共同参与的良好氛围。制订培训规划，组织开展各类培训，提高定点屠宰企业从业人员的专业素质。对肉品品质检验人员实行执业资格认定制度，经培训考核合格后，持证上岗。依托教育、科研单位，培养从事肉类科研和新产品开发的工程技术人员。

（七）发挥行业协会和有关中介组织作用

充分发挥行业协会和有关中介组织的桥梁纽带作用。商务主管部门要指导并支持各级行业协会和有关中介组织在加强行业自律、建设行业诚信体系、破除行业陋规、沟通行业信息、培育品牌和自主知识产权、加强国际交流、推广先进技术、组织专业培训、标准拟定和宣传贯彻等方面开展工作。各级行业协会和有关中介组织要积极提出工作建议，配合政府做好定点设置规划的制订和执行工作；要向政府有关部门反映行业问题和企业诉求，为企业提供优质服务，要求会员企业执行国家法律法规和制度标准，自觉遵守市场竞争规则，履行社会责任，保障肉品卫生和质量安全。

五、规划纲要的实施

本规划纲要是生猪屠宰行业发展的重要指导性文件。各级商务主管部门要在当地政府领导下，统筹规划，精心部署，分步达标，搞好综合协调，确保取得实效。要认真做好工作衔接，按照本规划纲要确定的原则、目标和任务措施，结合当地实际，于2010年4月底前制定（修订）并印发实施方案和生猪定点屠宰企业设置规划。各地设置规划要明确相应指标和要求，严格执行《生猪屠宰管理条例》相关规定，落实压缩定点屠宰企业数量的任务。地方制定的实施方案、规划以及实施过程中发现的情况和问题，应及时报送商务部畜禽屠宰管理办公室（设在市场秩序司）。

粮油仓储管理办法

（国家发展和改革委员会令 第5号 2010年1月7日）

第一章 总 则

第一条 为了规范粮油仓储单位的粮油仓储活动，维护粮食流通秩序，保障国家粮食安全，根据《粮食流通管理条例》、《中央储备粮管理条例》和相关法律法规，制定本办法。

第二条 中华人民共和国境内的粮油仓储单位从事粮油仓储活动，适用本办法。

第三条 粮油仓储单位必须遵守国家法律、法规和相关管理规定，执行国家和地方粮食流通政策和粮食应急预案，贯彻国家和地方制定的仓储管理制度和标准，接受粮食行政管理部门的业务指导，配合粮食行政管理部门依法开展监督检查。

第四条 粮油仓储单位应当建立健全粮油仓储管理制度，积极应用先进适用的粮油储藏技术，延缓粮油品质劣变，降低粮油损失损耗，防止粮油污染，确保库存粮油数量真实、质量良好、储存安全。

第五条 国家粮食行政管理部门负责全国粮油仓储监督管理工作，制定管理制度和标准，组织储粮安全检查工作。县级以上地方人民政府粮食行政管理部门负责本行政区域的粮油仓储监督管理工作。

第二章 粮油仓储单位备案管理

第六条 粮油仓储单位应当自设立或者开始从事粮油仓储活动之日起30个工作日内，向所在地粮食行政管理部门备案。备案应当包括单位名称、地址、法定代表人、主要仓储业务类型、仓（罐）容规模等内容。具体备案管理办法由省、自治区、直辖市人民政府粮食行政管理部门制定。

第七条 粮油仓储单位应当具备以下条件：

（一）拥有固定经营场地，并符合本办法有关污染源、危险源安全距离的规定；

（二）拥有与从事粮油仓储活动相适应的设施设备，并符合粮油储藏技术规范的要求；

（三）拥有相应的专业技术管理人员。

第八条 未经国家粮食行政管理部门批准，粮油仓储单位名称中不得使用“国家储备粮”和“中央储备粮”字样。

第三章 粮油出入库管理

第九条 粮油仓储单位应当按照国家粮油质量标准对入库粮油进行检验，建立粮油质量档案。成品粮油质量档案还应包括生产企业出具的质量检验报告、生产日期、保质期限等内容。

第十条 粮油仓储单位应当及时对入库粮油进行整理，使其达到储存安全的要求，并按照不同品种、性质、生产年份、等级、安全水分、食用和非食用等进行分类存放。粮油入库（仓）应当准确计量，并制作计量凭证。

第十一条 粮油仓储单位应当按货位及时制作“库存粮油货位卡”，准确记录粮油的品种、数量、产地、生产年份、粮权所有人、粮食商品属性、等级、水分、杂质等信息，并将卡片置于货位的明显位置。

第十二条 粮油仓储单位应当在粮油出库前按规定检验出库粮油质量。粮油出库应当准确计量，并制作计量凭证，做好出库记录。

第十三条 出库粮油包装物和运输工具不得对粮油造成污染。未经处理的严重虫粮、危险虫粮不得出库。可能存在发热危险的粮油不得长途运输。

第十四条 粮油仓储单位应当及时清除仓房、工作塔等仓储设施内的粉尘，按规定配置防粉尘设备，防止发生粉尘爆炸事故。禁止人员进入正在作业的烘干塔、立筒仓、浅圆仓等设施。

第四章 粮油储存管理

第十五条 粮油仓储单位负责人对全部库存粮油的数量真实、质量良好、储存安全负责。

粮油保管员、粮油质量检验员应当掌握必要的专业知识和职业技能，具备相应的职业资格。

第十六条 粮油储存区应当保持清洁，并与办公区、生活区进行有效隔离。在粮油储存区内开展的活动和存放的物品不得对粮油造成污染或者对粮油储存安全构成威胁。

第十七条 粮油仓储单位应当对仓房（油罐）编排号码，配备必要的仓储设备，建立健全设备使用、保养、维修、报废等制度。

第十八条 粮油仓储单位应当按照仓房（油罐）的设计容量和要求储存粮油，执行《粮油储藏技术规范》等技术标准，建立粮油仓储管理过程记录文件。

第十九条 粮油仓储单位仓储能力不足时，应当通过代储、租赁等方式，合理利用其他单位的现有粮油仓储设施，扩大仓储能力。粮油仓储单位应当与承储或者出租的单位签订规范的代储或者租赁合同，明确双方的权利义务。

现有仓储设施不足，确有必要露天储存粮油的，应当具备以下条件：

（一）打囤做垛应当确保结构安全，规格一致；

（二）囤垛应当满足防水、防潮、防火、防风、防虫鼠雀害的要求，并采取测温、通风等必要的仓储措施；

（三）用于堆放粮油的地坪和打囤做垛的器材不得对粮油造成污染。

第二十条 在常规储存条件下，粮油正常储存年限一般为小麦5年，稻谷和玉米3年，食用油脂和豆类2年。

第二十一条 粮油仓储单位应当按照本办法有关粮油储存损耗处置方法的规定处置粮油储存损耗。国家对政策性粮油储存损耗的处置方法另有规定的，从其规定。

第二十二条 储存粮油出库数量多于入库数量的溢余，不得冲抵其他货位或批次粮油的损耗和损失。

第二十三条 粮油仓储单位应当设立粮油保管账、统计账、会计账，真实、完整地反映库存粮油和资金占用情况，并按有关规定妥善保管。库存粮油情况发生变化的，粮油仓储单位应当在5个工作日内更新库存粮油货位卡和有关账目，确保账账相符、账实相符。

第二十四条 粮油仓储单位应当建立安全生产检查制度，定期对生产状况进行检查评估，及时消除安全隐患。

第二十五条 储粮化学药剂应当存放在专用的药品库内，实行双人双锁管理，并对药剂和包装物领用及回收进行登记。

进行熏蒸作业的，应当制订熏蒸方案，并报当地粮食行政管理部门备案。熏蒸作业中，粮油仓储单位应当在作业场地周围设立警示牌和警戒线，禁止无关人员进入熏蒸作业区。

第二十六条 库存粮油发生降等、损失、超耗等储存事故的，粮油仓储单位应当及时进行处置，避免损失扩大。属于较大、重大或者特大储存事故的，应当立即向所在地粮食行政管理部门报告。属于特大储存事故的，所在地粮食行政管理部门应当在接到事故报告24小时内，上报国家粮食行政管理部门。

粮油储存事故按照以下标准划分：

（一）一次事故造成10t以下粮食或2t以下油脂损失的为一般储存事故；

（二）一次事故造成10t以上100t以下粮食或2t以上20t以下油脂损失的为较大储存事故；

（三）一次事故造成100t以上1 000t以下粮食或20t以上200t以下油脂损失的为重大储存事故；

（四）一次事故造成1 000t以上粮食或200t以上油脂损失的为特别重大储存事故。

第二十七条 发生安全生产事故的，粮油仓储单位应当依法及时进行处理，并立即向所在地粮食行政管理部门报告。

第五章 法律责任

第二十八条 粮油仓储单位违反本办法第六条规定，未在规定时间向粮食行政管理部门备案，或者备案内容弄虚作假的，由负责备案管理的粮食行政管理部门责令改正，给予警告；拒不改正的，处1万元以下罚款。

第二十九条 粮油仓储单位不具备本办法第七条规定条件的，由负责备案管理的粮食行政管理部门责令改正，给予警告；拒不改正的，处1万元以上3万元以下罚款。

第三十条 粮油仓储单位的名称不符合本办法第八条规定的，由负责备案管理的粮食行政管理部门责令改正，给予警告。

第三十一条　粮油仓储单位违反本办法有关粮油出入库、储存等管理规定的，由所在地粮食行政管理部门责令改正，给予警告；情节严重的，可以并处3万元以下罚款；造成粮油储存事故或者安全生产事故的，按照有关法律法规和国家有关规定给予处罚。

第六章　附　　则

第三十二条　本办法所称粮油，包括各类粮食、植物油料和油脂。

本办法所称粮油仓储单位，是指仓容规模500t以上或者罐容规模100t以上，专门从事粮油仓储活动，或者在粮油收购、销售、运输、加工、进出口等经营活动过程中从事粮油仓储活动的法人和其他组织。

仓容规模500t以下或者罐容规模100t以下从事粮油仓储活动的经营者，其管理办法由省、自治区、直辖市人民政府粮食行政管理部门参照本办法制定。

第三十三条　本办法相关条款所称的“以上”包括本数，“以下”不包括本数。

第三十四条　本办法自公布之日起施行。原商业部1987年6月22日颁布的《国家粮油仓库管理办法》［（87）商储（粮）字第12号］同时废止。

附件：（略）

食品安全风险评估管理规定（试行）

（卫生部等七部门　卫监督发［2010］8号　2010年1月21日）

第一条　为规范食品安全风险评估工作，根据《中华人民共和国食品安全法》和《中华人民共和国食品安全法实施条例》的有关规定，制定本规定。

第二条　本规定适用于国务院卫生行政部门依照食品安全法有关规定组织的食品安全风险评估工作。

第三条　卫生部负责组织食品安全风险评估工作，成立国家食品安全风险评估专家委员会，并及时将食品安全风险评估结果通报国务院有关部门。

国务院有关部门按照有关法律法规和本规定的要求提出食品安全风险评估的建议，并提供有关信息和资料。

地方人民政府有关部门应当按照风险所在的环节协助国务院有关部门收集食品安全风险评估有关的信息和资料。

第四条　国家食品安全风险评估专家委员会依据国家食品安全风险评估专家委员会章程组建。

卫生部确定的食品安全风险评估技术机构负责承担食品安全风险评估相关科学数据、技术信息、检验结果的收集、处理、分析等任务。食品安全风险评估技术机构开展与风险评估相关工作接受国家食品安全风险评估专家委员会的委托和指导。

第五条　食品安全风险评估以食品安全风险监测和监督管理信息、科学数据以及其他有关信息为基础，遵循科学、透明和个案处理的原则进行。

第六条　国家食品安全风险评估专家委员会依据本规定及国家食品安全风险评估专家委员会章程独立进行风险评估，保证风险评估结果的科学、客观和公正。

任何部门不得干预国家食品安全风险评估专家委员会和食品安全风险评估技术机构承担的风险评估相关工作。

第七条　有下列情形之一的，由卫生部审核同意后向国家食品安全风险评估专家委员会下达食品安全风险评估任务：

（一）为制订或修订食品安全国家标准提供科学依据需要进行风险评估的；

（二）通过食品安全风险监测或者接到举报发现食品可能存在安全隐患的，在组织进行检验后认为需要进行食品安全风险评估的；

（三）国务院有关部门按照《中华人民共和国食品安全法实施条例》第十二条要求提出食品安全风险评估的建议，并按规定提出《风险评估项目建议书》（见附表1）；

（四）卫生部根据法律法规的规定认为需要进行风险评估的其他情形。

第八条　国务院有关部门提交《风险评估项目建议书》时，应当向卫生部提供下列信息和资料：

（一）风险的来源和性质；

（二）相关检验数据和结论；

（三）风险涉及范围；

（四）其他有关信息和资料。

卫生部根据食品安全风险评估的需要组织收集有关信息和资料，国务院有关部门和县级以上地方农业行政、质量监督、工商行政管理、食品药品监督管理等有关部门应当协助收集前款规定的食品安全风险评估信息和资料。

第九条 对于下列情形之一的，卫生部可以做出不予评估的决定：

（一）通过现有的监督管理措施可以解决的；

（二）通过检验和产品安全性评估可以得出结论的；

（三）国际政府组织有明确资料对风险进行了科学描述且适于我国膳食暴露模式的。

对做出不予评估决定和因缺乏数据信息难以做出评估结论的，卫生部应当向有关方面说明原因和依据；如果国际组织已有评估结论的，应一并通报相关部门。

第十条 卫生部根据本规定第七条的规定和国家食品安全风险评估专家委员会的建议，确定国家食品安全风险评估计划和优先评估项目。

第十一条 卫生部以《风险评估任务书》（见附表 2）的形式向国家食品安全风险评估专家委员会下达风险评估任务。《风险评估任务书》应当包括风险评估的目的、需要解决的问题和结果产出形式等内容。

第十二条 国家食品安全风险评估专家委员会应当根据评估任务提出风险评估实施方案，报卫生部备案。

对于需要进一步补充信息的，可向卫生部提出数据和信息采集方案的建议。

第十三条 国家食品安全风险评估专家委员会按照风险评估实施方案，遵循危害识别、危害特征描述、暴露评估和风险特征描述的结构化程序开展风险评估。

第十四条 受委托的有关技术机构应当在国家食品安全风险评估专家委员会要求的时限内提交风险评估相关科学数据、技术信息、检验结果的收集、处理和分析的结果。

第十五条 国家食品安全风险评估专家委员会进行风险评估，对风险评估的结果和报告负责，并及时将结果、报告上报卫生部。

第十六条 发生下列情形之一的，卫生部可以要求国家食品安全风险评估专家委员会立即研究分析，对需要开展风险评估的事项，国家食品安全风险评估专家委员会应当立即成立临时工作组，制订应急评估方案。

（一）处理重大食品安全事故需要的；

（二）公众高度关注的食品安全问题需要尽快解答的；

（三）国务院有关部门监督管理工作需要并提出应急评估建议的；

（四）处理与食品安全相关的国际贸易争端需要的。

第十七条 需要开展应急评估时，国家食品安全风险评估专家委员会按照应急评估方案进行风险评估，及时向卫生部提交风险评估结果报告。

第十八条 卫生部应当依法向社会公布食品安全风险评估结果。

风险评估结果由国家食品安全风险评估专家委员会负责解释。

第十九条 本规定用语定义如下：

危害：指食品中所含有的对健康有潜在不良影响的生物、化学、物理因素或食品存在状况。

危害识别：根据流行病学、动物试验、体外试验、结构-活性关系等科学数据和文献信息确定人体暴露于某种危害后是否会对健康造成不良影响、造成不良影响的可能性，以及可能处于风险之中的人群和范围。

危害特征描述：对与危害相关的不良健康作用进行定性或定量描述。可以利用动物试验、临床研究以及流行病学研究确定危害与各种不良健康作用之间的剂量-反应关系、作用机制等。如果可能，对于毒性作用有阈值的危害应建立人体安全摄入量水平。

暴露评估：描述危害进入人体的途径，估算不同人群摄入危害的水平。根据危害在膳食中的水平和人群膳食消费量，初步估算危害的膳食总摄入量，同时考虑其他非膳食进入人体的途径，估算人体总摄入量并与安全摄入量进行比较。

风险特征描述：在危害识别、危害特征描述和暴露评估的基础上，综合分析危害对人群健康产生不良作用的风险及其程度，同时应当描述和解释风险评估过程中的不确定性。

第二十条 食品安全风险评估技术机构的认定和资格管理规定由卫生部另行制订。

第二十一条 本办法由卫生部负责解释，自发布之日起实施。

附表：1. 风险评估项目建议书（略）

2. 风险评估任务书（略）

2010年食品安全整顿工作安排

（国务院 国办发［2010］17号 2010年3月2日）

为切实解决我国食品安全突出问题，全面提升食品安全水平，保障人民群众饮食安全，2009年2月国务院部署用两年左右时间，在全国集中开展食品安全整顿。一年来，各地区、各有关部门认真贯彻落实国务院决策部署，按照《国务院办公厅关于印发食品安全整顿工作方案的通知》（国办发［2009］8号）要求，切实加强领导，精心组织实施，清理和制（修）订食品安全标准，加强各环节食品安全监管，加大违法生产经营食品案件查处力度，推进食品工业企业诚信体系建设，食品安全整顿取得阶段性成效。为巩固前一阶段工作成果，全面落实食品安全整顿各项任务，现就2010年食品安全整顿工作作出以下安排：

一、2010年食品安全整顿工作主要任务

（一）加强违法添加非食用物质和滥用食品添加剂整顿

完善食品添加剂管理法规，修订食品添加剂使用标准。严格食品添加剂生产许可制度，加强食品添加剂标签标识管理，实行食品生产加工企业食品添加剂使用报告制度。开展食品中食品添加剂和非食用物质专项抽检和监测，整治超过标准限量和使用范围滥用食品添加剂的行为，查处和打击生产、销售、使用非法食品添加物的行为，严格食品添加剂及相关产品研制管理。

（二）加强农产品质量安全整顿

深入开展蔬菜、水果、茶叶、食用菌、畜禽产品、水产品中农兽药和禁用药物残留监测。加强生鲜乳质量安全监管，强化生鲜乳收购站日常监管与标准化管理，坚决取缔未经许可的非法收购站（点）。加大农药生产经营监管力度，加强农药质量监督抽查，依法查处违法违规生产经营单位，重点打击无证照生产"黑窝点"。加强饲料质量安全监测，打击在饲料原料和产品中添加有毒有害化学物质及养殖过程中使用"瘦肉精"等违禁药物行为。加强兽药GMP（良好生产规范）后续监管，积极推行兽药经营质量管理规范制度，实施动物产品兽药残留监控计划，打击制售假劣兽药违法行为。深入开展水产苗种专项整治，打击水产养殖环节违法使用硝基呋喃类、孔雀石绿等禁用药物和有毒有害化学物质行为。修订农药管理条例、饲料和饲料添加剂管理条例及相关管理办法，制（修）订饲料和饲料添加剂标准、兽药残留限量和检测方法标准。组织开展粮食收购、储存环节质量安全监测。

（三）加强食品生产加工环节整顿

严格食品生产许可制度，督促企业严格执行食品原料、食品添加剂、食品相关产品采购查验制度和出厂检验记录制度。加强生产加工环节食品安全监督抽检，督促企业建立健全食品可追溯制度和食品召回制度，查处企业生产不符合安全标准食品的行为。打击制售假冒伪劣食品、使用非食品原料和回收食品生产加工食品的行为。取缔无生产许可证、无营业执照的非法食品生产加工企业。大力整顿食品安全风险较高、投诉举报多的食品行业，建立对食品生产加工小作坊和食品摊贩加强监管的长效机制。

（四）加强食品进出口环节整顿

严格办理进出口食品海关相关手续，打击食品、食用农产品特别是疫区产品非法进出口行为。对已经备案的出口食品生产企业和出口食品原料种养殖场进行全面清查。加强进出口食品、食用农产品的检验检疫监管，重点加强对出口食品中食品添加剂和违法添加非食用物质检验检疫监管，严厉打击逃避检验检疫行为，完善进出口食品、食用农产品企业不良记录制度，将逃避检验检疫的企业一律列为不良记录企业。建立和完善进出口食品、食用农产品检验检疫监管的长效机制。加强进出口食品安全信息通报，完善风险预警和控制措施。

（五）加强食品流通环节整顿

严格食品流通许可制度，完善食品市场主体准入机制，完善流通环节食品安全抽样检验和退市制度，建立销售者主动退市和工商部门责令退市相结合的监管机制。加强流通环节食品安全日常监管，监督食品经营者依法落实食品进货查验和记录制度，督促食品经营者加强自律。完善食品市场监管和巡查制度，突出重点地区、重点场所和重点品种，深入开展专项执

法检查，加大食品市场分类监管和食品市场日常巡查力度，打击销售过期变质、假冒伪劣和不合格食品的违法行为。

（六）加强餐饮消费环节整顿

严格餐饮服务许可制度，查处餐饮单位无证经营行为。清理、修订餐饮消费环节相关食品监督管理规范办法，规范餐饮服务许可行为，提高餐饮服务准入门槛。制定并实施餐饮消费环节重点监督检查及抽检工作计划，以学校食堂、幼儿园食堂、建筑工地食堂、农家乐旅游点、小型餐饮单位为重点，加大对熟食卤味、盒饭、冷菜等高风险食品和餐具清洗消毒等重点环节的监督检查力度，开展餐饮消费环节专项整治和专项检查。督促餐饮服务单位建立食品原料采购索证索票制度，对其采购的重点品种开展专项抽查，查处采购和使用病死或者死因不明的畜禽及其制品、劣质食用油等行为。

（七）加强畜禽屠宰整顿

严把市场准入关，清理整顿生猪定点屠宰厂（场），加大对私屠滥宰行为的打击力度。加强对生猪（牛、羊）定点屠宰厂（场）的日常监管，查处违法屠宰注水或注入其他物质的猪（牛、羊）、出厂未经品质检验或经品质检验不合格的猪（牛、羊）肉产品等行为。强化活禽和生猪（牛、羊）产地和屠宰检疫，查处出售和屠宰病死畜禽的行为。督促企业建立和完善肉品质量安全全程监管体系，打击加工、销售病死病害畜禽肉和注水肉等行为，严防病死、注水或注入其他物质、未经检验检疫或检验检疫不合格肉品进入加工、流通、餐饮消费环节。加大生猪屠宰长效监管机制建设，进一步健全相关应急处置机制。

（八）加强保健食品整顿

依法对获批注册但未标明有效期的保健食品进行全面清理换证。开展保健食品违法添加药物专项检查，查处制售假劣保健食品行为。开展保健食品标签、说明书内容专项检查。查处通过公益讲座、健康诊疗、学术交流、会展销售等方式变相销售假冒伪劣保健食品的行为。整治普通食品声称具有特定保健功能和保健食品夸大宣传功能的行为。

（九）完善食品安全标准

制定清理现行食品安全标准的工作方案，对现行食品质量标准、卫生标准和行业标准中强制执行的标准进行清理，解决标准缺失、重复和矛盾问题。制（修）订食品中农药残留、有毒有害污染物、致病微生物、真菌毒素限量标准。公布国家乳品质量安全标准。组织开展食品安全标准的宣传贯彻，动员社会、企业和消费者积极参与食品安全标准实施工作，跟踪评价食品安全标准实施情况。跟踪研究有关国家和国际组织食品安全标准，积极开展对外交流和合作，借鉴国外先进研究成果，提高我国食品安全标准制定的效率和科学水平。

（十）加强食品安全风险监测和预警

建立国家食品安全风险监测制度，制定并实施国家食品安全风险监测计划，加强地区性食品安全风险监测，建立快速、方便的食品安全信息沟通机制和网络平台。发布年度食品安全风险监测评价报告，建立食源性疾病报告机制，构建食源性疾病和食物中毒报告信息采集网络，建立食品安全有害因素与食源性疾病监测数据库。实施食品安全风险评估制度，对相关食品安全风险和隐患进行风险评估。加大食品特别是乳品等高风险食品检验检测频次，定期公布检验检测结果。加强食品安全监测能力建设。加快推进检验检测机构改革，严格检验检测机构资质认定和检验人员管理，推进检验检测资源和信息共享。

（十一）推进食品生产企业诚信体系建设

制定食品生产企业诚信体系建设指导意见和诚信体系评价标准，选择若干企业开展诚信体系建设试点，及时总结推广试点经验。在企业中建立生产经营档案制度，鼓励支持食品企业建立食品安全可追溯系统，在食品行业全面推广。督促行业协会组织对食品企业从业人员培训、考核，培养具备良好职业道德、较高业务水平和较强实践能力的食品安全岗位专职人员。建立食品企业诚信不良记录收集、管理、通报制度和行业退出机制。加强食品生产企业和经营者质量信用建设和信用分类监管。

二、有关要求

（一）严格落实食品安全整顿工作责任

各地区、各有关部门要加强组织领导，认真履行职责，采取有力措施，依法加强治理整顿。要抓紧制定 2010 年整顿工作具体实施方案，分解整顿工作任务，明确各环节、各阶段的整顿目标和完成时限，落实责任单位和责任人员。要将集中整顿与日常工作相结合，及时总结整顿工作中的典型做法和经验，形成加强食品安全监管的长效机制。县级以上地方人民政府要切实承担起本行政区域食品安全整顿工作统一领导、组织、协调的责任，统筹安排监管力量，切实保障经费投入，全面抓好整顿任务落实；各有关部门要加强对本系统食品安全整顿工作的监督指导，坚持统一协调与分工负责相结合，各司其职，各负其责，密切协作，形成合力。国务院食品安全办要加强综合协调和督促指导，及时发现和协调解决有关问题。

（二）切实加大食品安全案件查处和责任追究

力度

各地区、各有关部门要重视投诉举报受理工作，注意发现食品安全事故和案件线索并及时进行调查处理。要完善快速反应机制，及时妥善处理食品安全事故。要进一步加强行政执法与刑事司法的衔接，规范和完善涉及食品安全刑事案件的鉴定程序，加大对食品安全领域违法犯罪行为的打击力度。强化行政监察和行政问责，严肃查处监管部门失职、渎职行为。严格实行重大食品安全事故报告、举报、通报制度，对行政机关迟报、漏报甚至瞒报、谎报食品安全事故的，依法依纪追究相关责任人责任。

（三）认真做好信息报告和新闻宣传工作

各地区、各有关部门要加强沟通协调，及时将食品安全整顿工作重要信息向国务院食品安全办、卫生部报告，并向相关部门通报。要统筹和规范食品安全整顿信息发布工作，对影响仅限于本行政区域的信息，由本级政府授权有关职能部门发布；对涉及两个以上省（自治区、直辖市）的信息，由国务院授权的食品安全整顿综合协调部门统一发布。要正确把握舆论导向，主动做好信息发布和政策解读；大力宣传《中华人民共和国食品安全法》及其实施条例，积极宣传食品安全整顿工作进展、成效和典型事例，支持新闻媒体开展舆论监督，引导新闻媒体客观准确报道，为食品安全整顿工作营造良好氛围。

（四）加强督促检查和评估考核

国务院食品安全委员会将组织对食品安全整顿工作进行检查，适时召开全体会议听取整顿工作情况汇报。地方人民政府也要将食品安全整顿工作作为重点督查内容，制定专项督查工作方案，逐级开展督查。国务院食品安全办要制订整顿工作评估考核办法，组织对各地区、各有关部门食品安全整顿工作进行评估考核。

餐饮服务许可管理办法

（卫生部令 第70号 2010年3月4日）

第一章 总 则

第一条 为规范餐饮服务许可工作，加强餐饮服务监督管理，维护正常的餐饮服务秩序，保护消费者健康，根据《中华人民共和国食品安全法》（以下简称《食品安全法》）、《中华人民共和国行政许可法》（以下简称《行政许可法》）、《中华人民共和国食品安全法实施条例》（以下简称《食品安全法实施条例》）等有关法律法规的规定，制定本办法。

第二条 本办法适用于从事餐饮服务的单位和个人（以下简称餐饮服务提供者），不适用于食品摊贩和为餐饮服务提供者提供食品半成品的单位和个人。

餐饮服务实行许可制度。餐饮服务提供者应当取得《餐饮服务许可证》，并依法承担餐饮服务的食品安全责任。

集体用餐配送单位纳入餐饮服务许可管理的范围。

第三条 国家食品药品监督管理局主管全国餐饮服务许可管理工作，地方各级食品药品监督管理部门负责本行政区域内的餐饮服务许可管理工作。

第四条 餐饮服务许可按照餐饮服务提供者的业态和规模实施分类管理。餐饮服务分类许可的审查规范由国家食品药品监督管理局制定。

《餐饮服务许可证》受理和审批的许可机关由各省、自治区、直辖市食品药品监督管理部门规定。

第五条 食品药品监督管理部门实施餐饮服务许可应当符合法律、法规和规章规定的权限、范围、条件与程序，遵循公开、公平、公正、便民原则。

第六条 食品药品监督管理部门应当建立餐饮服务许可信息和档案管理制度，定期公告取得或者注销餐饮服务许可的餐饮服务提供者名录。

第七条 食品药品监督管理部门应当加强对实施餐饮服务许可的监督检查。

第八条 任何单位和个人有权举报餐饮服务许可实施过程中的违法行为，食品药品监督管理部门应当及时核实、处理。

第二章 申请与受理

第九条 申请人向食品药品监督管理部门提出餐饮服务许可申请应当具备以下基本条件：

（一）具有与制作供应的食品品种、数量相适应的食品原料处理和食品加工、贮存等场所，保持该场所环境整洁，并与有毒、有害场所以及其他污染源保持规定的距离；

（二）具有与制作供应的食品品种、数量相适应的经营设备或者设施，有相应的消毒、更衣、洗手、采光、照明、通风、冷冻冷藏、防尘、防蝇、防鼠、防虫、洗涤以及处理废水、存放垃圾和废弃物的设备或者设施；

（三）具有经食品安全培训、符合相关条件的食品安全管理人员，以及与本单位实际相适应的保证食品安全的规章制度；

（四）具有合理的布局和加工流程，防止待加工食品与直接入口食品、原料与成品交叉污染，避免食品接触有毒物、不洁物；

（五）国家食品药品监督管理局或者省、自治区、直辖市食品药品监督管理部门规定的其他条件。

餐饮服务食品安全管理人员的条件和食品安全培训的有关要求由国家食品药品监督管理局制定。

第十条 申请《餐饮服务许可证》应当提交以下材料：

（一）《餐饮服务许可证》申请书；

（二）名称预先核准证明（已从事其他经营的可提供营业执照复印件）；

（三）餐饮服务经营场所和设备布局、加工流程、卫生设施等示意图；

（四）法定代表人（负责人或者业主）的身份证明（复印件），以及不属于本办法第三十六条、第三十七条情形的说明材料；

（五）食品安全管理人员符合本办法第九条有关条件的材料；

（六）保证食品安全的规章制度；

（七）国家食品药品监督管理局或者省、自治区、直辖市食品药品监督管理部门规定的其他材料。

第十一条 申请人提交的材料应当真实、完整，并对材料的真实性负责。

第十二条 食品药品监督管理部门依据《行政许可法》，对申请人提出的餐饮服务许可申请分别做出以下处理：

（一）申请事项依法不需要取得餐饮服务许可，或者依法不属于食品药品监督管理部门职权范围的，应当即时告知申请人不接收申请的原因；

（二）申请材料存在可以当场更正的错误的，应当允许申请人当场更正，申请人应当对更正内容签章确认；

（三）申请材料不齐全或者不符合法定形式的，应当当场或者在5个工作日内一次性告知申请人需要补正的全部内容，逾期不告知的，自收到申请材料之日起即为受理；

（四）申请事项属于食品药品监督管理部门职权范围，申请材料齐全且符合法定形式的，应当做出受理决定。

第三章 审核与决定

第十三条 食品药品监督管理部门受理申请人提交的申请材料后，应当审核申请人按照本办法第十条规定提交的相关资料，并对申请人的餐饮服务经营场所进行现场核查。

上级食品药品监督管理部门受理的餐饮服务许可申请，可以委托下级食品药品监督管理部门进行现场核查。

第十四条 食品药品监督管理部门应当根据申请材料和现场核查的情况，对符合条件的，做出准予行政许可的决定；对不符合规定条件的，做出不予行政许可的决定并书面说明理由，同时告知申请人享有依法申请行政复议或者提起行政诉讼的权利。

第十五条 食品药品监督管理部门应当自受理申请之日起20个工作日内做出行政许可决定。因特殊原因需要延长许可期限的，经本机关负责人批准，可以延长10个工作日，并应当将延长期限的理由告知申请人。

第十六条 食品药品监督管理部门做出准予行政许可决定的，应当自做出决定之日起10个工作日内向申请人颁发《餐饮服务许可证》。

第十七条 对于已办结的餐饮服务许可事项，食品药品监督管理部门应当将有关许可材料及时归档。

第四章 变更、延续、补发和注销

第十八条 餐饮服务提供者的名称、法定代表人（负责人或者业主）或者地址门牌号改变（实际经营场所未改变）的，应当向原发证部门提出办理《餐饮服务许可证》记载内容变更申请，并提供有关部门出具的有关核准证明。

餐饮服务提供者的许可类别、备注项目以及布局流程、主要卫生设施需要改变的，应当向原发证部门申请办理《餐饮服务许可证》变更手续。原发证部门应当以申请变更内容为重点进行审核。

食品药品监督管理部门根据本条第一款、第二款规定，准予变更《餐饮服务许可证》记载内容或者准予办理变更手续的，颁发新的《餐饮服务许可证》，原《餐饮服务许可证》证号和有效期限不变。

第十九条 餐饮服务提供者需要延续《餐饮服务

许可证》的，应当在《餐饮服务许可证》有效期届满30日前向原发证部门书面提出延续申请。逾期提出延续申请的，按照新申请《餐饮服务许可证》办理。

第二十条 申请延续《餐饮服务许可证》应当提供以下材料：

（一）《餐饮服务许可证》延续申请书；

（二）原《餐饮服务许可证》复印件；

（三）原《餐饮服务许可证》的经营场所、布局流程、卫生设施等内容有变化或者无变化的说明材料；

（四）省、自治区、直辖市食品药品监督管理部门规定的其他材料。

第二十一条 原发证部门受理《餐饮服务许可证》延续申请后，应当重点对原许可的经营场所、布局流程、卫生设施等是否有变化，以及是否符合本办法第九条的规定进行审核。准予延续的，颁发新的《餐饮服务许可证》，原《餐饮服务许可证》证号不变。

第二十二条 《餐饮服务许可证》变更、延续的程序按照本办法第二章、第三章的有关规定执行。

第二十三条 餐饮服务提供者在领取变更、延续后的新《餐饮服务许可证》时，应当将原《餐饮服务许可证》交回发证部门。

第二十四条 餐饮服务提供者遗失《餐饮服务许可证》的，应当于遗失后60日内公开声明《餐饮服务许可证》遗失，向原发证部门申请补发。《餐饮服务许可证》毁损的，凭毁损的原证向原发证部门申请补发。

第二十五条 有下列情形之一的，发证部门应当依法注销《餐饮服务许可证》：

（一）《餐饮服务许可证》有效期届满未申请延续的，或者延续申请未被批准的；

（二）餐饮服务提供者依法终止的；

（三）《餐饮服务许可证》依法被撤销、撤回或者被吊销的；

（四）餐饮服务提供者主动申请注销的；

（五）依法应当注销《餐饮服务许可证》的其他情形。

第二十六条 《餐饮服务许可证》被注销的，原持证者应当及时将《餐饮服务许可证》原件交回食品药品监督管理部门。食品药品监督部门应当及时做好注销《餐饮服务许可证》的有关登记工作。

第五章 许可证的管理

第二十七条 《餐饮服务许可证》应当载明单位名称、地址、法定代表人（负责人或者业主）、类别、备注、许可证号、发证机关（加盖公章）、发证日期、有效期限等内容。

第二十八条 《餐饮服务许可证》样式由国家食品药品监督管理局统一规定。

许可证号格式为：省、自治区、直辖市简称＋餐证字＋4位年份数＋6位行政区域代码＋6位行政区域发证顺序编号。

第二十九条 《餐饮服务许可证》有效期为3年。临时从事餐饮服务活动的，《餐饮服务许可证》有效期不超过6个月。

第三十条 同一餐饮服务提供者在不同地点或者场所从事餐饮服务活动的，应当分别办理《餐饮服务许可证》。

餐饮服务经营地点或者场所改变的，应当重新申请办理《餐饮服务许可证》。

第三十一条 餐饮服务提供者取得的《餐饮服务许可证》，不得转让、涂改、出借、倒卖、出租。

餐饮服务提供者应当按照许可范围依法经营，并在就餐场所醒目位置悬挂或者摆放《餐饮服务许可证》。

第六章 监督检查

第三十二条 上级食品药品监督管理部门发现下级食品药品监督管理部门违反规定实施餐饮服务许可的，应当责令下级食品药品监督管理部门限期纠正或者直接予以纠正。

第三十三条 食品药品监督管理部门及其工作人员履行餐饮服务许可职责，应当自觉接受餐饮服务提供者以及社会的监督。

食品药品监督管理部门接到有关违反规定实施餐饮服务许可的举报，应当及时进行核实；情况属实的，应当立即纠正。

第三十四条 食品药品监督管理部门及其工作人员违反本办法规定实施餐饮服务许可的，由上级食品药品监督管理部门责令限期整改，并通报批评；对有关工作人员追究行政责任，给予批评教育、离岗培训、调离执法岗位或者取消执法资格等处理。

追究有关人员行政责任时，按照下列原则：

（一）申请人不符合餐饮服务许可条件，承办人出具申请人符合餐饮服务许可条件的意见的，追究承办人行政责任；

（二）承办人认为申请人不符合餐饮服务许可条件，主管领导仍然批准发放《餐饮服务许可证》的，追究主管领导的行政责任；

（三）承办人和主管领导均有过错的，主要追究主管领导的行政责任。

第三十五条 有下列情形之一的，作出发放《餐饮服务许可证》决定的食品药品监督管理部门或者其上级食品药品监督管理部门，可以撤销《餐饮服务许可证》：

（一）食品药品监督管理部门工作人员滥用职权，玩忽职守，给不符合条件的申请人发放《餐饮服务许可证》的；

（二）食品药品监督管理部门工作人员超越法定职权发放《餐饮服务许可证》的；

（三）食品药品监督管理部门工作人员违反法定程序发放《餐饮服务许可证》的；

（四）依法可以撤销发放《餐饮服务许可证》决定的其他情形。

食品药品监督管理部门依照前款规定撤销《餐饮服务许可证》，对餐饮服务提供者的合法权益造成损害的，应当依法予以赔偿。

第七章 法律责任

第三十六条 申请人隐瞒有关情况或者提供虚假材料的，食品药品监督管理部门发现后不予受理或者不予许可，并给予警告；该申请人在1年内不得再次申请餐饮服务许可。

申请人以欺骗、贿赂等不正当手段取得《餐饮服务许可证》的，食品药品监督管理部门应当予以撤销；该申请人在3年内不得再次申请餐饮服务许可。

第三十七条 申请人被吊销《餐饮服务许可证》的，其直接负责的主管人员自处罚决定作出之日起5年内不得从事餐饮服务管理工作。

餐饮服务提供者违反《食品安全法》规定，聘用不得从事餐饮服务管理工作的人员从事管理工作的，由原发证部门吊销许可证。

第三十八条 食品药品监督管理部门发现已取得《餐饮服务许可证》的餐饮服务提供者不符合餐饮经营要求的，应当责令立即纠正，并依法予以处理；不再符合餐饮服务许可条件的，应当依法撤销《餐饮服务许可证》。

第八章 附 则

第三十九条 本办法下列用语的含义：

餐饮服务，指通过即时制作加工、商业销售和服务性劳动等，向消费者提供食品和消费场所及设施的服务活动。

经营场所，指与食品加工经营直接或者间接相关的场所，包括食品加工处理和就餐场所。

餐饮服务提供者的业态，指各种餐饮服务经营形态，包括餐馆、快餐店、小吃店、饮品店、食堂等。

集体用餐配送单位，指根据服务对象订购要求，集中加工、分送食品但不提供就餐场所的单位。

第四十条 国境口岸范围内的餐饮服务活动的监督管理由出入境检验检疫机构依照《食品安全法》和《中华人民共和国国境卫生检疫法》以及相关行政法规的规定实施。

铁路运营中餐饮服务许可的管理参照本办法。

根据《食品安全法》，食品摊贩的具体管理办法由省、自治区、直辖市人民代表大会常务委员会依法制定。

第四十一条 省、自治区、直辖市食品药品监督管理部门可以结合本地实际情况，根据本办法的规定制定实施细则。

第四十二条 本办法自2010年5月1日起施行，卫生部2005年12月15日发布的《食品卫生许可证管理办法》同时废止。餐饮服务提供者在本办法施行前已经取得《食品卫生许可证》的，该许可证在有效期内继续有效。

餐饮服务食品安全监督管理办法

（卫生部令 第71号 2010年3月4日）

第一章 总 则

第一条 为加强餐饮服务监督管理，保障餐饮服务环节食品安全，根据《中华人民共和国食品安全法》（以下简称《食品安全法》）、《中华人民共和国食品安全法实施条例》（以下简称《食品安全法实施条例》），制定本办法。

第二条　在中华人民共和国境内从事餐饮服务的单位和个人（以下简称餐饮服务提供者）应当遵守本办法。

第三条　国家食品药品监督管理局主管全国餐饮服务监督管理工作，地方各级食品药品监督管理部门负责本行政区域内的餐饮服务监督管理工作。

第四条　餐饮服务提供者应当依照法律、法规、食品安全标准及有关要求从事餐饮服务活动，对社会和公众负责，保证食品安全，接受社会监督，承担餐饮服务食品安全责任。

第五条　鼓励社会团体、基层群众性自治组织开展餐饮服务食品安全知识和相关法律、法规的普及工作，增强餐饮服务提供者食品安全意识，提高消费者自我保护能力；鼓励开展技术服务工作，促进餐饮服务提供者提高食品安全管理水平。

餐饮服务相关行业协会应当加强行业自律，引导餐饮服务提供者依法经营，推动行业诚信建设，宣传、普及餐饮服务食品安全知识。

第六条　鼓励和支持餐饮服务提供者为提高食品安全水平而采用先进技术和先进的管理规范，实施危害分析与关键控制点体系，配备先进的食品安全检测设备，对食品进行自行检查或者向具有法定资质的机构送检。

第七条　任何组织和个人均有权对餐饮服务食品安全进行社会监督，举报餐饮服务提供者违反本办法的行为，了解有关餐饮服务食品安全信息，对餐饮服务食品安全工作提出意见和建议。

第二章　餐饮服务基本要求

第八条　餐饮服务提供者必须依法取得《餐饮服务许可证》，按照许可范围依法经营，并在就餐场所醒目位置悬挂或者摆放《餐饮服务许可证》。

第九条　餐饮服务提供者应当建立健全食品安全管理制度，配备专职或者兼职食品安全管理人员。

被吊销《餐饮服务许可证》的单位，根据《食品安全法》第九十二条的规定，其直接负责的主管人员自处罚决定作出之日起5年内不得从事餐饮服务管理工作。

餐饮服务提供者不得聘用本条前款规定的禁止从业人员从事管理工作。

第十条　餐饮服务提供者应当按照《食品安全法》第三十四条的规定，建立并执行从业人员健康管理制度，建立从业人员健康档案。餐饮服务从业人员应当依照《食品安全法》第三十四条第二款的规定每年进行健康检查，取得健康合格证明后方可参加工作。

从事直接入口食品工作的人员患有《食品安全法实施条例》第二十三条规定的有碍食品安全疾病的，应当将其调整到其他不影响食品安全的工作岗位。

第十一条　餐饮服务提供者应当依照《食品安全法》第三十二条的规定组织从业人员参加食品安全培训，学习食品安全法律、法规、标准和食品安全知识，明确食品安全责任，并建立培训档案；应当加强专（兼）职食品安全管理人员食品安全法律法规和相关食品安全管理知识的培训。

第十二条　餐饮服务提供者应当建立食品、食品原料、食品添加剂和食品相关产品的采购查验和索证索票制度。

餐饮服务提供者从食品生产单位、批发市场等采购的，应当查验、索取并留存供货者的相关许可证和产品合格证明等文件；从固定供货商或者供货基地采购的，应当查验、索取并留存供货商或者供货基地的资质证明、每笔供货清单等；从超市、农贸市场、个体经营商户等采购的，应当索取并留存采购清单。

餐饮服务企业应当建立食品、食品原料、食品添加剂和食品相关产品的采购记录制度。采购记录应当如实记录产品名称、规格、数量、生产批号、保质期、供货者名称及联系方式、进货日期等内容，或者保留载有上述信息的进货票据。

餐饮服务提供者应当按照产品品种、进货时间先后次序有序整理采购记录及相关资料，妥善保存备查。记录、票据的保存期限不得少于2年。

第十三条　实行统一配送经营方式的餐饮服务提供者，可以由企业总部统一查验供货者的许可证和产品合格的证明文件等，建立食品进货查验记录。

实行统一配送经营方式的，企业各门店应当建立总部统一配送单据台账。门店自行采购的产品，应当遵照本办法第十二条的规定。

第十四条　餐饮服务提供者禁止采购、使用和经营下列食品：

（一）《食品安全法》第二十八条规定禁止生产经营的食品；

（二）违反《食品安全法》第四十八条规定的食品；

（三）违反《食品安全法》第五十条规定的食品；

（四）违反《食品安全法》第六十六条规定的进口预包装食品。

第十五条　餐饮服务提供者应当按照国家有关规定和食品安全标准采购、保存和使用食品添加剂。应当将食品添加剂存放于专用橱柜等设施中，标示“食品添加剂”字样，妥善保管，并建立使用台账。

第十六条 餐饮服务提供者应当严格遵守国家食品药品监督管理部门制定的餐饮服务食品安全操作规范。餐饮服务应当符合下列要求：

（一）在制作加工过程中应当检查待加工的食品及食品原料，发现有腐败变质或者其他感官性状异常的，不得加工或者使用；

（二）贮存食品原料的场所、设备应当保持清洁，禁止存放有毒、有害物品及个人生活物品，应当分类、分架、隔墙、离地存放食品原料，并定期检查、处理变质或者超过保质期限的食品；

（三）应当保持食品加工经营场所的内外环境整洁，消除老鼠、蟑螂、苍蝇和其他有害昆虫及其孳生条件；

（四）应当定期维护食品加工、贮存、陈列、消毒、保洁、保温、冷藏、冷冻等设备与设施，校验计量器具，及时清理清洗，确保正常运转和使用；

（五）操作人员应当保持良好的个人卫生；

（六）需要熟制加工的食品，应当烧熟煮透；需要冷藏的熟制品，应当在冷却后及时冷藏；应当将直接入口食品与食品原料或者半成品分开存放，半成品应当与食品原料分开存放；

（七）制作凉菜应当达到专人负责、专室制作、工具专用、消毒专用和冷藏专用的要求；

（八）用于餐饮加工操作的工具、设备必须无毒无害，标志或者区分明显，并做到分开使用，定位存放，用后洗净，保持清洁；接触直接入口食品的工具、设备应当在使用前进行消毒；

（九）应当按照要求对餐具、饮具进行清洗、消毒，并在专用保洁设施内备用，不得使用未经清洗和消毒的餐具、饮具；购置、使用集中消毒企业供应的餐具、饮具，应当查验其经营资质，索取消毒合格凭证；

（十）应当保持运输食品原料的工具与设备设施的清洁，必要时应当消毒。运输保温、冷藏（冻）食品应当有必要的且与提供的食品品种、数量相适应的保温、冷藏（冻）设备设施。

第十七条 食品药品监督管理部门依法开展抽样检验时，被抽样检验的餐饮服务提供者应当配合抽样检验工作，如实提供被抽检样品的货源、数量、存货地点、存货量、销售量、相关票证等信息。

第三章 食品安全事故处理

第十八条 各级食品药品监督管理部门应当根据本级人民政府食品安全事故应急预案制定本部门的预案实施细则，按照职能做好餐饮服务食品安全事故的应急处置工作。

第十九条 食品药品监督管理部门在日常监督管理中发现食品安全事故，或者接到有关食品安全事故的举报，应当立即核实情况，经初步核实为食品安全事故的，应当立即向同级卫生行政、农业行政、工商行政管理、质量监督等相关部门通报。

发生食品安全事故时，事发地食品药品监督管理部门应当在本级人民政府领导下，及时做出反应，采取措施控制事态发展，依法处置，并及时按照有关规定向上级食品药品监督管理部门报告。

第二十条 县级以上食品药品监督管理部门按照有关规定开展餐饮服务食品安全事故调查，有权向有关餐饮服务提供者了解与食品安全事故有关的情况，要求餐饮服务提供者提供相关资料和样品，并采取以下措施：

（一）封存造成食品安全事故或者可能导致食品安全事故的食品及其原料，并立即进行检验；

（二）封存被污染的食品工具及用具，并责令进行清洗消毒；

（三）经检验，属于被污染的食品，予以监督销毁；未被污染的食品，予以解封；

（四）依法对食品安全事故及其处理情况进行发布，并对可能产生的危害加以解释、说明。

第二十一条 餐饮服务提供者应当制定食品安全事故处置方案，定期检查各项食品安全防范措施的落实情况，及时消除食品安全事故隐患。

第二十二条 餐饮服务提供者发生食品安全事故，应当立即封存导致或者可能导致食品安全事故的食品及其原料、工具及用具、设备设施和现场，在2小时之内向所在地县级人民政府卫生部门和食品药品监督管理部门报告，并按照相关监管部门的要求采取控制措施。

餐饮服务提供者应当配合食品安全监督管理部门进行食品安全事故调查处理，按照要求提供相关资料和样品，不得拒绝。

第四章 监督管理

第二十三条 食品药品监督管理部门可以根据餐饮服务经营规模，建立并实施餐饮服务食品安全监督管理量化分级、分类管理制度。

食品药品监督管理部门可以聘请社会监督员，协助开展餐饮服务食品安全监督。

第二十四条 县级以上食品药品监督管理部门履行食品安全监督职责时，发现不属于本辖区管辖的，应当及时移送有管辖权的食品药品监督管理部门。接受移送的食品药品监督管理部门应当将被移送案件的处理情况及时反馈给移送案件的食品药品监督管理部门。

第二十五条 县级以上食品药品监督管理部门接到咨询、投诉、举报，对属于本部门管辖的，应当受理，并及时进行核实、处理、答复；对不属于本部门管辖的，应当书面通知并移交有管辖权的部门处理。

发现餐饮服务提供者使用不符合食品安全标准及有关要求的食品原料或者食用农产品、食品添加剂、食品相关产品，其成因属于其他环节食品生产经营者或者食用农产品生产者的，应当及时向本级卫生行政、农业行政、工商行政管理、质量监督等部门通报。

第二十六条 食品药品监督管理部门在履行职责时，有权采取《食品安全法》第七十七条规定的措施。

第二十七条 食品安全监督检查人员对餐饮服务提供者进行监督检查时，应当对下列内容进行重点检查：

（一）餐饮服务许可情况；

（二）从业人员健康证明、食品安全知识培训和建立档案情况；

（三）环境卫生、个人卫生、食品用工具及设备、食品容器及包装材料、卫生设施、工艺流程情况；

（四）餐饮加工制作、销售、服务过程的食品安全情况；

（五）食品、食品添加剂、食品相关产品进货查验和索票索证制度及执行情况、制定食品安全事故应急处置制度及执行情况；

（六）食品原料、半成品、成品、食品添加剂等的感官性状、产品标签、说明书及储存条件；

（七）餐具、饮具、食品用工具及盛放直接入口食品的容器的清洗、消毒和保洁情况；

（八）用水的卫生情况；

（九）其他需要重点检查的情况。

第二十八条 食品安全监督检查人员进行监督检查时，应当有2名以上人员共同参加，依法制作现场检查笔录，笔录经双方核实并签字。被监督检查者拒绝签字的，应当注明事由和相关情况，同时记录在场人员的姓名、职务等。

第二十九条 县级以上食品药品监督管理部门负责组织实施本辖区餐饮服务环节的抽样检验工作，所需经费由地方财政列支。

第三十条 食品安全监督检查人员可以使用经认定的食品安全快速检测技术进行快速检测，及时发现和筛查不符合食品安全标准及有关要求的食品、食品添加剂及食品相关产品。使用现场快速检测技术发现和筛查的结果不得直接作为执法依据。对初步筛查结果表明可能不符合食品安全标准及有关要求的食品，应当依照《食品安全法》的有关规定进行检验。

快速检测结果表明可能不符合食品安全标准及有关要求的，餐饮服务提供者应当根据实际情况采取食品安全保障措施。

第三十一条 食品安全监督检查人员抽样时必须按照抽样计划和抽样程序进行，并填写抽样记录。抽样检验应当购买产品样品，不得收取检验费和其他任何费用。

食品安全监督检查人员应当及时将样品送达有资质的检验机构。

第三十二条 食品检验机构应当根据检验目的和送检要求，按照食品安全相关标准和规定的检验方法进行检验，按时出具合法的检验报告。

第三十三条 对检验结论有异议的，异议人有权自收到检验结果告知书之日起10日内，向组织实施抽样检验的食品药品监督管理部门提出书面复检申请，逾期未提出申请的，视为放弃该项权利。

复检工作应当选择有关部门共同公布的承担复检工作的食品检验机构完成。

复检机构由复检申请人自行选择；复检机构与初检机构不得为同一机构。复检机构出具的复检结论为最终检验结论。

复检费用的承担依《食品安全法实施条例》第三十五条的规定。

第三十四条 食品药品监督管理部门应当建立辖区内餐饮服务提供者食品安全信用档案，记录许可颁发及变更情况、日常监督检查结果、违法行为查处等情况。食品药品监督管理部门应当根据餐饮服务食品安全信用档案，对有不良信用记录的餐饮服务提供者实施重点监管。

食品安全信用档案的形式和内容由省级食品药品监督管理部门根据本地实际情况作出具体规定。

第三十五条 食品药品监督管理部门应当将吊销《餐饮服务许可证》的情况在7日内通报同级工商行政管理部门。

第三十六条 县级以上食品药品监督管理部门依法公布下列日常监督管理信息：

（一）餐饮服务行政许可情况；

（二）餐饮服务食品安全监督检查和抽检的结果；

（三）查处餐饮服务提供者违法行为的情况；

（四）餐饮服务专项检查工作情况；

（五）其他餐饮服务食品安全监督管理信息。

第五章 法律责任

第三十七条 未经许可从事餐饮服务的，由食品药品监督管理部门根据《食品安全法》第八十四条的规定予以处罚。有下列情形之一的，按未取得《餐饮服务许可证》查处：

（一）擅自改变餐饮服务经营地址、许可类别、备注项目的；

（二）《餐饮服务许可证》超过有效期限仍从事餐饮服务的；

（三）使用经转让、涂改、出借、倒卖、出租的《餐饮服务许可证》，或者使用以其他形式非法取得的《餐饮服务许可证》从事餐饮服务的。

第三十八条 餐饮服务提供者有下列情形之一的，由食品药品监督管理部门根据《食品安全法》第八十五条的规定予以处罚：

（一）用非食品原料制作加工食品或者添加食品添加剂以外的化学物质和其他可能危害人体健康的物质，或者用回收食品作为原料制作加工食品；

（二）经营致病性微生物、农药残留、兽药残留、重金属、污染物质以及其他危害人体健康的物质含量超过食品安全标准限量的食品；

（三）经营营养成分不符合食品安全标准的专供婴幼儿和其他特定人群的主辅食品；

（四）经营腐败变质、油脂酸败、霉变生虫、污秽不洁、混有异物、掺假掺杂或者感官性状异常的食品；

（五）经营病死、毒死或者死因不明的禽、畜、兽、水产动物肉类及其制品；

（六）经营未经动物卫生监督机构检疫或者检疫不合格的肉类，或者未经检验或者检验不合格的肉类制品；

（七）经营超过保质期的食品；

（八）经营国家为防病等特殊需要明令禁止经营的食品；

（九）有关部门责令召回或者停止经营不符合食品安全标准的食品后，仍拒不召回或者停止经营的；

（十）餐饮服务提供者违法改变经营条件造成严重后果的。

第三十九条 餐饮服务提供者有下列情形之一的，由食品药品监督管理部门根据《食品安全法》第八十六条的规定予以处罚：

（一）经营或者使用被包装材料、容器、运输工具等污染的食品；

（二）经营或者使用无标签及其他不符合《食品安全法》、《食品安全法实施条例》有关标签、说明书规定的预包装食品、食品添加剂；

（三）经营添加药品的食品。

第四十条 违反本办法第十条第一款、第十二条、第十三条第二款、第十六条第（二）、（三）、（四）、（八）、（九）项的有关规定，按照《食品安全法》第八十七条的规定予以处罚。

第四十一条 违反本办法第二十二条第一款的规定，由食品药品监督管理部门根据《食品安全法》第八十八条的规定予以处罚。

第四十二条 违反本办法第十六条第十项的规定，由食品药品监督管理部门根据《食品安全法》第九十一条的规定予以处罚。

第四十三条 餐饮服务提供者违反本办法第九条第三款规定，由食品药品监督管理部门依据《食品安全法》第九十二条第二款进行处罚。

第四十四条 本办法所称违法所得，指违反《食品安全法》、《食品安全法实施条例》等食品安全法律法规和规章的规定，从事餐饮服务活动所取得的相关营业性收入。

第四十五条 本办法所称货值金额，指餐饮服务提供者经营的食品的市场价格总金额。其中原料及食品添加剂按进价计算，半成品按原料计算，成品按销售价格计算。

第四十六条 餐饮服务食品安全监督管理执法中，涉及《食品安全法》第八十五条、第八十六条、第八十七条适用时，"情节严重"包括但不限于下列情形：

（一）连续12个月内已受到2次以上较大数额罚款处罚或者连续12个月内已受到一次责令停业行政处罚的；

（二）造成重大社会影响或者有死亡病例等严重后果的。

第四十七条 餐饮服务提供者主动消除或者减轻违法行为危害后果，或者有其他法定情形的，应当依法从轻或者减轻处罚。

第四十八条 在同一违反《食品安全法》、《食品安全法实施条例》等食品安全法律法规的案件中，有两种以上应当给予行政处罚的违法行为时，食品药品监督管理部门应当分别裁量，合并处罚。

第四十九条 食品药品监督管理部门作出责令停业、吊销《餐饮服务许可证》、较大数额罚款等行政处罚决定之前，应当告知当事人有要求举行听证的权利。

当事人要求听证的，食品药品监督管理部门应当组织听证。

当事人对处罚决定不服的，可以申请行政复议或者提起行政诉讼。

第五十条 食品药品监督管理部门不履行有关法律法规规定的职责或者其工作人员有滥用职权、玩忽职守、徇私舞弊行为的，食品药品监督管理部门应当依法对相关负责人员或者直接责任人员给予记大过或者降级的处分；造成严重后果的，给予撤职或者开除的处分；其主要负责人应当引咎辞职。

第六章 附 则

第五十一条 省、自治区、直辖市食品药品监督管理部门可以结合本地实际情况，根据本办法的规定制定实施细则。

第五十二条 国境口岸范围内的餐饮服务活动的监督管理由出入境检验检疫机构依照《食品安全法》和《中华人民共和国国境卫生检疫法》以及相关行政法规的规定实施。

水上运营的餐饮服务提供者的食品安全管理，其始发地、经停地或者到达地的食品药品监督管理部门均有权进行检查监督。

铁路运营中餐饮服务监督管理参照本办法。

第五十三条 本办法自 2010 年 5 月 1 日起施行，卫生部 2000 年 1 月 16 日发布的《餐饮业食品卫生管理办法》同时废止。

2010 年流通环节食品安全整顿工作方案

（国家工商总局 工商食字［2010］51 号 2010 年 3 月 23 日）

为深入贯彻《食品安全法》及其实施条例，全面落实《国务院办公厅关于印发 2010 年食品安全整顿工作安排的通知》（国办发［2010］17 号）和全国工商行政管理工作会议、全国工商系统食品安全监管工作会议的部署，深入推进流通环节食品安全监管工作，切实维护食品市场秩序，现就 2010 年流通环节食品安全整顿工作提出如下方案：

一、指导思想

以邓小平理论和“三个代表”重要思想为指导，全面落实科学发展观，深入学习贯彻党的十七大、十七届三中、四中全会和中央经济工作会议精神，紧紧围绕落实中央保持经济平稳较快发展和加快经济发展方式转变的决策部署，认真贯彻国务院有关流通环节食品安全整顿工作的安排，切实落实全国工商行政管理工作会议和全国工商系统食品安全监管工作会议的要求，牢牢把握“四个只有”，努力做到“四个统一”，以保障流通环节食品安全为目标，巩固已有的专项整顿成果，在深化专项执法检查、强化日常规范监管、完善服务体系、创新机制手段、提升执法效能上狠下工夫，深入开展流通环节食品安全专项整顿，全面落实流通环节食品安全监管各项制度，切实维护食品市场秩序和促进经济社会又好又快发展。

二、整顿工作任务和重点

各级工商机关要在巩固去年整顿成果的基础上，继续集中执法力量，突出工作重点，强化专项执法检查，加大监管执法力度，着力解决流通环节食品安全突出问题，圆满完成国务院部署的 2010 年整顿工作安排和为期两年的食品安全整顿工作涉及流通环节食品安全整顿的各项任务。

（一）认真开展规范食品经营主体资格专项执法检查 各级工商机关要严格执行《食品安全法》及其实施条例和总局《关于食品流通许可证印制发放和管理有关问题的通知》的规定，认真开展规范食品经营主体资格专项执法检查。按照“谁登记、谁规范、谁负责”的原则，分别由各级食品流通许可、注册登记机构依法实施；按照“谁监管、谁清理、谁负责”的原则，由各省区市工商局统一部署和督查，由县级工商局组织，基层工商所采取逐户排查等办法依法实施，对发现存在食品主体准入方面的问题及时依法处理。在当地政府的统一领导和协调下，按照相关部门的职责分工和工商机关各职能机构的职责分工，依法查处和取缔无证无照经营食品违法行为。

（二）认真开展对重点食品和重点区域、重点场所食品经营以及季节性、节日性食品市场的专项执法

检查 各地要把开展重点食品专项执法检查作为整顿工作的重要任务，着力解决本地区食品市场存在的突出问题。一是认真开展对重点食品的专项执法检查。以消费者申诉举报多和与人民群众生活密切相关的食品品种为重点，突出抓好奶制品、肉制品、米面制品、禽蛋制品、儿童食品、老年食品、膨化食品、豆制品、糕点、月饼、调味品、食用油、酒类、腌制食品、冷冻食品等品种的专项执法检查，严厉打击销售过期霉变食品、“三无”食品等违法行为，切实解决人民群众反映强烈的突出问题。二是认真开展重点区域、重点场所食品经营的专项执法检查。以城乡结合部、社区、车站、码头、旅游景区为重点，依法抓好小食品店、小摊点、小市场的专项执法检查，坚决依法取缔无照商贩。严厉打击销售地沟油等假冒伪劣食品违法行为。以商场、超市等食品经营企业和批发市场、集贸市场及食品店为重点，突出抓好市场开办者和经营者的自查自纠和自律工作，由基层工商所按辖区逐户排查，认真监督食品经营者落实对食品安全的法定责任和义务，切实做到不进、不存、不销假冒伪劣食品和不符合食品安全标准的食品。三是认真开展季节性、节日性食品市场专项执法检查。以“五一”、中秋、“十一”、元旦、春节等为重点，突出抓好节日性、季节性重点食品品种及重点区域、场所的检查，针对节日和季节食品市场的消费特点，加大监管执法力度，重点整治不符合食品安全标准、过度包装、搭售商品、虚假宣传及欺诈消费者等问题，切实保障节日性、季节性食品市场消费安全。同时，按照各地和总局服务2010年上海世博会及2010年广州亚运会的总体部署，加强上海世博会和广州亚运会期间流通环节食品安全监管工作，完善食品安全预警防范和应急处置机制，切实维护世博会和广州亚运会期间流通环节食品市场秩序。

（三）认真开展打击流通环节违法添加非食用物质和滥用食品添加剂专项执法检查 按照全国食品安全整顿工作领导小组办公室公布的非食用物质和添加剂的品种名单，对重点食品、重点区域和重点食品经营者，认真开展集中执法检查行动，依法规范食品添加剂经营者主体资格，狠抓大要案件查办工作，配合有关部门查处和打击违法销售食品添加剂以及流通环节食品经营者在食品中添加非食用物质和滥用食品添加剂的行为。

（四）认真开展奶制品市场专项执法检查 深入贯彻《乳品质量安全监督管理条例》和《奶业整顿和振兴规划纲要》以及总局的实施意见，依法履行《条例》、《纲要》赋予工商机关的职责，严格监督奶制品销售者落实进货查验和进销货台账制度。强化对奶制品市场的专项执法检查，集中时间和执法力量对城乡市场奶制品经营者开展拉网式逐户清查，对辖区内经营者销售的不符合食品安全标准的奶制品，要依法监督或责令其全部停止销售、下架退市，不留死角。对下架退市的奶制品，在当地政府的领导和协调下，配合相关部门，分工协作，落实监管责任，该由生产企业召回的及时召回，该销毁的坚决依法销毁，严防再次流入市场。对进口的奶制品，重点检查食品合格证、中文标签和中文说明书及相关手续。

（五）认真开展农村食品市场专项执法检查 要结合农村食品市场特点，突出农民消费者日常食品消费的必需品种，加大对农村城镇、集镇、乡村举办的食品交易会、庙会等经营食品的监管力度，严格规范农村食品经营秩序。加大对农村和乡镇各类食品批发市场、集贸市场和食杂店的监管和整治力度，规范连锁配送和送货下乡经营食品行为，依法打击销售假冒、仿冒知名品牌食品的违法行为，切实保障农村食品市场消费安全。认真落实总局《流通环节食品安全示范店规范指导意见》，按照“两重点、三严格、四统一、五规范”的建设要求，加快推进农村食品安全示范店建设进程，充分发挥示范店的示范引导作用。

（六）认真开展对食品经营者履行法定责任义务的专项执法检查 按照《食品安全法》及其实施条例和总局《流通环节食品安全监督管理办法》的要求，严格依法监督食品经营者履行法定责任和义务。严格监督商场、超市等食品经营企业和食品店，在巩固索证索票、进货台账“两项制度”成果的基础上，切实履行进货查验和查验记录义务，严格落实企业内部食品质量管理责任，规范食品质量市场准入行为，切实把好食品进货关。鼓励和引导食品经营企业建立健全以食品进货把关、质量管理和退市等为主要内容的电子化台账及信息化网络管理体系。加强对食品经营者内部质量管理和质量控制的检查，督促经营者针对食品保质期的不同时间段采取有效的管理措施，引导其采取消费提示和食品有效期管理警示等防范措施，切实对消费者负责。监督食品经营者建立健全食品质量管理、食品退市、应急处置、消费纠纷解决、从业人员健康管理等制度，切实落实食品安全管理责任。

（七）加大食品广告监管执法力度 依法严厉查处含有虚假、夸大内容的食品广告，特别是保健食品广告。严厉查处涉及宣传疾病预防、治疗功能的违法食品广告；坚决制止和查处有关部门或者机构、协会违法推荐食品的广告。对广告宣传的产品功能和成分与标签、说明书不一致的，要责令停止发布，并依法查处。对于被确认为不符合食品安全标准的食品，要立即停止发布该食品的广告。

（八）加强食品安全监管执法协作配合工作 进一步加强与卫生、农业、质检、食品药品、工业和信息化、商务、公安等有关职能部门的协作与配合，在按照国务院《2010年食品安全整顿工作安排》做好流通环节食品安全整顿工作的同时，在当地党委政府统一领导和协调下，依据职能，依法积极配合有关部门开展其他整顿工作。一是依法配合商务、农业等部门加强畜禽屠宰整顿，严厉打击销售病死病害畜禽肉和注水肉等行为，严防病死、注水、未经检疫检验或检疫检验不合格肉品进入流通环节。二是依法配合有关部门开展包括食用农产品在内的农产品和农药市场的监管。三是依法配合食品药品监管部门整治普通食品声称具有特定保健功能和保健食品夸大宣传功能的行为。四是依法参与组织开展食品安全标准的宣传贯彻与食品安全标准实施等工作。五是依法配合工业和信息化部门建立食品企业诚信不良记录收集、管理、通报制度和行业退出机制，加强食品生产企业和经营者质量信用建设和信用分类监管。

三、整顿工作措施

要在开展食品安全专项整顿工作的同时，强化食品市场日常规范监管，加大食品市场巡查力度，严格食品市场主体准入管理，严格食品质量监管，严格食品经营行为的规范，依法查办食品大（要）案件，进一步创新监管机制和手段，积极构建流通环节食品安全监管保障体系。

（一）严格市场主体准入管理，依法规范证照核发行为 要严格按照法定条件、程序和有关规定核发《食品流通许可证》；坚持先证后照，对未获得相关许可文件的，登记注册机关不得核发营业执照。要严格执行总局《关于对食品经营主体予以特别标注的通知》的规定，对食品经营主体进行特别标注。建立许可证发放机关与登记注册机关的信息沟通机制，依托工商系统信息化网络体系，实现食品流通许可机构与登记注册机构信息共享，依法规范食品经营主体资格。

（二）严格食品质量监管，依法规范食品质量抽样检验行为 要严格落实《食品安全法》及其实施条例及总局有关规定和制度，依法开展流通环节食品抽样检验工作，认真执行当地政府年度食品安全监督管理计划中确定的流通环节食品抽样检验的安排，严格食品质量抽样检验工作程序和纪律，严格抽样检验信息和发布的规范管理及审核程序，认真落实总局《流通环节食品安全监督管理办法》和《食品抽样检验工作制度》。同时，要充分发挥食品抽样检验结果的作用，加强综合分析，按照有关规定和程序进行消费提示和警示，及时将有关情况通报相关职能部门和行业组织，促进食品安全的源头治理和行业自律。要监督食品经营者严格落实《食品安全法》的规定，对发现经营的食品不符合食品安全标准的，立即停止经营，履行通知相关生产者和消费者、记录停止经营和通知情况的责任和义务，配合生产者落实食品召回制度，对没有及时召回的不符合食品安全标准的食品，坚决依法彻底销毁，并作好销毁记录存档备查。同时，配合相关部门加强对不符合食品安全标准的食品退市后的跟踪监管，严防再次流入市场。

（三）严格食品市场巡查，依法规范食品市场监督检查行为 要按照法律法规的规定和食品市场巡查监管制度的要求，强化市场巡查，将监管重心下移，严格落实基层工商所食品安全日常巡查和属地监管责任制。基层工商所要突出巡查检查重点，通过增加巡查频次、强化巡查措施、完善巡查机制、创新巡查手段，有针对性地开展市场巡查，切实提高巡查效能，着力解决重点市场、重点区域和重点食品经营者的突出问题，建立健全制度规范、责任明晰、执法严格、反应迅速、措施有力的巡查机制。要如实记录巡查中发现、制止和查处食品经营者违法行为的情况，并将巡查记录纳入经营者食品安全监管档案和信用分类管理体系，激励守信者，查处违法者。要将食品市场巡查与经济户口管理、食品质量监管、食品市场分类监管等结合起来，加强对食品经营者食品安全违法行为记录与信用体系建设，完善监管档案，并加强对监管数据的统计和综合分析，切实提高日常巡查的针对性和有效性。

（四）严格落实监管制度和创新监管手段，依法规范行政执法行为 要突出流通环节食品安全监管关键环节、重点部位，结合专项执法检查和日常监管的实际情况，在建立健全监管制度和构建长效监管机制上下工夫，特别要抓好各项监管制度的实施和落实，切实用制度规范行政执法行为。要认真落实总局制定下发的流通环节食品安全监管八项制度，并在实践中不断细化、完善和创新，切实提高食品安全监管的制度化、规范化、程序化、法治化水平。同时，要认真落实总局《关于积极推进流通环节商品质量和食品安全信息化网络建设工作的意见》，强化网络信息技术在流通环节食品市场主体许可、登记注册、食品质量监管、市场巡查和执法办案等方面的综合应用。要加快建立流通环节食品经营主体、食品市场质量监管、食品抽样检验、食品安全监管和案件查办数据库，并与工商机关其他执法监管信息互联互通，实现数据信息共享。各地要加快推进基层工商所信息化网络体系建设和应用，充分运用无线网络执法平台、移动查询终端等现代科技手段，开展市场巡查和日常监管，有效开展网上预警防范和应急处置工作。要认真落实食品安全预警防范和应急处置各项工作，完善机制，严格责任制度，切实做到超前防范，及时有效应对和处置。

四、整顿工作要求

（一）进一步加强组织领导 各地要在地方党委政府的统一领导下，按照《食品安全法》等法律法规赋予的职能，切实履行法定职责，以保障流通环节食品安全为重点，切实加强组织领导，一把手亲自抓，主管领导具体抓，各内设机构按照职能分工负责，密切协作，切实抓好组织实施和落实工作。要落实各项市场监管制度，有效防范市场监管的系统性风险和区域性风险。各地要层层制定具体的整顿工作实施方案，明确目标任务和工作责任，精心组织和认真实施。

（二）进一步加强法制建设和队伍建设 各级工商机关要加大食品安全法制建设力度，严格监管执法、市场巡查和案件查办程序，严格规范行政执法行为，确保具体行政行为合法有效，经得起司法监督，切实完善食品安全监管法制体系。各地要按照建设学习型机关和基层的要求，采取学习、培训、岗位练兵、实践锻炼等方式，加大基层执法人员政治理论、业务知识、法规政策、管理技能的学习和培训力度，努力建设一支政治上、业务上、作风上过硬的干部队伍，为保障流通环节食品安全提供人才和素质保障。

（三）进一步健全责任制度和责任追究制度 各级工商机关要在当地党委政府领导下，严格流通环节食品安全监管责任，调整充实执法力量，改善监管执法条件。要按照《食品安全法》的要求，进一步建立健全工商行政管理机关对流通环节食品安全属地监管领导责任制、职能机构指导监督检查责任制和食品安全基层监管岗位责任制及其责任追究制。总局食品流通监督管理司负责流通环节食品安全整顿的综合协调工作。各地工商机关要明确一个内设机构牵头负责流通环节食品安全整顿的综合协调工作，并明确各内设机构的职能分工。企业登记注册、外资企业登记注册和个体私营经济监管机构要加强对食品生产经营主体的登记管理，严格特别标注管理，查处违反登记管理法律法规的行为，依法取缔无照经营；消费者权益保护机构要及时受理和依法分流、处理消费者的咨询和申诉举报，依法加强食品添加剂的质量监管，切实保护消费者合法权益；食品流通监管机构要依法加强流通环节食品质量监管，依法查处流通环节食品安全违法案件；市场监管机构要加强对批发市场、农贸市场、集贸市场食品安全的管理，依法查处农产品批发市场和销售企业的违法行为，依法配合有关部门加强农药市场管理，加强食品交易市场信用分类监管，规范食品市场秩序；竞争执法、直销监管、商标管理、广告监管等机构要依法分别加大对食品市场不正当竞争、传销、商标侵权、虚假广告违法行为的查处力度。纪检监察机构要对流通环节食品安全监管执法工作中发生的食品安全监管责任问题，依据法律法规和有关规定，严肃追究相关单位和人员的责任。

（四）进一步加强食品安全信息管理和新闻宣传工作 各省、自治区、直辖市工商局要按照国务院办公厅关于统筹和规范食品安全整顿信息发布工作的要求，在当地政府统一领导和协调下，加强流通环节食品安全监管信息的管理，建立健全食品安全日常监督管理信息公布制度。要依法依职责依程序公布食品安全日常监督管理信息，做到准确、及时、客观。对涉及其他食品安全监管部门职责的，要依据有关规定联合公布。要严格宣传纪律，适时宣传流通环节食品安全整顿工作进展、成效和典型事例，引导新闻媒体客观准确报道，为食品安全整顿工作营造良好舆论氛围和社会环境。

（五）进一步加强协作配合和检查落实工作 要加强工商机关内设机构之间以及与各有关部门的协作配合，及时通报有关情况，建立健全协调协作机制，切实形成监管合力。各级地方工商机关要在当地政府统一领导和协调下，积极配合有关部门依法履行食品安全监管职责，参与相关工作，开展联合执法检查。各省、自治区、直辖市工商局要层层加强对流通环节食品安全监管工作的指导、督查和考核，采取重点督查、专项督查、交叉检查、明察暗访等多种方式，一级抓一级，层层抓落实，确保组织领导、工作任务、工作措施、工作责任、人员力量和经费保障等落实到位。各级领导干部要深入基层，及时发现存在的问题和监管的薄弱环节，有针对性地加强指导，确保各项监管工作落到实处，取得实效。总局将适时组织开展流通环节食品安全整顿工作检查督查工作。

食品添加剂生产监督管理规定

（国家质检总局令　第127号　2010年4月4日）

第一章　总　　则

第一条　为了保障食品安全、加强对食品添加剂生产的监督管理，根据《中华人民共和国产品质量法》、《中华人民共和国食品安全法》及其实施条例和《中华人民共和国工业产品生产许可证管理条例》等有关法律法规，制定本规定。

第二条　在中华人民共和国境内从事食品添加剂生产、实施生产许可和监督管理，适用本规定。

本规定所称食品添加剂是指经国务院卫生行政部门批准并以标准、公告等方式公布的可以作为改善食品品质和色、香、味以及为防腐、保鲜和加工工艺的需要而加入食品的人工合成或者天然物质。

前款规定之外的其他物质，不得作为食品添加剂进行生产，不得作为食品添加剂实施生产许可。

第三条　国家质量监督检验检疫总局（以下简称"国家质检总局"）主管全国范围内生产食品添加剂的质量监督管理工作。

省级质量技术监督部门主管本行政区域内生产食品添加剂的质量监督管理工作，负责实施食品添加剂生产许可。

市、县级质量技术监督部门负责本行政区域内生产食品添加剂的质量监督管理工作。

第四条　生产者应当依照法律、法规、规章和有关标准的要求从事食品添加剂生产活动，保证产品质量持续稳定合格，对社会和公众负责，接受社会监督。

第五条　食品添加剂生产监督管理，应当遵循科学公正、便民高效的原则。

第二章　生产许可

第六条　生产者必须在取得生产许可后，方可从事食品添加剂的生产。

取得生产许可，应当具备下列条件：

（一）合法有效的营业执照；

（二）与生产食品添加剂相适应的专业技术人员；

（三）与生产食品添加剂相适应的生产场所、厂房设施；其卫生管理符合卫生安全要求；

（四）与生产食品添加剂相适应的生产设备或者设施等生产条件；

（五）与生产食品添加剂相适应的符合有关要求的技术文件和工艺文件；

（六）健全有效的质量管理和责任制度；

（七）与生产食品添加剂相适应的出厂检验能力；产品符合相关标准以及保障人体健康和人身安全的要求；

（八）符合国家产业政策的规定，不存在国家明令淘汰和禁止投资建设的工艺落后、耗能高、污染环境、浪费资源的情况；

（九）法律法规规定的其他条件。

第七条　生产食品添加剂的，申请人应当向生产所在地省级质量技术监督部门（以下简称"许可机关"）提交生产许可申请。

第八条　申请食品添加剂生产许可，应当提交下列材料：

（一）食品添加剂生产许可申请书；

（二）申请人营业执照复印件；

（三）申请生产许可的食品添加剂有关生产工艺文本；

（四）与申请生产许可的食品添加剂相适应的生产场所的合法使用权证明材料，及其周围环境平面图和厂房设施、设备布局平面图复印件；

（五）与申请生产许可的食品添加剂相适应的生产设备、设施的合法使用权证明材料及清单，检验设备的合法使用权证明材料及清单；

（六）与申请生产许可的食品添加剂相适应的质量管理和责任制度文本；

（七）与申请生产许可的食品添加剂相适应的专业技术人员名单；

（八）生产所执行的食品添加剂标准文本；

（九）法律法规规定的其他材料。

第九条　许可机关对申请人提出的许可申请，应当根据下列情况分别作出处理：

（一）申请事项依法不需要取得生产许可的，应当即时告知申请人不受理；

（二）申请事项依法不属于质量技术监督部门管理范围的，应当即时作出不予受理的决定，并告知申请人向有关行政机关申请；

（三）有《中华人民共和国行政许可法》第七十八条、第七十九条等规定情形的，应当即时作出不予受理的决定；

（四）申请材料存在可以当场更正的错误的，应当允许申请人当场更正；

（五）申请材料不完整或不符合法定形式的，应当当场或者五日内一次性告知予以补正的材料及要求，并向申请人发出许可申请材料补正告知书；逾期不告知的，视为受理；

（六）申请事项属于质量技术监督部门职权范围，申请材料齐全、符合法定形式，或者申请人按要求提交全部补正申请材料的，应当受理生产许可申请，并向申请人发出行政许可申请受理决定书。

许可机关受理或者不予受理许可申请，应当出具加盖本机关专用印章和注明日期的书面凭证。

第十条 许可机关受理申请后，应当组织对申请人是否具备持续生产合格产品的必备生产条件进行审查。

审查内容包括对申请的资料、生产场所进行实地核查以及产品质量检验。

第十一条 许可机关组织对申请人进行实地核查，应当组织核查组。核查组由二至四名有资质的核查人员组成，核查组工作实行组长负责制，并按照有关规定接受所在地质量技术监督部门的监督。

第十二条 许可机关组织对申请人进行实地核查应当制定实地核查计划，并于核查五日前向申请人发出实地核查通知书。

实地核查工作一般不超过二日。

第十三条 核查人员进行实地核查，不得刁难企业，不得索取、收受财物，不得谋取其他不正当利益。

申请人应当配合核查组的实地核查，因不可抗力等原因需要延长核查时间的，应当及时向许可机关提出延期申请。

第十四条 核查组应当按照核查计划以及规定的许可条件、程序等要求对申请人进行实地核查，并根据核查结果做出如下处理：

（一）实地核查合格的，按照规定抽取和封存样品，由申请人依法送交符合规定要求的检验机构进行检验；

（二）实地核查不合格的，不再进行产品抽样。

拒绝核查或无正当理由不予配合，导致实地核查无法在规定期限内实施的，视为实地核查不合格。

第十五条 实地核查工作应当由核查组组长填写实地核查记录，由核查人员签字并经申请人确认。

第十六条 许可机关应当自受理申请之日起三十日内，完成对申请人的实地核查和产品抽样工作，并向申请人发出实地核查结论告知书。核查不合格的，应当说明理由。

第十七条 承担发证检验工作的检验机构应当依据相关标准对食品添加剂进行检验，并在规定的时间内完成检验工作。

承担食品添加剂生产许可发证检验工作的检验机构，应当具备法定资质并由国家质检总局统一发布名录。

第十八条 检验机构完成检验工作后，应当出具产品检验报告。检验报告一式三份，一份送申请人，一份送许可机关，一份检验机构存档。

第十九条 对检验结果有异议的，申请人可以自接到检验报告之日起五日内向原许可机关提出复检申请。

复检应在原检验机构以外的符合规定要求的检验机构进行，复检结论为最终结论。

复检结论与原检验结论一致的，复检费用由申请人承担；复检结论与原检验结论不一致的，复检费用由原检验机构承担。

第二十条 许可机关应当自受理申请之日起六十日内，根据审查结果作出如下处理：

（一）申请人符合发证条件的，依法作出准予生产许可的书面决定，并于作出决定之日起十日内向申请人颁发食品添加剂生产许可证书；

（二）申请人不符合发证条件的，依法作出不予生产许可的书面决定，并说明理由，告知申请人享有依法申请行政复议或者提起行政诉讼的权利。

产品检验时间不计入许可期限。

第二十一条 省级质量技术监督部门应当及时将获得食品添加剂生产许可证书的生产者名单向国家质检总局备案，并向社会公布。

第二十二条 获得食品添加剂生产许可证书的生产者需要增加产品品种的，应当依照本规定提出申请。原许可机关应当依照本规定对申请增加的产品品种组织审查。

第二十三条 在食品添加剂生产许可证书有效期内，生产者生产条件、检验手段、生产技术或者工艺发生较大变化的，生产者应当及时向原许可机关提出审查申请，原许可机关应当依照本规定重新组织审查。

第二十四条 生产者名称等发生变化而生产者生产条件、检验手段、生产技术或者工艺未发生较大变化的，食品添加剂生产者应当在变更后一个月内向原许可机关提出生产许可变更申请。原许可机关按照有关规定办理变更手续。

第二十五条 在生产许可证有效期内，国家有关法律法规、产品标准及技术要求发生较大改变的，国家质检总局可以根据需要作出相应的规定，原许可机关根据规定重新组织审查。

第二十六条 许可机关应当将办理食品添加剂生产许可的有关资料及时归档。档案材料的保存期限为五年。

第二十七条 食品添加剂生产许可证有效期为五年。

有效期届满，生产者需要继续生产的，应当在生产许可证有效期届满六个月前向原许可机关提出换证申请。

逾期未申请换证或申请不予批准的，食品添加剂生产许可证自有效期届满之日起失效。

第二十八条 食品添加剂生产许可证书分为正本和副本。

证书应当载明生产者名称、住所、生产地址、食品添加剂名称、证书编号、发证日期、有效期、发证机关（加盖公章）等内容。

第二十九条 食品添加剂生产许可证书格式和编号规则由国家质检总局统一规定。

第三十条 食品添加剂生产许可证书遗失或者损毁，生产者应当及时向原许可机关提出补领生产许可证申请，并同时在省级以上媒体发布原生产许可证书遗失和作废声明。原许可机关按照有关规定办理补证手续。

第三十一条 许可决定作出前，申请人要求退回食品添加剂生产许可申请的，应当说明理由，并提交申请书；退回许可申请的，许可机关以书面形式予以确认，许可自然终止。

第三十二条 生产者要求终止食品添加剂生产许可的，应当说明理由，并向原许可机关提交申请书；原许可机关按照有关规定依法办理注销手续。

第三十三条 食品添加剂生产许可的撤销、撤回、注销，依照有关规定执行。

第三十四条 任何单位和个人不得伪造、变造食品添加剂生产许可证书和编号。

取得生产许可证的食品添加剂生产者不得出租、出借或者以其他方式转让生产许可证书和编号。

第三章 生产者质量义务

第三十五条 生产者应当对出厂销售的食品添加剂进行出厂检验，检验合格后方可销售。

第三十六条 生产食品添加剂，应当使用符合相关质量安全要求的原辅材料、包装材料及生产设备。

第三十七条 生产者应当建立原材料采购、生产过程控制、产品出厂检验和销售等质量管理制度，并做好以下生产管理记录：

（一）生产者从业人员的培训和考核记录；

（二）厂房、设施和设备的使用、维护、保养检修和清洗消毒记录；

（三）生产者质量管理制度的运行记录，其中包括原辅材料进货验收记录、生产过程控制记录、产品出厂检验记录、产品销售记录等。

上述记录应当真实、完整，生产者对其真实性和完整性负责。记录的保存期限不得少于二年；产品保质期超过二年的，保存期限应当不短于产品保质期。

第三十八条 食品添加剂应当有标签、说明书，并在标签上载明“食品添加剂”字样。

标签、说明书，应当标明下列事项：

（一）食品添加剂产品名称、规格和净含量；

（二）生产者名称、地址和联系方式；

（三）成分或者配料表；

（四）生产日期、保质期限或安全使用期限；

（五）贮存条件；

（六）产品标准代号；

（七）生产许可证编号；

（八）食品安全标准规定的和国务院卫生行政部门公告批准的使用范围、使用量和使用方法；

（九）法律法规或者相关标准规定必须标注的其他事项。

第三十九条 食品添加剂标签、说明书不得含有不真实、夸大的内容，不得涉及疾病预防、治疗功能。

食品添加剂的标签、说明书应当清楚、明显，容易辨认识读。

有使用禁忌或安全注意事项的食品添加剂，应当有警示标志或者中文警示说明。

第四十条 食品添加剂应当有包装并保证食品添加剂不被污染。

第四十一条 受他人委托加工食品添加剂的，受委托生产者应当具有委托生产范围内的食品添加剂生产许可证。

委托加工的食品添加剂，除应当按照产品质量和食品安全法律法规以及本规定的要求进行食品添加剂标识标注外，还应标明受委托生产者的名称、地址和联系方式等内容。

第四十二条 生产的食品添加剂存在安全隐患的，生产者应当依法实施召回。

生产者应当将食品添加剂召回和召回产品的处理情况向质量技术监督部门报告。

第四十三条 生产者应当建立生产管理情况自查制度，按照有关规定对食品添加剂质量安全控制等生产管理情况进行自查。

第四章　监督管理

第四十四条　质量技术监督部门应当建立本行政区域内获得生产许可的食品添加剂生产者档案，详细记录生产许可或者监督检查结果、违法行为查处等情况。

第四十五条　质量技术监督部门应当根据监督管理工作计划，对本行政区域内食品添加剂生产者进行监督检查，并按照规定做好记录。

第四十六条　对生产者实施现场监督检查，应有二名以上工作人员参加。监督检查人员实施监督检查时，应当出示有效证件。

第四十七条　对生产者实施监督检查应当重点检查生产者质量管理制度的运行记录，核实生产者自查报告的疑点问题；并依法对生产者实施召回的情况进行监督管理。

被监督检查的生产者应当指定工作人员配合质量技术监督部门的监督检查工作，如实提供有关资料。

第四十八条　任何单位和个人可以向各级质量技术监督部门投诉举报生产许可审查人员、检验机构及其工作人员以及监督检查工作人员的违法违规行为。

各级质量技术监督部门接到投诉举报，应当及时调查处理并向投诉举报者及时反馈处理结果。

第五章　法律责任

第四十九条　生产者违反本规定第六条第一款、第二十二条、第二十三条、第二十四条、第三十四条、第三十五条、第三十八条、第三十九条、第四十条、第四十一条等规定，构成《中华人民共和国食品安全法》、《中华人民共和国产品质量法》、《中华人民共和国工业产品生产许可证管理条例》等有关法律法规规定的违法行为的，依照有关法律法规的规定予以处罚。

第五十条　生产者违反本规定第二条第三款、第三十六条、第三十七条、第四十二条等规定，构成有关法律法规规定的违法行为的，按照有关法律法规的规定处罚；未构成有关法律法规规定的违法行为的，由县级以上地方质量技术监督部门责令限期改正，处三万元以下罚款。

第五十一条　县级以上质量技术监督部门有关工作人员违反本规定或者滥用职权、玩忽职守、徇私舞弊的，依法追究相关法律责任。

第五十二条　当事人对行政机关依据本规定所给予的行政处罚不服的，可以依法提起行政复议或者行政诉讼。

第六章　附　　则

第五十三条　本规定所规定的实施生产许可的食品添加剂的品种的划分，按照法律法规和国家质检总局有关规定执行。

第五十四条　本规定由国家质检总局负责解释。

第五十五条　本规定自2010年6月1日起施行。国家质检总局在本规定施行前公布的有关食品添加剂生产监督管理的规章、规范性文件与本规定不一致的，以本规定为准。

食品生产许可管理办法

（国家质检总局令　第129号　2010年4月7日）

第一章　总　　则

第一条　为了保障食品安全，加强食品生产监管，规范食品生产许可活动，根据《中华人民共和国食品安全法》和其实施条例以及产品质量、生产许可等法律法规的规定，制定本办法。

第二条　在中华人民共和国境内，企业从事食品生产活动以及质量技术监督部门实施食品生产许可，必须遵守本办法。

第三条　企业未取得食品生产许可，不得从事食品生产活动。

第四条　国家质量监督检验检疫总局（以下简称国家质检总局）在职责范围内负责全国食品生产许可管理工作。

县级以上地方质量技术监督部门在职责范围内负

责本行政区域内的食品生产许可管理工作。

第五条 食品生产许可必须严格按照法律、法规和规章规定的程序和要求实施，遵循公开、公平、公正、便民原则。

第二章 程 序

第六条 设立食品生产企业，应当在工商部门预先核准名称后依照食品安全法律法规和本办法有关要求取得食品生产许可。

第七条 县级以上地方质量技术监督部门是食品生产许可的实施机关，但按照有关规定由国家质检总局实施的食品生产许可除外。

省级质量技术监督部门按照有关法律法规和国家质检总局有关规定要求，确定本行政区域内质量技术监督部门分别实施许可的品种范围。

第八条 取得食品生产许可，应当符合食品安全标准，并符合下列要求：

（一）具有与申请生产许可的食品品种、数量相适应的食品原料处理和食品加工、包装、贮存等场所，保持该场所环境整洁，并与有毒、有害场所以及其他污染源保持规定的距离；

（二）具有与申请生产许可的食品品种、数量相适应的生产设备或者设施，有相应的消毒、更衣、盥洗、采光、照明、通风、防腐、防尘、防蝇、防鼠、防虫、洗涤以及处理废水、存放垃圾和废弃物的设备或者设施；

（三）具有与申请生产许可的食品品种、数量相适应的合理的设备布局、工艺流程，防止待加工食品与直接入口食品、原料与成品交叉污染，避免食品接触有毒物、不洁物；

（四）具有与申请生产许可的食品品种、数量相适应的食品安全专业技术人员和管理人员；

（五）具有与申请生产许可的食品品种、数量相适应的保证食品安全的培训、从业人员健康检查和健康档案等健康管理、进货查验记录、出厂检验记录、原料验收、生产过程等食品安全管理制度。

法律法规和国家产业政策对生产食品有其他要求的，应当符合该要求。

第九条 拟设立食品生产企业申请食品生产许可的，应当向生产所在地质量技术监督部门（以下简称许可机关）提出，并提交下列材料：

（一）食品生产许可申请书；

（二）申请人的身份证（明）或资格证明复印件；

（三）拟设立食品生产企业的《名称预先核准通知书》；

（四）食品生产加工场所及其周围环境平面图和生产加工各功能区间布局平面图；

（五）食品生产设备、设施清单；

（六）食品生产工艺流程图和设备布局图；

（七）食品安全专业技术人员、管理人员名单；

（八）食品安全管理规章制度文本；

（九）产品执行的食品安全标准；执行企业标准的，须提供经卫生行政部门备案的企业标准；

（十）相关法律法规规定应当提交的其他证明材料。

申请食品生产许可所提交的材料，应当真实、合法、有效。申请人应在食品生产许可申请书等材料上签字确认。

第十条 许可机关对收到的申请，应当依照《中华人民共和国行政许可法》第三十二条等有关规定进行处理。

对申请决定予以受理的，应当出具《受理决定书》。决定不予受理的，应当出具《不予受理决定书》，并说明不予受理的理由，告知申请人享有依法申请行政复议或者提起行政诉讼的权利。

第十一条 许可机关受理申请后，应当依照有关规定组织对申请的资料和生产场所进行核查（以下简称现场核查）。

现场核查应当由许可机关指派二至四名核查人员组成核查组并按照国家质检总局有关规定进行，企业应予以配合。

第十二条 许可机关应当根据核查结果，在法律法规规定的期限内作出如下处理：

（一）经现场核查，生产条件符合要求的，依法作出准予生产的决定，向申请人发出《准予食品生产许可决定书》，并于作出决定之日起十日内颁发设立食品生产企业食品生产许可证书。

（二）经现场核查，生产条件不符合要求的，依法作出不予生产许可的决定，向申请人发出《不予食品生产许可决定书》，并说明理由。

除不可抗力外，由于申请人的原因导致现场核查无法在规定期限内实施的，按现场核查不合格处理。

第十三条 拟设立的食品生产企业必须在取得食品生产许可证书并依法办理营业执照工商登记手续后，方可根据生产许可检验的需要组织试产食品。

第十四条 新设立的食品生产企业应当按规定实施许可的食品品种申请生产许可检验。

许可机关接到生产许可检验申请后，应当及时按照有关规定抽取和封存样品，并告知申请企业在封样后七日内将样品送交具有相应资质的检验机构

第十五条 检验机构收到样品后，应当按照规定

要求和标准进行检验，并准确、及时地出具检验报告。

第十六条 检验结论合格的，许可机关根据检验报告确定食品生产许可的品种范围，并在食品生产许可证副页中予以载明。

在未经许可机关确定食品生产许可的品种范围之前，禁止出厂销售试产食品。

第十七条 检验结论为不合格的，可以按照有关规定申请复检。

复检结论为部分食品品种不合格的，不予确定该类食品的生产许可范围，在食品生产许可证副页中不予载明；禁止出厂销售该类食品。

复检结论为全部食品品种不合格的，应当按照有关规定注销食品生产许可；禁止出厂销售全部品种的食品。

第十八条 已经设立的企业申请取得食品生产许可的，应当持合法有效的营业执照，按照本章规定的有关条件和要求办理许可申请手续。

许可机关按照本章规定的有关条件和要求，受理已经设立的企业从事食品生产的许可申请，并根据现场核查结果和检验报告决定是否准予许可以及确定食品生产许可的品种范围，颁发食品生产许可证书。

第十九条 食品生产许可证有效期为三年。

有效期届满，取得食品生产许可证的企业需要继续生产的，应当在食品生产许可证有效期届满六个月前，向原许可机关提出换证申请；准予换证的，食品生产许可证编号不变。

期满未换证的，视为无证；拟继续生产食品的，应当重新申请，重新发证，重新编号，有效期自许可之日起重新计算。

第二十条 食品生产许可证有效期内，有以下情形之一的，企业应当向原许可机关提出变更申请：

（一）企业名称发生变化的；

（二）住所、生产地址名称发生变化的；

（三）生产场所迁址的；

（四）生产场所周围环境发生变化的；

（五）设备布局和工艺流程发生变化的；

（六）生产设备、设施发生变化的；

（七）法律法规规定的应当申请变更的其他情形。

有前款第（三）项至第（六）项情形之一的，原许可机关应当按照本办法的规定组织进行核查和检验；符合条件的，依法办理变更手续。

第二十一条 企业提出变更食品生产许可申请，应当提交下列申请材料：

（一）变更食品生产许可申请书；

（二）食品生产许可证书正、副本；

（三）与变更食品生产许可事项有关的证明材料。

申请变更食品生产许可所提交的材料，应当真实、合法、有效，符合相关法律法规的规定。申请人应当在变更食品生产许可申请书等材料上签字确认，并对其内容的合法性、真实性负责。

第二十二条 食品生产许可有效期内，有关法律法规、食品安全标准或技术要求发生变化的，原许可机关可以根据国家有关规定重新组织核查和检验。

第二十三条 有下列情形之一的，原许可机关应当依法办理食品生产许可证书注销手续：

（一）生产许可被依法撤回、撤销，或者生产许可证书被依法吊销的；

（二）企业申请注销的或者生产许可证有效期满未换证的；

（三）企业依法终止的；

（四）因不可抗力导致生产许可事项无法实施的；

（五）法律法规规定的应当注销生产许可证书的其他情形。

第二十四条 企业申请注销食品生产许可证书的，应当向原许可机关提交下列申请材料：

（一）注销食品生产许可申请书；

（二）食品生产许可证书正、副本；

（三）与注销食品生产许可事项相关的证明材料。

第三章 证书与标识

第二十五条 食品生产许可证书分为正本和副本，证书及其副页式样由国家质检总局统一规定。

第二十六条 企业应当妥善保管食品生产许可证书，并在生产场所显著位置予以悬挂或者摆放。食品生产许可证书遗失或者损毁的，企业应当及时在省级以上媒体声明，并及时申请补证。

第二十七条 企业应当在其食品或者其包装上标注食品生产许可证编号和标志；没有食品生产许可证编号和标志的，不得出厂销售。

第二十八条 食品生产许可证编号和标志均属企业获得食品生产许可的标识。食品生产许可证编号规则和标志式样由国家质检总局统一规定。

第二十九条 企业不得出租、出借或者以其他形式转让食品生产许可证书和编号。禁止伪造、变造食品生产许可证书、食品生产许可证编号和食品生产许可证标志。

第四章 监督检查

第三十条 企业应当在食品生产许可的品种范围

内从事食品生产活动，不得超出许可的品种范围生产食品

第三十一条 企业应当保证生产条件持续符合规定要求，并对其生产的食品安全负责。

第三十二条 各级质量技术监督部门在各自职责范围内依法对企业食品生产活动进行定期或不定期的监督检查。

第三十三条 各级质量技术监督部门应当建立食品生产许可和监督检查档案管理制度。档案保存期限按国家有关规定执行。

第三十四条 各级质量技术监督部门应当建立食品生产许可和监督检查信息平台，便于公民、法人和其他社会组织查询。

第五章 法律责任

第三十五条 违反本办法第三条、第十六条第二款、第十七条第二款、第十七条第三款、第三十条等规定，或者已取得食品生产许可但被依法注销的，按照《中华人民共和国食品安全法》第八十四条规定处罚。

第三十六条 违反本办法第二十条、第二十七条、第二十九条等规定，构成有关法律法规规定的违法行为的，按照有关法律法规的规定实施行政处罚。

第三十七条 各级质量技术监督部门及有关工作人员、核查人员、检验机构及检验人员在食品生产许可管理工作中，滥用职权、玩忽职守、徇私舞弊的，依法追究相关法律责任。

第三十八条 本办法规定的行政处罚由县级以上地方质量技术监督部门在职权范围内决定并实施决定吊销食品生产许可证的，应当在作出行政处罚决定之前逐级上报许可机关核准。

第三十九条 当事人对依据本办法所实施的行政许可和行政处罚不服的，可以依法提出行政复议或者行政诉讼。

第六章 附 则

第四十条 本办法所称食品是指《中华人民共和国食品安全法》第九十九条等规定的食品，但不包括食用农产品、声称具有保健功能的食品。

法律、行政法规对乳品、转基因食品、生猪屠宰、酒类和食盐的食品生产许可另有规定的，依照其规定。

第四十一条 本办法规定的实施生产许可的食品品种的划分，按照法律法规和国家质检总局有关规定执行。

第四十二条 取得餐饮服务许可的餐饮服务提供者在其餐饮服务场所制作加工食品，不需要取得本办法规定的食品生产许可。

第四十三条 小作坊等其他食品生产者从事食品生产活动，按照有关法律法规的规定执行

第四十四条 本办法所规定的核查人员、检验机构资质及其管理，按照有关规定执行。

第四十五条 本办法由国家质检总局负责解释。

第四十六条 本办法自 2010 年 6 月 1 日起施行。国家质检总局在本办法施行前公布的有关食品生产许可的规章、规范性文件与本办法不一致的，以本办法为准。

关于认真开展农村食品市场专项整治行动工作方案

（国家工商总局　工商食字［2010］85 号　2010 年 4 月 26 日）

为了规范农村食品市场秩序，根据《国务院办公厅关于印发 2010 年食品安全整顿工作安排的通知》（国办发［2010］17 号）、国务院领导同志批示以及国家工商行政管理总局《关于印发〈2010 年流通环节食品安全整顿工作方案〉的通知》（工商食字［2010］51 号）的要求，国家工商行政管理总局决定，把农村食品市场整顿工作作为流通环节食品安全整顿工作的重点，集中力量开展农村食品市场专项整治行动，现提出如下方案：

一、总体目标

按照国务院的总体部署和国家工商行政管理总局关于流通环节食品安全整顿工作的要求，以保障农村食品市场消费安全为目标，坚持防打结合、标本兼治、综合治理，突出重点，严厉打击销售假冒伪劣食

品等违法行为，着力解决当前农村食品市场安全存在的突出问题，切实维护农村食品市场秩序。

二、专项整治行动任务和重点

（一）以城乡结合部、乡（村）镇、农村旅游景区景点为重点区域，集中整治销售假冒、仿冒食品等违法行为 重点查处无证无照经营食品，销售假冒伪劣食品，仿冒知名食品特有的名称、包装、装潢，以及印制食品假包装、假标识、假商标等案件，严厉打击违法行为。

（二）以农村批发市场、集贸市场等市场为重点场所，集中整治农村市场食品经营者的经营行为，监督落实市场开办者的责任 监督市场开办者和食品经营者严格落实内部食品质量管理制度，规范食品质量市场准入行为，严把食品质量进货关，确保食品质量安全。依法监督批发市场、集贸市场、食品店等食品经营者，履行食品进货查验和查验记录制度，确保依法规范经营。

（三）以农村商场、超市和食品（杂）店为重点单位，集中整治不落实自律制度的行为，建立健全经营者自律机制 认真落实《流通环节食品安全示范店规范指导意见》，按照“两重点、三严格、四规范、五统一”的建设要求，加大工作力度，推进示范店建设进程。结合示范店建设，监督食品经营者落实查验和查验记录制度，依法建立健全食品质量管理体系和食品经营者长效自律机制。监督食品经营者落实对食品安全的法定责任和义务，促使食品经营者切实做到不进、不存、不销假冒伪劣和不符合食品安全标准的食品。

（四）以节日性、季节性食品和地方特色食品为重点品种，集中整治农村食品市场销售不合格食品和过期食品等违法行为 要加强“五一”、中秋、“十一”、元旦、春节等节日食品市场的监管，重点整治不符合食品安全标准、过度包装、搭售商品、虚假宣传及欺诈消费者等问题，切实保障食品市场消费安全。针对本地区食品市场的消费特点，加大对地方特色食品的监管力度，严把食品质量准入关，监督食品经营者按照食品标签标注的条件贮存食品、及时清理变质或者超过保质期的食品。

（五）以全国食品安全整顿工作领导小组办公室公布的非食用物质和添加剂的品种为重点，集中开展打击农村食品市场违法添加非食用物质和滥用食品添加剂专项执法检查 要对重点区域、重点场所、重点食品和重点食品经营者，集中开展执法检查行动，配合有关部门查处和打击违法销售食品添加剂以及农村市场食品经营者在食品中添加非食用物质和滥用食品添加剂的行为。

三、专项整治行动工作措施

（一）突出农村市场食品安全监管重点，集中力量开展专项执法检查 各地要按照本方案确定的五个方面的专项整治任务和重点，集中力量、集中时间，有针对性地开展专项整治行动。重点整治农民群众反映强烈、社会影响面大、侵害农村消费者合法权益的违法行为，着力解决农村食品市场经营存在的突出问题。

（二）加大农村食品市场日常监管和巡查力度，严格市场准入和食品经营行为 各地要对农村市场各类食品经营主体进行一次全面清理检查，对不符合条件的，依法吊销证照或限期办理变更登记；对违法经营的，依法进行查处；对无证、无照经营的，在当地政府的统一领导和协调下，按照相关部门的职责分工和工商机关各内设职能机构的职责分工，依法查处和取缔。要认真贯彻《食品市场巡查监管制度》，按照“六查六看”要求，将监管重心下移，严格落实基层工商所食品安全日常巡查和属地监管责任制，突出重点区域、重点场所、重点经营者，采取增加巡查频次、完善巡查内容、提高巡查效能等措施，及时发现和查处违法违章行为，切实规范食品经营者的经营行为。

（三）加大食品质量监管力度，依法开展食品抽样检验 各地要按照《食品安全法》及其实施条例和《流通环节食品安全监督管理办法》以及《食品抽样检验工作制度》的规定和要求，认真执行当地政府年度食品安全监督管理计划中确定的流通环节食品抽样检验的安排，以与农民群众日常生活消费关系密切的食品品种为重点，加大农村食品市场抽样检验力度。要加强对食品抽样检验结果的综合分析和利用，严格信息管理，依法依程序进行消费提示和警示，及时将有关情况通报相关职能部门和行业组织，促进源头治理和行业自律。要监督食品经营者严格落实法律法规的规定，对发现经营的食品不符合食品安全标准的，立即停止经营，配合生产者落实食品召回制度。配合相关部门加强对不符合食品安全标准的食品退市后的跟踪监管，严防再次流入市场。

（四）加大案件查办力度，严厉查处各类违法行为 要强化案件查办工作，尤其要抓好对农村食品市场大要案件的排查和督办工作。对大要案件要挂牌督办，限期办结。同时要严格办案程序，规范行政执法行为，严肃执法纪律，既有效惩处违法行为，又依法保护消费者和经营者的合法权益，促进农村食品市场健康有序发展。

（五）加大农村食品市场分类监管力度，建立健全长效监管机制 要针对农村商场、超市、批发市场、集贸市场和食品（杂）店经营食品的不同特点和不同经营管理状况，有针对性地采取分类监管措施，切实提高食品安全监管执法效能。严格监督农村批发市场、集贸市场等市场履行食品安全管理责任，确保市场开办者承担法定义务。严格监督农村商场、超市加强自律管理，确保入市食品质量合格。严格监督农村食品（杂）店履行进货查验义务，确保食品来源合法。

四、专项整治行动实施步骤

各地要坚持边整治与边规范、边整改相结合，集中整治与日常规范相结合，整改与建章立制、建立健全长效监管机制相结合，监督经营者自查自纠与加强检查督促相结合，从4月份到年底，集中执法力量和时间，认真开展专项整治行动，确保取得实效。4月至6月，为集中整治阶段；7月至9月，为自查自纠和整改阶段；10月至12月中旬，为建章立制和检查督查阶段。

五、专项整治行动要求

（一）提高认识，统一思想 各级工商行政管理机关务必高度重视，提高认识，进一步增强开展农村食品市场专项整治工作的紧迫感、责任感，结合完成流通环节食品安全整顿各项工作任务，切实把开展农村食品市场专项整治行动作为市场监管工作的重点，抓紧抓好，切实抓出成效。

（二）严格责任制度，加强协作配合 各地要按照《食品安全法》的要求，进一步建立健全工商行政管理机关对流通环节食品安全属地监管领导责任制、职能机构指导监督检查责任制和食品安全基层监管岗位责任制及其责任追究制。要强化各级食品安全监管牵头协调部门和内设机构的职能作用，切实落实监管责任。要将监管重心下移，把日常监管的任务和责任落实到基层，落实到基层执法岗位，落实到每一个执法人员。要加强工商机关内设机构之间以及与卫生、质监、农业、商务、食品药品监管、公安等有关职能部门协作与配合，强化信息共享，发挥整体优势，形成监管合力。在当地政府统一领导和协调下，加强专项整治行动期间农村食品市场食品安全信息的管理，及时上报和通报专项整治工作情况，对重要的专项整治信息，要按照国务院办公厅《关于印发2010年食品安全整顿工作安排的通知》，配合有关部门做好发布工作。

（三）加强宣传工作，努力营造良好舆论环境 各地要充分发挥新闻媒体的宣传引导和舆论监督作用，广泛宣传工商行政管理机关开展的农村食品市场专项整治行动工作，引导新闻媒体加强正面宣传和客观准确报道，重点宣传专项整治行动工作进展、成效和典型经验，支持新闻媒体开展舆论监督，为农村食品市场专项整治行动工作营造良好氛围。国家工商行政管理总局拟邀请人民日报、新华社、光明日报、经济日报、中央人民广播电台、中央电视台、法制日报、中国政府网、新华网、人民网、新浪网和搜狐网等新闻媒体，以及中国工商报、中国消费者报、《工商行政管理》半月刊、《中国工商管理研究》及国家工商行政管理总局政府网站，共同做好宣传报道工作。

（四）加强组织领导，狠抓检查落实 各级工商行政管理机关要按照国家工商行政管理总局的要求，在地方人民政府的统一领导和协调下，认真部署和安排专项整治行动工作。要切实加强组织领导，一把手亲自抓，主管领导具体抓，各内设机构按照职能分工负责抓，密切协作，形成齐抓共管的工作格局。要结合当地实际，研究制定具体的实施方案，层层分解任务，精心组织和认真实施，确保专项整治行动取得实效。要加强对农村食品市场专项整治行动工作的指导，坚持上级指导下级，对整治过程中存在的问题和薄弱环节，及时指导，及时解决，不留隐患。要狠抓督促检查落实，采取重点督查、明察暗访等方式，层层抓检查，一级抓一级，全力抓落实，确保专项整治行动各项任务落到实处。

全国奶业发展规划（2009—2013年）

（农业部 2010年6月8日）

奶业是现代农业的重要组成部分。促进奶业持续健康发展，是优化农业结构、增加农民收入、改善居民膳食结构、增强国民体质的需要。为切实保障奶业持续健康发展，根据《国务院关于促进奶业持续健康发展的意见》、《乳品质量安全监督管理条例》和《奶业整顿和振兴规划纲要》，特制定本规划，规划期为2009—2013年。

一、我国奶业发展现状及面临的形势

进入新世纪以来，我国奶业以市场为导向，强化政策支持，实施优势产业布局，推进发展方式转变，产业规模、产业结构和生产水平得到大幅提升，实现了持续快速发展。

（一）奶牛存栏快速增加，奶类总产量大幅增长

2008年，全国奶牛存栏达到1 233.5万头，是2000年的2.5倍；奶类产量3 781.5万t,是2000年的4.1倍。我国奶类产量已跃居世界第三位,成为奶类生产大国。

（二）奶牛生产区域化进程加快，产业集中度明显提高

2008年，内蒙古、黑龙江、河北等13个优势省（自治区、直辖市）奶牛存栏占全国84.3%，与2000年基本持平；牛奶产量占全国88.3%，比2000年提高了10个百分点，产业集中度进一步提高。同时，优势区域内部布局也进一步优化，涌现了一大批奶牛养殖大县。

（三）奶牛规模养殖加快推进，发展质量进一步提升

2008年，全国存栏20头以上的奶牛规模养殖比例达到36%，比2003年提高了9个百分点；奶牛单产水平达到4 800kg，比2000年提高了40%。挤奶机械化水平显著提高，2008年底达到66%

（四）乳制品加工业飞速发展，生产规模迅速扩大

2008年，规模以上乳制品企业达到791家，比2000年增加414家；实现工业产值1 555.8亿元，是2000年的8倍；前10家大型骨干企业乳制品工业产值占全行业的47.5%。

（五）乳制品产量持续增加，产品种类丰富多样

2008年，全国规模以上企业乳制品产量1 810.6万t，其中液态乳产量1 525.2万t，分别是2000年的7.7倍和11.2倍。目前，市场上巴氏杀菌乳、超高温灭菌乳、酸乳、乳粉、干酪、奶油、炼乳等产品种类齐全，基本满足了城乡居民多样化的消费需求。

（六）乳品消费同步增长，城乡居民消费水平不断提高

2008年，城镇居民人均乳品消费量22.72kg，比2000年增长56.8%；农村居民人均4.81kg，为2000年的3.9倍；城镇居民家庭人均乳品消费金额比2000年增长了1.8倍。

但是，我国奶业在快速发展的同时，一些长期积累的矛盾和问题日益凸显。一是养殖方式落后。小规模散养户仍是生鲜乳生产的主体，专用饲草饲料缺乏，饲养方式粗放，高产奶牛比例不高，单产水平与国外发达国家相比差距较大，成母牛平均单产不足5t。二是乳品质量安全监管依然薄弱。生鲜乳收购站点数量多，条件参差不齐，开办主体复杂，监管难度大；乳品质量安全保障体系不健全，监管力量不足。三是乳制品市场秩序不规范。一些乳制品企业缺乏稳定的奶源基地，淡季压价、旺季争抢奶源的现象时有发生；部分乳制品企业为抢市场打价格战和广告战，炒作概念，不落实复原乳标识制度，误导消费者。四是原料奶定价机制不合理。奶农组织化程度低，乳制品企业单方面决定生鲜乳价格，奶农利益难以保证。五是消费市场培育滞后。科学消费的观念和习惯尚未形成，乳品消费市场培育滞后于奶业发展。这些深层次矛盾和问题，与婴幼儿乳粉事件、国际金融危机等多重因素叠加，交互影响，使得2008年下半年以来，我国乳品消费萎缩，乳粉进口大幅增加，出口下降，乳制品企业经营困难，生鲜乳价格持续下行，奶牛养殖亏损严重，奶业面临前所未有的严峻挑战。

当前，我国奶业正处于从数量扩张向整体优化、全面提高产业素质转变的关键时期，还有很大的发展空间和潜力。从消费市场看，城镇居民的人均乳品消费量只有世界平均水平的1/4，农村居民的人均乳品消费量只有城镇居民的1/5，随着人口增长特别是城镇人口大量增加、城乡居民收入持续较快增长和消费结构不断改善，乳品消费需求增长空间巨大。从资源条件看，奶牛存栏已突破1 200万头，还有1 000多万头牦牛、2 000多万头水牛和500多万只奶山羊资源可供开发，农区种植业结构调整和饲草产业稳步发展，牧区生态逐步恢复，近7亿t可用作饲料的农作物秸秆还有40%左右的利用空间，奶业发展相关资源还有较大的开拓潜力。从政策环境看，《国务院关于促进奶业持续健康发展的意见》、《乳品质量安全监督管理条例》和《奶业整顿和振兴规划纲要》、《乳制品工业产业政策》相继出台，国家扶持奶业发展的政策日趋完善，规范奶业发展的管理制度逐步健全。各级政府把发展奶业摆在重要位置，加大政策落实和资金扶持力度。只要采取有效措施，因势利导，就能化危机为机遇，促进奶业持续健康发展。

二、保障奶业持续健康发展的指导思想和基本目标

（一）指导思想

全面贯彻落实党的十七大精神，以邓小平理论和

"三个代表"重要思想为指导，深入贯彻落实科学发展观，以市场为导向，以质量安全为核心，以促进产业链各环节协调发展为根本，推动科技进步，转变发展方式，夯实奶业基础，强化乳品质量安全监管，加快建设现代奶业，满足城乡居民日益增长的乳品消费需求。

切实保障奶业持续健康发展，必须坚持以下原则：

——着眼当前和立足长远相结合。既要采取有效措施，帮助奶农和企业渡过难关，恢复消费信心，稳定奶业生产；又要立足长远，着力强化奶业发展基础建设，解决制约奶业发展的深层次矛盾和问题，全面提高科技含量和产业素质，促进产业升级。

——市场调节和政府扶持相结合。充分发挥市场配置资源的基础性作用，利用市场机制，推动企业和奶农提高自身素质，促进产业升级。同时，通过政府扶持，帮助企业和奶农克服困难，增强奶业抗御风险的能力，保护奶业基本生产能力，巩固奶业发展的基础，加快转变奶业发展方式。

——强化监管和规范引导相结合。把保障乳品质量安全放在优先地位，坚定不移推进乳品行业清理整顿，全面加强以质量安全为核心的制度建设，消除产业链各环节的监管漏洞。规范市场秩序，鼓励企业和奶农建立各种形式的利益联结机制，构建互利共赢的产业化经营新格局。

——突出重点与全面发展相结合。扶持奶业重点产区，发挥区域优势，提高准入门槛，培育骨干企业，促进养殖、加工与消费协调发展。同时，兼顾地方品种和民族特色，实现奶业全面发展，满足多样化的消费需求。

（二）基本目标

——生鲜乳生产能力稳定增长。2013 年，全国奶牛存栏达到 1 500 万头，奶类产量达到 4 800 万 t，成母牛平均单产水平提高到 5.7t；100 头以上奶牛规模养殖比例达到 35%，奶牛粗饲料质量显著提高。奶水牛和奶山羊发展取得突破。

——乳品质量安全水平显著提高。生鲜乳生产符合《生鲜乳生产技术规程（试行）》，乳制品企业实行《乳制品企业良好生产规范（GB 12693）》，婴幼儿乳粉生产企业全面实施危害分析与关键控制点（HACCP）（GB/T 27342）管理，质量安全保障机制更加健全，产品质量全部符合法律法规及相关标准的要求。

——生鲜乳收购站全面规范。2013 年，生鲜乳收购站 100%实现持证收购和标准化管理，偏远牧区、山区的牛奶收购点和山羊奶收购点 100%纳入监管范围。

——奶源生产和乳制品加工衔接更加合理。乳制品企业奶源基地和加工产能合理配置，符合《乳制品工业产业政策》的要求。2013 年乳制品企业稳定可控奶源达到 70%以上，初步建立生鲜乳质量第三方检测体系。

——乳制品流通条件进一步优化。2013 年，生产经营低温产品的乳制品企业拥有完善冷链体系的比例达到 90%以上。配送网络覆盖全部中小城市和 90%以上乡村。

——乳品消费群体不断壮大。全国城镇居民人均乳品消费不断提高，农村居民人均乳品消费大幅度增长，"学生饮用奶计划"在全国中小学校的覆盖率进一步提高。

三、保障奶业持续健康发展的主要任务和建设重点

（一）优化奶业区域布局

根据市场需求、资源环境、消费习惯和现有产业基础等因素，重点发展五大奶业产区，建立生产、加工、销售协调发展的产业格局。五大奶业产区以加快奶牛品种改良，加强优质饲草料生产，提高奶牛单产水平，发展适度规模标准化养殖为重点，不断提高奶牛生产水平和养殖效益；按照《乳制品工业产业政策》，合理布局加工企业，淘汰落后产能，全面提升乳制品质量，不断提高乳制品企业自主创新能力，基本实现奶源基地建设和乳制品工业协调发展。

——东北内蒙古产区包括黑龙江、吉林、辽宁和内蒙古等 4 省（自治区），以培育奶牛大户（家庭牧场）、规范化养殖小区、适度规模养殖场为重点，重点发展乳粉、干酪、奶油、超高温灭菌乳等，根据市场需要适当发展巴氏杀菌乳、酸乳等产品。

——华北产区包括河北、河南、山东、山西等 4 省，在发展规模养殖场（小区）的同时，兼顾奶山羊生产，探索资源综合利用新模式，重点发展乳粉、干酪、超高温灭菌乳、巴氏杀菌乳、酸乳等产品。

——西部产区包括陕西、甘肃、青海、宁夏、新疆和西藏等 6 省（自治区），着力发展奶牛规模养殖场（小区），培育山羊奶、牦牛奶、马奶、驼奶和驴奶等特色奶源基地，扩大优质饲草饲料种植，推广舍饲、半舍饲养殖，重点发展乳粉、干酪、奶油、干酪素等乳制品，适度发展超高温灭菌乳、酸乳、巴氏杀菌乳等产品，鼓励发展具有地方特色的乳制品。

——南方产区包括湖北、湖南、江苏、浙江、福建、安徽、江西、广东、广西、海南、云南、贵州、四川等 13 个省（自治区），重点发展适度规模养殖

场，广西、云南及其他有条件的省（自治区）鼓励开展奶水牛品种改良与水牛奶产品开发，重点发展巴氏杀菌乳、干酪、酸乳等产品，适度发展炼乳、超高温灭菌乳、乳粉等乳制品，大力开发水牛奶加工等具有地方特色的乳制品。

——大城市周边产区包括北京、天津、上海和重庆等4个直辖市，着力培育高产奶牛核心群，提高奶牛育种选育水平，推进标准化生产，全面开展粪污无害化处理和资源化利用，大力发展都市型乳业，主要发展巴氏杀菌乳、酸乳等低温产品，适当发展干酪、奶油、功能性乳制品。

（二）加强良种繁育及推广

实施奶牛群体遗传改良计划，建立高产奶牛核心群，开展奶牛生产性能测定和种公牛遗传评估，加快实行奶牛良种登记、标识管理制度。加强对奶牛改良工作的指导，推广人工授精、胚胎移植等繁育技术，不断提高奶牛单产水平，改善生鲜乳质量。

——构建高产奶牛核心群。以种牛引进、遗传资源开发利用、基础设施建设为重点，加强奶牛原良种场建设，选育高产奶牛核心群，提高核心养殖场的生产水平和供种能力。

——提升种公牛站生产经营能力。加大种公牛站设施改造和先进生产设备配备力度，健全种公牛遗传评定和后裔测定体系，加快推进种公牛站改制，成为自主经营、自负盈亏的经济实体，提高种公牛自主培育能力和优质冻精供应能力。

——健全生产性能测定体系。加强奶牛生产性能测定中心、奶牛改良中心基础设施建设和仪器设备更新，完善有关奶牛生产性能测定、品种登记和改良的技术及管理标准，奠定奶牛品种改良的技术基础，加强对奶牛改良工作的指导。

——完善优质冻精推广体系。加强奶牛配种站点液氮罐、液氮运输车、改良配种器材配置以及配套基础设施建设，开展人工授精技术人员培训，进一步完善奶牛优质冻精推广体系。

（三）发展奶源生产基地

以奶牛养殖大县为依托，带动奶源基地发展，构建稳定的奶源生产集群。加强标准化规模养殖场（小区）建设和优质饲草料基地建设，加快推进奶源基地生产方式转变。发展奶农专业合作社，提高奶农组织化程度和生产经营能力。推动龙头企业建设自有奶源基地和学生饮用奶奶源基地。

——增强奶牛养殖大县综合生产能力。以奶牛养殖大县为依托，发展标准化规模养殖，规范投入品使用，增强防疫服务能力，加强环境保护，从源头上保证生鲜乳质量安全。

——发展奶牛标准化规模养殖场（小区）。加强养殖场和养殖小区圈舍、水、电、路等基础设施建设，粪污处理、疫病防控、饲草料贮存（或青贮）等配套设施建设，全混合日粮（TMR）饲养、挤奶、良种繁育、生鲜乳质量检测等设备配置，推进规模化奶牛养殖场良好农业规范（GAP）认证，提高标准化生产水平。

——建立优质饲草料生产基地。建立奶牛青绿饲料生产基地，示范推广全株玉米青贮，鼓励发展专业性青贮生产经营企业和大户，为奶牛养殖提供充足的青绿饲料资源。充分利用中低产地、退耕地、秋冬闲地等土地资源，大力发展苜蓿等高产优质牧草种植。在有条件的地区发展人工饲草地。

——发展奶农专业合作社。积极安排资金，扶持奶农专业合作社发展，发挥其为奶农提供服务和维护奶农利益等方面的作用。继续推进科技入户，开展实用技术培训，提高奶农素质。

（四）完善乳品质量安全监管体系

继续推进生鲜乳收购站清理整顿，规范生鲜乳收购站建设，改善基础设施条件，推行标准化、规范化经营。完善乳品质量安全标准体系，建立健全检验检测和监管体系，提高执法能力，严厉打击违禁添加行为，保障乳品质量安全。

——建设标准化生鲜乳收购站。支持乳制品企业、奶农专业合作社、奶牛养殖场对个体和流动生鲜乳收购站点进行改造、合并或重组，加大生鲜乳收购站挤奶设备、专用生鲜乳运输车等设施设备的更新改造力度。推进生鲜乳收购站标准化管理，配备必要的检验检测仪器设备和监控设备。

——完善生鲜乳质量监测体系。建立国家生鲜乳质量安全中心，健全由国家、区域、省和县四级检测机构组成的检验检测体系，提高检测能力。实施生鲜乳质量安全监测计划，开展质量安全监测和风险评估，严厉打击生鲜乳收购环节添加违禁添加物的行为。建立全国生鲜乳收购站监督管理信息系统，初步建立生鲜乳第三方检测制度。

——提高乳制品企业质量安全管理水平。乳制品加工企业根据原料检测、生产过程动态检测、产品出厂检测的需要，配置在线检测、快速检测及其他先进检验设备。对乳制品生产实施全程标准化管理和质量控制，实行《乳制品企业良好生产规范(GB 12693)》，婴幼儿奶粉生产企业实施危害分析与关键控制点(HACCP)（GB/T 27342）管理。

——完善乳制品质量安全监管制度。建立和完善乳制品检验制度、产品质量可追溯及责任追究制度、问题产品召回和退市制度、食品质量安全申诉投诉处理制度。加强乳品质量安全风险评估，完善国家乳品质量安全标准体系。加强乳制品工业企业诚信体系建设。全面清理乳制品添加剂和非法添加物，严厉打击乳制品加工中添加违禁物的行为。

（五）提升乳制品加工与流通能力

全面落实乳制品工业产业政策，严格行业准入，提升装备水平，加强冷链体系建设，培育一批骨干企业，形成资源配置合理、技术水平先进、产品结构优化、市场应对得力的现代乳制品加工与流通产业体系。

——有序发展乳制品工业。乳制品工业新建和改扩建项目，必须符合《乳制品工业产业政策》中规定的行业准入条件，项目建设按国家有关规定履行手续，防止盲目投资和重复建设。已建加工项目（企业）未达到《乳制品工业产业政策》要求的应限期整改。鼓励企业通过兼并、重组等方式整合资源，形成以市场为导向的合理经营规模，加快淘汰落后产能。

——提升技术与装备水平。推进乳品加工设备国产化，重点研发大型乳粉生产、低温喷雾干燥、干酪生产、膜过滤、灭菌及无菌灌装成套设备等关键设备。发展和应用膜分离技术、生物技术、冷杀菌技术、直投发酵剂技术等高新技术，以及纸塑复合无菌包装、多层共挤高阻隔性复合材料、可持续性绿色包装等材料。

——优化乳制品产品结构。大力发展干酪、发酵乳、功能肽产品等适合不同消费需求的产品，逐步改变以液态乳为主的产品单一局面。积极发展高品质、市场需求量大的乳制品，如脱脂乳粉、乳清综合利用产品等。根据市场需求开发乳蛋白、乳糖等精深加工产品。

——改善乳制品冷链流通条件。加强大中型乳制品企业、专业化物流企业低温设施建设，建设以原料奶收购、加工及乳制品储藏、运输、销售等全部环节实行低温控制的冷链物流体系。建立健全乳制品标准化冷链管理制度。

四、保障奶业持续健康发展的主要政策和措施

（一）加大对奶业发展的投入

大力实施奶牛良种补贴、饲草收贮加工、粪污处理和挤奶机械购置补贴以及种奶牛场和标准化规模养殖场（小区）建设等各项扶持政策，加强对奶业的扶持和保护。完善奶牛保险制度，降低养殖风险。加大对奶牛养殖大县的扶持。鼓励和扶持牧草良种推广和优质饲草料基地建设。加强对奶牛养殖农户、奶农专业合作社和乳制品企业的信贷支持。积极发挥公共财政资金的引导作用，吸引社会资本投资奶业，建立多元化投融资机制，为奶业持续健康发展注入活力。

（二）加快奶业科技研发与推广应用

进一步提高奶业科技研发和应用水平，不断完善现代奶牛产业技术体系建设，加强奶业技术服务平台与推广体系建设。鼓励相关部门、大专院校、科研院所和企业，依托国家科技计划和重大工程项目，联合开展奶业领域的重大科技研发活动，加快奶业科技进步。扩大奶牛科技推广服务实施范围，大力推广科学饲养等先进适用技术。扶持奶农专业合作组织，加强生鲜乳收购、人员培训、疫病防治、良种繁育等社会化服务。

（三）切实加强奶牛疫病防控

坚持生产发展和防疫保护并重的方针，加强奶牛的疫病防控，健全奶牛布氏杆菌病、结核病和口蹄疫等传染病的国家扑杀制度，积极开展奶牛疫病的净化，提高奶牛疫病扑杀补贴。强化定期监测和重大传染病强制免疫，建立奶牛免疫档案。指导奶牛养殖户实施科学的防疫措施，建立完善的消毒防疫制度。加强乳房炎、蹄病等常见病的防治，通过转变饲养方式、推广新疫苗和兽药等措施，逐步降低奶牛常见病的发病率。

（四）强化奶业监管能力

贯彻落实食品安全、乳品质量安全监督有关规定，加强乳品质量安全监管能力建设，健全国家、省、市、县四级监督管理体系，完善乳品质量安全监督管理制度，明确监管人员，保障工作经费，提高执法能力。各部门按照职责分工，各负其责，密切合作，形成合力，确保乳品质量安全监管无缝对接。建立健全乳品质量安全举报投诉工作机制，畅通社会监督渠道。

（五）做好奶业发展的调控和引导服务

加强生鲜乳生产、乳品市场和乳制品进出口等预警预测系统建设，强化信息发布，引导奶牛养殖场户和乳制品加工企业适时调整生产结构。采取多种措施，支持奶农专业生产合作社建设，通过引导散养户“进区入园”等方式，发展适度规模化生产。进一步扩大国产乳粉收储规模，完善乳粉临时收储政策，合理运用国际通行规则，减缓乳粉进口冲击，开展产业损害调查，建立救助补偿机制。完善生鲜乳价格协调机制和收购合同制度，鼓励各地推行生鲜乳第三方检测和按质论价。严格执行鲜乳、纯乳和复原乳标识制度，规范液态奶生产经营秩序。充分发挥各级奶业协会的作用，加强行业自律，推动企业诚信体系建设。

（六）提振消费信心，扩大乳品消费

加强正面报道，加大宣传力度，主动引导舆论，

为奶业发展营造良好的舆论氛围。及时、主动、客观公布加强乳品质量安全监管的政策措施和乳品质量安全状况，科学回应社会关切，提振消费信心。继续推行“学生饮用奶计划”，加大推广力度，完善管理体制和运行机制，扩大学生饮用奶覆盖范围。积极开拓中小城市和农村奶类消费市场，普及乳制品知识，倡导乳品科学消费，依托企业购销网点和“万村千乡”等工程，加大乳制品采购力度，做好配送工作。

五、环境保护

贯彻落实国务院《关于加快发展循环经济的若干意见》，以及国务院办公厅转发的《关于加强农村环境保护工作的意见》，遵循预防为主、防治结合、综合利用的原则，推行奶业废弃物减量化、无害化和资源化利用。通过全面规划，合理布局，加强监管，推动粪便等废弃物污染防治和综合利用设施建设，实现奶业与生态环境的协调发展。

（一）区域布局符合环境条件要求 充分考虑各地环境状况，不在环境敏感的水源保护区、风景名胜区、自然保护区的核心区和缓冲区、城镇居民区等人口集中区域和法律法规规定的其他禁养区发展规模化养殖场（小区）。新建、改扩建乳制品加工项目和奶源基地建设应依法进行环境影响评价，落实环境保护“三同时”要求。

（二）提高资源利用率，减少废弃物产生量和环境污染 严格执行土地管理制度，推进养殖场（小区）标准化改造，推广清洁养殖模式，推广应用粪便耗氧堆肥和沼气处理等综合利用技术，提高乳制品加工厂和奶源基地废弃物无害化处理和资源化利用率。提倡乳制品包装简洁化、多样化，鼓励企业使用可回收、易降解的环保包装材料，减少包装材料使用量，控制包装废弃物的产生量和排放量。

（三）充分考虑环境承载能力 农区要充分考虑周边土地消纳能力和粪污处理能力，大力推进农牧结合，确定适当的养殖规模。牧区和半牧区大力推行舍饲、半舍饲圈养，严格实行草畜平衡制度，实现草原生态保护和生产发展相协调。

（四）加强环境监管 严格执行国家和地方相关环保及清洁生产等法律法规和标准，建立奶业产地环境监测体系，及时监督和跟踪规划实施后的环境效果。

农产品冷链物流发展规划

（国家发展和改革委员会　发改经贸［2010］1304号　2010年6月8日）

农产品冷链物流是指使肉、禽、水产、蔬菜、水果、蛋等生鲜农产品从产地采收（或屠宰、捕捞）后，在产品加工、贮藏、运输、分销、零售等环节始终处于适宜的低温控制环境下，最大限度地保证产品品质和质量安全、减少损耗、防止污染的特殊供应链系统。近年来，随着农业结构调整和居民消费水平的提高，生鲜农产品的产量和流通量逐年增加，全社会对生鲜农产品的安全和品质提出了更高的要求。加快发展农产品冷链物流，对于促进农民持续增收和保障消费安全具有十分重要的意义。为落实《物流业调整和振兴规划》，促进农产品冷链物流快速健康发展，特制订本规划。规划期为2010—2015年。

一、现状与形势

（一）发展现状

我国现代农产品储藏、保鲜技术起步于20世纪初，自20世纪六七十年代开始在生鲜农产品产后加工、储藏及运输等环节逐步得到应用。进入新世纪以来，我国农产品储藏保鲜技术迅速发展，农产品冷链物流发展环境和条件不断改善，农产品冷链物流得到较快发展。

1. 农产品冷链物流初具规模 我国是农业生产和农产品消费大国，目前蔬菜产量约占全球总产量的60%，水果和肉类产量占30%，禽蛋和水产品产量占40%。近年来我国生鲜农产品产量快速增加，每年约有4亿t生鲜农产品进入流通领域，冷链物流比例逐步提高，目前我国果蔬、肉类、水产品冷链流通率分别达到5%、15%、23%，冷藏运输率分别达到15%、30%、40%，冷链物流的规模快速增长。

2. 农产品冷链物流基础设施逐步完善 目前全国有冷藏库近2万座，冷库总容量880万t，其中冷却物冷藏量140万t，冻结物冷藏量740万t；机械冷藏列车1 910辆，机械冷藏汽车20 000辆，冷藏船吨

位 10 万 t，年集装箱生产能力 100 万标准箱。

3. *冷链物流技术逐步推广*　生鲜农产品出口企业率先引进国际先进的 HACCP（危害分析和临界控制点）认证、GMP（良好操作规范）等管理技术，普遍实现了全程低温控制。大型肉类屠宰企业开始应用国际先进的冷链物流技术，从屠宰、分割加工、冷却成熟等环节低温处理起步，逐渐向储藏、运输、批发和零售环节延伸，向着全程低温控制的方向快速发展。适应我国国情的低能耗、低成本的冷链处理技术广泛推广，推动水产品和反季节果蔬为代表的高价值量农产品冷链迅速兴起。

4. *冷链物流企业不断涌现*　中外运、中粮等社会化第三方物流企业强化与上下游战略合作与资源整合建立国际先进的冷链设施和管理体系，积极拓展冷链物流业务；双汇、众品、光明乳业等食品生产企业，加快物流业务与资产重组，组建独立核算的冷链物流公司，积极完善冷链网络；大型连锁商业企业完善终端销售环节的冷链管理，加快发展生鲜食品配送。我国冷链物流企业呈现出网络化、标准化、规模化、集团化发展态势。

5. *农产品冷链物流发展环境逐步完善*　国家高度重视冷链物流发展，在近几年下发的中央 1 号文件中均强调要加快农产品冷链物流系统建设，促进农产品流通。一些冷链物流的国家标准、行业标准和地方标准先后颁布实施，(食品安全法》等重要法律法规逐步完善。农产品冷链物流的重要性进一步被消费者认识，全社会对“优质优价”农产品的需求不断增长。

但是，我国农产品冷链物流发展仍处于起步阶段，规模化、系统化的冷链物流体系尚未形成，与发展现代农业、居民消费和扩大农产品出口的需求相比仍有差距。突出表现在：一是鲜活农产品通过冷链流通的比例仍然偏低。目前我国鲜活农产品冷链流通的比例远低于欧美发达国家水平（欧、美、加、日等发达国家肉禽冷链流通率已经达到 100%，蔬菜、水果冷链流通率也达 95%以上），大部分生鲜农产品仍在常温下流通；冷链物流各环节缺乏系统化、规范化、连贯性的运作，部分在屠宰或储藏环节采用了低温处理的产品，在运输、销售等环节又出现“断链”现象，全程冷链的比率过低。二是冷链物流基础设施能力严重不足。我国设施整体规模不足，人均冷库容量仅 7kg，冷藏保温车占货运汽车的比例仅 0.3%，与发达国家差距较大；现有冷冻冷藏设施普遍陈旧老化，国有冷库中近一半已使用 30 年以上；区域分布不平衡，中部农牧业主产区和西部特色农业地区冷库严重短缺，承担全国 70%以上生鲜农产品批发交易功能的大型农产品批发市场、区域性农产品配送中心等关键物流节点缺少冷冻冷藏设施。三是冷链物流技术推广滞后。生鲜农产品产后预冷技术和低温环境下的分等分级、包装加工等商品化处理手段尚未普及，运输环节温度控制手段原始粗放，发达国家广泛运用的全程温度自动控制没有得到广泛应用。四是第三方冷链物流企业发展滞后。在农产品冷链物流发展过程中，优质优价的机制仍没有形成，冷链物流的服务体系尚未完全建立，服务水平有待进一步提高，第三方冷链物流企业发展滞后。现有冷链物流企业以中小企业为主，实力弱，经销规模小，服务标准不统一，具备资源整合和行业推动能力的大型冷链物流企业刚刚起步。五是冷链物流法律法规体系和标准体系不健全。规范冷链物流各环节市场主体行为的法律法规体系尚未建立。冷链物流各环节的设施、设备、温度控制和操作规范等方面缺少统一标准，冷链物流各环节的信息资源难以实现有效衔接，在发达国家普遍推行的相关管理办法和操作规范在我国尚处于推广的起步阶段。

（二）面临的形势

从国际农产品流通产业发展的经验看，发达国家已经建立了“从田间到餐桌”的一体化冷链物流体系，不仅确保了产品质量，而且提高了农业效益。随着我国经济和社会的快速发展，对加快发展农产品冷链物流提出了更高的要求。

1. *加快冷链物流发展是适应农产品大规模流通的客观需要*　经过改革开放 30 年的发展，我国农业结构调整取得显著成效，区域和品种布局日益优化使农产品流通呈现出了大规模、长距离、反季节的特点，对农产品物流服务规模和效率提出了更高的要求。一是随着农产品区域生产布局的细化，农业特色产区加快发展，生鲜农产品的区域规模化产出迫切需要加快发展农产品跨地区保鲜运输；二是农产品反季节销售加快发展，急需进一步提高低温储藏保鲜水平。从今后一段时期农业结构加快调整优化的需要看，加快发展农产品冷链物流也是适应我国生鲜农产品大规模流通的客观需要。

2. *加快冷链物流发展是满足居民消费的必要保证*　随着城乡居民消费水平和消费能力的不断提高，我国生鲜农产品的消费规模快速增长，居民对农产品的多样化、新鲜度和营养性等方面提出了更高要求，特别是对食品安全的关注程度不断提高。加快发展农产品冷链物流已经成为提升农产品消费品质，减少营养流失，保证食品安全的必要手段是满足居民消费需求的必要保证。

3. *加快冷链物流发展是促进农民增收的重要途*

径 长期以来，我国农产品产后损失严重，果蔬、肉类、水产品流通腐损率分别达到20%～30%、12%、15%，仅果蔬一类每年损失就达到1 000亿元以上；同时，受到生鲜农产品集中上市后保鲜储运能力制约，农产品“卖难”和价格季节性波动的矛盾突出，农民增产不增收的情况时有发生。发展农产品冷链物流，既是减少农产品产后损失，间接节约耕地等农业资源，促进农业可持续发展的重要举措，也是带动农产品跨季节均衡销售，促进农民稳定增收的重要途径。

4. *加快冷链物流发展是提高我国农产品国际竞争力的重要举措* 我国生鲜农产品生产具有较强的比较优势，但是由于冷链发展滞后，我国蔬菜、水果出口量仅占总产量的1%～2%，且其中80%是初级产品，在国际市场上缺乏竞争力。特别是随着近年来欧盟、日本、美国等发达国家不断提高进口农产品准入标准，相关质量、技术和绿色壁垒已经成为制约我国农产品出口的重要障碍。加快发展农产品冷链物流，已经成为提高出口农产品质量，突破贸易壁垒，增强国际竞争力的重要举措。

二、指导思想、基本原则和发展目标

（一）指导思想

按照全面贯彻落实科学发展观、推进社会主义新农村建设和构建和谐社会的要求，紧紧围绕构建农业增产增效和农民持续增收的长效机制，适应城乡居民生活水平提高和保障居民食品安全的需要，以市场为导向，以企业为主体，加快冷链物流技术、规范、标准体系建设，完善冷链物流基础设施，培育冷链物流企业，建设一体化的冷链物流服务体系，以降低农产品产后损失和流通成本，促进农民增收，确保农产品品质和消费安全。

（二）基本原则

1. *科学规划，合理布局* 根据农产品生产规模与布局状况，分析产品流量、流向及其储运的技术要求，综合考虑居民消费水平、消费习惯以及交通区位等条件，制定农产品冷链物流发展规划，优化冷链物流发展布局。

2. *因地制宜，分类指导* 针对我国东中西部地区、大中城市和广大农村、产地与销地之间，在经济社会发展、居民收入水平、消费习惯方面的差异，结合果蔬、肉类、水产品等生鲜农产品的不同特点，因地制宜发展特色农产品冷链物流。

3. *市场运作，政府扶持* 充分发挥企业的主体作用，坚持投资主体多元化、经营管理企业化、运作方式市场化。政府要加强发展规划、法律法规体系、标准体系和检验检测体系建设，对重点冷链物流项目给予扶持，为冷链物流发展营造良好环境。

4. *重点突破，扶优扶强* 借鉴发达国家冷链物流发展经验，选择对消费安全影响大以及价值量高、生产规模相对集中的农产品优先发展冷链物流。当前要优先发展猪肉等肉类产品和水产品冷链物流，鼓励果蔬产品根据国内市场消费变化和出口产品品质要求逐步发展。要集中资金重点支持经营规模大、带动作用强的大型冷链物流企业，鼓励冷链物流企业做强做大。

（三）发展目标

到2015年，建成一批效率高、规模大、技术新的跨区域冷链物流配送中心，冷链物流核心技术得到广泛推广，形成一批具有较强资源整合能力和国际竞争力的核心冷链物流企业，初步建成布局合理、设施先进、上下游衔接、功能完善、管理规范、标准健全的农产品冷链物流服务体系。肉类和水产品冷链物流水平显著提高，食品安全保障能力显著增强；果蔬冷链物流进一步加快发展。果蔬、肉类、水产品冷链流通率分别提高到20%、30%、36%以上，冷藏运输率分别提高到30%、50%、65%左右，流通环节产品腐损率分别降至15%、8%、10%以下。

三、主要任务

（一）推广现代冷链物流理念与技术

进一步加大对全程冷链重要性的宣传力度，提高公众对生鲜农产品冷链的认知度，营造促进品牌生鲜农产品销售的商业氛围，促进优质优价，扩大销售规模。鼓励农产品生产企业利用冷链物流理念与技术，在产后商品化处理、屠宰加工环节实现低温控制，促进生鲜农产品质量等级化、包装规格化，加强与下游企业的冷链对接，稳妥推进冷链物流服务外包。鼓励流通和冷链物流服务企业运用供应链管理技术与方法，实现生鲜农产品从产地到销地的一体化冷链物流运作。加强各相关企业温度监控和追溯体系建设，实现农产品在生产流通各环节的品质可控性和安全性。

（二）完善冷链物流标准体系

重点制定和推广一批农产品冷链物流操作规范和技术标准，建立以HACCP为基础的全程质量控制体系，积极推行质量安全认证和市场准入制度。一是制订各类生鲜农产品原料处理、分选、加工与包装、冷却冷冻、冷库储藏、包装标识、冷藏运输、批发配送、分销零售等环节的保鲜技术和制冷保温技术标准。制定冷链各环节有关设施设备、工程设计安装标准；二是围绕生鲜农产品质量全程监控和质量追溯制度的建立和发展，制定数据采集、数据交换、信息管理等信息类标准；三是建立符合国际规范的HACCP、GMP、GAP（良好农业规范）、ISO（国际标准化组织）等质量安全认证制度和市场准入制度。四是对于肉类、水产品等密切关系居民消费安全的产品，执行国家强制性标准。

（三）建立主要品种和重点地区农产品冷链物流体系

1. 鼓励肉类农产品冷链物流发展　积极发展覆盖生产、储存、运输及销售整个环节的冷链，建立全程“无断链”的肉类冷链物流体系。重点发展猪肉冷链物流，减少生猪活体的跨区域运输，积极发展从中部、华南地区到珠三角、长三角、港澳等沿海地区，从东北地区到京津地区的冷链物流体系。围绕肉类屠宰加工企业，加快大中城市猪肉冷链配送发展，推广品牌冷鲜肉消费。积极发展牛羊肉冷链物流，逐步完善从中部地区到京津、环渤海和长三角地区，西北地区到中亚和中东市场，西南地区到华南地区的牛羊肉冷链物流体系。

2. 加快推广水产品冷链物流体系建设　积极培育长三角、珠三角和环渤海地区为重点的水产品产销集中区，进一步完善水产品超低温储藏、运输、包装和加工体系，促进远洋等高端水产品消费。积极推动黄淮海、东南沿海、长江流域等水产品优势产区到中西部大中城市的水产品冷链物流体系，提高内陆居民水产品消费量。

3. 逐步推进果蔬冷链物流发展　适应市场需要，选择部分高价值的特色蔬菜、水果推广产后预冷、初加工、储存保鲜和低温运输技术，发展一体化冷链物流，建立跨地区长途调运的冷链物流体系，促进反季节销售。积极推动苹果、柑橘、葡萄、香梨、热带水果等特色水果产区到大中城市的水果冷链物流体系，以及蒜薹、芦笋等反季节蔬菜和特色蔬菜的南菜北运、东菜西输冷链物流体系建设。积极推进乳制品、冰激凌及速冻产品等其他产品的冷链物流发展。

（四）加快培育第三方冷链物流企业

培育一批经济实力雄厚、经营理念和管理方式先进、核心竞争力强的大型冷链物流企业。鼓励大型生鲜农产品生产企业从生产源头实现低温控制，积极发展冷链运输和低温销售，建立以生产企业为核心的冷链物流体系。鼓励企业在产地、销地建设低温保鲜设施，实现产地市场和销地市场冷链物流的高效对接。鼓励大型零售企业加快生鲜食品配送中心建设，在做好企业内部配送的基础上逐步发展为社会提供公共服务的第三方冷链物流中心。

（五）加强冷链物流基础设施建设

鼓励冷链物流企业加快各类保鲜、冷藏、冷冻、预冷、运输、查验等冷链物流基础设施建设。从关键环节入手，重点加强批发市场等重要农产品物流节点的冷藏设施建设，在大中城市周边加快规划布局一批生鲜农产品低温配送和处理中心；大力改善农产品加工环节的温控设施，建设经济适用的农产品预冷设施；配备节能、环保的长短途冷链运输车辆，推广全程温度监控设备；完善与冷链物流相配套的查验与检测基础设施建设推广应用快速准确的检测设备和试剂。

（六）加快冷链物流装备与技术升级

加快节能环保的各种新型冷链物流技术的自主研发、引进消化和吸收，重点加强各种高性能冷却、冷冻设备自动化分拣、清洗和加工包装设备，冷链物流监控追溯系统、温控设施以及经济适用的农产品预冷设施、移动式冷却装置、节能环保的冷链运输工具、先进的陈列销售设备等冷链物流装备的研发与推广，完善科技成果转化的有效机制，不断提高冷链物流产业的自主创新能力和技术水平。

（七）推动冷链物流信息化

依托各类生鲜农产品优势产区、重要集散地区和大中城市等集中消费地区，建立区域性各类生鲜农产品冷链物流公共信息平台，实现数据交换和信息共享，优化配置冷链物流资源，为建立冷链物流产品监控和追溯系统奠定基础。鼓励市场信息、客户服务、库存控制和仓储管理、运输管理和交易管理等应用系统软件开发，健全冷链物流作业的信息收集、处理和发布系统，全面提升冷链物流业务管理的信息化水平。推广应用条形码、RFID（无线射频识别）、GNSS（全球定位系统）、传感器技术、移动物流信息技术、电子标签等技术，建立全国性和区域性的生鲜农产品质量安全全程监控系统平台。明确冷链物流信息报送和信息交换的责任机制，提高政府监管部门的冷链信息采集和处理能力，提高行业监管和质量保证水平

四、重点工程

（一）冷库建设工程

鼓励肉类和水产品生产企业、专业冷链物流企业、农业产业化龙头企业、农产品批发市场、大型零售企业等经营主体，在技术改造和充分利用现有低温储藏设施的基础上，加快建设一批设施先进、节能环保、高效适用的冷库，满足全社会对储藏设施的急需。到2015年，推动全社会通过改造、扩建和新建，

增加冷库库容 1 000 万 t。

（二）低温配送处理中心建设工程

鼓励冷链物流企业在大中城市周边规划建设一批具有低温条件下中转和分拨功能的配送中心，集中完成肉类和水产品分割、果蔬分拣以及包装、配载等处理流程，形成冷链长短途有效衔接、生产与流通环节紧密联系的物流体系，促进其与上游的屠宰加工企业、批发市场以及下游的超市等零售市场协同推进冷链发展。

（三）冷链运输车辆及制冷设备工程

鼓励大型冷链物流企业购置冷藏运输车辆，到 2015 年，争取全社会新增冷藏运输车 4 万辆，大幅度提升冷链物流企业的冷链运输能力，提高我国生鲜农产品的冷链运输率；鼓励肉类和水产品加工、流通和销售企业购置预冷保鲜、冷藏冷冻、低温分拣加工、冷藏运输工具等冷链设施设备，提高冷链处理能力，逐步减少“断链”现象的发生。

（四）冷链物流企业培育工程

根据我国生鲜农产品生产、流通、消费格局，重点培育一批发展潜力大、经营效益好、辐射带动能力强的农产品冷链物流企业。采用政策倾斜等方式，鼓励其创新物流服务模式，加强资源整合，拓展物流服务网络，强化资产重组与战略合作，力争到 2015 年在中央及地方企业中形成 30～50 个大型冷链物流企业集团。

（五）冷链物流全程监控与追溯系统工程

按照规范化、标准化运作的要求，选择 50 个果蔬、肉类、水产品等大型农产品生产及物流企业，率先建设全程温控和可追溯系统，充分利用现有的企业管理和市场交易信息平台，建立便捷、高效、低成本的农产品冷链物流信息追溯系统。

（六）肉类和水产品冷链物流工程

加快肉类特别是猪肉，以及水产品的冷链物流体系建设。鼓励大型肉类和水产品企业改造生产流水线及温控设施，加强产品排酸、预冷等低温初加工设施建设，积极推广肉类和水产品冷藏运输和全程监控技术，推动零售环节超市、大卖场冷柜销售方式，形成“无缝化”连接的肉类冷链物流体系。加强中央直属猪肉储备冷库和地方猪肉储备冷库建设，依托企业冷库完善猪肉储备体系，提高政府对猪肉市场的调控能力。

（七）果蔬冷链物流工程

加强果蔬冷链物流体系建设，重点加强分级、包装、预冷等商品化处理和冷藏储存环节建设，推动主要产区果蔬产品冷链物流设施条件的改善；大力发展冷藏运输，逐步提高果蔬产品冷藏运输能力；完善主销区果蔬冷链配送设施建设，发展具有集中采购、跨区域配送能力的现代化果蔬配送中心。鼓励大型果蔬农产品批发市场、连锁超市、果蔬储运营销企业加快冷链物流设施建设，积极培育具有一定规模和竞争力的第三方果蔬冷链物流服务企业。

（八）冷链物流监管与查验体系工程

完善冷链物流生产、加工、储存、运输、中转、进出口等主要环节的监管和查验基础设施建设。在冷链建设重点工程中，同步建设监管和检测设施。依托现有监管和检测资源，进一步提高主要生产基地、加工基地、配送中心、中转中心、进出口口岸的查验和检测能力，提高监管水平，保障产品质量和安全。

五、保障措施

（一）加强协调

农产品冷链物流体系建设环节多、产业链长，是一个跨部门、跨行业、跨区域的系统工程，需要多方面的配合与支持。由国家发展改革委会同有关部门，加强协调配合，形成合力统一组织规划实施，协调解决冷链物流发展中的突出矛盾和重大问题，确保规划目标的实现。

（二）完善政策

兼顾农产品第三方冷链物流企业的特点，完善企业营业税差额纳税试点办法，扩大政策享受范围。对冷库建设新增用地，要在提高土地集约利用的基础上，合理安排用地。简化冷链物流企业设立时的前置审批手续，放宽对冷链运输车辆的城市交通管制；充分考虑冷链运输车辆因增加保温车厢和制冷机组使自重增加的特殊情况，合理确定运输车辆的载重量；支持冷藏运输车辆跨区域加盟，在车辆审验、车辆管理等方面提供支持。对冷链物流企业的用水、用电、用气价格与工业企业基本实现同价。

（三）整合资源

通过企业兼并重组、参股控股、合资合作等方式，整合现有生鲜农产品生产加工企业、批发市场、冷链物流企业以及港口、码头、航空航运交通枢纽的冷链物流资源，加快升级改造步伐和配套协作，建立全国性和区域性的大型低温物流中心，并采用现代经营理念、管理手段和运作模式，提高冷链物流整体质量与效率。

（四）增加投入

冷链物流设施建设要充分发挥市场机制的作用，鼓励企业加大投入，多渠道筹集建设资金。中央和地方政府可对大型冷藏保鲜设施、冷藏运输工具、产品质量认证及追溯、企业信息化等重要项目给予必要的引导和扶持。要多方面拓宽农产品冷链物流企业的融资渠道。银行业金融机构对符合条件的农产品冷链物流企业，要加大融资支持，并做好配套金融服务。

（五）鼓励创新

加强对冷却冷冻、冷藏和信息化管理等冷链物流技术和设备的创新与研发，对农产品冷链物流新工艺新技术、新型高效节能的大容量冷却冷冻机械、移动式冷却装置、大型冷藏运输设备、冷藏运输车辆专用保温厢和质量安全追溯装置等进行集中攻关与研制。

（六）培养人才

引导和推动高等学校设置冷链物流相关学科专业、开设相关课程，发展农产品冷链物流职业教育，并建立交叉研究机构，鼓励扶持行业协会、企业及有关高校结合国内外实践，开展冷链物流职业技术培训和继续教育，形成多层次的人才教育、培训体系。建立农产品冷链物流行业的人才激励与柔性机制，推动高素质人才队伍建设。将“农产品冷链物流”作为“农产品营销与储运”专业的专业（技能）方向增加至新修订的《中等职业学校专业目录》。

（七）完善法规与监督

完善冷链物流的法律法规体系，进一步加大强制性国家标准的制定力度；建立以HACCP为基础的全程质量控制体系，制定与国际接轨的冷链物流操作规范和技术标准，充分发挥现有部门和机构的作用，补充完善检测项目和内容，建立全程质量检查与监督机制。

餐饮服务食品安全百千万示范工程建设指导意见

（国家食品药品监督管理局等　国食药监食［2010］235号　2010年6月25日）

为建立健全餐饮服务食品安全责任落实的有效机制，充分发挥餐饮服务食品安全示范单位的引领带动辐射作用，进一步提高餐饮服务食品安全保障水平，国家食品药品监督管理局和商务部决定在全国开展餐饮服务食品安全百千万示范工程建设（以下简称“百千万示范工程”建设）活动。现提出如下意见：

一、充分认识百千万示范工程建设的重大意义

餐饮服务食品安全关系着人民群众的身体健康和生命安全，关系着经济健康发展、社会和谐稳定、政府形象声誉。近年来，随着监管力度不断加大，餐饮服务食品安全形势总体稳定。但由于餐饮服务单位多、小、散、低特征明显，一些深层次的问题仍然存在，餐饮服务食品安全状况仍不容乐观。餐饮服务是食品安全保障的最后一道关口，责任重大。在全国范围内开展百千万示范工程建设，建设一批示范单位，树立一批先进典型，推广一批先进经验，有利于进一步增强餐饮服务单位食品安全意识和自律意识，推动餐饮服务单位升级和健康发展；有利于创新餐饮服务食品安全监管机制，落实食品安全责任，规范食品安全秩序，提升食品安全水平；有利于动员社会各界参与餐饮服务食品安全监督，创造安全放心的消费环境，不断满足人民群众日益提高的餐饮服务食品安全需求。

二、科学把握百千万示范工程建设的目标任务

开展百千万示范工程建设，以科学发展观为指导，大力践行科学监管理念，坚持政府推动与企业争创相结合、分类指导与分级联创相结合、逐步推进与滚动发展相结合、突出重点与全面统筹相结合、政策扶持与资金扶助相结合，从2010年开始，力争在“十二五”期间，在全国创建数百个餐饮服务食品安全示范县（含县级市、区）、数千条餐饮服务食品安全示范街，数万个餐饮服务食品安全示范单位（店、食堂），形成点线面相结合的多层次、全方位、全业态的餐饮服务食品安全示范群体，充分发挥示范单位的引领带动辐射作用，促进餐饮服务食品安全保障水平的稳步提高。

三、认真执行百千万示范工程建设的基本标准

（一）餐饮服务食品安全示范县

餐饮服务食品安全示范县应将餐饮服务食品安全

监管工作纳入政府目标考核体系，建立创建餐饮服务食品安全示范县领导与工作机构，独立设置食品药品监督管理部门，执法监督队伍配备有力，应急管理体系组织健全，财政支持保障充足，辖区内建立餐饮服务食品安全社会监督员队伍，设立投诉举报网络，及时处理群众投诉举报，广泛开展多种形式的食品安全宣传教育，监管工作扎实有效，达到以下基本要求：辖区内餐饮服务单位量化分级管理达到100%，其中B级以上达到80%；辖区内餐饮服务食品及餐具抽检合格率达到95%以上；农村集体聚餐备案率达到90%以上；辖区食品安全应急网络覆盖面达100%；辖区内连续三年以上未发生重大食品安全事故；辖区政府食品安全工作考核目标达到100%；公众对餐饮服务食品安全满意率达到70%以上。

（二）餐饮服务食品安全示范街

餐饮服务食品安全示范街应选择餐饮服务单位相对集中、基础好或影响大的街区开展创建工作，并满足下列基本要求：街区内不存在无证经营的现象；街区内所有餐饮服务经营单位均应诚信守法经营；配备餐饮服务食品安全社会监督员；街区内餐饮服务经营单位量化分级管理均达到B级以上；街区内餐饮服务食品安全示范单位比例达到50%以上；街区内连续两年以上未发生重大食品安全事故；公众对餐饮服务食品安全满意率达到80%以上。

（三）餐饮服务食品安全示范单位

餐饮服务食品安全示范单位应当诚信守法经营，内部管理制度健全并有效实施，各项措施符合餐饮服务食品安全操作规范，能够有效控制食品安全风险，食品安全保障水平较高，从业人员食品安全管理规范，能够全面承担食品安全责任，并达到以下基本要求：建立并执行索证索票制度，食品原料、食品添加剂、食品相关产品的可追溯率达到100%；量化分级管理被列为B级以上；从业人员健康证持证率达到100%；积极采用“五常法”或“六T法”等先进管理方法；连续三年以上未发生食物中毒事件。

四、全力做好百千万示范工程建设的组织实施

（一）制订方案

各省级食品药品监督管理部门和商务部门要按照统一部署和总体要求，结合本地实际，制订示范工程建设方案，组织开展示范工程建设。各地可结合本地实际情况，在示范工程建设基本标准的基础上，对示范县、示范街、示范单位建设标准进行补充，并积极开展省级示范县、示范街、示范单位的创建工作。在省级示范县基础上，国家食品药品监督管理局和商务部遴选国家级示范县。有关实施方案另行制定。

（二）实施步骤

2010年6月下发指导意见，启动百千万示范工程建设活动。各地迅速宣传发动，组织制定实施方案，10月底报送启动情况。各地结合实际，组织开展辖区内示范单位、示范街、示范县建设活动，并组织年度考核。每年12月底前上报年度建设活动进展情况。。

2011年开始，每年第二季度各地上报国家级示范县候选名单，第三季度国家食品药品监督管理局和商务部组织开展国家级示范县遴选工作。

五、全面推进百千万示范工程建设的基本要求

（一）提高认识，加强领导

百千万示范工程建设是国家食品药品监督管理局和商务部积极创新机制，推动落实食品安全责任的重要举措。各级食品药品监督管理部门和商务部门要从全面履行法定职责，确保公众饮食安全的高度出发，统一思想，明确任务，科学规划，精心组织，扎实推进，确保示范工程建设取得显著成效。

（二）沟通协调，齐抓共建

各地食品药品监督管理部门和商务部门要积极争取地方政府的大力支持，在当地政府的统一领导下，扎实开展示范工程建设工作。要积极协调有关部门，尤其要加强与教育行政部门、住房和城乡建设部门、旅游部门的沟通协作，共同做好学校示范食堂、建筑工地示范食堂、旅游景点餐饮示范店的建设工作。

（三）注重实效，大胆创新

各地要结合本地实际，积极创新示范工程建设的方式方法，把握好示范工程建设的代表性和示范性，及时研究解决建设过程中出现的新情况、新问题，不断推进示范工程建设向纵深发展，确保示范工程建设取得实效。

（四）典型带动，整体提高

要通过示范工程建设活动，将一批食品安全责任意识强、食品安全水平高的单位、街、县向社会进行展示和宣传，使示范工程创建在更大范围、更宽领域、更深层次开展起来，切实发挥餐饮安全示范的引领带动辐射作用，不断提高餐饮服务食品安全水平，让群众看到实实在在的成效。

（五）广泛宣传，营造氛围

各地要充分争取报刊、广播、电视和互联网等媒体的支持，采取多种形式，广泛宣传餐饮服务食品安

全示范工程的目的意义，及时宣传报道创建工作动态、进展和成效，及时总结和推广创建经验，营造创建工作的浓厚舆论氛围。

关于推进纺织产业转移的指导意见

（工信部消费品司 2010年7月2日）

为贯彻落实《纺织工业调整和振兴规划》，优化区域布局，促进纺织工业结构调整和产业升级，增强纺织工业国际竞争力和可持续发展能力，现就推进纺织产业转移提出如下意见：

一、纺织产业转移对促进结构调整具有重要意义

纺织工业是我国国民经济的传统支柱产业和重要的民生产业，也是国际竞争优势明显的产业。多年来实现了快速发展，但长期积累的结构性矛盾和问题也日渐凸显。特别是受国际金融危机的影响，占我国纺织产业规模85%的东部沿海地区要素制约加剧，成本上涨较快，竞争优势减弱，而中西部地区比较优势尚未得到充分发挥。推进纺织产业转移，对推动纺织结构调整，优化产业布局，促进纺织行业持续发展显得尤为紧迫。

推进纺织产业转移，有利于发挥东部沿海地区人才、技术、市场和信息等优势，突破土地资源匮乏、环境压力加大和人力成本上升等制约因素，提高技术创新、品牌建设和供应链管理能力，加速产业升级的步伐；有利于发挥中西部和东北地区土地、劳动力、原料、能源等比较优势，通过承接纺织和服装制造业转移，发展经济并扩大就业；有利于充分利用我国地缘广阔、区域经济互补性强的综合优势，进一步增强纺织工业的国际竞争力。

二、纺织产业转移的指导思想和基本原则

（一）指导思想

全面贯彻落实党的十七大精神，以科学发展观为指导，坚持走新型工业化道路，按照“政府引导、市场运作、优势互补、互利共赢”的方针，推进纺织产业转移，发挥区域比较优势，提高资源整合和利用能力，优化产业区域布局，提高产业竞争力，实现新一轮纺织产业发展。

（二）基本原则

1. 坚持政府引导与市场运作相结合 发挥市场配置资源的功能，突出企业主体作用，政府因势利导，创造条件，调动各方面积极性，形成企业主动、政府引导、行业协调推进产业转移和产业承接的机制，推动纺织产业转移的有序实施。

2. 坚持产业转移与产业升级相结合 产业转移要与培育优势企业、优势产业相结合，与淘汰落后、兼并重组相结合，支持企业在转移中提升，在承接中发展，增强自主创新能力，培育自主品牌，促进产业升级。

3. 坚持优势互补与互利共赢相结合 统筹兼顾东中西部特色优势，因地制宜，扬长避短，形成地区之间优势互补、互利共赢、协同发展的产业分工协作关系和错位竞争、互相依存的产业布局。

4. 坚持节能环保与持续发展相结合 产业转移要充分考虑环境要求，严格执行行业准入条件，注重节能环保，避免污染转移。禁止列入淘汰目录的生产、工艺、设备和产品的转移，防止低水平产能的无序扩张，增强后发地区可持续发展能力，实现区域经济与生态环境的协调发展。

三、纺织产业转移和区域发展重点

（一）东部地区加速产业升级步伐

东部地区发挥市场、人才、资金、信息等优势，以“优化结构、强化创新、增强服务、培育品牌”为原则，引导纺织产业向高端领域转移，加速产业升级步伐。

1. 推进中心城市都市产业建设 东部中心城市重点发展纺织服装的研发设计、品牌营销、市场推广等生产性服务业和纺织总部基地，培育建设全球或区域性纺织服装时尚创意中心、营销中心、贸易中心、品牌中心和购物（消费）中心，以贸易、商业流通带动周边地区和全行业的生产制造。

2. 促进产业集群转型升级　用高新技术改造传统产业，提升现有纺织产业集群水平，培育特色区域品牌；进一步加强产业集群区公共服务平台建设，增强服务功能，提高服务水平；重视发挥东部纺织服装专业市场作用，满足国内外客户一站式采购的服务需求。

3. 发展纺织服装高端制造业　进一步细化产业分工，发展高技术、高附加值、时尚化、差异化终端产品制造业；发展资金密集型、技术密集型、科技含量高的化纤、产业用纺织品、纺织机械制造业。

4. 因地制宜推进纺织产业转移　通过兼并重组或新增投资等方式将纺纱、缫丝、织造、制品等部分制造环节转移到具有一定产业基础的中西部和东北地区；支持有订单的纺织企业通过采购和经营合作等方式，加强与中西部和东北地区纺织企业合作；鼓励优势纺织企业以技术和管理方式加强与中西部和东北地区纺织企业的对接。

（二）中部地区完善纺织产业制造体系

中部地区发挥区位、人才、资源等优势，以“发挥优势、积极承接、加强配套、完善体系”为原则，抓住中部崛起战略机遇，重点发展棉纺织、麻纺织、针织、服装、家纺、产业用纺织品等加工制造，逐步建立和完善纺织产业制造体系。

1. 利用产业基础优势发展特色产业　河南、湖北、安徽等棉产区可利用资源优势重点承接东部棉纺织产业转移；湖南、湖北、江西等地应加快麻纺织生产基地建设；江西、河南可依托粘胶纤维产业的基础，重点推进功能化、差别化粘胶纤维开发生产。

2. 发挥比较优势发展终端产品制造业　利用紧邻东部沿海的区位优势和劳动力充裕优势发展服装、家纺等终端产品制造业，提升车用、医用等产业用纺织品制造水平，加快完善产业配套体系，壮大纺织服装生产规模。

3. 充分发挥中心城市的辐射作用带动自主品牌建设　中部地区中心城市要以发展生产型服务业为重点，优化商贸流通环境，加快专业市场建设，积极培育纺织服装自主品牌。

（三）西部地区重点发展特色产业

西部地区发挥资源、能源、劳动力等优势，以“立足资源、发展边贸、突出重点、强化特色”为原则，抓住西部开发战略机遇，发展棉纺织、丝绸、服装及其他特色产业。

1. 加快资源优势向产业优势转化　新疆应利用棉花资源优势，进一步加快优质棉纱、棉布和棉纺织品生产基地建设；内蒙古、新疆、宁夏、青海、甘肃和西藏可利用羊绒羊毛资源优势发展特色毛制品；四川、广西、云南等地发展蚕桑生产，扩大茧丝绸加工，提高产品附加值；四川、重庆、陕西等省市可适度发展棉纺织、服装业。

2. 发展民族艺术和民间工艺特色产业　利用西部地区少数民族多、文化多元、旅游资源丰富等优势，大力发展民族服装服饰、藏区藏毯、贵州蜡染、江南蓝印花布等特色产业。

3. 适度建设纺织服装加工区　新疆、西藏、云南、广西等省区应利用区位优势，结合边境地区贸易需求，建设纺织服装加工区。

（四）东北地区加快发展优势产业

东北地区利用特色原料资源、产业基础和资源枯竭型城市转型的机遇，以“发挥优势，立足提升，整合资源，拓展贸易”为原则，响应东北老工业基地振兴战略，加快发展化纤、亚麻、服装等优势产业。

1. 加快发展优势产业　黑龙江省应利用亚麻资源和加工优势，进一步提升麻纺织加工水平；辽宁、吉林应利用化工产业优势，提升腈纶、粘胶、碳纤维和产业用纺织品加工能力和水平。

2. 适度发展纺织、服装业　资源枯竭型城市发展接续产业，可以园区建设为主，发展纺织（针织）、服装等劳动密集型产业。大连、沈阳、哈尔滨等中心城市，要整合优势资源，发展服装设计、品牌营销等服务业。

四、完善纺织产业转移条件

（一）做好发展规划，促进有序转移

各地区应立足长远发展，结合纺织产业现状，做好本地区纺织发展规划。东部地区立足纺织产业升级，积极引导产业转移。中西部和东北地区充分发挥自身优势，创造条件，促进并承接纺织产业有序转入。

（二）加强合作共建，实现共同发展

东部地区应加强与中西部和东北地区的合作，按照优势互补、产业配套以及利益共享原则，探索在中西部或东北地区共建产业园区和特色产业基地，利用双方优势促进纺织产业集聚发展。

（三）培育承接载体，完善产业配套

承接地区要选择部分产业基础好、物流成本低、配套能力强的产业基地或工业园区进行重点培育，加强基地或园区的基础设施建设，完善公共服务体系，培育优势主导产业，吸引同类及关联度高的项目向基地或园区集中，提高专业配套服务的能力和效率，促进产业集群的形成与发展。

（四）稳定政策体系，营造公平环境

建立稳定、透明的政策体系，特别是承接地区应营造良好的投资环境，在招商引资、工商注册、金融服务、员工培训等方面建立健全配套服务机制，为实现纺织产业持续发展提供保障。

（五）制定承接门槛，注重节能环保

承接地区要充分考虑本地区的资源禀赋和环境承载能力，坚持集约发展，注重提升产业技术水平。要将承接产业转移与结构调整、节能减排紧密结合，制定承接门槛，将资源节约、生态环保和循环经济的理念贯穿于承接产业转移的整个过程。

五、政策保障措施

（一）发挥现有政策的引导作用

充分用好中部崛起、西部大开发、振兴东北老工业基地有关政策，完善基础设施、物流环境建设，降低运营成本，营造有利于产业转移的政策环境。现有中央预算内专项资金对符合行业规划和产业政策要求的产业转移项目要给予支持，特别支持东部与中西部、东北地区企业兼并重组的项目，促进资源优化配置。

（二）加强对产业转移项目的金融服务

积极鼓励和引导银行业金融机构为符合条件的纺织产业转移项目提供必要的金融支持，按照法律法规规定进一步拓宽贷款抵押担保物范围，不断改善和完善金融服务。

（三）各地区可制定相关的支持政策

各产业转移地区、承接地区根据国家政策和本地区实际，在符合世界贸易组织规则前提下，可制定鼓励产业转移或产业承接的地方政策，并保持政策的连续性、稳定性。

（四）加强协调，促进区域互动

加强部门间、地区间的协调，发挥行业协会、商会等中介组织作用，建立省际间产业转移信息发布平台，促进产业转移和承接双方的对接。选择具备一定基础的产业园区作为产业承接的示范园区，总结产业转移的成功经验，加强宣传引导，推进纺织产业有序转移。

放心粮油示范加工企业和示范主食厨房质量安全管理规则

（中国粮食行业协会　中粮协［2010］10号　2010年7月9日）

第一条　为规范放心粮油示范企业质量安全管理，确保产品质量合格、卫生安全，制定本规则。

第二条　本规则适用于中国粮食行业协会和各省（区、市）粮食行业协会认定的放心粮油示范加工企业和示范主食厨房（以下称“示范企业”）。

第三条　示范企业必须严格遵守国家关于产品质量和食品安全的各项法律法规，严格执行相关产品质量标准、卫生标准，建立健全质量安全管理体系，实施从原辅材料到最终产品全过程的质量安全控制。

第四条　示范企业质量安全管理体系应当包括下列基本内容：

（一）质量安全管理的方针和目标

（二）质量安全管理机构及其职责

（三）生产、质量管理人员的要求

（四）环境卫生的要求

（五）车间及设施卫生的要求

（六）原料、辅料卫生的要求

（七）生产加工卫生的要求

（八）包装、储存、运输卫生的要求

（九）有毒有害物品的控制

（十）检验的要求

（十一）保证质量安全管理体系有效运行的要求

第五条　示范企业应当建立与生产规模相适应的产品质量安全管理机构，并明确规定其职责和权限。

第六条　示范企业的生产、质量管理人员应当符合下列要求：

（一）配备足够数量的、具备相应资格的专业人员从事质量安全管理工作；

（二）企业负责人应当熟悉产品质量和食品安全法律法规；生产技术人员应当具有相关的专业技术知识；生产操作人员和检验人员上岗前应当经过培训考核，持证上岗；企业所有人员均应具有必要的食品质量安全知识；

（三）生产人员、质量管理人员每年进行一次健康检查，必要时做临时健康检查，体检合格后方可上岗；凡患有影响食品卫生疾病的人员，必须调离食品生产岗位；

（四）生产人员、质量管理人员保持个人清洁，不得将与生产无关的物品带入车间；工作时不得戴首饰、手表，不得化妆；进入车间时洗手、消毒并穿着工作服、帽、鞋，工作服、帽、鞋应当定期消毒。

第七条 示范企业的环境卫生应当符合下列要求：

（一）不得建在有碍食品卫生的区域，企业周围无有害气体、烟尘、灰尘、放射性物质及其他扩散性污染源；

（二）厂区、生产加工车间、原辅材料与成品库房、储运工具的卫生条件和企业环保措施应当符合国家规定，厂区内不得兼营、生产、存放有碍食品卫生的其他产品；

（三）厂区路面平整、无积水，厂区无裸露地面；

（四）厂区卫生间应当有冲水、洗手、防蝇、防虫、防鼠设施，墙裙以浅色、平滑、不透水、无毒、耐腐蚀的材料修建，并保持清洁；

（五）生产中产生的废水、废料及气体的排放符合国家有关规定；

（六）厂区建有与生产能力相适应的符合卫生要求的原料、辅料、化学物品、包装物料等储存设施和废物、垃圾暂存设施；

（七）生产区与生活区隔离。

第八条 示范企业生产车间及设施的卫生应当符合下列要求：

（一）必须具备与保证产品质量安全相适应的生产设施、设备；

（二）车间面积与生产能力相适应，布局合理，排水畅通；车间地面用防滑、坚固、不透水、耐腐蚀的无毒材料修建，平坦、无积水并保持清洁；车间出口及与外界相连的排水、通风处应当安装防鼠、防蝇、防虫等的设施；

（三）车间内墙壁、屋顶或者天花板使用无毒、浅色、防水、防霉、不脱落、易于清洗的材料修建；

（四）车间门窗用浅色、平滑、易清洗、不透水、耐腐蚀的坚固材料制作，结构严密；

（五）车间内位于食品生产线上方的照明设施装有防护罩，工作场所以及检验台的照度符合生产、检验的要求，光线以不改变被加工物的本色为宜；

（六）有温度要求的工序和场所安装温度显示装置，车间温度按照产品工艺要求控制在规定的范围内，并保持良好通风；

（七）车间供电、供气、供水满足生产需要；

（八）在适当的地点设足够数量的洗手、清洁消毒设备或者用品，洗手水龙头为非手动开关；

（九）根据产品加工需要，车间入口处设有鞋、靴和车轮消毒设施；

（十）设有与车间相连接的更衣室，不同清洁程度要求的区域设有单独的更衣室，视需要设立与更衣室相连接的卫生间，更衣室、卫生间应当保持清洁卫生，其设施和布局不得对车间造成潜在的污染风险；

（十一）车间内的设备、设施和工器具用无毒、耐腐蚀、不生锈、易清洗消毒、坚固的材料制作，其构造易于清洗消毒。

第九条 生产用原料、辅料的卫生应当符合下列要求并得到有效控制：

（一）生产用原料、辅料必须符合相应的质量标准和卫生标准，避免来自空气、土壤、水、肥料中的农药、重金属或者其他有害物质的污染；不得使用非食品用原料、辅料生产食品；

（二）生产用原料、辅料有检验合格证，经进厂验收合格后方准使用；采购实施生产许可证管理的产品作为原料、辅料的，应当索取该产品的生产许可证复印件并查验其有效性；

（三）超过保质期的原料、辅料不得用于食品生产；

（四）食品添加剂和营养强化剂必须符合GB 2760《食品添加剂使用卫生标准》和GB 14880《食品营养强化剂使用卫生标准》，严禁超量或超范围使用食品添加剂和营养强化剂；

（五）加工用水应当符合GB 5749《生活饮用水卫生标准》，对水质的卫生防疫检测每年不得少于两次。

第十条 生产加工过程应当符合下列要求：

（一）生产设备布局合理，并保持清洁和完好；

（二）生产设备、工具、容器、场地等严格执行清洗消毒制度，盛装熟食品的容器不得直接接触地面；

（三）班前班后进行卫生清洁工作，专人负责检查，并做检查记录；

（四）原料、辅料、半成品、成品以及生、熟品分别存放在不会受到污染的区域；

（五）按照生产工艺的先后次序和产品的特点，将原料处理、产品加工、成品包装、成品检验和成品储存等不同清洁卫生要求的区域分开设置，防止交叉污染；

（六）对加工过程中产生的不合格品、跌落地面的产品和废弃物，在固定地点用有明显标志的专用容器分别收集盛装，并在检验人员监督下及时处理，其容器和运输工具及时消毒；

（七）对不合格产品的原因进行分析，并及时采取纠正措施。

第十一条 食品的包装、储存、运输过程应当符合下列要求并得到有效控制：

（一）用于包装食品的物料必须符合卫生标准并保持清洁卫生，不得含有有毒、有害物质，不易褪色；

（二）定量包装食品的净含量应当符合《定量包装商品计量监督管理办法》，标签标识应符合GB 7718《预包装食品标签通则》或GB 13432《预包装特殊膳食用食品标签通则》；

（三）包装物料间干燥通风，内、外包装物料分别存放，不得有污染；

（四）运输工具符合卫生要求，并根据产品特点配备防雨、防尘、冷藏、保温等设施；

（五）成品库内保持清洁，定期消毒，有防霉、防鼠、防虫设施，库内物品与墙壁、地面保持一定距离，库内不得存放有碍卫生的物品；同一库内不得存放可能造成相互污染的食品。

第十二条 严格执行有毒有害物品的储存和使用管理规定，确保厂区、车间和化验室使用的洗涤剂、消毒剂、杀虫剂、燃油、润滑油和化学试剂等有毒有害物品得到有效控制，避免对食品、食品接触表面和食品包装物料造成污染。

第十三条 质量、卫生检验应当符合下列要求并得到有效控制：

（一）企业应对原料进厂、生产加工、成品出厂全过程进行检验，不合格原料不得进厂，不合格产品不得出厂；

（二）企业有与生产能力相适应的内设检验机构，具备相应资格的检验人员，检验机构应能够独立行使检验职权；

（三）企业内设检验机构具备检验工作所需要的标准资料（相关质量、卫生标准目录见附录1）、检验设施和仪器设备（必备检验仪器设备目录见附录2），检验仪器设备按规定进行计量检定；

（四）使用外部检验机构承担企业质量、卫生检验工作的，该机构应当具有相应的资格，并签订合同。

第十四条 示范企业应当保证质量安全体系能够有效运行，达到如下要求：

（一）制定并有效执行原料、辅料、包装物、半成品、成品及生产过程质量安全控制程序，做好记录；

（二）建立严于国家标准和行业标准的企业内控标准并有效执行；

（三）建立并执行质量、卫生标准操作程序并做好记录，确保加工用水、食品接触表面、有毒有害物质、虫害防治等处于受控状态；

（四）对影响质量安全的关键工序，要制定明确的操作规程并得到连续的监控，同时必须有监控记录；

（五）制定并执行对不合格品的控制制度，包括不合格品的标识、记录、评价、隔离处置和可追溯性等内容；

（六）制定产品质量追溯和召回制度，确保出厂产品在出现质量安全问题时能够及时召回；

（七）制定并执行加工设备、设施的维护程序，保证加工设备、设施处于良好状态，满足生产加工的需要；

（八）制定并实施职工培训计划并做好培训记录，保证不同岗位的人员熟练完成本职工作；

（九）建立内部审核制度，每半年进行一次内部审核，每年进行一次管理评审，并做好记录；

（十）对反映产品质量安全情况的有关记录，应当制定并执行标记、收集、编目、归档、存储、保管和处理等管理规定。所有质量安全记录必须真实、准确、规范并具有可追溯性，保存期不少于2年。

第十五条 本规则由中国粮食行业协会提出，自发布之日起施行。

第十六条 本规则由中国粮食行业协会秘书处解释。

附录：1. 质量安全相关法律、法规、标准目录（略）

2. 示范加工企业必备检验仪器设备目录（略）

保健食品审评专家管理办法

（国家食品药品监督管理局　国食药监许［2010］282号　2010年7月19日）

第一条　为加强和规范保健食品审评专家（以下简称审评专家）的聘用与管理，促进审评工作科学化和规范化，保证技术审评的公正、公平、公开，根据《保健食品注册管理办法（试行）》，制定本办法。

第二条　国家食品药品监督管理局负责审评专家的聘用和管理，并设立保健食品审评专家库（以下称审评专家库）。国家食品药品监督管理局委托保健食品审评中心承担审评专家库的日常管理工作。

第三条　审评专家库由食品科学与工程、基础医学、临床医学、公共卫生与预防医学、中医学、中西医结合、药学、中药学、化学等相关领域的专家组成。

第四条　审评专家应当具备以下基本条件：

（一）作风正派、科学公正、认真负责、坚持原则；

（二）熟悉掌握食品安全、保健食品及相关领域的法律法规、标准规范等；

（三）具备大学本科以上（含大学本科）学历；

（四）具有相应专业的正高级专业技术职称或具有博士学位副高级专业职称；

（五）在本专业具有较高的学术造诣和丰富的实践工作经验，在相应专业岗位工作5年以上；

（六）身体健康，原则上年龄在65周岁以下（院士除外）；

（七）能正常参加保健食品的技术审评会议，并能按要求承担和完成保健食品技术审评工作；

（八）本人不在保健食品相关企业任职或兼职。

第五条　国家食品药品监督管理局聘任审评专家时，可由专家所在单位推荐、专家署名推荐或省级食品药品监督管理部门推荐，也可由国家食品药品监督管理局直接提名，征得本人及所在单位同意，由国家食品药品监督管理局组织遴选，符合要求的，予以聘任并进入审评专家库。

第六条　国家食品药品监督管理局对审评专家实施动态管理，审评专家聘用期为5年。聘用期届满后，经考核合格者，可以续聘。

第七条　审评专家的主要职责是：

（一）参加保健食品审评会议，对保健食品产品进行技术审评，提出审评意见；

（二）受国家食品药品监督管理局委托，开展保健食品注册相关政策的研究；

（三）开展保健食品技术审评咨询工作；

（四）承担国家食品药品监督管理局交付的保健食品注册技术方面的其他任务。

第八条　参加保健食品审评的专家由国家食品药品监督管理局食品许可司和保健食品审评中心共同从保健食品审评专家库中选取。

按照随机原则，分专业从审评专家库中选取参加保健食品审评会议的审评专家和备选专家，组成保健食品审评会议专家委员会。备选专家人数不少于审评专家人数。

第九条　审评会议分审评大会和审评小会。审评大会负责审核首次申报产品、大会再审产品以及复审产品。审评小会负责审核补充资料产品、变更产品。

审评大会专家委员会由配方、毒理、功能、工艺、卫生学企标等相关领域的专家组成，每个领域专家不少于3名。专家委员会设主任委员1名，副主任委员1至2名。

审评小会专家委员会根据审评内容确定有关专家，人数不少于3名。专家委员会应设主任委员1名，一般由曾担任过审评大会的主任或副主任委员、资深专家担任。

第十条　主任委员和副主任委员应当由来自不同单位的审评专家担任，评委会秘书由审评专家担任。

第十一条　主任委员负责主持审评会议，副主任委员协助主任委员工作，秘书负责整理审评会议记录。

第十二条　保健食品审评中心应当在审评会议开始前5个工作日内通知参会专家。入选审评专家因故不能参加审评会议时，审评专家应当从备选专家名单中按专业依次选取。

第十三条　每次审评大会应当至少更换四分之一的审评专家，审评专家不得连续三次参加保健食品审评大会。特殊情况须经国家食品药品监督管理局同意。

第十四条　审评专家应当遵守以下规定：

（一）按照国家有关法律法规、标准规范对保健食品申报资料进行技术审评，独立、客观地提出审评意见，并对所提出的审评意见负责。

（二）以科学、公正、公平的态度从事技术审评工作，认真履行职责，廉洁自律，不得借审评之机谋取私利。

（三）按时全程参加审评会议，会议期间原则上不得请假，遇到特殊情况应当经审评委员会主任委员同意并得到保健食品审评中心批准后方可离会。

（四）对申报资料、审评意见和有关审评情况予以保密，不得抄录和外传。

（五）不得向保健食品注册申请人公开本人参加会议的信息或透露其他参加审评会议的专家名单及会议日程等。

（六）不得参与任何可能影响审评公正性的活动。

（七）有下列情形之一的，审评专家应当主动向国家食品药品监督管理局食品许可司申明并申请回避：

1. 涉及审评专家本单位参与研制产品的；

2. 审评专家签字的试验报告产品的；

3. 作为国家食品药品监督管理局认定的检验机构法人代表，遇有本单位试验产品的。

（八）接受国家食品药品监督管理局的培训、考核及监督。

（九）不得以国家食品药品监督管理局审评专家名义进行保健食品商业性活动。

（十）签署保健食品技术审评专家承诺书并履行承诺。

第十五条 国家食品药品监督管理局定期对审评专家进行考核。一次考核不合格者，半年内不得再次参加审评会议。两次考核不合格者，予以解聘。

第十六条 审评专家有下列情况之一的，国家食品药品监督管理局应当中止其审评工作，将有关情况通报审评专家所在单位，直至予以解聘；有违法行为的，按有关规定处理。被解聘的专家，国家食品药品监督管理局不再聘任其作为审评专家。

（一）违反本办法第十四条规定的；

（二）被通知参加审评会议无故不出席会议或会议期间擅自离会的；

（三）审评中出现差错并造成不良后果的；

（四）因其他原因不适于参加审评工作的。

第十七条 本办法由国家食品药品监督管理局负责解释。

第十八条 本办法自发布之日起施行。

餐饮服务食品安全监督抽检工作规范

（国家食品药品监督管理局 国食药监食［2010］342号 2010年8月23日）

第一章 总 则

第一条 为加强餐饮服务食品安全监管，规范餐饮服务食品安全监督抽检工作，根据《食品安全法》、《食品安全法实施条例》和《餐饮服务食品安全监督管理办法》等法律、法规和规章，制定本规范。

第二条 餐饮服务食品安全监督抽检是指餐饮服务食品安全监管部门对餐饮服务提供者所使用的食品（含原料、半成品和成品）、食品添加剂、食品相关产品、餐饮服务场所和环境等依法进行抽样和检验的活动。

第三条 食品药品监管部门开展餐饮服务食品安全监督抽检工作，应当坚持依法、科学、客观、公正的原则，严格遵守本规范。

第四条 餐饮服务食品安全监督抽检应当按成本价购买所抽取的样品，不得收取被抽检单位的检验费和其他任何费用。

第二章 计划和方案

第五条 餐饮服务食品安全监督抽检的重点是：

（一）餐饮服务提供者使用的主要食品原、辅料。

（二）餐饮服务提供者使用的食品添加剂和食品相关产品。

（三）餐饮服务食品加工经营的重点环节。

（四）食物中毒事件报告较多的业态和场所。

（五）对人体有潜在危害、对其安全性必须严格控制的物质。

第六条 国家食品药品监督管理局根据国家食品安全风险监测结果和食品安全监管部门食品安全风险

通报、食品安全调查与评价结果以及餐饮服务食品安全监管工作需要，制定国家餐饮服务食品安全监督抽检工作计划。

第七条 省级食品药品监管部门应当根据国家餐饮服务食品安全监督抽检工作计划和本区域餐饮服务食品安全监管工作中发现的突出问题，有针对性地制定本区域餐饮服务食品安全监督抽检工作方案，开展餐饮服务食品安全监督抽检工作。

省级食品药品监管部门应当在规定时间内将本区域餐饮服务食品安全监督抽检方案报送国家食品药品监督管理局。

第八条 餐饮服务食品安全监督抽检工作方案至少应当包括下列内容:。

（一）承担抽样任务的监管机构、负责人及其负责的抽样区域等。

（二）承担检验任务的技术机构、负责人及其负责的检验任务等。

（三）抽检样品的种类、来源、批次、频次和检验项目等。

（四）采样方法、抽样量、样品封装、传递和储运条件等。

（五）检验方法标准和检验依据或其他判定标准等。

（六）结果汇总和报送机构。

（七）完成时间和结果报送日期。

第九条 建立餐饮服务食品安全调查评价与监督抽检联动机制。国家食品药品监督管理局及时将食品安全调查与评价执行过程中发现的餐饮服务食品安全隐患通报省级食品药品监管部门。省级食品药品监管部门应当根据通报，确定重点地区、重点环节、重点产品和重点危害因素，及时开展监督抽检。

国家食品药品监督管理局根据餐饮服务食品安全监督抽检中发现的问题和隐患，结合社会经济发展需要，可适时调整食品安全调查与评价的区域、环节、品种、项目和频率等。

第十条 建立餐饮服务食品安全监督抽检与执法联动机制。对经确认不合格的样品或按程序进行复检后仍不合格的样品，食品药品监管部门应当及时依法查处。

第三章 抽 样

第十一条 监督抽检实行抽、检分离制度。抽样任务主要由当地食品药品监管部门或其执法机构负责。检验任务主要由依法取得资质认定的食品检验机构负责。根据需要，食品药品监管部门可以要求检验机构协助进行抽样和样品预处理等工作。

第十二条 抽样人员不得少于2名。抽样人员在抽样前应当向被抽检单位出示证件和监督抽检通知书，并告知监督抽检的性质和抽样内容等。

抽样人员应当准确、客观、完整填写《产品样品采样记录》或《非产品样品采样记录》，并分别加盖食品药品监管部门和被抽检单位公章，且由抽样人员和被抽检单位在场人员签字。被抽检单位无公章或无法现场盖章的，由被抽检单位负责人或者其授权的人员签字确认。

现场无法抽取到样品的，应当由被抽检单位出具抽样未果证明。

第十三条 抽取样品时，抽样量应当不少于检验需要量的3倍。对于均匀性较好的样品，应当现场分为三份，一份检验，两份留样；对于均匀性不好的样品，抽样量应当满足实验室处理分样的需要，检验前将抽取的样本分为三份，一份检验，两份留样，并做好分样操作记录。

食品安全国家标准对抽样量有特别规定的，依照其规定。

第十四条 被抽检单位遇有下列情况之一的，可以拒绝接受抽样：

（一）抽样人员少于2人。

（二）抽样人员应当携带的监督抽检通知书和证件等材料不齐全。

（三）被抽检单位或抽检品种等与监督抽检通知书不一致。

（四）抽样日期超过监督抽检通知书有效期限。

第十五条 被抽检单位无正当理由而拒绝抽样，抽样人员应当向被抽检单位告知拒绝抽样的后果和处理措施。如果被抽检单位仍拒绝抽样，抽样人员应当现场填写拒绝抽样说明书并签字，及时向当地食品药品监管部门报告，由当地食品药品监管部门按抽检不合格处理。

第十六条 抽取的样品应当严格按照样品的物理、化学和生物学等特性，或其标签标识上注明的储运条件储藏运输，以确保样品在检测前的完整性和原始性。在样品储运过程中，应当配备温、湿度测量仪表，建立温、湿度测量记录。

第四章 检 验

第十七条 承检机构应当具备食品检验机构资质，并由制定餐饮服务食品安全监督抽检工作方案的食品药品监管部门遴选和公告。

第十八条 食品检验机构接收样品时应当有专人

负责检查、记录样品的外观、状态、封条有无破损及其他可能对检验结果或者综合判定产生影响的情况，并确认样品与采样记录是否相符，对检验样品和备份样品分别加贴相应标识后入库。必要时，在不影响样品检验结果的情况下，可以将样品进行分装或者重新包装编号。

第十九条 样品的前处理应当严格按照检验方法标准的要求进行，样品处理量应当能满足方法检测限的要求。

第二十条 食品检验机构应当遵循检验规程，按照监督抽检方案中规定的方法和依据进行检验和判定。检验方法应当采用食品安全国家标准中规定的方法或其他具有法律效力的检验方法。

第二十一条 承检的食品检验机构应当按照相关要求，对检测方法进行方法学验证，按照相应标准建立本实验室的标准操作程序，并经食品检验机构技术负责人审核发布。

第二十二条 在餐饮服务食品安全监督抽检工作中，可以采用国家食品药品监督管理局认定的快速检测方法进行初步筛查。

对初步筛查结果表明不符合相关食品安全标准的，可采取临时控制措施，并依照《食品安全法》第六十条第三款的规定进行检验。

快速检测方法的认定办法另行规定。经认定的快速检测方法，由国家食品药品监督管理局公告。

第二十三条 食品检验机构未经委托检验部门同意，不得分包、转包餐饮服务食品安全监督抽检任务。

第二十四条 检验过程中遇有样品失效或者其他致使检验无法进行的情况时，必须如实记录，经食品检验机构的质量负责人签字确认，并具有相应的证明材料。

第二十五条 检验数据处理应当遵循测量误差与数据处理技术规程。

第二十六条 检验结果接近限量标准的临界值时，承检的食品检验机构应当重新选择实验室备份样品安排复检，复检结果为最终结果。

第二十七条 食品检验机构应当将检验结果及时报送委托检验的食品药品监管部门。对检验结果不合格的，还应当附具检验报告。

第二十八条 被抽检单位对检验结果有异议的，应当自收到检验结果告知书之日起 10 日内，向委托检验的食品药品监管部门提出书面复检申请，逾期则视为认同结果。

复检依照《食品安全法实施条例》第三十四条、第三十五条的规定执行。

第五章 监督管理

第二十九条 省级食品药品监管部门执行国家食品药品监督管理局下达的监督抽检任务，应当按照相关要求向国家食品药品监督管理局提交样品登记汇总表、抽检结果汇总表、不合格样品汇总表和不合格被抽检单位名录等材料，并编制监督抽检年度总结报告。

第三十条 监督抽检的结果公开应当严格遵循《食品安全法》和《食品安全法实施条例》中关于食品安全信息管理的规定，并按照本规范规定的程序，对不合格样品进行确认后方可发布。

抽检不合格产品涉及其他监管环节的，应当按照法律法规要求，将抽检结果通报有关监管部门。

第三十一条 省级食品药品监管部门应当根据相关要求，对项目执行情况进行绩效自评，并在项目总结时，将自评报告报送国家食品药品监督管理局。

国家食品药品监督管理局在项目完成 3 个月内，组织开展项目绩效评价与考核。

第三十二条 参与监督抽检的工作人员应当严格遵守国家法律法规，恪守职业道德，秉公执法，廉洁公正，不得弄虚作假。检验人员应当独立按时完成任务，保证出具的检验数据和结论客观、公正，不得出具虚假的检验报告。

第三十三条 承担监督抽检任务的单位和人员应当严格遵守国家相关保密规定。监督抽检结果未经管理部门许可，不得向任何单位和个人泄露。

第三十四条 任何单位和个人对餐饮服务食品安全监督抽检工作中的违规违法行为，有权向食品药品监管部门举报，接受举报的部门应当及时组织调查处理，并将调查处理的情况告知举报人。

第三十五条 对违反抽样工作规定的，由抽样单位做出相应的处理，并报上级食品药品监管部门备案。如抽样单位明知有违纪行为而不做处理的，由上级食品药品监管部门责成其做出处理并给予通报批评。

对违反检验工作规定，伪造检验结果，或因出具检验结果不实而造成损失的，依照《食品安全法》及相关法律法规的规定做出处理。

第三十六条 地方食品药品监管部门无正当理由未按时间要求上报数据结果的，由上级食品药品监管部门责令整改。

第六章 附 则

第三十七条 本规范由国家食品药品监督管理局

负责解释。

第三十八条 食品药品监管部门开展其他相关监督抽检工作，参照本规范执行。

第三十九条 本规范自发布之日起施行。

关于进一步加强乳品质量安全工作的通知

（国务院 国办发［2010］42号 2010年9月16日）

各省、自治区、直辖市人民政府，国务院各部委、各直属机构：

为切实加强乳品质量安全工作，严格乳品质量安全监管，提升乳品质量安全水平，保障人民群众身体健康，经国务院同意，现就有关事项通知如下：

一、严把生产经营许可关

（一）严格乳制品行业管理 各省（自治区、直辖市）要认真执行乳制品工业产业政策，对新建和改（扩）建乳制品工业项目严格进行核准，突出对起始规模、配套奶源基地、布局合理性和出资人必备条件的审核，防止盲目投资和重复建设；不符合条件的项目，不得予以核准。对已建乳制品工业项目，要于2010年年底前组织完成重新审核清理工作，届时达不到有关行业核准条件的，由质检部门依法注销生产许可证。

（二）严格乳制品生产许可 要按照从严管理的原则，进一步严格乳制品生产许可审查条件，禁止以承包、转包或租赁乳制品生产企业等方式逃避监管，禁止将乳粉再还原生产乳粉，依法严格限制乳粉分装生产行为。质检总局要于2010年10月底前修订完成乳制品生产许可审查细则。对新建乳制品生产企业，省级质检部门要严格审核把关，不符合条件的一律不予发放生产许可证；对已获得生产许可证的企业，要于2011年2月底前按照修订后的生产许可审查条件进行重新审核，对不符合条件的企业责令停止生产销售、限期整改；整改不合格的，依法撤销或吊销其生产许可证并公告名单；对撤销或吊销生产许可证的企业，当地政府要采取吊销营业执照、收回税务发票、拆除设备设施等措施，防止企业非法开工生产。

（三）加强生鲜乳收购运输许可管理 畜牧兽医主管部门要加强对生鲜乳收购站和运输车辆的许可管理，严格审核相关资质和条件，禁止向经工商登记的乳制品生产企业、奶畜养殖场、奶农专业生产合作社之外的单位和个人发放许可证；鼓励通过并购重组等方式推动生鲜乳收购站的标准化建设。对已被责令关停的生鲜乳收购站，要采取封存、拆除设备设施等措施，防止其暗自收购，并将关停信息及时通报同级质检部门及辖区内的奶牛养殖户和乳制品生产企业。

（四）强化乳制品流通许可管理 工商部门要细化和完善乳制品流通许可制度，进一步明确对乳制品经营单位的资质要求；将乳制品列为食品流通许可项目核定类别单独审核，严格按照许可项目登记营业执照的经营范围；发现销售三聚氰胺超过临时管理限量值乳制品的，一律依法吊销流通许可证。对未取得流通许可非法经营乳制品的，要依法进行处罚。

（五）严格三聚氰胺生产流通管理 工业和信息化部要尽快会同工商总局等有关部门制定三聚氰胺生产流通管理办法，进一步完善和落实三聚氰胺生产企业出厂销售用户登记制度、承诺制度和销售台账制度，并在从三聚氰胺批发商到零售商的流通全程建立销售实名登记等制度，防止三聚氰胺产品及其废料流向食品生产加工企业和饲料生产加工企业。

二、强化检验检测和监测评估

（一）加强对生鲜乳、原料乳粉和奶畜饲料的检验 畜牧兽医主管部门要以非企业自建生鲜乳收购站和生鲜乳运输车辆为重点，加大对生鲜乳的抽检频次和范围，对饲料加工厂、奶畜养殖场的奶畜饲料加强监督抽检。食品加工企业对购入的生鲜乳和原料乳粉要批批进行三聚氰胺检验，并严格执行索证索票制度。当地质检部门要对企业购入的生鲜乳、原料乳粉加强监督抽检，抽检比例不得少于所有批次的15%。

（二）加强乳制品出厂和流通环节的检验 乳制品企业必须对每批出厂产品进行三聚氰胺等检验。当地质检部门要对企业出厂产品每周进行抽检。各地工商、食品药品监管部门要加大对流通和餐饮服务环节乳制品、含乳食品质量安全的抽检范围和频次。

（三）切实做好风险监测和评估 卫生部要会同有关部门强化监测手段，合理布局食品安全风险监测点，重点加大对乳品中三聚氰胺等危害人体健康物质的监测频次；有关部门要及时向卫生部通报抽检、监测信息，卫生部要及时汇总分析相关疾病信息和抽检、监测信息，一旦在乳品中发现其他可能危害人体健康的物质，要立即组织风险评估，科学发布预警；各相关部门要采取有效措施，尽早消除隐患，防止演变为系统风险。

（四）切实提高检验效率 地方各级政府要结合本地实际，统一调配检验资源，促进资源共享和信息互通，集中力量做好重点环节、重点企业、重点产品的监督检验。各类抽检要随机进行，不得事先告知企业，特别要加大对中小企业的检查力度。农业、质检部门要建立健全本系统乳品质量安全异地抽检制度。要不断健全相关标准，完善检测方法，加快推广三聚氰胺等非食用物质的快速检测技术，提高检验质量和效率。

三、完善乳品追溯制度

（一）建立健全验证验票查询系统 质检、工商、商务部门要加快建立全国统一的乳制品生产经营单位信息数据库，详细收录包括银行开户名和账号在内的相关信息，从2011年6月开始向有关乳制品进货单位提供验证验票查询服务。相关检验机构要在检验报告上注明查询方式，并向有关进货单位提供查询服务。

（二）完善进货查验制度 农业、商务、工商、质检、食品药品监管等部门要进一步细化对乳品生产经营记录和进货查验的具体要求，并做好各环节的衔接，增强记录的可追溯性。食品生产经营单位在购入乳制品时，应核实销售乳制品的生产企业、经营单位、检验报告、发票等方面的信息，不得购入无法验证真伪的产品，确保购入产品来源正规、渠道可靠；需要质检、工商部门和有关检验机构协助确认供货者资质以及产品合格证明文件的，相关部门和机构应协助提供所需信息。发现虚假票证的，食品生产经营单位要立即向当地有关监管部门报告。监管部门发现乳品生产经营单位未按规定记录、造成产品无法准确溯源的，或未验证产品真伪即购进的，情节严重的依法责令停产停业，直至吊销许可证。

（三）建立电子信息追溯系统 质检总局、工商总局、农业部、商务部、食品药品监管局要会同有关部门抓紧研究以婴幼儿配方乳粉和原料乳粉为试点推行电子信息追溯系统，实现从奶源、采购、生产、出厂、运输到销售终端的全程有效监管，确保对产品在任何环节都能快速辨别真伪。2011年年底前完成婴幼儿配方乳粉和原料乳粉电子信息追溯系统建设和相关标准、法规的制定，并逐步在乳品行业推行电子信息追溯系统。

四、强化婴幼儿配方乳粉监管

（一）加大危害分析与关键控制点体系审核力度 质检部门要根据《乳品质量安全监督管理条例》等的有关规定，组织对婴幼儿配方乳粉生产企业推行危害分析与关键控制点体系情况进行全面检查审核，对达不到要求的企业，立即责令停业、限期整改，整改后仍达不到要求的，依法吊销生产许可证，并在当地主要媒体上公告。

（二）严格落实驻厂监督制度 各市、县级政府要指定监管部门对辖区内婴幼儿配方乳粉生产企业派员驻厂监督，监督、指导企业落实质量安全主体责任，特别要监督企业对进厂原料和出厂产品批批检验，保障婴幼儿配方乳粉质量安全。质检总局等有关部门要加强监督指导，确保驻厂监督制度落实到位。

（三）强化流通环节监管 各地工商部门要加大对婴幼儿配方乳粉经营单位的监督检查力度，以婴幼儿配方乳粉批发企业、大中型超市为重点对象，明确监管责任人，实行每周抽检；对小超市、食杂店、零售商等经常抽检。质检部门要将所有婴幼儿配方乳粉生产企业及产品名录上网公布并及时更新；工商部门要督促所有婴幼儿配方乳粉经营单位严格按照公布的生产企业和产品名录进货，对不在名录内的婴幼儿配方乳粉要立即检查、发出消费警示，并追查来源、依法打击。

五、加大对非法生产经营乳品行为的打击惩处力度

（一）全面清剿非法生产经营乳品“黑窝点” 在省级政府统一领导下，各市、县要明确政府分管负责人牵头，统筹协调有关部门，全面彻底清剿非法生产经营乳品“黑窝点”、非法制售三聚氰胺及其调和物“黑窝点”以及藏匿三聚氰胺超过临时管理限量值乳粉“黑窝点”；要保持高压打击态势，对农村及城乡结合部、城镇临时建筑、出租库房等重点区域进行经常性排查，及时发现、取缔各类“黑窝点”。辖区内出现“黑窝点”且未被及时清剿的，或发现仍有藏匿三聚氰胺超过临时管理限量值乳粉未被清缴且重新流入食品生产、经营、消费环节的，要严肃追究当地政府和有关部门负责人的责任。

（二）加大案件侦办力度 食品生产经营单位及

食品检验检测机构在乳品或含乳食品中检出三聚氰胺等非食用物质的，要立即向监管部门报告，监管部门要及时查清来源；检出三聚氰胺超过临时管理限量值的，有关监管部门要立即向当地政府报告，并向当地公安机关及有关部门通报。公安机关要及时介入，对涉嫌犯罪的要迅速立案侦查；对跨省份的案件，公安部要挂牌督办。地方政府要加强统一领导，由政府负责人统筹协调案件查处工作，确保部门工作衔接顺畅，案件查处及时有力。

（三）加大惩处力度 要加强行政执法与刑事司法的衔接，加大对乳品生产经营违法犯罪行为的刑事处罚力度。农业、工商、质检、食品药品监管等部门要尽快研究制定有关规定，对违法生产经营乳品的责任单位和人员在法律法规规定的幅度内从重进行行政处罚。

（四）充分发挥社会监督作用 各地区、各有关部门要建立健全食品安全有奖举报制度，切实落实对举报人的奖励，保护举报人合法权益，特别要鼓励生产经营单位内部人员举报和提供线索；逐步建立食品安全协防员、信息员队伍，构建食品安全投诉网络。要支持新闻媒体开展舆论监督，畅通信息交流渠道，高度重视、认真研究处理新闻媒体反映的食品安全问题，及时发布权威信息，同时要引导媒体客观公正报道，防止不实炒作。

六、严格落实乳品质量安全各方责任

（一）企业要切实履行食品安全主体责任 乳品及含乳食品生产经营单位要完善质量安全控制体系，严格执行进货查验、生产经营记录、检验检测、停开业报告、产品召回和质量安全自查自纠制度，配备专兼职食品安全管理人员，加强从业人员质量安全培训，进一步提高守法意识和诚信意识，提高质量安全管理能力和水平。工业和信息化、商务等部门要研究制定激励惩戒措施，积极推动乳品生产经营单位诚信体系建设。有关监管部门要抓紧建立所有乳品生产经营单位信用档案，及时向社会公告违法企业及其法定代表人“黑名单”，同时向投资、国土资源、建设、银行、证券等主管部门通报，对其投资、用地、融资、信贷等予以严格限制。

（二）地方政府对本地区乳品质量安全负总责 地方各级政府要建立健全乳品质量安全监管责任制，明确政府负责人及有关部门的职责；要将乳品质量安全监管列为食品安全监管的重点，切实加大人力、财力投入，依法落实各项监管及检验监测经费，保障乳品质量安全监管工作正常开展。省级财政要切实做好质监、工商等省以下垂直管理部门的相关经费保障工作。市、县级政府要进一步完善和落实对乳制品企业的政府及相关部门领导定点包厂质量安全负责制，根据日常监管情况和诚信记录，确定本地区重点乳品生产经营单位名单，明确有关部门对其实施重点监管。要将定点包厂负责人、“黑窝点”清剿负责人、驻厂监督员等责任人名单和监管及检验监测经费保障办法、重点生产经营单位监管办法等报上级政府。对工作落实不力的，严肃追究责任。

（三）有关部门要各负其责、密切配合 农业、卫生、工商、质检、食品药品监管等有关部门要切实依法履行监管职责，密切协调配合。各级食品安全综合协调机构要加强综合协调和督查指导。发展改革委、财政部要会同有关部门研究制定相关规划，加快基层农业、工商、质检、食品药品监管等部门快速检测能力建设。中央财政要在保证本级乳品质量安全监管经费的同时，继续加大对地方特别是中西部地区的支持力度。监察机关要加大行政监察和问责力度，对监管中的失职、渎职等行为，依法依纪严肃追究相关责任人的责任。

国家粮食质量检验监测机构管理暂行办法

（国家粮食局 国粮发［2010］161号 2010年10月14日）

第一条 为推进国家粮食质量检验监测体系建设，规范国家粮食质量检验监测机构行为，做好粮食质量安全监管工作，根据《中华人民共和国食品安全法》、《粮食流通管理条例》、《中华人民共和国标准化法实施条例》等法律法规及《国家粮食局关于建立国家粮食质量监测体系的通知》的有关规定，制定本办法。

第二条 国家粮食局根据开展粮食质量检验监测工作的需要，依托现有粮食检验资源，择优选用，建立国家粮食质量检验监测体系，直接承担国家粮食局委托的检验监测任务。

国家粮食质量检验监测机构（以下简称“国家监测机构”）的原隶属关系不变，人、财、物管理关系不变（中央财政给予投入且另有规定的除外）。

第三条 国家粮食局质量管理部门具体负责国家监测机构管理工作。

第四条 国家监测机构分为省级监测中心、区域监测站和综合检验中心三类，实行统一命名挂牌。省级监测中心按“省名＋国家粮食质量监测中心”命名，区域监测站按“省名＋所在地名＋国家粮食质量监测站”命名，综合检验中心按“所在地名＋国家粮食检验中心”命名。

第五条 国家监测机构应当具备下列基本条件：

（一）独立法人。科研院所、大专院校的粮食检验机构等属于非独立法人的，须经本单位法人代表授权，能够承担相应的法律责任。

（二）有稳定的公益性事业经费保障。

（三）计量认证有效。

（四）具有与承担的粮食检验监测任务相适应的人员、场所、检验仪器设备、配套设施和环境条件。

（五）具有与承担的粮食检验监测任务相适应的质量管理体系。

第六条 国家监测机构应当具备下列检验能力：

（一）省级中心：能够依据国家和行业粮油标准以及国家有关规定，检验各类粮油产品的质量、内在品质和卫生安全项目；具有结合本省（自治区、直辖市）实际，开展主要粮油产品质量跟踪和标准研究验证检验的能力。

（二）区域监测站：能够依据国家和行业粮油标准以及国家有关规定，检验当地主要粮油品种的各项质量、内在品质和主要卫生安全项目。

（三）综合检验中心：具有比较全面和完备的粮油产品品质和质量安全专业化检验能力，具有较强的粮油标准研究和参与国际验证检验的能力。主要依托有关科研院所、大专院校的粮食检验机构建设。

第七条 国家监测机构应当履行下列职责：

（一）协助当地粮食行政管理部门制订粮食质量安全管理制度，做好有关法律法规、方针政策和粮油标准的宣传贯彻工作。

（二）协助当地粮食行政管理部门制订粮食质量安全监测计划和经费预算，提供相应的技术支持。

（三）承担粮食行政管理部门委托的储备粮及其他政策性粮食的例行监测、质量监督抽查与普查工作。

（四）开展收获粮食的质量调查、品质测报和原粮卫生监测，提出粮食质量安全监管的重点区域、重点环节、重点项目、重点监管对象，以及粮食收购质量控制、当地粮食出库必检项目与强制检验的政策建议。

（五）在当地粮食行政管理部门的组织协调下，指导粮食经营者建立粮食质量安全内部管理制度，包括岗位责任制度、粮食出（入）库检验制度、出证索证制度、储粮药剂使用与管理制度、质量档案制度等；协助开展对粮食经营者履行粮食质量安全责任、执行国家粮油质量安全标准与技术规范情况的监督检查；指导农户科学储粮，减少产后粮食损失。

（六）承担收购、储存环节粮食质量安全的监督检验和超过正常储存年限粮食的出库检验工作。

（七）承担粮食质量安全重大事故与纠纷的调查、鉴定和评价，接受委托、仲裁等检验工作。

（八）收集、报送当地粮食质量安全信息，提出有关工作建议和意见。

（九）开展有关粮食质量安全检验技术、检验方法、检验设备等技术研究，承担国家、行业和地方粮油标准的制修订及验证工作。

（十）开展有关技术培训与咨询服务。

第八条 国家监测机构应当承担下列义务：

（一）按照国家有关法律、法规、政策和标准开展检验工作，客观、公正、及时地出具检验报告，妥善保管备份样品和检验档案，并做到随时备查，可以溯源。

（二）履行检验数据保密义务，未经委托方同意，不得擅自公开或者向他人提供检验数据。

（三）不得从事可能影响检验公正性的经营活动或其他业务，管理与检验技术人员不得在粮食经营企业兼职。

第九条 实行定期监督评审制度。国家粮食局定期组织对国家监测机构的监督评审。

（一）优选粮食质量管理、粮食检验和计量认证等高级专业技术人员，经培训并考核合格后，颁发《国家粮食质量检验监测机构监督评审员聘书》，纳入监督评审专家库。

（二）定期从监督评审专家库中抽调专家，组成监督评审组，对国家监测机构进行监督评审。每个国家监测机构在3年内，至少接受1次监督评审。

（三）监督评审内容主要包括国家监测机构的基本条件、检验能力、工作业绩和履行职责义务等情况，评定结果的认定，按照《国家粮食质量检验监测机构监督评审（自查）表》（见附件）的要求执行。

第十条 国家监测机构应于每年12月30日前向国家粮食局报送年度工作总结，并附《国家粮食质量检验监测机构监督评审（自查）表》。发现重大粮食质量安全问题以及发生领导班子成员变更情况时，应当及时报告。

第十一条 实行检验技术人员考核制度。国家监测机构应建立检验技术人员考核档案，记录检验技术人员业务培训、技能培训及考核情况，检验技术人员每年参加业务培训和技能培训时间不少于80个学时。国家粮食局定期组织国家监测机构的检验技术比对考核。

第十二条 国家粮食局为授权挂牌的国家监测机构颁发《国家粮食质量检验监测机构证书》（以下简称机构证书），并予以公告。机构证书有效期为3年。

国家监测机构在机构证书有效期满前3个月，须报省级粮食行政管理部门同意，向国家粮食局提出换证申请。国家粮食局根据申请机构完成任务、机构自身建设和专家评审考核结果等情况，确定是否延续授权。准予延续的，核发新的机构证书。

对申请机构的性质、资质、办公场地、检验能力等发生重大变化的，必须重新考核。

第十三条 国家粮食局为国家监测机构颁发“国家粮食质量检验监测机构检验专用章”（以下简称国家检验专用章）。国家检验专用章应当在机构证书有效期内使用。

国家监测机构应专门登记国家检验专用章使用情况，严格审批程序，注明使用事项、时间、经办人和审批人等。国家检验专用章的使用登记应长期保存。

第十四条 国家检验专用章仅限用于执行政府部门下达的检验、监测、抽查等任务时使用，不得用于出具企业委托检验报告和证明等其他业务。

第十五条 国家监测机构存在下列情形之一的，国家粮食局将予以警告、要求限期整改，直至撤销授权挂牌名称并收回机构证书和国家检验专用章：

（一）计量认证失效仍向社会提供数据的。

（二）出具虚假报告的。

（三）监督评审不合格的。

（四）比对考核连续两年出现不满意结果的。

（五）检验能力下降，不适应检验工作要求，或检验数据出现较大错误造成严重影响的。

（六）管理不规范，效率低下，或未履行职责义务的。

（七）瞒报、迟报或不报重大粮食质量安全事件的。

（八）违规使用国家监测机构名称和国家检验专用章的。

（九）违规开展影响检验监测结果公正性业务活动的。

（十）发生严重泄密事件的。

（十一）其他违规行为造成严重后果的。

第十六条 国家粮食局按本办法第十五条做出处罚的，由相关省级粮食行政管理部门负责监督落实。

第十七条《国家粮食质量检验监测机构监督评审（自查）表》为本办法的组成部分。

第十八条 本办法自印发之日起施行。

附件：国家粮食质量检验监测机构监督评审（自查）表（略）。

食品安全国家标准管理办法

（卫生部令　第77号　2010年10月20日）

第一章　总　　则

第一条 为规范食品安全国家标准制（修）订工作，根据《中华人民共和国食品安全法》及其实施条例，制定本办法。

第二条 制定食品安全国家标准应当以保障公众健康为宗旨，以食品安全风险评估结果为依据，做到科学合理、公开透明、安全可靠。

第三条 卫生部负责食品安全国家标准制（修）订工作。

卫生部组织成立食品安全国家标准审评委员会（以下简称审评委员会），负责审查食品安全国家标准草案，对食品安全国家标准工作提供咨询意见。审评委员会设专业分委员会和秘书处。

第四条 食品安全国家标准制（修）订工作包括规划、计划、立项、起草、审查、批准、发布以及修改与复审等。

第五条 鼓励公民、法人和其他组织参与食品安全国家标准制（修）订工作，提出意见和建议。

第二章　规划、计划和立项

第六条　卫生部会同国务院农业行政、质量监督、工商行政管理和国家食品药品监督管理以及国务院商务、工业和信息化等部门制定食品安全国家标准规划及其实施计划。

第七条　食品安全国家标准规划及其实施计划应当明确食品安全国家标准的近期发展目标、实施方案和保障措施等。

第八条　卫生部根据食品安全国家标准规划及其实施计划和食品安全工作需要制定食品安全国家标准制（修）订计划。

第九条　各有关部门认为本部门负责监管的领域需要制定食品安全国家标准的，应当在每年编制食品安全国家标准制（修）订计划前，向卫生部提出立项建议。立项建议应当包括要解决的重要问题、立项的背景和理由、现有食品安全风险监测和评估依据、标准候选起草单位，并将立项建议按照优先顺序进行排序。

任何公民、法人和其他组织都可以提出食品安全国家标准立项建议。

第十条　建议立项的食品安全国家标准，应当符合《食品安全法》第二十条规定。

第十一条　审评委员会根据食品安全标准工作需求，对食品安全国家标准立项建议进行研究，向卫生部提出制定食品安全国家标准制（修）订计划的咨询意见。

第十二条　卫生部在公布食品安全国家标准规划、实施计划及制（修）订计划前，应当向社会公开征求意见。

第十三条　食品安全国家标准制（修）订计划在执行过程中可以根据实际需要进行调整。

根据食品安全风险评估结果和食品安全监管中发现的重大问题，可以紧急增补食品安全国家标准制（修）订项目。

第三章　起　　草

第十四条　卫生部采取招标、委托等形式，择优选择具备相应技术能力的单位承担食品安全国家标准起草工作。

第十五条　提倡由研究机构、教育机构、学术团体、行业协会等单位组成标准起草协作组共同起草标准。

第十六条　承担标准起草工作的单位应当与卫生部食品安全主管司局签订食品安全国家标准制（修）订项目委托协议书。

第十七条　起草食品安全国家标准，应当以食品安全风险评估结果和食用农产品质量安全风险评估结果为主要依据，充分考虑我国社会经济发展水平和客观实际的需要，参照相关的国际标准和国际食品安全风险评估结果。

第十八条　标准起草单位和起草负责人在起草过程中，应当深入调查研究，保证标准起草工作的科学性、真实性。标准起草完成后，应当书面征求标准使用单位、科研院校、行业和企业、消费者、专家、监管部门等各方面意见。征求意见时，应当提供标准编制说明。

第十九条　起草单位应当在委托协议书规定的时限内完成起草和征求意见工作，并将送审材料及时报送审评委员会秘书处（以下简称秘书处）。

第四章　审　　查

第二十条　食品安全国家标准草案按照以下程序审查：

（一）秘书处初步审查；

（二）审评委员会专业分委员会会议审查；

（三）审评委员会主任会议审议

第二十一条　秘书处对食品安全国家标准草案进行初步审查的内容，应当包括完整性、规范性、与委托协议书的一致性。

第二十二条　经秘书处初步审查通过的标准，在卫生部网站上公开征求意见。公开征求意见的期限一般为两个月。

第二十三条　秘书处将收集到的反馈意见送交起草单位，起草单位应当对反馈意见进行研究，并对标准送审稿进行完善，对不予采纳的意见应当说明理由。

第二十四条　专业分委员会负责对标准科学性、实用性审查。审查标准时，须有三分之二以上（含三分之二）委员出席。审查采取协商一致的方式。在无法协商一致的情况下，应当在充分讨论的基础上进行表决。参会委员四分之三以上（含四分之三）同意的，标准通过审查。

专业分委员会应当编写会议纪要，记录讨论过程、重大分歧意见及处理情况。

未通过审查的标准，专业分委员会应当向标准起草单位出具书面文件，说明未予通过的理由并提出修改意见。标准起草单位修改后，再次送审。

审查原则通过但需要修改的标准，由秘书处根据审查意见进行修改；专业分委员会可以根据具体情况决定对修改后的标准再次进行会审或者函审。

第二十五条 专业分委员会审查通过的标准，由专业分委员会主任委员签署审查意见后，提交审评委员会主任会议审议。

第二十六条 审评委员会主任会议审议通过的标准草案，应当经审评委员会技术总师签署审议意见。

审议未通过的标准，审评委员会应当出具书面意见，说明未予通过的理由。

审议决定修改后再审的，秘书处应当根据审评委员会提出的修改意见组织标准起草单位进行修改后，再次送审。

第二十七条 标准审议通过后，标准起草单位应当在秘书处规定的时间内提交报批需要的全部材料。

第二十八条 秘书处对报批材料进行复核后，报送卫生部卫生监督中心。

第二十九条 卫生部卫生监督中心应当按照专业分委员会审查意见和审评委员会主任会议审议意见，对标准报批材料的内容和格式进行审核，提出审核意见并反馈秘书处。

审核通过的标准由卫生部卫生监督中心报送卫生部。

第三十条 遇有特殊情况，卫生部可调整食品安全国家标准草案公开征求意见的期限，并可直接由专业分委员会会议、审评委员会主任会议共同审查。

第三十一条 食品安全国家标准草案按照规定履行向世界贸易组织（WTO）的通报程序。

第五章 批准和发布

第三十二条 审查通过的标准，以卫生部公告的形式发布。

第三十三条 食品安全国家标准自发布之日起20个工作日内在卫生部网站上公布，供公众免费查阅。

第三十四条 卫生部负责食品安全国家标准的解释工作。食品安全国家标准的解释以卫生部发文形式公布，与食品安全国家标准具有同等效力。

第六章 修改和复审

第三十五条 食品安全国家标准公布后，个别内容需作调整时，以卫生部公告的形式发布食品安全国家标准修改单。

第三十六条 食品安全国家标准实施后，审评委员会应当适时进行复审，提出继续有效、修订或者废止的建议。对需要修订的食品安全国家标准，应当及时纳入食品安全国家标准修订立项计划。

第三十七条 卫生部应当组织审评委员会、省级卫生行政部门和相关单位对标准的实施情况进行跟踪评价。

任何公民、法人和其他组织均可以对标准实施过程中存在的问题提出意见和建议。

第七章 附 则

第三十八条 食品安全国家标准制（修）订经费纳入财政预算安排，并按照国家有关财经制度和专项资金管理办法管理。

第三十九条 发布的食品安全国家标准属于科技成果，并作为标准主要起草人专业技术资格评审的依据。

第四十条 食品中农药、兽药残留标准制（修）订工作应当根据卫生部、农业部有关规定执行。

食品安全国家标准的编号工作应当根据卫生部和国家标准委的协商意见及有关规定执行。

第四十一条 食品安全地方标准制（修）订可参照本办法执行。

第四十二条 本办法自2010年12月1日起施行。

食品工业企业诚信体系建设工作实施方案

（2010—2012年）

（工信部 工信部消费［2010］549号 2010年10月21日）

为落实国务院食品安全委员会工作部署，贯彻实施《食品工业企业诚信体系建设工作指导意见》，加快推进食品工业企业诚信体系建设，增强企业食品质量安全主体责任意识，提高企业诚信保障能力和食品质量安全管理水平，促进行业健康发展，特制定本方案。

一、指导思想和工作原则

1. 指导思想　全面贯彻落实科学发展观，以保障食品质量安全和促进行业健康发展为目标，以加强质量安全诚信为核心，以守法遵章为准绳、社会道德为基础、企业自律为重点，通过政府指导和推动，行业协会加强自律，企业履行主体责任，社会各界参与并监督，逐步建立起企业责任为基础、社会监督为约束、诚信效果可评价、诚信奖惩有制度的食品工业企业诚信体系。

2. 工作原则　食品工业企业诚信体系建设坚持制度建设与教育宣传相结合、企业履行责任与行业实行自律相结合、政府指导推动与社会监督作用相结合以及失信惩戒与诚信褒奖相结合的原则。

二、工作目标

从2010年开始，用3年左右时间，初步建立起食品工业企业诚信管理体系、企业诚信信息征集体系、企业诚信评价体系和政府部门协同推动、行业协会组织实施、食品企业积极参与、诚信责任有效落实的食品工业企业诚信体系运行机制。

通过加快推进食品工业企业诚信体系建设，食品工业企业质量信誉水平和责任意识明显提高，企业普遍建立诚信的职业道德规范和依法经营的管理规章制度，违约、违规、违法等行为得到有效遏制；食品行业协会在统一、规范的诚信标准下，基本建立起符合自身特点的行业诚信自律机制；食品工业质量管理水平和产品质量稳步提高。

三、实施思路

建立组织机构和部门协调工作机制，制定工作制度文本体系；从选择部分地区和行业试点开始，指导企业建立诚信管理体系、开展诚信自查自纠；通过统筹规划、资源整合，建立健全国家、地方及行业、企业三级信息平台，逐步形成全国统一的食品工业企业诚信信息管理系统；实行企业诚信评价及失信曝光制度，运用市场机制，发挥社会监督作用，激励企业加快诚信体系建设；总结试点经验，扩大试点范围，逐步形成诚信体系推广模式，并在全国食品行业全面推广。

四、主要任务

（一）建立诚信体系建设协调工作机制　一是建立部门联席会议制度。由工业和信息化部牵头，会同发展改革委、科技部、财政部、人力资源社会保障部、农业部、商务部、卫生部、人民银行、工商总局、质检总局、食品药品监管局、国家认监委、中国轻工业联合会、中国食品工业协会等部门（单位），建立部门联席会议制度，确定任务分工，共同推动食品工业企业诚信体系建设。二是成立食品工业企业诚信体系建设办公室。承担制定工作实施计划、组织专家指导地方和企业开展诚信管理体系试点建设、审核并管理企业诚信信息、建立并维护国家食品工业企业诚信信息平台、组织开展标准升级等工作。三是组建食品工业企业诚信体系建设专家队伍，建立专家库。发挥专家在指导企业建立诚信管理体系、开展诚信管理培训、参与企业诚信评价等方面的作用，形成诚信咨询和管理服务机制。四是建立部与省、与行业组织间的联系机制。明确各省、行业组织的职责分工及负责人，落实地方政府负总责，行业组织加强自律的责任。五是建立食品工业企业诚信体系建设工作督察及信息报送制度。定期检查食品工业企业诚信体系建设执行情况，对地方工作进行指导和督促检查。建立简报和半年、年度诚信报告制度。

（二）建立诚信建设制度和标准体系　一是发布实施《食品工业企业诚信管理体系（CMS）建立及实施通用要求》和《食品工业企业诚信评价准则》；分行业编写诚信管理体系建立及实施指南，制定诚信评价实施细则。二是制定诚信信息征集与使用管理办法，明确信息征集项目、渠道、方式，规范信息的使用和披露。三是制定诚信服务机构管理办法，规范诚信服务机构行为，培育诚信服务市场。

（三）建立企业诚信管理体系　一是开展诚信建设相关标准宣贯，指导试点企业建立诚信管理体系。二是督促企业完善检验检测手段，提升质量检测能力；加强食品生产原料管理，建立健全企业生产经营档案，完善食品安全可追溯体系。三是开展企业诚信建设自查自纠，建立企业内部诚信管理自律机制。四是总结经验，扩大试点。

（四）建立诚信信息征集和披露体系　一是建立全国统一的食品工业企业诚信信息管理平台和查询披露系统。实现部门间诚信信息资源共建共享，及时向社会公布企业诚信体系建设信息。二是加快地方、行业、企业诚信信息平台建设，促进两化融合。三是严格执行管理制度，依法采集及披露企业诚信信息（包括其他有效的信用评价信息)。

(五) 建立企业诚信评价体系 一是组织企业开展自查自评活动。指导企业依据评价准则和评价实施细则开展对标达标自我评价。二是开展试点企业诚信评价。由工业主管部门组织行业协会或第三方服务机构，选择诚信体系建设基础较好的试点企业开展试评价，并逐步向食品工业企业全面推开。三是规范诚信服务机构管理，健全诚信服务机构的服务监督、考核制度，推动诚信服务机构发展。

(六) 加强行业自律机制建设 行业协会加强自律机制建设，制定和完善行规行约，在行业内开展诚信宣言、公约、自查或互查等自律活动。企业配备专职或兼职食品安全和诚信管理人员，开展重合同、守信誉、依法生产经营的活动，倡导文明诚信经商，提高企业和员工的诚信意识和诚信水平，形成有效的企业自律机制。同时，建立企业失信举报制度，充分发挥社会监督作用。

(七) 加强诚信宣传与诚信文化建设 一是制定年度宣传计划。结合年度工作重点确定宣传主题，明确采用的媒体形式和宣传的范围等内容。二是宣传食品工业企业诚信试点工作。跟踪宣传试点进展，宣传试点地区、行业及企业的好做法和取得的成效。三是开展专题宣传活动。举办食品安全高层论坛、3·15诚信宣传和诚信兴商宣传月等活动，警示失信行为，褒扬诚信企业；组织开展知识培训、法制讲座、技术咨询、企业诚信文化国际交流等活动。

(八) 加强诚信奖惩机制建设 一是利用现有政策及资金渠道，支持国家级食品工业企业诚信信息管理平台建设、企业诚信管理体系建设和宣传、培训等工作，提高食品企业诚信保障能力。二是在国家食品储备、政府采购、招投标管理、公共服务、项目核准、技术改造、融资授信、有关资金政策、信用担保、社会宣传等方面参考使用企业诚信信息及评价结果，对诚信企业给予重点支持和优先安排。同时，以法律法规为依据，通过失信曝光、分类监管和市场退出机制等手段加大对失信企业惩戒力度，促进行业健康发展。

五、工作安排

2010年1月至2012年12月，按工作内容侧重可分为三个阶段：

(一) 建立组织机构，制定工作标准 (2010年1月至2011年12月)

由工业和信息化部牵头，会同发展改革委、科技部、财政部、人力资源社会保障部、农业部、商务部、卫生部、人民银行、工商总局、质检总局、食品药品监管局、国家认监委、中国轻工业联合会、中国食品工业协会等部门(单位)，建立部门联席会议制度。设立食品工业企业诚信体系建设工作办公室。制定企业诚信建设行业标准、实施指南、评价细则、管理办法、工作方案等制度、标准，指导和规范企业诚信体系建设工作。

(二) 组织开展试点，形成工作机制 (2010年1月—2012年12月)

选择具有一定工作基础的黑龙江省乳制品行业和河南省肉类食品行业作为诚信试点。组织试点省制订工作方案及实施计划，组织召开启动会，开展人员培训，完善管理制度，指导企业建立诚信管理体系，构建国家食品工业企业诚信信息管理平台，组织专家对企业开展食品企业诚信试评价工作。

组织召开试点阶段总结交流会，开展试点企业诚信体系建设绩效评估，总结工作经验，有序扩大试点范围。在北京、福建、广东、河北等省(市)分别开展调味品、罐头、饮料和葡萄酒及乳制品行业标准宣贯和分行业实施指南编制，扩大诚信体系建设试点范围。

(三) 总结试点经验，逐步全面推广 (2011年1月—2012年12月)

总结试点省食品企业诚信体系建设经验和做法，形成可在全国范围内推广实施的模式，统一部署，在食品行业全面推广。

在三年的诚信体系建设过程中，各部门要加强对地方的工作指导，发挥行业协会的作用，督促食品工业企业不断完善内部制度，理顺工作流程，健全食品安全可追溯体系，改进诚信管理状况，初步建立起一个自我完善，自我约束，诚信履责的良性循环长效机制，稳步提高食品工业企业诚信保障能力，全面提升我国食品行业诚信水平。

附表：2010—2012年食品工业企业诚信体系建设工作任务表(略)

中央储备粮代储资格认定办法实施细则

（国家粮食局 2010年10月26日）

为规范中央储备粮代储资格的认定行为，依据《中央储备粮管理条例》和《中央储备粮代储资格认定办法》，制定本细则。

第一章 中央储备粮代储资格的申请

第一条 中央储备粮代储资格认定受理实行属地管理。各省、自治区、直辖市及新疆生产建设兵团粮食行政管理部门（以下简称省级粮食行政管理部门）负责本行政区域内企业的中央储备粮代储资格申请受理工作。

中粮集团有限公司、中国华粮物流集团公司、中国中纺集团公司、黑龙江省农垦总局以及其他由国务院国有资产监督委员会管理的从事粮食仓储业务的企业集团公司（以下简称“企业集团”）直属企业申请中央储备粮代储资格，由企业集团负责进行现场考察，汇总后报至国家粮食局，同时抄报申请企业所在地省级粮食行政管理部门。

第二条 中央储备粮代储资格包括粮食类和油脂类中央储备粮代储资格。粮食类、油脂类中央储备粮代储资格均需单独申请。

第三条 申请企业提交中央储备粮代储资格的申请材料应使用中央储备粮代储资格认定申请软件制作，包括纸制文本（三份）和电子文本（一份），其中纸质文本应使用A4纸印制（总平面示意图除外）。

申请企业应保证申请材料的真实性。

第四条 中央储备粮代储资格认定申请软件可从国家粮食局政府网站（www.chinagrain.gov.cn）下载。

第五条 申请企业有多个独立库区的，每个独立库区的仓容量、交通条件、设备种类和数量、化验室、检化验仪器品种和数量等条件必须符合中央储备粮代储资格认定条件。其中，每个独立库区提出申请的有效仓容不得低于2.5万t或者有效罐容不得低于0.3万t。

第六条 申请企业的粮油保管员和粮油质量检验员应取得国家职业技能鉴定证书，且数量满足以下规定：

粮食类：2.5万～5万t（含2.5万t，不含5万t，下同）仓容，粮油质量检验员不少于2人，粮油保管员不少于4人；5万～10万t仓容，粮油质量检验员不少于3人，粮油保管员不少于7人；10万t及以上仓容，粮油质量检验员不少于4人，粮油保管员不少于10人。

油脂类：0.3万～5万t（含0.3万t，不含5万t，下同）容量，粮油质量检验员不少于2人，粮油保管员不少于2人；5万t及以上容量，粮油质量检验员不少于3人，粮油保管员不少于3人。

第七条 含有地下仓（含洞库）的申请企业除满足通用条件外，地下仓仓门前应有能满足80t额定载重量货车进出的场地。

第二章 中央储备粮代储资格的受理核报

第八条 省级粮食行政管理部门应建立规范的中央储备粮代储资格受理工作制度，并以一定方式向社会公布负责中央储备粮代储资格受理工作的机构名称、联系方式和工作流程。

第九条 中央储备粮代储资格认定受理工作于每年五月和十月的第三个星期一开始的5个工作日内进行，如受理时间发生变化，国家粮食局提前向社会公告。

省级粮食行政管理部门在收到企业书面申请材料后5个工作日内做出是否受理的决定，并向申请企业发出行政许可受理通知书。

第十条 省级粮食行政管理部门受理企业申请后应直接派人到现场复核企业申报材料的真实性。

第十一条 省级粮食行政管理部门应对企业提交的申请材料进行初步审查，并在受理时间截止后10个工作日内将有关材料报送至国家粮食局。省级粮食行政管理部门需要上报的资料包括：

（一）企业申请材料（二份）。

（二）行政许可受理通知书、中央储备粮代储资格认定审查意见表、省级粮食行政管理部门现场核查情况表（各一份）。

（三）中央储备粮代储资格认定申请企业汇总表、本地区开展中央储备粮代储资格认定工作情况说明（各一份）。

（四）通过中央储备粮代储资格认定省级受理软件制作的电子数据（一份）。

（五）省级粮食行政管理部门正式文件（二份）。

（六）其他应说明的情况。

企业集团也应按照本条规定的要求向国家粮食局提交材料（行政许可受理通知书、中央储备粮代储资格认定审查意见表除外）。

第十二条 取得中央储备粮代储资格后连续 3 年未承储中央储备粮的企业，其中央储备粮代储资格自动失效。企业再代储中央储备粮时，需要重新申请中央储备粮代储资格。

第十三条 中央储备粮代储资格的有效期为 5 年。企业应在有效期届满前 30 个工作日按照《中央储备粮代储资格延续申请办法》的规定提出延续申请。

第十四条 出现《中央储备粮代储资格认定办法》第三条规定的特殊情况，由中国储备粮管理总公司在粮食入库后 15 个工作日内向国家粮食局备案。备案内容包括：执行代储任务的企业名称、所有制性质、代储中央储备粮的数量等。

第三章 中央储备粮代储资格的审核

第十五条 国家粮食局负责对省级粮食行政管理部门和企业集团提交的申请材料实行预审。预审内容包括：申请企业是否属于本批认定范畴，企业名称是否符合有关规定，省级粮食行政管理部门和企业集团是否直接派人到现场复核。预审通过后交评审专家组审核。

第十六条 中央储备粮代储资格需要经过专家评审。专家评审组对企业的申请材料进行评审并提出是否授予企业中央储备粮代储资格的建议，然后由国家粮食局决定是否授予企业中央储备粮代储资格。

第十七条 国家粮食局建立由粮油储藏、粮油检验、粮库建设、仓储管理和财务管理等方面的专业人员组成的专家库。根据评审工作需要，组成专家评审组。专家评审组由不少于 5 人的单数组成。

第十八条 国家粮食局在接到省级粮食行政管理部门上报资料后 20 个工作日内完成审核工作。如不能按期完成，经局长批准可适当延长审核时间，但最长不能超过 30 个工作日，并告知申请企业。

第十九条 中央储备粮代储资格认定审核实行公示制度。国家粮食局将审核结果在国家粮食局政府网上公示，公示期限为 7 个工作日。

国家粮食局鼓励实名举报并保护举报人信息，对于匿名举报信息，将视情况处理。

第二十条 各级粮食行政管理部门及相关单位、申请企业和其他有关单位有义务对公示期间反映的问题进行核实和澄清。

第二十一条 国家粮食局向社会公告取得中央储备粮代储资格企业名单，并向企业颁发中央储备粮代储资格证书。符合政务公开规定的信息同时在国家粮食局政府网及相关媒体上公布。

第二十二条 国家粮食局向未取得中央储备粮代储资格的企业发出不予行政许可决定书，并抄送相关省级粮食行政管理部门和企业集团。

第二十三条 中央储备粮代储资格申请企业如果对审核过程或结果有异议，可依法申请行政复议或提起行政诉讼。

第四章 中央储备粮代储资格的管理

第二十四条 国家粮食局应加强对中央储备粮代储资格企业的监督检查，省级粮食行政管理部门和企业集团有责任协助国家粮食局加强对中央储备粮代储资格企业的监督检查，并及时向国家粮食局报告检查结果。

第二十五条 中国储备粮管理总公司应定期对承储中央储备粮的资格企业仓储管理行为进行检查，并在每年 6 月 30 日、12 月 30 日向国家粮食局通报有关检查结果。

第二十六条 中央储备粮代储资格企业的资格条件发生重要变化，企业应及时报告。资格企业需要报告的变更事项有：

（一）企业名称、法定代表人、所有制性质已经发生变化。

（二）取得中央储备粮代储资格的仓房灭失。

（三）申请中央储备粮代储资格时申报的设备、设施及检验仪器损坏、灭失后数量已不能满足中央储备粮代储资格认定条件。

（四）粮油保管员、粮油质量检验员数量减少后已不能满足中央储备粮代储资格认定条件。

（五）企业库区环境及交通条件发生变化后已不能满足中央储备粮代储资格认定条件或出现了可能危及库存粮食储存安全的危险源、污染源。

第二十七条 企业变更中央储备粮代储资格的程序：企业应在变更事项发生后 30 个工作日内报告省级粮食行政管理部门或企业集团。涉及企业名称、法定代表人、所有制性质变化的，企业应同时上报企业法人营业执照等有关变更证明资料的复印件；省级粮食行政管理部门或企业集团对企业报告的变更事项进行核实，汇总后随同每年的中央储备粮代储资格申请资料一并上报国家粮食局；国家粮食局确认变更事项。

涉及企业名称、资格仓容、资格仓号等变化的，国家粮食局应同时将变更情况向社会公告。涉及证书内容变化的，国家粮食局应重新向企业颁发资格证书。

第二十八条　中央储备粮代储资格企业出现下列情况，企业应在5个工作日内报告省级粮食行政管理部门或企业集团，省级粮食行政管理部门或企业集团应在接到报告后3个工作日内将有关情况报至国家粮食局。

（一）企业出现违反粮食法规、政策的事件。

（二）企业发生较大及以上等级储粮安全事故，发生人员死亡或3人及以上重伤的安全生产事故。

第五章　中央储备粮代储资格证书的管理

第二十九条　中央储备粮代储资格证书由国家粮食局颁发。证书包含以下内容：证书编号、资格类别、企业名称、取得中央储备粮代储资格的仓容仓号、有效期等。

第三十条　有效期届满或因其他原因被国家粮食局注销的中央储备粮代储资格证书不再具有法律效力，由省级粮食行政管理部门或企业集团负责收回并销毁。

第三十一条　中央储备粮代储资格证书遗失或损坏，企业可向省级粮食行政管理部门或企业集团提出补发中央储备粮代储资格证书的书面申请。经省级粮食行政管理部门或企业集团核实后，报国家粮食局核准补发。

第六章　附　　则

第三十二条　本细则自2011年1月1日起施行。国家粮食局2004年3号通告、2006年1号通告、2006年第2号公告、2007年第1号公告同时废止。

第三十三条　以下附件为本细则的组成部分：

附件：（略）

食品安全信息公布管理办法

（卫生部等六部门　卫监督发［2010］93号　2010年11月3日）

第一条　为规范食品安全信息公布行为，根据《食品安全法》及其实施条例等法律法规，制定本办法。

第二条　本办法所称食品安全信息，是指县级以上食品安全综合协调部门、监管部门及其他政府相关部门在履行职责过程中制作或获知的，以一定形式记录、保存的食品生产、流通、餐饮消费以及进出口等环节的有关信息。

第三条　食品安全信息公布应当准确、及时、客观，维护消费者和食品生产经营者的合法权益。

第四条　食品安全信息分为卫生行政部门统一公布的食品安全信息和各有关监督管理部门，依据各自职责公布的食品安全日常监督管理的信息。

第五条　县级以上卫生行政、农业行政、质量监督、工商行政管理、食品药品监管以及出入境检验检疫部门应当建立食品安全信息公布制度，通过政府网站、政府公报、新闻发布会以及报刊、广播、电视等便于公众知晓的方式向社会公布食品安全信息。各地应当逐步建立统一的食品安全信息公布平台，实现信息共享。

第六条　县级以上卫生行政、农业行政、质量监督、工商行政管理、食品药品监督管理、商务行政以及出入境检验检疫部门应当相互通报获知的食品安全信息。各有关部门应当建立信息通报的工作机制，明确信息通报的形式、通报渠道和责任部门。接到信息通报的部门应当及时对食品安全信息依据职责分工进行处理。对食品安全事故等紧急信息应当按照《食品安全法》有关规定立即进行处理。

第七条　国务院卫生行政部门负责统一公布以下食品安全信息：

（一）国家食品安全总体情况。包括国家年度食品安全总体状况、国家食品安全风险监测计划实施情况、食品安全国家标准的制订和修订工作情况等。

（二）食品安全风险评估信息。

（三）食品安全风险警示信息。包括对食品存在或潜在的有毒有害因素进行预警的信息；具有较高程度食品安全风险食品的风险警示信息。

（四）重大食品安全事故及其处理信息。包括重大食品安全事故的发生地和责任单位基本情况、伤亡人员数量及救治情况、事故原因、事故责任调查情况、应急处置措施等。

（五）其他重要的食品安全信息和国务院确定的需要统一公布的信息。

各相关部门应当向国务院卫生行政部门及时提供获知的涉及上述食品安全信息的相关信息。

第八条 省级卫生行政部门负责公布影响仅限于本辖区的以下食品安全信息：

（一）食品安全风险监测方案实施情况、食品安全地方标准制订、修订情况和企业标准备案情况等。

（二）本地区首次出现的，已有食品安全风险评估结果的食品安全风险因素。

（三）影响仅限于本辖区全部或者部分的食品安全风险警示信息，包括对食品存在或潜在的有毒有害因素进行预警的信息；具有较高程度食品安全风险食品的风险警示信息及相应的监管措施和有关建议。

（四）本地区重大食品安全事故及其处理信息。

上述信息由省级卫生行政部门自行决定并公布。

第九条 县级以上卫生行政、农业行政、质量监督、工商行政管理、食品药品监管、商务行政以及出入境检验检疫部门应当依法公布相关信息。日常食品安全监督管理信息涉及两个以上食品安全监督管理部门职责的，由相关部门联合公布。各有关部门应当向社会公布日常食品安全监督管理信息的咨询、查询方式，为公众查阅提供便利，不得收取任何费用。

第十条 发生重大食品安全事故后，负责食品安全事故处置的省级卫生行政部门会同有关部门，在当地政府统一领导下，在事故发生后第一时间拟定信息发布方案，由卫生行政部门公布简要信息，随后公布初步核实情况、应对和处置措施等，并根据事态发展和处置情况滚动公布相关信息。对涉及事故的各种谣言、传言，应当迅速公开澄清事实，消除不良影响。

第十一条 各相关部门在公布食品安全信息前，可以组织专家对信息内容进行研究和分析，提供科学意见和建议。在公布食品安全信息时，应当组织专家解释和澄清食品安全信息中的科学问题，加强食品安全知识的宣传、普及，倡导健康生活方式，增强消费者食品安全意识和自我保护能力。

第十二条 县级以上食品安全各监督管理部门公布食品安全信息，应当及时通报各相关部门，必要时应当与相关部门进行会商，同时将会商情况报告当地政府。各食品安全监管部门对于获知涉及其监管职责，但无法判定是否属于应当统一公布的食品安全信息的，可以通报同级卫生行政部门；卫生行政部门认为不属于统一公布的食品安全信息的，应当书面反馈相关部门。

第十三条 依照本办法负有食品安全信息报告、通报、会商职责的有关部门，应当依法及时报告、通报和会商食品安全信息，不得隐瞒、谎报、缓报。

第十四条 地方各级卫生行政部门和有关部门的上级主管部门应当组织食品安全信息公布情况的监督检查，不定期对食品安全监管各部门的食品安全信息公布、报告和通报情况进行考核和评议。必要时有关部门可以纠正下级部门发布的食品安全信息，并重新发布有关食品安全信息。

第十五条 各地、各部门要充分发挥新闻媒体信息传播和舆论监督作用，积极支持新闻媒体开展食品安全信息报道，畅通与新闻媒体信息交流渠道，为采访报道提供相关便利，不得封锁消息、干涉舆论监督。对重大食品安全问题要在第一时间通过权威部门向新闻媒体公布，并适时通报事件进展情况及处理结果，同时注意做好舆情收集和分析。对于新闻媒体反映的食品安全问题，要及时调查处理，并通过适当方式公开处理结果，对不实和错误报道，要及时予以澄清。

第十六条 任何单位和个人有权向有关部门咨询和了解有关情况，对食品安全信息管理工作提出意见和建议。

任何单位或者个人未经政府或有关部门授权，不得发布食品安全信息。

第十七条 公民、法人和其他组织对公布的食品安全信息持有异议的，公布食品安全信息的部门应当对异议信息予以核实处理。经核实确属不当的，应当在原公布范围内予以更正，并告知持有异议者。

第十八条 公布食品安全信息的部门应当根据《食品安全法》规定的职责对公布的信息承担责任。任何单位或个人违法发布食品安全信息，应当立即整改，消除不良影响。

第十九条 国务院有关食品安全监管部门应当根据本办法制订本部门的食品安全信息公布管理制度。

第二十条 本办法自公布之日起施行。国家食品药品监督管理局等部门联合印发的《食品安全监管信息发布暂行管理办法》（国食药监协〔2004〕556号）同时废止。

中央储备粮油质量检查扦样检验管理办法

（国家粮食局　国粮发［2010］190号　2010年12月2日）

第一章　总　　则

第一条　为加强中央储备粮管理，规范中央储备粮质量检查扦样检验活动，推进质量检查工作制度化、规范化，根据《中华人民共和国食品安全法》、《中华人民共和国农产品质量安全法》、《粮食流通管理条例》和《中央储备粮管理条例》等有关法律法规，制定本办法。

第二条　开展中央储备粮（包括中央储备油和国家临时存储油，下同）质量检查扦样检验工作，应当遵守本办法。

第三条　中央储备粮质量检查工作由国家粮食局组织，必要时由国家粮食局会同有关部门联合组织。中国储备粮管理总公司及其分支机构，应配合做好质量检查工作。中央储备粮承储企业（以下简称承储企业）应为检查扦样提供便利条件。

地方粮食行政管理部门，应按在地监管原则，将中央储备粮及其他中央事权粮食的卫生安全状况列为日常监管内容。

第四条　国家粮食局质量管理部门具体负责组织实施中央储备粮质量检查的扦样检验工作，包括制定扦样检验方案，确定检验方式，委托有资质的检验机构承担扦样检验任务等。

第五条　承担中央储备粮扦样和检验任务的机构（以下简称"承检机构"），应取得国家粮食质量检验监测机构资质。扦样、检验人员，应当熟悉有关法律法规与政策业务知识，具有粮食质量检查扦样、检验实际工作经验。

第六条　扦样、检验要严格执行国家有关标准和规定，并符合委托任务书的要求。

第二章　扦样与送样

第七条　检验机构接到委托任务书后，应做好以下工作：

（一）准备扦样器（含深层）、分样器、记录夹、样品袋（瓶）、封条（标签）等工具和用具，复制《中央储备粮质量检查扦样登记表》（见附件2-1A、2-1B，以下简称《扦样登记表》），做好扦样人员的技术培训工作。

（二）收集和整理本省（自治区、直辖市）和中储粮分支机构粮食质量管理和粮食安全储存水分规定等文件，并报送国家粮食局质量管理部门备案。

（三）制定样品集并和转送工作方案，明确专人和车辆，确保样品按时送达。

（四）指派专业技术人员赴承储企业扦样，到每个库点的扦样人员不得少于2人。扦样人员到达承储企业后，应出示国家粮食局质量管理部门出具的委托任务书原件或复印件，按要求实施扦样、分样和封样，做好样品记录。

（五）指定专人负责核对、录入检查样品的原始信息。

第八条　承储企业应如实提供粮食库存数量、品种、货位分布、产地或来源、收获及入库年度、检验记录、粮温变化、虫害及施药情况、储粮技术措施等资料，供扦样人员查阅和记录，并派人协助扦样。

第九条　散装粮食扦样。

大型仓房和圆仓均以不超过2 000t为一个检验单位，分区扦样，每增加2 000t应增加一个检验单位。扦样点的布置应以扦取的样品能够反映被扦区域粮食质量的整体状况为原则。分区及扦样布点要求见附件1。扦样人员可根据实际情况对扦样点位置进行适当调整。同一检验单位的各扦样点应扦取等量的样品（每个取样点的样品一般不大于0.5kg，下同）并合并，充分混合均匀后分样，形成检验样品。

小型仓房可在同品种、同等级、同批次、同生产年份、同储存条件下，以代表数量不超过2 000t为原则，按权重比例从各仓房扦取适量样品合并，充分混合均匀后分样，形成检验样品。

第十条　包装粮食扦样。在同品种、同等级、同批次、同生产年份、同储存条件下，以不超过2 000t为一个检验单位，分区扦样。扦样点的布置应以确保人身安全和尽量避免破坏既有储粮形态为前提，在粮包质量分布很不均匀的情况下，可以翻包打井，扦取中层样品；如翻包打井确有困难，可在粮垛边缘和上层设点扦样。各点等量样品合并，充分混合均匀后分样，形成检验样品。

第十一条 食用植物油扦样。散装油以一个油池、一个油罐、一个车槽为一个检验单位。

扦样按从上至下的位置顺序进行，在罐内油深1/10、1/2、9/10处分别扦取顶部、中部、底部检样。顶部取样点距油面、底部取样点距罐底的距离应不少于50cm。顶部、中部、底部三层扦样质量比为1∶3∶1。将各层检样混合，充分摇匀缩分后，形成代表该油罐（池、车槽）的检验样品。

第十二条 委托任务书对扦样有特殊要求的，按其要求进行扦样。发现受潮、发热、结块、生霉、严重生虫、色泽气味异常等情况，应单独扦样和记录。

正在实施熏蒸的仓房一般不安排扦样。但应查验熏蒸记录。

第十三条 扦取的检验样品应在承储企业进行现场封样、编号，经扦样人和承储企业代表签字认可后加贴封口条。样品编号应按国家粮食局质量管理部门的统一要求执行。样品袋中应放入该样品的唯一编号条。食用植物油样品编号条应粘贴在样品瓶外。

第十四条 扦样人应核实承储企业的有关记录和凭证，现场填写《扦样登记表》和扦样布点图，详细记录相关原始信息，表中无填写内容的空格以斜杠填充，所填信息须由扦样人和承储企业负责人签字确认。《扦样登记表》一式两份，一份留承储企业，一份交承检机构。

第十五条 扦取样品应集并到承检机构，由其对照《样品登记表》逐一清点核对样品，填写《粮食质量检查样品登统表》（见附件2-2，以下简称《样品登统表》），按照《粮食质量检查专用软件》规定的内容录入样品基本信息，并将纸质文档和电子文档报国家粮食局质量管理部门。

实行跨省交叉检验或集中检验的样品，承担扦样任务的机构应在扦样工作完成后2日内，安排专人专车将样品送达指定的承检机构，并附《样品登统表》。

第十六条 运送样品，应采取低温、密闭和避光等必要措施，防止雨淋，尽量缩短在途时间，确保样品包装完好，确保样品在运送和保管期间不发生质量异常变化。备检样品应在低温条件下保存3个月。

第十七条 承检机构接收样品时，应认真检查样品包装和封条有无破损，样品在运送过程中是否受到雨淋、污染，是否存在其他可能对检验结果产生影响的情况，确认样品编号与《样品登统表》是否相符，并填写样品签收单。

第三章 检验与判定

第十八条 承检机构应做好样品接收、保存、检验场地、仪器设备、药剂和样品统一编号等前期准备工作，对检验人员进行专业培训考核，指定专人负责检验数据的录入和汇总分析。

第十九条 承检机构接收样品后应及时检验。样品的领用、传递和处理要严格执行实验室管理规程，全部过程应有翔实记录。

第二十条 原粮质量检验的主要项目为：水分、杂质、色泽气味；稻谷的出糙率、整精米率、黄粒米；小麦的容重、硬度、不完善粒、降落数值；玉米的容重、不完善粒、生霉粒；大豆的完整粒率（进口大豆为破碎粒）；其他需要增加的项目。

食用植物油质量检验的主要项目为：气味滋味、水分及挥发物、不溶性杂质、酸值、过氧化值、溶剂残留量，其他需要增加的项目。

第二十一条 质量检验项目有一项不符合国家标准或国家有关规定的，综合判定为不达标。评判是否达标时，对下列指标，应按照相应的国家检验方法标准扣除允许偏差。即：

原粮“杂质”的允许偏差不大于0.3个百分点。

稻谷“黄粒米”的允许偏差不大于0.3个百分点。

小麦“不完善粒”的允许偏差不大于0.5个百分点。

玉米“不完善粒”的允许偏差不大于1.0个百分点。

水分按当地安全储存水分判定。常规储存条件下水分超过安全储存水分的，判定为不达标。当地安全储存水分没有明确规定的，按照国家粮食质量标准规定的水分判定。待烘干新粮不作水分评价，但应加以说明并对代表数量进行单独统计。

第二十二条 稻谷、小麦、玉米和大豆、食用植物油储存品质分别按《谷物储存品质判定规则》、《粮油储存品质判定规则》国家标准及有关文件规定的项目进行检验和判定。判定结果为宜存、轻度不宜存或重度不宜存。

第二十三条 卫生检验项目按照国家粮食、油料、食用植物油卫生标准（安全标准）进行检验和判定，有一项超过卫生标准限量的，即判定为不合格。

第二十四条 承检机构收到样品后，一般应在10～20个工作日内完成检验工作，以纸质文档和电子文档两种形式向国家粮食局质量管理部门报送检验结果。纸质文档格式见附件2-3；电子文档格式应符合《粮食质量检查专用软件》的汇总格式要求。

承检机构对临界值和超标样品，要认真进行复查，确保检验数据准确、可靠。

第二十五条　国家粮食局质量管理部门负责审核、汇总质量检查检验数据，编写质量检查报告，按照有关规定向有关部门和单位通报。

第二十六条　中国储备粮管理总公司可向国家粮食局质量管理部门查询、复制质量检查扦样检验的详细资料。对检查检验结果有异议的，应自接到通报之日起 10 日内，以书面形式提出复检申请。

第二十七条　国家粮食局质量管理部门收到复检申请后，认为需要复检的，检验机构应当复检；必要时，可另行安排检验机构进行复检。复检样品原则上调用原承检机构留存的备份样品，不重新扦样。

如有充分证据证明承检机构扦样和检验不规范或存在失误的，应撤销该样品的检验报告。

第四章　工作纪律

第二十八条　扦样检验机构的工作人员在执行扦样和检验任务时，必须严格遵守国家有关法律法规，廉洁自律，客观公正，认真负责，如实记录和反映中央储备粮质量状况，发现重大质量安全问题，要立即向国家粮食局质量管理部门报告。

第二十九条　承检机构应如实上报检查检验结果，不得弄虚作假；禁止以任何方式将委托任务对外分包。

承检机构应对委托检验数据承担保密义务，未经许可不得向外提供。

第三十条　国家粮食局质量管理部门发现承检机构承担委托任务时出现重大失误或发生违规、违纪问题，应向其上级行政主管部门通报，要求限期纠正和整改，依法依纪追究有关人员的责任。

第五章　附　　则

第三十一条　国家临时储存粮、最低收购价粮、临时储存进口粮和地方储备粮（油）等政策性购销粮食质量检查的扦样和检验可参照本办法执行。

国家标准和有关文件有新规定的，按新规定执行。

第三十二条　本办法自发布之日起施行。原《中央储备粮油质量抽查扦样检验管理办法（试行）》（国粮发［2003］158 号）同时废止。

附件：（略）

4 第四部分

国内综合统计资料

国内综合统计资料
简 要 说 明

1. 本部分统计资料主要包括农林牧渔业主要产品产量、农产品加工机械拥有量及农产品加工行业固定资产投资情况、按国民经济行业分类统计有关农产品加工业现状、农产品加工业主要产品产量、农产品加工业主要产品出口创汇情况、农产品加工业部分行业与企业排序，以及我国西部地区综合统计等7部分统计数据。

2. 香港和澳门特别行政区的统计是构成国家统计总体的一部分，但根据中华人民共和国“香港特别行政区基本法”和“澳门特别行政区基本法”的有关原则，香港、澳门与内地是相对独立的统计区域。根据各自不同的统计制度和法律规定，独立进行统计工作。本部分中所涉及的统计数据均未包括香港、澳门特别行政区和台湾省。这三部分相关统计数据，另在本年鉴附录中列出。

3. 本部分统计资料数据，除已注明“资料来源”之外，其余均采用国家统计局公布的数据。

4. 本部分采用的统计数据，基本上以2009年数据为主，为了保持与上卷年鉴提供数据的连续性，有一部分统计数据在上卷基础上延续列出。

5. 本部分有关表所示“规模以上非国有企业”是指年产品销售收入500万元以上的非国有企业。

6. 本部分有关表中所示工业产值、工业增加值、工业产品销售产值、利税总额等数据未单独标注者，均按当年价格计算（当年价格即为现行价格）。

7. 本部分统计资料数据所使用的计量单位，均采用国际统一标准计量单位。对有关行业未按国际统一标准计量单位提供的数据，编辑部均按国际统一标准计量单位进行了相应换算。

8. 本部分中同一类、同一行业统计数据，由于管理渠道、统计范围、数据采集方法、时间等略有不同，加之有些行业与相关管理部门交叉较多，因此数据也略有不同。但来自同一系统的数据基本上还是一致的。

9. 本部分统计资料，依据于国家统计局、农业部、国家林业局、中国食品工业协会、中国轻工联合会、中国纺织工业协会等部门、行业提供的相关数据。开辟了“我国西部地区综合统计”专栏。由于时间短促，难免有误，请给予批评指正。

10. 本部分统计资料中符号使用说明：“空格”表示该项统计指标数据不详或无该项数据；“*”或“①”表示本表下有注解。

农林牧渔业主要产品产量统计

表1 我国主要农产品产量（2005—2009年） 单位：万t

年份	粮食						
	合计	谷物				豆类	薯类
		小计	稻谷	小麦	玉米		
2005	48 402	42 776	18 059	9 745	13 937	2 158	3 469
2006	49 804	45 099	18 172	10 847	15 160	2 004	2 701
2007	50 160	46 632	18 603	10 930	15 230	1 720	2 808
2008	52 871	47 847	19 190	11 246	16 591	2 043	2 980
2009	53 082	48 156	19 510	11 512	16 397	1 930	2 996

年份	棉花	油料				麻类	
		小计	花生	油菜籽	芝麻	小计	黄红麻
2005	571.4	3 077	1 434	1 305	62.5	110.5	8.3
2006	753.3	2 640	1 289	1 097	66.2	89.1	8.7
2007	762.4	2 569	1 303	1 057	55.7	72.8	9.9
2008	749.2	2 953	1 429	1 210	58.6	62.5	8.4
2009	637.7	3 154	1 471	1 366	62.2	38.8	7.5

年份	糖料			茶叶	烟叶	
	小计	甘蔗	甜菜		小计	烤烟
2005	9 452	8 664	788	93.5	268.3	244
2006	10 460	9 709	751	102.8	245.6	226
2007	12 188	11 295	893	116.5	239.5	218
2008	13 419	12 415	1 004	125.8	283.8	262
2009	12 277	11 559	718	135.9	306.6	281

年份	水果						蔬菜
	合计	苹果	柑橘	梨	葡萄	香蕉	
2005	16 120	2 401	1 592	1 132	579	652	56 452
2006	17 102	2 606	1 790	1 199	627	690	58 326
2007	18 136	2 786	2 058	1 290	670	780	56 452
2008	19 220	2 985	2 331	1 354	715	784	59 240
2009	20 396	3 168	2 521	1 426	794	883	61 824

注：蔬菜产量含菜用瓜。

表 2 各地区主要农产品产量（2009 年） 单位：万 t

地区	一、粮食								
	总产	其中:夏收粮食	1. 谷物						
			总产	(1) 稻谷				(2) 小麦	
				总产	早稻	中稻	晚稻	总产	其中:春小麦
全国总计	**53 082.1**	**12 348.5**	**48 156.3**	**19 510.3**	**3 335.5**	**12 660.6**	**3 514.3**	**11511.5**	**714.2**
北京	124.8	31.1	121.5	0.2		0.2		31.0	0.1
天津	156.3	54.0	154.1	11.3		11.3		54.0	3.5
河北	2 910.2	1 243.2	2 801.8	57.5		57.5		1 229.8	1.5
山西	942.0	212.9	895.8	0.5		0.5		211.1	0.2
内蒙古	1 981.7		1 677.2	64.8		64.8		171.2	171.2
辽宁	1 591.0	40.3	1 517.2	506.0		506.0		4.5	4.5
吉林	2 460.0		2 348.0	505.0		505.0		1.0	1.0
黑龙江	4 353.0		3 641.7	1 574.5		1 574.5		116.3	116.3
上海	121.7	27.9	119.5	90.0		90.0		22.1	
江苏	3 230.1	1 103.2	3 100.3	1 802.9		1 800.1	2.8	1 004.4	
浙江	789.2	58.5	716.1	666.7	67.9	498.1	100.7	23.2	
安徽	3 069.9	1 182.2	2 895.9	1 405.6	150.4	1 111.5	143.7	1 177.2	
福建	666.9	31.6	532.7	515.3	125.5	276.1	113.7	1.1	
江西	2 002.6	8.0	1 916.1	1 905.9	793.8	262.8	849.3	1.9	
山东	4 316.3	2 047.7	4 088.1	112.0		112.0		2 047.3	0.1
河南	5 389.0	3 065.0	5 159.9	451.0		451.0		3 056.0	
湖北	2 309.1	398.5	2 179.8	1 591.9	208.3	1 132.8	250.8	331.7	
湖南	2 902.7	49.5	2 750.4	2 578.6	809.7	850.3	918.6	6.4	
广东	1 314.5	100.3	1 136.7	1 058.1	519.4		538.7	0.2	
广西	1 463.2	20.3	1 373.8	1 145.9	553.3	84.7	507.9	0.6	
海南	187.6	14.9	153.9	145.9	69.9		76.0		0.6
重庆	1 137.2	155.2	813.0	511.3		511.3		51.7	
四川	3 194.6	552.8	2 632.2	1 520.2	0.8	1 519.0	0.4	423.3	1.7
贵州	1 168.3	226.5	922.5	453.2		449.6	3.5	44.5	
云南	1 576.9	236.5	1 274.4	636.2	36.4	591.7	8.1	92.3	0.7
西藏	90.5		87.8	0.5		0.5		24.6	5.1
陕西	1 131.4	426.0	1 012.9	82.5		82.5		383.1	
甘肃	906.2	341.3	681.1	3.9		3.9		261.1	114.3
青海	102.7		53.6					39.0	39.0
宁夏	340.7	76.3	298.4	64.6		64.6		73.6	53.7
新疆	1 152.0	645.0	1 099.8	48.3		48.3		627.2	200.7

（续）

地　区	一、粮　食						
	1. 谷　物				2. 豆　类		
	（3）玉米	（4）谷子	（5）高粱	（6）其他谷物	总　产	（1）大豆	（2）杂豆
全国总计	**16 397.4**	**122.5**	**167.7**	**447.0**	**1 930.3**	**1 498.2**	**432.1**
北　京	89.8	0.3	0.1	0.1	1.6	1.5	0.1
天　津	88.7		0.1		1.7	1.6	0.1
河　北	1 465.2	37.2	5.2	7.0	34.9	28.5	6.4
山　西	654.3	15.7	4.1	10.2	21.5	13.8	7.7
内蒙古	1 341.3	14.4	48.5	47.0	143.2	114.4	28.8
辽　宁	963.1	15.1	22.9	5.6	32.1	30.0	2.1
吉　林	1 810.0	3.0	25.0	4.0	85.0	82.0	3.0
黑龙江	1 920.2	4.5	21.6	4.5	618.5	591.9	26.6
上　海	2.4			5.0	1.9	1.0	0.9
江　苏	216.2			76.8	87.2	60.9	26.3
浙　江	11.7			14.6	31.2	13.6	17.6
安　徽	304.7		0.2	8.3	127.2	124.7	2.5
福　建	14.6		0.6	1.0	18.0	14.1	3.9
江　西	7.3		0.4	0.6	26.9	19.7	7.2
山　东	1 921.5	4.4	2.1	0.8	41.9	39.6	2.3
河　南	1 634.0	11.0	0.4	7.5	93.0	86.0	7.0
湖　北	244.1		1.3	10.8	44.5	25.6	18.9
湖　南	159.9		1.4	4.1	38.1	21.7	16.4
广　东	74.7	0.1		3.5	18.1	13.6	4.5
广　西	225.2	0.7	0.7	0.7	25.6	16.7	8.9
海　南	8.0				1.9	0.8	1.1
重　庆	244.5		3.5	2.0	39.8	17.0	22.8
四　川	643.0		17.2	28.5	100.3	50.4	49.9
贵　州	405.2	0.2	10.9	8.5	36.9	15.9	21.0
云　南	542.7		0.2	3.0	130.4	29.1	101.3
西　藏	2.6			60.2	2.4	0.1	2.3
陕　西	526.1	12.3	2.9	6.0	46.5	42.4	4.1
甘　肃	312.6	2.9	6.7	93.9	33.7	14.3	19.4
青　海	4.3			10.3	10.8		10.8
宁　夏	156.4	0.4		3.5	3.3	1.0	2.3
新　疆	403.4	0.3	1.6	19.0	32.2	26.5	5.7

(续)

地区	一、粮食		二、油料						三、棉花
	3. 薯类		总产	1. 花生	2. 油菜籽	3. 芝麻	4. 胡麻籽	5. 向日葵	总产
	总产	其中:马铃薯							
全国总计	**2 995.5**	**1 464.6**	**3 154.3**	**1 470.8**	**1 365.7**	**62.2**	**31.8**	**195.6**	**637.7**
北京	1.7		1.8	1.8					0.1
天津	0.5		0.5	0.3				0.2	7.1
河北	73.4	23.7	143.3	133.9	2.9	1.0	1.6	3.1	60.5
山西	24.7	19.4	17.0	2.2	0.7	0.4	5.0	5.7	8.4
内蒙古	161.3	157.2	119.6	2.9	22.4	0.2	2.9	90.0	0.1
辽宁	41.7	29.6	55.3	53.5	0.1	0.1		1.1	0.1
吉林	27.0	23.0	50.4	30.5		0.8		17.2	0.2
黑龙江	92.9	89.4	28.2	5.9	0.3	0.2		11.8	
上海	0.3		3.4		3.1				0.3
江苏	42.6		162.2	38.7	121.7	1.8			25.5
浙江	41.8	18.5	43.2	5.4	37.0	0.8			2.8
安徽	46.7	5.3	240.3	75.1	157.8	6.6			34.6
福建	116.1	26.5	26.3	24.6	1.5	0.2			
江西	59.5		102.0	38.2	60.9	2.8		0.1	12.5
山东	186.3		334.5	330.9	3.1	0.1			92.1
河南	136.1		532.9	412.6	93.1	26.2		1.2	51.8
湖北	84.8	50.0	314.1	62.6	216.5	14.2		0.7	48.1
湖南	114.2	32.2	179.2	24.7	153.4	1.1			21.2
广东	159.8	17.2	84.6	83.6	0.8	0.2			
广西	63.8	5.8	42.1	39.8	1.3	0.6		0.4	0.2
海南	31.8		9.1	8.8		2.6			
重庆	284.4	107.0	40.5	8.2	30.9	0.8		0.4	
四川	462.1	210.3	261.8	60.1	199.9	0.5		0.4	1.5
贵州	208.8	153.5	78.7	7.3	70.4			0.9	0.1
云南	172.2	151.8	50.2	7.1	41.4			0.9	
西藏	0.3	0.3	5.8		5.8				
陕西	72.0	55.2	54.4	9.7	35.6	2.0	0.5	4.8	8.6
甘肃	191.4	191.4	58.5	0.2	33.1		14.4	7.0	9.5
青海	38.3	38.3	36.6		36.2		0.4		
宁夏	39.1	39.1	13.6				5.1	8.1	
新疆	20.0	20.0	63.9	1.8	15.7	1.2	1.9	41.4	252.4

注：薯类产量按5∶1折粮计算，下同。

（续）

地区	四、麻类					五、糖料		
	总产	1. 黄红麻	2. 苎麻	3. 大麻	4. 亚麻	总产	1. 甘蔗	2. 甜菜
全国总计	**38.8**	**7.5**	**21.2**	**1.24**	**8.6**	**12 276.6**	**11 558.7**	**717.9**
北京								
天津								
河北	0.1	0.1				30.7		30.7
山西						15.4		15.4
内蒙古	1.0				1.0	109.6		109.6
辽宁						6.2		6.2
吉林	0.1					6.6		6.6
黑龙江	4.5			0.1	4.4	110.0		110.0
上海						1.6	1.6	
江苏	0.3		0.2			11.6	11.6	
浙江	0.1	0.1				81.4	81.4	
安徽	2.3	1.2	0.6	0.5		21.8	21.8	
福建						65.9	65.9	
江西	1.1	0.1	1.0			62.2	62.2	
山东	0.1					0.1		0.1
河南	4.6	4.6		0.1		28.3	28.3	
湖北	3.8	0.1	3.7			34.4	34.4	
湖南	7.7	0.1	7.6			78.2	78.2	
广东	0.1	0.1				1 253.5	1 253.5	
广西	1.0	0.9	0.1			7 509.4	7 509.4	
海南	0.1	0.1				479.2	479.2	
重庆	1.6		1.5			11.6	11.6	
四川	6.6	0.3	6.3			94.1	93.9	0.2
贵州	0.1		0.1			64.3	64.2	0.1
云南	1.8			0.1	1.5	1 761.4	1 761.3	0.1
西藏								
陕西	0.1					0.2	0.2	
甘肃	0.4			0.4		20.4		20.4
青海						0.1		0.1
宁夏								
新疆	1.6				1.6	418.4		418.4

（续）

地区	六、烟叶		七、蔬菜、瓜类			
	总产	其中：烤烟	1. 蔬菜（含菜用瓜）	2. 瓜类		
				总产	（1）西瓜	（2）甜瓜
全国总计	**306.60**	**281.40**	**61 823.8**	**8 149.1**	**6 478.5**	**1 215.3**
北京			317.1	34.6	32.8	1.2
天津			373.9	35.3	30.7	2.5
河北	0.67	0.41	6 742.1	474.6	369.0	56.9
山西	0.97	0.92	893.1	66.6	57.2	8.6
内蒙古	1.18	0.97	1 380.6	179.2	117.0	48.9
辽宁	3.15	2.92	2 604.4	178.4	102.8	38.5
吉林	6.65	3.45	968.4	189.4	129.1	58.1
黑龙江	8.29	7.32	701.2	218.3	148.1	55.5
上海			394.1	59.5	47.7	9.9
江苏	0.05	0.01	3 837.8	480.3	380.1	55.2
浙江	0.37		1 764.8	326.9	281.5	21.2
安徽	2.94	2.89	2 028.1	530.0	453.0	43.9
福建	14.56	14.46	1 521.5	81.0	67.5	8.9
江西	4.33	4.14	1 088.6	170.4	149.5	10.8
山东	11.69	11.60	8 937.2	1 309.2	1 045.3	178.1
河南	29.73	29.73	6 370.4	1 472.2	1 279.4	164.5
湖北	15.21	10.89	2 979.6	325.0	278.9	43.8
湖南	21.78	20.99	2 844.2	315.9	282.4	31.0
广东	5.36	4.80	2 567.2	98.9	71.7	10.1
广西	3.74	3.13	2 063.1	236.1	217.2	18.3
海南			410.0	82.5	62.0	3.6
重庆	9.99	8.23	1 177.4	32.3	29.9	0.2
四川	25.96	21.04	3 227.3	121.2	103.9	2.0
贵州	39.03	36.92	1 079.5	55.5	49.4	2.0
云南	91.69	88.03	1 238.2	38.9	31.4	1.7
西藏			55.1	0.4	0.4	
陕西	7.50	7.31	1 257.6	215.6	175.0	29.9
甘肃	1.23	1.02	1 145.4	182.3	145.8	13.2
青海	0.19		118.9	1.9	1.8	
宁夏	0.21	0.21	354.0	145.7	134.1	10.7
新疆	0.10	0.04	1 383.2	491.2	204.2	286.3

表 3 我国玉米主产区生产情况（2008—2009 年）

单位：万 t

地 区	2008 年	2009 年	同比增长（%）
河 北	1 442.1	1 465.2	1.61
山 西	682.8	654.3	−4.17
内蒙古	1 410.8	1 341.3	−4.93
辽 宁	1 189.0	963.1	18.99
吉 林	2 082.9	1 810.0	−13.10
黑龙江	1 822.1	1 920.2	5.38
山 东	1 887.5	1 921.5	1.80
河 南	1 615.0	1 634.0	1.18
陕 西	483.6	526.1	8.79
其 他	3 975.8	4 161.7	4.68
总 计	16 591.6	16 379.4	−1.17

表 4 各地区水果产量（2009 年）

单位：t

地 区	水 果	其中					
		苹 果	梨	柑 橘	桃	猕猴桃	葡 萄
全国总计	**122 463 930**	**31 680 788**	**14 262 979**	**25 211 024**	**10 040 200**	**875 125**	**7 940 612**
北 京	855 022	119 676	155 889		408 517	123	40 618
天 津	317 991	63 405	33 131		61 544		104 560
河 北	11 040 692	2 767 973	3 640 682		1 444 854	89	1 050 802
山 西	3 825 564	2 384 775	479 790		260 852	177	129 413
内蒙古	294 503	78 576	78 399				46 983
辽 宁	4 772 144	1 948 100	1 103 509		506 750	250	642 124
吉 林	640 620	145 764	142 198		720		144 685
黑龙江	493 241	140 670	41 164				42 206
上 海	451 590	139	32 733	235 776	95 098	352	77 123
江 苏	2 354 138	572 333	662 410	59 765	437 898	2 937	278 506
浙 江	3 854 784		382 379	1 975 382	365 679	12 491	390 359
安 徽	2 157 169	368 978	867 949	23 264	380 300	1 400	214 046
福 建	5 640 848	300	183 967	2 668 299	229 173	3 692	98 817
江 西	3 270 764		117 653	2 993 721	45 745	10 484	24 564
山 东	14 190 856	7 710 497	1 166 317		2 442 602	2 786	935 686
河 南	7 559 013	3 886 253	922 590	40 068	938 641	211 085	461 083
湖 北	4 008 568	11 445	468 461	2 747 010	566 623	10 906	123 644
湖 南	3 998 119		128 561	3 384 746	112 055	39 530	83 892
广 东	10 618 918		55 116	3 220 505	78 011		
广 西	7 746 463		193 990	2 892 339	155 297	2 198	180 790
海 南	2 679 486			44 461			
重 庆	1 807 076	6 887	259 982	1 263 348	78 000	3 876	31 124
四 川	5 683 280	408938	845 236	2 773 464	410 342	59 560	206 370
贵 州	642 161	16 177	167 719	194 240	84 796	11 783	41 734
云 南	3 038 481	269 289	278 681	383 120	173 082	992	167 090
西 藏	8 747	4 427	1 420	365	1 250		1 286
陕 西	11 504 464	8 051 728	629 939	308 028	485 471	500 286	258 829
甘 肃	2 775 594	1 856 204	320 461	3 124	161 822	128	116 185
青 海	14 575	5 729	4 835		533		109
宁 夏	567 573	327 487	22 831		18 239		115 827
新 疆	5 651 495	535 058	874 988		96 306		1 932 157

（续）

地 区	其		中			
	红 枣	柿 子	香 蕉	菠 萝	荔 枝	龙 眼
全国总计	**4 247 773**	**2 834 165**	**8 833 904**	**1 042563**	**1 695 586**	**1 259 799**
北 京	11 333	57 295				
天 津	31 134	13 843				
河 北	1 077 928	418 102				
山 西	395 660	71 476				
内蒙古						
辽 宁	115 873					
吉 林						
黑龙江						
上 海	1 721	2 751				
江 苏	13 868	51 541				
浙 江		48 671				
安 徽	18 537	164 975				
福 建	18	192 705				
江 西		18 837	906 006	41 031	127 126	234 378
山 东	1 077 117	158 520				
河 南	387 830	415 736				
湖 北	27 499	52 980				
湖 南	24 093	18 440				
广 东		122 969				
广 西	19 978	586 415	3 578 810	636 154	945 561	571 279
海 南			1 556 342	32 330	492 894	388 926
重 庆	3 580	10 558	1 595 792	296 554	110 822	34 387
四 川	11 768	42 101	1 620		307	1 905
贵 州	1 370	12 770	31 499		9 045	17 378
云 南	8 651	49 902	7 916		250	430
西 藏			1 155 919	36 494	9 581	11 116
陕 西	594 350	299 547				
甘 肃	94 108	24 031				
青 海						
宁 夏	41 407					
新 疆	289 950					

表 5　各地区茶叶产量（2009 年）　　单位：t

地　区	茶　叶	其		中		
		红毛茶	绿毛茶	乌龙毛茶	紧压茶原料	其他茶叶
全国总计	**1 358 642**	**71 944**	**1 006 302**	**159 062**	**45 096**	**76 236**
北　京						
天　津						
河　北						
山　西						
内蒙古						
辽　宁						
吉　林						
黑龙江						
上　海						
江　苏	15 721	2 337	12 958			426
浙　江	167 411	168	165 709	151	356	1 027
安　徽	82 032	3 995	72 287	72		5 678
福　建	265 659	6 545	109 187	139 082	10	10 835
江　西	26 359	3 680	19 658			3 021
山　东	11 049		11 049			
河　南	35 519		35 519			
湖　北	144 244	11 830	119 853		10 252	2 309
湖　南	98 516	17 608	51 903	628	19 879	8 498
广　东	51 410	1 780	24 966	18 731	30	5 903
广　西	36 622	710	30 468	142		5 302
海　南	1 084	75	965			44
重　庆	22 569	2 330	17 116			3 123
四　川	154 666	1 240	123 771	106	14 306	15 243
贵　州	41 883	225	28 691	4	249	12 714
云　南	182 948	19 421	161 253	146	14	2 113
西　藏	1					
陕　西	20 153		20 153			
甘　肃	796		796			
青　海						
宁　夏						
新　疆						

表 6　我国农垦系统主要农产品产量（2008—2009 年）

项　目	产　　量（万 t）		
	2008 年	2009 年	同比增减（%）
一、粮食	2 421.50	2 773.10	14.52
夏收粮食	210.20	283.40	34.82
1. 稻谷	1 240.40	1 354.30	9.18
其中：早稻	41.30	45.30	9.69
2. 小麦	258.40	382.20	47.91
其中：春小麦	129.50	216.60	67.26
3. 玉米	574.20	721.90	25.72
4. 谷子	0.66	0.35	－46.97
5. 高粱	5.40	8.05	49.07
6. 大豆	170.80	205.80	20.49
7. 薯类（折粮）	48.90	33.30	－31.84
二、棉花	163.60	141.20	－13.69
三、油料	78.50	81.10	3.31
其中：花生	9.97	9.22	－7.52
油菜籽	29.45	41.99	42.58
向日葵	29.70	25.80	－13.13
四、糖料	846.03	758.22	－10.38
其中：甘蔗	584.11	543.30	－6.99
甜菜	261.92	214.92	－17.94
五、麻类	11.70	3.60	－69.23
六、烟叶	0.68	0.36	－47.06
七、药材	2.89	1.49	－58.82
八、蔬菜、瓜类	971.69	1 216.83	25.23
九、其他农作物			
十、水果	250.63	307.77	22.80
十一、茶叶	4.97	4.68	－5.84
十二、干胶	28.17	31.70	12.53
十三、剑麻（折纤维）	3.22	3.23	0.31

表 7 各地区农垦系统主要农产品产量（2009 年） 单位：万 t

地区	粮食	棉花	油料	糖料	大豆	干胶
全国总计	**2 773.15**	**141.22**	**81.14**	**758.22**	**205.76**	**61.89**
北京	0.50					
天津	1.48	0.15			0.03	
河北	39.30	2.55	0.19	0.15	0.20	
山西	2.31	0.02	0.03	0.38	0.02	
内蒙古	159.47	0.02	27.27	1.59	15.36	
辽宁	116.83		1.00	0.13	1.50	
吉林	61.77		1.10		1.38	
黑龙江	1 652.63		3.29	46.20	171.86	
上海	21.58		0.02			
江苏	98.17	0.15	0.31	0.08	0.42	
浙江	1.51		0.03		0.32	
安徽	34.07	0.66	0.59		2.63	
福建	7.08		0.44	3.16	0.20	
江西	49.84	0.90	2.09	0.67	0.33	
山东	4.78	0.63	0.06		0.33	
河南	24.00	0.25	1.10		2.03	
湖北	87.02	6.35	9.71	1.04	1.80	
湖南	57.82	2.53	4.57	12.46	0.75	
广东	5.44		0.76	216.28	0.05	1.30
广西	1.19		0.36	220.15	0.06	0.04
海南	14.37		0.66	44.99	0.07	30.71
重庆						
四川	0.18		0.05			
贵州	0.61		0.07			
云南	4.89		0.03	44.55		29.84
西藏						
陕西	6.49	0.43	0.15		0.22	
甘肃	19.59	0.98	0.89	0.18		
青海	2.39		1.44			
宁夏	31.69		0.51		0.10	
新疆（兵团）	212.10	113.43	18.63	145.33	4.33	
新疆（农业）	22.15	7.10	1.08	6.84	0.32	
新疆（畜牧）	31.77	5.06	4.71	14.04	1.43	
热作两院	0.14					
广州						
南京						
昆明						
哈尔滨						

表 8　我国农垦系统茶、桑、果、林生产情况（2008—2009 年）

指　　标	单　位	2008 年	2009 年	同比增长（%）
一、年末实有茶园面积	khm^2	31.5	31.3	－0.6
茶叶总产量	万 t	5.0	4.7	－5.4
二、年末实有桑园面积	khm^2	1.9	1.9	
三、年末实有果园面积	khm^2	296.7	322.6	8.7
水果总产量	万 t	250.6	307.8	22.8
其中：苹果	万 t	32.4	40.6	25.2
梨	万 t	41.6	48.8	17.3
柑橘	万 t	27.8	29.0	4.2
四、年末实有橡胶园面积	khm^2	471.8	465.2	－1.4
当年橡胶开割面积	khm^2	315.3	317.4	0.7
每公顷产干胶	kg	894.4	998.8	11.7
全年干胶总产量	万 t	28.2	31.7	12.4
五、当年造林面积	khm^2	63.7	95.3	49.5
用材林	khm^2	21.7	18.7	－13.9
经济林	khm^2	11.9	17.1	43.4
防护林	khm^2	28.0	55.2	97.2
薪炭林	khm^2	0.4	0.5	16.8
特种用材林	khm^2	0.9	1.8	112.8

表 9　我国热带、亚热带作物产量（2009 年）

项　　目	单位	总计	福建	广东	广西	海南	云南
一、橡胶总产量（干胶片）	t	618 866		13 008	382	307 062	298 414
二、咖啡豆总产量（干咖啡豆）	t	70 405				202	70 203
三、椰子（按果实计）	万个	23 891		153		23 697	41
四、腰果总产量（干果）	t	370				369	1
五、香料作物（按香料油计）	t	1 119					1 119
其中：香茅草(按香料油计)	t	1 034					1 034
六、剑麻（番麻）（按纤维计）	t	97 061		33 274	57 735	6 052	

表 10　我国棉花主产区生产情况（2008—2009 年） 单位：万 hm^2、万 t

地　　区	面　　积			产　　量		
	2008 年	2009 年	同比增长（%）	2008 年	2009 年	同比增长（%）
新　疆	171.86	140.93	－17.99	302.6	352.4	16.46
山　东	88.83	80.04	－9.90	104.1	92.1	－11.53
河　南	60.60	53.73	－11.34	65.1	51.7	－20.58
河　北	69.00	62.00	－10.14	73.7	60.5	－17.91
湖　北	54.30	46.01	－15.27	51.3	48.1	－6.24
江　苏	30.05	25.23	－16.04	32.6	25.5	－21.78
安　徽	39.01	35.17	－9.84	36.3	34.6	－4.68
湖　南	18.30	15.26	－16.61	24.7	21.2	－14.17
主产区总计	531.95	458.37	－13.83	690.4	586.1	－0.62
全国总计	**575.41**	**495.18**	**－13.94**	**749.2**	**637.7**	**－7.63**
主产区占全国比重（%）	92.45	92.57	0.13	92.15	91.91	8.61

表 11　各地区蔬菜产量增减情况（2008—2009 年）

单位：万 t

地　　区	2008 年	2009 年	同比增长（%）
全国总计	**59 240.3**	**61 823.8**	**4.36**
北　京	321.3	317.1	－1.31
天　津	314.2	373.9	19.00
河　北	6 684.6	6 742.1	0.86
山　西	852.8	893.1	4.73
内蒙古	1 360.8	1 380.6	1.46
辽　宁	2 438.3	2 604.4	6.81
吉　林	857.6	968.4	12.92
黑龙江	1 057.9	701.2	－33.72
上　海	409.9	394.1	－3.85
江　苏	3 544.7	3 837.8	8.27
浙　江	1 757.9	1 764.8	0.39
安　徽	1 923.5	2 028.1	5.44
福　建	1 480.3	1 521.5	2.78
江　西	1 084.9	1 088.6	0.34
山　东	8 634.9	8 937.2	3.54
河　南	6 394.3	6 370.4	－0.37
湖　北	2 890.6	2 979.6	3.08
湖　南	2 578.2	2 844.2	10.32
广　东	2 431.4	2 567.2	5.59
广　西	2 015.2	2 063.1	2.38
海　南	379.2	410.0	8.12
重　庆	994.5	1 177.4	18.39
四　川	3 078.3	3 227.3	4.84
贵　州	991.1	1 079.5	8.92
云　南	1 166.6	1 238.2	6.14
西　藏	48.1	55.1	14.55
陕　西	1 067.1	1 257.6	17.85
甘　肃	1 082.3	1 145.4	5.83
青　海	110.1	118.9	7.99
宁　夏	318.9	354.0	11.01
新　疆	970.7	1 383.2	42.50

表 12　我国主要林产品产量（2005—2009 年）

单位：万 t

年　份	木材（万 m^3）	生　漆	油桐籽	油茶籽	松　脂	核　桃	橡　胶
2005	5 560.3	1.43	36.87	87.50	76.71	49.91	51.36
2006	6 611.8	2.08	38.30	91.99	90.88	47.55	53.80
2007	6 976.6	1.29	36.13	93.91	96.56	62.99	58.84
2008	8 108.3	1.55	37.10	98.99	84.92	82.86	54.79
2009	7 068.3	2.05	36.73	116.93	104.66	97.94	61.89

表 13　各地区主要林产品产量（2009 年）　　单位：t

地　区	生漆	油桐籽	油茶籽	乌桕籽	五倍子	棕片	松脂	竹笋干	核桃	板栗	紫胶（原胶）
全国总计	**20 498**	**367 287**	**1169 289**	**33 171**	**14 431**	**77 314**	**1046579**	**465 340**	**979 366**	**1 627 656**	**3 694**
北　京									15 808	31 494	
天　津									654	615	
河　北									70 518	211 619	
山　西									70 399	259	
内蒙古											
辽　宁									67 845	86 045	
吉　林									11 861	826	
吉林集团									4 796		
黑龙江									350		
龙江集团											
上　海								214			
江　苏			174					3 887		29 356	
浙　江		68	47 048			481	992	126 061	20 731	77 526	
安　徽	257	2 656	29 973	146	49	953	13 569	14 281	15 317	108 715	
福　建	217	20897	89 294	521	132	13 868	74762	78 418	11	72 085	23
江　西	758	12 433	268 966	285	161	3450	57 306	9 979	501	25 616	4
山　东									48 242	247 937	
河　南	1 563	72 416	19 347	11 426	3 350		2 673	40	44 816	237 725	
湖　北	7 752	13 617	65 991	9 399	1 867	2 365	38 382	20 278	4 951	190 677	
湖　南	2 801	37 178	418 982	1 117	1 145	32 738	36 994	37 634	5 158	71 033	877
广　东		6 254	55 144	517		2 217	168 542	28 849		11 429	298
广　西	31	69 872	133 363	116	101	2 977	469 878	22 008	631	62 530	
海　南							2 211				
重　庆	617	19 761	1 967	6 170	2 303	744	749	52 668	8 990	7 214	
四　川	819	24 236	3 426	1 344	644	3 987	10 848	51 349	123 683	21 987	61
贵　州	1 983	54 669	28 264	1 866	1 354	3 129	7 067	10 283	13 546	18 225	59
云　南	519	16 611	6 616	97	122	9 358	161 745	7 198	191 213	58 710	2 372
西　藏									1 750		
陕　西	3 151	16 567	734	217	3 067	3 026	858	2 185	89 648	52 434	
甘　肃	30	52			136	21		8	48 184	3 599	
青　海									272		
宁　夏									47		
新　疆									124 240		

表 14 我国主要牲畜饲养情况（2005—2009 年） 单位：万头（只）

年份	合计	大牲畜年底存栏头数				
		牛	马	驴	骡	骆驼
2005	15 948	14 158	740	777	360	26.9
2006	12 287	10 465	719	730	345	26.9
2007	12 309	10 595	703	689	299	24.2
2008	12 251	10 576	682	673	296	24.0
2009	12 357	10 726	679	648	279	24.8

年份	肉猪出栏头数	牛出栏头数	猪年底存栏头数	羊年底存栏只数			羊出栏只数
				合计	山羊	绵羊	
2005	66 099	5 288	50 335	37 266	19 876	17 390	30 805
2006	61 207	4 222	41 850	28 309	13 768	14 601	24 734
2007	56 508	4 360	43 990	28 565	14 337	14 228	25 571
2008	61 017	4 446	46 291	28 085	15 229	12 856	26 172
2009	64 527	4 602	46 983	28 453	15 800	12 653	26 588

表 15 我国主要畜产品产量（2005—2009 年）

年份	肉类产量（万 t）					奶类产量（万 t）		禽蛋产量（万 t）
	总产量（万 t）	猪牛羊肉				总产量	其中:牛奶	
		小计	猪肉	牛肉	羊肉			
2005	7 741.3	6 157.6	5 010.6	711.5	435.5	2 864.8	2 753.4	2 879.5
2006	7 089.0	5 591.0	4 650.5	576.7	363.8	3 302.5	3 193.4	2 424.0
2007	6 865.7	5 283.8	4 287.8	613.4	382.6	3 633.4	3 525.2	2 529.0
2008	7 278.7	5 614.0	4 620.5	613.2	380.3	3 718.5	3 555.8	2 702.2
2009	7 649.9	5 915.5	4 890.5	635.5	389.5	3 734.6	3 520.9	2 740.6

年份	蜂蜜(万 t)	蚕茧（万 t）		绵羊毛（万 t）			山羊毛总产（t）	羊绒总产（t）
		总产	其中:桑蚕茧	总产	细羊毛	半细羊毛		
2005	29.3	78.0	71.3	39.3	13.8	12.3	36 904	15 435
2006	33.3	88.2	82.0	38.9	13.2	11.6	40 512	16 395
2007	35.4	94.7	87.9	36.3	12.4	10.7	38 382	18 483
2008	40.0	90.9	83.1	36.8	12.4	10.5	44 406	17 184
2009	40.2	83.2	76.1	36.4	12.7	11.3	49 453	16 964

表 16　各地区奶类产量（2008—2009 年）　　单位：万 t

地区	2008 年		2009 年	
	奶类产量	其中：牛奶	奶类产量	其中：牛奶
全国总计	**3 781.5**	**3 555.8**	**3 732.6**	**3 518.8**
北　京	66.5	66.4	67.4	67.4
天　津	70.1	69.8	68.7	68.3
河　北	515.3	504.5	461.0	451.5
山　西	70.0	68.2	74.1	72.5
内蒙古	921.3	912.2	934.0	903.1
辽　宁	107.3	101.2	115.6	110.0
吉　林	39.7	39.7	44.5	44.5
黑龙江	512.8	508.4	534.7	528.7
上　海	23.3	23.3	21.2	21.2
江　苏	61.1	61.1	55.4	55.4
浙　江	22.5	22.5	19.9	19.9
安　徽	18.1	18.1	20.1	20.1
福　建	14.9	14.5	15.6	15.2
江　西	11.2	11.2	11.2	11.2
山　东	254.9	230.5	258.1	236.3
河　南	298.6	279.1	301.3	281.9
湖　北	33.2	15.5	28.3	15.5
湖　南	15.2	7.7	7.7	7.7
广　东	13.3	12.9	14.4	14.0
广　西	7.5	7.5	8.1	8.1
海　南	0.5	0.2	0.4	0.2
重　庆	7.8	7.8	7.9	7.9
四　川	66.6	66.1	68.7	68.2
贵　州	4.3	4.3	4.5	4.5
云　南	97.3	44.7	105.9	48.4
西　藏	52.4	22.9	28.7	23.0
陕　西	182.3	149.0	185.8	149.2
甘　肃	34.7	34.7	37.7	37.7
青　海	27.2	25.3	25.3	25.3
宁　夏	89.2	89.2	81.1	81.1
新　疆	142.3	137.4	125.2	120.9

表 17　我国农垦系统主要畜产品产量（2008—2009 年）　　单位：万 t

项　目	2008 年	2009 年	同比增长（%）
1. 肉类总产量	192.0	223.4	16.34
其中：猪肉	120.6	136.9	13.54
牛肉	18.8	21.0	11.98
羊肉	17.8	14.7	－17.41
2. 牛奶	320.8	344.7	7.43
3. 羊毛	2.5	2.5	0.59
4. 蜂蜜	0.6	0.7	9.81
5. 禽蛋	25.6	31.3	22.38

表 18 我国水产品产量（2005—2009 年） 单位：kt

年 份	总产量	1. 海水产品	其中		2. 内陆产品	其中	
			捕 捞	养 殖		捕 捞	养 殖
2005	51 017	28 381	14 533	13 848	22 636	2 551	20 085
2006	45 836	25 096	12 455	12 642	20 739	2 204	18 536
2007	47 475	25 509	11 360	13 073	21 966	2 256	19 710
2008	48 956	25 983	11 496	13 403	22 973	2 248	20 725
2009	51 164	26 816	11 786	14 052	24 349	2 184	22 165

表 19 各地区水产品产量（2009 年） 单位：kt

地 区	总产量	1. 海水产品	其中		2. 内陆产品	其中	
			捕 捞	养 殖		捕 捞	养 殖
全国总计	**51 164.0**	**26 815.6**	**11 786.1**	**14 052.2**	**24 348.5**	**2 183.9**	**22 164.6**
北 京	58.2	3.9	3.9		54.3	4.0	50.3
天 津	334.0	39.5	25.4	14.1	294.6	8.7	285.8
河 北	1 004.1	553.9	253.3	300.6	450.2	87.7	362.5
山 西	31.0				31.0	0.7	30.3
内蒙古	106.0				106.0	29.6	76.4
辽 宁	4 006.1	3 275.3	1 132.1	2 143.2	730.8	56.3	674.5
吉 林	165.2				165.2	19.2	146.0
黑龙江	380.7				380.7	43.1	337.6
上 海	309.0	156.4	156.4		152.6	4.8	147.9
江 苏	4 432.2	1 305.0	570.0	735.0	3 127.3	320.7	2 806.5
浙 江	4 403.1	3 538.1	2 773.5	764.6	865.1	90.3	774.7
安 徽	1 831.5				1 831.5	307.3	1 524.2
福 建	5 675.2	4 958.1	2 027.9	2 930.3	717.1	78.1	639.0
江 西	2 010.5				2 010.5	227.5	1 783.0
山 东	7 535.9	6 263.9	2 449.6	3 814.3	1 272.0	128.3	1 143.7
河 南	537.7				537.7	30.6	507.1
湖 北	3 338.9				3 338.9	262.2	3 076.7
湖 南	1 880.6				1 880.6	110.2	1 770.4
广 东	7 026.0	3 871.5	1 525.4	2 346.2	3 154.5	126.5	3 027.9
广 西	2 622.8	1 490.2	667.7	822.5	1 132.6	112.6	1 020.0
海 南	1 454.9	1 142.8	961.1	181.7	312.1	19.2	292.9
重 庆	203.9				203.9	9.9	194.0
四 川	1 001.3				1 001.3	57.7	943.6
贵 州	80.3				80.3	11.0	69.3
云 南	271.2				271.2	23.4	247.8
西 藏	0.5				0.5	0.4	0.1
陕 西	56.0				56.0	4.2	51.8
甘 肃	11.9				11.9		11.9
青 海	1.4				1.4		1.4
宁 夏	81.9				81.9	0.2	81.7
新 疆	95.0				95.0	9.2	85.8

表 20 我国沿海地区海洋捕捞水产品产量（按品种分）（2009 年） 单位：kt

地区	海洋捕捞产量	按水产品种类分					
		1. 鱼类	带鱼	鳀鱼	蓝圆鲹	鲐鱼	鲅鱼
全国总计*	**11 786.1**	**8 040.3**	**1 172.4**	**521.9**	**539.9**	**397.0**	**429.1**
天津	16.5	8.6		0.9		1.6	0.4
河北	253.3	136.8	5.7	31.9			8.3
辽宁	995.3	554.5	23.3	71.8		40.9	62.3
上海	21.9	11.5	0.4				
江苏	562.7	347.3	73.6	1.7		25.9	7.3
浙江	2 666.4	1 843.9	495.9	5.6	100.1	160.2	70.4
福建	1 859.3	1 412.3	168.2	63.8	220.8	72.2	42.2
山东	2 370.9	1 514.5	103.7	299.0		44.8	177.8
广东	1 415.9	987.2	133.1	35.1	110.7	28.3	25.7
广西	662.9	399.6	34.2		69.0	13.6	2.4
海南	961.1	824.1	134.3	12.1	39.3	9.4	32.3

地区	鱼类						
	鲳鱼	小黄鱼	海鳗	金线鱼	沙丁鱼	石斑鱼	金枪鱼
全国总计	**373.1**	**372.9**	**340.6**	**306.5**	**134.4**	**86.0**	**31.4**
天津	0.02	1.6				0.2	
河北	1.0	7.6					
辽宁	5.5	105.8	0.4	0.2	1.8	4.8	
上海	0.4	0.2	0.5				
江苏	35.1	31.6	9.4		3.5		
浙江	126.9	89.6	83.9	2.8	20.9	1.3	6.0
福建	53.9	8.1	62.4	9.8	11.7	15.1	2.6
山东	51.5	87.8	18.4		11.9		0.7
广东	50.9	25.2	71.9	84.4	61.4	25.2	7.5
广西	11.6		14.2	35.8	13.9	6.0	
海南	36.3	15.5	79.3	173.5	9.3	33.3	14.5

* 海洋捕捞产量不含远洋捕捞产量。

（续）

地　区	2. 甲壳类	虾	毛　虾	对　虾	鹰爪虾	蟹	其中：梭子蟹
全国总计	**2 018.9**	**1 475.4**	**588.7**	**107.6**	**282.6**	**543.5**	**332.8**
天　津	2.8	1.9	0.1	0.1		0.9	0.3
河　北	54.9	43.9	11.9	2.1	2.3	11.0	9.4
辽　宁	194.0	155.1	49.4	1.8	12.5	38.9	14.6
上　海	9.9	3.9		0.08	1.2	5.9	2.8
江　苏	114.1	52.7	26.3	2.8	8.2	61.5	49.2
浙　江	672.8	557.4	235.8	14.8	147.2	115.4	71.2
福　建	276.2	155.6	56.7	16.7	38.9	120.6	74.3
山　东	315.1	271.8	122.8	5.2	42.5	43.3	28.7
广　东	227.2	152.9	53.8	43.9	17.4	74.3	44.9
广　西	113.5	65.1	27.1	16.8	8.3	48.4	28.3
海　南	38.3	15.1	4.7	3.2	4.1	23.2	8.9

地　区	3. 贝类	4. 藻类	5. 头足类	鱿　鱼	章　鱼	6. 其他类	海　蜇
全国总计	**669.7**	**27.6**	**643.3**	**351.8**	**118.3**	**386.3**	**223.2**
天　津	3.9		1.2				
河　北	18.9		12.8	0.7	7.5	29.9	21.9
辽　宁	119.9	0.1	49.9	28.4	7.1	76.8	50.5
上　海			0.2	0.1	0.08	0.2	0.1
江　苏	43.8	0.9	20.1	11.6	5.7	36.5	22.3
浙　江	13.3	1.9	114.4	64.8	24.5	20.2	2.9
福　建	50.9	1.1	97.6	53.3	11.4	21.1	13.0
山　东	260.5	1.8	157.3	95.4	33.6	121.8	61.4
广　东	70.2	10.2	76.6	33.4	17.7	44.4	21.7
广　西	63.5		52.3	22.4	5.9	34.1	28.2
海　南	25.0	11.6	60.7	41.6	4.8	1.4	0.8

表 21 我国沿海地区海水养殖水产品产量（按品种分）（2009 年） 单位：kt

地 区	海水养殖产量	1. 鱼类	鲈 鱼	鲆 鱼	大黄鱼	美国红鱼	石斑鱼
全国总计	**14 052.2**	**767.9**	**101.9**	**86.7**	**66.0**	**49.1**	**44.2**
天 津	14.1	2.1		1.4			0.2
河 北	300.6	14.7	1.1	2.7			1.1
辽 宁	2 143.2	40.0	1.2	23.6			
上 海							
江 苏	734.9	43.1	1.3	1.9			
浙 江	764.6	32.3	9.8	0.1	3.4	6.8	0.1
福 建	2930.3	158.9	12.8	2.4	58.6	10.9	9.8
山 东	3 814.3	127.6	25.1	53.7	0.2	3.5	0.1
广 东	2 346.2	279.6	40.4	0.8	3.8	22.9	18.0
广 西	822.5	26.1	7.7			2.8	2.3
海 南	181.7	43.4	2.5			2.0	12.6

地 区	鱼 类					2. 甲壳类	虾
	鲷 鱼	军曹鱼	狮 鱼	河 鲀	鲽 鱼		
全国总计	**40.3**	**29.1**	**19.4**	**18.9**	**11.5**	**1 016.9**	**796.5**
天 津					0.1	11.9	11.9
河 北				3.4		18.0	15.6
辽 宁				4.9	0.4	25.8	24.9
上 海							
江 苏				0.2	1.1	66.5	44.1
浙 江	3.6		0.1		0.1	79.5	34.4
福 建	16.1	0.3	4.5	1.1	0.5	88.5	48.7
山 东	1.7			5.3	8.8	120.9	85.8
广 东	11.2	18.3	14.0	3.8	0.6	335.5	285.7
广 西	5.3	0.2				168.6	155.9
海 南	2.3	10.3	0.8	0.1		101.8	89.3

（续）

地区	甲壳类						
	虾				蟹	梭子蟹	青蟹
	南美对白虾	斑节对虾	中国对虾	日本对虾			
全国总计	**580.8**	**60.2**	**44.4**	**50.4**	**220.5**	**95.8**	**115.9**
天津	11.8						
河北	7.3		4.1	4.2	2.4	2.2	0.1
辽宁	10.1		11.9	2.3	0.8	0.8	
上海							
江苏	24.0	0.6	5.7	1.5	22.4	21.1	0.7
浙江	21.9	0.9	2.9	3.1	45.1	22.5	22.4
福建	30.4	5.3	3.4	7.0	39.7	13.4	24.3
山东	44.4	1.6	10.8	27.3	35.1	33.9	0.1
广东	215.4	36.4	5.5	4.9	49.8	1.8	43.2
广西	135.9	13.3		0.2	12.6		12.6
海南	79.5	1.9			12.4	0.1	12.4

地区	3. 贝类	牡蛎	蛤	扇贝	蛏	贻贝	蚶
全国总计	**10 530.5**	**3 503.8**	**3 192.5**	**1 276.8**	**683.8**	**637.4**	**276.7**
天津							
河北	264.0		80.9	174.1	0.1	0.3	8.4
辽宁	1 663.5	130.7	771.6	312.6	22.4	35.1	29.8
上海							
江苏	591.3	10.9	365.9		87.8	54.3	15.4
浙江	611.6	105.2	52.5	1.9	215.4	71.9	109.0
福建	2 125.8	1 449.5	278.9	10.2	180.1	63.6	40.7
山东	2 964.7	581.5	1 165.2	702.3	149.9	215.9	19.5
广东	1 665.0	864.3	270.5	74.7	26.9	87.6	48.1
广西	625.1	360.3	197.8	0.7	1.0	8.6	5.3
海南	19.4	1.3	8.9				0.6

（续）

地　区	贝　类				4. 藻类	海　带	裙带菜
	螺	蚶	鲍	江　珧			
全国总计	**203.8**	**276.7**	**42.4**	**15.4**	**1 456.5**	**827.9**	**132.4**
天　津							
河　北		8.4					
辽　宁		29.8	0.9		248.2	138.8	103.1
上　海							
江　苏	55.4	15.4			32.6	5.9	0.1
浙　江	12.4	109.0	0.4		40.3	12.2	
福　建	3.0	40.7	29.1		554.3	431.6	0.7
山　东	9.1	19.5	6.5		505.7	236.3	28.2
广　东	92.6	48.1	4.9	15.4	58.5	2.9	0.4
广　西	29.4	5.3					
海　南	1.8	0.6	0.6		16.8		

地　区	藻　类		5. 其他	海　参	海　胆 (kg)	海水珍珠 (kg)	海　蜇
	江　蓠	紫　菜					
全国总计	**125.4**	**107.5**	**280.4**	**102.2**	**6 086 131.0**	**22 713.0**	**62.9**
天　津							
河　北			3.8	1.5			
辽　宁			165.6	36.1	2 891 000.0		50.8
上　海							1.3
江　苏		26.5	1.4	0.1			1.3
浙　江	0.1	20.9	0.8	0.1			
福　建	67.1	49.4	2.8	1.3			0.4
山　东	2.3	2.4	95.4	62.8	3 112 003.0		8.3
广　东	45.3	8.3	7.5	0.2	83 128.0	13 791.0	1.6
广　西			2.7			7 222.0	0.6
海　南	10.5		0.3			1 700.0	

表 22 各地区农垦系统水产品养殖面积与产量（2009 年） 单位：hm^2、t

地 区	水产养殖面积	水产品总产量	其中：养殖产量	对虾养殖面积	对虾产量
全国总计	**319 431**	**1 077 235**	**947 813**	**16 569**	**42 080**
北 京					
天 津	793	7 875	7 875		
河 北	12 501	73 952	67 192	3 912	10 574
山 西	8	6	6		
内蒙古	4 276	4 727	2 215		
辽 宁	106 941	282 308	236 519	5 750	6 692
吉 林	669	1 644	1 594		
黑龙江	25 711	23 555	18 958		
上 海	2 995	14 755	14 755		
江 苏	4 820	40 322	27 814	388	2 446
浙 江	1 140	7 231	5 775	584	2 409
安 徽	1 148	4 635	4 213		
福 建	2 001	32 107	24 354	192	801
江 西	19 609	34 518	25 949		
山 东	4 538	4 948	2 354	3 060	506
河 南	577	6 736	6 555		
湖 北	43 200	332 622	332 622		
湖 南	33 554	78 684	43 697		
广 东	4 101	29 475	29 475	1 618	10 078
广 西	1 375	15 487	15 487	278	2 025
海 南	5 330	41 827	41 208	787	6 549
重 庆	26	154	154		
四 川	51	794	794		
贵 州	107	32	32		
云 南	1 723	6 248	6 248		
西 藏					
陕 西	33	42	42		
甘 肃	139	20	20		
青 海					
宁 夏	6 167	6 714	6 714		
新疆（兵团）	32 481	23 569	22 969		
新疆（农业）	3 218	1 882	1 882		
新疆（畜牧）	169	222	222		
热作两院	23	120	120		
广 州					
南 京	8	26			
昆 明					

表 23　我国按人口平均的主要农畜产品产量（2005—2009 年） 单位：kg/人

年　份	粮　食	棉　花	油　料	水　果	茶　叶	猪、牛、羊肉
2005	371	4.4	23.6	123.7	0.72	41.9
2006	379	5.8	20.1	130.5	0.78	42.7
2007	381	5.8	19.5	137.6	0.88	40.1
2008	399	5.7	22.3	144.7	0.95	40.3
2009	398	4.8	23.2	153.2	1.01	44.3
年　份	**禽　蛋**	**牛　奶**	**水产品**	**糖　料**	**烤　烟**	**黄红麻**
2005	22.0	21.1	33.9	72.5	1.86	0.06
2006	22.4	24.4	34.9	79.8	1.89	0.07
2007	19.1	26.7	36.0	92.5	1.65	0.08
2008	20.3	26.8	37.0	101.1	1.98	0.06
2009	20.5	26.4	38.4	91.4	2.10	0.06

表 24　我国城乡居民家庭人均食品消费量比较（2005—2009 年） 单位：kg/人

年　份	粮　食		蔬　菜		食用油(植物油)		猪牛羊肉		家　禽		水产品	
	农村	城市	农村	城市	农村	城市	农村	城市	农村	城市	农村	城市
2005	208.8	77.0	102.3	118.6	6.0	9.3	17.1	23.9	3.7	9.0	4.9	12.6
2006	205.6	75.9	100.5	117.6	5.8	9.4	17.0	23.8	3.5	8.3	5.0	13.0
2007	199.5	77.6	98.9	117.8	5.1	9.6	14.9	22.1	3.9	9.7	5.4	14.2
2008	199.1		99.7	123.2	5.4	10.3	13.9	22.7	4.4	8.0	5.3	
2009	189.3	81.3	98.4	120.5	5.4	9.8	15.3	24.2	4.3	10.5	5.3	

资料来源：表中数据出自国家统计局。

表 25　我国城镇和农村人口人均食品消费支出情况（2005—2009 年） 单位：元/人

项　目	2005	2006	2007	2008	2009
全国人均	**2 038.28**	**2 164.46**	**2 508.51**	**2 850.48**	**2 960.56**
城镇居民	2 914.39	3 111.92	3 628.03	4 259.81	4 478.54
农村居民	1 162.16	1 216.99	1 388.99	1 598.75	1 636.04
人均增长	167.52	126.18	344.05	341.97	110.08
城镇居民增长	204.79	197.53	516.11	631.78	218.73
农村居民增长	130.25	54.83	172.00	209.76	37.29

资料来源：表中数据出自 2010 年版《中国统计年鉴》。

表 26　我国人口增长情况（2005—2009 年） 单位：万人

项　目	2005	2006	2007	2008	2009
人口数	130 756	131 448	132 129	132 802	133 474
增长人数	768	692	681	673	672
其中：城镇人口	56 212	57 706	59 379	60 667	62 186
农村人口	74 544	73 742	72 750	72 135	71 288

农产品加工机械拥有量及农产品加工行业固定资产投资情况

表 27　农业部系统农产品初加工机械年末拥有量（2009 年）

地　区	农产品初加工动力机械		初加工作业机械（万台）	畜牧养殖机械（万台）	渔业机械（万台）	林果机械（万台）
	万台	（万 kW）				
全国总计	**1 296.64**	**8 066.05**	**1 157.83**	**577.05**	**216.56**	**13.36**
北　京	0.88	6.76	0.90	1.07	1.14	0.37
天　津	2.42	9.26	0.86	0.58	3.54	0.01
河　北	98.72	869.79	49.98	11.49	3.79	0.14
山　西	19.87	166.06	13.32	5.80	0.07	0.08
内蒙古	9.53	84.60	6.25	20.74	0.10	0.16
辽　宁	17.63	122.59	15.65	18.02	4.57	0.45
吉　林	14.45	132.53	12.08	8.07	0.45	0.02
黑龙江	11.20	119.40	5.84	24.60	0.31	0.07
上　海	0.44	3.93	0.44	0.18	2.11	0.06
江　苏	24.81	228.58	20.53	9.71	22.62	0.36
浙　江	20.70	137.56	38.25	5.43	15.64	1.39
安　徽	41.24	324.25	45.05	6.82	4.86	0.94
福　建	56.08	197.63	57.19	3.35	12.10	1.44
江　西	51.57	521.16	38.70	5.88	6.56	1.08
山　东	95.22	842.68	47.81	16.26	10.58	1.09
河　南	78.57	566.42	47.79	20.34	2.22	0.14
湖　北	82.23	394.76	87.56	34.17	26.28	0.21
湖　南	113.16	616.23	111.21	22.67	9.64	0.91
广　东	27.86	228.33	21.57	9.02	61.27	0.86
广　西	77.40	432.33	70.34	32.01	5.82	0.24
海　南	2.17	24.51	2.01	0.52	6.08	0.02
重　庆	85.64	295.46	97.66	41.28	5.03	0.46
四　川	125.99	538.45	155.13	56.27	9.00	
贵　州	105.24	448.85	103.88	40.47	0.21	0.44
云　南	64.01	368.87	65.36	122.79	0.98	0.04
西　藏			1.14	0.18		
陕　西	36.47	185.59	21.87	25.32	0.56	0.32
甘　肃	24.00	101.27	13.31	13.50	0.03	
青　海	1.38	14.05	1.27	1.72		
宁　夏	2.58	26.26	2.08	11.55	0.77	0.87
新　疆	5.18	57.90	2.80	7.24	0.23	0.87

表 28 我国农产品加工行业固定资产投资情况（2009 年） 单位：亿元、%

行　业	投资额	新增固定资产	固定资产交付使用率（平均值）
合　计	**13 099.6**	**9 495.6**	**70.9**
农副食品加工业	2 830.1	2 046.6	72.3
食品制造业	1 509.5	1 107.2	73.4
饮料制造业	1 078.8	783.9	72.7
烟草制品业	216.6	104.4	48.2
纺织业	1 764.4	1 310.1	74.3
纺织服装、鞋、帽制造业	1 050.6	788.4	75.0
皮革、毛皮、羽毛（绒）及其制品业	518.2	365.3	70.5
木材加工及木、竹、藤、棕、草制品业	1 016.5	837.2	82.4
家具制造业	645.2	527.2	81.7
造纸及纸制品业	1 244.1	776.8	62.4
印刷业和记录媒介的复制	567.4	417.2	73.5
橡胶制品业	658.2	431.3	65.5

表 29 我国农产品加工行业新增固定资产后主要产品新增生产能力（2008—2009 年）

产品名称	单　位	2008 年	2009 年
轮胎外胎	万条/年	5 913	3 519
轮胎内胎	万条/年	4 137	7 082
化学纤维	t/年	2 817 572	1 923 430
棉 纺 锭	锭	9 816 359	10 249 173
毛 纺 锭	锭	352 621	161 190
啤　酒	万 t/年	551	240
白　酒	万 t/年	179	182
其 他 酒	万 t/年	44	67
卷　烟	箱 /年	820 000	1 315 007
机制纸浆	万 t/年	192	267

表 30 我国农产品加工行业 50 万元以上施工、投产项目数（2009 年）

行　业	施工项目（个）		全部建成投产项目（个）	项目建成投产率（%）
	总　计	其中：新开工		
合　计	**49 916**	**38 312**	**33 897**	**66.6**
农副食品加工业	11 412	9 052	7 784	68.2
食品制造业	5 375	4 083	3 596	66.9
饮料制造业	3 662	2 798	2 364	64.6
烟草制品业	422	281	234	55.5
纺织业	6 734	4 963	4 543	67.5
纺织服装、鞋、帽制造业	4 805	3 548	3 141	65.4
皮革、毛皮、羽毛（绒）及其制品业	2 138	1 425	1 337	62.5
木材加工及木、竹、藤、棕草制品业	5 146	4 248	3 816	74.2
家具制造业	2 936	2 360	2 112	71.9
造纸及纸制品业	3 522	2 785	2 455	69.7
印刷业和记录媒介的复制	2 241	1 668	1516	67.7
橡胶制品业	1 523	1 101	999	65.6

表 31　林业系统森工固定资产投资完成情况（2008—2009 年）　单位：万元

项　　目	2008 年	2009 年	同比增长（%）
一、森工固定资产投资完成额（按构成划分）	1 506 249	2 351 488	56.12
1. 基本建设	1 245 733	1 786 595	43.42
2. 更新改造	197 183	453 854	130.17
3. 其他投资	6 333	111 039	75.33
二、当年新增固定资产	1 017 950	1 209 179	18.79

表 32　林业系统各地区森工固定资产投资完成情况（2009 年）　单位：万元

地　　区	合　　计	基本建设	更新改造	其他投资
全国总计	**2 351 488**	**1 786 595**	**453 854**	**111 039**
北　　京				
天　　津				
河　　北				
山　　西				
内 蒙 古	18 274	1 152		17 122
辽　　宁				
吉　　林	190 524	176 432	8 980	5 112
黑 龙 江	337 774	331 077	6 697	
上　　海				
江　　苏				
浙　　江	150	150		
安　　徽				
福　　建	2 373	1 524	564	285
江　　西	500		500	
山　　东				
河　　南				
湖　　北	5 840	4 530	300	1 010
湖　　南	3	3		
广　　东				
广　　西	1 699 210	1 193 511	423 960	81 739
海　　南				
重　　庆				
四　　川	5 432	4 032	1 300	100
贵　　州				
云　　南	7 126	4 811		2 315
西　　藏				
陕　　西	230		230	
甘　　肃				
青　　海				
宁　　夏				
新　　疆	865	718		147
局直属单位	83 187	68 655	11 323	3 209

表 33 我国农垦系统固定资产投资完成情况（2008—2009 年） 单位：万元

项 目	2008 年	2009 年	同比增长（%）
固定资产投资总额	9 312 162	13 578 956	45.82
当年新增固定资产	6 647 125	11 079 135	66.68

表 34 我国水产行业固定资产投资情况（2008—2009 年） 单位：亿元

项 目	2008 年	2009 年	同比增长（%）
一、投资总额	102.4	129.9	26.86
二、本年新增固定资产	85.5	95.6	11.81
三、固定资产交付使用率（%）	83.5	73.6	－11.86

资料来源：表中数据出自 2010 年版《中国统计年鉴》。

按国民经济行业分类统计农产品加工业现状

表 35 我国农产品加工业全部国有及规模以上非国有工业企业主要指标（2009 年）

行 业	单位数（个）	工业总产值（亿元）	资产总计（亿元）	主营业务收入（亿元）	利润总额（亿元）	从业人员年平均人数（万人）
合 计	**136 160**	**114 607.8**	**76 174.1**	**112 167.2**	**7501.4**	**2 525.2**
农副食品加工业	24 550	27 961.0	13 344.9	27 624.7	1 501.2	337.7
食品制造业	8 735	9 219.2	6 155.0	8 865.0	716.8	162.7
饮料制造业	5 904	7 465.0	6 589.7	7 464.9	728.8	119.0
烟草制品业	158	4 924.9	4 940.1	4 870.9	650.4	20.0
纺织业	32 412	22 971.4	16 330.2	22 470.5	1 091.2	617.0
纺织服装、鞋、帽制造业	18 265	10 444.8	5 946.1	10 140.5	611.2	449.3
皮革、毛皮、羽毛（绒）及其制品业	8 520	6 425.6	3 295.9	6 241.4	408.9	257.6
木材加工及竹、藤、棕、草制品业	10 765	5 759.6	2 979.4	5 618.9	345.5	130.7
家具制造业	5 576	3 431.1	2 126.6	3 353.3	184.1	98.6
造纸及纸制品业	9 937	8 264.4	8 084.4	8 001.9	504.7	152.6
印刷业和记录媒介的复制	6 618	2 972.9	2 855.9	2 873.1	236.5	82.1
橡胶制品业	4 720	4 767.9	3 525.9	4 642.1	322.1	97.9

表 36 我国农产品加工业全部国有及规模以上非国有工业企业主要经济效益指标(2009 年)

行业	总资产贡献率（%）	资产负债率（%）	流动资产周转次数（次/年）	工业成本费用利润率（%）	产品销售率（%）
平均值	**21.12**	**50.32**	**2.78**	**9.51**	**97.88**
农副食品加工业	17.93	53.76	4.06	5.83	97.86
食品制造业	18.96	50.24	2.95	8.89	97.64
饮料制造业	21.39	50.61	2.28	11.23	97.25
烟草制品业	70.64	23.88	1.48	33.61	99.67
纺织业	12.43	56.95	2.67	5.15	97.89
纺织服装、鞋、帽制造业	16.98	52.16	2.85	6.46	97.31
皮革、毛皮、羽毛（绒）及其制品业	19.99	52.73	3.09	7.08	97.55
木材加工及竹、藤、棕、草制品业	20.58	48.18	4.05	6.68	97.41
家具制造业	14.78	53.22	2.79	5.90	98.02
造纸及纸制品业	11.32	57.62	2.39	6.76	98.14
印刷业和记录媒介的复制	13.29	48.69	2.02	9.00	97.61
橡胶制品业	15.18	55.75	2.69	7.54	98.16

表 37 我国农产品加工业国有及国有控股工业企业主要指标（2009 年）

行业	单位数（个）	工业总产值（亿元）	资产总计（亿元）	主营业务收入（亿元）	利润总额（亿元）	从业人员年平均人数（万人）
合计	**3 334**	**10 949.1**	**12 436.6**	**10 977.2**	**1 069.6**	**158.7**
农副食品加工业	817	1 509.4	1 089.3	1 553.3	52.2	18.5
食品制造业	368	670.8	753.6	664.6	39.7	13.8
饮料制造业	330	1 290.9	1 820.9	1 447.6	213.3	22.9
烟草制品业	123	4 891.8	4 899.3	4 838.8	646.1	19.2
纺织业	424	584.0	882.9	615.6	6.1	31.6
纺织服装、鞋、帽制造业	185	141.9	153.9	143.8	8.2	9.1
皮革、毛皮、羽毛（绒）及其制品业	31	25.3	35.2	26.9	1.6	1.2
木材加工及竹、藤、棕、草制品业	168	138.9	176.0	142.9	3.7	5.8
家具制造业	40	79.7	54.7	81.7	6.3	1.0
造纸及纸制品业	179	637.3	1 379.7	625.2	18.3	11.2
印刷业和记录媒介的复制	551	387.8	580.9	384.9	41.9	12.9
橡胶制品业	118	590.3	610.1	621.7	32.2	11.5

表 38 我国农产品加工业国有及国有控股工业企业主要经济效益指标（2009 年）

行业	总资产贡献率（%）	资产负债率（%）	流动资产周转次数（次/年）	工业成本费用利润率（%）	产品销售率（%）
平均值	**15.38**	**57.60**	**1.77**	**8.85**	**98.41**
农副食品加工业	9.41	61.74	2.88	3.46	97.92
食品制造业	10.75	62.17	1.85	6.23	95.03
饮料制造业	22.06	40.71	1.48	17.96	99.64
烟草制品业	71.08	23.73	1.48	33.88	99.69
纺织业	4.12	62.24	1.63	0.99	99.68
纺织服装、鞋、帽制造业	8.17	67.56	1.37	5.95	96.82
皮革、毛皮、羽毛（绒）及其制品业	7.20	68.55	1.33	6.50	101.80
木材加工及竹、藤、棕、草制品业	6.70	63.45	1.94	2.62	95.83
家具制造业	18.91	64.19	2.48	8.21	99.12
造纸及纸制品业	5.03	68.50	1.27	2.95	98.73
印刷业和记录媒介的复制	11.32	39.61	1.55	11.90	97.64
橡胶制品业	9.84	68.73	2.02	5.51	98.99

表 39 我国农产品加工业外商投资和港澳台商投资工业企业主要指标（2009 年）

行业	单位数（个）	工业总产值（亿元）	资产总计（亿元）	主营业务收入（亿元）	利润总额（亿元）	从业人员年平均人数（万人）
合计	**25 331**	**31 555.4**	**24 960.7**	**31 075.4**	**2 028.44**	**813.1**
农副食品加工业	2 600	6 880.6	3 955.3	6 980.9	350.0	68.3
食品制造业	1 601	3 158.1	2 410.5	3 113.7	283.6	48.1
饮料制造业	818	2 515.1	2 238.4	2 492.8	238.7	31.4
烟草制品业	3	3.5	8.3	3.5	0.5	0.1
纺织业	5 673	5 014.5	4 452.1	4 880.8	236.5	152.2
纺织服装、鞋、帽制造业	6 319	4 158.6	2 673.5	4 055.7	255.9	212.7
皮革、毛皮、羽毛（绒）及其制品业	2 670	2 867.7	1 732.8	2 783.4	178.0	145.7
木材加工及竹、藤、棕、草制品业	1 002	728.6	597.6	718.9	30.6	17.8
家具制造业	1 361	1 182.9	927.4	1 155.2	62.3	40.5
造纸及纸制品业	1 494	2 544.9	3 570.9	2 467.2	180.2	37.1
印刷业和记录媒介的复制	785	762.7	839.9	727.4	83.2	22.1
橡胶制品业	1 005	1 738.2	1 554.0	1 695.9	128.9	37.1

表 40　我国农产品加工业外商投资和港澳台商投资工业企业主要经济效益指标（2009 年）

行　　业	总资产贡献率（%）	资产负债率（%）	流动资产周转次数（次/年）	工业成本费用利润率（%）	产品销售率（%）
平　均　值	**13.58**	**49.39**	**2.11**	**8.42**	**98.53**
农副食品加工业	13.58	60.77	2.93	5.33	97.74
食品制造业	19.21	49.00	2.43	10.03	98.35
饮料制造业	19.97	52.60	2.45	10.78	99.43
烟草制品业	11.33	23.70	0.77	17.07	103.68
纺织业	9.37	50.58	2.02	5.11	97.14
纺织服装、鞋、帽制造业	15.18	49.24	2.45	6.74	97.49
皮革、毛皮、羽毛（绒）及其制品业	16.20	52.50	2.47	6.85	97.17
木材加工及竹、藤、棕、草制品业	10.87	51.17	2.18	4.45	97.81
家具制造业	10.95	53.16	2.04	5.72	98.17
造纸及纸制品业	8.88	54.68	1.72	7.85	98.68
印刷业和记录媒介的复制	13.92	43.01	1.54	12.84	97.49
橡胶制品业	13.47	52.25	2.36	8.24	99.20

表 41　我国农产品加工业私营工业企业主要指标（2009 年）

行　　业	企业数（个）	工业总产值（亿元）	资产总计（亿元）	主营业务收入（亿元）	利润总额（亿元）	从业人员年平均人数（万人）
合　　计	**83 649**	**49 113.9**	**24 664.4**	**47 839.4**	**2 818.3**	**1 081.8**
农副食品加工业	16 169	12 558.3	4 893.3	12 287.1	718.1	160.9
食品制造业	4 825	2 971.6	1 569.1	2 877.4	203.7	60.6
饮料制造业	3 387	2 037.8	1 261.2	1 964.7	145.4	34.8
烟草制品业	8	4.1	9.3	3.7	0.5	0.1
纺织业	22 201	12 894.6	7 696.3	12 605.8	634.4	312.2
纺织服装、鞋、帽制造业	9 764	4 565.1	2 149.8	4 426.4	239.1	174.6
皮革、毛皮、羽毛（绒）及其制品业	4 880	2 516.0	1 079.5	2 444.8	157.6	79.8
木材加工及竹、藤、棕、草制品业	6 211	3 879.8	1 543.3	3 781.6	247.8	85.4
家具制造业	3 396	1 734.1	905.8	1 692.5	100.1	44.4
造纸及纸制品业	6 250	3 198.6	1 844.4	3 093.1	193.2	66.1
印刷业和记录媒介的复制	3 808	1 213.4	912.9	1 178.9	74.1	31.4
橡胶制品业	2 750	1 540.5	799.5	1 483.4	104.3	31.5

表 42 我国农产品加工业私营工业企业主要经济效益指标（2009 年）

行业	总资产贡献率（%）	资产负债率（%）	流动资产周转次数（次/年）	工业成本费用利润率（%）	产品销售率（%）
平均值	**19.5**	**50.55**	**3.60**	**7.42**	**97.58**
农副食品加工业	23.38	46.46	5.40	6.33	97.97
食品制造业	21.48	45.64	4.15	7.85	97.99
饮料制造业	22.44	50.58	3.44	8.44	96.52
烟草制品业	7.16	34.90	0.74	13.38	96.29
纺织业	15.11	59.34	3.15	5.37	98.07
纺织服装、鞋、帽制造业	19.58	54.28	3.60	5.78	97.48
皮革、毛皮、羽毛（绒）及其制品业	24.81	53.89	4.02	6.99	98.06
木材加工及竹、藤、棕、草制品业	27.40	43.45	5.50	7.19	97.51
家具制造业	18.88	51.54	3.59	6.44	97.89
造纸及纸制品业	18.16	56.01	3.36	6.74	97.66
印刷业和记录媒介的复制	14.26	56.68	2.64	6.82	97.83
橡胶制品业	21.37	53.86	3.59	7.74	97.72

表 43 我国农产品加工业大中型工业企业主要指标（2009 年）

行业	企业数（个）	工业总产值（亿元）	资产总计（亿元）	主营业务收入（亿元）	利润总额（亿元）	从业人员年平均人数（万人）
合计	**11 655**	**54 181.6**	**44 736.0**	**53 333.0**	**4 071.5**	**1 139.3**
农副食品加工业	1 610	10 874.2	6 418.9	10 906.2	579.4	140.1
食品制造业	955	5 122.8	3 597.8	4 915.9	451.3	82.3
饮料制造业	745	4 598.0	4 520.4	4 743.2	521.7	70.8
烟草制品业	97	4 872.5	4 860.8	4 819.6	640.9	19.1
纺织业	3 056	10 554.8	9 268.2	10 340.0	531.3	297.4
家具制造业	1 659	4 465.4	3 175.7	4 302.0	356.5	171.7
纺织服装、鞋、帽制造业	983	3 245.6	1 933.5	3 141.7	240.0	138.1
皮革、毛皮、羽毛（绒）及其制品业	390	1 244.4	958.4	1 225.9	82.3	27.9
木材加工及竹、藤、棕、草制品业	493	1 292.4	992.4	1 270.9	78.2	42.5
造纸及纸制品业	776	4 028.8	5 386.1	3 883.5	271.2	66.7
印刷业和记录媒介的复制	408	1 008.1	1 165.3	966.5	114.2	28.8
橡胶制品业	483	2 874.6	2 458.5	2817.6	204.5	53.9

表 44 我国农产品加工业大中型工业企业主要经济效益指标（2009 年）

行业	总资产贡献率（%）	资产负债率（%）	流动资产周转次数（次/年）	工业成本费用利润率（%）	产品销售率（%）
平均值	**20.06**	**51.12**	**2.29**	**10.61**	**97.87**
农副食品加工业	14.89	56.76	3.24	5.63	97.78
食品制造业	20.16	51.93	2.73	10.12	97.81
饮料制造业	22.61	50.30	2.02	12.77	97.96
烟草制品业	71.51	23.88	1.48	33.85	99.70
纺织业	10.73	56.87	2.23	5.41	97.77
纺织服装、鞋、帽制造业	16.68	51.62	2.19	9.00	96.40
皮革、毛皮、羽毛（绒）及其制品业	18.69	51.68	2.57	8.29	97.21
木材加工及竹、藤、棕、草制品业	15.51	52.88	2.68	7.18	97.18
家具制造业	12.68	56.52	2.15	6.56	98.18
造纸及纸制品业	9.29	59.33	1.96	7.44	98.46
印刷业和记录媒介的复制	14.13	43.68	1.70	13.17	97.42
橡胶制品业	13.82	57.93	2.48	7.88	98.52

表 45 2009/2010 年度制糖期全国制糖行业主要经济技术指标

行业实现销售收入（亿元）	实现利税总额（亿元）	平均含糖（%）		平均单产（t/hm²）		平均产糖率（%）	
		甘蔗糖	甜菜糖	甘蔗糖	甜菜糖	甘蔗糖	甜菜糖
576.64	122.82	14.38	15.50	57.0	41.70	12.54	12.10

资料来源：表中数据由中国糖业协会提供。

表 46 我国食品和包装机械经济运行情况（2005—2009 年）

年份	类别	年销售情况（亿元）		占食品工业比重（%）	占机械工业比重（%）
		销售收入	同比增长（%）		
2005	**总计**	**673.70**	**20.71**	**3.31**	**1.63**
	其中：食品机械	341.70	20.06		
	包装机械	332.00	21.39		
2006	**总计**	**828.37**	**22.96**	**3.24**	**1.51**
	其中：食品机械	422.47	23.64		
	包装机械	405.90	22.26		
2007	**总计**	**987.15**	**19.17**	**3.02**	**1.33**
	其中：食品机械	503.45	19.17		
	包装机械	483.70	19.17		
2008	**总计**	**1 262.00**	**27.84**	**3.16**	**1.39**
	其中：食品机械	620.66	23.28		
	包装机械	641.34	32.59		
2009	**总计**	**1 484.00**	**17.59**	**2.99**	**1.38**
	其中：食品机械	756.80	21.93		
	包装机械	727.20	13.39		

表 47　我国机械工业、食品工业、食品与包装机械行业经济增长情况（2005—2009 年）

类　别	2005 年	2006 年	2007 年	2008 年	2009 年	年均增长（%）
机械工业	41 400.00	54 717.80	74 000.00	90 700.00	107 500.00	
同比增长（%）	21.60	32.17	35.24	22.57	16.07	25.53
食品工业	20 344.80	25 540.00	32 666.00	40 320.00	49 698.71	
同比增长（%）	26.53	25.54	27.90	23.43	17.86	24.25
食品与包装机械	673.70	828.37	987.15	1 262.00	1 484.00	
同比增长（%）	20.71	22.96	19.17	27.84	17.59	21.65

注：表中数据为年销售收入，单位为亿元。

表 48　林业系统农产品加工业总产值（2008—2009 年）

行　业	工业总产值（万元）		
	2008 年	2009 年	同比增长（%）
总　计	**66 681 082**	**84 675 292**	**26.99**
1. 非木质林产品加工制造业	5 748 231	6 781 363	17.97
2. 木材加工及竹、藤、棕、草制品业	32 323 297	39 292 789	21.56
锯材、木片加工业	5 799 236	7 135 579	23.04
人造板制造业	16 729 526	20 496 082	22.51
木制品制造业	7 172 890	8 887 931	23.91
竹、藤、棕、草制品制造业	2 621 645	2 773 197	5.78
3. 木、竹、藤家具制造业	10 580 559	14 814 538	40.02
4. 木、竹、苇浆造纸	11 793 724	16 636 054	41.06
5. 林产化学产品制造业	2 024 490	2 197 610	8.55
6. 木、竹、藤工艺品制造业	2 031 320	2 026 270	0.25
7. 其　他	2 179 461	2 926 668	34.28

表 49　林业系统农产品加工业国有独立核算大中型工业企业主要经济效益指标（2009 年）

指　标　名　称	单　位	2009 年
总资产贡献率	%	3.8
资本保值增值率	%	99.2
资产负债率	%	54.9
流动资产周转率	次/年	0.7
成本费用利润率	%	14.6
全员劳动生产率	元/人	13 555.0
产品销售率	%	92.5

表50 林业系统各地区农产品加工业总产值（2009年）

单位：万元

地区	总计	非木质林产品加工制造业	木材加工及竹、藤、棕、草制品业				
			合计	锯材、木片加工业	人造板制造业	木制品制造业	竹藤棕草制品制造业
全国总计	**84 675 292**	**6 781 363**	**39 292 789**	**7 135 579**	**20 496 082**	**8 887 931**	**2 773 197**
北京	56 446		56 446		17 033	39 413	
天津	24 138		24 138		24 138		
河北	2 535 123	661 283	3 569 199	133 937	1 366 702	57 893	10 667
山西	104 365	94 658	5 767	4 999	400	210	158
内蒙古	480 730	20 661	325 526	238 674	85 452	1 333	67
辽宁	2 067 214	119 040	1 139 592	334 477	403 520	394 816	6 779
吉林	3 557 092	1 274 887	1 567 084	366 748	520 420	660 048	19 868
黑龙江	2 063 741	28 726	1 369 423	678 846	318 202	369 672	2 703
上海	296 992		269 660	4 727	35 465	251 468	
江苏	6 867 471	127 838	5 718 482	353 543	4 390 334	944 892	29 713
浙江	7 735 565	882 812	4 110 049	426 428	1 114 553	1 845 719	723 349
安徽	2 593 115	239 956	2 083 363	267 242	1 154 080	373 893	288 148
福建	10 402 658	1 173 378	3 330 069	363 444	1 473 059	859 216	634 350
江西	3 122 684	326 350	1 776 111	390 700	758 427	486 984	140 000
山东	4 491 604	358 871	3 109 740	857 227	1 819 665	345 451	87 397
河南	2 248 872	375 703	1 240 990	230 065	884 230	102 167	24 528
湖北	2 451 080	129 733	1 167 310	290 796	606 227	242 727	27 560
湖南	4 007 797	218 101	1 975 298	628 491	720 794	298 453	327 560
广东	18 155 001	98 205	3 543 841	252 941	2 001 300	1 054 519	235 081
广西	4 572 947	162 201	2 330 096	594 074	1 394 052	246 878	95 092
海南	956 028	96 888	246 612	193 235	52 818		559
重庆	523 838	50 058	203 172	38 833	89 163	59 624	15 552
四川	3 517 981	32 478	1 139 851	173 246	798 705	88 582	79 318
贵州	393 605	18 817	279 573	64 426	174 641	24 212	16 294
云南	803 808	94 156	278 179	156 212	158 657	61 346	1 964
西藏	13 334		12 616	12 501	112		3
陕西	146 031	5 050	122 016	20 442	80 536	15 437	5 601
甘肃	34 219	5 956	7 645	2 358	2 984	1 417	886
青海							
宁夏	210 243	136 836					
新疆	78 382	43 494	28 546	12 341	12 342	3 863	
大兴安岭	163 188	5 227	140 395	44 626	38 071	57 698	

（续）

地　区	木质、竹、藤家具制造业	木、竹、苇浆造纸及纸制品业	林产化学产品制造业	木、竹、藤工艺品制造业	其　他
全国总计	**14 814 538**	**16 636 054**	**2 197 610**	**2 026 270**	**2 926 668**
北　京					
天　津					
河　北	193 168	20 133	12 211	1 630	77 499
山　西	2 264		778		898
内蒙古	974		894	1700	130 975
辽　宁	614 160	36 663	3 054	26 386	128 319
吉　林	149 705	426 963	16 437	20 696	101 320
黑龙江	189 238	238 332	33 305	17 184	187 533
上　海	5 332				
江　苏	397 761	381 000	178	41 980	200 232
浙　江	1 534 465	259 343	125 201	813 695	
安　徽	129 532	29 328	21 173	38 045	51 718
福　建	1 153 318	3 393 670	321 719	601 737	428 767
江　西	424 317	204 111	203 416	65 737	122 642
山　东	349 876	419 970	11 289	151 811	90 047
河　南	290 782	249 636	3 967	11 273	76 521
湖　北	359 497	575 066	55 542	23 501	140 431
湖　南	304 917	1 094 812	120 470	81 784	212 415
广　东	6 917 316	7 025 472	487 142	65 699	17 326
广　西	277 344	852 595	577 859	23 572	349 280
海　南	8 120	599 439	4 714		255
重　庆	111 321	33 282	9 515	17 488	99 002
四　川	1 332 611	619 177	16 319	16 494	361 051
贵　州	34 266	25 447	4 677	2 982	27 843
云　南	13 319	95 493	128 082	1 408	93 171
西　藏					718
陕　西	10 438		594	1 340	6 593
甘　肃	5 081			120	15 417
青　海					
宁　夏	5 207	46 122	21 616		462
新　疆	101			8	6 233
大兴安岭	108		17 458		

表 51　我国水产品加工业发展情况（2008—2009 年）

项　　目	单　位	2008 年	2009 年	同比增长（%）
一、水产品加工企业	个	9 971.0	9 635.0	−3.37
水产品加工能力	万 t/年	2 197.0	2 209.2	0.55
二、水产品冷库	座	7 439.0	7 548.0	1.47
冻结能力	万 t/d	43.1	49.9	15.78
冷藏能力	万 t/次	335.7	360.4	7.36
制冰能力	万 t/d	23.2	21.3	−8.19
冷藏总量	万 t·d			
制冰总量	万 t			
三、水产品加工总量	万 t	1 367.8	1 477.3	8.74
其中：淡水加工产品	万 t	200.8	227.9	13.50
海水加工产品	万 t	1 166.9	1 249.4	7.07
（一）水产品冷冻	万 t	850.9	941.1	10.60
其中：冷冻加工品	万 t	424.7	451.4	6.29
（二）鱼糜制品及干腌制品	万 t	193.5	223.5	15.50
其中：鱼糜制品	万 t	81.9	84.8	3.54
干腌制品	万 t	111.6	138.7	24.28
藻类制品	万 t	81.7	90.5	10.77
（三）罐制品	万 t	22.0	22.1	0.45
（四）饲料	万 t			
其中：鱼粉	万 t	147.9	136.5	−7.71
（五）鱼油制品	万 t	9.2	2.5	−72.83
（六）其他水产加工品	万 t	62.4	61.2	−1.92
其中：助剂和添加剂	万 t	5.4	7.1	31.48
珍珠	Kg	390 114.0	700 363.0	79.53
四、用于加工的水产品总量	万 t	1 637.4	1 822.2	11.29
其中：淡水产品	万 t	323.3	393.6	9.19
海水产品	万 t	1 314.1	1 428.5	8.71

表 52　我国水产品加工业加工能力、产量及产值（2006—2009 年）

年　份	加工企业数（个）	加工能力（万 t/年）	水产品加工总产量		折合水产品原料（万 t）	总产值（亿元）	占水产品总产值比率（%）
			总产量（万 t）	同比增长（%）			
2006	9 549	1 799.4	1 332.5	11.46	1 634.8		
2007	9 796	2 124.0	1 337.8	0.40	1 676.9		
2008	9 971	2 197.5	1 367.8	2.24	1 637.4	1 971.0	37.88
2009	9 635	2 209.2	1 477.3	8.74	1 822.2	2 026.6	36.02

表 53　我国沿海省、自治区、直辖市水产品加工业生产情况（2009 年）

单位：万 t

地区	水产品加工企业		水产品加工品总量	其中					
	企业数（个）	加工能力（万 t/年）		冷冻水产品	鱼糜及干腌制品	罐制品	鱼粉	鱼油制品	其他
全国总计	**9 635**	**2 209.2**	**1 477.3**	**941.1**	**223.5**	**22.1**	**136.5**	**2.5**	**61.2**
天津	5	0.2	0.2	0.2					
河北	266	49.1	13.9	5.9	1.4	0.6	5.8		0.2
辽宁	833	241.7	186.0	120.6	15.6	1.6	6.0	0.2	13.2
上海	30	4.9	15.4	15.4					
江苏	947	113.0	77.8	49.9	3.6	1.4	19.6		1.7
浙江	2 133	245.7	200.1	153.9	24.7	2.9	13.7	0.2	4.1
福建	.1 202	219.1	213.4	78.1	44.1	2.7	44.1	0.3	11.1
山东	1 881	647.5	436.6	296.4	60.8	3.6	29.3	1.7	20.6
广东	1 173	427.0	141.8	95.6	22.3	6.1	11.2	0.1	6.2
广西	212	32.6	48.7	45.2	2.4				1.0
海南	237	88.0	46.4	39.6	2.6		1.4		1.9
11 省份小计	8 919	2 068.8	1 380.3	900.9	177.5	18.9	131.1	2.4	60.0
占全国比率（%）	92.57	93.64	93.43	95.73	79.42	85.61	96.07	97.36	98.08

表 54　我国乡镇企业规模以上农产品加工企业基本情况（2009 年）

项目	单位	2009 年
企业个数	个	136 000
从业人员	万人	2 525
工业总产值	万元	950 000 000
工业增加值	万元	153 149 035
营业收入	万元	598 757 665
利税总额	万元	33 539 748
上交税金	万元	31 000 000

资料来源：表中数据由农业部农产品加工局提供。

表 55　轻工业系统农产品加工业分行业主要经济指标（2008 年）

单位：亿元

行业	企业单位数（个）		工业总产值	主营业务收入	利税总额	流动资产年均余额	固定资产净值年均余额	出口交货值
	合计	其中亏损						
轻工业总计	**122 145**	**18 012**	**95 673.2**	**93 201.6**	**9 101.3**	**31 673.7**	**17 177.0**	**18 457.3**
有关农产品加工行业小计	64 499	8 576	56 594.1	55 176.1	5 547.0	17 149.4	12 240.2	6 601.6
1. 农副食品加工业	22 800	2 318	23 917.4	23 565.8	1 860.4	5 422.1	3 663.1	1 693.8
2. 食品制造业	8 108	1 178	7 716.5	7 463.7	832.5	2 381.8	1 855.5	653.9
3. 饮料制造业	5 411	720	6 250.5	6 137.6	1 106.5	2 737.2	1 897.4	184.1
4. 制盐	209	18	253.2	248.3	40.7	123.8	134.1	5.3
5. 皮革、毛皮、羽毛制品业	8 622	1 174	5 871.4	5 692.8	547.3	1 738.9	775.0	2 130.7
6. 木、竹、藤、棕草制品业	1 914	234	581.6	563.7	55.5	144.5	97.9	161.1
7. 家具制造业	5 386	982	3 072.8	3 001.3	246.9	1 051.3	557.9	1 109.9
8. 造纸及纸制品业	10 011	1 642	7 873.9	7 501.2	740.3	3 012.1	3 040.9	536.2
9. 轻工专用设备制造业	2 038	310	1 056.8	1 001.7	116.9	527.7	218.4	126.6

表 56 轻工业系统食品工业分行业主要经济指标（2008 年） 单位：亿元

行业	企业单位数（个）		工业总产值	主营业务收入	利税总额	流动资产年均余额	固定资产净值年均余额	从业人员（万人）
	合计	其中亏损						
食品工业合计*	**36 528**	**4 234**	**38 137.6**	**37 415.4**	**3 840.1**	**10 664.9**	**7 550.1**	**592.6**
一、农副食品加工业	22 800	2 318	23 917.4	23 565.8	1 860.4	5 422.1	3 663.1	315.1
谷物磨制	5 633	259	3 699.3	3 632.7	322.2	665.0	545.8	43.8
饲料加工	3 293	344	3 761.3	3 696.1	287.0	624.7	392.5	34.0
植物油加工	2 205	304	4 659.9	4 675.1	344.3	1 192.7	510.4	26.2
其中：食用植物油加工	2 078	285	4 589.6	4 606.6	336.9	1 180.0	501.1	25.4
制糖业	318	117	627.8	580.9	54.8	392.6	249.9	15.5
屠宰及肉类加工	3 593	402	4 900.6	4 977.9	351.8	879.4	742.6	76.4
水产品加工	2 341	339	2 393.2	2 284.9	161.8	711.1	404.9	46.8
蔬菜、水果及坚果加工	3 112	309	1 764.7	1 690.4	164.9	440.8	317.9	39.7
其他农副食品加工	2 305	244	2 110.6	2 027.6	173.5	515.7	499.1	32.7
二、食品制造业	8 108	1 178	7 716.5	7 463.7	832.5	2 381.8	1855.5	154.6
焙烤食品制造业	1 320	164	812.6	804.2	103.8	220.4	194.3	23.4
糖果、巧克力及蜜饯制造业	736	63	553.6	558.4	84.3	186.1	138.2	13.2
方便食品制造业	1 201	165	1 310.7	1 267.8	142.8	350.2	280.8	29.3
液体乳及乳制品制造业	815	223	1 490.7	1 431.0	103.9	408.9	317.1	21.2
罐头制造业	915	144	609.3	587.3	53.1	232.1	139.7	17.9
调味品、发酵品制造业	1 154	147	1 156.3	1 104.5	132.8	388.2	355.6	20.3
其他食品制造业	1 967	272	1 783.3	1 710.4	211.9	595.8	429.9	29.2
三、饮料制造业	5 411	720	6 250.5	6 137.6	1 106.5	2 737.2	1 897.4	113.0
酒精制造业	204	52	437.9	390.0	41.9	127.6	145.8	4.9
酒的制造业	2 485	350	3 181.2	3 112.7	721.2	1 636.4	1 055.5	67.5
软饮料制造业	1 599	224	2 258.6	2 487.5	296.5	831.8	613.4	31.2
精制茶加工业	1 123	94	372.7	347.4	46.9	141.4	82.7	9.5
四、制盐业	229	18	253.2	248.3	40.7	123.8	134.1	9.9

* 食品工业合计数据中未包括烟草加工业统计数据；表中数据由中国轻工业信息中心提供。

表 57 我国食品工业总产值增长情况（2005—2009 年） 单位：亿元

类别	2005 年	2006 年	2007 年	2008 年	2009 年
总计	**20 324.31**	**24 801.03**	**32 425.61**	**42 373.0**	**49 570.1**
农副食品加工业	10 614.95	12 973.49	17 496.08	23 917.0	27 961.0
食品制造业	3779.35	4 714.25	6 070.96	7 717.0	9 219.2
饮料制造业	3 089.27	3 899.21	5 082.34	6 250.0	7 465.0
烟草加工业	2 840.74	3 214.08	3 776.23	4 489.0	4 924.9

表 58　我国食品工业焙烤糖制食品行业主要经济指标（2008 年）

行业	产量（万 t）		工业总产值（亿元）		新产品产值（亿元）		出口交货值（亿元）	
	2008 年	比上年增减（%）	2008 年	比上年增减（%）	2008 年	比上年增减（%）	2008 年	比上年增减（%）
合　计	**1 188.96**	**8.19**	**2 721.85**	**26.19**	**260.61**		**122.26**	**1.04**
糖果巧克力	121.37	15.82	386.16	23.66	54.22	33.77	35.05	20.32
糕点面包	79.91	26.21	246.34	38.23	23.04	39.15	11.03	−20.26
饼干	282.70	30.82	544.38	39.26	55.81	37.50	14.54	−1.70
米面制品			286.24	40.16	22.00	62.00	10.50	8.26
速冻食品			248.60	30.24	16.12	8.77	25.92	−19.84
方便面	499.45	5.34	693.76	24.13	66.23	32.23	11.02	15.56
蜜饯			133.99	29.77	10.63	28.90	13.45	9. 57
冷冻饮品	205.53	4.84	182.38	22.41	12.56	31.97	0.75	36.48

资料来源：表中数据由中国焙烤食品糖制品工业协会提供。

表 59　我国饮料行业主要经济指标（2008—2009 年）

指　　标	单　　位	2008 年	2009 年	同比增长（%）
企业单位数	个	5 411.0	5 904.0	9.11
总产量	万 t	6 503.1	8 086.2	24.33
工业总产值	亿 元	6 250.5	7 460.5	19.43
主营业务收入	亿 元	6 137.6	7 464.9	21.63
利润总额	亿 元	558.9	728.8	30.40
职工人数	万 人	113.0	119.0	5.31
资产总计	亿 元	5 946.2	6 589.7	10.82
负债合计	亿 元	3 019.7	3 335.2	10.45

注：表中数据出自 2010 年版《中国统计年鉴》，为规模以上工业企业的指标。

表 60　我国酒精工业主要经济指标（2008—2009 年）

指　　标	单　位	2008 年	2009 年	同比增长（%）
产品产量	万 kL	681.3	731.7	7.40
主营业务收入	亿元	380.6		
利润总额	亿元	15.3	11.3	−26.14
税金总额	亿元	19.0	16.9	−11.05
出口总量	万 kL	10.8		

资料来源：表中数据由中国酿酒协会酒精分会提供。

表 61　我国乳制品行业主要经济指标（2008—2009 年）

指　标	单　位	2007 年	2008 年	同比增长（%）
全年奶牛存栏	万头	1 233.0	1 218.5	−1.18
全年奶类总产量	万 t	3 633.4	3 650.0	0.46
其中：牛奶产量	万 t	3 557.1	3 518.0	−1.10
全国乳制品产量	万 t	1 714.3	1 935.1	12.88
其中：液态奶	万 t	1 525.2	1 641.6	7.63
干乳制品	万 t	267.9	293.5	9.56
乳制品工业总产值	亿元	1 468.4	1 650.2	12.38
主营业务收入	亿元	1 282.4	1 456.8	13.60
乳制品加工利润总额	亿元	47.7	82.4	72.75
城镇居民人均消费	kg	25.5	25.3	−0.60
乳制品进口量	万 t	35.1	59.7	70.10
乳制品进口额	亿美元	8.6	10.3	19.31
乳制品出口量	万 t	12.1	3.7	−69.50
乳制品出口额	亿美元	3.0	0.6	−81.00

资料来源：表中数据由中国奶业协会、中国乳制品工业协会提供。

表 62　轻工业系统农产品加工机械重点企业主要经济指标（2008 年）

行　业	企业数（个）	工业总产值（亿元）	主营业务收入（亿元）	利润总额（亿元）	应交增值税（亿元）	从业人员（万人）
轻工机械合计	**1 757**	**1 033.9**	**992.9**	**965.9**	**69.9**	**23.4**
农产品加工机械合计	**1 083**	**672.8**	**651.9**	**640.0**	**48.8**	**12.1**
食品及包装机械	362	234.7	228.1	224.3	19.2	5.4
农副食品加工机械	336	206.6	200.1	195.6	12.5	1.9
制浆造纸机械	273	166.5	160.9	157.8	13.1	3.6
制革制鞋机械	54	22.6	22.3	20.3	0.6	0.6
其他日用品加工机械	58	42.4	40.5	42.0	3.4	0.6

资料来源：表中数据由中国轻工业协会信息中心提供。

表 63　我国烟草工业主要经济指标（2008—2009 年）

指　标	单　位	2008 年	2009 年	同比增长（%）
企业数	个	156.0	158.0	1.28
工业总产值	亿元	4 488.9	4 924.9	9.71
主营业务收入	亿元	4 259.7	4 870.9	14.35
利润总额	亿元	712.9	650.4	−8.77
职工人数	万人	19.8	20.0	1.01
资产总计	亿元	4 428.5	4 940.1	11.55
负债合计	亿元	1 042.1	1 179.6	13.19

表 64　我国纺织工业主要经济指标（2008—2009 年）

指　标	单　位	2008 年	2009 年	同比增长（%）
企业数	个	33 133.0	32 412.0	−2.18
工业总产值	亿元	21 393.1	22 971.4	7.38
主营业务收入	亿元	18 318.8	22 470.5	22.66
利润总额	亿元	927.4	1 091.2	17.66
职工人数	万人	652.1	617.0	−5.38
资产总计	亿元	15 336.6	16 330.2	6.48
负债合计	亿元	8 935.3	9 299.9	4.08

表 65　我国纺织服装、鞋、帽制造业主要经济指标（2008—2009 年）

指　　标	单　位	2008 年	2009 年	同比增长（%）
企业数	个	18 237.0	18 265.0	0.15
工业总产值	亿元	9 435.8	10 444.8	10.69
主营业务收入	亿元	9 074.1	10 140.5	11.75
利润总额	亿元	487.3	611.2	25.43
职工人数	万人	458.7	449.3	−2.05
资产总计	亿元	5 655.9	5 946.1	5.13
负债合计	亿元	3 068.4	3 101.8	1.09

表 66　我国皮革工业经济运行情况（2008—2009 年）

指　　标	单　位	2008 年	2009 年	同比增长（%）
企业数	个	8 622.0	8 520.0	−1.18
工业总产值	亿元	5 871.4	6 425.6	9.44
主营业务收入	亿元	5 692.8	6 241.4	9.64
利润总额	亿元	333.1	408.9	22.76
职工人数	万人	273.3	257.6	−5.74
资产总计	亿元	3 025.1	3 295.9	8.95
负债合计	亿元	1 622.7	1 738.1	7.11

注：表 65～表 67 中数据，出自 2010 年版《中国统计年鉴》。

表 67　我国家具行业经济运行情况（2008—2009 年）

指　　标	单　位	2008 年	2009 年	同比增长（%）
家具总产值	亿元	3 003.6	3 409.1	13.5
家具销售产值	亿元	2 944.3	3 338.8	13.4
家具出口交货值	亿元	1 072.1	1 007.8	−6.0

资料来源：表中数据由中国家具协会提供。

表 68　我国造纸工业主要经济指标（2008—2009 年）

指　　标	单　位	2008 年	2009 年	同比增长（%）
企业数	个	3 494	3 686	5.50
工业总产值	亿元	4 190	4 162	−0.67
主营业务收入	亿元	3 970	3 998	0.71
利税总额	亿元	364.1	341.3	−6.26
利润总额	亿元	228.2	210.0	−7.98
资产总计	亿元	4 697.0	5 016.0	6.79
资产负债率	%	59.74	58.69	−1.76
从业人员平均人数	万人	75.20	71.10	−5.45

注：表中数据为中国造纸协会提供的年销售收入 500 万元以上的造纸企业统计数据。

表 69　我国新闻出版业产业基本情况（2007—2008 年）

	类　别	单　位	2007 年	2008 年	同比增长（%）
总计	图书、期刊、报纸总印张	亿印张	2 354.2	2 649.3	12.97
	折合用纸量	万 t	542.7	613.0	12.95
	其中：书籍用纸量	万 t	58.7	71.0	20.95
	课本用纸量	万 t	55.5	60.6	9.19
	期刊用纸量	万 t	37.1	37.1	
	报纸用纸量	万 t	391.2	444.1	13.52
	图片用纸量	万 t	0.2	0.2	−10.00
图书	图书出版总量	种	248 283.0	275 668.0	11.03
	其中：新版图书	种	136 226.0	149 988.0	10.10
	重版重印图书	种			
	总印数	亿册（张）	62.9	69.4	10.33
	总印张	亿印张	486.5	560.7	15.25
	折合用纸量	万 t	114.4	131.9	15.30
	定价金额	亿元	576.7	791.4	37.10
期刊	期刊出版总数	种	9 468.0	9 549.0	0.86
	平均期印数	万 册	16 697.0	16 767.0	0.42
	总印数	亿 册	30.4	31.1	2.30
	总印张	亿印张	157.9	158.0	0.06
	折合用纸量	万 t	37.1	37.1	
	定价金额	亿元	170.9	187.4	9.65
报纸	出版种数	种	1 938.0	1 943.0	0.26
	平均期印数	万 份	20 545.4	21 154.8	2.97
	总印数	亿 份	437.9	442.9	1.14
	总印张	亿印张	1 700.8	1 930.6	13.51
	折合用纸量	万 t	391.2	444.0	13.50
	定价金额	亿元	306.5	317.9	3.72
音像制品及电子出版物	出版种数	种	40 607.0	23 493.0	−42.15
	出版数量	亿盒（张）	6.3	4.33	−31.27
	发行数量	亿盒（张）	4.4	4.10	−6.82
	发行金额	亿 元	31.5	18.44	−41.46
出版物进出口	出　口				
	图书、期刊、报纸	种次	1 155 765.0	947 204.0	−18.05
	出口数量	万册（份）	1 027.8	801.8	−21.99
	出口金额	万美元	3 787.5	3 487.3	−7.93
	进　口				
	图书、期刊、报纸	种次	815 233.0	703 787.0	−13.67
	进口数量	万册（份）	2 385.9	3 452.5	44.70
	进口金额	万美元	21 105.4	24 061.4	14.01

表 70 我国 130 个书刊印刷企业（含其他印刷）主要经济指标（2008—2009 年）

指　　标		单　　位	2008 年	2009 年	同比增长（%）
工业经济效益综合指数		%	100.3	89.2	−11.07
总资产贡献率		%	5.3	4.5	−15.09
资本保值增值率		%	104.0	78.1	−24.90
资产负债率		%	47.4	49.4	4.22
流动资产周转率		%	1.7	1.5	−11.76
成本费用利润率		%	0.6	−0.7	−16.67
会员劳动生产率		元/人	565 521.0	55 266.0	−90.23
工业产品销售率		%	99.2	100.6	1.41
利税总额		万元	679.0	614.0	−9.57
利润总额		万元	202.0	154.0	−23.76
企业平均从业人数		人	450.0	458.0	1.78
工资总额		万元	1 117.0	1 181.0	5.73
人均工资		万元	2.4	2.6	7.85
主要产品	书刊印刷	万令	19	20	5.26
	胶印印刷	万色令	84	89	5.95
	书刊装订	万令	30	31	3.33
	纸板	4K 块	211 384	21 826	−89.67

资料来源：表中数据由中国印刷及设备器材工业协会书刊印刷专业委员会等单位提供。

表 71 我国 62 个印刷机械企业主要经济指标（2008—2009 年）

指　　标	单　　位	2008 年	2009 年	同比增长（%）
工业总产值	万元	598 249.0	562 223.0	−6.0
工业销售产值	万元	574 233.0	582 720.0	1.5
工业增加值	万元	179 484.0	165 418.0	−7.8
产品销售收入	万元	564 616.0	574 129.0	1.7
利润总额	万元	8 488.0	14 061.0	扭亏
成本费用总额	万元	543 157.0	524 590.0	−3.4
出口交货值	万元	103 906.0	60 837.6	−41.4
新产品产值	万元	317 676.0	305 000.0	−4.0
经济效益综合指数	%	101.9	125.7	23.8
总资产贡献率	%	2.6	5.9	3.3
资产保值增值率	%	96.0	99.6	3.6
资产负债率	%	51.6	49.7	−1.9
流动资金年周转率（次）	次/年	0.9	1.0	8.6
成本费用利润率	%	−1.6	2.7	4.2
全员劳动生产率	元/人	93 469.0	93 056.9	−0.5
产品销售率	%	96.0	103.7	7.7

资料来源：表中数据出自 2010 年版《印刷工业》杂志第 6 期。

表 72 我国橡胶工业主要经济指标（2008—2009 年）

指标	单位	2008 年	2009 年	同比增长（%）
企业数	个	346	337	−2.6
工业总产值	亿元	1 275.9	1 921	9.4
工业增加值	亿元	146.6	186.2	27.0
销售收入	亿元	1 785.7	1 905.3	6.7
实现利润	亿元			
实现利税	亿元	78.4	151.2	92.8
出口交货值	亿元	489.9	463.4	−5.4
橡胶总消耗量	万 t	550.0	588.0	6.9

资料来源：表中数据出自 2010 年版《中国橡胶》杂志第 5 期。

表 73 我国橡胶工业全部独立核算工业企业主要经济指标（2007—2008 年）

行业	企业数（个）		工业总产值（万元）	
	2007 年	2008 年	2007 年	2008 年
橡胶制品业	3 622	3 909	34 567 171	41 072 558
其中：1. 轮胎制造业	373	398	16 449 443	20 267 500
2. 力车胎制造业	84	90	703 799	780 028
3. 橡胶板管带制造业	773	818	3 912 985	4 845 962
4. 橡胶零件制造业	795	872	3 134 938	4 029 579
5. 再生橡胶制造业	178	209	972 032	1 376 011
6. 橡胶靴鞋制造业	617	622	4 843 625	4 186 435
7. 日用橡胶制品业	239	247	1 767 827	1 911 463
8. 其他橡胶制品业	520	598	2 604 471	3 438 691
9. 橡胶制品翻修业	43	55	178 051	236 890
其中：轮胎翻修业	43	55	178 051	236 890
橡胶工业专用设备制造业	171	177	1 047 090	1 235 469

行业	工业销售产值（万元）		出口交货值（万元）	
	2007 年	2008 年	2007 年	2008 年
橡胶制品业	33 964 744	40 259 244	8 490 728	9 154 982
其中：1. 轮胎制造业	16 255 981	19 979 342	4 749 408	5 207 447
2. 力车胎制造业	689 944	777 852	76 674	97 487
3. 橡胶板管带制造业	9 808 257	4 707 043	393 813	460 287
4. 橡胶零件制造业	3 035 407	3 905 405	674 410	794 400
5. 再生橡胶制造业	956 502	1 337 648	28 247	23 813
6. 橡胶靴鞋制造业	4 774 266	4 070 333	1 443 674	1 126 419
7. 日用橡胶制品业	1 744 495	1 879 375	627 963	789 418
8. 其他橡胶制品业	2 525 825	3 370 335	494 734	655 422
9. 橡胶制品翻修业	174 066	231 911	1 787	289
其中：轮胎翻修业	174 066	231 911	1 787	289
橡胶工业专用设备制造业	998 668	1 171 831	85 258	127 317

资料来源：表中数据出自 2009 年版《中国橡胶工业年鉴》。

表 74　我国中药行业经济效益情况（2009 年）

行　业	工业总产值（亿元）	产品销售产值（亿元）	实现利润（亿元）	出口总额（亿美元）
全国医药工业合计	**9 684.9**	**9 915.9**	**942.9**	**319.9**
其中：中药工业	2 560.8	2 509.7	229.4	6.3
中成药工业	2 041.6	1 998.0	197.5	1.6
中药饮片工业	519.2	511.7	31.9	5.2
中药工业占我国医药工业比例（%）	26.4	25.3	24.3	2.2

表 75　我国农产品加工业能源消费总量和主要能源品种消费量（2008 年）

行　业	能源消费总量（万 t 标准煤）	煤炭消费量（万 t）	焦炭消费量（万 t）	原油消费量（万 t）	汽油消费量（万 t）	煤油消费量（万 t）	柴油消费量（万 t）	燃料油消费量（万 t）	天然气消费量（亿 m^3）	电力消费量（亿 kW·h）
合　计	**20 028.9**	**11 340.4**	**43.9**	**3.1**	**124.3**	**5.5**	**319.7**	**136.7**	**8.4**	**3 042.2**
农副食品加工业	2 731.3	1 641.6	13.2	0.1	17.6	0.4	59.3	10.9	0.5	362.3
食品制造业	1 544.7	1 071.9	7.9	0.1	9.9	0.3	30.2	15.4	2.1	166.4
饮料制造业	1 161.9	856.5	1.1	0.6	9.1	0.5	20.6	11.4	1.0	111.0
烟草加工业	232.6	94.9	0.8		0.9		6.7	1.1	0.4	38.6
纺织业	6 396.4	2 529.1	5.3	0.2	22.5	1.4	51.2	36.0	1.5	1 126.4
纺织服装、鞋、帽制造业	725.3	229.4	3.2	0.3	12.6	0.5	38.1	7.0	0.2	130.1
皮革、毛皮、羽毛（绒）及其制品业	388.7	85.6	0.2	0.1	6.1	0.2	20.5	11.1	0.1	77.0
木材加工及竹、藤、棕草制品业	981.9	440.0	2.6	0.2	7.9	0.5	16.8	2.0	0.2	175.4
家具制造业	181.8	33.5	1.1	0.1	4.0	0.2	13.8	0.3	0.4	34.9
造纸及纸制品业	3 998.7	3 858.1	5.7	0.6	12.0	0.9	36.3	25.9	1.1	471.8
印刷业和记录媒介复制	349.8	41.5	0.3		8.2	0.5	17.2	1.8	0.5	77.3
橡胶制品业	1 335.8	458.4	2.5	0.9	13.7	0.2	9.1	15.9	0.5	271.1

农产品加工业主要产品产量

表 76　我国农产品加工业主要产品产量（2008—2009 年）

产品名称	单　位	2008 年	2009 年	同比增长（%）
纱	万 t	2 170.9	2 393.5	10.25
布	亿 m	723.1	753.4	4.19
机制纸及纸板	万 t	8 404.3	8 956.1	6.67
成品糖	万 t	1 432.6	1 338.4	−6.58
卷烟	亿支	22 199.2	22 901.5	3.16

（续）

产品名称	单 位	2008 年	2009 年	同比增长（%）
罐头	万 t	764.8	811.7	6.13
啤酒	万 kL	4 156.9	4 162.2	0.13
原盐	万 t	6 664.4	6 662.8	−0.02
精制食用植物油	万 t	2 850.1	3 433.4	22.40
中成药	万 t	177.8	200.8	12.94
合成橡胶	万 t	296.0	274.9	−7.13
橡胶轮胎外胎	万条	51 956.9	65 601.6	26.26

表 77 轻工业系统农产品加工业主要产品产量（2007—2008 年）

产 品	单 位	2007 年	2008 年	同比增长（%）
原盐	万 t	5 797.5	5 952.8	2.68
成品糖	万 t	1 271.4	1 449.5	14.01
糖果	万 t	98.3	121.4	23.50
糕点	万 t	63.8	79.9	25.24
饼干	万 t	225.0	282.7	25.64
方便面	万 t	507.7	499.5	−1.62
罐头	万 t	513.6	595.3	15.91
乳制品	万 t	1 771.6	1 810.6	2.20
其中：液体乳	万 t	1 574.3	1 525.2	−3.12
味精	万 t	191.3	184.4	−3.61
酱油	万 t	324.1	367.1	13.27
饮料酒	万 kL	4 601.7	4 882.3	6.10
其中：白酒（折 65 度）	万 kL	483.9	569.3	17.65
啤酒	万 kL	3 931.4	4 103.1	4.37
黄酒	万 kL	75.7	80.9	6.87
葡萄酒	万 kL	66.5	69.8	4.96
软饮料	万 t	5 032.6	6 415.1	27.47
其中：碳酸饮料	万 t	1 001.6	1 107.4	10.56
果汁及果汁饮料	万 t	1 017.8	1 182.5	16.18
瓶(罐)装饮用水	万 t	1 785.9	2 475.6	38.62
冷冻饮品	万 t	212.4	205.5	−3.25
轻革	亿 m^2	5.9	6.4	8.47
皮鞋	亿双	32.3	33.2	2.79
皮革服装	万件	5 270.5	5 653.2	7.26
毛皮服装	万件	271.2	385.3	42.07
家具	亿件	4.9	5.2	6.12
其中：木制家具	万件	17 466.9	18 946.9	8.47
软体家具	万件	2 663.0	3 252.6	22.14
纸浆	万 t	2 082.4	2 058.5	−1.15
机制纸及纸板	万 t	7 581.5	8 390.9	10.68
其中：新闻纸	万 t	425.8	461.5	8.38
纸制品	万 t	2 734.3	3 191.4	16.72
造纸机械	台	52 361.0		

资料来源：表中数据由中国轻工业协会信息中心提供。

表 78　我国粮油工业主要产品产量（2008—2009 年）　　单位：万 t

产　品	2008 年	2009 年	同比增长（%）
大米	4 783.0	5 723.8	19.67
其中：特等米	1 466.0	1 606.5	9.58
标准一等米	2 944.6	3 565.4	21.11
标准二等米	266.0	370.6	39.32
其他	48.0	181.3	377.71
小麦粉	5 505.6		
其中：特制一等粉	2 415.2		
特制二等粉	1 368.9		
标准粉	705.2		
专用粉	702.6		
其他	313.6		
食用植物油	2 293.6	2 355.5	2.70
按品种分：大豆油	1 243.5	1 405.6	13.04
菜籽油	276.0	556.2	101.52
花生油		144.8	
棉籽油		83.1	
其他		165.8	
按等级分：一级油		1 250.8	7.43
二级油	1 164.3	83.7	
三级油		171.5	
四级油		564.4	
其他		118.7	

表 79　我国淀粉产量及品种情况（2008—2009 年）　　单位：万 t

品　种	2008 年	2009 年	同比增长（%）	占总淀粉（%）
合　　计	**1 818.37**	**1 802.70**	**−0.86**	**100.00**
玉米淀粉	1 685.23	1 725.52	2.39	95.72
木薯淀粉	89.54	47.43	−47.03	2.63
马铃薯淀粉	32.15	16.72	−47.99	0.93
甘薯淀粉	7.20	9.00	25.00	0.50
小麦淀粉	4.25	4.03	−5.18	0.22

表 80　我国淀粉深加工品产量（2008—2009 年）　　单位：万 t

主要品种	2008 年	2009 年	同比增长（%）	占深加工品（%）
合　计	**895.15**	**1 027.26**	**14.76**	**100.00**
变性淀粉	85.28	112.93	32.42	10.99
结晶葡萄糖	210.35	238.78	13.52	23.24
液体淀粉糖	518.52	588.88	13.57	57.33
糖　醇	81.00	86.67	7.00	8.44

表 81　我国淀粉产量分布及生产规模情况（2009 年）

地　区	淀粉产量（万 t）	占淀粉总产量（%）	生产规模情况	
			企业数(10 万 t/年)	企业最大淀粉产量（万 t/年）
合　计	**1 802.11**	**100.00**	**33**	
山　东	812.40	45.07	11	213.66
吉　林	385.35	19.88	6	159.61
河　北	260.50	14.45	8	56.37
河　南	105.86	5.87	5	28.00
陕　西	77.20	4.28	2	62.84
广　西	41.00	2.27		
其他 15 个省份合计	147.40	8.18	1	63.50

注：其他 15 个省份为：山西、内蒙古、辽宁、黑龙江、江苏、浙江、湖北、四川、广东、海南、云南、甘肃、宁夏、青海、新疆。

表 82　我国玉米淀粉生产规模情况（2008—2009 年）

项　目	单位	2008 年	2009 年	同比增长（%）
年产 100 万 t 以上的企业	个	5	5	
年产 100 万 t 以上的企业总产量	万 t	694.92	718.54	3.40
占全国玉米淀粉总产量	%	41.24	41.64	0.97
年产 40 万 t 以上的企业	个	9	8	−11.11
年产 40 万 t 以上的企业总产量	万 t	504.22	439.44	−12.85
占全国玉米淀粉总产量	%	29.92	25.47	−14.87
年产 30 万 t 以上的企业	个	4	2	−50.00
年产 30 万 t 以上的企业总产量	万 t	123.33	66.10	−46.40
占全国玉米淀粉总产量	%	7.32	3.83	−47.68
年产 10 万 t 以上的企业	个	12	18	50.00
年产 10 万 t 以上的企业总产量	万 t	362.76	312.82	−13.77
占全国玉米淀粉总产量	%	21.52	18.13	−15.76

表83　我国部分淀粉深加工品生产规模情况（2008—2009年）

类别	项　目	单位	2008年	2009年	同比增长（%）
变性淀粉	年产5万t以上的企业	个	6	88	33.33
	年产5万t以上的企业总产量	万t	48.49	67.74	39.70
	占全国总产量	%	56.86	59.98	5.49
	年产3万t以上的企业	个	5	3	−40.00
	年产3万t以上的企业总产量	万t	20.03	11.83	−40.94
	占全国总产量	%	23.49	10.48	−55.39
	年产1万t以上的企业	个	7	15	114.29
	年产1万t以上的企业总产量	万t	12.20	28.08	130.16
	占全国总产量	%	14.31	24.86	73.72
结晶葡萄糖	年产20万t以上的企业	个	2	3	50.00
	年产20万t以上的企业总产量	万t	107.66	140.23	30.25
	占全国总产量	%	51.18	58.73	14.75
	年产10万t以上的企业	个	4	5	25.00
	年产10万t以上的企业总产量	万t	58.86	66.57	13.10
	占全国总产量	%	27.98	66.57	137.92
	年产5万t以上的企业	个	5	3	−40.00
	年产5万t以上的企业总产量	万t	35.57	21.15	−47.54
	占全国总产量	%	16.91	8.86	−47.60
	年产2万t以上的企业	个	1	3	200.00
	年产2万t以上的企业总产量	万t	3.05	10.82	254.75
	占全国总产量	%	1.45	4.53	212.41
液体葡萄糖	年产100万t以上的企业	个	2	2	
	年产100万t以上的企业总产量	万t	255.62	240.30	−5.99
	占全国总产量	%	49.30	40.81	17.22
	年产10万t以上的企业	个	8	12	50.00
	年产10万t以上的企业总产量	万t	116.43	244.46	109.96
	占全国总产量	%	22.45	41.51	84.90
	年产5万t以上的企业	个	9	8	−11.11
	年产5万t以上的企业总产量	万t	103.92	53.21	−48.80
	占全国总产量	%	20.04	9.04	−54.89

表 84　我国食品添加剂主要产品产量（2007—2008 年）　单位：万 t

产　品　名　称	2007 年	2008 年	同比增长（%）
总　计	**524.0**	**586.0**	**11.83**
食用香精香料	9.1	10.2	12.08
食用着色剂	33.0	32.4	−1.82
增稠乳化品质改良剂	25.0	27.0	8.00
增稠乳化剂	13.0	14.0	7.60
品质改良剂	12.0	13.0	8.30
防腐抗氧保鲜剂	17.9	20.0	11.73
高倍甜味剂	16.0	17.4	8.75
糖醇类甜味剂	100.0	108.0	8.00
营养强化剂	18.0	20.0	11.11
味精	172.1	169.5	−1.51

资料来源：其中数据由中国食品添加剂和配料协会提供。

表 85　我国饮料行业主要产品产量（2008—2009 年）

产品名称	单位	2008 年	2009 年	同比增长（%）
软饮料总产量	万 t	6 503.9	8 086.2	24.33
其中：碳酸饮料	万 t	1 171.2	1 254.2	7.09
果汁及果汁饮料	万 t	1 051.4	1 447.6	37.68
瓶（罐）装饮用水	万 t	2 535.3	3 159.0	24.60
饮料酒总产量（不含果露酒）	万 kL	5 504.5	5 188.6	−5.74
其中：白酒	万 kL	570.9	706.9	23.82
啤酒	万 kL	3 955.6	4 236.4	7.10
葡萄酒	万 kL	75.2	96.0	27.63
黄酒	万 kL	87.7	100.0	14.00

资料来源：表中数据出自 2010 年版《中国饮料》杂志第 4 期。

表 86　我国牛奶与乳制品产量（2008—2009 年）

产品名称	单位	2008 年	2009 年	同比增长（%）
牛奶	万 t	3 650.0	3 518.0	−3.6
乳制品	万 t	1 734.6	1 935.1	11.56
其中：液态奶	万 t	1 449.2	1 641.6	13.28
干乳制品	万 t	285.4	293.5	2.84
城镇居民人均消费	kg	25.5	26.4	3.46

表 87 我国饮料行业各地区主要产品产量（2008 年） 单位：t

地区	软饮料	碳酸饮料	果汁及果汁饮料	瓶（罐）装饮用水	其他饮料
全国总计	**64 151 038**	**11 074 011**	**11 825 120**	**24 755 767**	**16 496 140**
北京	2 159 924	674 056	458 977	609 339	417 552
天津	1 698 625	472 736	44 233	206 034	975 622
河北	1 626 007	7 949	450 907	358 111	809 040
山西	391 573	154 713	215 658	21 202	
内蒙古	1 148 574	25 665	79 772	141 464	901 673
辽宁	3 215 099	539 891	145 707	2 027 612	501 889
吉林	3 048 895	595 357	153 035	2 289 966	10 537
黑龙江	1 194 836	344 143	513 762	327 898	9 033
上海	2 522 921	1 123 832	89 930	992 396	316 763
江苏	2 255 345	537 635	525 356	392 012	800 342
浙江	6 419 168	845 114	962 738	1 685 995	2 925 321
安徽	892 397	133 469	42 617	229 178	487 133
福建	2 243 407	427 223	295 895	494 721	1 025 568
江西	925 580	196 338	216 466	388 143	151 633
山东	3 428 874	519 528	962 869	1 433 921	512 556
河南	4 911 519	384 963	1 156 178	1 607 597	1 762 781
湖北	2 929 715	509 701	623 632	728 938	1 067 444
湖南	488 253		14 474	406 554	67 225
广东	12 133 263	2 214 359	1 989 754	5 696 724	2 242 426
广西	1 292 143	200 675	19 158	838 871	233 439
海南	313 413	53 616	53 848	164 757	41 192
重庆	1 426 450	376 418	381 571	444 961	223 500
四川	2 468 850	261 835	349 757	1 411 263	445 995
贵州	312 206		72 091	229 298	10 817
云南	1 196 457	127 573	40 102	765 196	263 586
西藏	38 491			38 491	
陕西	1 806 433	319 157	1 293 090	194 186	
甘肃	925 540	275	467 537	249 243	208 485
青海	27			27	
宁夏	112 267		24 268	87 999	
新疆	597 787	27 790	191 740	293 669	84 588

资料来源：表中数据由中国饮料工业协会提供。

表 88 我国烟草工业主要产品产量（2008—2009 年）

年 份	烟叶（万 t）	烤烟（万 t）	卷烟（亿支）
2008	283.8	262.3	22 199.2
2009	306.6	281.4	22 901.5
同比增长（%）	8.03	7.28	3.16

资料来源：表中数据由农业部、国家烟草专卖局提供。

表 89 我国酒精工业产品产量（2008—2009 年）

单位：万 kL

年 份	2008 年	2009 年	同比增长（%）
产 量	681.3	731.7	7.40

资料来源：表中数据由中国酿酒工业协会提供。

表 90 我国酒精工业各地区产品产量（2007—2008 年）

单位：万 kL

地区	2007 年	2008 年	同比增长（%）
全国总计	**654.2**	**681.3**	**4.13**
吉 林	123.2	136.5	10.79
河 南	64.4	81.8	26.92
广 西	55.6	66.3	19.17
黑龙江	52.3	56.9	8.94
安 徽	56.5	54.9	−2.62
内蒙古	49.5	53.9	8.76
山 东	46.5	49.2	5.85
江 苏	73.8	48.9	−33.74
四 川	31.6	38.9	23.08
天 津	32.3	26.2	−18.84
云 南	20.3	20.2	平
广 东	15.3	13.9	−9.41
河 北	11.0	12.6	14.29
湖 北	3.1	5.3	72.03
山 西	7.7	4.5	−40.90
新 疆	2.7	3.9	45.50
辽 宁	4.7	3.1	−34.96
湖 南	0.8	1.3	62.50
甘 肃	0.6	1.3	116.67
宁 夏	0.8	0.5	−37.50
海 南	0.47	0.46	−2.13
陕 西	1.10	0.42	−60.23
贵 州	0.21	0.21	平
浙 江	0.07	0.08	14.29

资料来源：表中数据由中国酿酒工业协会酒精分会提供。

表 91 我国各地区味精产量（2008 年） 单位：万 t

地 区	2008 年	占全国总产量比重（%）
全国总计	**184.39**	**100.00**
天 津	0.13	0.07
河 北	16.56	9.00
辽 宁	3.79	2.05
上 海	1.08	0.59
江 苏	5.06	2.74
浙 江	11.03	5.98
安 徽	9.10	4.93
福 建	6.71	3.64
江 西	0.76	0.41
山 东	57.87	31.38
河 南	38.17	20.70
湖 北	2.37	1.29
湖 南	1.60	0.87
广 东	9.58	5.20
广 西	0.08	0.04
重 庆	4.85	2.63
四 川	7.01	3.80
云 南	1.16	0.63
甘 肃	0.10	0.06
宁 夏	6.67	3.61
新 疆	0.69	0.37

资料来源：表中数据由中国发酵工业协会提供。

表 92 我国焙烤食品糖制品主要产区产量（2008 年） 单位：万 t

地 区	糖果巧克力	糕点面包	饼干及其他烤烤食品	方便面及其他焙烤食品	冷冻饮品	米面制品（亿元）	速冻食品（亿元）	蜜饯制品（亿元）
全国总计	**121.37**	**79.91**	**282.69**	**499.45**	**205.53**	**286.24**	**248.57**	**133.99**
北 京	7.18	5.01			9.90			2.53
河 北		3.30		52.49				16.58
内蒙古					47.52			
辽 宁					17.99		9.15	
吉 林					15.97		14.17	
上 海	12.71	4.31					8.82	
江 苏							8.63	
浙 江		4.44		28.97	9.14			6.21
安 徽				24.01				
福 建	23.22	6.56	26.08			14.98	8.53	22.56
江 西			11.09			17.56		
山 东	3.83	13.28	36.93	38.33	15.25	27.87	60.51	37.42
河 南	8.08	8.00	88.42	136.82	23.94	63.87	86.59	8.25
湖 南	9.14					37.73		
湖 北	9.10		8.91			12.67		
广 东	30.86	15.03	40.22	39.66	8.29	18.18	16.08	24.94
四 川			15.98			30.57		
陕 西			14.51	19.27				2.98

资料来源：表中数据由中国焙烤食品糖制品工业协会提供。

表93 我国各地区啤酒产量（2008—2009年） 单位：万kL

地 区	2008年	2009年	同比增长（%）
全国总计	**3 955.9**	**4 236.4**	**7.09**
北 京	154.7	161.4	4.30
天 津	30.1	31.7	5.27
河 北	131.9	111.6	−15.40
山 西	21.9	25.4	15.98
内蒙古	98.3	110.4	12.30
辽 宁	239.5	246.9	3.09
吉 林	115.4	125.2	8.49
黑龙江	168.9	175.4	3.85
上 海	72.7	67.4	−7.29
江 苏	248.1	236.5	−4.68
浙 江	237.1	247.5	4.39
安 徽	140.1	156.5	11.71
福 建	197.2	190.5	−3.40
江 西	86.9	106.3	22.32
山 东	418.8	507.8	21.25
河 南	371.4	382.1	2.88
湖 北	214.2	250.6	16.99
湖 南	71.8	82.6	15.04
广 东	321.4	351.7	9.42
广 西	113.8	124.4	9.31
海 南	15.4	17.1	11.04
重 庆	67.9	72.8	7.22
四 川	154.0	159.1	3.31
云 南	41.0	47.4	15.61
贵 州	22.8	27.5	20.61
西 藏	9.0	11.3	25.56
陕 西	83.7	90.0	7.53
甘 肃	52.5	59.5	13.33
青 海	9.4	10.5	11.70
宁 夏	11.0	12.0	9.09
新 疆	34.8	37.5	7.76

资料来源：表中数据由中国酿酒工业协会啤酒分会提供。

表94 我国罐头工业产值与产品产量（2008年）

总产量（万t）	同比增长（%）	总产值（亿元）	同比增长（%）
595.3	17.44	589.4	31.08

资料来源：表中数据由中国罐头工业协会提供。

表 95　我国各地区白酒产量（2008—2009 年）　　单位：万 kL

地　区	2008 年	2009 年	同比增长（%）
全国总计	**570.90**	**706.90**	**23.82**
北　京	17.61	18.03	2.36
天　津	4.64	4.11	−11.42
河　北	19.96	23.45	17.48
山　西	10.29	9.91	−3.69
内蒙古	24.93	34.36	37.83
辽　宁	43.13	47.32	9.71
吉　林	20.18	34.48	70.86
黑龙江	7.22	10.32	42.94
上　海	0.68	0.77	13.24
江　苏	30.83	34.14	10.70
浙　江	2.81	2.40	−14.59
安　徽	26.95	29.71	10.23
福　建	2.34	3.09	31.95
江　西	11.66	15.36	31.73
山　东	72.19	86.87	20.33
河　南	60.98	71.96	18.00
湖　北	33.33	43.54	30.63
湖　南	7.07	12.45	76.10
广　东	10.26	9.39	−8.48
广　西	3.53	3.70	4.81
海　南	0.54	0.99	82.28
重　庆	12.05	17.01	41.16
四　川	110.85	155.96	40.69
贵　州	16.75	13.79	−17.67
云　南	3.78	4.75	25.66
陕　西	6.80	7.04	3.53
甘　肃	3.45	3.78	9.57
青　海	1.02	1.06	3.92
宁　夏	0.67	2.29	241.79
新　疆	4.40	4.91	11.47

资料来源：表中数据出自 2010 年版《酿酒》杂志第 3 期。

表 96　我国饲料工业产品产量（2006—2009 年）　单位：万 t

年　　份	饲料产量	其中：1. 配（混）合饲料	2. 浓缩饲料	3. 预混合饲料
2006	11 100	8 117	2 456	486
2007	12 300	9 319	2 491	521
2008	13 667	10 590	2 531	546
2009	13 999	10 696	2 708	595

资料来源：表中数据由全国饲料工作办公室提供。

表 97　2009/2010 年度制糖期糖料与食糖生产情况

地　　区	糖料种植面积（khm^2）	糖料入榨量（万 t）	产糖量（万 t）	开工工厂数（个）
全国合计	**1 608.51**	**8 591.99**	**1 073.83**	**276**
甘蔗糖合计	**1 468.15**	**8 100.83**	**1013.83**	**240**
广　　东	126.00	834.00	85.77	32
其中：湛江	108.00	733.94	73.03	22
广　　西	963.33	5560.00	710.20	102
云　　南	305.17	1364.87	177.15	77
海　　南	62.67	262.00	31.81	20
福　　建	3.61	32.24	3.48	2
四　　川				
其　　他	7.37	47.72	5.42	7
甜菜糖合计	**140.36**	**491.16**	**60.00**	**36**
黑 龙 江	44.18	83.20	9.89	9
新　　疆	64.67	321.00	38.44	14
内 蒙 古	24.40	53.50	7.01	5
其　　他	13.78	33.46	4.66	8

资料来源：表中数据由中国糖业协会提供。

表 98 我国食用菌产量、产值、出口情况（2009 年）

地 区	产 量（t）	产 值（万元）	出口量（t）	创 汇（万美元）	主要品种产量（t）		
					香 菇	平 菇	双孢菇
全国总计	**20 205 988**	**11 033 109**	**528 600**	**130 700**	**3435 447**	**4928 662**	**2183 053**
北 京	140 436	98 263	1 200	42	42 671	48 064	3676
天 津	68 050				15600	26 200	1350
河 北	1907 685	1 003 886	162 712	15 518	341 604	794 939	75 673
山 西	98 670	56 500	2 850	410	5150	71 000	5 200
内蒙古							
辽 宁	690 786	343 917	79 186	10 365	310 293	205 579	12 049
吉 林	937 030	556000	16 000	1 500	20 000	180 000	100
黑龙江	1642 690	667 680	16 000	8 176	81 660	86 300	
上 海	88 280	79 179			5 571	4 000	18 872
江 苏	1576 161	652 896	63 182	6 318	66 560	626 274	488 748
浙 江	950 000	650 000	50 000	15 000	410 000	110 000	40 000
安 徽	625 769	201 945			50 264	173 257	33 349
福 建	1 969 752	868 244			415 526	54 992	306 237
江 西	600 000	212000	5000	160	115 000	170 000	100 000
山 东	2 061 400	1 236800	200 000	21 000	150 003	715 400	244 700
河 南	2260 694	1132 996	70 275	7 196	416 378	767 952	223 043
湖 北	869 808	391 414	156 000	21 100	438 600	112 050	34 050
湖 南	650 000	390000	12 000	2 800	136 600	137 620	44 100
广 东	701 952	678 541	211 000	24 278	24 900	185 004	7210
广 西	758 497	424 193	233	196	94 169	78489	430 977
海 南							
重 庆	52 780	22 167			7 660	18 757	8 350
四 川	937 800	422 000			75 500	181 000	82 300
贵 州	30 940	282 400			4 500	7 200	1 200
云 南	69753	350 000	4 737	7 812	4 800	23 000	4800
西 藏							
陕 西	466 019	280 900	28 000	2 000	198 925	124 608	8465
甘 肃							
青 海							
宁 夏	16 287	8116			1 713	6 977	4 404
新 疆	34 749	23 072			1 800	20000	2200

（续）

地 区	主要品种产量（t）						
	金针菇	草 菇	黑木耳	毛木耳	银 耳	滑 菇	猴头菇
全国总计	**1567 748**	**401 901**	**2 697 316**	**889 988**	**312 725**	**310 467**	**127 069**
北 京	15 186	890	4 867				
天 津	5200		800				
河 北	194 946	6 826	57 464			968	
山 西	2 740	350	2160				350
内蒙古							
辽 宁	12 808		10142			151 358	100
吉 林	7 000		685000			10 000	200
黑龙江	7 600		1 242 500			136 700	77 660
上 海	26 946	5 803					
江 苏	258 748	40 968	4 068	23223	11420		
浙 江	140 000	4 000	70 000	5000			2 000
安 徽	60 669	553	9 486	8 160	70		
福 建	47 163	26 672	31 489	211 075	290 730	8 769	21 210
江 西	20 000	9 000	8 000	12 000			1 000
山 东	272 200	93 200	115 500	50 100	2 300	2 400	12 800
河 南	79 308	61 888	208 322	210 216	3660		4 016
湖 北	33 500	120	145 240	4 560	300	40	30
湖 南	94 000	5 200	8 050	23 870	4 230		1 140
广 东	173 768	151 908		7 022			6 210
广 西	16 334	3 393	19 132	23 193			85
海 南							
重 庆	7517		3971	3 525			200
四 川	78 500			305 000			
贵 州	400		50	800		30	
云 南	6000	130	450	460	15	140	20
西 藏							
陕 西	2 015		70 607	434		62	40
甘 肃							
青 海							
宁 夏							
新 疆	520 0			1 200			3

（续）

地　区	主要品种产量（t）						
	鸡腿菇	白灵菇	杏鲍菇	茶薪菇	小平菇	姬　菇	袖珍菇
全国总计	**440 714**	**204 829**	**322 289**	**416 360**	**132 525**	**442 325**	**219 706**
北　京	1 339	5 282	6 376	2 807			1 004
天　津		14 200	3250	200		480	350
河　北	43 610	39 594	29 902			183 392	
山　西	100	4 160	2350		4 860	610	
内蒙古							
辽　宁	3 047	700	1999			104	800
吉　林	1800	500	800		40		
黑龙江			780		830		
上　海		200	2 895	216		4 000	6 347
江　苏	36 092		7 896	2 425		540	
浙　江	15 000	5 000	50 000	20 000	15 000	10 000	40 000
安　徽	546	412	4 775	3 000		1 446	1678
福　建	26 367	109	48 245	236 079			86 944
江　西	13 000		20 000	76 000	15 000		5 000
山　东	125 500	45 800	63 300	47 900	22 100	28 500	19 400
河　南	108 487	79 659	14 239	385		10 163	
湖　北	165	1350	950	2 400	37 800		8 150
湖　南	4 120	2 300	23 100	9 460	32 300	67 110	22 280
广　东	28 486	1580	40 150	8 413		2549	7 846
广　西	10 321		699	3 360			19 797
海　南							
重　庆	2 500			300			
四　川	18 500					131 000	
贵　州	500	20	30	1500	4 000	1 000	100
云　南	140	130	138	1 500	1100	450	10
西　藏							
陕　西	494	233	295	415	365	961	
甘　肃							
青　海							
宁　夏							
新　疆	600	3 600	120			20	

（续）

地　区	主要品种产量（t）									
	灰树花	竹荪	姬松茸	松茸	牛肝菌	羊肚菌	灵芝	天麻	茯苓	其他菇
全国总计	**6 423**	**52 827**	**34 539**	**6 200**	**11 659**	**210**	**114 437**	**121 743**	**293 314**	**378 100**
北　京	750						14			7 510
天　津							120			150
河　北							780			
山　西						21	39	10		
内蒙古										
辽　宁				150	1926	30	245	30		12 115
吉　林	10		30	50	200		1 000	300		30 000
黑龙江			530				660			
上　海										
江　苏							10			10
浙　江							9 000	3 000	2 000	
安　徽			20				3 786	10 000	243 040	21 259
福　建	200	40 705	24 089				1 543		1321	90 277
江　西	1 000	1 000					12 000	1 000	1 000	20000
山　东	1 200						36 500	2100	200	10 000
河　南		707					3 985	24 493	3 000	40 793
湖　北	3	95	3 200		315	65	1 420	22 500	22600	305
湖　南	3 200	770	4 090		70	20	10 300	4 870	11 200	
广　东			750				31 482		1570	23 104
广　西		500	180				1 363		7 133	49 373
海　南										
重　庆										
四　川										66 000
贵　州		9 000	50		10	10	80	300	150	10
云　南	60	50	1 450	6000	8 800	50	50	5 500	10	4 500
西　藏										
陕　西			150		338	8	60	47 640	90	9 816
甘　肃										
青　海										
宁　夏										3 193
新　疆						6	2			

资料来源：1. 表中数据根据各省、自治区、直辖市食用菌协会、农业、供销及科研部门上报的资料汇总而成，由中国食用菌协会提供。

2. 表中 2009 年食用菌产品出口数量与金额，为国家海关总署提供的数据。

3. 表中产品数据均按鲜品统计，干品折鲜品比例按 1∶10 计算。

表 99　我国农垦系统农产品加工业主要产品产量（2008—2009 年）

产　　品	单　位	2008 年	2009 年	同比增长（%）
粮食商品量	万 t	2 094.3	2 416.5	15.39
粮食商品率	%	86.49	87.14	0.65
食用植物油	万 t	110.4	170.5	54.42
机制糖	万 t	190.1	178.8	−5.93
乳制品	万 t	187.9	207.1	10.20
其中：液体奶	万 t	159.9	178.1	11.41
饮料酒	万 t	192.8	184.8	−4.17
其中：葡萄酒	万 t	7.9	6.5	−18.31
纱	万 t	45.6	42.2	−7.48
布	亿 m	4.9	6.5	33.27
配（混）合饲料	万 t	383.5	417.8	8.95
机制纸及纸板	万 t	137.7	107.8	−21.74

表 100　农垦系统各地区农产品加工业主要产品产量（2009 年）

地　区	混配合饲料（t）	机制纸及纸板（t）	纱（万 t）	布（万 m）	机制糖（t）	饮料酒（t）	乳制品（t）	食用植物油（t）
全国合计	**4 178 077**	**1 077 642**	**42.16**	**65 339**	**1 788 222**	**1847850**	**2 070908**	**1 704 508**
北　　京						16	235 618	
天　　津		8 109				40 558	84 669	
河　　北	100 466	607 336	0.02	6 250		3 846	333 931	28 950
山　　西	350						735	
内 蒙 古	21 190	3 640				911	23 418	40 131
辽　　宁	80 411	3 075				292 174	99 484	2 200
吉　　林		6 800				5		
黑 龙 江	312 788	47 924			32 127	38 989	357 241	794 751
上　　海					185 598	112 546	360 675	
江　　苏	98 447		2.76					12 534
浙　　江	234 117			35 309		534 668	2 380	
安　　徽	63 332		1.38			4 250	15 910	4 170
福　　建	7 750	66 164		86		1 551	1 186	792
江　　西	26 970	95 736	2.00	2 285		28 630		9 209
山　　东	2 003						160	
河　　南	91 167	1 751	1.68	21		26 920	11 778	1 982
湖　　北	729 015	16 238	11.94	12 812		388 153	76 525	470 475
湖　　南	940 000	36 000			3 500	3 843	5 400	3 000
广　　东	4 059	22 293			557 015	1 961	68 300	1 750
广　　西	182 355	40 242			764 009	3 079	2 926	491
海　　南					45 700	107		115
重　　庆	426 827						184 428	
四　　川						6 823	2 532	
贵　　州	21 227					24	30 127	
云　　南					61 522	74		
西　　藏								
陕　　西	11 867						1 798	2 432
甘　　肃	8 570		0.01			142 951		
青　　海							13 367	
宁　　夏	23 884					126 361	19 572	57
新疆（兵团）	773 076	120 131	20.16	8 576	138 751	85 392	72 773	315 236
新疆（农业）	13 797		2.15			4 018	505	10 198
新疆（畜牧）	1 209	2 203	0.06				44 168	6 035

表101 我国森林工业主要产品产量（2008—2009年）

主要产品	单 位	2008年	2009年	同比增长（%）
锯材	万 m^3	2 841.0	3 229.8	13.69
木片（实积）	万 m^3	1 000.8	1 285.8	28.48
人造板	万 m^3	9 410.0	11 546.7	22.71
胶合板	万 m^3	3 540.9	4 451.2	25.71
纤维板	万 m^3	2 906.6	3 488.6	20.02
刨花板	万 m^3	1 142.2	1 431.0	25.28
其他人造板	万 m^3	1 820.3	2 175.9	19.54
胶合木	万 m^3	295.4	325.9	10.32
木地板	万 m^2	37 689.4	37 753.2	0.17
卫生筷子	标准箱	9 231 247	10 409 774	12.77
人造板表面装饰板	万 m^2	22 738.2	25 327.1	11.39
热固性树脂装饰层压板	万 m^2	660.1	1 640.0	148.45
单板	万 m^3	2 284.0	2 714.4	18.84
林产化学产品				
松香类产品	t	1 067 293	1 117 030	4.66
松节油类产品	t	128 036	157 506	23.02
樟脑	t	10 215	9 700	−5.04
冰片	t	1 057	986	−6.72
栲胶类产品	t	9 337	11 000	17.81
紫胶类产品	t	2 899	2 755	−4.97
木材热解产品				
其中：木炭	t	285 408	316 612	10.93
活性炭	t	185 243	226 529	22.29
软木制品				
其中：软木砖	m^3	30 270	8 200	−72.91
软木纸	m^3	218 784	45 747	−79.09

表 102 各地区森林工业主要产品产量（2009 年）

单位：万 m³

地 区	锯材	木片（实积）	人造板						胶合木	木地板（万 m²）
			合计	热带材人造板	胶合板	纤维板	刨花板	其他人造板		
全国总计	**3 229.8**	**1 285.8**	**11 546.7**	**595.5**	**4451.2**	**3488.6**	**1 431.0**	**2 175.9**	**325.9**	**37 753.2**
北 京			12.2			12.2				328.4
天 津			5.6		2.8		2.8			
河 北	168.9	39.3	1 097.8		347.0	278.8	198.3	273.8	0.5	51.5
山 西	0.1	0.01	55.5		0.3	31.6	23.6			
内蒙古	391.7	13.6	69.3		32.4	13.9	20.1	2.9	1.4	0.7
辽 宁	161.4	56.3	194.8		67.1	36.8	28.9	61.9	20.7	3 082.9
吉 林	96.5	24.2	192.9		73.6	35.8	54.9	28.6	11.8	2 515.8
黑龙江	126.5	47.2	98.3	0.3	13.5	30.8	29.6	24.5	3.7	217.6
上 海			15.8		3.9	11.9				2 890.1
江 苏	56.9	67.9	2 195.9	237.6	903.1	506.7	345.8	440.2	3.7	6 106.9
浙 江	271.9	58.9	487.1	2.7	143.9	119.5	13.7	210.1	49.5	7 223.9
安 徽	124.2	32.7	670.6		344.0	197.2	39.3	90.2	5.2	2 726.7
福 建	133.9	66.2	702.1		268.9	170.3	129.9	132.9	102.4	1 247.7
江 西	126.4	32.1	320.7		116.1	85.3	34.8	84.6	22.2	1 172.9
山 东	364.7	326.4	1 163.0	45.0	516.2	400.1	82.7	163.9	50.9	1 681.9
河 南	115.6	85.1	1 422.6		598.5	345.6	263.9	214.6	5.4	278.0
湖 北	27.7	24.1	248.7		37.5	149.1	8.4	53.8	1.7	2 604.8
湖 南	229.7	22.9	430.8		241.6	55.5	17.9	115.8	20.9	1 183.0
广 东	76.4	97.6	577.5	116.1	132.6	322.2	75.2	47.5		2 220.4
广 西	389.3	144.8	864.9	140.4	380.5	317.5	19.9	147.0	6.9	89.2
海 南	31.0	60.0	42.5	42.5	22.0	15.5	3.0	2.0	1.5	
重 庆	5.3	3.4	38.9		30.1	5.7	1.7	1.5	0.2	1.0
四 川	117.6	14.0	419.4		120.1	222.8	25.8	50.8	11.3	1 699.0
贵 州	41.2	2.9	47.0		28.6	7.8	0.9	9.9	0.9	59.9
云 南	125.9	33.0	112.9	10.1	22.6	71.2	8.3	10.8	3.7	356.2
西 藏	19.4	18.6	0.01					0.01	0.1	
陕 西	1.6	0.1	33.9		1.5	31.8	0.4	0.2		
甘 肃			2.4	0.8	1.4	0.8	0.2			
青 海										
宁 夏										
新 疆	1.1	0.1	0.2		0.2					
大兴安岭	24.7	13.9	22.9		1.0	12.5	1.0	8.5	1.4	14.9

（续）

地区	卫生筷子（标准箱）	人造板表面装饰板（万 m²）	热固性树脂装饰层压板（万 m²）	单板（万 m²）	松香类产品（t）	松节油类产品（t）	樟脑（t）	冰片（t）	栲胶类产品（t）	紫胶类产品（t）	木材热解产品（t）		软木制品（m³）	
											木炭	活性炭	软木砖	软木纸
全国总计	**10 409 774**	**25 327.1**	**1 640**	**2714.4**	**1 117 030**	**157 506**	**9 700**	**986**	**11 000**	**2 755**	**316 612**	**226 529**	**8 200**	**45 747**
北京														
天津														
河北	570	1 099.1		408.5					1 500					
山西		38.0										324		
内蒙古	149 949			0.1					1 334					
辽宁				2.9	300						13 018	1 530		
吉林	553 600	1 356.9		27.1							2 030			
黑龙江	2 147 652	94.4		12.8							9 120			28 250
上海														
江苏		234.5		956.4							60			
浙江	1 327 961	20 235.9		3.4	13 550	6 570					20 011	57 852		
安徽	218 855		40	55.7	5 008	1 061					28 443	6 545		
福建	831 801	0.1		0.01	76 925	15 660	6 690			6	14 686	95 066		
江西	1 667 863				84 556	32 209	586	2		4	29 298	42 610		
山东	11 380	154.5		653.5							52 503	520		
河南	17 930			226.9	2 500						3 321			
湖北	24 750	2.7	1 600	19.9	13 516	3 020					20			
湖南	865 545	30.1		20.9	26 689	3 140	24	320	10	862	26 377	17 145		8 888
广东	200 200	2 070.7		16.3	108 918	10 739	2 309	464		337	6 060		8 200	8 200
广西	665 657			283.2	649 010	43 507	15		7 161		2 340	876		
海南		2.5		8.3	2 993						22 000			
重庆	200				1 160	15 231					20	1 200		
四川	319 460	7.5		3.5	2 571	298	55	200		61	6 080			
贵州	27 290			0.9	3 825	26 071					39 211	160		4
云南	35 840	0.3		7.5	125 509		21		845	1 485	22 039	284		
西藏														
陕西									150					405
甘肃														
青海														
宁夏														
新疆														
大兴安岭	1 343 271			1.4							19 975	2 417		

表 103 我国水产品加工产品的主要种类与产量（2006—2009 年） 单位：万 t

年 份	冷冻制品	干制品	腌熏制品	鱼糜及其制品	动物蛋白饲料	罐制品	其他
2006	819.8	77.9	29.9	56.5	171.6	22.4	84.5
2007	806.6	92.3	25.3	74.9	188.1	18.3	62.4
2008	850.9	111.6		81.9	148.0	22.0	62.4
2009	941.1	138.8		84.8	136.5	22.1	61.2

表 104 纺织工业主要产品产量（规模以上企业）（2008—2009 年）

产品名称	单 位	2008 年	2009 年	同比增长（%）
纤维	万 t	2 405.0	2 726.0	13.35
纱	万 t	2 149.0	2 406.0	11.96
布	亿 m	528.0	568.0	7.58
服装	亿件	207.0	237.5	14.73
全行业加工总量	万 t			

资料来源：表中数据由国家工信部提供。

表 105 我国皮革行业主要产品产量（2008—2009 年）

主要产品	单位	2008 年	2009 年	同比增长（%）
轻革	亿 m^2	687.00	6.90	0.40
皮鞋	亿双	33.20	35.90	8.13
皮革服装	万件	5 265.00	5 612.00	6.60
毛皮服装	万件	385.00	468.50	21.70
皮革皮包、袋	亿只	7.70	7.03	−8.70

资料来源：表中数据出自 2010 年版《中国皮革》杂志。

表 106 我国家具工业主要产品产量（2008—2009 年） 单位：万件

产品名称	单位	2008 年	2009 年	同比增长（%）
总 计	**万件**	**58 001.3**	**60 814.4**	**4.85**
木质家具	万件	19 618.2	20 501.1	4.50
软体家具（含床垫沙发）	万件	3 462.8	3 683.4	6.37
金属家具	万件	31 573.1	33 366.5	5.68

表 107 我国家具工业分地区主要产品产量（2009 年） 单位：万件

地 区	家 具	地 区	家 具
全国总计	**60 814.4**	河 南	2 179.3
北 京	719.4	湖 北	174.1
天 津	516.4	湖 南	351.9
河 北	602.0	广 东	15 696.9
山 西	9.5	广 西	82.8
内蒙古	150.9	海 南	19.0

（续）

地 区	家 具	地 区	家 具
辽 宁	1 923.7	重 庆	454.2
吉 林	153.0	四 川	834.1
黑龙江	351.3	贵 州	23.5
上 海	2 738.6	云 南	6.3
江 苏	2 107.0	西 藏	
浙 江	17 106.5	陕 西	50.2
安 徽	125.8	甘 肃	5.3
福 建	8 318.2	青 海	
江 西	512.3	宁 夏	4.6
山 东	5 457.8	新 疆	139.7

资料来源：表中数据由中国家具工业协会提供。

表 108 我国造纸工业纸浆消耗情况（2007—2009 年） 单位：万 t

品 种	2007 年		2008 年		2009 年		同比增长(%)
	消耗	所占比例（%）	消 耗	所占比例（%）	消 耗	所占比例（%）	
纸浆消耗量	**6 769**	**100.00**	**7 360**	**100.00**	**7 980**	**100.00**	**8.42**
1. 木浆	1 450	22.00	1 624	22.00	1 866	23.00	14.90
其中：进口木浆	845	12.00	952	13.00	1 315	16.00	38.13
国产木浆	605	10.00	672	9.00	551	7.00	18.00
2. 非木浆	1 302	19.00	1 297	18.00	1 175	15.00	−9.41
3. 废纸浆	4 017	59.00	4 439	60.00	4 939	62.00	11.26
其中：国产废纸浆	2 212	32.00	2 503	34.00	2 739	34.00	9.43
进口废纸浆	1 805	27.00	1 936	26.00	2 200	28.00	13.64

注：表中数据出自 2010 年版《中华纸业》杂志第 31 卷第 11 期，表中废纸浆＝废纸量×0.8。

表 109 我国废纸回收利用情况（2004—2008 年）

年 份	废纸回收量（万 t）	废纸回收率（%）	废纸浆用量（万 t）	废纸浆利用率（%）	废纸进口量（万 t）
2004	1 651.0	30.40	2 305	51.7	1 230
2005	1 809.0	31.50	2 810	54.0	1 703
2006	2 367.0	35.90	3 380	56.0	1 962
2007	2 765.0	37.90	2 212	59.3	2 256
2008	3 127.7	39.50	4 439	69.5	2 421

资料来源：表中数据出自 2010 年版《国际造纸》杂志第 1 期。

表 110 我国各类造纸纤维原料所占比重（2008—2009 年） 单位：万 t

名 称	木 浆		草类纤维		废纸浆		总 量	
	2008 年	2009 年	2008 年	2009 年	2008 年	2009 年	2008 年	2009 年
我国造纸纤维原料消耗量	1 624	1866	1 297	1 175	4 439	4 939	7 360	7 980
造纸纤维原料中所占比重（%）	22	23	18	15	60	62	100	100

表 111　我国机制纸及纸板主要品种产量（2008—2009 年）　　单位：万 t

品　种	2008 年	2009 年	同比增长（%）
纸及纸板合计	**7 980**	**8 640**	**8.27**
一、纸			
1. 新闻纸	460	480	4.35
2. 未涂布印刷书写纸	1 400	1 510	7.86
3. 涂布印刷纸	550	590	7.27
4. 生活用纸	550	580	5.45
5. 包装用纸	560	575	2.68
二、纸板			
1. 白纸板	1 120	1 150	2.68
2. 箱纸板	1 530	1 730	13.07
3. 瓦楞原纸	1 520	1 715	12.83
三、特种纸及纸板	140	150	7.14
四、其他纸及纸板	150	160	6.67

资料来源：表中数据出自 2010 年版《中华纸业》杂志第 31 卷第 11 期。

表 112　我国纸和纸板消费结构情况（2007—2008 年）　　单位：万 t

产品名称	2007 年					2008 年				
	生产量	进口量	出口量	消费量	比重（%）	生产量	进口量	出口量	消费量	比重（%）
机制纸及纸板	**7 350**	**401**	**461**	**7 290**	**100.0**	**7 980**	**358**	**403**	**7 935**	**100.0**
一、机制纸										
1. 新闻纸	450	2	59	393	5.4	460	2	36	426	5.4
2. 未涂布印刷书写纸	1 340	45	53	1 332	18.3	1 400	39	54	1 385	17.5
其中：书刊印刷纸										
书写纸										
3. 涂布纸	510	56	140	426	5.8	550	54	137	467	5.9
其中：铜版纸	420	40	93	367	5.0	460	38	97	401	5.1
4. 生活用纸	520	4	48	476	6.5	550	5	52	503	6.3
5. 包装用纸	530	10	3	537	7.4	560	12	3	569	7.2
6. 白纸板纸板	1 050	70	58	1 062	14.5	1 120	64	53	1 131	14.3
其中：涂布白纸板	1 000	70	58	1 012	13.9	1 070	64	53	1 081	13.6
7. 箱纸板	1 360	103	25	1 438	19.7	1 530	88	13	1 605	20.2
8. 瓦楞原纸	1 340	53	39	1 354	18.6	1 520	45	13	1 552	19.6
其中：高强度瓦楞原纸										
9. 特种纸和纸板	120	43	27	136	1.9	140	38	34	144	6.8
10. 其他纸和纸板	130	15	9	136	1.9	150	11	8	153	1.9

资料来源：表中数据出自 2009 年版《中国造纸年鉴》。

表 113　我国造纸工业主要产品生产及消费情况（2008—2009 年）

单位：万 t

产品名称	生产量			消费量		
	2008 年	2009 年	同比（%）	2008 年	2009 年	同比（%）
总　量	**7 980**	**8 640**	**8.27**	**7 935**	**8 569**	**7.99**
1. 新闻纸	460	480	4.35	426	461	8.22
2. 未涂布印刷书写纸	1 400	1 510	7.86	1 385	1 497	8.09
3. 涂布印刷纸	550	590	7.27	467	463	−0.86
其中：铜版纸	460	500	8.70	401	399	−0.50
4. 生活用纸	550	580	5.45	503	529	5.17
5. 包装用纸	560	575	2.68	569	587	3.16
6. 白纸板	1 120	1 150	2.68	1 131	1 160	2.56
其中：涂布白纸板	1 070	1 100	2.80	1 081	1 110	2.68
7. 箱纸板	1 530	1 730	13.07	1 605	1 809	12.71
8. 瓦楞原纸	1 520	1 715	12.83	1 552	1 758	13.27
9. 特种纸及纸板	140	150	7.14	144	144	
10. 其他纸及纸板	150	160	6.67	153	161	5.23

资料来源：表中数据出自 2010 年版《中华纸业》杂志，第 31 卷第 11 期。

表 114　我国纸和纸板生产、消费及进口量与人均消费量（2005—2009 年）

年　份	纸和纸板总产量（万 t）	纸和纸板总消费量（万 t）	纸和纸板进口量（万 t）	人均消费量（kg）
2005	5 600	5 930	524	45
2006	6 500	6 600	441	50
2007	7 350	7 290	401	55
2008	7 980	7 935	359	60
2009	8 391	8 331	352	64

表 115　我国 136 个重点书刊印刷（含其他印刷）企业主要产品产量（2007—2008 年）

年　份	照相排字（亿字）	书刊印刷（万令）	胶印印刷（万对开色令）	书刊装订（万令）
2007	41.6	2 267	9 240	2 347
2008	49.4	2 135	10 253	2 503
同比增长（%）	18.75	−5.82	10.96	6.65

表 116　我国纸和纸板人均消费量与美国的比较（2005—2009 年）

单位：kg/（人·年）

年　份	2005 年	2006 年	2007 年	2008 年	2009 年
我国人均消费量	45	50	55	60	64
美国人均消费量	301	301	288	266	234

表 117 我国橡胶工业主要产品产量（2008—2009 年）

产品名称	单 位	2008 年	2009 年	同比增长（%）
轮 胎	万条	35 000.0	38 000.0	8.57
摩托车胎	万条	21 872.0	22 800.0	4.24
自行车胎	万条	58 400.0	56 706.0	−2.90
输送带	万 m^2	21 946.0	21 200.0	−3.40
胶 鞋	万双	34 421.0	32 700.0	−5.00
安全套	亿只	34.5	32.9	−4.64
助 剂	万 t	51.8	59.5	15.00
炭 黑	万 t	174.3	206.7	18.60
再生胶	万 t	50.1	55.9	11.50
钢丝帘线	万 t	69.6	91.6	31.70

注：表中数据为 44 个轮胎分会会员企业、23 个力车车胎分会会员企业、84 个胶管胶带分会会员企业、29 个胶鞋分会会员企业、27 个乳胶分会会员企业、38 个炭黑分会会员企业、42 个废橡胶综合利用分会会员企业以及橡胶助剂、骨架材料分会会员企业的统计数据。

资料来源：表中数据出自 2010 版《中国橡胶》杂志第 5 期。

表 118 我国人均主要工农业产品产量（2005—2009 年）

产品名称	单 位	2005 年	2006 年	2007 年	2008 年	2009 年
粮 食	kg	371.26	379.89	380.61	399.13	398.70
棉 花	kg	4.38	5.75	5.78	5.66	4.80
油 料	kg	23.60	20.14	19.49	22.29	23.70
糖 料	kg	72.50	79.78	92.48	101.31	92.20
茶 叶	kg	0.72	0.78	0.88	0.95	1.02
水 果	kg	123.65	130.45	137.62	145.10	153.20
猪牛羊肉	kg	41.98	42.65	40.09	42.38	44.32
水产品	kg	33.90	34.96	36.02	36.96	38.50
布	m	37.15	45.66	51.24	53.60	55.60
机制纸及纸板	kg	47.60	52.35	59.13	63.34	64.73
纱	kg	11.13	13.29	15.69	16.03	17.93

农产品加工业主要产品出口创汇情况

表 119 我国海关出口农产品及加工品数量与金额（2008—2009 年） 单位：万美元

产 品 名 称	单 位	2008 年		2009 年	
		数 量	金 额	数 量	金 额
活猪	万头	164	38 270	169	33 008
活家禽	万只	1 166	3 399	696	2 608
牛肉	万 t	2	9 550	1	6 121
猪肉	万 t	8	27 565	9	26 272
冻鸡	万 t	7	15 666	7	13 627

（续）

产品名称	单位	2008年		2009年	
		数量	金额	数量	金额
水海产品	万t	175	517 708	209	680 851
鲜蛋	百万个	1 216	8 013	1 111	7 889
谷物及谷物粉	万t	181	75 857	132	71 620
稻谷和大米	万t	97	48 326	79	52 506
玉米	万t	27	7 942	13	3 171
蔬菜	万t	624	216 654	636	499 576
鲜或冷藏蔬菜	万t	415	155 138	424	218 760
橘、橙	t	748 814	36 227	985 127	50 640
苹果	t	1 153 325	69 834	1 171 805	71 213
松子仁	t	4 178	4 768	7 862	14 297
大豆	万t	47	35 146	35	23 714
花生及花生仁	万t	23	30 652	24	21 823
食用值物油（含棕榈油）	t	247 623	40 156	114 019	15 149
食糖	t	58 403	2 708	63 886	3 365
天然蜂蜜	t	84 865	14 711	71 831	12 570
茶叶	t	296 940	68 226	302 952	70 495
辣椒干	t	96 476	17 997	91 025	14 262
猪肉罐头	t	31 563	8 747	36 133	9 765
蘑菇罐头	t	422 371	65 206	285 791	36 014
啤酒	万L	24 170	12 952	21 030	12 269
肠衣	t	67 642	84 141	69 219	78 798
填充用羽毛、羽绒	t	29 846	29 618	27 030	24 825
药材	t	188 296	45 145	199 552	48 488
烤烟	t	116 127	33 430	99 449	41 148
纸烟	万条	6 834	24 869	8 078	27 960
锯材	万m^3	69	40 142	56	34 509
生丝	t	13 431	33 379	9 227	24 352
山羊绒	t	2 421	19 621	2 125	13 783
棉花	t	16 361	3 410	8 249	1 812
中式成药	t	13 180	17 435	13 367	16 596
烟花、爆竹	t	313 849	49 500	297 107	55 690
松香及树脂酸	t	276 517	27 194	193 505	18 202
新的充气橡胶轮胎	万条	31 227	806 031	30 214	768 493
纸及纸板（末切成形）	万t	361	327 914	362	313 604
棉纱线	t	547 247	197 312	537 527	181 593
丝织物			82 242		77 572
棉机织物			1 021 657		850 718
亚麻及苎麻机织物	万m	19 642	41 992	19 980	44 363
合成短纤及棉混纺机织物	万m	276 913	229 411	237 282	182 384
地毯	万m^2	41 757	160 752	45 725	149 126
塑料编织袋（周转袋除外）	万条	474 191	80 453	508 453	71 238
纺织机械及零件			156 548		121 151
家具及其零件			2 691 118		2 532 923

（续）

产品名称	单位	2008年		2009年	
		数量	金额	数量	金额
非针织或钩编织物制服装			4 676 329		4 265 440
针织或钩编织服装			5 455 564		4 806 802
皮鞋	万双	112 586	980 903	88 241	835 620
橡胶或塑料底布鞋（包括球鞋）	万双	138 050	394 376	142 355	412 858
足球、篮球、排球	万个	19 652	34 676	18 493	32 804
竹编结品	t	70 845	22 250	41 641	14 253
藤编结品	t	31 642	17 624	17 905	10 983
草编结品	t	53 580	21 917	38 350	16 682
柳编结品	t	143 387	60 257	93 775	40 014

表 120　我国农产品进出口状况（2008—2009 年）　　单位：亿美元

项目	2008年	2009年
农产品进出口额	985	921.3
农产品出口额	402	395.9
农产品进口额	583	525.4

资料来源：表中数据出自 2010 年版《中国统计年鉴》。

表 121　我国海关进口农产品及加工品数量与金额（2008—2009 年）

单位：万美元

产品名称	单位	2008年		2009年	
		数量	金额	数量	金额
谷物及谷物粉	万 t	154	73 179	315	89 807
小麦	万 t	4	1 480	90	21 117
稻谷和大米	万 t	33	2 0841	36	21 558
大豆	万 t	3 744	2 181 265	4 255	1 878 728
食用植物油	万 t	816	897 734	816	589 519
食糖	万 t	78	31 850	106	37 840
天然橡胶（包括乳胶）	万 t	168	430182	171	281 371
合成橡胶（包括乳胶）	万 t	120	334 031	147	300 042
原木	万 m^3	2 957	518 362	2 806	408 652
锯材	万 m^3	709	202 416	988	231 927
纸浆	万 t	952	670 556	1 368	684 370
羊毛及毛条	万 t	30	180 193	33	154 048
棉花	万 t	211	349 238	153	211 464
纺织用合成纤维	万 t	32	74 615	35	69 965
聚脂纤维	万 t	15	23 206	15	20 298
聚丙烯腈纤维	万 t	15	37291	18	37 835
纸及纸板（未切成形）	万 t	352	352 458	331	314 578
制冷设备用压缩机	万台	1 464	95 793	1 184	84 156

表 122　我国畜产品进出口状况（2009 年）

产品名称	单位	出口		进口		出口同比（%）		进口同比（%）	
		数量	金额（万美元）	数量	金额（万美元）	数量	金额（万美元）	数量	金额（万美元）
活　猪	万头	1 627.3	33 007.5			−37.59	−13.8		
活家禽	万只	950.2	2 608.3	9.9	3 052.1	−18.5	−23.3	−9.5	1.5
鲜冻牛肉	万 t	1.3	6 120.5	1.4	4 404.6	−41.1	−35.9	234.6	144.1
鲜冻猪肉	万 t	8.7	26 272.1	13.5	13 613.3	6.3	−4.7	−63.9	−74.0
冻　鸡	万 t	7.1	13 627.2	72.2	94 697.1	−3.2	−13.0	−8.3	−8.3
鲜冻兔肉	万 t	1.0	4 147.8			21.5	26.0		
鲜　蛋	百万个	1 111.0	7 888.6	0.1	50.0	−8.6	−1.6	−16.2	−46.5
乳　品	万 t	3.7	5 689.0	59.7	102 799.2	−69.5	−81.1	70.2	19.3
天然蜂蜜	万 t	7.2	12 569.7	0.2	532.5	−15.4	−14.6	24.0	13.9
猪　鬃	万 t	0.7	7 148.3		4.1	−16.9	−30.7		
肠　衣	万 t	6.9	78 798.0	8.6	14 159.7	2.3	−6.4	5.2	28.7
羽毛羽绒	万 t	2.7	24 825.0	0.6	5 180.6	−9.4	−16.2	−29.1	−26.7
皮　张	t	27.3	49.5	32 755.4	26 064.0	−70.1	−81.8	−0.7	18.6
山羊绒	t	2 123.6	13 777.4	3 581.6	4 264.0	−12.3	−29.8	234.6	79.8
兔　毛	t	1.0	0.7	5.0	9.2			−80.2	−78.27
羊　毛	万 t	1.1	3 825.3	30.8	146 590.1	−28.4	−28.1	7.9	−13.7
猪肉罐头	万 t	3.6	9 764.6		40.0	14.5	11.6	−25.5	−26.3
饲料用鱼粉	万 t	0.4	339.7	130.8	130 181.7	89.6	66.4	−3.0	−6.9
配合饲料	万 t	54.9	87 288.8	12.8	19 598.5	−17.5	5.3	1.7	−6.4

资料来源：表中数据出自 2010 年版《中国畜牧业通讯》杂志第 10 期。

表 123　我国主要粮食产品进出口情况（2009 年）

单位：万 t

主要粮食产品	进　口	出　口	顺　差
谷　物	315.1	137.10	−178.00
大　米	33.8	78.40	44.60
小　麦	89.4	0.84	−88.56
玉　米	174.0		
大　麦	5.4	13.0	7.60
大　豆	4 255.2	35	−4 220.2

资料来源：表中数据由农业部提供。

表 124 我国林产品进出口数量（2008—2009 年）

产品名称		贸易	单位	2008 年	2009 年
原木	针叶原木	出口 进口	m^3	100 18 577 008	851 20 302 606
	阔叶原木	出口 进口	m^3	2 725 10 992 626	11 885 7 756 655
	合计	出口 进口	m^3	2 825 29 569 634	12 736 28 059 621
锯材		出口 进口	m^3	717 475 7 181 828	561 106 9 935 167
单板		出口 进口	m^3	146 283 91 894	114 327 72 327
特形材		出口 进口	t	310 052 12 333	251 560 7 953
刨花板		出口 进口	m^3	193 171 374 137	124 944 446 543
纤维板		出口 进口	m^3	2 382 562 504 505	2 031 141 452 979
胶合板		出口 进口	m^3	7 185 060 293 937	5 634 800 179 178
木制品		出口 进口	t	1 750 049 60 187	1 563 994 39 734
家具		出口 进口	件	242 633 034 3 147 981	247470 421 3 298 999
木片		出口 进口	t	73 014 1 056 387	7 247 2 766 012
木浆		出口 进口	t	10 628 9 460 349	35 045 13 578 483
废纸		出口 进口	t	24 205 826 1356 450	220 27 501 707
纸和纸制品		出口 进口	t	1 356 450 3 735 959	4 802 753 3 495 948
木炭		出口 进口	t	50 976 136 266	54 922 156 678
松香		出口 进口	t	276 517 1 076	193 291 2 927

（续）

产品名称		贸易	单位	2008 年	2009 年
水果	柑橘类	出口	t	862 105	1 113 022
		进口		79 946	91 652
	鲜苹果	出口	t	1 153 326	1 174 191
		进口		42 395	54 116
	鲜梨	出口	t	446 656	463 159
		进口		9	13
	鲜葡萄	出口	t	63 303	100 225
		进口		51 613	89 775
	山竹果	出口	t		
		进口		41 084	91 719
	鲜榴莲	出口	t		
		进口		138 929	196 147
	鲜龙眼	出口	t	2 221	945
		进口		196 451	256 037
坚果	核桃	出口	t	26 179	10 582
		进口		9 033	21 102
	板栗	出口	t	40 920	46 640
		进口		11 890	10 820
	松子仁	出口	t	4 178	7 862
		进口		882	935
	开心果	出口	t	7 691	2 469
		进口		29 605	21 545
干果	梅干及李干	出口	t	475	551
		进口		1 552	3 034
	龙眼干、肉	出口	t	222	232
		进口		76 117	133 616
	柿饼	出口	t	5 660	5 001
		进口		7	
	红枣	出口	t	7 884	5 668
		进口		17	5
	葡萄干	出口	t	30 620	41 345
		进口		12 570	11 743
果汁	柑橘类果汁	出口	t	16 895	20 220
		进口		47 566	65 108
	苹果汁	出口	t	692 574	799 505
		进口		2 270	467

表 125 我国林产品进出口金额（2008—2009 年）

单位：千美元

产品名称		贸易	2008 年	2009 年
总计		**出口**	**33 488 310**	**36 316 317**
		进口	**38 439 466**	**33 902 486**
原木	针叶原木	出口	21	274
		进口	2 414 186	2 234 430
	阔叶原木	出口	965	4 306
		进口	2 769 073	1 852 088
	合计	**出口**	**986**	**4 580**
		进口	**5 183 259**	**4 086 518**
锯材		出口	412 265	346 344
		进口	2 039 427	2 327 863
单板		出口	243 925	172 678
		进口	98 504	63 736
特形材		出口	448 662	371 345
		进口	19 774	15 547
刨花板		出口	45 873	32 712
		进口	91 859	88 913
纤维板		出口	1 094 538	884 401
		进口	140 415	119 570
胶合板		出口	3 400 530	2 523 949
		进口	167 469	89 042
木制品		出口	3 522 246	3 324 597
		进口	75 033	84 081
家具		出口	11 017 339	12 035 202
		进口	311 952	297 671
木片		出口	9 034	887
		进口	182 490	353 802
木浆		出口	6 916	22 351
		进口	6 660 933	6 795 615
废纸		出口	1	48
		进口	5 556 926	3 796 054
纸和纸制品		出口	2 070 567	6 129 326
		进口	4 363 240	3 879 784
木炭		出口	22 979	26 065
		进口	14 663	17 552
松香		出口	271 944	181 729
		进口	4 739	6 104

（续）

产品名称		贸易	2008年	2009年
水果	柑橘类	出口	437 373	592 697
		进口	67 312	74 224
	鲜苹果	出口	698 398	713 518
		进口	45 188	54 108
	鲜梨	出口	215 087	220 716
		进口	27	23
	鲜葡萄	出口	47 437	85 926
		进口	95 018	172 077
	山竹果	出口		
		进口	69 565	144 383
	鲜榴莲	出口		
		进口	92 850	124 373
	鲜龙眼	出口	2 770	857
		进口	124 192	157 334
坚果	核桃	出口	60 224	19 849
		进口	12 624	28 502
	板栗	出口	62 981	68 208
		进口	18 531	18 108
	松子仁	出口	47 675	142 974
		进口	6 955	7 875
	开心果	出口	13 098	5 622
		进口	76 554	77 461
干果	梅干及李干	出口	1 942	2 311
		进口	1 783	2 865
	龙眼干、肉	出口	1 005	1 249
		进口	53 530	88 737
	柿饼	出口	10 630	9 098
		进口		
	红枣	出口	12 187	17 399
		进口	14	20
	葡萄干	出口	47 225	65 311
		进口	19 686	18 340
果汁	柑橘类果汁	出口	14 424	14 218
		进口	97 790	106 311
	苹果汁	出口	1 130 079	655 526
		进口	4 634	718
其他		出口	8 116 983	7 640 042
		进口	7 559 270	6 718 656

表 126 轻工业系统农产品加工业主要出口产品创汇情况（2008 年）

主要产品名称	单 位	出口产品		同比增长（%）	
		数 量	金 额	数 量	金 额
轻工业产品出口总额	**万美元**		**30 922 906**		**14.48**
有关农产品加工业产品合计	**万美元**		**11 799 957**		**12.96**
纸浆	万 t、万美元	7.23	9 838	−35.18	7.03
纸张	万 t、万美元	412.05	415 129	−13.47	5.67
纸制品	万 t、万美元	127.31	213 593	0.73	12.56
香料香精	万 t、万美元	3.44	27 047	20.81	25.69
制盐	万 t、万美元	96.70	6 060	25.77	70.55
糖	万 t、万美元	6.24	2 846	−43.55	−41.15
乳品	万 t、万美元	12.06	30 170	−10.38	24.54
罐头	万 t、万美元	252.78	285 039	−2.11	10.74
可可制品	万 t、万美元	5.04	20 025	6.74	35.93
调味品、发酵品	万 t、万美元	144.21	177 520	4.82	32.25
冷冻饮品	万 t、万美元	0.88	1 688	−29.10	−25.42
酒	万 L、万美元	42 867.00	44 885	1.13	12.73
软饮料	万美元		139 867		−5.78
茶	万 t、万美元	29.69	68 234	2.49	12.86
其他食品、饮料	万美元		2 082 151		11.70
皮革及其制品	万美元		4 165 689		10.77
毛皮及其制品	万美元		88 885		−5.32
木制品及其他天然植物制品	万美元		333 257		−0.86
家具	万美元		2 758 280		21.94
抽丝刺绣工艺品	万美元		192 393		−0.09
地毯	万 m^2、万美元	41 877.00	161 185	30.37	22.23
烟花爆竹	万 t、万美元	31.38	49 500	−12.54	0.01
天然植物编织工艺品	万 t、万美元	42.63	157 505	3.08	29.13
轻工机械	万美元		211 313		27.87
羽绒制品	万美元		157 958		−0.53

表 127 轻工业系统农产品加工业主要进口产品情况（2008 年）

主要产品名称	单 位	进口产品		同比增长（%）	
		数 量	金 额	数 量	金 额
轻工业产品进口总额	**万美元**		**7 999 067**		**15.68**
有关农产品加工业产品合计	**万美元**		**4 464 884**		**29.52**
纸 浆	万 t、万美元	952.12	670 530	12.40	20.87
纸 张	万 t、万美元	356.95	370 190	−11.24	2.59
纸制品		12.51	35 244	−8.34	−1.80
香料香精	万 t、万美元	2.34	36 636	3.23	20.64
制 盐	万 t、万美元	194.40	7 994	21.83	45.75
糖	万 t、万美元	77.99	31 850	−34.64	−16.09
乳 品	万 t、万美元	35.07	86 165	17.45	15.79
罐 头	万 t、万美元	1.73	1 966	48.80	60.75
可可制品	万 t、万美元	5.00	17 222	10.45	25.99
调味品、发酵品	万 t、万美元	4.56	13 538	−15.59	−1.02
冷冻饮品	万 t、万美元	0.41	1 566	21.88	40.41
酒	万 L、万美元	24 865.00	108 229	9.45	32.76
软饮料	万美元		17 688		−8.18
茶	万 t 万美元	0.54	1 775	1.32	38.62
其他食品、饮料	万美元		1 966 982		32.24
皮革及其制品	万美元		521 723		−1.17
毛皮及其制品	万美元		23 541		24.11
木制品及其他天然植物制品	万美元		6 812		7.35
家具	万美元		122 167		10.70
抽丝刺绣工艺品	万美元		12 474		−2.55
地毯	万 m^2、万美元	1 032.58	10 142	−3.30	11.38
烟花爆竹	万 t、万美元		1	−99.90	−93.59
天然植物编织工艺品	万 t、万美元	0.29	697	−21.74	−19.23
轻工机械	万美元		398 381		24.81
羽绒制品	万美元		1 371		−3.61

资料来源：表 126、表 127 中数据由中国轻工业信息中心提供。

表 128 我国淀粉及部分深加工品进出口情况（2009 年）

单位：t

主要品种	进口量	同比增加（%）	出口量	同比增加（%）
合 计	**1 034 399**	**60**	**486 642**	**−37**
玉米淀粉	965	−72	289 787	−35
本薯淀粉	831 987	80	464	51
马铃薯淀粉	35 004	182	8 712	−56
小麦淀粉	1 243	−29	11 978	−41
山梨醇	1 877	大幅度减少	50 078	−21
甘露糖醇	505	−39	4 444	持平
肌醇	11	−21	2 647	9
糊精及变性淀粉	160 872	12	117 522	−46
化学醇果糖	1 935	−56	1 010	大幅度增长

表 129　我国食糖进出口与贸易方式情况（2007—2009 年）　单位：万 t

进　口

年 份	合　计	一般贸易	进料加工	保税仓库进出境货物	边境小额贸易
2007	119.34	99.18	13.28	5.22	
2008	77.99	61.91	8.89	3.67	
2009	106.45	83.02	9.93	12.77	0.47

出　口

年 份	合　计	一般贸易	进料加工	来料加工	边境小额贸易
2007	11.05	2.24	5.99	2.79	0.03
2008	6.24	1.76	1.53	2.15	0.80
2009	6.39	2.21	3.15	0.91	0.12

资料来源：表中数据由中国糖业协会提供。

表 130　我国乳制品进口情况（2009 年）　单位：万 t、万美元

产 品 名 称		进口		同 比（%）	
		数　量	金　额	数　量	金　额
乳制品合计		**60.00**	**103 000**	**70.24**	**19.31**
液体乳		1.28	1 970	71.90	57.30
乳粉	合　计	24.70	58 041	144.28	45.79
	脱脂乳粉	7.04	15 601	28.20	−27.40
	全脂乳粉	17.50	41 953	298.20	140.00
	调味乳粉	0.14	486	−35.20	−41.50
炼乳		0.17	398	103.20	27.00
酸乳		0.15	436	94.40	51.90
乳清粉		28.9	28 422	35.50	−8.90
奶油		2.84	6 566	109.90	11.20
干酪		1.70	6 966	22.10	−5.60
其他乳制品合计		14.07	74 046	30.60	38.70
乳糖类		5.96	3 441	7.10	−21.40
零售包装婴幼儿乳粉		6.24	60 452	47.90	52.60
酪蛋白类		0.63	4 299	39.80	−22.80
白蛋白类		1.24	5 854	130.70	53.10

表 131 我国乳制品出口情况（2009 年） 单位：万 t、万美元

产品名称		出口		同比（%）	
		数量	金额	数量	金额
乳制品合计		3.68	5 689	−69.51	81.14
液体乳		2.00	1 334	−47.90	−54.90
乳粉	小计	0.97	3 086	−84.70	−87.90
	脱脂乳粉		0.1	−99.98	−99.99
	全脂乳粉	0.81	2 561	−86.40	−88.40
	调味乳粉	0.17	525	−45.40	−48.90
炼乳		0.37	571	−54.20	−51.20
酸乳		0.08	115	−23.60	−33.30
乳清粉		0.03	34	−92.70	−93.00
奶油		0.20	501	−58.80	−70.80
干酪		0.01	48		
其他乳制品合计		0.17	863	−69.00	−74.30
乳糖类		0.01	22	−82.70	−47.70
零售包装婴幼儿乳粉		0.02	88	31.50	77.40
酪蛋白类		0.14	730	−70.50	−77.50
白蛋白类		0.01	23	47.90	19.40

资料来源：表 130、表 131 中的数据，由中国乳制品工业协会提供。

表 132 我国罐头产品主要类别及品种出口情况（2008 年）

单位：万 t、万美元

产品名称	出口量	出口额
肉类罐头	41 230	10 677
猪肉罐头	31 563	8 747
牛肉罐头	7 449	1 487
水产罐头	114 496	57 003
鲭鱼	20 735	4 545
金枪鱼、鲣鱼	35 457	11 579
蔬菜罐头	1 804 332	208 566
芦笋罐头	76 252	12 289
蚕豆罐头	49 647	2 499
竹笋罐头	153 384	14 574
番茄酱罐头	814 792	78 687
小白蘑菇罐头	336 332	42 226
清水马蹄罐头	45 402	3 615
其他伞菌属蘑菇罐头	60 348	16 136
脱荚豇豆及菜豆罐头	27 105	2 012
干果罐头	18 075	5 864
水果罐头	788 704	69 171
梨罐头	62 078	5 378
桃罐头	148 268	14 420
菠萝罐头	76 766	6 251
柑橘罐头	353 297	28 271
什棉水果罐头	57 718	5 784
荔枝罐头	26 032	2 402
狗猫饲料罐头	5 685	1 930

资料来源：表中数据由海关总署提供。

表 133 我国罐头产品出口情况（2007—2008 年）

年　份	出 口 量（t）	同比增长（%）	出口金额（万美元）	同比增长（%）
2007	2 777 900	21.84	304 600	30.17
2008	3 000 000	8.00	350 000	14.90

资料来源：表中数据由中国罐头工业协会提供。

表 134 我国蜂蜜生产及出口情况（2006—2009 年）

年　份	世界产量（万 t）	我国产量（万 t）	占世界比例（%）	出口量（万 t）	出口率（%）	出口创汇（万美元）
2006	141.7	33.30	23.50	8.11	24.35	10 500
2007	135.4	35.35	26.10	6.44	18.10	9438
2008	107.3	40.00	37.28	8.49	21.25	14 720
2009	149.6	36.70	24.53	7.19	19.59	12 600

表 135 我国蜂产品出口情况（2008—2009 年）

主 要 产 品	数量、金额、单价	2008 年	2009 年	同比增长（%）
金额总计	**金额（万美元）**	**19 106**	**16 151**	**−15.47**
蜂　蜜	数量（t）	84 900	72 000	−15.19
	金额（万美元）	14 720	12 600	−14.40
	平均单价（美元/kg）	1.73	1.75	0.93
鲜王浆	数量（t）	903	542	−40.00
	金额（万美元）	1 908	1 202	−37.00
	平均单价（美元/kg）	21.15	22.00	4.00
鲜蜂王浆冻干粉	数量（t）	231	249	8.00
	金额（万美元）	1 487	1 546	4.00
	平均单价（美元/kg）	64.58	62.00	−4.00
鲜蜂王浆制剂	数量（t）	724	644	−11.00
	金额（万美元）	991	803	−18.00
	平均单价（美元/kg）	13.04	12.00	−8.00

资料来源：表中数据出自 2010 年版《中国蜂业》杂志第 4 期。

表 136 我国水产品进出口贸易情况（2006—2009 年）

年　　份	出口量（万 t）	出口额（亿美元）	进口量（万 t）	进口额（亿美元）
2006	301.5	93.6	332.2	43.0
2007	306.4	97.4	346.4	47.2
2008	296.5	106.1	388.4	54.1
2009	294.2	107.0	373.7	52.6

注：2009 年我国水产品进出口总量达 667.9 万 t，进出口总额达 159.6 亿美元，实现贸易顺差 54.4 亿美元，出口额继续位居大宗农产品首位，占全国农产品出口总额（395.9 亿美元）的 27%，较上年提高 0.8 个百分点。

表 137　我国食品和包装机械进出口情况（2005—2009 年）　单位：万美元

项　目	2005 年	2006 年	2007 年	2008 年	2009 年
进出口总额	**260 694**	**278 500**	**356 700**	**486 614**	**417 400**
食品机械进出口	57 499	76 300	115 300	156 685	141 500
食品机械进口	40 008	43 800	62 000	80 885	76 000
食品机械出口	17 491	32 500	53 300	75 800	65 500
包装机械进出口	203 195	202 200	241 400	329 929	275 900
包装机械进口	159 951	153 300	165 200	231 529	194 600
包装机械出口	43 243	48 900	76 200	98 400	81 300

资料来源：表中数据由中国食品和包装机械工业协会提供。

表 138　我国鞋类产品进出口情况（2008—2009 年）

进　出　口	单　位	2008 年		2009 年	
		数 量	金 额	数 量	金　额
出　口	亿双、亿美元	85.3	296.6	81.7	265.7
进　口	万双、亿美元	3 446.9	7.3	2 871.3	6.3

资料来源：表中数据出自 2010 年版《中国皮革》杂志。

表 139　我国纺织品服装出口情况（2008—2009 年）

产 品 名 称	单　位	2008 年	2009 年	同比增长（%）
纺织品服装出口总额	**亿美元**	**1 851.7**	**1 670.2**	**−9.80**
其中：纺织品	亿美元	653.8	599.7	−8.27
服装	亿美元	1 197.9	1 070.5	−10.64

资料来源：表中数据出自海关总署。

表 140　我国家具工业主要产品进出口情况（2009 年）　单位：万美元

主要产品	单　位	进		口	
		数　量	同比增长（%）	金　额	同比增长（%）
家具	**万美元**			**129 679.5**	**6.22**
木家具	万件	273.9	−0.40	23 141.2	−3.60
金属家具	万件	42.9	−9.71	2 955.1	−19.99
塑料家具	万件	37.6	52.02	1 136.1	90.43
其他材料制家具	万件	0.6	−39.39	13 982.2	1 210.80
坐具及其零件	万美元			81 035.7	7.88
牙科、理发椅及其零件	万美元			407.6	7.69
医用家具	万件	3.05	−15.51	6 390.4	3.91
床垫	万个	2.81	6.04	631.0	18.43
家具零件	t				

主要产品	单　位	出		口	
		数　量	同比增长（%）	金　额	同比增长（%）
家具	**万美元**			**2 595 804**	**−6.00**
木家具	万件	16 945.3	1.43	758 844.9	11.18
金属家具	万件	21 400.4	−29.34	313 072.4	−22.30
塑料家具	万件	2 269.3	−4.66	33 961.6	−0.15
其他材料制家具	万件	164.6	32.05	270 793.2	213.46
坐具及其零件	万美元			1 167 472.0	−11.59
牙科、理发椅及其零件	万美元			4 466.6	−29.02
医用家具	万件	458.0	−60.47	23 544.6	1.68
床垫	万个	594.3	−6.99	23 648.9	−4.90
家具零件	t				

表 141 我国皮革工业主要产品进出口情况（2009 年） 单位：万美元

主要产品	单位	数量	同比增长（%）	金额	同比增长（%）
出口					
皮面皮鞋	万双	88 242	−21.8	835 619.7	−14.9
旅行用品及箱包	万美元			1 279 068.5	−9.2
皮革服装	万件	1 875	−16.0	78 083.4	−21.3
毛皮服装	万件	209	16.7	60 336.9	138.5
皮革手套	万双	52 342	−34.4	67 968.4	−18.4
足、篮、排球	万个	18 493	−12.6	32 803.5	−8.4
生皮	kt	4	180.7	338.5	72.6
成品及半成品革	kt	30	−17.1	23 819.5	−40.0
靴鞋零件及类似品	kt	297	−27.6	144 506.8	−9.9
制革、制鞋机械	万台	40	−18.9	4 643.5	−29.5
总　计	**万美元**			**2 527 188.7**	**−11.0**
进口					
主要产品	单位	数量	同比增长（%）	金额	同比增长（%）
生　皮	kt	1 280	17.1	144 060.5	−22.0
成品及半成品	kt	815	−15.4	302 179.7	−20.3
靴鞋零件及类似品	kt	20	−23.5	24 722.5	−13.3
制革、制鞋机械	台	4 688	15.8	3 056.5	32.4
制革机械零件	t	146	−70.1	327.5	−61.0
旅行用品及箱包	万美元			56 993.9	4.6
皮革服装	万件	12.7	20.2	3 727.4	−10.1
皮面皮鞋	万双	1 314	−26.5	43 147.4	−15.1
皮革手套	万双	107.9	67.5	59.40	131.5
毛皮服装	万件	1.7	−72.5	647.2	2.4
足球、篮球、排球	万个	120.4	60.6	470.8	37.4
总　计	**万美元**			**579 927.2**	**−18.1**

表 142 我国纸浆、废纸、纸、纸板、纸制品进出口情况（2007—2009 年） 单位：万 t

产品名称	2007 年		2008 年		2009 年	
	进口	出口	进口	出口	进口	出口
一、纸浆	845	11	952	7	1 367	9
二、废纸	2 256		2 421		2 750	
三、纸及纸板	401	461	358	403	334	405
1. 新闻纸	2	59	2	36	2	21
2. 未涂布印刷书写纸	45	53	39	54	38	51
3. 涂布纸	56	140	54	137	36	163
其中：铜版纸	40	93	38	97	31	132
4. 包装用纸	10	3	12	3	15	3
5. 箱纸板	103	25	88	13	86	7
6. 白纸板	70	58	64	53	71	61
其中：涂布白纸板	70	58	64	53	71	61
7. 生活用纸	4	48	5	52	5	56
8. 瓦楞原纸	53	39	45	13	46	3
9. 特种纸及纸板	43	27	38	34	27	33
10. 其他纸及纸板	15	9	11	8	8	7
四、纸制品	19	156	18	211	16	195
总　计	**3 521**	**628**	**3 749**	**621**	**4 467**	**609**

资料来源：表中数据出自 2010 年版《中华纸业》杂志，第 31 卷第 11 期。

表 143 我国印刷机械进出口统计（2007—2008 年） 单位：万美元

产品名称	出口			进口		
	2007 年	2008 年	同比增长（%）	2007 年	2008 年	同比增长（%）
合 计	**69 500**	**98 052**	**41.60**	**177 921**	**172 987**	**−2.77**
印前机械	10 930	8 599	−21.33	7 045	7 531	6.90
印刷机械	38 168	43 232	13.35	140 003	125 729	−10.20
印后机械	11 203	16 280	45.22	13 464	17 214	27.85
常规印机附件	5 404	5 975	10.57	8 243	6 905	−16.23
数码印机附件	3 331	23 947	525.08	9 165	15 609	70.31

表 144 我国机械工业产品进出口情况（2005—2009 年） 单位：万美元

项目	2005 年	2006 年	2007 年	2008 年	2009 年
产品进出口总额	2 229	2 840	3 568	4 373	3 767
产品进口总额	1 184	1 416	1 661	1 948	1 958
产品出口总额	1 045	1 424	1 907	2 425	1 809

表 145 我国中药行业进出口情况（2008—2009 年） 单位：万美元、%

年份	行业	进出口		出口		进口	
		总额	同比增长（%）	总额	同比增长（%）	总额	同比增长（%）
2008	全国医药合计	484.10	25.45	317.4	29.08	166.70	19.07
	中药合计	17.52	15.71	13.1	11.02	4.42	22.78
2009	全国医药合计	531.50	9.80	329.1	3.70	202.40	21.50
	中药合计	12.28	−29.91	6.88	−47.48	5.40	22.17

表 146 我国橡胶工业制品出口量与出口额（2007—2008 年）

产品名称	单位	2007 年		2008 年	
		出口量	出口额	出口量	出口额
新充气橡胶轮胎	万条、万美元	17 032			
其中：机动小客车用新充气轮胎	万条、万美元	9 928	251 435	10 980	314 035
客、货机动车辆新充气轮胎	万条、万美元	4 491	344 598	4 000	375 988
航空器用的新充气轮胎	万条、万美元	0.3	128	0.6	187
摩托车用的新充气轮胎	万条、万美元	1 187	5993	1 385	8 706
自行车用的新充气轮胎	万条、万美元	11 443	15 580	9 981	17 108
其他新人字形等胎面充气轮胎	万条、万美元	152.7	3 005	469	3 213
未列名新充气轮胎	万条、万美元	1 299	20 595	882	22 362
橡胶内胎	万条、万美元				
其中：客、货运机动车辆用橡胶内胎	万条、万美元	13 632	19 167	7 274	23 431
自行车用橡胶内胎	万条、万美元	19 935	10 698	21 265	14 593

（续）

产品名称	单位	2007年		2008年	
		出口量	出口额	出口量	出口额
未列名橡胶内胎	万条、万美元	6 186	4 973	11 598	10 701
翻新轮胎	万条、万美元	12	628	32	725
汽车用旧轮胎	万条、万美元	3	33	4	86
实心或半实心轮胎、胎面及轮胎衬带	t、万美元	45 788	8 683	52 615	11 337
橡胶输送带、三角带、传动带	t、万美元	146 555	36 742	141 742	41 529
橡胶卫生医疗用品	t、万美元	13 731	6 197	14 325	7 146
外科手套及其他手套	万双、万美元	385 551	32 140	373 897	34 576
橡胶杂件	t、万美元	335 534	104 918	334 481	111 564
橡胶管	t、万美元	85 505	27 034	92 852	33 109
橡胶医疗用衣着用品	t、万美元	4 198	2 305	5 429	1 592
未硫化橡胶板、片、带及制品	t、万美元	40 643	7 186	29 897	6 521
硫化橡胶线、绳、板、片、带及型材	t、万美元	146 217	16 278	154 004	18 287
硬质橡胶及制品	t、万美元	17 789	3 931	14 026	3 799
再生胶等	t、万美元	53 605	3 177	45 921	3 673
胶鞋	万双、万美元				
其中：防水鞋靴	万双、万美元	6 311	27 367	6 639	33 315
滑雪鞋、防护鞋等	万双、万美元	460 231	916 403	424 748	1 062 180
运动鞋、网球鞋、篮球鞋等	万双、万美元	144 533	342 807	138 036	394 343

表147 我国橡胶工业制品出口量与出口额（2007—2008年）

产品名称	单位	2007年		2008年	
		进口量	进口额	进口量	进口额
新的充气橡胶轮胎	万条、万美元	638	27 542		
其中：机动小客车用新充气橡胶轮胎	万条、万美元	199	11 365	282	17 525
客、货机动车辆用新充气橡胶轮胎	万条、万美元	53	8 480	54	10 860
航空器用的新充气橡胶轮胎	万条、万美元	4	1 555	4	1 773
摩托车用的新充气橡胶轮胎	万条、万美元	6	61	4	46
自行车用的新充气橡胶轮胎	万条、万美元	243	694	231	806
其他新人字形等胎面充气轮胎	万条、万美元		15		10
未列名新充气橡胶轮胎	万条、万美元	124	1 004	96	571
橡胶内胎	万条、万美元	241	292		
其中：客、货运机动车辆用橡胶内胎	万条、万美元	12	159	103	148
航空器用橡胶内胎	万条、万美元		1		1
自行车用橡胶内胎	万条、万美元	120	85	103	72
未列名橡胶内胎	万条、万美元	108	47	65	27

（续）

产品名称	单位	2007年		2008年	
		进口量	进口额	进口量	进口额
翻新轮胎	万条、万美元	1	87	1	115
汽车用旧轮胎	万条、万美元	6	122	4	86
实心或半实心轮胎、胎面以 及轮胎衬带	t、万美元	3 893	1 432	3 954	1 301
橡胶输送带、三角带、传动带	万 m、万美元	13 626	20 981	15 675	21 397
橡胶卫生医疗用品	t、万美元	1 725	2 215	2 193	2 751
外科手套及其他手套	万双、万美元	68 800	3 333	97 904	3 856
橡胶杂件	t、万美元	60 329	113 172	56 621	129 861
橡胶管	t、万美元	30 022	31 866	33 957	42 808
橡胶医疗用衣着用品	t、万美元	467	626	453	763
未硫化橡胶板、片、带及制品	t、万美元	564 975	120 084	559 038	155 525
硫化橡胶线、绳、板、片、带及型材	t、万美元	58 225	23 832	61 918	24 551
硬质橡胶及制品	t、万美元	1 255	2 243	763	1 686
再生胶等	t、万美元	13 150	1 129	20 532	2 455
胶鞋	万双、万美元				
其中：防水鞋靴	万双、万美元	17	77	15	151
滑雪鞋、防护鞋等	万双、万美元	670	6 332	900	9 042
运动鞋、网球鞋、篮球鞋等	万双、万美元	287	5 033	703	12 042

资料来源：表中数据出自2009年版《中国橡胶工业年鉴》。

表148 我国胶鞋产品进出口情况（2008年） 单位：双、万美元

产品名称	进口		出口	
	数量	金额	数量	金额
装金属护头的塑料或橡胶制外底及鞋面的防水鞋靴	6 734	23.1	255 782	1 799.6
橡胶、塑料制底及面的中、短统防水靴	58 860	65.4	56 871 937	26 955.0
其他橡胶或塑料制外底及鞋面的防水靴	87 089	63.4	6 978 447	4 561.7
橡胶或塑料制外底及鞋面的滑雪靴	15 905	68.0	2 335 075	3 404.2
橡胶或塑料制外底及鞋面的其他运动鞋靴	895 652	1 299.8	196 591 695	109 714.3
鞋面条带拴塞在鞋底上的鞋	756 367	251.3	1 110 002 904	91 291.6
其他橡胶、塑料短统靴（过踝）	209 211	445.1	55 002 465	38 499.9
其他橡胶、塑料鞋靴（橡胶或塑料制外底及鞋面）	7 167 400	6 980.0	2 883 268 021	819 272.6
纺织材料制鞋面的运动鞋靴（橡胶或塑料制外底）	698 750	1 597.0	132 676 504	109 577.3
纺织材料制鞋面的其他鞋靴	6 347 458	10 446.2	1 247 694 485	284766.7

资料来源：表中数据出自2009年版《中国橡胶工业年鉴》。

表 149　我国主要胶鞋企业出口创汇情况（2007—2008 年）

单位：万双、万美元

企业名称	出口创汇			出口胶鞋数量		
	2008 年	2007 年	同比（%）	2008 年	2007 年	同比（%）
青岛双星集团有限公司	14 968.0	14 769.0	1.35	713.7	932.3	－23.45
荣光集团有限公司	5 652.0	6 587.0	－14.19	2 175.0	1789.0	21.58
威海中威橡胶有限公司	1 095.1	1 008.4	8.55	113.1	133.4	－15.19
瑞安市大桥鞋厂	1 120.0	1 060.0	5.66	569.5	592.3	－38.5
上海回力鞋业有限公司	733.7	672.5	9.10			
常州鸿福鞋业有限公司	560.0	634.0	－11.67	103.0	180.0	－42.78
滁州胶鞋总厂	559.0	428.8	30.36	63.5	69.7	－8.88
际华 3517 厂	393.0	322.0	22.05			
丹东橡胶厂	344.0	307.0	12.05	101.0	95.0	6.32

资料来源：表中数据出自 2009 年版《中国橡胶工业年鉴》。

表 150　我国天然橡胶、合成橡胶进口情况（2006—2009 年）

产　品	2006 年		2007 年		2008 年		2009 年	
	数量（万 t）	金额（万美元）	数量（万 t）	金额（万美元）	数量（万 t）	金额（万美元）	数量（万 t）	金额（万美元）
天然橡胶	161.0	371 478	165.0	346 500	168.2	420 937	171.0	281 371.4
合成橡胶	130.0	185 224	150.0	263 500	120.2	334.000	147.2	300 041.5

农产品加工业部分行业与企业排序

表 151　轻工业系统农产品加工业分行业主要经济指标（2008 年）

序号	按工业总产值排序			序号	按工业销售产值排序		
	行　业	工业总产值（亿元）	行业占轻工系统比重（%）		行　业	工业销售产值（亿元）	行业占轻工系统比重（%）
	全国轻工行业合计	**95 673.2**	**100.00**		**全国轻工行业合计**	**93 236.7**	**100.00**
1	农副食品加工业	23 917.4	25.00	1	农副食品加工业	23 373.9	25.07
2	造纸及纸制品业	7 873.9	8.23	2	造纸及纸制品业	7 651.7	8.21
3	食品制造业	7 716.5	8.07	3	食品制造业	7 461.4	8.00
4	饮料制造业	6 250.5	6.53	4	饮料制造业	6 068.5	6.51
5	皮革、毛皮、羽毛（绒）及其制品业	5 871.4	6.14	5	皮革、毛皮、羽毛（绒）及其制品业	5 757.8	6.18
6	家具制造业	3 072.8	3.21	6	家具制造业	3 003.7	3.22
7	木竹藤棕草制品业	581.6	0.61	7	木竹藤棕草制品业	564.3	0.61
8	制盐	253.2	0.26	8	制盐	246.2	0.26

（续）

序号	按利税总额排序 行业	利税总额（亿元）	行业占轻工系统比重（%）	序号	按利润总额排序 行业	利润总额（亿元）	行业占轻工系统比重（%）
	全国轻工行业合计	**9 101.3**	**100.00**		**全国轻工行业合计**	**5 413.8**	**100.00**
1	农副食品加工业	1 860.4	20.44	1	农副食品加工业	1 213.9	22.42
2	饮料制造业	1 106.5	12.16	2	饮料制造业	558.9	10.32
3	食品制造业	832.5	9.15	3	食品制造业	489.6	9.04
4	造纸及纸制品业	740.3	8.13	4	造纸及纸制品业	434.8	8.03
5	皮革、毛皮、羽毛（绒）及其制品业	547.3	6.01	5	皮革、毛皮、羽毛（绒）及制品业	333.1	6.15
6	家具制造业	246.9	2.71	6	家具制造业	139.9	2.58
7	木竹藤棕草制品业	55.5	0.61	7	木竹藤棕草制品业	32.1	0.59
8	制盐	40.7	0.45	8	制盐	19.9	0.37

序号	按出口交货值排序 行业	出口交货值（亿元）	行业占轻工系统比重（%）	序号	按主营业务收入排序 行业	主营业务收入（亿元）	行业占轻工系统比重（%）
	全国轻工行业合计	**18 457.4**	**100.00**		**全国轻工行业合计**	**93 201.6**	**100.00**
1	皮革、毛皮、羽毛（绒）及制品业	2 130.7	11.54	1	农副食品加工业	23 565.8	25.28
2	农副食品加工业	1 693.8	9.18	2	造纸及纸制品业	7 501.2	8.05
3	家具制造业	1 109.9	6.01	3	食品制造业	7 463.7	8.01
4	食品制造业	653.9	3.54	4	饮料制造业	6 137.6	6.59
5	造纸及纸制品业	536.2	2.91	5	皮革、毛皮、羽毛（绒）及制品业	5 692.8	6.11
6	饮料制造业	184.1	1.00	6	家具制造业	3 001.3	3.22
7	木竹藤棕草制品业	161.1	0.87	7	木竹藤棕草制品业	563.7	0.60
8	制盐	5.3	0.03	8	制盐	248.3	0.27

序号	按资产总计排序 行业	资产总计（亿元）	行业占轻工系统比重（%）	序号	按全部从业人员平均人数排序 行业	从业人员（万人）	行业占轻工系统比重（%）
	全国轻工行业合计	**61 796.3**	**100.00**		**全国轻工行业合计**	**2 243.9**	**100.00**
1	农副食品加工业	10 977.2	17.76	1	农副食品加工业	315.1	14.04
2	造纸及纸制品业	7 448.8	12.05	2	皮革、毛皮、羽毛（绒）及制品业	273.3	12.18
3	饮料制造业	5 946.2	9.62	3	食品制造业	154.6	6.89
4	食品制造业	5 244.1	8.49	4	造纸及纸制品业	151.9	6.77
5	皮革、毛皮、羽毛（绒）及制品业	2 025.1	4.90	5	饮料制造业	113.0	5.04
6	家具制造业	1 941.2	3.14	6	家具制造业	104.4	4.65
7	制盐	344.2	0.56	7	木竹藤棕草制品业	23.6	1.05
8	木竹藤棕草制品业	294.1	0.48	8	制盐	9.9	0.44

资料来源：表中数据由中国轻工业信息中心提供。

表 152 轻工业系统农产品加工业分行业进出口总额（2008 年）

序号	按出口总额排序			序号	按进口总额排序		
	行 业	出口总额（亿美元）	行业占轻工系统比重（%）		行 业	进口总额（亿美元）	行业占轻工系统比重（%）
	全国轻工行业合计	**3 992.3**	**100.00**		**全国轻工行业合计**	**799.9**	**100.00**
1	皮革、毛皮、羽毛（绒）及其制品业	425.5	13.76	1	食品、饮料	224.7	28.09
2	食品饮料	285.2	9.22	2	纸浆、纸及纸制品	107.6	13.45
3	家具	275.8	8.92	3	皮革、毛皮、羽毛（绒）及其制品业	54.5	6.82
4	纸浆、纸及纸制品	63.9	2.07	4	轻工机械	39.8	4.98
5	木制品及其他天然植物制品	33.3	1.08	5	家具	12.2	1.53
6	轻工机械	21.1	0.68	6	制盐	0.8	0.10
7	制盐	0.6	0.02	7	木制品及其他天然植物制品	0.7	0.09

资料来源：表中数据由中国轻工业信息中心提供。

表 153 我国农产品进出口额前 10 位省、直辖市排序（2009 年）

单位：亿美元

出口额前 10 位省、直辖市			进口额前 10 位省、直辖市		
排名	省、直辖市	出口额	排名	省、直辖市	进口额
1	山 东	97.6	1	山 东	83.9
2	广 东	48.6	2	广 东	79.9
3	福 建	34.2	3	江 苏	66.6
4	辽 宁	30.7	4	上 海	61.8
5	浙 江	30.1	5	北 京	51.4
6	江 苏	19.7	6	浙 江	27.0
7	上 海	12.1	7	福 建	26.1
8	北 京	10.6	8	天 津	24.9
9	河 北	10.2	9	辽 宁	20.4
10	天 津	8.2	10	河 北	18.1

资料来源：表中数据出自 2010 年版《国际农产品贸易》杂志第 1 期。

表 154 我国十大最具增长潜力白酒品牌（2010 年）

排序	品 牌	生 产 企 业
1	红花郎	四川郎酒集团有限公司
2	泸州老酒坊	泸州老窖股份有限公司
3	董 酒	贵州董酒股份有限公司
4	酒 鬼	酒鬼酒股份有限责任公司
5	古井贡	安徽古井贡酒股份有限公司
6	国色清香	宝丰酒业有限公司
7	宣酒特贡	安徽宣酒集团股份有限公司
8	江口醇	四川江口醇酒业（集团）有限公司
9	双沟珍宝坊	江苏双沟酒业股份有限公司
10	稻花香	湖北稻花香酒业股份有限公司

注：资料来源于中国酒类流通协会，表中排名不分先后。

表 155　选入我国 500 个最具价值品牌的酿酒企业拥有的品牌（2009 年）

序号	500 个品牌中的排名	品牌名称	品牌拥有企业	品牌价值（亿元）
1	22	五粮液	四川宜宾五粮液集团有限公司	398.2
2	23	青岛啤酒	青岛啤酒股份有限公司	366.3
3	33	茅　台	贵州茅台酒厂有限责任公司	273.3
4	75	郎	四川郎酒集团有限责任公司	87.8
5	78	燕　京	北京燕京啤酒股份有限公司	81.9
6	82	泸州老窖	泸州老窖股份有限公司	81.1
7	88	剑南春	四川剑南春股份有限公司	78.9
8	89	沱　牌	四川沱牌曲酒股份有限公司	78.3
9	121	长　城	中粮酒业有限公司	67.6
10	125	洋　河	江苏洋河酒厂股份有限公司	64.6
11	136	金六福	华泽集团有限公司	60.4
12	146	稻花香	湖北稻花香集团	55.9
13	175	古井贡	安徽古井贡有限责任公司	46.6
14	182	杏花村	山西杏花村汾酒集团有限责任公司	44.9
15	199	王　朝	中法合营王朝葡萄酿酒公司	41.9
16	233	牛栏山	北京顺鑫农业股份有限公司牛栏山酒厂	35.1
17	255	张　裕	烟台张裕葡萄酿酒股份有限公司	33.1
18	269	哈尔滨	哈尔滨啤酒集团有限公司	31.3
19	276	通　化	通化葡萄酒股份有限公司	30.9
20	370	水井坊	四川水井坊股份有限公司	18.2
21	376	古越龙山	浙江古越龙山绍兴酒股份有限公司	16.9
22	392	威　龙	烟台威龙葡萄酒股份有限公司	16.0
23	394	枝　江	湖北枝江酒业有限公司	15.8
24	395	舍　得	四川舍得酒业有限公司	15.7
25	457	金种子	安徽金种子集团有限公司	11.1
26	489	河　套	内蒙古河套酒业集团股份有限公司	9.7

资料来源：表中数据出自 2010 年版《酿酒科技》杂志第 5 期。

表 156　我国啤酒产量 20 万 kL 以上企业（2009 年）

序号	企业名称	产量（kL）	序号	企业名称	产量（kL）
1	华润雪花啤酒(中国)有限公司	8 398 450	15	哈尔滨啤酒有限公司	421 265
2	青岛啤酒集团有限公司	5 903 478	16	三得利啤酒（中国）投资有限公司	418 136
3	北京燕京啤酒集团有限公司	4 672 479	17	百威（武汉）集团啤酒有限公司	409 616
4	河南金星啤酒集团有限公司	1 908 559	18	新疆乌苏啤酒有限责任公司	333 590
5	重庆啤酒集团有限公司	1 770 166	19	浙江英博石梁啤酒有限公司	261 318
6	英博雪津啤酒有限公司	1 176 116	20	南昌亚洲啤酒有限公司	254 408
7	广州珠江啤酒集团有限公司	1 137 698	21	河南蓝牌集团商丘啤酒有限公司	236 713
8	金威啤酒（中国）有限公司	821 502	22	河南省月山啤酒股份有限公司	227 620
9	江苏大富豪啤酒有限公司	493 834	23	河南维雪啤酒有限公司	221 580
10	湖北金龙泉啤酒集团公司	487 216	24	兰州黄河嘉酿啤酒有限公司	209 865
11	英博双鹿啤酒集团	470 410	25	大连大雪啤酒股份有限公司	209 311
12	蓝贝酒业集团有限公司	467 527	26	云南澜沧江企业集团有限公司	207 024
13	四平金士百啤酒股份有限公司	440 790	27	河南奥克啤酒实业有限公司	205 000
14	山东新银麦啤酒有限公司	430 839	28	百威啤酒（佛山）有限公司	204 687

注：全国 20 万 kL 以上啤酒企业总产量 32 399 179kL，占全国总产量 4 236.38 万 kL 的 76.48%（国家统计局数据）。

表 157　我国啤酒销售收入 3 亿元以上企业（2008 年）

单位：万元

序号	企　业　名　称	销售收入	序号	企　业　名　称	销售收入
1	青岛啤酒集团有限公司	1 0577 062	17	四平金士百啤酒有限公司	66 299
2	华润雪花啤酒（中国）有限公司	1 471 956	18	上海亚太酿酒有限公司	66 221
3	北京燕京啤酒集团公司	1 167 177	19	海南亚洲太平洋酿酒有限公司	58 775
4	河南金星啤酒集团有限公司	416 568	20	河南月山啤酒股份有限公司	50 964
5	百威（武汉）国际啤酒有限公司	341 966	21	河南维雪啤酒有限公司	50 617
6	广州市珠江啤酒集团有限公司	330 707	22	浙江英博石梁啤酒有限公司	49 458
7	重庆啤酒（集团）有限责任公司	323 818	23	云南澜沧江啤酒企业（集团）有限公司	46 844
8	英博雪津啤酒有限公司	303 589	24	河南蓝牌集团商丘啤酒有限公司	45 401
9	河北蓝贝酒业集团有限公司	166 859	25	南昌亚洲啤酒有限公司	43 845
10	三得利啤酒（中国）投资有限公司	144 278	26	浙江英博浙东啤酒有限公司	38 512
11	金威啤酒（中国）有限公司	134 357	27	珠海麒麟啤酒有限公司	35 762
12	哈尔滨啤酒集团有限公司	96 157	28	大连大雪啤酒股份有限公司	34 180
13	江苏大富豪啤酒有限公司	96 128	29	杭州西湖啤酒朝日（股份）有限公司	33 625
14	英博双鹿啤酒集团有限公司	94 023	30	生力（广东）啤酒有限公司	32 022
15	山东新银麦啤酒有限公司	93 164	31	济南卢堡啤酒有限公司	30 443
16	湖北金龙泉啤酒集团公司	77 874			

资料来源：表中数据由中国酿酒工业协会啤酒分会提供。

表 158　我国葡萄酒产量前 10 位省、直辖市主要经济运行情况（2008 年）

地　区	产量总计（kL）	同比增长（%）	工业总产值（万元）	同比增长（%）	工业销售产值（万元）	同比增长（%）
山　东	280 853.3	16.00	1 086 280.0	27.12	1 045 719.1	18.50
吉　林	110 120.8	90.92	139 076.3	108.31	127 915.0	99.80
河　北	99 290.7	7.47	198 567.2	12.83	188 843.9	16.83
河　南	68 791.3	43.95	91 615.2	21.47	91 450.5	24.79
天　津	45 379.0	6.43	126 350.0	−3.69	135 343.0	15.44
新　疆	17 280.6	90.65	44.631.2	24.57	40 797.3	51.82
北　京	15 871.9	−10.48	33 575.2	8.03	20 613.8	−6.59
甘　肃	14 142.8	31.89	56 977.2	36.89	49 368.2	35.53
辽　宁	13 482.0	123.56	44 028.4	54.86	39 207.1	55.27
陕　西	7 039.6	40.93	10 719.0	48.90	9 926.5	32.99
合　计	**672 251.9**		**1 821 819.7**		**1 749 184.4**	
占行业比重（%）	96.3		95.1		95.5	

资料来源：表中数据由中国酿酒工业协会葡萄酒分会提供。

表 159 我国饮料工业 20 强企业（2008 年）

序 号	企 业 名 称
1	杭州娃哈哈集团有限公司
2	康师傅饮品控股有限公司
3	统一企业（中国）投资有限公司
4	北京汇源饮料食品集团有限公司
5	农夫山泉股份有限公司
6	惠尔康集团有限公司
7	杭州中萃食品有限公司
8	华润怡宝食品饮料（深圳）有限公司
9	椰树集团有限公司
10	红牛维他命饮料有限公司
11	河北承德露露股份有限公司
12	深圳百事可乐饮料有限公司
13	厦门银鹭食品有限公司
14	国投中鲁果汁股份有限公司
15	广东键力宝集团有限公司
16	深圳达能益力泉饮料有限公司
17	乐百氏（广东）食品饮料有限公司
18	上海百事可乐饮料有限公司
19	四川蓝剑饮品集团有限公司
20	深圳市景田食品饮料有限公司

资料来源：表中信息由中国饮料工业协会提供。

表 160 我国饮料行业按产量分地区前 8 位情况（2008 年） 单位：万 t

名 次	地 区	产 量	占全国总产量（%）
1	广 东	12 133 263	18.90
2	浙 江	6 419 168	10.00
3	河 南	4 911 519	7.65
4	山 东	3 428 874	5.30
5	辽 宁	3 215 099	5.00
6	吉 林	3 048 895	4.70
7	湖 北	2 929 715	4.50
8	上 海	2 522 921	3.90
	合 计	38 609 454	60.20

资料来源：表 160～表 162 中数据由中国饮料工业协会提供。

表 161 我国瓶（罐）装饮用水分地区产量前 5 位情况（2008 年） 单位：万 t

名 次	地 区	产 量	占全国比重（%）
1	广 东	5 696 724	23.00
2	吉 林	2 289 966	9.30
3	辽 宁	2 027 612	8.20
4	浙 江	1 685 995	6.80
5	河 南	1 607 597	6.50

表 162 我国果汁及果汁饮料产量分地区前 5 位情况（2008 年）

单位：t

名 次	地 区	产 量	占全国比重（%）
1	广 东	1 979 754	16.70
2	陕 西	1 293 090	10.90
3	河 南	1 156 178	9.80
4	山 东	962 869	8.10
5	浙 江	962 738	8.10

表 163 我国乳制品生产企业销售收入居前列的企业（2009 年）

单位：万元

序 号	企 业 名 称	销售收入
1	内蒙古蒙牛乳业（集团）股份有限公司	2 549 821
2	内蒙古伊利实业集团股份有限公司	2 378 206
3	杭州娃哈哈集团有限公司	1 886 389
4	维维集团	899 200
5	光明乳业服分有限公司	794 316
6	多美滋婴幼儿食品有限公司	364 759
7	黑龙江完达山乳业股份有限公司	635 742
8	黑龙江乳业集团	308 423
9	黑龙江飞鹤乳业有限公司	300 000
10	美赞臣营养食品（中国）有限公司	295 425
11	黑龙江摇篮乳业股份有限公司	255 677
12	圣元营养食品有限公司	243 441
13	北京三元食品股份有限公司	237 959
14	西安银桥生物科技有限责任公司	237 591
15	福州明一乳业有限公司	208 213
16	济南佳宝乳业有限公司	190 855
17	沈阳乳业有限责任公司	175 670
18	新希望乳业控股有限公司	169 441
19	广东雅士利集团有限公司	164 613
20	山西古城乳业集团有限公司	149 554

资料来源：表中数据由中国乳制品工业协会提供。

表 164 我国液体乳产量位居前列的企业（2009 年） 单位：万 t

序 号	企 业 名 称	产量
1	内蒙古蒙牛乳业（集团）股份有限公司	268.6
2	内蒙古伊利实业集团股份有限公司	175.4
3	光明乳业股份有限公司	70.0
4	维维集团	47.3
5	北京三元食品股份有限公司	34.5
6	西安银桥生物科技有限责任公司	33.3
7	黑龙江乳业集团	30.7
8	黑龙江省完达山乳业股份有限公司	29.3
9	济南佳宝乳业有限公司	29.3
10	沈阳乳业有限责任公司	25.1
11	新希望乳业控股有限公司	24.3
12	石家庄君乐宝乳业有限公司	19.7
13	南京卫岗乳业有限公司	17.3
14	山东亚奥特乳业有限公司	17.2
15	山东得益乳业有限公司	15.9
16	山西古城乳业集团有限公司	14.4
17	徐州绿健乳业有限责任公司	11.3
18	浙江李子园牛奶食品有限公司	9.9
19	浙江金华市佳乐乳业有限公司	8.3
20	宁夏夏进乳业集团股份有限公司	8.1

资料来源：表中数据由中国乳制品工业协会提供。

表 165 我国酒精产量 9 万 t 以上酒精企业和产量 11 万 t 以上燃料乙醇企业（2008 年）

产量 9 万 t 以上酒精企业

序 号	企 业 名 称	产 量（万 t）
1	吉林省新天龙酒业有限公司	29.2
2	梅河口市阜康酒精有限责任公司	23.0
3	天津市冠达实业总公司	17.8
4	吉安生化乾安酒精有限责任公司	14.1
5	承德避暑山庄企业集团有限责任公司	9.5

产量 11 万 t 以上燃料乙醇企业

序 号	企 业 名 称	产 量（万 t）
1	吉林燃料乙醇有限公司	48.0
2	河南天冠企业集团有限公司	47.0
3	安徽丰原生化股份有限公司	39.8
4	黑龙江中粮生化能源（肇东）有限公司	15.0
5	广西中粮生物质能源有限公司	11.7

资料来源：表中数据由中国酿酒工业协会酒精分会提供。

表 166　我国味精产量 2 万 t 以上企业（2008 年）

序号	企业简称	产量（万 t）	序号	企业简称	产量（万 t）
1	山东阜丰	49.44	7	福建武夷	8.54
2	河北梅花	36.97	8	江苏天香	8.41
5	河南莲花	22.44	9	重庆飞亚	6.38
4	山东信乐	16.61	10	沈阳红梅	5.20
5	山东菱花	15.17	11	广州奥桑	4.26
6	山东齐鲁	14.46			

资料来源：表中数据由中国发酵工业协会提供。

表 167　2009 年中国蜂产品行业第二批信用等级评价结果

序号	企业名称	信用级别
1	湖南省明园蜂业有限公司	AAA
2	杭州天厨蜜源保健品有限公司	AAA
3	东莞市养生源蜂业有限公司	AA
4	颐寿园（北京）蜂产品有限公司	AA
5	杭州常青蜂业公司	AA
6	北京中蜜科技发展有限公司	AA
7	安徽鸿汇食品（集团）有限公司	AA
8	河南长兴蜂业有限公司	AA
9	北京绿纯有机生物科技开发中心	A
10	大连大阁保健品有限公司	A
11	天津市蜂产品公司	A

资料来源：表中信息由中国蜂产品协会提供，排名不分先后。

表 168　2009/2010 年度我国纺织工业各行业“企业竞争力”排名前列企业

棉纺织、色织			
序号	企业名称	序号	企业名称
1	山东魏桥创业集团有限公司	11	华芳集团棉纺有限公司
2	鲁泰集团	12	淄博兰雁集团有限责任公司
3	百隆东方有限公司	13	宁波雅戈尔日中纺织印染有限公司
4	德州华源生态科技有限公司	14	际华三五四二纺织有限公司
5	淄博银仕来纺织（集团）有限公司	15	石家庄常山纺织集团有限责任公司
6	安徽华茂集团有限公司	16	山东华乐实业集团有限公司
7	天虹纺织集团有限公司	17	三阳纺织有限公司
8	广东溢达纺织有限公司	18	海宁八方布业有限公司
9	无锡市第一棉纺织厂	19	河南新野纺织集团股份有限公司
10	许昌裕丰纺织有限公司	20	山东昊龙集团有限公司

（续）

印 染 业

序号	企 业 名 称	序号	企 业 名 称
1	盛虹集团有限公司	6	浙江宝纺印染有限公司
2	浙江航民股份有限公司	7	浙江美欣达印染集团有限公司
3	青岛凤凰印染有限公司	8	浙江永通染织集团有限公司
4	浙江富润印染有限公司	9	三元控股集团有限公司
5	宜兴乐祺纺织集团有限公司	10	济宁如意印染有限公司

毛 纺 织、毛 针 织

序号	企 业 名 称	序号	企 业 名 称
1	江苏阳光集团有限公司	6	浙江新奥纺织股份有限公司
2	山东南山纺织服饰有限公司	7	宁波雅戈尔毛纺织染整有限公司
3	山东如意科技集团有限公司	8	云幅投资控股有限公司
4	内蒙古鄂尔多斯羊绒集团有限责任公司	9	内蒙古鹿王羊绒有限公司
5	泰安康平纳毛纺织集团公司	10	宁夏中银绒业国际集团有限公司

麻 纺

序号	企 业 名 称	序号	企 业 名 称
1	湖南华升企集团公司	6	金达集团控股有限公司
2	常州美源亚府纺织有限公司	7	浙江金鹰集团有限公司
3	新申集团有限公司	8	铜陵华源麻业有限公司
4	江西恩达家纺有限公司	9	湖北精华纺织集团有限公司
5	黑龙江圆宝纺织股份有限公司	10	郴州湖南麻业有限公司

丝 绸

序号	企 业 名 称	序号	企 业 名 称
1	江苏新民纺织科技股份有限公司	6	万事利集团有限公司
2	江苏华佳投资集团有限公司	7	金富春集团有限公司
3	达利（中国）有限公司	8	广东省丝绸纺织集团有限公司
4	安徽京九丝绸有限责任公司	9	达利丝绸（浙江）有限公司
5	鑫缘茧丝集团股份有限公司	10	浙江嘉欣丝绸股份有限公司

针 织

序号	企 业 名 称	序号	企 业 名 称
1	宁波申州针织有限公司	6	常州老三集团有限公司
2	江苏东渡纺织集团有限公司	7	浙江袜业有限公司
3	青岛即发集团控股有限公司	8	福建凤竹纺织科技股份有限公司
4	上海嘉麟杰纺织品股份有限公司	9	江苏 AB 集团有限责任公司
5	泉州海天材料科技股份有限公司	10	上海三枪集团有限公司

（续）

服装			
序号	企业名称	序号	企业名称
1	新郎希努尔集团股份有限公司	6	虎都（中国）服饰有限公司
2	波司登股份有限公司	7	雅鹿集团股份有限公司
3	庄吉集团有限公司	8	耶莉娅集团
4	报喜岛集团有限公司	9	拜丽德集团有限公司
5	江苏虎豹集团有限公司	10	青岛红领集团有限公司

化纤			
序号	企业名称	序号	企业名称
1	恒力集团有限公司	6	浙江富丽达纤维有限公司
2	浙江华峰氨纶股份有限公司	7	盛虹集团有限公司
3	桐昆集团股份有限公司	8	长乐力恒锦纶科技有限公司
4	吉林化纤集团有限责任公司	9	广东新会美达锦纶股份有限公司
5	浙江荣盛控股集团有限公司	10	新乡白鹭化纤集团有限责任公司

资料来源：此排名由中国纺织工业协会等9个专业协会于2010年9月10日发布，表中排名按主营业务收入由高到低排序。

表169　2008—2009年获“中国驰名商标”的家具企业

序号	商标	生产企业	年份
1	联邦	广东联邦家私集团有限公司	2008
2	八益	成都八一家具股份有限公司	2008
3	晚安	湖南省晚安家居实业有限公司	2008
4	全友	成都市全友家私有限公司	2008
5	双虎	成都市双虎实业有限公司	2009
6	浪度	成都浪度家私有限公司	2009
7	缘梦圆	重庆市缘梦圆家俱有限公司	2009
8	强力	北京市强力家具有限公司	2009
9	Kinwai	江门健威家具装饰有限公司	2009
10	双叶	七台河市双叶家具有限责任公司	2009
11	罗浮宫	广东罗浮宫国际家具博览中心有限公司	2009
12	恒友	大兴安岭恒友家具有限公司	2009
13	光明	光明集团家具股份有限公司	2009
14	QUAMA	广州市至盛冠美家具有限公司	2009
15	皖宝	合肥皖宝集团床垫有限公司	2009

资料来源：表中信息由国家工商总局商标局提供。

表 170　2009 年中国皮革行业 10 强企业

序　号	企　业　名　称	综合得分
1	百丽鞋业股份有限公司	95.50
2	泉州市三兴体育用品有限公司	79.65
3	奥康集团有限公司	76.52
4	康奈集团有限公司	74.00
5	石狮市富贵鸟集团公司	70.81
6	安踏（中国）有限公司	70.06
7	兴业皮革科技股份有限公司	66.32
8	雪豹集团	64.00
9	浙江中辉皮革有限公司	63.53
10	嘉兴新秀箱包制造有限公司	63.19

资料来源：表中信息，由中国皮革协会提供。

表 171　2009 年中国真皮名鞋、名装品牌

2009 年中国真皮名鞋

序　号	企　业　名　称	品　牌
1	杰豪集团有限公司	杰　豪
2	成都艾民儿皮制品有限责任公司	艾民儿
3	石狮市吉祥鸟鞋业有限公司	吉祥鸟
4	青岛孚德鞋业有限公司	孚　德
5	浙江圣帝罗阑鞋业有限公司	圣帝罗阑
6	日泰集团有限公司	日　泰
7	浙江邦赛鞋业有限公司	邦　赛
8	南京万里集团有限公司	万　里
9	海弘鞋业有限公司	海　弘
10	兽霸鞋业有限公司	兽　霸
11	嘉兴市圣丹丽鞋业有限公司	圣·丹丽
12	浙江卡帝奥尼鞋业有限公司	卡帝·奥尼
13	重庆科而士实业（集团）有限公司	科而士
14	青岛雄虎鞋业有限公司	雄　虎
15	扬州金自豪鞋业有限公司	凯　森
16	浙江路标鞋业有限公司	路　标

2009 年中国真皮名装

序　号	企　业　名　称	品　牌
1	河北东明制衣有限公司	DONGMING
2	北京奥豹国际投资有限公司	奥　豹
3	河北佰立特皮业有限公司	佰立特
4	北京湫斯迪服饰有限公司	湫斯迪

资料来源：表中信息由中国轻工业联合会、中国皮革协会提供，真皮标志排名不分先后。

表 172　纸及纸板产量 100 万 t 以上的省、自治区主营业务收入（2007—2008 年）

地　区	企业个数（个）		主营业务收入（亿元）		
	2007 年	2008 年	2007 年	2008 年	同比增长（%）
山　东	345	343	1 051	1 206	15.00
浙　江	667	658	429	479	12.00
广　东	380	410	421	532	26.00
江　苏	216	215	453	490	8.00
河　南	248	251	371	474	28.00
河　北	188	151	139	132	−5.00
福　建	168	189	103	127	23.00
湖　南	204	211	148	180	22.00
四　川	148	159	76	101	33.00
安　徽	86	84	50	72	45.00
广　西	81	107	44	56	26.00
湖　北	101	93	56	76	37.00
江　西	69	71	61	69	13.00

注：表中数据出自 2008 年度造纸工业报告。

表 173　我国纸及纸板产量 100 万 t 以上的省、自治区（2007—2009 年）

单位：万 t

地　区	产　　量		
	2007 年	2008 年	2009 年
山　东	1 280	1 350	1 430
浙　江	1 209	1 283	1 372
广　东	1 029	1 154	1 316
江　苏	893	930	1 026
河　南	685	806	864
河　北	425	379	367
福　建	288	297	313
湖　南	223	280	300
四　川	177	211	227
安　徽	137	185	205
重　庆		82	174
湖　北	119	132	157
广　西	131	150	139
江　西	106	114	120
合　计	6 702	7 353	8 010

资料来源：表中数据出自 2010 年版《中华纸业》杂志第 11 期。

表 174　我国重点造纸企业产量排名前 30 名企业（2008—2009 年）

序号	企业名称	产量（万 t）		
		2008 年	2009 年	同比增长（%）
1	玖龙纸业（控股）有限公司	442.9	652.0	47.21
2	德文造纸有限公司	299.0	355.0	18.74
3	山东晨鸣纸业集团股份有限公司	307.3	299.3	−2.58
4	金东纸业（江苏）有限公司	230.5	228.9	−0.68
5	山东太阳纸业股份有限公司	164.5	220.0	33.71
6	华泰集团有限公司	154.3	155.0	0.47
7	宁波中华纸业有限公司	144.7	147.8	2.14
8	海南金海浆纸业有限公司（纸浆）	123.2	112.1	−9.03
9	中冶纸业集团有限公司	89.4	100.6	12.58
10	湖南泰格林纸集团	87.4	93.8	7.32
11	安徽山鹰纸业股份有限公司	62.9	82.5	31.17
12	山东博汇纸业股份有限公司	74.2	80.5	8.56
13	芬欧汇川（常熟）纸业有限公司	74.8	80.1	7.03
14	中国纸业投资总公司	41.0	75.4	83.90
15	浙江景兴纸业股份有限公司	66.6	74.9	12.62
16	森叶（清新）纸业有限公司	42.7	74.6	74.90
17	河南银鸽实业投资集团	65.3	72.8	11.58
18	广州造纸集团有限公司	78.0	72.1	−7.58
19	吉安纸容器有限公司	51.9	66.5	28.19
20	东莞建辉纸业有限公司	65.6	64.2	−2.09
21	山东泉林纸业有限责任公司	56.1	64.1	14.18
22	金华盛纸业（苏州工业园区）有限公司	60.2	59.1	−1.74
23	中国阳光纸业控股有限公司	41.8	54.9	31.45
24	新乡新亚纸业集团股份有限公司	55.0	51.3	−6.73
25	山东华金集团有限公司	46.9	47.5	1.26
26	山东贵和纸业集团有限公司	39.8	46.2	15.95
27	福建优兰发集团实业有限公司	27.5	42.6	54.91
28	河南省龙源纸业有限公司	35.0	42.5	21.23
29	金红叶纸业（苏州）有限公司	31.3	42.3	35.46
30	上海中隆纸业有限公司	39.0	40.7	4.26

资料来源：表中数据出自 2010 年版《中华纸业》杂志第 31 卷第 11 期。

表 175 我国印刷机械企业实现销售收入前 10 名企业（2009 年）

序 号	企 业 名 称	销售收入（万元）
1	北人集团公司	97 342
2	上海高斯印刷设备有限公司	51 080
3	辽宁大族冠华印刷科技股份有限公司	35 862
4	上海光华印刷机械有限公司	34 298
5	天津长荣印刷设备有限公司	30 221
6	陕西北人印刷机械有限责任公司	24 002
7	江西中景集团有限公司	21 990
8	潍坊华光精工设备有限公司	21 390
9	中山市松德包装机械股份有限公司	20 158
10	江苏昌昇集团股份有限公司	18 956

表 176 我国印刷机械企业出口交货值前 10 名企业（2009 年）

序 号	企 业 名 称	出口交货值（万元）
1	上海高斯印刷设备有限公司	15 192
2	北人集团公司	7 193
3	上海亚华印刷机械有限公司	4 426
4	神力集团有限公司	3 875
5	青岛瑞普电气有限责任公司	2 774
6	浙江蓝宝机械有限公司	2 678
7	天津长荣印刷设备有限公司	2 226
8	上海德拉根印刷机械有限公司	2 156
9	陕西北人印刷机械有限责任公司	2 004
10	威海滨田印刷机械有限公司	1 905

表 177 我国重点造纸机械企业实现销售收入 5 000 万元以上的企业（2008 年）

序 号	企 业 名 称	销售收入（万元）
1	许昌中亚造纸设备有限公司	
2	山东诸城市金日东造纸机械有限公司	5 000～10 000
3	湖北沙市轻工机械有限公司	
4	辽宁辽阳造纸机械股份有限公司	
5	山东凯信机械有限公司	
6	山东晨钟机械股份有限公司	10 000～20 000
7	沙市轻工机械有限公司	
8	山东长星机械集团公司	
9	淄博恒星股份有限公司	
10	山东海天造纸机械有限公司	
11	山东昌华造纸机械有限公司	20 000～30 000
12	汶瑞机械（山东）有限公司	
13	西安中 造纸机械集团	30 000 以上

资料来源：表 177～表 179 中数据出自 2009 版《中国造纸年鉴》。

表 178 我国重点造纸机械企业实现利税总额 500 万元以上的企业（2008 年）

序号	企业名称	利税总额（万元）
1	山东诸城市金日东造纸机械有限公司	
2	福建省轻工机械设备有限公司	500～1 000
3	山东海天造纸机械有限公司	
4	辽阳造纸机械股份有限公司	
5	山东凯信机械有限公司	
6	山东晨钟机械股份有限公司	1 000～2 000
7	山东滕州力华米泰克斯胶辊有限公司	
8	湖北沙市轻工机械有限公司	
9	山东昌华造纸机械有限公司	
10	汶瑞机械（山东）有限公司	2 000 以上
11	山东长星机械集团公司	

表 179 劳动生产率在 10 万元以上的重点造纸机械企业（2008 年）

单位：万元/（人・年）

序号	企业名称	劳动生产率
1	辽阳造纸机械股份有限公司	
2	山东昌华造纸机械有限公司	10～20
3	盐城市宏宇造纸机械有限公司	
4	福建省轻工机械设备有限公司	
5	福建省轻工机械设备有限公司	20～30
6	许昌中亚造纸设备有限公司	
7	湖北沙市轻工机械有限公司	
8	山东诸城市金日东造纸机械有限公司	30～50
9	山东潍坊凯业信机械有限公司	50 以上
10	汶瑞机械（山东）有限公司	

表 180 我国橡胶工业协会会员企业按销售收入排序（2009 年）

序号	轮胎行业	序号	力车胎行业
	企业名称		企业名称
1	杭州中策橡胶有限公司	1	厦门正新橡胶工业有限公司
2	三角集团有限公司	2	杭州中策橡胶有限公司
3	山东玲珑橡胶有限公司	3	江苏飞驰股份有限公司
4	佳通轮胎（中国）有限公司	4	山东新东岳集团有限公司
5	中国正新橡胶公司	5	山东正兴轮胎有限公司
6	光源轮胎股份有限公司	6	青岛喜盈门双驼轮胎有限公司
7	双钱集团股份有限公司	7	四川远星橡胶有限公司
8	青岛双星轮胎工业有限公司	8	广州广橡企业集团公司
9	风神轮胎股份有限公司	9	天津万达集团公司
10	固铂成山（山东）轮胎有限公司	10	江苏通用科技有限公司

（续）

序号	胶鞋行业	序号	炭黑行业
	企业名称		企业名称
1	解放军3537工厂	1	江西黑猫炭黑股份有限公司
2	四川资阳市征峰胶鞋厂	2	河北龙星化工集团有限公司
3	浙江荣光集团有限公司	3	台湾中橡公司
4	解放军35172厂	4	山东华东橡胶材料有限公司
5	张家港贝顺橡胶有限公司	5	苏州宝化炭黑有限公司
6	解放军3544工厂	6	石家庄市新星化炭有限公司
7	解放军3539工厂	7	大石桥市辽滨炭黑厂
8	鹤壁飞鹤股份有限公司	8	河北大光明实业集团有限公司
9	上海回力鞋业有限公司	9	山东贝斯特化工有限公司
10	浙江人本鞋业有限公司	10	青州市博奥炭黑有限责任公司

序号	乳胶行业	序号	橡胶制品行业
	企业名称		企业名称
1	桂林乳胶厂	1	安徽中鼎密封件有限公司
2	北京华腾橡塑乳胶制品有限公司	2	际华3517橡胶制品有限公司
3	镇江苏惠乳胶制品有限公司	3	衡水橡胶股份有限公司
4	广州广橡集团有限公司双一乳胶厂	4	中南橡胶集团有限责任公司
5	安徽豪杰塑胶制品有限公司	5	上海华问橡胶制品有限公司
6	青岛双蝶集团股份有限公司	6	山东美晨科技股份有限公司
7	北京瑞京乳胶制品有限公司	7	凯迪西北橡胶有限公司
8	苏州嘉乐威企业发展有限公司	8	石家庄第一橡胶股份公司
9	大连乳胶有限责任公司	9	铁岭华晨橡塑制品有限公司
10	天津中生乳胶有限公司	10	南京金三力橡胶有限公司

资料来源：表中信息由中国橡胶工业协会提供。

表181　我国中成药按出口金额排序前10名企业（2009年）

序号	企业名称	序号	企业名称
1	北京同仁堂股份有限公司	6	上海医药（集团）有限公司
2	漳州片仔癀药业股份有限公司	7	厦门虎标医药有限公司
3	广州市医药进出口公司	8	培力（南宁）药业有限公司
4	北京同仁堂科技发展股份有限公司进出口分公司	9	深圳金活利生有限公司
5	天津中新药业集团股份有限公司	10	梁介福（广东）药业有限公司

我国西部地区综合统计

表 182　我国西部地区主要农产品产量（2008—2009 年）　单位：万 t

主要农产品	2008 年	2009 年	同比增长（%）
一、粮食作物	13 951.9	14 245.4	2.10
（一）谷物	11 639.5	11 926.6	2.47
稻谷	4 482.0	4 531.4	1.10
小麦	1 963.4	2 192.1	11.65
玉米	4 749.9	4 807.1	1.20
谷子	45.6	31.2	−31.58
高粱	85.8	82.3	−4.08
（二）豆类	602.1	605.1	−0.50
大豆	305.4	327.8	7.33
杂豆	276.7	277.4	−6.50
（三）薯类	1 710.3	1 731.6	0.19
马铃薯	1 095.6	1 129.9	3.13
二、油料作物	754.1	825.7	9.49
花生	127.3	137.2	7.78
油菜籽	435.6	492.8	13.13
芝麻	5.7	5.3	−7.02
胡麻籽	24.8	25.2	1.61
向日葵籽	139.4	154.3	10.69
三、棉花	327.1	272.5	−16.69
四、麻类	20.8	14.1	−32.21
黄红麻	1.4	1.2	−14.29
五、糖料	10 943.3	9 989.5	−8.71
甘蔗	10 313.8	9 440.7	−8.47
甜菜	629.4	548.8	−12.81
六、烟叶	170.5	180.8	6.04
烤烟	158.4	166.9	5.37
七、茶叶	39.7	46.0	15.87
八、水果	4 766.5	5 673.6	19.03

表 183 我国西部地区主要农产品单位面积产量（2008—2009 年）

单位：kg/hm²

主要农产品	2008 年	2009 年	同比增长（%）
一、粮食作物	4 286.0	4 258.0	−0.65
（一）谷物	4 911.4	4 877.9	−0.68
稻谷	6 479.3	6 513.7	0.53
小麦	3 418.0	3 481.6	1.86
玉米	5 171.7	5 044.4	−2.46
谷子	1 854.5	1 214.8	−34.49
高粱	3 925.0	3 378.0	−13.94
（二）豆类	1 774.3	1 754.6	−1.11
大豆	1 814.3	1 733.3	−4.46
杂豆	1 735.0	1 780.4	2.62
（三）薯类	3 132.3	3 083.9	−1.55
马铃薯	3 064.9	2 877.3	−6.12
二、油料作物	1 859.4	1 895.5	1.94
花生	2 233.7	2 261.5	1.24
油菜籽	1 778.8	1 813.8	1.97
芝麻	1 215.9	1 019.3	−16.17
胡麻籽	1 113.2	1 116.4	0.29
向日葵籽	2 034.7	2 300.6	13.07
三、棉花	1 720.7	1 760.2	2.30
四、麻类	2 583.6	2 144.4	−16.99
黄红麻	1 995.9	1 855.1	−7.05
五、糖料	69 774.2	66 716.4	−4.38
甘蔗	71 446.3	67 640.9	−5.33
甜菜	50 433.4	54 021.8	7.12
六、烟叶	2 095.8	2 141.8	3.98
烤烟	2 062.4	2 144.4	3.98

表 184 我国西部地区茶叶产量（2009 年）

单位：t

地 区	茶 叶 总产量	其 中				
		红毛茶	绿毛菜	乌龙毛菜	紧压茶原料	其他茶
全国总计	**1 358 642**	**71 944**	**1 006 302**	**159 062**	**45 096**	**76 236**
地区小计	459 638	24 256	382 248	398	14 569	38 495
占全国比重（%）	33.83	33.72	37.99	0.25	32.31	50.49
内蒙古						
广 西	36 622	710	30 468	142		5 302
重 庆	22 569	2 330	17 116			3 123
四 川	154 666	1 240	123 771	106	14 306	15 243
贵 州	41 883	225	28 691	4	249	12 714
云 南	182 948	19 421	161 253	146	14	2 113
西 藏	1					
陕 西	20 153		20 153			
甘 肃	796		796			
青 海						
宁 夏						
新 疆						

表 185　我国西部地区水果产量（2008—2009 年）　　单位：kt

品　种	2008 年	2009 年	同比增长（%）
全国总计	**113 389.2**	**122 464**	**8.00**
地区小计	29 920.9	39 156.0	23.39
占全国比重（%）	26.39	31.97	17.92
苹果	10 287.0	11 560.5	12.38
柑橘	7 126.8	7 434.8	4.32
梨	3 400.8	3 678.1	8.15
香蕉	1 946.8	6 363.7	226.88
菠萝	55.8	969.3	1 637.10
荔枝	335.2	1 075.6	220.87
龙眼	409.9	636.5	55.28
桃	1 521.7	1 663.8	9.34
猕猴桃	417.2	578.8	38.73
葡萄	2 664.7	3 098.5	16.28
红枣	807.2	1 065.2	31.96
柿子	947.8	1 024.9	8.13

表 186　我国西部地区森林工业主要产品产量（2009 年）

产　品	单　位	全国产量	地区产量	占全国比重（%）
木　材	万 m^3	7 068.3	2 245.1	31.76
竹　材	万根	135 649.9	42 237.3	31.14
紫　胶	t	3 694.0	2 492.0	67.46
生　漆	t	20 498.0	7 150.0	34.88
油桐籽	t	367 287.0	201 768.0	54.93
乌桕籽	t	33 171.0	9 760.0	29.42
五倍子	t	14 431.0	7 727.0	54.68
棕　片	t	77 314.0	23 342.0	30.06
松　脂	t	1 046 579.0	651 115.0	62.21
竹笋干	t	465 340.0	145 699.0	31.31
核　桃	t	979 366.0	603 728.0	61.64
板　栗	t	1 627 656.0	224 699.0	13.81
油茶籽	t	1 169 289.0	174 370.0	14.91

表 187 我国西部地区热带、亚热带作物面积和产量（2009 年）

项　目	单　位	全国产量	地区产量	占全国比重（%）
一、橡胶（按干橡胶片计算）				
收获面积	khm^2	2 014.41	1 664.57	82.63
产量	t	618 866.00	298 796.00	48.28
二、咖啡豆（按干咖啡豆计算）				
收获面积	khm^2	22.53	22.44	99.60
产量	t	70 405.00	70 203.00	99.71
三、椰子（按果实计算）				
收获面积	khm^2	27.41	0.05	0.18
产量	万个	23 891.00	41.00	0.17
四、腰果				
收获面积	khm^2	0.28		
产量	t	370.00	1.00	0.27
五、香料作物				
收获面积	khm^2	3.40	3.40	100.00
产量	t	1 119.00	1 119.00	100.00
其中：香茅草				
收获面积	khm^2	2.65	2.65	100.00
产量	t	1 034.00	1 034.00	100.00
六、剑麻（番麻）（折纤维）				
收获面积	khm^2	15 713.52	15 706.00	99.95
产量	t	97 061.00	57 735.00	59.48

表 188 我国西部地区主要畜产品产量（2008—2009 年）

产品名称	单　位	2008 年	2009 年	同比增长（%）	占全国比重（%）
一、肉类总产量	万 t	2 154.1	2 273.4	5.54	29.72
猪　肉	万 t	1 371.2	1 455.0	6.11	29.75
牛　肉	万 t	208.8	221.3	5.99	34.82
羊　肉	万 t	219.6	223.8	1.91	57.47
禽　肉	万 t	303.5	314.3	3.56	19.71
兔　肉	万 t	26.0	29.1	11.92	45.75
二、其他畜产品产量					
奶　类	万 t	1 632.9	1 613.0	−1.22	43.21
牛　奶	万 t	1 501.1	1 477.3	−1.59	41.98
蜂　蜜	万 t	7.9	8.4	6.33	20.90
禽　蛋	万 t	371.1	375.7	1.24	13.70
山羊毛	t	22 852.1	29 805.0	30.43	60.27
羊　绒	t	11 581.3	11 525.0	−0.49	67.94
绵羊毛	t	246 377.0	243 624.0	−1.12	66.93
细羊毛	t	87 299.1	93 641.0	7.26	73.53
半细羊毛	t	47 058.0	49 753.0	5.73	44.02

表 189 我国西部地区水产品产量（2008—2009 年） 单位：kt

产品名称	2008 年	2009 年	同比增长（%）	占全国比重（%）
水产品总产量	**4 305.6**	**4 532.2**	**5.26**	**8.86**
按海水、内陆分				
海水产品产量	1 440.7	1 490.2	3.44	5.56
内陆水产品产量	2 864.9	3 042.0	6.18	12.49
按生产性质分				
捕捞产量	918.2	925.9	0.84	6.19
养殖产量	3 387.4	3 606.3	6.46	9.96

表 190 我国西部地区人均主要农产品、畜产品、水产品产量（2008—2009 年）

单位：kg/人

产品名称	2008 年	2009 年	同比增长（%）
一、主要农产品			
（一）粮食	385.1	388.9	0.99
1. 谷物	321.3	325.6	1.34
稻谷	123.7	123.7	平
小麦	54.2	59.9	10.52
玉米	131.1	131.2	0.08
谷子	1.3	0.9	−30.77
高粱	2.4	2.2	−8.33
2. 豆类	16.6	16.5	−0.60
大豆	8.4	8.9	5.95
杂豆	8.2	7.6	−7.32
3. 薯类	47.2	46.8	−0.85
马铃薯	30.2	30.8	1.99
（二）油料	20.8	22.5	8.17
花生	3.5	3.7	5.71
油菜籽	12.0	13.5	12.50
芝麻	0.2	0.1	−50.00
胡麻籽	0.7	0.7	平
向日葵籽	3.8	4.2	10.53
（三）棉花	9.0	7.4	−17.78
（四）麻类	0.6	0.4	−33.33
黄红麻			
（五）糖料	302.1	272.7	−9.73
甘蔗	284.7	257.8	−9.45
甜菜	17.4	15.0	−13.79
（六）水果	139.5	154.9	11.04
（七）烟叶	4.7	4.9	4.26
烤烟	4.4	4.6	4.55
二、畜产品			
（一）猪牛羊肉	49.4	51.9	5.06
猪肉	37.7	39.7	5.31
牛肉	5.7	6.0	5.26
羊肉	6.0	6.1	1.67
（二）奶类	44.8	44.0	−1.79
牛奶	41.2	40.3	−2.18
（三）禽蛋	10.2	10.3	0.98
三、水产品	11.8	12.4	5.08
鱼类	8.8	9.3	5.68
虾蟹类	0.8	0.8	平

表 191　我国西部地区农林牧渔业总产值、增加值及构成（2008—2009 年）

名　　称	总　产　值		增　加　值	
	2008 年	2009 年	2008 年	2009 年
一、绝对数（亿元）				
合　计	**14 860.3**	**15 137.4**	**9 008.3**	**9 194.9**
1. 农业	7 465.2	8 104.6	4 970.0	5 347.6
2. 林业	642.8	701.2	445.0	473.6
3. 牧业	5 886.3	5 372.5	3 114.9	2 847.5
4. 渔业	405.6	452.1	273.5	295.9
二、构成（%）				
农林牧渔业合计	**100.0**	**100.0**	**100.0**	**100.0**
1. 农业	50.2	53.5	55.2	58.2
2. 林业	4.3	4.6	4.9	5.2
3. 牧业	39.6	35.3	34.6	31.0
4. 渔业	2.7	3.0	3.0	3.2
三、西部占全国的比重（%）				
农林牧渔业总产值合计	**25.6**	**25.1**	**26.7**	**26.1**
1. 农业	26.6	26.5	27.4	27.1
2. 林业	29.9	29.7	30.5	28.2
3. 牧业	28.6	27.6	31.2	33.1
4. 渔业	7.8	8.0	8.6	8.0

表 192　我国西部地区林业产业总产值（2009 年）

单位：万元

地　区	总　　计	第一产业	第二产业	第三产业
全国总计	**174 937 336**	**72 252 565**	**87 179 183**	**15 505 588**
地区小计	35 820 867	20 077 160	11 348 473	4 368 600
占全国比重（%）	20.48	27.97	13.02	28.17
内蒙古	1 795 755	1 030 362	542 705	222 688
广　西	8 817 723	3 904 590	4 572 947	313 552
重　庆	2 117 564	1 304 557	526 916	286 091
四　川	9 533 984	3 701 272	3 600 236	2 232 476
贵　州	2 475 936	1 235 314	690 065	550 557
云　南	4 598 691	3 524 784	905 360	168 547
西　藏	128 798	115 464	13 334	
陕　西	1 977 672	1 711 147	152 064	114 461
甘　肃	1 178 477	1 006 415	54 388	117 674
青　海	59 043	56 493		2 550
宁　夏	610 314	314 629	210 243	85 442
新　疆	2 526 910	2 172 133	80 215	274 562

表 193　我国西部地区林业系统森林工业固定资产投资（2009 年）

单位：万元

地　区	总　　计	其中：基本建设	更新改造	其他投资	本年新增固定资产
全国总计	**2 351 488**	**1 786 595**	**453 854**	**111 039**	**1 209 179**
地区小计	1 731 437	1 204 224	425 490	101 423	886 336
占全国比重（%）	73.63	67.40	93.75	91.34	73.30
内 蒙 古	18 274	1 152		17 122	14 137
广　西	1 699 210	1 193 511	423 960	81 739	867 147
重　庆					
四　川	5 432	4 032	1 300	100	125
贵　州					
云　南	7 126	4 811		2 315	4 090
西　藏					
陕　西	230		230		230
甘　肃					
青　海					
宁　夏					
新　疆	865	718		147	607

表 194 我国西部地区林业系统农产品加工业总产值（2009 年）

单位：万元

地 区	非木质林产品加工制造业	木材加工及竹、藤、棕、草制品业			
		合 计	锯材木片加工业	人造板制造业	木制品制造业
全国总计	**6 781 363**	**39 292 789**	**7 135 579**	**20 496 082**	**8 887 931**
地区小计	563 707	4 827 223	1 313 108	2 796 644	502 692
占全国比重（%）	8.31	12.29	18.40	13.64	5.66
内蒙古	20 661	325 526	238 674	85 452	1 333
广 西	162 201	2 330 096	594 074	1 394 052	246 878
重 庆	50 058	203 172	38 833	89 163	59 624
四 川	32 478	1 139 853	173 246	798 705	88 582
贵 州	12 817	279 573	64 426	174 641	24 212
云 南	94 156	378 179	156 212	158 657	61 346
西 藏		12 616	12 501	112	
陕 西	5 050	122 016	20 442	80 536	15 437
甘 肃	5 956	7 645	2 358	2 984	1 417
青 海					
宁 夏	136 836				
新 疆	43 494	28 546	12 342	12 342	3 863

地 区	竹、藤、棕草制品业	木质、竹藤家具制造业	木、竹、苇浆造纸及纸制品业	林产化学产品制造业	木、竹藤工艺品制造业	其 他
全国总计	**2 773 197**	**14 814 538**	**16 636 054**	**2 197 610**	**2 026 270**	**2 926 668**
地区小计	214 777	1 790 662	1 672 116	759 556	65 112	1 080 745
占全国比重（%）	7.74	12.09	10.05	34.56	3.21	36.93
内蒙古	67	974		894	1 700	130 975
广 西	95 092	277 344	852 595	577 859	23 572	349 280
重 庆	15 552	111 321	33 282	9 515	17 488	89 002
四 川	79 318	1 332 611	619 177	16 319	16 494	361 051
贵 州	16 294	34 266	25 447	4 677	2 982	27 843
云 南	1 964	13 319	95 493	128 082	1 408	93 171
西 藏	3					718
陕 西	5 601	10 438		594	1 340	6 593
甘 肃	886	5 081			120	15 417
青 海						
宁 夏		5 207	46 122	21 616		462
新 疆		101			8	6 233

表 195 我国西部地区森林工业主要产品产量（2009 年）

地　区	锯材（万 m^3）	木片（万实积 m^3）	胶合板（万 m^3）	纤维板（万 m^3）	刨花板（万 m^3）	胶合木（万 m^3）	木地板（万 m^2）	卫生筷子（标准箱）
全国总计	**3 229.8**	**1 285.8**	**4451.2**	**3 488.6**	**1431.0**	**325.9**	**37 753.2**	**10 409 774**
地区小计	1 093.1	230.5	617.4	671.5	77.3	24.5	2 206.0	1 198 396
占全国比重(%)	33.84	17.39	13.87	19.25	5.40	7.52	5.84	11.51
内蒙古	391.7	13.6	32.4	13.9	20.1	1.4	0.7	149 949
广　西	389.3	144.8	380.5	317.5	19.9	6.9	89.2	665 657
重　庆	5.3	3.4	30.1	5.7	1.7	0.2	1.0	200
四　川	117.6	14.0	120.1	222.8	25.8	11.3	1699.0	319 460
贵　州	41.2	2.9	28.6	7.8	0.9	0.9	59.9	27 290
云　南	125.9	33.0	22.6	71.2	8.3	3.7	356.2	35 840
西　藏	19.4	18.6				0.1		
陕　西	1.6	0.1	1.5	31.8	0.4			
甘　肃			1.4	0.8	0.2			
青　海								
宁　夏								
新　疆	1.1	0.1	0.2					

地　区	人造板表面装饰板（万 m^2）	单板（万 m^2）	松香类产品（t）	松节油类产品（t）	樟脑（t）	冰片（t）	栲胶类产品（t）	紫胶类产品（t）	木材热解产品(t)		软木制品(m^3)	
									木炭	活性炭	软木砖	软木纸
全国总计	**25 327.1**	**2 714.4**	**1 117 030**	**157 506**	**9 700**	**986**	**11 000**	**2 755**	**316 612**	**226 529**	**8 200**	**45 747**
地区小计	7.8	295.2	782 075	144 143	91	200	9 490	1 546	69 690	1 644		1 285
占全国比重(%)	0.03	10.88	70.01	91.52	0.94	20.28	86.27	56.12	22.01	0.73		2.81
内蒙古		0.1					1 334					
广　西		283.2	649 010	43 231	15		7 161		2 340			876
重　庆			1 160						20	1 200		
四　川	7.5	3.5	2 571	15 231	55	200		61	6 080			
贵　州		0.9	3 825	298					39 211	160		4
云　南	0.25	7.5	125 509	26 071	21		845	1 485	22 039	284		
西　藏												
陕　西							150					405
甘　肃												
青　海												
宁　夏												
新　疆												

表 196　我国西部地区农垦系统主要农产品加工企业产品产量（2009 年）

地　区	配混合饲料（t）	机制纸及纸版（t）	纱（万 t）	布（万 m）	机制糖（t）	饮料酒（t）	乳制品（t）	食用植物油（t）
全国总计	**4 178 077**	**1 077 642**	**42.16**	**65 339**	**1 788 222**	**1 847 850**	**2 070 908**	**1 704 508**
地区小计	1 484 002	166 216	22.38	8 576	964 282	369 633	395 614	374 580
占全国比重(%)	35.52	15.42	53.08	13.13	53.92	20.00	19.10	21.98
内蒙古	21 190	3 640				911	23 418	40 131
广　西	182 355	40 242			764 009	3 079	2 926	
重　庆	426 827						184 428	491
四　川						6 823	2 532	
贵　州	21 227					24	30 127	
云　南					61 522	74		
西　藏								
陕　西	11 867						1 798	2 432
甘　肃	8 570					142 951		
青　海							13 367	
宁　夏	23 884					126 361	19 572	57
新疆（兵团）	773 076	120 131	20	8 576	138 751	85 392	72 773	315 236
新疆（农业）	13 797		2			4 018	505	10 198
新疆（畜牧）	1 209	2 203					44 168	6 035

表 197　我国西部地区轻工业系统农产品加工业产品产量（2008 年）

地　区	纸　浆（万 t）	机制纸、纸板（万 t）	纸制品（万 t）	原　盐（万 t）	机制糖（万 t）	糖　果（万 t）	方便面（万 t）
全国总计	**2 058.5**	**8390.9**	**3 191.4**	**5 952.8**	**1 449.5**	**121.4**	**499.5**
地区小计	248.0	696.9	324.8	1 410.0	1 226.0	3.03	60.8
占全国比重（%）	12.05	8.31	10.18	23.69	84.58	2.50	12.17
内蒙古	21.4	35.5	36.1	236.8	22.4		2.8
广　西	83.7	149.7	41.1	4.0	931.1	0.2	4.2
重　庆	3.9	81.5	40.6	122.4		0.4	13.6
四　川	60.6	211.2	120.6	559.7	5.8	1.7	13.7
贵　州	9.1	2.4	23.9		1.2	0.1	1.1
云　南	19.7	36.7	16.9	91.1	210.1	0.5	2.1
西　藏			0.2				
陕　西		73.5	27.3	41.3		0.1	19.8
甘　肃	1.2	14.1	8.3	4.3	1.6		0.1
青　海			0.2	235.7			
宁　夏	22.3	69.0	0.3				
新　疆	26.1	23.3	9.2	114.7	53.8		3.4

（续）

地　　区	乳制品（万 t）	液体乳（万 t）	罐头（万 t）	味精（万 t）	冷冻饮品（万 t）	饮料酒（万 kL）	软饮料（万 kL）	饼干（万 t）
全国总计	**1 810.6**	**1 525.2**	**595.3**	**184.4**	**205.5**	**4 882.3**	**6 415.1**	**282.7**
地区小计	620.4	541.7	121.34	20.7	63.63	985.9	1 132.6	32.3
占全国比重（%）	34.26	35.52	20.38	11.23	30.96	20.19	17.66	11.44
内蒙古	355.9	325.7			47.5	123.2	114.9	0.4
广　西	32.2	31.9	25.1	0.1	2.7	120.6	129.2	1.1
重　庆	9.3	9.1	3.9	4.9	4.9	78.1	142.6	0.2
四　川	35.1	30.7	23.4	7.0	3.1	350.7	246.9	16.0
贵　州	3.6	3.5	0.9		2.8	41.7	31.2	0.1
云　南	24.9	23.5	2.5	1.2		45.1	119.7	
西　藏	0.6					9.0	3.9	
陕　西	110.9	79.5	1.5		0.7	92.9	180.6	14.5
甘　肃	7.7	6.4	7.3	0.1		56.2	92.6	
青　海	6.4	6.2				10.5		
宁　夏	13.1	9.4		6.7		13.0	11.2	
新　疆	20.7	15.8	56.7	0.7	1.9	44.9	59.8	0.1

地　　区	轻　革（万 m^2）	皮　鞋（万双）	皮革服装（万件）	毛皮服装（万件）	天然皮革、手提包、袋（万个）	家　具（万件）	造纸机械（台）
全国总计	**64 203.5**	**331533.5**	**5 653.2**	**385.3**	**76 980.0**	**51 867.2**	**39 250**
地区小计	4 690.6	15 291.1	172.5	1.5	25.0	1 456.0	114
占全国比重（%）	7.31	4.61	3.05	0.39	0.032	2.81	0.29
内蒙古	0.6			0.2		118.5	
广　西	1 953.0	644.5			25.0	59.4	61
重　庆	38.6	2 473.9	7.5			358.2	
四　川	2 145.5	12 042.1	158.5			707.6	45
贵　州		0.5				31.0	
云　南						9.0	
西　藏		2.6	0.4				
陕　西		113.0	0.1			45.0	8
甘　肃	147.9		5.9	1.3		5.9	
青　海	7.9	4.0					
宁　夏						1.1	
新　疆	397.1	10.5				120.3	

资料来源：表中数据由中国轻工业信息中心提供。

其 他

表 198 我国食品卫生抽样监测情况（2008 年） 单位：万件

食品名称	合计			生产加工业			经营和餐饮服务		
	监测件数	合格件数	合格率（%）	监测件数	合格件数	合格率（%）	监测件数	合格件数	合格率（%）
全国总计	**1 150 766**	**1 053 990**	**91.6**	**321 089**	**297 466**	**92.6**	**829 677**	**756 524**	**91.2**
粮食及其制品	96 732	90 955	94.0	36 169	34 342	95.0	60 563	56 613	93.5
肉及肉制品	175 667	153 930	87.6	50 316	45 098	89.6	125 351	108 832	86.8
乳和乳制品	42 585	40 027	94.0	9 899	9 224	93.2	32 686	30 803	94.2
蛋及蛋制品	16 706	15 618	93.5	6 989	6 468	92.6	9 717	9 150	94.2
糖及糖果制品	26 100	24 942	95.6	9 177	8 665	94.4	16 923	16 277	96.2
冷冻饮料	37 882	34 577	91.3	10 563	9 438	89.4	27 319	25 139	92.0
（软）饮料	58 145	54 098	93.0	14 304	12 812	89.6	43841	41 286	94.2
酒类	56 296	55 049	97.8	21 435	20 844	97.2	34 861	34 205	98.1
焙烤食品	124 595	115 205	92.5	62 537	58 199	93.1	62 058	57 006	91.9
水产品	20 185	18 966	94.0	5 084	4 717	92.8	15 101	14 249	94.4
豆制品	34 316	31 043	90.5	16 098	14 590	90.6	18 218	16 453	90.3
调味品	60 922	57 558	94.5	12 194	11 339	93.0	48 728	46 219	94.9
果蔬制品	19 468	18 245	93.7	4 630	4 257	91.9	14 838	13 988	94.3
罐头	12 964	12 543	96.8	3 778	3 702	98.0	9186	8 841	96.2
茶叶	15 483	15 061	97.3	5 114	4 989	97.6	10 369	10 072	97.1
食用油脂	48 893	46 816	95.8	12 120	11 568	95.5	36 773	35 248	95.9
酱腌菜	19 279	17 768	92.2	6 981	6 399	91.7	12 298	11 369	92.5
婴幼儿食品	11 792	11 316	96.0	1 186	1 112	93.8	10 606	10 204	96.2
保健食品	11 020	10 561	95.8	2 471	2 344	94.9	8 549	8 217	96.1
新资源食品	387	367	94.8	152	141	92.8	235	226	96.2
食品添加剂	6 856	6 568	95.8	2 041	1 976	96.8	4 815	4 592	95.4
其他食品	254 493	222 777	87.5	27 581	25 242	90.6	226 642	197 535	87.2

资料来源：表中数据出自 2009 年版《中国卫生统计年鉴》。

表 199 轻工业系统农产品加工行业十大质量品牌当选企业（2008 年）

产品类别	品 牌	生产企业名称
酱 醋	海 天	佛山市海天调味品有限公司
	李锦记	南方李锦记有限公司
	保 宁	四川保宁醋有限公司
	恒顺牌食醋	江苏恒顺醋业股份有限公司
	东湖牌老陈醋	山西老陈醋集团
	太太乐	上海太太乐食品有限公司
	岐江桥	广东美味鲜调味食品有限公司
	味事达	广东开平市味事达调味品有限公司
	水塔牌食醋	山西水塔老陈醋股份有限公司
	珠江桥	珠江桥生物科技股份有限公司
黄酒、保健酒	古越龙山	浙江古越龙山绍兴酒股份有限公司
	中国劲酒	中国劲酒有限公司
	椰岛鹿龟酒	海南椰岛酒业有限公司
	佳善黄酒	浙江佳善黄酒股份有限公司
	竹叶青酒	山西杏花村汾酒集团有限责任公司
	女儿红	浙江绍兴女儿红酿酒总公司
	古岭神酒	广西柳州市古岭神酒厂
	塔牌黄酒	浙江塔牌绍兴酒有限公司
	金枫黄酒	上海金枫酿酒公司
	鹿鞭酒	山东淄博福禄酒业有限公司
白 酒	五粮液	四川省五粮液集团有限公司
	泸州老窖	泸州老窖集团有限责任公司
	贵州茅台	贵州茅台酒厂（集团）有限责任公司
	生力源	山东泰山生力源集团股份有限公司
	稻花香	湖北稻花香集团
	西 凤	陕西西凤酒业有限公司
	全兴	四川成都全兴集团有限公司
	水井坊	四川水井坊股份有限公司
	彩山特曲	山东金彩山酒业有限公司
	国 渝	重庆国渝酒业有限公司

（续）

产品类别	品　牌	生产企业名称
啤　酒	青岛啤酒	青岛牌酒集团有限公司
	燕京啤酒	北京燕京牌酒集团公司
	雪花啤酒	华润雪花牌酒（中国）有限公司
	山城啤酒	重啤酒集团宜宾有限公司
	金星啤酒	金星啤酒集团有限公司
	金威啤酒	金威啤酒（中国）有限公司
	哈尔滨啤酒	哈尔滨啤酒集团有限公司
	珠江啤酒	广州市珠江啤酒集团有限公司
	百威啤酒	百威（武汉）国际啤酒有限公司
	雪津啤酒	英博雪津啤酒有限公司
红　酒	长城葡萄酒	中国长城葡萄酒有限公司
	张裕葡萄酒	烟台张裕葡萄酿酒有限公司
	王朝葡萄酒	天津王朝葡萄酿酒有限公司
	禧吉红	
	龙威葡萄酒	河北龙威葡萄酒业有限公司
	通化葡萄酒	吉林通化葡萄酒有限公司
	新天葡萄酒	新天国际葡萄酒业股份有限公司
	丰收葡萄酒	北京丰收葡萄酒有限公司
	香格里拉葡萄酒	云南香格里拉葡萄酒业股份有限公司
	华夏五千年葡萄酒	华夏五千年（北京）葡萄酒有限公司
饮　料	康师傅冰红茶	康师傅控股有限公司
	汇源果汁	北京汇源饮料食品集团有限公司
	椰树牌椰汁	海南椰树集团
	统一鲜橙多	上海统一企业集团
	红牛饮料	海南红牛饮料有限公司
	可口可乐	可口可乐饮料有限公司
	百事可乐	广州百事可乐饮料有限公司
	露露杏仁露	河北承德露露股份有限公司
	农夫果园	福建永安农夫果园公司
	王老吉	广州王老吉药业股份有限公司

（续）

产品类别	品　牌	生产企业名称
饮用水	怡　宝	怡宝食品饮料（深圳）有限公司
	景　田	深圳景田实业集团公司
	益　力	深圳达能益力泉饮品有限公司
	农夫山泉	农夫山泉股份有限公司
	鼎湖爱森山泉	肇庆市鼎湖山泉饮用水有限公司
	娃哈哈	杭州娃哈哈集团有限公司
	乐百事	乐百事（广东）食品饮料有限公司
	依　云	深圳依云矿泉水配送站
	滔达饮料	哈尔滨滔达饮料有限公司
	屈臣氏	广州屈臣氏食品饮料有限公司
大　米	北大荒	黑龙江北大荒米业有限公司
	五　常	黑龙江五常市健洋有限公司
	金　健	湖南金健米业股份有限公司
	金　佳	江西金佳谷物有限公司
	梧　桐	黑龙江泰丰粮油食品有限公司
	好　雨	吉林裕丰企业股份公司
	玉　珠	江西樟树粮油公司
	白　湖	安徽白湖大米有限公司
	粮　丰	潮阳市粮丰集团有限公司
	金　苗	广东金福米业有限公司
方便米面制品	康师傅方便面	天津顶益国际食品有限公司
	统一100	统一企业集团
	白　象	白象集团食品有限公司
	华　龙	河北华龙集团
	华祥方便面	陕西华祥食品（集团）有限公司
	锦丰方便面	广东锦丰集团公司
	亚　兰	新乡市亚特兰食品有限责任公司
	鸡蓉公仔面	鸡蓉公仔面（食品）公司
	福满多	河北福满多食品有限公司
	华　丰	武汉金鼎食品有限公司

（续）

产品类别	品 牌	生产企业名称
食用油	金龙鱼	辽宁营口渤海油脂工业有限公司
	福临门	中粮粮油有限公司
	鲁 花	山东鲁花集团有限公司
	胡姬花	嘉里粮油（青岛）有限公司
	美洲王	广州市至润油脂食品工业有限公司
	海 狮	上海市油脂公司
	禧万年	南通宝港油脂发展有限公司
	刀 唛	深圳南顺油脂有限公司
	口 福	益海集团
	长 康	长康集团公司湖南长康实业有限公司
月 饼	荣 华	佛山市顺德区苏氏荣华食品有限公司
	金九饼业	广东金九饼业有限公司
	好利来 月饼	好利来北京食品工业园
	杏花楼月饼	上海杏花楼（集团）有限公司
	裕海月饼	上海克莉丝汀食品有限公司
	米旗月饼	西安米旗食品有限公司
	金源月饼	吴川市金源大厦、吴川市南方月饼业有限公司
	元祖月饼	上海元祖食品有限公司
	稻香村饼	北京稻香村食品集团稻香村月饼生产有限公司
	华美月饼	东莞华美食品有限公司
饼 干	达 能	上海达能饼干食品有限公司
	康师傅	天津顶益国际食品有限公司
	太 平	纳贝斯克食品（苏州）有限公司
	旺 旺	旺旺食品集团
	嘉士利	广东嘉士利食品有限公司
	达 利	福建达利食品集团有限公司
	好吃点	福建达利食品集团有限公司
	徐福记	东莞徐福记食品有限公司
	嘉 顿	香港嘉顿公司
	丹麦蓝罐	深圳全记十力贸易有限公司

（续）

产品类别	品　牌	生产企业名称
速冻食品	思念速冻食品	郑州思念食品有限公司
	三全速冻食品	郑州三全食品股份有限公司
	龙凤速冻食品	浙江龙凤食品有限公司
	金城食品	佛山金城速冻食品有限公司
	佑康速冻食品	杭州佑康食品集团有限公司
	科迪速冻食品	河南科迪速冻食品有限公司
	湾仔码头	美国通用磨坊食品公司
	大娘水饺	江苏大娘水饺餐饮有限公司
	狗不理	天津狗不理集团速冻食品有限公司
	海霸王	海霸王（汕头）食品有限公司
肉制品	双　汇	河南省漯河市双汇实业集团有限责任公司
	金　锣	山东临沂新程金锣肉制品集团有限公司
	科尔沁	内蒙古科尔沁牛业股份有限公司
	鹏中宝	江门市鹏中宝食品有限公司
	得利斯	得利斯集团
	唐人神	湖南唐人神肉制品有限公司
	雨　润	江苏雨润食品产业集团有限公司
	鹏　程	北京鹏程食品有限公司
	银　宝	山东满地香食品有限公司
	皓月	吉林省长春皓月清真肉业股份有限公司
休闲食品	箭牌口香糖	箭牌糖果（中国）有限公司
	喜之郎果冻	广东喜之郎集团有限公司
	旺　旺	旺旺食品集团
	珍奇味	广州市珍奇味有限公司
	蜡笔小新果冻	蜡笔小新（福建）食品工业有限公司
	洽洽瓜子	合肥华泰食品有限公司
	佳宝凉果	广东佳宝集团有限公司
	好丽友蛋黄派	好丽友食品有限公司
	乐事薯片	上海乐事薯片公司
	益达木糖醇	香港益达糖果有限公司

（续）

产品类别	品 牌	生产企业名称
茶 业	张一元	北京张一元茶业有限责任公司
	吴裕泰	北京吴裕泰茶业股份公司
	雪青绿茶	山东雪青茶场有限公司
	八马茶业	厦门八马茶业有限公司
	华龙茶业	浙江华龙茶业有限公司
	午子绿茶	陕西省午子绿茶有限责任公司
	绿剑茶业	浙江绿剑茶业有限公司
	通天香	广西通天香茶业有限公司
	云峰茶业	福建南安市云峰茶业有限公司
	望海茶业	浙江宁波望海茶业发展有限公司
卷 烟	中华卷烟	上海烟草（集团）公司
	熊猫卷烟	上海烟草（集团）公司
	玉溪卷烟	红塔集团玉溪卷烟厂
	娇子卷烟	川渝中烟工业公司
	红塔山卷烟	红塔山烟草（集团）有限责任公司
	云烟卷烟	红云烟草（集团）有限责任公司
	芙蓉王卷烟	湖南中烟工业有限责任公司
	红河卷烟	红河烟草（集团）有限责任公司
	利群卷烟	浙江中烟工业有限责任公司
	双喜卷烟	广东中烟工业有限责任公司
中成药	江中药业	江中药业股份有限公司
	三精制药	哈药集团三精制药有限公司
	三九医药	三九医药股份有限公司
	中一药业	广州中一药业有限公司
	西南药业	西南药业股份有限公司
	九芝堂	湖南九芝堂（集团）有限公司
	双鹭药业	北京双鹭药业股份有限公司
	同仁堂	北京同仁堂（集团）有限责任公司
	片仔癀	漳州片仔癀药业股份有限公司
	云南白药	云南白药集团股份有限公司

（续）

产品类别	品　牌	生产企业名称
羽绒服	波司登羽绒服	江苏波司登羽绒服装有限公司
	艾莱依羽绒服	浙江艾莱依羽绒制品有限公司
	雅鹿羽绒服	江苏雅鹿实业股份有限公司
	鸭宝宝羽绒服	哈尔滨鸭宝宝羽绒服有限公司
	鸭鸭羽绒服	江西共青鸭鸭集团
	雪中飞羽绒服	江苏雪中飞制衣有限公司
	冰洁羽绒服	上海冰洁服饰有限公司
	雪驰羽绒服	湖北普雅特尔雪驰服饰有限公司
	红豆羽绒服	江苏红豆实业股份有限公司
	雪伦羽绒服	雪伦国际时装（北京）有限公司
衬　衫	雅戈尔	雅戈尔集团股份有限公司
	步　森	浙江诸暨市步森集团有限公司
	七匹狼	福建七匹狼实业股份公司
	红豆集团	红豆集团有限公司
	报喜乌	浙江报喜乌服饰股份有限公司
	木才衬衫	福建才子服饰股份有限公司
	绅士衬衫	北京绅士服饰股份有限公司
	罗　蒙	罗蒙集团股份有限公司
	洛　兹	宁波洛兹集团有限公司
	太平鸟	宁波太平鸟股份有限公司
皮　鞋	森　达	江苏森达集团有限公司
	达芙尼	永恩实业（上海）有限公司
	百丽	深圳百丽鞋业有限公司
	红蜻蜓	浙江红蜻蜓鞋业股份有限公司
	小灵猪	高明市港星鞋业有限公司
	香香莉	浙江香香莉鞋业有限公司
	奇　迪	上海奇迪鞋业有限公司
	展　风	浙江华都鞋业有限公司
	戈美其	浙江戈其美鞋业有限公司
	中国巨康	温州巨康鞋业有限公司

资料来源：表中信息由中国轻工业信息中心提供。

表 200 我国农产品加工创业基地第一批名单（2009 年）

序号	基地名称	所在地	序号	基地名称	所在地
1	北京经纬农产品加工创业基地	北京	31	黑龙江建三江经济开发区	黑龙江
2	北京民族农产品加工创业基地	北京	32	庆安县农产品加工园区	黑龙江
3	北京榆垡农产品加工创业基地	北京	33	绥化市苗氏特种稻产业化示范基地	黑龙江
4	天津市农产品加工专业园区蓟县园区	天津	34	鹤岗市米业集团农产品加工创业基地	黑龙江
5	天津市农产品加工专业园区宝坻园区	天津	35	虎林市农产品加工创业基地	黑龙江
6	魏县回隆糖果加工创业基地	河北	36	海伦市海北镇农产品加工基地	黑龙江
7	藁城市（增村）卤制品加工创业基地	河北	37	上海市孙桥现代农业园区	上海
8	石家庄乐盈食品加工创业基地	河北	38	上海浦东临空出口农业园区	上海
9	河北华宇肠衣有限公司肠衣加工基地	河北	39	江苏兴化农副产品加工创业基地	江苏
10	柳林三交红枣基地	山西	40	江苏省沛县农产品加工创业基地	江苏
11	山西忻州农产品加工创业富民基地	山西	41	江苏泗洪绿色农产品加工创业基地	江苏
12	山西神池县农产品加工创业绿宇基地	山西	42	高邮鸭及绿色农产品加工创业基地	江苏
13	山西平顺县农产品加工创业基地	山西	43	如皋市肠衣加工创业基地	江苏
14	山西永济市双孢菇加工创业基地	山西	44	望江经济开发区农产品加工创业基地	安徽
15	盛乐经济园区	内蒙古	45	砀山果蔬加工创业基地	安徽
16	通辽市科尔沁区农产品创业基地	内蒙古	46	安徽亳州工业园区	安徽
17	内蒙古察右前旗哈尔工业园区	内蒙古	47	淮北市凤凰山现代食品加工园	安徽
18	内蒙古杭锦后旗农产品加工创业基地	内蒙古	48	和县盛家口麻油产业集中区	安徽
19	托克托工业园区农产品加工创业基地	内蒙古	49	淮南市夏集大米加工园区	安徽
20	内蒙古小肥羊锡林郭勒盟基地	内蒙古	50	丽水市莲都区农产品加工示范基地	浙江
21	沈阳辉山农业开发区农产品加工基地	辽宁	51	舟山市干览镇食品工业专业区	浙江
22	大连瓦房店农产品加工创业基地	辽宁	52	福鼎市农产品加工创业基地	福建
23	清源满族自治县农产品加工基地	辽宁	53	福建省漳浦县农产品加工创业基地	福建
24	本溪五女山北江农产品加工基地	辽宁	54	漳平台湾农民创业园乌龙茶加工基地	福建
25	东港市农产品加工创业基地	辽宁	55	福建省长汀县腾飞工业园区	福建
26	朝阳市建平县杂粮加工创业基地	辽宁	56	华安县大地茶叶加工创业基地	福建
27	吉林省榆树市产品加工创业基地	吉林	57	连成县红心地瓜干加工创业基地	福建
28	吉林省洮南农产品加工创业基地	吉林	58	江西南昌小蓝农产品加工创业基地	江西
29	吉林省东丰县农产品加工创业基地	吉林	59	江西省新余农产品加工创业基地	江西
30	吉林省永吉农产品加工创业基地	吉林	60	年万贡米加工创业基地	江西

（续）

序号	基地名称	所在地	序号	基地名称	所在地
61	浮梁县茶叶加工创业基地	江西	95	成都市新都区农产品加工基地	四川
62	江西乐平蔬菜加工创业基地	江西	96	大理开发区绿色食品工业园	云南
63	山东金乡东运农产品加工创业基地	山东	97	丘北辣椒系列产品加工基地	云南
64	山东卒县朝城镇畜禽肉食加工基地	山东	98	迪庆州香格里拉绿色产业园区	云南
65	山东诸成市农产品（食品）加工基地	山东	99	呈贡绿色产业基地	云南
66	山东荣成好当家食品加工创业园	山东	100	大理自治州祥云农产品加工基地	云南
67	山东莱阳市食品工业园	山东	101	元谟县特色农产品加工基地	云南
68	胶东镇农产品加工区	山东	102	贵阳市乌当区农产品加工基地	贵州
69	武汉食品工业加工区	湖北	103	中国食品工业（西秀）示范基地	贵州
70	潜江市优质水产品出口创业基地	湖北	104	黎平县农产品加工创业基地	贵州
71	京山县粮食加工工业园	湖北	105	遵义县农产品加工创业基地	贵州
72	三里岗镇香菇产业加工创业基地	湖北	106	石阡县泉都旅游产品加工集聚区	贵州
73	汉川市农产品加工创业基地	湖北	107	惠水县农产品加工创业基地	贵州
74	枝江安福寺工业园	湖北	108	贵州省湄潭县绿色食品加工基地	贵州
75	湖南平江工业园区	湖南	109	西安市临潼区农副产品加工基地	陕西
76	湖南宁乡农产品加工创业基地	湖南	110	杨陵农产品加工创业基地	陕西
77	湖南怀化工业园区	湖南	111	陕西澄城县农产品加工创业基地	陕西
78	湖南湘乡工业园区	湖南	112	陕西汇生源农副产品加工基地	陕西
79	湖南资兴市农产品加工创业基地	湖南	114	陕西扶风工业基地	陕西
80	广西良庆开发区农产品加工基地	广西	113	清涧县乡镇企业红枣加工创业基地	陕西
81	那阳工业集中区茉莉产业园	广西	114	天水农产品加工创业基地	甘肃
82	广西柳州市柳城县工业集中区	广西	115	甘肃驿马农产品加工创业基地	甘肃
83	广西贵港市南区桥圩镇羽绒城	广西	116	甘肃张掖东北郊科技产业园	甘肃
84	贺州旺高工业区农产品加工基地	广西	117	会宁县农业产业园区	甘肃
85	铜梁县侣俸小企业创业基地	重庆	118	青海省循化撒拉族县辣椒加工基地	青海
86	江津区油溪镇小企业创业基地	重庆	119	银川德胜工业园农产品加工创业园	宁夏
87	重庆市忠县水坪工业园农产品加工区	重庆	120	青河县特色农业产业化园区	新疆
88	万州区农副产品加工创业基地	重庆	121	新疆吐鲁番科技特色产业园	新疆
89	石柱县辣椒产业基地	重庆	122	喀什地区疏勒县南疆齐鲁工业园	新疆
90	中国（重庆）国际食品工业城	重庆	123	察布查尔锡伯自治县伊南工业园地	新疆
91	四川遂宁市船山农产品加工创业基地	四川	124	伊宁县伊工业园城南产业区	新疆
92	乐至县农副产品加工园区	四川	125	石河子北泉镇农产品加工基地	新疆
93	雅安市农产品加工创业基地	四川	126	奇台农场农产品加工创业基地	新疆
94	梓潼县经济技术产业园区	四川	127	石河子西营镇农产品加工创业基地	新疆

资料来源：表中信息出自 2009 年版《中国乡镇企业与农产品加工年鉴》。

表 201　我国粮油加工行业首批获 AAA 级、AA 级、A 级信用等级企业（2009 年）

信用等级	企 业 名 称	信用等级	企 业 名 称
AAA	嘉里粮油（天津）有限公司（天津市）	AAA	河北黑马粮油工业有限责任公司（河北辛集）
AAA	江苏省银河面粉有限公司（江苏通州市）	AAA	惠民县宇东面粉有限公司（山东惠民县）
AAA	湖北国宝桥米有限公司（湖北京山县）	AAA	内蒙古恒丰食品工业集团股份有限公司
AAA	湖南金浩茶油股份有限公司（湖南祁阳县）	AAA	青岛长生集团股份有限公司（山东青岛市）
AAA	安徽皖王面粉集团有限公司（安徽肃县）	AAA	武汉福达食用油调料有限公司（湖北武汉市）
AAA	安徽丰大股份有限公司（安徽合肥市）	AAA	安徽家乐米业有限公司（安徽广德县）
AAA	江苏三零面粉有限公司（江苏泰兴市）	AAA	口口香米业股份有限公司（湖南益阳市）
AAA	江西金佳谷物股份有限公司（江西南昌市）	AAA	河南丰盛粮油食品有限责任公司（河南西平）
AAA	江苏省淮安新丰面粉有限公司（江苏淮安市）	AAA	哈尔滨方正绿宝石优质米有限公司（哈尔滨）
AAA	河南粮油阳光油脂有限公司（河南荥阳市）	AAA	菏泽华瑞食品责任有限公司（山东菏泽市）
AAA	山东鲁花集团有限公司（山东莱阳市）	AAA	湖南益阳粒粒晶粮食购销有限公司（益阳）
AAA	洪湖市洪湖粮米业有限责任公司（洪湖市）	AA	济宁鲁鑫油脂有限公司（山东济宁市）
AAA	安徽大平工贸集团有限公司（安徽巢湖市）	AA	山东莱阳春雪食品有限公司（山东莱阳市）
AAA	郑州海嘉食品有限公司（河南郑州市）	AA	湖南银光粮油股份有限公司（湖南祁阳县）
AAA	光明面业股份有限公司（湖南南县）	AA	扎兰屯市淳江油脂有限责任公司（内蒙古）
AAA	陕西老牛面粉有限公司（陕西眉县）	AA	重庆市油脂公司（重庆市）
AAA	安徽槐祥工贸集团有限公司（安徽巢湖市）	AA	湖南盈成油脂工业有限公司（湖南常德市）
AAA	山东香驰粮油有限公司（山东博兴县）	AA	江苏省农垦米业有限公司（江苏南京市）
AAA	湖北襄樊万宝粮油有限公司（湖北襄樊市）	AA	天津市津沽粮食工业有限公司（天津市）
AAA	北京古船食品有限公司（北京市）	AA	湖南金山粮油食品有限公司（湖南长沙市）
AAA	中粮北海粮油工业（天津）有限公司（天津市）	AA	江苏金太阳油脂有限责任公司（江苏如东县）
AAA	宜兴市粮油集团大米有限公司（江苏宜兴市）	AA	潍坊风筝面粉有限责任公司（山东潍坊市）
AAA	中粮东海粮油工业（张家港）有限公司	AA	九三集团天津大豆科技有限公司（天津市）
AAA	湖南省天龙米业有限公司（湖南祁阳县）	AA	凤阳县凤宝粮油食品有限公司（安徽凤阳县）
AAA	济南民天面粉有限责任公司（山东济南市）	AA	合肥金润米业有限公司（安徽合肥市）
AAA	陕西陕富面业有限责任公司（陕西富平县）	AA	西安市群众面粉厂（陕西西安市）
AAA	安徽燕之坊食品有限公司（安徽合肥市）	AA	天津市金卢米业有限公司（天津市）
AAA	和县金城米业有限责任公司（安徽和县）	AA	明光市鸿达油脂有限公司（安徽明光市）
AAA	山东半球面粉有限公司（山东广饶县）	AA	上海福新面粉有限公司（上海市）
AAA	江苏苏南面粉有限公司（江苏金坛市 ）	AA	维维六朝松面粉产业有限公司（江苏徐州市）
AAA	邹平三星油脂工业有限公司（山东邹平县）	AA	肥城富世康制粉有限公司（山东肥城市）
AAA	安徽双福粮油工贸集团有限公司（安徽庐江）	AA	上海良友海狮油脂实业有限公司（上海市）
AAA	河南爱厨植物油有限公司（河南郑州市）	AA	山东鲁王集团有限公司（山东鱼台）
AAA	湖南金霞粮食产业有限公司（湖南长沙市）	AA	上海乐惠米业有限公司（上海市）
AAA	江苏楚龙面粉有限公司（江苏兴化市）	A	重庆粮油集团大足粮油购销有限责任公司
AAA	黑龙江泰丰粮油食品有限公司（黑龙江鹤岗）		

注：表中信息由中国粮食行业协会提供。

表 202　我国轻工业系统列入国家 500 强的农产品加工企业（2009 年）

序号	500 强企业中名次	企 业 名 称	地 区	营业收入（万元）
		食 品 业		
1	41	光明食品（集团）有限公司	上海	4 646 035
2	114	天津天狮集团有限公司	天津	2 308 093
3	215	中国盐业总公司	北京	1 248 843
4	248	上海良友（集团）有限公司	上海	1 076 718
5	336	广西南华糖业集团有限公司	广西	753 573
6	353	北京二商集团有限责任公司	北京	714 516
7	492	天津二商集团有限公司	天津	448 600
		乳 制 品 业		
1	119	内蒙古蒙牛乳业（集团）股份有限公司	内蒙古	2 118 375
2	132	内蒙古伊利实业集团股份有限公司	内蒙古	1 920 800
3	484	北京三元集团有限责任公司	北京	452 118
		饮料制造业		
1	103	杭州娃哈哈集团有限公司	浙江	2 581 196
2	253	维维集团股份有限公司	江苏	1 053 590
3	400	今麦郎食品有限公司	河北	597 577
		酿 酒 工 业		
1	104	四川省宜宾五粮液集团有限公司	四川	2 523 807
2	189	青岛啤酒股份有限公司	山东	1 370 922
3	258	北京燕京啤酒集团公司	北京	1 038 393
4	295	中国贵州茅台酒厂有限责任公司	贵州	924 700
		肉食品加工业		
1	83	江苏雨润食品产生集团有限公司	江苏	3 102 726
2	86	河南省漯河市双汇集团有限责任公司	河南	3 033 400
3	330	诸城外贸有限责任公司	山东	783 211
4	485	北京顺鑫农业股份有限公司	北京	452 113
		烟草加工业		
1	50	上海烟草（集团）公司	上海	4 068 678
2	53	红塔烟草（集团）有限责任公司	云南	3 987 997
3	70	湖南中烟工业有限责任公司	湖南	3 501 103
4	81	红云烟草（集团）有限责任公司	云南	3 153 312
5	112	浙江中烟工业有限责任公司	浙江	2 322 139
6	130	湖北中烟工业有限责任公司	湖北	1 930 843
7	141	河南中烟工业公司	河南	1 780 236
8	180	贵州中烟工业公司	贵州	1391 969
9	187	红河烟草（集团）有限责任公司	云南	1 378 139
10	333	广西中烟工业公司	广西	765 164
11	366	江西中烟工业公司	江西	679 081
12	406	厦门烟草工业有限责任公司	福建	577 411
13	417	重庆烟草工业有限责任公司	重庆	564 756

（续）

序号	500强企业中名次	企业名称	地区	营业收入（万元）
纺织、印染				
1	29	山东魏桥创业集团有限公司	山东	6 656 603
2	100	上海纺织控股（集团）公司	上海	2 611 973
3	109	江苏阳光集团有限公司	江苏	2 350 218
4	121	华芳集团有限公司	江苏	2 095 615
5	183	山东如意科技集团有限公司	山东	1 386 211
6	202	天津纺织集团（控股）有限公司	天津	1 315 958
7	341	浙江华孚集团有限公司	浙江	748 684
8	354	澳洋集团有限公司	江苏	710 680
9	388	北京纺织股份有限责任公司	北京	623 268
10	444	兴惠化纤集团有限公司	浙江	512 979
11	462	浙江天圣控股集团有限公司	浙江	489 446
纺织品、服装鞋帽（含皮革、毛、绒等制造业）				
1	143	雅戈尔集团股份有限公司	浙江	1 840 866
烟草加工业				
1	136	红豆集团有限公司	江苏	1 814 242
2	159	海澜集团有限公司	江苏	1 614 930
3	223	波司登股份有限公司	江苏	1 171 680
4	234	杉杉投资控股有限公司	浙江	1 123 321
5	243	内蒙古鄂尔多斯羊绒集团有限责任公司	内蒙古	1 092 340
6	262	维科控股集团股份有限公司	浙江	1 032 597
7	450	青岛即龙集团控股有限公司	山东	501 841
8	451	孚日集团股份有限公司	山东	501 631
9	454	江苏梦兰集团有限公司	江苏	500 572
造纸及纸制品加工业				
1	165	山东晨鸣纸业集团股份有限公司	山东	1 516 474
2	204	华泰集团有限公司	山东	1 305 195
3	278	金东纸业（江苏）股份有限公司	江苏	996 150
4	279	九龙纸业（控股）有限公司	广东	983 766
5	390	湖南泰格林纸业集团有限责任公司	湖南	620 634
6	486	芬欧汇川（常熟）纸业有限公司	江苏	451 900
7	490	胜达集团有限公司	浙江	450 020
橡胶制品业				
1	198	杭州橡胶（集团）公司	浙江	1 337 160
2	249	双星集团有限责任公司	山东	1 075 687
3	276	三角集团有限公司	江苏	1 003 806
4	318	山东珍珑橡胶有限公司	山东	820 245
5	332	双钱集团股份有限公司	上海	773 077
6	398	风神轮胎股份有限公司	河南	601 858
7	440	安徽佳通轮胎有限公司	安徽	518 110
8	491	厦门正新橡胶工业有限公司	福建	448 829

资料来源：表中信息由中国轻工业信息中心提供。

5

第五部分

标准、专利

农产品加工业部分国家标准（2010年）

标准号	标准名称	代替标准
GB 4404.2—2010	粮食作物种子　第2部分：豆类	GB 4404.2—1996 等
GB 4404.3—2010	粮食作物种子　第3部分：荞麦	GB 4404.3—1999
GB 4404.4—2010	粮食作物种子　第4部分：燕麦	GB 4404.4—1999
GB/T 12529.5—2010	粮油工业用图形符号、代号　第5部分：仓储工业	GB/T 12529.5—1990
GB/T 24852—2010	大米及米粉糊化特性测定　快速粘度仪法	
GB/T 24853—2010	小麦、黑麦及其粉类和淀粉糊化特性测定　快速粘度仪法	
GB/T 25226—2010	大米　蒸煮过程中米粒糊化时间的评价	
GB/T 25227—2010	粮食加工、储运设备现场监测装置技术规范	
GB/T 25229—2010	粮油储藏　平房仓气密性要求	
GB 25461—2010	淀粉工业水污染物排放标准	
GB/T 25733—2010	藕粉	
GB/T 25866—2010	玉米干全酒糟（玉米DDGS）	
GB/T 25868—2010	早熟马铃薯　预冷和冷藏运输指南	
GB/T 25872—2010	马铃薯　通风库贮藏指南	
GB/T 26433—2010	粮油加工环境要求	
GB/T 5490—2010	粮油检验　一般规则	GB/T 5490—1985
GB/T 5517—2010	粮油检验　粮食及制品酸度测定	GB/T 5517—1985
GB/T 24870—2010	粮油检验　大豆粗蛋白质、粗脂肪含量的测定　近红外法	
GB/T 24871—2010	粮油检验　小麦粉粗蛋白质含量测定　近红外法	
GB/T 24872—2010	粮油检验　小麦粉灰分含量测定　近红外法	
GB/T 24896—2010	粮油检验　稻谷水分含量测定　近红外法	
GB/T 24897—2010	粮油检验　稻谷粗蛋白质含量测定　近红外法	
GB/T 24898—2010	粮油检验　小麦水分含量测定　近红外法	
GB/T 24899—2010	粮油检验　小麦粗蛋白质含量测定　近红外法	
GB/T 24900—2010	粮油检验　玉米水分含量测定　近红外法	
GB/T 24901—2010	粮油检验　玉米粗蛋白质含量测定　近红外法	
GB/T 24902—2010	粮油检验　玉米粗脂肪含量测定　近红外法	
GB/T 24903—2010	粮油检验　花生中白藜芦醇的测定　高效液相色谱法	
GB/T 25219—2010	粮油检验　玉米淀粉含量测定　近红外法	
GB/T 25221—2010	粮油检验　粮食中麦角甾醇的测定　正相高效液相色谱法	
GB/T 25222—2010	粮油检验　粮食中磷化物残留量的测定　分光光度法	
GB/T 24892—2010	动植物油脂　在开口毛细管中熔点（滑点）的测定	
GB/T 24893—2010	动植物油脂　多环芳烃的测定	
GB/T 24894—2010	动植物油脂　甘三酯分子2-位脂肪酸组分的测定	
GB/T 24904—2010	粮食包装　麻袋	
GB/T 24905—2010	粮食包装　小麦粉袋	
GB/T 24854—2010	粮油机械　产品包装通用技术条件	
GB/T 24855—2010	粮油机械　装配通用技术条件	
GB/T 24856—2010	粮油机械　铸件通用技术条件	
GB/T 24857—2010	粮油机械　板件、板型钢构件通用技术条件	
GB/T 25218—2010	粮油机械　产品涂装通用技术条件	
GB/T 25230—2010	粮油机械　打麸机	
GB/T 25231—2010	粮油机械　喷风碾米机	

（续）

标准号	标准名称	代替标准
GB/T 25232—2010	粮油机械　刷麸机	
GB/T 25233—2010	粮油机械　袋式除尘器	
GB/T 25234—2010	粮油机械　叶轮闭风器	
GB/T 25235—2010	粮油机械　组合清理筛	
GB/T 25236—2010	粮油机械　检验用锤片粉碎机	
GB/T 25237—2010	粮油机械　淀粉洗涤旋流器	
GB/T 25238—2010	粮油机械　重力曲筛	
GB/T 25239—2010	粮油机械　微量喂料器	
GB/T 25727—2010	粮油机械　螺旋脱水机	
GB/T 25728—2010	粮油机械　气压磨粉机	
GB/T 25729—2010	粮油机械　撞击松粉机	
GB/T 25730—2010	粮油机械　清粉机	
GB/T 25731—2010	粮油机械　长管蒸发器	
GB/T 25732—2010	粮油机械　液压榨油机	
GB/T 25416—2010	棉籽脱绒成套设备	
GB/T 25736—2010	棉花加工企业生产环境及安全管理要求	
GB/T 25247—2010	饲料添加剂　糖萜素	
GB/T 26441—2010	饲料添加剂　没食子酸丙酯	
GB/T 26442—2010	饲料添加剂　亚硫酸氢烟酰胺甲萘醌	
GB/T 25735—2010	饲料添加剂　L-色氨酸	
GB/T 25865—2010	饲料添加剂　硫酸锌	
GB/T 17817—2010	饲料中维生素 A 的测定　高效液相色谱法	GB/T 17817—1999
GB/T 17818—2010	饲料中维生素 B_3 的测定　高效液相色谱	GB/T 17818—1999
GB/T 26425—2010	饲料中产气荚膜梭菌的检测	
GB/T 26426—2010	饲料中副溶血性弧菌的检测	
GB/T 26427—2010	饲料中蜡样芽孢杆菌的检测	
GB/T 26428—2010	饲用微生物制剂中枯草芽孢杆菌的检测	
GB 26434—2010	饲料中锡的允许量	
GB/Z25008—2010	饲料和食品链的可追溯性　体系设计与实施指南	
GB/T 25698—2010	饲料加工工艺术语	
GB/T 25699—2010	带式横流颗粒饲料干燥机	
GB/T 10498—2010	糖料甘蔗	GB/T 10498—1989
GB 16715.1—2010	瓜菜作物种子　第 1 部分：瓜类	GB 4862—1984 等
GB 16715.2—2010	瓜菜作物种子　第 2 部分：白菜类	GB 16715.2—1999
GB 16715.3—2010	瓜菜作物种子　第 3 部分：茄果类	GB 16715.3—1999
GB 16715.4—2010	瓜菜作物种子　第 4 部分：甘蓝类	GB 16715.4—1999
GB 16715.5—2010	瓜菜作物种子　第 5 部分：绿叶菜类	GB 16715.5—1999
GB/T 24700—2010	大蒜冷藏	
GB/T 25393—2010	葡萄栽培和葡萄酒酿制设备　葡萄收获机　试验方法	
GB/T 25394—2010	葡萄栽培和葡萄酒酿制设备　果浆泵　试验方法	
GB/T 25395—2010	葡萄栽培和葡萄酒酿制设备　葡萄压榨机　试验方法	
GB/T 25504—2010	冰葡萄酒	
GB/T 25867—2010	根菜类　冷藏和冷藏运输	

（续）

标准号	标准名称	代替标准
GB/T 25869—2010	洋葱　贮藏指南	
GB/T 25870—2010	甜瓜　冷藏和冷藏运输	
GB/T 25871—2010	结球生菜　预冷和冷藏运输指南	
GB/T 25873—2010	结球甘蓝　冷藏和冷藏运输指南	
GB/T 26430—2010	水果和蔬菜　形态学和结构学术语	
GB/T 26431—2010	甜椒	
GB/T 26432—2010	新鲜蔬菜贮藏与运输准则	
GB/T 24861—2010	水产品流通管理技术规范	
GB/T 24862—2010	畜禽体细胞库检测技术规程	
GB/T 24863—2010	畜禽细胞体外培养与冷冻保存技术规程	
GB/T 24864—2010	鸡胴体分割	
GB/T 25009—2010	蛋制品生产管理规范	
GB/T 25734—2010	牦牛肉干	
GB 5413.30—2010	乳和乳制品杂质度的测定	
GB 5413.33—2010	生乳相对密度的测定	
GB 5413.34—2010	乳和乳制品酸度的测定	
GB 5413.37—2010	乳和乳制品中黄曲霉毒素 M_1 的测定	
GB 5413.38—2010	生乳冰点的测定	
GB 5413.39—2010	乳和乳制品中非脂乳固体的测定	
GB 5420—2010	干酪	
GB 11674—2010	乳清粉和乳清蛋白粉	
GB 12693—2010	乳制品良好生产规范	
GB 13102—2010	炼乳	
GB 19301—2010	生乳	
GB 19302—2010	发酵乳	
GB 19644—2010	乳粉	
GB 19645—2010	巴氏杀菌乳	
GB 19646—2010	稀奶油、奶油和无水奶油	
GB 21703—2010	乳和乳制品中苯甲酸和山梨酸的测定	
GB 22031—2010	干酪及加工干酪制品中添加的柠檬酸盐的测定	
GB 25190—2010	灭菌乳	
GB 25191—2010	调制乳	
GB 25192—2010	再制干酪	
GB 25595—2010	乳糖	
GB/T 26176—2010	豆浆机	
GB 1975—2010	食品添加剂　琼脂（琼胶）	
GB 1900—2010	食品添加剂　二丁基羟基甲苯（BHT）	
GB 3150—2010	食品添加剂　硫磺	
GB 4479.1—2010	食品添加剂　苋菜红	
GB 4481.1—2010	食品添加剂　柠檬黄	
GB 4481.2—2010	食品添加剂　柠檬黄铝色淀	
GB 6227.1—2010	食品添加剂　日落黄	
GB 7912—2010	食品添加剂　栀子黄	

（续）

标 准 号	标 准 名 称	代替标准
GB 8820—2010	食品添加剂　葡萄糖酸锌	
GB 8821—2010	食品添加剂　β-胡萝卜素	
GB 12487—2010	食品添加剂　乙基麦芽酚	
GB 12489—2010	食品添加剂　吗啉脂肪酸盐果蜡	
GB 13481—2010	食品添加剂　山梨醇酐单硬脂酸酯（司盘 60）	
GB 13482—2010	食品添加剂　山梨醇酐单油酸酯（司盘 80）	
GB 14750—2010	食品添加剂　维生素 A	
GB 14751—2010	食品添加剂　维生素 B_1（盐酸硫胺）	
GB 14752—2010	食品添加剂　维生素 B_2（核黄素）	
GB 14753—2010	食品添加剂　维生素 B_6（盐酸吡哆醇）	
GB 14754—2010	食品添加剂　维生素 C（抗坏血酸）	
GB 14755—2010	食品添加剂　维生素 D_2（麦角钙化醇）	
GB 14756—2010	食品添加剂　维生素 E（DL-α-醋酸生育酚）	
GB 14757—2010	食品添加剂　烟酸	
GB 14758—2010	食品添加剂　咖啡因	
GB 14759—2010	食品添加剂　牛磺酸	
GB 14888.1—2010	食品添加剂　新红	
GB 14888.2—2010	食品添加剂　新红铝色淀	
GB 15570—2010	食品添加剂　叶酸	
GB 15571—2010	食品添加剂　葡萄糖酸钙	
GB 17512.1—2010	食品添加剂　赤藓红	
GB 17512.2—2010	食品添加剂　赤藓红铝色淀	
GB 17779—2010	食品添加剂　L-苏糖酸钙	
GB 25531—2010	食品添加剂　三氯蔗糖	
GB 25532—2010	食品添加剂　纳他霉素	
GB 25533—2010	食品添加剂　果胶	
GB 25534—2010	食品添加剂　红米红	
GB 25535—2010	食品添加剂　结冷胶	
GB 25536—2010	食品添加剂　萝卜红	
GB 25537—2010	食品添加剂　乳酸钠（溶液）	
GB 25538—2010	食品添加剂　双乙酸钠	
GB 25539—2010	食品添加剂　双乙酰酒石酸单双甘油酯	
GB 25540—2010	食品添加剂　乙酰磺胺酸钾	
GB 25541—2010	食品添加剂　聚葡萄糖	
GB 25542—2010	食品添加剂　甘氨酸（氨基乙酸）	
GB 25543—2010	食品添加剂　L-丙氨酸	
GB 25544—2010	食品添加剂　DL-苹果酸	
GB 25545—2010	食品添加剂　L（+）-酒石酸	
GB 25546—2010	食品添加剂　富马酸	
GB 25547—2010	食品添加剂　脱氢乙酸钠	
GB 25548—2010	食品添加剂　丙酸钙	
GB 25549—2010	食品添加剂　丙酸钠	
GB 25550—2010	食品添加剂　L-肉碱酒石酸盐	

（续）

标准号	标准名称	代替标准
GB 25551—2010	食品添加剂　山梨醇酐单月桂酸酯（司盘20）	
GB 25552—2010	食品添加剂　山梨醇酐单棕榈酸酯（司盘40）	
GB 25553—2010	食品添加剂　聚氧乙烯(20)山梨醇酐单硬脂酸酯(吐温60)	
GB 25554—2010	食品添加剂　聚氧乙烯（20）山梨醇酐单油酸酯（吐温80）	
GB 25555—2010	食品添加剂　L-乳酸钙	
GB 25556—2010	食品添加剂　酒石酸氢钾	
GB 25557—2010	食品添加剂　焦磷酸钠	
GB 25558—2010	食品添加剂　磷酸三钙	
GB 25559—2010	食品添加剂　磷酸二氢钙	
GB 25560—2010	食品添加剂　磷酸二氢钾	
GB 25561—2010	食品添加剂　磷酸氢二钾	
GB 25562—2010	食品添加剂　焦磷酸四钾	
GB 25563—2010	食品添加剂　磷酸三钾	
GB 25564—2010	食品添加剂　磷酸二氢钠	
GB 25565—2010	食品添加剂　磷酸三钠	
GB 25566—2010	食品添加剂　三聚磷酸钠	
GB 25567—2010	食品添加剂　焦磷酸二氢二钠	
GB 25568—2010	食品添加剂　磷酸氢二钠	
GB 25569—2010	食品添加剂　磷酸二氢铵	
GB 25570—2010	食品添加剂　焦亚硫酸钾	
GB 25571—2010	食品添加剂　活性白土	
GB 25572—2010	食品添加剂　氢氧化钙	
GB 25573—2010	食品添加剂　过氧化钙	
GB 25574—2010	食品添加剂　次氯酸钠	
GB 25575—2010	食品添加剂　氢氧化钾	
GB 25576—2010	食品添加剂　二氧化硅	
GB 25577—2010	食品添加剂　二氧化钛	
GB 25578—2010	食品添加剂　滑石粉	
GB 25579—2010	食品添加剂　硫酸锌	
GB 25580—2010	食品添加剂　稳定态二氧化氯溶液	
GB 25581—2010	食品添加剂　亚铁氰化钾（黄血盐钾）	
GB 25582—2010	食品添加剂　硅酸钙铝	
GB 25583—2010	食品添加剂　硅铝酸钠	
GB 25584—2010	食品添加剂　氯化镁	
GB 25585—2010	食品添加剂　氯化钾	
GB 25586—2010	食品添加剂　碳酸氢三钠（倍半碳酸钠）	
GB 25587—2010	食品添加剂　碳酸镁	
GB 25588—2010	食品添加剂　碳酸钾	
GB 25589—2010	食品添加剂　碳酸氢钾	
GB 25590—2010	食品添加剂　亚硫酸氢钠	
GB 25591—2010	食品添加剂　复合膨松剂	
GB 25592—2010	食品添加剂　硫酸铝铵	
GB 25593—2010	食品添加剂　N，2，3-三甲基-2-异丙基丁酰胺	

（续）

标 准 号	标 准 名 称	代替标准
GB 25594—2010	食品工业用酶制剂	
GB 5413.3—2010	婴幼儿食品和乳品中脂肪的测定	
GB 5413.5—2010	婴幼儿食品和乳品中乳糖、蔗糖的测定	
GB 5413.6—2010	婴幼儿食品和乳品中不溶性膳食纤维的测定	
GB 5413.9—2010	婴幼儿食品和乳品中维生素 A、D、E 的测定	
GB 5413.10—2010	婴幼儿食品和乳品中维生素 K_1 的测定	
GB 5413.11—2010	婴幼儿食品和乳品中维生素 B_1 的测定	
GB 5413.12—2010	婴幼儿食品和乳品中维生素 B_2 的测定	
GB 5413.13—2010	婴幼儿食品和乳品中维生素 B_6 的测定	
GB 5413.14—2010	婴幼儿食品和乳品中维生素 B_{12} 的测定	
GB 5413.15—2010	婴幼儿食品和乳品中烟酸和烟酰胺的测定	
GB 5413.16—2010	婴幼儿食品和乳品中叶酸（叶酸盐活性）的测定	
GB 5413.17—2010	婴幼儿食品和乳品中泛酸的测定	
GB 5413.18—2010	婴幼儿食品和乳品中维生素 C 的测定	
GB 5413.19—2010	婴幼儿食品和乳品中游离生物素的测定	
GB 5413.21—2010	婴幼儿食品和乳品中钙、铁、锌、钠、钾、镁、铜和锰的测定	
GB 5413.22—2010	婴幼儿食品和乳品中磷的测定	
GB 5413.23—2010	婴幼儿食品和乳品中碘的测定	
GB 5413.24—2010	婴幼儿食品和乳品中氯的测定	
GB 5413.25—2010	婴幼儿食品和乳品中肌醇的测定	
GB 5413.26—2010	婴幼儿食品和乳品中牛磺酸的测定	
GB 5413.27—2010	婴幼儿食品和乳品中脂肪酸的测定	
GB 5413.29—2010	婴幼儿食品和乳品溶解性的测定	
GB 5413.35—2010	婴幼儿食品和乳品中 β-胡萝卜素的测定	
GB 5413.36—2010	婴幼儿食品和乳品中反式脂肪酸的测定	
GB 10765—2010	婴儿配方食品	
GB 10767—2010	较大婴儿和幼儿配方食品	
GB 10769—2010	婴幼儿谷类辅助食品	
GB 10770—2010	婴幼儿罐装辅助食品	
GB 23790—2010	粉状婴幼儿配方食品良好生产规范	
GB 25596—2010	特殊医学用途婴儿配方食品通则	
GB 4789.1—2010	食品微生物学检验　总则	
GB 4789.2—2010	食品微生物学检验　菌落总数测定	
GB 4789.3—2010	食品微生物学检验　大肠菌群计数	
GB 4789.4—2010	食品微生物学检验　沙门氏菌检验	
GB 4789.10—2010	食品微生物学检验　金黄色葡萄球菌检验	
GB 4789.15—2010	食品微生物学检验　霉菌和酵母计数	
GB 4789.18—2010	食品微生物学检验　乳与乳制品检验	
GB 4789.30—2010	食品微生物学检验　单核细胞增生李斯特氏菌检验	
GB 4789.35—2010	食品微生物学检验　乳酸菌检验	
GB 4789.40—2010	食品微生物学检验　阪崎肠杆菌检验	
GB 5009.3—2010	食品中水分的测定	
GB 5009.4—2010	食品中灰分的测定	

（续）

标准号	标准名称	代替标准
GB 5009.5—2010	食品中蛋白质的测定	
GB 5009.12—2010	食品中铅的测定	
GB 5009.24—2010	食品中黄曲霉毒素 M_1 和 B_1 的测定	
GB 5009.33—2010	食品中亚硝酸盐与硝酸盐的测定	
GB 5009.93—2010	食品中硒的测定	
GB 7189—2010	食品级石蜡	GB 7189—1994
GB/T 9289—2010	制糖工业术语	GB/T 9289—1988
GB/T 25005—2010	感官分析方便面感官评价方法	
GB/T 25007—2010	速冻食品生产 HACCP 应用准则	
GB/T 25345—2010	食品金属探测器	
GB 25462—2010	酵母工业水污染物排放标准	
GB/T 27320—2010	食品防护计划及其应用指南　食品生产企业	
GB/T 15269.1—2010	雪茄烟　第 1 部分：产品分类和抽样技术要求	GB 15269—1994
GB/T 25240—2010	烟草包衣丸化种子	
GB/T 25241.1—2010	烟草集约化育苗技术规程　第 1 部分：漂浮育苗	
GB/T 25241.2—2010	烟草集约化育苗技术规程　第 2 部分：托盘育苗	
GB/T 25241.3—2010	烟草集约化育苗技术规程　第 3 部分：砂培育苗	
GB/T 4122.2—2010	包装术语　第 2 部分：机械	GB/T 4122.2—1996
GB/T 4122.3—2010	包装术语　第 3 部分：防护	GB/T 4122.3—1997
GB/T 4122.4—2010	包装术语　第 4 部分：材料与容器	GB/T 13039—1991 等
GB/T 4122.5—2010	包装术语　第 5 部分：检验与试验	GB/T 4122.5—2002
GB/T 4122.6—2010	包装术语　第 6 部分：印刷	GB/T 13483—1992
GB/T 25159—2010	包装术语　非危险货物用中型散装容器	
GB/T 16716.2—2010	包装与包装废弃物　第 2 部分：评估方法和程序	
GB/T 16716.3—2010	包装与包装废弃物　第 3 部分：预先减少用量	
GB/T 16716.4—2010	包装与包装废弃物　第 4 部分：重复使用	
GB/T 16716.5—2010	包装与包装废弃物　第 5 部分：材料循环再生	
GB/T 18455—2010	包装回收标志	GB 18455—2001
GB/T 23156—2010	包装　包装与环境术语	
GB/T 25160—2010	包装　卡纸板折叠纸盒结构尺寸	
GB/T 17858.2—2010	包装袋　术语和类型　第 2 部分：热塑性软质薄膜袋	GB/T 17858.2—1999
GB/T 25161.1—2010	包装袋　尺寸允许偏差　第 1 部分：纸袋	
GB/T 25161.2—2010	包装袋　尺寸允许偏差　第 2 部分：热塑性软质薄膜袋	
GB/T 25162.1—2010	包装袋　跌落试验　第 1 部分：纸袋	
GB/T 25162.2—2010	包装袋　跌落试验　第 2 部分：热塑性软质薄膜袋	
GB/T 17876—2010	包装容器　塑料防盗瓶盖	GB/T 17876—1999
GB/T 25164—2010	包装容器　25.4mm 口径铝气雾罐	GB 13042—1998
GB/T 25006—2010	感官分析　包装材料引起食品风味改变的评价方法	
GB/T 12703.4—2010	纺织品　静电性能的评定　第 4 部分：电阻率	
GB/T 12703.5—2010	纺织品　静电性能的评定　第 5 部分：摩擦带电电压	GB/T 12703—1991
GB/T 12703.6—2010	纺织品　静电性能的评定　第 6 部分：纤维泄漏电阻	
GB/T 12703.7—2010	纺织品　静电性能的评定　第 7 部分：动态静电压	
GB/T 22970—2010	纺织面料编码　化纤部分	

（续）

标准号	标准名称	代替标准
GB/T 25874.1—2010	纺织机械与附件　筘齿用钢片　第1部分：冷轧钢片	
GB/T 25874.2—2010	纺织机械与附件　筘齿用钢片　第2部分：淬硬钢片	
GB/Z24987—2010	纸、纸板和纸浆　测试方法不确定度的评定	
GB/T 24988—2010	复印纸	
GB/T 24989—2010	装饰原纸	
GB/T 24990—2010	纸、纸板和纸浆　铬含量的测定	
GB/T 24991—2010	纸、纸板和纸浆　铅含量的测定　石墨炉原子吸收法	
GB/T 24992—2010	纸、纸板和纸浆　砷含量的测定	
GB/T 24997—2010	纸、纸板和纸浆　镉含量的测定　原子吸收光谱法	
GB/T 25001—2010	纸、纸板和纸浆　7种多氯联苯（PCBs）含量的测定	
GB/T 25002—2010	纸、纸板和纸浆　水抽提液中五氯苯酚的测定	
GB/T 24998—2010	纸和纸板　碱储量的测定	
GB/T 24999—2010	纸和纸板　亮度（白度）最高限量	
GB/T 26203—2010	纸和纸板　内结合强度的测定（Scott型）	
GB/T 24993—2010	造纸湿部Zeta电位的测定	
GB/T 24994—2010	造纸湿部溶解电荷量的测定	
GB/T 24995—2010	铸涂原纸	
GB/T 24996—2010	纸张中脱墨回用纤维的判定	
GB/T 26202—2010	纸管纸板	
GB/T 25675—2010	印刷机械　资源利用技术条件	
GB/T 25676.1—2010	印刷机械　宽幅面喷绘机　第1部分:卷材型宽幅面喷绘机	
GB/T 25677—2010	印刷机械　卷筒纸平版印刷机	
GB/T 25678—2010	印刷机械　卷筒纸平版商业印刷机	
GB/T 25679—2010	印刷机械　卷筒料机组式柔性版印刷机	
GB/T 25680—2010	印刷机械　卧式平压模切机	
GB/T 25681—2010	印刷机械　胶粘装订联动机	

农产品加工业农业行业标准（2010年）

标准号	标准名称	代替标准
NY/T 372—2010	重力式种子分选机质量评价技术规范	NY/T 372—1999
NY/T 460—2010	天然橡胶初加工机械干燥车	NY/T 460—2001
NY/T 461—2010	天然橡胶初加工机械推进器	NY/T 461—2001
NY/T 494—2010	魔芋粉	NY/T 494—2002
NY/T 528—2010	食用菌菌种生产技术规程	NY/T 528—2002
NY/T 676—2010	牛肉等级规格	NY/T 676—2003
NY/T 1834—2010	茭白等级规格	
NY/T 1835—2010	大葱等级规格	
NY/T 1836—2010	白灵菇等级规格	
NY/T 1837—2010	西葫芦等级规格	
NY/T 1838—2010	黑木耳等级规格	
NY/T 1840—2010	露地蔬菜产品认证申报审核规范	
NY/T 1841—2010	苹果中可溶性固形物、可滴定酸无损伤快速测定近红外光谱法	
NY/T 1842—2010	人参中皂苷的测定	

（续）

标准号	标准名称	代替标准
NY/T 1843—2010	葡萄无病毒母本树和苗木	
NY/T 1845—2010	食用菌菌种区别性鉴定拮抗反应	
NY/T 1846—2010	食用菌菌种检验规程	
NY/T 1871—2010	黄羽肉鸡饲养管理技术规程	
NY/T 1872—2010	种羊遗传评估技术规范	
NY/T 1878—2010	生物质固体成型燃料技术条件	
NY/T 1879—2010	生物质固体成型燃料采样方法	
NY/T 1880—2010	生物质固体成型燃料样品制备方法	
NY/T 1881.1—2010	生物质固体成型燃料试验方法 第1部分：通则	
NY/T 1881.2—2010	生物质固体成型燃料试验方法 第2部分：全水分	
NY/T 1881.3—2010	生物质固体成型燃料试验方法 第3部分：一般分析样品水分	
NY/T 1881.4—2010	生物质固体成型燃料试验方法 第4部分：挥发分	
NY/T 1881.5—2010	生物质固体成型燃料试验方法 第5部分：灰分	
NY/T 1881.6—2010	生物质固体成型燃料试验方法 第6部分：堆积密度	
NY/T 1881.7—2010	生物质固体成型燃料试验方法 第7部分：密度	
NY/T 1881.8—2010	生物质固体成型燃料试验方法 第8部分：机械耐久性	
NY/T 1882—2010	生物质固体成型燃料成型设备 技术条件	
NY/T 1883—2010	生物质固体成型燃料成型设备 试验方法	
NY/T 471—2010	绿色食品 畜禽饲料及饲料添加剂使用准则	NY/T 471—2001
NY/T 844—2010	绿色食品 温带水果	NY/T 844—2004
NY/T 1041—2010	绿色食品 干果	NY/T 1041—2006
NY/T 1884—2010	绿色食品 果蔬粉	
NY/T 1885—2010	绿色食品 米酒	
NY/T 1886—2010	绿色食品 复合调味料	
NY/T 1887—2010	绿色食品 乳清制品	
NY/T 1888—2010	绿色食品 软体动物休闲食品	
NY/T 1889—2010	绿色食品 烘炒食品	
NY/T 1890—2010	绿色食品 蒸制类糕点	
NY/T 1891—2010	绿色食品 海洋捕捞水产品生产管理规范	
NY/T 1892—2010	绿色食品 畜禽饲养防疫准则	
NY/T 1893—2010	加工用花生等级规格	
NY/T 1894—2010	茄子等级规格	
NY/T 1895—2010	豆类、谷类电子束辐照处理技术规范	
NY/T 1902—2010	饲料中单核细胞增生李斯特氏菌的微生物学检验	
NY/T 1904—2010	饲草产品质量安全生产技术规范	
NY/T 1915—2010	生物质固体成型燃料术语	
NY/T 1930—2010	秸秆颗粒饲料压制机质量评价技术规范	
NY/T 1960—2010	茶叶中磁性金属物的测定	
NY/T 1961—2010	粮食作物名词术语	
NY/T 1963—2010	马铃薯品种鉴定	
NY/T 1968—2010	玉米干全酒糟（玉米DDGS）	
NY/T 1969—2010	饲料添加剂产朊假丝酵母	
NY/T 1970—2010	饲料中伏马毒素的测定	

（续）

标 准 号	标 准 名 称	代替标准
NY/T 1933—2010	大豆等级规格	
NY/T 1934—2010	双孢蘑菇、金针菇贮运技术规范	
NY/T 1939—2010	热带水果包装、标识通则	
NY/T 1940—2010	热带水果分类和编码	
NY/T 1944—2010	饲料中钙的测定 原子吸收分光光谱法	
NY/T 1945—2010	饲料中硒的测定 微波消解-原子荧光光谱法	
NY/T 1946—2010	饲料中牛羊源性成分检测 实时荧光聚合酶链反应法	
NY 5359—2010	无公害食品 香辛料产地环境条件	
NY 5360—2010	无公害食品 可食花卉产地环境条件	
NY 5361—2010	无公害食品 淡水养殖产地环境条件	
NY 5362—2010	无公害食品 海水养殖产地环境条件	
NY/T 5363—2010	无公害食品 蔬菜生产管理规范	
SC/T 1004—2010	鳗鲡配合饲料	SC/T 1004—2004
SC/T 3046—2010	冻烤鳗良好生产规范	
SC/T 3047—2010	鳗鲡储运技术规程	
SC/T 3101—2010	鲜大黄鱼、冻大黄鱼、鲜小黄鱼、冻小黄鱼	SC/T 3101—1984
SC/T 3102—2010	鲜、冻带鱼	SC/T 3102—1984
SC/T 3103—2010	鲜、冻鲳鱼	SC/T 3103—1984
SC/T 3104—2010	鲜、冻蓝圆鲹	SC/T 3104—1986
SC/T 3106—2010	鲜、冻海鳗	SC/T 3106—1988
SC/T 3107—2010	鲜、冻乌贼	SC/T 3107—1984
SC/T 3119—2010	活鳗鲡	
SC/T 3302—2010	烤鱼片	SC/T 3302—2000

农产品加工业机械行业标准（2010 年）

标 准 号	标 准 名 称	代替标准
JB/T 5284—2010	隔爆型刮刀卸料离心机	JB/T 5284—1991
JB/T 6418—2010	分离机械 清洁度测定方法	JB/T 6418—1992
JB/T 7241—2010	进动卸料离心机	JB/T 7241—1994
JB/T 7243—2010	离心萃取机型号编制方法	JB/T 7243—1994
JB/T 8101—2010	离心卸料离心机	JB/T 8101—1999
JB/T 8865—2010	活塞推料离心机用滤网	JB/T 8865—2001
JB/T 8866—2010	筒式加压过滤机	JB/T 8866—2001
JB/T 7881.1—2010	剪羊毛机 第 1 部分：术语	JB/T 7881.1—1999
JB/T 7881.2—2010	剪羊毛机 第 2 部分：型式与基本参数	JB/T 7881.2—1999
JB/T 7881.3—2010	剪羊毛机 第 3 部分：技术条件	JB/T 7881.3—1999
JB/T 7881.4—2010	剪羊毛机 第 4 部分：试验方法	JB/T 7881.4—1999
JB/T 7881.5—2010	剪羊毛机 第 5 部分：刀片	JB/T 7881.5—1999
JB/T 8581—2010	畜牧机械 产品型号编制规则	JB/T 8581—1997
JB/T 9868.1—2010	散装饲料运输车 第 1 部分：型式与基本参数	JB/T 9868.1—1999
JB/T 9868.2—2010	散装饲料运输车 第 2 部分：技术条件	JB/T 9868.2—1999
JB/T 9868.3—2010	散装饲料运输车 第 3 部分：试验方法	JB/T 9868.3—1999
JB/T 10950—2010	多功能软袋装箱机	

（续）

标 准 号	标 准 名 称	代替标准
JB/T 10951—2010	重袋充填包装机	
JB/T 10952—2010	粉、粒听装包装生产线	
JB/T 10953—2010	透明膜三维包装机	
JB/T 10965—2010	肉类加工机械　真空定量灌装机	
JB/T 3090—2010	印刷机械　产品命名与型号编制方法	JB/T 3090—1999
JB/T 3789—2010	印刷机械　磨刀机	JB/T 3789—1997
JB/T 8115—2010	印刷机械　切纸机	JB/T 8115.1—2000
JB/T 8585—2010	印刷机械　卷筒料复合机	JB/T 8585—1997
JB/T 8586—2010	印刷机械　上光机	JB/T 8586—1997
JB/T 9110—2010	印刷机械　三面切书机	JB/T 9110—1999
JB/T 9115.1—2010	印刷机械　平压平烫印机　第1部分：卧式机	JB/T 9115.1—1999
JB/T 9115.2—2010	印刷机械　平压平烫印机　第2部分：立式机	JB/T 9115.2—1999
JB/T 9123—2010	印刷机械　热熔胶订包封皮机	JB/T 9123—1999
JB/T 10978—2010	印刷机械　书帖堆积机	
JB/T 11012—2010	印刷机械　切纸机刀片	JB/T 8115.2—2000
JB/T 11015—2010	印刷机械　瓦楞纸板卧式平压模切机	
JB/T 11016—2010	印刷机械　耗电技术条件	
JB/T 11118—2010	印刷机械　丝网涂布机	
JB/T 11119—2010	印刷机械　绷网机	
JB/T 11120—2010	印刷机械　网版印刷紫外线光固机	
JB/T 11121—2010	印刷机械　分切收牌机	
JB/T 11122—2010	印刷机械　局部上光机	
JB/T 11123—2010	印刷机械　润版循环水箱	
JB/T 11124—2010	印刷机械　单张纸平版印刷机　收纸装置	
JB/T 11125—2010	印刷机械　辊式粘单页机	
JB/T 11126—2010	印刷机械　热敏型直接制版冲版机	
JB/T 11127—2010	印刷机械　光敏光聚合型直接制版冲版机	
JB/T 11128—2010	印刷机械　玻璃印刷机	
JB/T 20133—2010	中药煎药机	
JB/T 20134—2010	药用料斗提升机	

农产品加工业轻工行业标准（2010年）

标 准 号	标 准 名 称	代替标准
QB/T 1012—2010	胶版印刷纸	QB/T 1012—1991
QB/T 1014—2010	食品包装纸	QB 1014—1991
QB/T 1319—2010	气相防锈纸	QB 1319—1991
QB/T 1313—2010	中性包装纸	QB/T 1313—1991
QB/T 1349—2010	制革机械　电子量革机	QB/T 1349—1991
QB/T 1710—2010	食品羊皮纸	QB/T 1710—1993
QB/T 2367—2010	制革机械　辊印涂饰机	QB/T 2367—1998
QB/T 2801—2010	皮革　验收、标志、包装、运输和贮存	QB/T 2801—2006 等
QB/T 4003—2010	食用香精标签通用要求	
QB/T 4012—2010	淀粉基塑料	

（续）

标 准 号	标 准 名 称	代替标准
QB/T 4026—2010	真空搅拌锅	
QB/T 4027—2010	炊饭机	
QB/T 4028—2010	洗碗碟机	
QB/T 4033—2010	餐盒原纸	
QB/T 4034—2010	壁纸	
QB/T 4039—2010	造纸用原料　芦苇	
QB/T 4040—2010	液体包装用纸板	
QB/T 4044—2010	防护鞋用合成革	
QB/T 4049—2010	塑料饮水口杯	
QB/T 4067—2010	食品工业用速溶茶	
QB/T 4068—2010	食品工业用茶浓缩液	
QB/T 4069—2010	饮料制造综合能耗限额	
QB/T 4072—2010	木制衣架	
QB/T 4073—2010	烫衣板	
QB/T 4087—2010	食用明胶	
QB/T 4092—2010	糖霜	
QB/T 4093—2010	液体糖	
QB/T 4095—2010	黄砂糖	
QB/T 4098—2010	家用和类似用途的速热式饮水机	
QB/T 4099—2010	电饭锅及类似器具	QB/T 3899—1999
QB/T 4100—2010	饮水机专用净水器	
QB/T 4110—2010	不锈钢无菌储运罐	
QB/T 4111—2010	食品工业企业诚信管理体系(CMS)建立及实施通用要求	
QB/T 4112—2010	食品工业企业诚信评价准则	
QB/T 4115—2010	皮革专业市场管理技术规范	
QB/T 4124—2010	造纸毯通用规范	
QB/T 4125—2010	纸浆　亮度（白度）最高限量	
QB/T 4135—2010	家用和类似用途全自动面包机	
QB/T 4153—2010	书写白板	

农产品加工业国内贸易行业标准（2010 年）

标 准 号	标 准 名 称	代替标准
SB/T 10559—2010	主食加工配送中心建设规范	
SB/T 10560—2010	中央储备边销茶储存库资质条件	
SB/T 10561—2010	散装水泥罐式集装箱	
SB/T 10562—2010	豆沙馅料	
SB/T 10563—2010	莲蓉馅料	
SB/T 10564—2010	果仁馅料	
SB/T 10567—2010	餐饮企业品牌竞争力评估	
SB/T 10569—2010	冷藏库门	
SB/T 10570—2010	片猪肉激光灼刻标识码、印应用规范	
SB/T 10571—2010	病害畜禽及其产品焚烧设备	
SB/T 10572—2010	黄瓜流通规范	

（续）

标准号	标准名称	代替标准
SB/T 10573—2010	青椒流通规范	
SB/T 10574—2010	番茄流通规范	
SB/T 10575—2010	豇豆流通规范	
SB/T 10576—2010	冬瓜流通规范	
SB/T 10577—2010	鲜食马铃薯流通规范	
SB/T 10578—2010	洋葱流通规范	

农产品加工业出入境检验检疫行业标准（2010年）

标准号	标准名称	代替标准
SN/T 0076—2010	进出口毛皮褥子检验规程	SN/T 0076—2003
SN/T 0874—2010	进出口纸和纸板检验规程	SN/T 0874—2000
SN/T 0917—2010	进出口茶叶品质感官审评方法	SN/T 0917—2000 等
SN/T 1233—2010	进出口非织造布检验规程	SN/T 1233—2003
SN/T 2460—2010	出口橡子淀粉检验检疫规程	
SN/T 2461—2010	纺织品中苯氧羧酸类农药残留量的测定	
SN/T 2462—2010	棉花曲叶病毒检疫鉴定方法	
SN/T 2463—2010	纺织品中多氯联苯的测定方法　气相色谱法	
SN/T 2464—2010	洋葱条黑粉病菌检疫鉴定方法	
SN/T 2468—2010	进出口纺织品酚黄变试验方法	
SN/T 2470—2010	纺织品颜色迁移测试方法	
SN/T 2478—2010	进出口面粉检疫操作规程	
SN/T 2546—2010	进境木薯干检验检疫规程	
SN/T 2548—2010	出口冻章鱼检验规程	
SN/T 2549—2010	食品接触材料检验规程　辅助材料类	
SN/T 2567—2010	食品及包装品无菌检验	
SN/T 2595—2010	食品接触材料检验规程　软木、木、竹制品类	
SN/T 2606—2010	进出口食品检验中食品添加剂摄入量的简要评估方法指南	
SN/T 2611—2010	食品接触材料　木制品中游离甲醛的测定　气相色谱法	

农产品加工业烟草行业标准（2010年）

标准号	标准名称	代替标准
YC/T 146—2010	烟叶　打叶复烤　工艺规范	YC/T 146—2001
YC/T 147—2010	打叶烟叶　质量检验	YC/T 147—2001
YC/T 366—2010	打叶烟叶　烤烟质量均匀性评价	
YC/T 336—2010	烟叶工作站设计规范	
YC/T 335—2010	卷烟物流配送中心设计规范	
YC/T 348—2010	卷烟　主流烟气中氮氧化物的测定　离子色谱法	
YC/T 349—2010	卷烟　测流烟气气相中一氧化碳的测定	
YC/T 350—2010	卷烟　测流烟气中氰化氢的测定　连续流动法	
YC/T 353—2010	卷烟　加料均匀性的测定	
YC/T 377—2010	卷烟　主流烟气中氨的测定　离子色谱法	
YC/T 378—2010	卷烟　侧流烟气中羰基化合物的测定　高效液相色谱法	
YC/T 351—2010	卷制过程烟丝破碎度的测定	

（续）

标准号	标准名称	代替标准
YC/T 354—2010	卷烟和滤棒物理性能的测定　热塌陷	
YC/T 355—2010	卷烟工业企业物流作业规范	
YC/T 356—2010	工商卷烟物流在途信息系统数据交换	
YC/T 357—2010	卷烟生产过程产品安全卫生保障通则	
YC/T 340.4—2010	烟草害虫预测预报调查规程　第4部分：斜纹夜蛾	
YC/T 340.7—2010	烟草害虫预测预报调查规程　第7部分：白粉病	
YC/T 339—2010	烟草及烟草制品　转基因测定的取样方法	
YC/T 343—2010	烟草及烟草制品　磷酸盐的测定　连续流动法	
YC/T 345—2010	烟草及烟草制品　水分的测定　气相色谱法	
YC/T 346—2010	烟草及烟草制品　果胶的测定　离子色谱法	
YC/T 382—2010	烟草及烟草制品　质体色素的测定　高效液相色谱法	
YC/T 352—2010	烟草加工介质湿含量的测定	
YC/T 365—2010	烟草病毒的测定　逆转录-聚合酶链反应法	
YC/T 367—2010	烟草种子　雄性不育系种子生产技术规程	
YC/T 368—2010	烟草种子　催芽包衣丸化种子生产技术规程	
YC/T 338—2010	白肋烟栽培技术规程	
YC/T 358—2010	烟用二醋酸纤维素片	
YC/T 359—2010	烟用添加剂　甲醛的测定　高效液相色谱法	
YC/T 360—2010	烟用添加剂　焦炭酸二乙酯的测定　色谱-质谱联用法	
YC/T 361—2010	烟用添加剂　β-细辛醚的测定　气相色谱-质谱联用法	
YC/T 375—2010	烟用添加剂　环已基氨基磺酸钠的测定　离子色谱法	
YC/T 376—2010	烟用添加剂　β-萘酚的测定　气相色谱-谱联用法	
YC/T 362—2010	烟草机械　设备噪声声压级测量	
YC/T 363—2010	烟草机械　卷接机组　卷烟材料工艺损耗率及其测定	
YC/T 364—2010	烟草机械　钢铁制件工序间防腐蚀保护	

农产品加工业纺织行业标准（2010年）

标准号	标准名称	代替标准
FZ/T 20014—2010	毛织物干热熨烫尺寸变化试验方法	FZ/T 20014—1997
FZ/T 20017—2010	毛纱试验方法	FZ/T 20017—2001
FZ/T 20018—2010	毛纺织品中二氯甲烷可溶性物质的测定	FZ/T 20018—2000
FZ/T 21003—2010	分梳山羊绒	FZ/T 21003—1998
FZ/T 21006—2010	丝光防缩毛条	
FZ/T 22001—2010	精梳机织毛纱	FZ/T 22001—2002
FZ/T 22002—2010	粗梳机织毛纱	FZ/T 22002—2002
FZ/T 24005—2010	座椅用毛织品	FZ/T 24005—1993
FZ/T 24007—2010	粗梳羊绒织品	FZ/T 24007—1998
FZ/T 24009—2010	精梳羊绒织品	FZ/T 24009—1999
FZ/T 24011—2010	羊绒机织围巾、披肩	
FZ/T 24012—2010	拒水、拒油、抗污羊绒针织品	
FZ/T 24013—2010	耐久型抗静电羊绒针织品	
FZ/T 32003—2010	涤麻（亚麻）纱	FZ/T 32003—1994
FZ/T 32007—2010	气流纺苎麻棉混纺本色纱	FZ/T 32007—2000

（续）

标 准 号	标 准 名 称	代替标准
FZ/T 32012—2010	气流纺亚麻棉混纺纱线	
FZ/T 33001—2010	亚麻本色布	FZ/T 33001—1998
FZ/T 33009—2010	苎麻色织布	FZ/T 33009—1999
FZ/T 40003—2010	桑蚕绢丝试验方法	FZ/T 40003—1997
FZ/T 41003—2010	桑蚕绵球	FZ/T 41003.1—1999 等
FZ/T 42002—2010	桑蚕绢丝	FZ/T 42002—1997
FZ/T 43001—2010	桑蚕丝织物	FZ/T 43001—1991
FZ/T 54028—2010	蛋白质粘胶短纤维	
FZ/T 54029—2010	蛋白质粘胶长丝	
FZ/T 60021—2010	织带产品物理机械性能试验方法	FZ/T 60021—1996
FZ/T 63005—2010	机织腰带	FZ/T 63005—1993
FZ/T 63006—2010	松紧带	FZ/T 63006—1996
FZ/T 63013—2010	涤纶长丝民用丝带	
FZ/T 64007—2010	机织树脂衬	FZ/T 64007—2000
FZ/T 70013—2010	天然彩色棉针织制品标志	
FZ/T 72010—2010	针织摇粒绒面料	
FZ/T 73013—2010	针织泳装	FZ/T 73013—2004
FZ/T 73019.1—2010	针织塑身内衣　弹力型	FZ/T 73019.1—2004
FZ/T 73035—2010	针织彩棉内衣	
FZ/T 73036—2010	吸湿发热针织内衣	
FZ/T 73037—2010	针织运动袜	
FZ/T 73038—2010	涂胶尼龙手套	
FZ/T 73039—2010	涂胶防振手套	
FZ/T 73040—2010	高温高热作业防护手套	
FZ/T 92055—2010	进布装置通用技术条件	FZ/T 92055—1998
FZ/T 92056—2010	织物对中、对边装置	FZ/T 92056—1998
FZ/T 92057—2010	卷布装置通用技术条件	FZ/T 92057—1998
FZ/T 92058—2010	落布装置通用技术条件	FZ/T 92058—1998
FZ/T 93015—2010	转杯纺纱机	FZ/T 93015—2001
FZ/T 93017—2010	精纺梳毛机	FZ/T 93017—1993
FZ/T 93048—2010	针刺用针	FZ/T 93048—1998
FZ/T 93052—2010	棉纺滤尘设备	FZ/T 93052—1999
FZ/T 93053—2010	转杯纺纱机　转杯	FZ/T 93053—1999
FZ/T 93054—2010	转杯纺纱机　分梳辊	FZ/T 93054—1999
FZ/T 93067—2010	环锭细纱机用锭带	
FZ/T 93068—2010	集聚纺纱用网格圈	
FZ/T 93069—2010	转杯纺纱机　转杯轴承	
FZ/T 93070—2010	转杯纺纱机　分梳辊轴承	
FZ/T 94056—2010	数字化簇绒地毯织机	
FZ/T 94057—2010	无梭织带机	

农产品加工业发明专利（2009年）

［2009年农产品加工业（含加工制品、加工技术与设备）部分专利选摘］

申请或批准号	发明名称	申请人	通讯地址	发明人
200920081808.1	农产品实地证据收集、打印设备	黄晓维	（610000）四川省成都市锦江区横九龙巷30号2幢2单元2号	黄晓维
200920169146.3	可遥控的自动转换农产品初加工机械组合机	陈 硕 李 红	（613100）四川省乐山市井研县研城镇研溪巷36号	陈 硕； 李 红
200910095275.7	带全封闭加热或制冷装置的罐装食品容器	李小卿	（325000）浙江省温州市鹿城区五马街道朔门街105号	李小卿
200910110865.2	营养儿童鱼肉调理食品及制备工艺	林向阳	（350000）福建省福州市鼓楼区光荣路282号25座704	林向阳； 卞智英等
200910058157.9	一种芫根食品的制备方法	徐 宁	（626000）四川省康定县炉城镇新市前街117号	徐 宁
200910037175.9	方便食品	王树林	（528000）广东省佛山市禅城区汾江中路144号科华大厦9楼	王树林
200910094096.1	一种清咽、抗氧化的保健功能食品	陶国闻	（650106）云南省昆明市高新技术开发区海源北路6号高新招商大厦九楼	陶国闻
200910094116.5	乌天麻保健胶囊食品及其制备方法	陶国闻	（650106）云南省昆明市高新技术开发区海源北路6号高新招商大厦九楼	陶国闻
200910010573.1	以野鸡为基料的食品制备方法	张立波	（134300）吉林省白山市邮局50信箱	张立波
200910113865.8	真空脱水食品及其生产方法	郭 伟； 郭 强等	（537400）广西壮族自治区北流市城西一路0180号	郭 伟 郭强等
200910036639.4	液体食品加热、搅拌、发泡杯	蔡坚明	（524018）广东省湛江市椹川大道中46号湛江豪捷电器有限公司	蔡坚明
200910010574.6	以蛤士蟆为基料的食品制备方法	张立波	（134300）吉林省白山市邮局50信箱	张立波
200910096580.8	一种蜗牛食品	沈福良	（314000）浙江省嘉兴市南湖区余新镇曹庄人民路8号嘉兴潜福食品公司	沈福良
200910096581.2	一种蜗牛即食食品	沈福良	（314000）浙江省嘉兴市南湖区余新镇曹庄人民路8号嘉兴潜福食品公司	沈福良
200910048223.4	食品和饲料中猫源性成分的检测方法和试剂盒	张舒亚	（200135）上海市民生路1208号	张舒亚； 刘月明等
200910059008.4	新型方便食品的加工工艺及方法	张昆华	（614100）四川省夹江县沔城镇西河路133号2单元3楼2号	张昆华
200910136192.8	一种生鲜食品的无害化处理方法	刘传林	（101200）北京市平谷区文乐胡同工会楼4单元408房	刘传林； 王海鹰
200910011167.7	魔芋食品减肥胶囊及制备方法	孙吉良	（116012）辽宁省大连市西岗区八一路174号-2	孙吉良

（续）

申请或批准号	发明名称	申请人	通讯地址	发明人
200910043012.1	一种含银杏果仁的组合食品及其制备方法	严 安	（225411）江苏省泰兴市黄桥镇柳苑小区3栋4号	严 安
200910000254.2	太阳能风能炊事食品加工和供暖锅炉	钟显亮	（123000）辽宁省阜新市辽宁工程技术大学东区833信箱	钟显亮；黄福元等
200910140547.0	高速渗透设备与民用15分钟速成蛋类食品腌制器	孟令松	（301611）天津市静海县唐官屯镇小郝庄	孟令松
200910066604.5	食品及环境有机污染物荧光检测卡及检测方法	于源华 侯巍等	（130021）吉林省长春市自由大路108号461医院检验科	于源华 侯 巍等
200910103735.6	一种食品调色酱制作方法及食品调色酱	石 勇	（408000）重庆市涪陵区兴华中路宏富大厦C904	石 勇
200910064825.9	食品级高活力β-淀粉酶的生产方法	卢强福	（451450）河南省中牟县向阳路南段郑州市福源生物科技有限公司	卢强福
200910303132.0	一种保健食品瘦身粉	谭秋娥	（412000）湖南省株洲市芦淞区人民中路55号京鹰华府	谭秋娥；鲁 毅等
200910009458.2	一种降低高血压和糖尿病的食品及其制备方法	田向东	（032300）山西省孝义市省级农业科技示范园山西金绿禾生物科技有限公司	田向东；田伟民
200910009459.7	防治高血脂高血糖的食品及其制备方法	田向东	（032300）山西省孝义市省级农业科技示范园山西金绿禾生物科技有限公司	田向东；田伟民
200910132791.2	复合营养膳食纤维食品	袁维理	（518020）广东省深圳市罗湖区太安路东乐花园17B-1B	袁维理
200910117007.0	一种食品或饮料的自热式密封容器	邢学峰	（234000）安徽省宿州市埇桥区西关大街218号8栋1单元302室	邢学峰
200910136125.6	一种手持食用的米饭类快餐食品及其制作方法	杨 斌	（100085）北京市海淀区上地西路38号5楼	杨 斌
200910136006.0	一种提高人类机体功能的纯天然食品	莫以贤 任志杰	524044广东省湛江市海滨大道北91号（湛江市贤博科技有限公司）	莫以贤
200910136007.5	一种促进人类健康的纯天然食品	莫以贤 任志杰	（524044）广东省湛江市海滨大道北91号（湛江市贤博科技有限公司）	莫以贤
200910143273.0	肿瘤患者用的特膳营养食品	刘志伟	（430000）湖北省武汉市武汉工业学院东校区博士楼1-1-301	刘志伟
200910203313.6	一种生产铁食品营养强化剂的方法	石惠民	（643011）四川省自贡市大安区马冲口街高峒居委会10栋2单元6号	石惠民
200910074784.1	一种食品添加剂及使用方法	郭计秋	（052362）河北省石家庄市辛集市张古庄镇张古庄村南郭家街2号	郭计秋
200910147858.X	双参营养保健食品	邓振全	（454003）河南省焦作市工业东路299号百合园31号	邓振全；仝太云
200910143269.4	产后及人流术后康复用特膳营养食品	刘志伟	（430000）湖北省武汉市武汉工业学院东校区博士楼1-1-301	刘志伟
200910087267.8	宠物食品	丁淑绿	（100076）北京市丰台区南苑北里4区3号楼5门402	丁淑绿
200910065240.9	一种大豆营养食品加工方法	孔红忠	（221000）江苏省徐州市民和小区23号楼1单元502室	孔红忠

（续）

申请或批准号	发明名称	申请人	通讯地址	发明人
200910147651.2	一种具有清热、防暑作用的营养食品及其制备方法	邵　伟	（130052）吉林省长春市宽城区柳影路农安南街新月花园15栋506室	邵　伟
200910147652.7	一种具有健身、防寒作用的营养食品及其制备方法	邵　伟	（130052）吉林省长春市宽城区柳影路农安南街新月花园15栋506室	邵　伟
200910094614.X	定型生鲜食品及其制备方法	李荣祥	（650300）云南省安宁市连然镇大凹子村	李荣祥
200910021214.6	土豆糍粑食品加工机	唐　科	（721600）陕西省太白县咀头镇咀头街村四组青年南路南端	唐　科
200910108306.8	一种多功能食品烹饪炉	周红卫	（518000）广东省深圳市福田区莲花二村12栋2单元203房	周红卫；傅玉颖
200910010800.0	食品中三种产芽孢菌的检测试剂盒及其检测方法	郑秋月	（116000）辽宁省大连市中山区人民路39号	郑秋月
200910102661.4	油炸食品用面粉及加工方法	鲁仕忠	（551102）贵州省贵阳市息烽县青山苗族乡大林村三口洞组	鲁仕忠
200910089368.9	一种保健食品	郭景龙	（650000）云南省昆明市五华区建设路112号紫薇苑2单元701室	郭景龙
200910144085.X	一种魔芋系列食品	罗发明	（241000）安徽省芜湖市安徽师范大学镜湖区凤凰山1幢506室	罗发明
200910023328.4	一种板栗休闲食品的加工方法	魏四海	（726200）陕西省丹凤县龙驹寨镇县委路朝阳街	魏四海
200910060108.9	葛根营养免疫食品	王丽杰	（610066）四川省成都市锦江区牛市口无缝钢管厂一区48幢1单元12号	王丽杰；马千雯
200910157424.8	一种清体营养组合固体食品及其制备方法	刘泉来	（102300）北京市门头沟区城子大街40号	刘泉来
200910113380.9	日常保健食品本草添加剂及其应用	薛万里	（833200）新疆维吾尔自治区奎屯市农七师看守所转	薛万里
200910129034.X	用银杏叶制备食品添加剂的方法	孔赟荣	（315207）浙江省宁波市镇海区蛟川街道炼化公司居民区184幢601室	孔赟荣
200910108811.2	具有保健功能的鱼头食品及其制作方法	蒋崇国	（518172）广东省深圳市龙岗区龙岗街道爱联村嶂背路170号	蒋崇国
200910101166.1	工业级和食品级液体二氧化碳的联产方法及装置	申屠晶	（310009）浙江省杭州市上城区江城路887号联银大厦西楼906室	申屠晶；沈建冲等
200910114247.5	一种罗汉果口味的保健食品	胡银安	（530021）广西壮族自治区南宁市桃源路59号商贸宾馆1楼	胡银安
200910157355.0	一种利用竹叶黄酮生产的新型天然食品防腐剂	孙爱东	（100083）北京市海淀区清华东路35号北京林业大学112信箱	孙爱东；游辉等
200910163110.9	一种蜂蜜王浆复配食品及其制作工艺	刘富海	（100084）北京市海淀区农大南路1号硅谷亮城5号楼206	刘富海
200910163111.3	一种适用于糖尿病人食用的蜂蜜食品及其制作工艺	刘富海	（100084）北京市海淀区农大南路1号硅谷亮城5号楼206	刘富海；陈振强等

（续）

申请或批准号	发明名称	申请人	通讯地址	发明人
200910065653.7	一种调节内分泌的食品及制备方法	耿辰通	（457000）河南省濮阳市濮上路第二工程处	耿辰通
200910055468.X	一种用于航空食品柜安全装置和监管方法	盛骏；马旻	（200062）上海市普陀区白兰路169弄12号1002室	盛骏；马旻
200910044025.0	一种预防高血压、降血脂、降血糖的营养保健食品	唐健鹏	（425200）湖南省双牌县紫阳路37号	唐健鹏
200910069566.9	一种含有发酵虫草和灵芝的保健食品及其制备方法	丁友昉	（300222）天津市河西区柳苑公寓4-2-201	丁友昉
200910017287.8	富含浒苔多糖的可食性食品包装膜的制备和应用	刘畅	（266071）山东省青岛市市南区福州南路38号7号楼3单元501户	刘畅
200910056466.2	营养果蔬食品	周耀清	（200050）上海市长宁区镇宁路9号2号楼20层C座	周耀清
200910065828.4	一种规模化生产冰糖葫芦食品的工艺	张二军	（450000）河南省尉氏县城关镇南街163号	张二军
200910159362.4	一种果蔬脆片休闲食品及其制作工艺	高世乐	（266100）山东省青岛市四方区兴元一路18号2单元701	高世乐
200910059006.5	一种商店式餐馆的中式快餐食品	朱明华	（611330）四川省大邑县晋原镇迎春大道235号鲢鱼庄	朱明华
200910016973.3	方便无污染食品车	孟兆强	（257091）山东省东营市府前街104号A楼513	孟兆强
200910031624.9	香酥麦片系列食品	赵彩玲	（221100）江苏省铜山县房村镇驻地徐州国花食品厂	朱月恒
200910072775.9	谷-豆型营养食品配方与制备工艺	秦慧生	（150040）黑龙江省哈尔滨市香坊区哈平路107-2号2单元401室	秦慧生；于卫平
200910070386.2	食品处理机粉碎刀具结构	王晓东	（300191）天津市南开区红旗南路水上温泉花园9-3-501	王晓东
200910161839.2	一种含魔芋粉、螺旋藻粉的解酒、保健双功能食品	陆伟	（617065）四川省攀枝花市西区河门口北街石灰石矿20栋83-14号	陆伟
200910169993.4	怀山药和面粉制做的保健食品	邓振全	（454003）河南省焦作市工业东路299号百合园31号	邓振全
200910094928.X	一种降血糖增强免疫力的功能食品	陶国闻	（650106）云南省昆明市海源北路6号高新招商大厦9楼	陶国闻
200910029705.5	清除人体内毒素毒垢的功能性食品及制备方法	韩友强	（221000）江苏省徐州市九里区张集沛南工人村4楼301室	韩友强
200910192369.6	一种多喷头食品浇注机	黎泽荣	（528200）广东省佛山市南海区西樵山旅游度假区白西管理区大地村	黎泽荣
200910010799.1	食品中5种新出现致病菌的检测试剂盒及检测方法	曹际娟	（116000）辽宁省大连市中山区人民路39号	曹际娟

（续）

申请或批准号	发明名称	申请人	通讯地址	发明人
200910180549.2	一种耐热巧克力食品的制备方法	吴文团	（362200）福建省晋江市新塘湖格西路88号	吴文团
200910307044.8	荠菜营养食品	庞建中	（474350）河南省内乡县湍东镇菊韵花园4号楼	庞建中
200910019104.6	一种有催乳作用的保健食品	王俊茹；张　敏	（264400）山东省文登市环山东路10号10-14306室	王俊茹；张　敏
200910307650.X	肉类食品的蒸卤加工方法	廖开太	（610017）四川省成都市青羊区草市街123号时代锋尚大厦906室	廖开太
200910034459.2	一种宠物保健食品	韩　勇	（221011）江苏省徐州市贾汪区青山泉冶金工业园恒信球墨铸管有限公司	韩　勇
200910091160.0	一种含有豆科植物种子的食品	郭景龙	（650000）云南省昆明市五华区建设路112号紫薇苑2单元701室	郭景龙
200910024045.1	一种富硒功能食品的制备方法	杨林伟	（710027）陕西省西安市东郊新合街1号西安东方乳业有限公司	杨林伟
200910059790.X	多型鱼肉食品	唐　剑	（610000）四川省成都市一环路东五段108号	唐　剑
200910175097.9	根皮苷在制备保肝药物或保健食品中的用途	汪鋆植	（443002）湖北省宜昌市大学路8号	汪鋆植；薛冰洁等
200910307043.3	马齿苋营养食品	庞建中	（474350）河南省内乡县湍东镇菊韵花园4号楼	庞建中
200910167952.1	荞麦芦丁食品生产方法	郑鉴忠	（615000）四川省西昌市沿河路红烛苑2西昌山林食疗研究所3单元4号	郑鉴忠
200910019592.0	一种降脂保健食品	闫聿逊	（257300）山东省广饶县月河路27号广饶县中医院	闫聿逊
200910210746.4	一种预消化的大豆食品	张正生	（102208）北京市昌平区霍营天鑫家园16号楼1单元401室	张正生；梁　超等
200910167889.1	预防糖尿病的保健食品	寇开勤	（621000）四川省绵阳市安昌路18号爱喜嘉年华物业服务中心转A817	寇开勤
200910035756.9	食品级可发性聚苯乙烯颗粒及其制备方法	华啸威	（214101）江苏省无锡市锡山区东亭镇新明中路88号（兴达泡塑）	许　铭；杨　琪等
200910167993.0	一种杂粮米制成的糖尿病保健食品的配方	胡金玉	（620000）四川省眉山市东坡区下西街47号1栋4单元301号	胡金玉
200910210880.4	真空包装动物熟血制品食品工艺	向明强	（100071）北京市丰台区新村鸿业兴园10-1-1203	向明强
200910075281.6	一种包装食品的自加热方法及装置	刘永录	（052360）河北省辛集市建设街东段57号辛集市第二医院	刘永录
200910193812.1	一种淀粉烘焙食品及其生产方法	陈世翰	（515000）广东省汕头市龙湖区长平路新世纪花园2幢402室	陈世翰；许其然

（续）

申请或批准号	发 明 名 称	申请人	通 讯 地 址	发明人
200910221088.9	带旋转式消除泡沫装置的食品处理机	王晓东	(300191) 天津市南开区红旗南路水上温泉花园 9-3-501	王晓东
200910246662.6	一种卫生、易清洗的食品加工机	顾永洪	(528425) 广东省中山市东凤镇同乐工业园中山美斯特电器有限公司	顾永洪
200910172677.2	低温加工芝麻油脂及蛋白食品的方法	王瑞体	(456476) 河南省滑县高平镇后子厢村	王瑞体
200910172792.X	一种辣椒食品及其加工方法	刘兰顺	(456400) 河南省滑县留固镇前庄村 73 号	刘兰顺
200910172793.4	枣杞多果保健食品	李太普	(456400) 河南省滑县道口镇太行小区 46 号	李太普
200910250639.4	营养补充食品用于孕期女性的饮食补充配方及方法	刘建敏	(452470) 河南省登封市送表矿区刘楼村二组	刘建敏
200910166032.8	一种食品物料冰点的测定方法	林向东	(570228) 海南省海口市人民大道 58 号	林向东；张 琪等
200910185660.0	一种苔菜食品加工方法	左 营	(233600) 安徽省涡阳县义门镇工业园安徽义门苔干有限公司	左 营；于成继
200910101882.X	大米为原料的方便食品的制作方法	李本章	(316000) 浙江省嵊泗县菜园镇横山园 5 弄 9 号	李本章
200910248502.5	自动食品切片切丝机	赵 罡	(116021) 辽宁省大连市甘井子区红旗街祥满园 2 号楼 4-203	赵 罡
200910259852.1	一种土豆方便食品的加工工艺	张 礼	(076750) 河北省张家口市尚义县南壕堑镇安宁街工行家属楼 1 单元 113 号	张 礼；王国山
200910249616.1	蛋白能量营养食品	杨春庆	(100031) 北京市西城区太仆寺街 33 号 4-3-301	杨春庆
200910241658.0	一种食品组合物	郭景龙	(650000) 云南省昆明市五华区建设路 112 号紫薇苑 2 单元 701 室	郭景龙
200910176937.3	碱性食品及其制备工艺	李大鹏	(250101) 山东省济南市高新开发区正丰路中段环保科技园 E 座南 6004	李大鹏
200910265808.1	一种食品灌装装置	杨 艺	(201101) 上海市闵行区七莘路 2855 弄 135 号 502 室	杨 艺
200910255775.2	一种滋补养生海参食品及其加工方法	郑 波	(264003) 山东省烟台市福山区天府街 18 号富豪新天地	郑 波；崔 樱
200910220771.0	蜂胶林蛙卵磷脂胶囊保健食品	白万钧	(118200) 辽宁省宽甸县过街楼西街 64 号	白万钧
200910251711.5	牛肉口味膨化食品及其制备方法	郭 欣	(236500) 安徽省界首市华美路东段	郭 欣
200910265807.7	一种食品快速离心脱水机	杨 艺	(201101) 上海市闵行区七莘路 2855 弄 135 号 502 室	杨 艺
200910028643.6	一种蔬菜食品的制备方法	乔维汉；乔梁等	(224055) 江苏省盐城市盐都区开元西路 168 号	乔维汉；乔梁等
200910001756.7	食品包装方法	金 英	(214062) 江苏省无锡市梁清路 501 号天景花园 13 号 301 室	金 英；程学贤

（续）

申请或批准号	发明名称	申请人	通讯地址	发明人
200910060867.5	一种冲泡型食品及其制作方法	张五一	（435500）湖北省黄梅县黄梅镇五祖大道138号	张五一
200910019826.1	一种黄豆食品及其加工方法	周丕义	（265600）山东省蓬莱市钟楼南路123号	周丕义
200910079872.0	一种多功能扩展式食品安全快速检测设备	桑华春	（100871）北京市海淀区北京大学生命科学学院	桑华春；付晓春等
200910180878.7	太空人造良田及其生产功能性有机食品方法	王海文	（102423）北京市房山区韩村河镇韩村河西小区1号楼3单元101室	王海文
200910210907.X	一种干锅食品配方及其加工方法	邱建忠	（100066）北京市崇文区法华南里34号5层007	邱建忠
200910010252.1	一种菊苣胶囊食品及其生产方法	马　俊	（111008）辽宁省辽阳市弓长岭区政府城建局马玉欣转	马　俊
200910217420.4	一种环保纸膜食品包装及其制造工艺	王福刚	（150056）黑龙江省哈尔滨市南岗区红旗新区26-2栋6单元-1层3号	王福刚
200910021073.8	一种具有养生保健特殊功效的食品山葛醋液	张　仟	（710001）陕西省西安市碑林区安居巷4号	张　仟
200910096149.3	一种面粉食品的加工方法	王亦坤	（311323）浙江省临安市清凉峰镇乾山村横店里12号	王亦坤
200910118049.6	一种绿豆食品	叶其胜	（523009）广东省东莞市莞太路8号南城路段精明汉	叶其胜
200910007485.6	电热食品营销柜（俗称太阳柜）	刘定能	（422412）湖南省武冈市大田乡船田村7组9号	刘定能
200910245090.X	具有降脂、利心和助眠作用的山楂食品及制备方法	王福起	（300451）天津市塘沽区杭州道毓园1栋1门301	王福起
200910010719.2	气动力肉灌制食品原料吸送机	王正飞	（110042）辽宁省沈阳市大东区小河沿路150-3，7号楼5-1-1	王正飞
200910119560.8	一种红糖姜枣的食品制备工艺	薛　青	（033210）山西省吕梁市临县碛口镇尧昌里村097号	薛　青
200910106064.9	多功能食品加工机	励春亚	（315725）浙江省宁波市象山县新桥镇东溪村4组75号	励春亚
200910106070.4	易清洗食品加工机	励春亚	（315725）浙江省宁波市象山县新桥镇东溪村4组75号	励春亚
200910131913.6	一种治疗便秘的保健食品及制备工艺	刘东华；刘遂余	（037006）山西省大同市城区新建北路25号院4楼1单元7号	刘东华；刘遂余
200920095213.1	食品包装检测前处理浸泡装置	王利兵	（300042）天津市河西区浦口道6号天津出入境检验检疫局	王利兵；周　磊等
200920105298.7	食品叉	张洪滨	（100007）北京市东城区东四十条甲22号南新仓国际商务大厦B座1711B	张洪滨

（续）

申请或批准号	发明名称	申请人	通讯地址	发明人
200920083275.0	颗粒食品包装盒	潘光振	(443000) 湖北省宜昌市西陵区新世纪广场A座807室	潘光振
200920019497.6	食品旋切机	杨国通	(100070) 北京市丰台区花乡郑王坟万柳桥南97号3119室	杨国通
200920105883.7	一种自加热方便食品盒	蒋学军	(100020) 北京市朝阳区朝外大街吉庆里小区12号楼天诺物业	蒋学军
200920023006.5	一种悬挂式供鼻饲食品装置	闫香芹	(272031) 山东省济宁市传染病医院	闫香芹
200920126145.0	可重复启闭的食品包装袋	夏梦珣	(408000) 重庆市涪陵区兴华中路7号种子大厦1单元5楼2号	夏梦珣
200920112236.9	带全封闭加热或制冷装置的罐装食品容器	李小卿	(325000) 浙江省温州市鹿城区五马街道朔门街105号	李小卿
200920088079.2	穆斯林清真食品信誉标牌	沙金波	(475001) 河南省开封市顺河回族自治区财政厅东街99号	沙金波
200920140487.8	真空脱水食品加工生产系统	郭　伟；郭　强等	(537400) 广西壮族自治区北流市城西一路0180号	郭　强；郭　伟等
200920001454.5	食品包装装置	金　英	(214062) 江苏省无锡市梁清路501号天景花园13号301室	金　英；程学贤
200920148063.6	一种保温食品罩	巩　剑	(321306) 浙江省武义县泉溪镇巩宅村中心二路1弄15号	巩　剑
200920019646.9	一种精神病人吃流质食品饮药液装置	吴士玲	(272051) 山东省济宁市精神病防治院	吴士玲；郭　萍等
200920079818.1	食品的竹材质包装体	王　骏	(610041) 四川省成都市高新区神仙树南路55号	王　骏
200920101873.6	食品药品生产经营监管黑匣子	闫宝奎	(030000) 山西省太原市体育西路成豪宛1号楼1单元801	高国顺；赵光国等
200920116231.3	一种食品加工机的杯体	高洽伸	(315312) 浙江省慈溪市范市镇工业开发区慈溪市环球电器有限公司	高洽伸
200920096229.4	多功能环保复合食品袋	李民利	(300132) 天津市红桥区丁字沽新村八段48楼201	李民利
200920114128.5	油炸食品的减油装置	叶文明	(322000) 浙江省义乌市北苑工业区三凯路10-2号C座4楼	叶文明
200920037392.3	吉祥双芯肠类食品	张炳华	(116300) 辽宁省瓦房店市文全街大华楼1-301-1	张炳华
200920107922.7	一种将固体食品加入半流质食品中的装置	张汉生	(510600) 广东省广州市越秀区共和西路28号303室	张汉生
200920113405.0	食品纸卡包装机	吴伟杰	(316000) 浙江省舟山市普陀区沈家门街道食品厂路1号楼601室	吴伟杰；王坚强

（续）

申请或批准号	发明名称	申请人	通讯地址	发明人
200920021930.X	一种新型食品包装袋	史晓磊	（430000）湖北省武汉市南湖狮子山特一号华中农业大学食品科技学院	史晓磊
200920102197.4	药品、食品库用智能温湿度监控仪	李 斌；温旭民	（030006）山西省太原市长治路111号世贸中心B座2311室	李 斌；温旭民等
200920024489.0	一种食品过油器	王燕燕	（250014）山东省济南市历下区经十东路155号	王燕燕
200920023555.2	食品快检试管架	王传成	（271219）山东省新泰市新汶矿业集团卫生防疫站	王传成；范洁琼等
200920117353.4	一种食品防尘罩	吴碧峰	（321000）浙江省金华市金东区东孝街道戴店小区5幢2单元302室	吴碧峰
200920153921.6	肉禽类食品焖烤窖	苏连才	（065000）河北省廊坊市广阳区北旺乡东户屯村3排60号	苏连才
200920099700.5	一种食品加工机的空心食品成型装置	沈风焕	（157000）黑龙江省牡丹江市西安区华隆一区一号楼5单元202	沈风焕
200920144644.2	空芯或加芯条状食品加工装置	赵希春	（063500）河北省滦南县滦化家属楼	赵希春
200920131943.2	一种液体食品搅拌容器	熊兴剑	（518104）广东省深圳市宝安区沙井镇洪田金源工业区A14栋	熊兴剑；陈玉水
200920150241.9	新型食品有害细菌检验操作箱	沈 燕	（256100）山东省淄博市沂源县胜利路8号沂源县疾病控制中心检验科	沈 燕
200920130668.2	食品包装盒	陈林光	（515600）广东省汕头市潮安县庵埠镇文里村文西路东巷2号	陈林光
200920014379.6	一种新型蝠翼式电子食品保鲜器	王慧超	（110000）辽宁省沈阳市皇姑区黄河北大街98-8号4-5-1	王慧超
200920185336.4	一种环保食品袋	杜 兵	（315400）浙江省余姚市梨洲街道南雷里新村22幢202室	杜 兵
200920033566.9	线形食品搓散机	乔养正	（710500）陕西省蓝田县蓝关镇东场村一组	乔养正
200920028794.7	一种用于食品烘干的变频调速器	丁相军	（276300）山东省沂南县工业园临沂市运通食品有限公司	丁相军
200920089914.4	铝塑易开式食品罐	李利民	（453000）河南省新乡市卫滨区新原路司法干部学校2单元6号	李利民
200910064188.5	长期储存粮食不变质的方法及其设备	胡屹博；靳 策等	（473000）河南省南阳市梅溪宾馆家属院1号楼601室	胡屹博；靳 策等
200910013434.4	粮食磁化植物酒配方发酵酿造的方法及设备	王铁军	（112503）辽宁省铁岭市昌图县下二台乡西大五组	王铁军
200910162676.X	多用途粮食取样针	许修武	（239500）安徽省全椒县仙鹤街仙鹤巷12号	许修武

（续）

申请或批准号	发明名称	申请人	通讯地址	发明人
200910222398.2	多功能粮食烘干机	杨庆询	（236057）安徽省阜阳市中央储备粮阜阳直属库（颍东区阜胡路17号）	杨庆询
200910114672.4	全封闭节能三叠联动式粮食作物快速烘干除尘机	王志军；赵艳平	（530000）广西壮族自治区南宁市西乡塘区园艺路北湖村27号	王志军；赵艳平
200910229507.3	粮食烘干装置	张琳	（271000）山东省泰安市泰山区更新小区3号楼5单元6楼602	崔芳华
200910229724.2	粮食储存装置	张琳	（271000）山东省泰安市泰山区更新小区3号楼5单元6楼602	崔志远
200910072027.0	多彩高营养合成颗粒粮食	孙年超	（164031）黑龙江省北安市铁北十委二组139号	孙年超
200920099144.1	带有喂料圆盘的粮食自动计量包装机	周利臣	（154624）黑龙江省七台河市茄子河区中心河乡中心河村利臣摩托车商店	周利臣
200920101545.6	一种粮食扒送装置	齐进	（072250）河北省保定市顺平县蒲阳镇北下叔村	齐进
200920037565.1	粮食电力烘干控制器	李安民	（223400）江苏省淮安市涟水县保滩工业集中区涟淮路6号	李安民
200920092867.9	气压差粮食干燥塔	于春海	（130118）吉林省长春市新成大街2888号农大工程学院机制教研室	于春海；赵清来等
200920021768.1	粮食储存罐	刘文娇	（264000）山东省烟台市芝罘区南大街130号烟台第三中学	刘文娇
200920154026.6	蔬菜、水果、粮食真空冷藏结构	张保金	（048400）山西省高平市福利公司院内高平第一家总部	张保金
200910071369.0	同时获取大豆中蛋白和油脂的方法	初景涛	（163316）黑龙江省大庆市高新区创业园C座514室	初景涛
200910184813.X	一种利用餐厨废弃物生产微生物油脂的方法	曹媛媛；姚建铭	（230031）安徽省合肥市蜀山湖路350号中国科学院等离子体物理研究所	曹媛媛；姚建铭等
200910214169.6	一种油脂加注器	杨盛林	（523000）广东省东莞市东城新世纪豪园博客公寓B232	刘余明
200910227842.X	用动物油脂和鲜薯类制备生物柴油的方法	张建旺	（036000）山西省朔州市职业技术学院家属楼南楼3单元102	张建旺；张立航等
200910227846.8	用动物油脂制备动物脂肪酸的方法	张建旺	（036000）山西省朔州市职业技术学院家属楼南楼3单元102	张建旺；张立航等
200910008809.8	一种保留黄豆油天然营养的饲料油脂的生产方法	洪平	（201615）上海市松江区九亭镇龙高路363号	洪平
200910014125.9	一种油脂酸价的便携检测方法	解振清	（253015）山东省德州市禹城市伦镇镇解水村	解振清

（续）

申请或批准号	发 明 名 称	申请人	通 讯 地 址	发明人
200920196388.1	双速自动脱油脂离心机	蔡体勇	（315104）浙江省宁波市鄞州区启明路78号宁波东港紧固件制造有限公司	蔡体勇；陆昱森
200930304166.2	油脂杂物分离机	王维燊	（510010）广东省广州市越秀区机务段大街100号403房	王维燊
200910102413.X	一种茶香型白酒的配方及其制作方法	吴　海	（550004）贵州省贵阳市中华北路242号5号楼7楼708	吴　海
200910058453.9	一种提高酿造固态白酒陈香味的大曲药制备方法	李家民	（629209）四川省射洪县柳树镇中街149号	李家民
200910303080.7	一种酱香型白酒的制备工艺	龙则河	（564500）贵州省仁怀市新景城市花园9271	龙则河
200910115645.9	家用白酒蒸馏器	方缺法	（318020）浙江省台州市黄岩区宁溪镇上桧村233号	方缺法
200910309310.0	暴马丁香白酒	纪念军	（134005）吉林省通化市二道江区鸭园镇二道沟村六队	纪念军
200910178260.7	一种白酒的生产方法	郭凌云	（010020）内蒙古自治区呼和浩特市大学西路36号学府康都A座1502室	郭凌云
200930128506.0	瓶贴（盘龙青纯粮白酒）	杨跃平	（663000）云南省文山州文山县河滨路4幢6号	杨跃平
200930188049.4	白酒包装盒（特酒老窖）	邹国辉	（330000）江西省南昌市西湖区十字街467号4门506室	邹国辉
200930165466.7	标贴（江津白酒外包装图案）	阙基林	（400000）重庆市江津市几江镇布市街1号	阙基林
200930122365.1	包装瓶（白酒）	杨克秀	（300380）天津市西青区杨柳青镇明清街E21号宜成轩	杨克秀；韩广霖
200930265168.5	白酒瓶	能学廷	（276300）山东省沂南县玉泉路50号5排502号	能学廷
200910005212.8	葡萄酒储藏柜	陈善荣	（518000）广东省深圳市布吉坂田岗头亚洲工业园2栋2层	陈善荣
200910014171.9	紫珍香葡萄酒的酿造工艺	王华涛	（262400）山东省潍坊市昌乐县昌盛花园14号楼2单元	孙炳东
200910009344.8	一种玛咖葡萄酒及其制备方法	杨勇武；刘佑贤等	（100083）北京市海淀区东王庄4号楼1107	杨勇武；刘佑贤等
200910064413.5	一种银杏葡萄酒及其酿制方法	李洪磊；王　伟等	（476600）河南省永城市双桥乡李林村李林东组032号	赵　雨；李道德等
200910165808.4	一种冬虫夏草葡萄酒的制作方法	刘文宝	（014030）内蒙古自治区包头市青山区呼得木林大街11号街坊23栋27号	刘文宝

（续）

申请或批准号	发 明 名 称	申请人	通 讯 地 址	发明人
200910013497.X	一种葡萄酒的生产方法	李 静	(112003) 辽宁省铁岭市清河区杨木乡中心小学	李 静
200910256046.9	一种低醇甜型白葡萄酒的生产技术	屈慧鸽	(265500) 山东省烟台市福山区观月里小区1号楼2单元401号	屈慧鸽；邓军哲等
200920017624.9	一种气压式的葡萄酒软木塞提取器	张玉来	(265400) 山东省招远市罗峰路办事处北关西335号	张玉来
200920000276.4	葡萄酒储藏柜	陈善荣	(518000) 广东省深圳市布吉坂田岗头亚洲工业园2栋2层	陈善荣
200920035535.7	一种葡萄酒醒酒器	王胜杰	(515071) 广东省汕头市潮阳区和平镇中寨蔡厝埕巷4号101户	王胜杰
200920318196.3	葡萄酒发酵罐上的取样装置	罗建峰	(623104) 四川省阿坝州理县薛城镇上孟乡塔斯村塔斯酒庄有限公司	罗建峰；唐渝成
200920318197.8	用于葡萄酒酿造的发酵罐上的进排料装置	罗建峰	(623104) 四川省阿坝州理县薛城镇上孟乡塔斯村塔斯酒庄有限公司	罗建峰；唐渝成
200920267249.3	相变自调温母子葡萄酒桶	张吉庆	(066003) 河北省秦皇岛市海港区耀北里5-3-1302室	张吉庆
200920272607.X	简易葡萄酒架	曾 宇	(610000) 四川省成都市高新区神仙树南路11号2栋2单元2号	曾 宇
200930066934.5	包装箱（葡萄酒干红）	余秉足	(362000) 福建省永春县桃城镇洋上村837号	余秉足
200910063450.4	带面皮的果味糕点	胡志伟	(433000) 湖北省仙桃市沙嘴路十一墩新村河小区	胡志伟
200910101696.6	绿色糕点及制作方法	王雅琳	(315800) 浙江省宁波市北仑区新碶街道华山新村16幢602室	王雅琳
200920052020.8	一种糕点铲	林 齐	(529500) 广东省阳江市江城区创业路联新街3号	林 齐
200920225745.2	一种糕点加工机	胡美东	(273200) 山东省济宁市泗水县古城路山东泗水创新机械有限公司	胡美东
200930183340.2	迷你型夹心糕点制作机	战宝松	(266600) 山东省莱西市水集街道办事处青岛路86号1033户	战宝松
200930010702.8	糕点（熊猫）	苗 建	(110013) 辽宁省沈阳市沈河区热闹路60-6号473	苗 建
200930222313.1	糕点	胡志伟	(433000) 湖北省仙桃市沙嘴路十一墩新村河小区	胡志伟
200930055782.9	包装袋（糕点系列）	王兆玲	(221145) 江苏省铜山县黄集镇谢庄村村委会2组	王兆玲
200910030685.3	果蔬汁趣味饼干	韩婷婷	(221011) 江苏省徐州市贾汪区汴塘镇政府宿舍18号	韩婷婷

（续）

申请或批准号	发 明 名 称	申请人	通 讯 地 址	发明人
200910099312.1	天然植物性营养压缩饼干及其制备方法	徐新月	(310053) 浙江省杭州市滨江区临江花园21幢601室	徐新月
200910160364.5	健脑饼干	杨贵成	(425600) 湖南省宁远县老建委大院陈勇家	杨贵成
200910144440.3	一种发芽糙米营养饼干的生产方法	彭常安	(241006) 安徽省芜湖市镜湖区康复路111号5幢2户	彭常安
200910029861.1	饼干机燃气供热装置	张勤英	(210029) 江苏省南京市建邺区茶南小区露园19幢73号303室	张勤英
200910249013.1	一种以黑木耳和白菜汁为原料的保健饼干	周福铎	(116600) 辽宁省大连市开发区管委会西侧楼309房间	周福铎
200910029789.2	一种饼干龟饲养料的配制方法	许吉雷	(221100) 江苏省铜山县汉王镇虎腰村39号	许吉雷
200910180662.0	具有促进消化功能的饼干	吕学栋	(056004) 河北省邯郸市丛台区和平里4号楼1单元2号	吕学栋
200920148252.3	饼干合排装置	刘 翔	(519000) 广东省珠海市香洲区香洲兴柠街57号9栋1单元201房	刘 翔
200920251617.5	小饼干三明治冷冻饮品	杨 明	(300143) 天津市河北区宜清花园3-6-202	杨 明
200920185831.5	夹心饼干机	卢礼权	(528300) 广东省佛山市顺德区勒流镇江义工业区江义大道日成机械厂	卢礼权

第六部分

大事记

1 月

11 日 《全国生猪屠宰行业发展规划纲要(2010—2015)》暨猪肉市场运行新闻发布会在北京举行。商务部畜禽屠宰管理办公室主任、市场秩序司司长向欣同志就全国生猪屠宰行业基本情况、《纲要》的主要内容以及近期猪肉市场运行情况作了介绍。向欣指出，为落实党中央、国务院保民生、促消费、调结构、的总体要求，保障肉品卫生和质量安全，促进生猪屠宰行业健康发展，商务部制订了《全国生猪屠宰行业发展规划纲要（2010—2015)》。《纲要》肯定了自1998年国务院《生猪屠宰管理条例实施办法》实施以来，生猪屠宰行业发展取得的成绩，分析了面临的新形势和存在的问题，提出了促进屠宰行业发展的主要任务和保障措施，是未来几年全国生猪屠宰行业发展的重要指导性文件。《纲要》提出，要以保障肉品卫生质量安全为宗旨，在科学发展观指导下，以优化布局、减控总量、升级改造和规范经营为着力点，推动屠宰行业布局调整和结构优化，适度提高产业集中度，提升定点屠宰企业的技术装备和管理水平，更好满足人民群众对安全优质猪肉产品的消费需求。到2015年，全国逐步形成以跨区域流通的现代化屠宰加工企业为主体，区域性肉品加工、配送企业发挥重要功能作用，以供应本地市场的定点屠宰企业为补充，梯次配置、布局合理、有序流通的产业布局。未来几年内，我国生猪屠宰行业发展的主要任务是完善设置规划，严格执行标准、调整优化行业布局，实施企业分级管理；加快行业升级改造，提升技术和管理水平；推动企业兼并重组、延伸产业链条、培育自主品牌、发展清洁生产；提倡科学消费，积极调整产品结构；建设诚信体系，推动信用分类管理；加强国际合作，提升企业国际竞争力。纲要强调，各级商务主管部门要在当地政府领导下，统筹规划，切实负起责任，共同推动《纲要》的组织实施。商务主管部门将会同有关部门加强屠宰行业标准和制度建设；加大投入，深入开展“放心肉”服务体系建设；规范流通秩序，营造开放、公平、竞争、有序的市场环境；加强部门、地区间协调配合，建立健全屠宰监管体系；广泛开展宣传、培训，充分发挥行业协会和有关中介组织作用，加强行业自律，沟通行业信息，维护企业利益。

11～12 日 国家粮食局在北京召开“全国粮食局长会议”。会议的主要任务是，深入学习贯彻党的十七大、十七届三中、四中全会和中央经济工作会议、中央农村工作会议精神，总结2009年粮食流通工作，分析当前面临的新形势，研究部署2010年粮食流通工作。国家粮食局局长、党组书记聂振邦在会上作了题为《大力发展现代粮食流通产业，加强和改善粮食宏观调控，切实保障国家粮食安全》的工作报告。会议认为，2009年粮食部门深入学习实践科学发展观，认真贯彻落实党中央、国务院关于粮食工作的方针政策，在国家发展改革委的指导和有关部门的大力支持下，努力克服国际金融危机的冲击和影响，顺利完成年初部署的“抓好收购促增收，充实储备强基础，清仓查库摸家底，加强调控稳市场，深化改革促发展”等重点工作任务，粮食依法行政能力、服务水平和行业整体素质进一步提高，粮食流通各项工作取得新进展，保证了全国粮食市场和价格基本稳定，保护了种粮农民利益，保障了国家粮食安全，为保增长、保民生、保稳定做出了积极贡献。会议指出，2010年是实施“十一五”规划的最后一年，是巩固和发展粮食流通体制改革成果，进一步完善宏观调控政策措施，继续推进现代粮食流通产业发展的关键之年。2010年粮食流通工作的总体要求是：全面贯彻党的十七大和十七届三中、四中全会精神，高举中国特色社会主义伟大旗帜，以邓小平理论和“三个代表”重要思想为指导，深入贯彻落实科学发展观，认真落实中央经济工作会议、中央农村工作会议的部署和全国发展改革工作会议的要求，按照“发展产业壮实力、加强调控保安全”的基本思路，以加强宏观调控、深化体制改革、发展流通产业、推进依法管粮、加强行业建设为着力点，实现抓好收购、促农增收、保证供应、稳定市场、统筹发展、保障安全的目标，促进粮食流通事业科学发展，为巩固经济回升向好势头、促进国民经济平稳较快发展发挥特有优势，作出新的贡献。要抓好以下七项工作：一是加强和改善粮食宏观调控，维护粮食市场和价格基本稳定；二是充分利用清仓查库成果，健全粮食库存管理长效机制；三是深化粮食流通体制改革，促进粮食企业健康发展；四是积极推进现代粮食流通产业发展，壮大粮食流通产业实力；五是加强粮食法制建设，积极推进依法管粮；六是总结粮食行业发展经验，认真研究制订“十二五”发展规划；七是深入贯彻落实十七届四中全会精神，着力加强粮食行业自身建设。各省、自治区、直辖市、计划单列市及新疆生产建设兵团粮食局和黑龙江省农垦总局主要负责同志参加了会议。中央、国务院有关部门、单位和大型国有粮食企业的有关负责同志参加了会议。

20 日 “第一届食品安全国家标准审评委员会成立大会”在京举行。全国人大常委会、国防大学、国家发展和改革委员会、工业和信息化部、农业部、商务部、卫生部、国家工商总局、国家质量监督检验检疫总局、国务院新闻办、食品药品监管局等部门有关领导和负责同志出席会议。会议由卫生部副部长陈啸宏主持。第一届食品安全国家标准审评委员会由10个专业分委员会的350名委员和工业和信息化、农业、商务、工商、质检、食品药品监管等20个单位委员组成，主要职责是审评食品安全国家标准，提出实施食品安全国家标准的建议，对食品安全国家标准的重大问题提供咨询，承担食品安全标准其他工作。委员会下设食品产品、微生物、生产经营规范、营养与特殊膳食食品、检验方法与规程、污染物、食品添加剂、食品相关产品、农药残留、兽药残留10个专业分委员会。卫生部部长陈竺担任主任委员，卫生部副部长陈啸宏担任常务副主任委员，农业部副部长陈晓华、中国疾病预防控制中心陈君石院士、中国农业科学院茶叶研究所陈宗懋院士、中国检验检疫科学研究院庞国芳院士和中国疾病预防控制中心主任王宇同志担任副主任委员，陈君石院士兼任审评委员会技术总师。陈啸宏宣读了《卫生部关于成立第一届食品安全国家标准审评委员会的通知》，并向委员代表颁发了聘书。卫生部部长陈竺作重要讲话。为做好食品安全国家标准审评工作，陈竺提出3点要求：一是认真学法，进一步提高食品安全标准重要性的认识。他强调，做好食品安全标准工作是切实维护公众身体健康的需要，是强化食品安全监管的需要，是促进经济健康发展的需要。二是要科学分析食品安全标准工作形势，明确工作任务。按照国务院的统一部署，卫生部已经采取了一系列措施加强食品安全标准工作。包括清理完善现有食品安全标准，加强食品安全标准基础研究工作，加强食品安全标准体系建设，成立食品安全国家标准审评委员会，完善食品安全标准管理制度等方面。三是要团结协作，认真履行食品安全国家标准审评委员会职责。一方面是要坚持标准工作的原则，做好标准审评工作，另一方面要通过完善工作机制，提高审评工作效率。

2 月

3日 “2010年全国餐饮服务食品安全监督管理工作会议”在上海召开，这是食品药品监管系统承担餐饮服务食品安全监管新职能后召开的第一次全国性专题会议。会议总结了2009年全国工作，分析了当前餐饮服务食品安全监管工作面临的新形势，明确了2010年全国餐饮服务食品安全监管工作思路和工作重点。国家食品药品监督管理局副局长边振甲出席会议并作重要讲话。边振甲表示，食品药品监管体制的重大调整和《食品安全法》的颁布实施，标志着我国食品安全监管理念和监管模式的重大变革。食品链上游各环节存在的安全隐患都可能累积到餐饮服务环节，这使我们面临的风险更为复杂和严重；广大消费者每天都有可能接触餐饮消费，这使我们所承受的风险更为现实和广泛；餐饮服务涉及面宽、影响人群广，情况十分复杂，监管任务十分繁重。边振甲强调，2010年是深入开展餐饮服务食品安全整顿的关键之年，各级食品药品监管部门要深入落实2010年全国食品药品监管工作暨党风廉政建设工作会议精神，深入贯彻实施《食品安全法》，认真履行餐饮服务食品安全监管新职责，全面加强监管制度和队伍建设，深入开展餐饮服务食品安全整顿，严厉打击违法违规行为，确保餐饮服务食品安全监管工作扎实稳步推进。自《食品安全法》实施以来，全国食品药品监管部门开始履行餐饮服务食品安全监管职责，地方食品药品监管体制改革全面启动，为期两年的食品安全整顿工作正在逐步深入。据统计，自从整顿工作开展以来，截至2009年12月，各地餐饮服务监管部门检查各类餐饮单位248万多户次，收集违法违规线索11万多条，警告和责令整改23万多户，吊销许可证1 400多户，取缔无证经营24 000多户，移送司法机关处理案件119件。此外，食品药品监管部门覆盖全国31个省（自治区、直辖市）的食品安全调查与评价工作也已开展，对全国餐饮服务环节8大类18个品种的食品原辅料及高风险自制食品开展了54项化学性危害和4项生物性危害的调查评价。会议明确了2010年全国餐饮服务食品安全监管工作思路和工作重点。积极推动《餐饮服务许可管理办法》、《餐饮服务食品安全监督管理办法》以及餐饮服务许可、审批、信息管理、操作规范等制度出台；强化学校食堂、工地食堂、旅游景区餐饮单位等重点场所餐饮服务监管；研究制定餐饮服务监管基本能力建设标准；启动餐饮服务食品安全示范工程，推进各地创建食品安全示范区（县）、街、店；启动编制餐饮服务食品安全状况报告；开展餐饮服务环节食品安全风险因素分析，提出预防和降低风险防控措施，指导餐饮服务单位全面加强食品安全管理；研究建立餐饮服务食品安全风险监测体系、检验检测体系、信息系统和应急体系；全力做好上海世博会等重大活动食品安全保障工作。

9日 国务院食品安全委员会召开第一次全体会议。中共中央政治局常委、国务院副总理、国务院食品安全委员会主任李克强出席会议并讲话，国务院食品安全委员会全体成员及有关部门和单位负责人参加了会议。会议听取了卫生部、农业部、国家质检总局、国家工商总局、工业和信息化部负责人关于开展食品安全整顿工作情况的汇报，审议并原则通过了《国务院食品安全委员会工作规则》、《2010 年深入开展食品安全整顿工作的安排》等文件。李克强副总理指出，党中央、国务院高度重视食品安全，并采取了一系列政策措施，目前我国食品安全总体比较稳定。同时也要清醒地看到，食品安全的基础还较薄弱，形势依然严峻。他要求各级政府：一是要进一步完善和强化责任制度与问责制度，推动食品安全监管工作迈上新台阶；二是要完善食品安全标准，健全食品安全检测检验体系、食品安全风险评估与食品安全事故预防和应急处置机制，加快食品安全诚信体系建设；三是要采取有效措施，坚决打击食品安全领域各种违法生产经营的行为，严肃查处并追究监管不力的行为。李克强副总理强调，2010 年将重点治理食品添加剂、食用农产品、食品生产加工、食品流通和进出口、禽畜屠宰、餐饮消费、保健食品等方面存在的突出问题。同时，进一步加强对重点部位、重点环节、重点场所的清查，不留死角，净化市场。国务院食品安全委员会作为国务院食品安全工作的高层次议事协调机构，有 15 个部门参加，主要职责包括：一是分析食品安全形势，研究部署、统筹指导食品安全工作；二是提出食品安全监管的重大政策措施；三是督促落实食品安全监管责任。另外，设立国务院食品安全委员会办公室，具体承担委员会的日常工作。

26 日 “农产品加工技术推广专家座谈会”在京举行。会议由农业部农产品加工局科教质量处杨泽钊处长主持，项目承担单位的领导和专家参加会议。会议围绕如何做好优势农产品加工重大技术推广工作展开研讨，各位专家积极发言，献计献策。专家一致认为，本项目符合时代发展要求，在成功破解农产品加工行业技术发展瓶颈问题方面取得了显著成效。但是，目前项目资金规模较小，推广模式较单一，示范带动作用有限等问题日益凸现。因此，专家建议，在现有资金条件下，应做好项目前期准备工作，包括项目拟示范推广技术的收集、筛选和论证工作；同时，要不断完善和创新项目实施的形式和内容，使本项目取得更好的示范带动作用。针对农产品加工实用技术示范推广，专家认为在粮油、果蔬、畜禽产品加工 3 大领域，应选择节能减排、质量安全、综合利用等方面共性的成熟、实用、新型的农产品加工技术组织示范推广；同时，应考虑到中小型农产品加工企业普遍存在的规模较小、资金薄弱的现状，示范推广技术的投资不能太大，要真正起到四两拨千斤的效果。针对农产品加工技术对接活动，专家认为应通过调研选择粮油、果蔬、畜禽产品加工 3 大领域中小型企业实际生产中存在的共性问题汇编成册进行重点讲解，再组织相关专家和企业深入到代表性企业进行现场答疑，效果将更好。最后，杨泽钊处长总结指出，本项目经过 3 年的实施，实现了 3 个转变，一是实现了从小规模到比较大规模的转变；二是实现了从原来的不会做、不知道怎么做，到现在的比较会做的转变；三是从没有财政专项、没有固定资金安排，到形成一个财政专项的转变。这些成绩的取得是项目承担单位和各位专家共同努力的结果，实属不易，希望大家继续努力，集思广益，统筹规划，积极谋划，力争使本项目“做大、做实”。

3　月

11 日 农业部农产品加工局在广西桂林召开“2010 年优势农产品加工重大技术推广项目启动会”。农业部农产品加工局副局长王秀忠，广西壮族自治区农业厅巡视员韦吉田出席会议。会议由农产品加工局科教质量处杨泽钊处长主持。王秀忠强调，农产品加工业的发展靠技术推广。近 3 年推广工作建立了 3 个平台，即资源转化平台，促进了产业发展；难题解决平台，促进了中小企业的发展；产学研合作平台，提供了坚实的技术支撑。同时，取得了良好的技术推广效果：即提高了加工质量、企业效益和生产效率，降低了能耗、物耗和污染，突破了关键技术制约，提升了产业竞争力，技术创新能力有所提高。王秀忠对 2010 年的技术推广工作提出了四点建议：一是统筹安排项目实施及培训的时间。二是重视组织实施。事先调查研究，摸准需求，组织细致，是 2010 年工作效果的重要保证。三是注重开拓创新，无论工作方式还是推广模式，都要有所突破，有所创新。四是加大宣传力度，建立良好的工作机制。农产品加工局科教质量处调研员姜倩对 2010 年项目经费的使用及注意事项做了详尽的说明。农业部规划设计研究院和中国农业科学院分别对承担项目的实施方案和地方工作任务进行阐述，明确地方项目实施单位的工作范畴和职责。

16 日 农业部农产品加工局在北京召开了“2010 年农产品加工预警工作会议”。会议由农业部农产品加工局规划统计处傅金凯处长主持，各预警分中心负责人参加了会议。会议对 2009 年全国农产品加工预警工作进行了总结：一是进一步加大了预警工作的力度和广度；二是进一步完善了全国农产品加工预警服务体系。2009 年虽然在基本建设、产业调研、指标体系建设、信息化服务平台建设方面取得了一定成绩，但仍然存在主管机构不稳定、组织机构不完备、资金投入有缺口等问题。各预警分中心负责人分别就本省本产业2009年农产品加工预警工作情况作了详细的汇报，提出了工作中存在的问题以及相关的意见和建议。针对工作中的困难、结合2010年工作内容，分中心代表展开了热烈的讨论，在信息采集方式、工作运行机制等方面提出了许多切实可行的解决方法。本次会议还确定了新疆、陕西、河南、黑龙江、江西、吉林6个重点加工产业预警中心；会上布置了2010年预警工作的任务、规划了本年度预警项目建设方向。最后，傅金凯处长指出：一是农产品加工预警工作任重道远，我们要认清形势，看清方向，明确任务，共同努力；二是在现有工作基础上，应拓展预警体系网络，以省中心拓宽产业、以产业为中心扩大预警范围，真正建立起全国农产品加工预警体系；三是加强对突发事件的预警能力。新疆、陕西、河南、黑龙江、江西、吉林、内蒙等分中心负责人及专家参加了会议。

18～19日 “全国‘三品一标’工作会议”在昆明召开。会议的主要任务是贯彻落实2010年中央1号文件、全国农业工作会议和全国农产品质量安全监管工作会议精神，研究部署无公害农产品、绿色食品、有机农产品和农产品地理标志（统称“三品一标”）工作。农业部副部长陈晓华作重要讲话。陈晓华充分肯定了“三品一标”工作成效。他指出，“三品一标”是政府主导的安全优质农产品公共品牌，是当前和今后一个时期农产品生产消费的主导产品。“三品一标”经过这些年的积极推动，已有一定的总量规模和发展基础，各自形成了一套行之有效的生产方式和发展模式，呈现出几个特点：一是发展速度快。自2001年“无公害食品行动计划”实施以来，“三品一标”工作呈现出快速、健康的发展势头。截止到2009年底，全国认证无公害农产品已达到49 000个，认定无公害农产品产地已超过51 000个；认定的种植业产地面积0.45亿hm^2，占全国耕地面积35%左右。全国有效使用绿色食品标志企业6 000个，获证产品15 700多个，产地监测面积为0.17亿hm^2，农作物种植面积0.11亿hm^2。经农业系统认证的有机生产基地1 000余个，产品接近5 000个，实物总量210多万t，生产面积280多万hm^2。已获国家农产品地理标志登记保护的产品211个，与2008年启动之初比，登记的速度快、质量高、效果好，深受各地政府高度重视和生产者欢迎。二是产品质量稳定可靠。“三品一标”通过推行标准化生产和全程控制，实施严格的产地认定和产品认证制度，加上认证后的有效监督，较好地实现了上市产品“生产有记录、流向可追踪、信息可查询、质量可追溯”，保证了生产的规范化和产品的安全性。2008年在部里组织的“保质量、保安全、助奥运”活动抽检中，供京供奥无公害农产品、绿色食品、有机农产品质量抽检合格率分别达到99.2%、100%和100%；在2009年农产品质量安全专项整治暨执法年活动抽检中，无公害农产品、绿色食品、有机农产品质量抽检合格率分别达到99.1%、98.8%和100%。三是生产组织化程度高。“三品一标”认证的前提条件都要求规模化生产和产业化经营，申请者必须是面向生产和消费的生产经营主体。在已认定的无公害农产品种植业产地中，每个产地平均规模都在0.07万hm^2左右，带动农户200多个、600多人。获证的“三品一标”产品，基本上都实现了规模化生产、产业化经营，有稳定的标准化生产基地。在“三品一标”获证单位中，企业化的主体占85%以上，生产企业、行业协会和农民专业合作社已成为“三品一标”获证的主流。绿色食品获证企业中，有250多个为国家级农业产业化龙头企业，1 100个为省级农业产业化龙头企业，分别占国家级和省级农业产业化龙头企业总数的三分之一和五分之一。四是品牌影响力大幅提升。“三品一标”作为安全优质农产品的代表和政府公共品牌，权威性已基本建立，品牌公信力已基本形成，品牌认知度全面提升。无公害农产品已成为安全农产品的代名词和各级政府推动农产品质量安全监管的重要抓手；绿色食品作为安全优质精品品牌，推行标准化生产，倡导健康消费，品牌形象深得社会各界的推崇，美誉度不断增强；农产品地理标志作为推动特色农业和区域优势经济发展的载体，已成为各级政府保护产地环境、传承农耕文化、彰显区位优势、营销特色产品、壮大产业集群、提升市场竞争力的重要途径，深得广大农产品生产者与消费者的青睐。五是促进农业增效和农民增收作用明显。“三品一标”产品与普通农产品相比，表现出明显的市场优势和价格优势。无公害农产品市场售价比同类未认证产品要高出10%左右；绿色食品平均增幅达到20%～30%；有机食品大多出口和供应高端市场，价格提升更加明显，部分产品市场售价甚至高出常规产品好几倍；地理标志农产品市场价格和品牌价值得到大规模、全地域双重提升。本次会议由农业部农产品质量安全中心和中国绿色食品发展中心联合召开。农业部农产品质量安全监管局副局长徐肖君主持会议并作总结。各省、自治区、直辖市、计划单列市及新疆生产建设兵团无公害农产品（农产品地理标志）工作机构，绿色食品（有机食品）工作机构，相关检测机构负责人共200余人参加了会议。

4 月

1日 商务部在哈尔滨市召开“全国商务系统食品安全暨屠宰行业管理工作会议”，部署商务系统贯彻落实《食品安全法》及《食品安全法实施条例》以及国务院食品安全委员会第一次全体会议精神，抓好流通领域食品安全行业管理及生猪屠宰管理工作。商务部副部长姜增伟出席会议并讲话，黑龙江省副省长孙尧在会议上致辞。会议总结回顾了2009年全国生猪屠宰管理工作取得的成效。一是政策法规标准体系充实完善。出台了《全国生猪屠宰行业发展规划纲要（2010—2015）》等重要文件，为调整行业结构，优化行业布局提供了重要依据。二是行业监管成效显著。各级商务主管部门加强监管能力建设，已有80%的市、县成立了专（兼）职屠宰执法队伍，狠抓日常监管，肉品质量安全状况进一步改善。监管制度不断完善，部门和地区间的配合得到了有效地加强。组织开展严厉打击病死、病害猪及其猪肉非法交易等专项整治成效明显，有效净化了市场秩序。三是屠宰行业取得较快发展。2009年，全国生猪定点屠宰企业屠宰量达到3.16亿头，比上年增加12.8%，其中规模以上屠宰企业屠宰量达2.1亿头，较上年增加11%，规模化程度提升明显。四是“放心肉”服务体系建设积极推进。2009年商务部、财政部在北京、上海、山东、广州等10个省、直辖市开展了“放心肉”服务体系建设试点，安排3亿元资金用于试点屠宰监管技术系统、肉品质量安全信息可追溯系统和大型企业冷链建设，取得了阶段性的成效。会议指出，2010年，生猪屠宰管理工作要紧紧围绕《全国生猪屠宰行业发展规划纲要（2010—2015）》，以保障肉品卫生和质量安全为核心，着力抓好五项重点工作：一是淘汰落后产能，优化行业布局。严格执行国务院《生猪屠宰管理条例》，按照《纲要》和《商务部办公厅关于严格执行标准做好生猪定点屠宰企业审核换证工作的通知》要求，对所有的生猪定点屠宰企业的资质条件进行审核，淘汰落后产能，进一步调整优化行业布局。二是切实加强行业监管，建立行业信用分类监管制度。按照国务院2010年食品安全整顿计划和统一部署，组织开展畜禽屠宰专项整顿，采取有效措施，切实加强行业监管，促进肉品安全形势根本好转。同时，要创新监管机制，建立实行屠宰企业信用分类监管。三是加快推进分级管理。2010年将全面推行生猪定点屠宰厂（场）分级管理，推动行业发展、规范行业秩序。四是继续推动“放心肉”服务体系建设。五是加强对从业人员的资质等级管理。会议要求，各级商务主管部门要加强对企业的教育培训，提高其食品安全责任意识，自觉将有关法律法规要求转变为企业内部管理制度；要推动完善食品安全行业标准，积极扶持行业协会发展，充分发挥行业自律作用；建立政府投资为引导、企业投资为主体的多元投入机制，加快建设现代食品流通体系，改善流通企业食品安全设施，提高食品安全保障能力；积极配合有关部门，督促企业履行食品安全社会责任；建立健全应急处置机制，及时妥善处理食品安全突发事件。各类食品流通、餐饮服务和生猪定点屠宰企业，要牢固树立第一责任人意识，严格按照相关法律法规要求，建立健全食品安全管理制度，改善食品安全设施，切实承担起保障食品安全的社会责任。

12日 商务部食品安全领导小组召开第一次全体会议。商务部副部长姜增伟、钟山同志出席会议并讲话。部长助理房爱卿同志主持会议。商务部食品安全领导小组全体成员及联络员参加了会议。会议指出，食品安全工作事关人民群众的身体健康和生命安全，关系到社会的和谐稳定和人民的家庭幸福，是一项保民生的重要工作，商务部门要高度重视。商务部作为国务院食品安全委员会的成员单位，要认真贯彻落实国务院食品安全委员会第一次全体会议精神，切实履行好流通领域行业管理部门对食品安全的职责，抓好生猪屠宰监管和酒类流通管理，促进食品经营行业健康发展，努力提高流通行业食品安全保障能力和水平。会议要求，商务部食品安全领导小组要按照部党组的要求，健全工作机制，处理好日常工作和应急处置工作的关系，确保工作高效、有序运转；各成员单位要加强协调配合，按照职责分工，做好各自工作；要将食品安全融入各项业务工作，在业务工作中要提出提升食品安全保障能力的新问题；要制订切实可行的应急预案，妥善处理涉及商务部门的食品安全突发事件。会议宣布了调整后的商务部食品安全领导小组组成人员名单，讨论并原则通过了《商务部食品安全领导小组工作规则》和《2010年商务部食品安全工作要点》。

16日 农业部农产品加工局在京组织召开了“国家农产品加工技术研发体系建设工作座谈会”。200名来自国家农产品加工技术研发分中心的代表参加了会议。农业部农产品加工局甘士明局长作了题为：“加大研发力度，提高自主创新能力，努力开创农产品加工技术研发工作新局面”的讲话。甘士明指出，现代农业发展、农产品竞争力提升、居民营养膳食结构的平衡和市场消费结构的调整提升要靠加工业支撑；农产品加工质量稳定控制、资源有效利用与开发、产品创新、利用现代技术提升传统产业、前瞻性技术的储备等方面存在的问题，对新时期农产品加工业及其技术研发带来很大的挑战；农产品加工技术研发的准确定位、科研院所与企业协作研发的创新机制建立，农产品加工研究院所联谊平台、行业科技支撑平台、科技对接平台和研发体系等四大平台打造，以及农产品加工科研项目，都为农产品加工技术研发提供了良好的发展机遇。2009 年，新认定 76 个技术研发中心。目前，在粮油加工、肉畜产品加工、水产加工、果蔬加工等重大领域建设研发中心 201 个，研发体系的框架基本形成。2009 年组建了粮油加工、畜牧加工、果蔬加工等 5 个专业委员会，以优化研发体系的运行机制；积极发展农产品加工重大关键共性技术筛选，大力推动技术研发与联合攻关。据不完全统计，研发中心承担省部级以上项目 734 项，国家发明专利 189 项，技术成果推广 333 项。农业部农产品加工局王秀忠副局长对 2009 年研发体系建设工作总结中指出：2009 年，研发中心不仅在技术创新上取得明显成效，而且积极参与农产品加工重大技术推广、农产品加工国际标准跟踪、人才培养和技术服务。当前农产品加工技术研发工作，正面临国家高度重视新兴战略型产业发展，重视低碳经济、绿色经济、循环经济发展等机遇，也面临质量安全事件频发、行业恶性竞争和国际贸易保护主义的制约。对于 2010 年农产品加工技术研发体系的工作重点，王秀忠强调，应进一步加大建设力度，突出抓好研发体系的完善；突出公益性、关键性、战略性，突出质量安全控制、环保节能、资源节约等领域的技术攻关，继续做好重大关键共性技术筛选，为“十二五”农产品加工技术攻关、技术引进、技术推广指明方向；继续抓好重大关键共性技术的联合攻关，扎实推进技术研发工作；完善好研发体系工作机制、研发机制和管理机制。与会代表一致认为：国家农产品加工技术研发体系，是以企业为主体，以科研院所、高等院校为技术依托，产学研相结合的农产品加工科技创新平台。通过建设这个平台，对农产品加工重大关键共性技术进行攻关、熟化和示范推广，将对提升我国农产品加工业的整体技术水平，促进农产品加工业的发展发挥重要作用。

5　月

7 日　由中国粮食行业协会、中国储备粮管理总公司、中国农业发展银行、中粮集团有限公司、郑州粮食批发市场有限公司、郑州商品交易所、大连商品交易所共同主办，五得利面粉集团有限公司协办的第十三届中国粮食论坛在北京隆重举行。来自全国各地的重点粮油加工企业、贸易公司、粮食批发市场、粮库的负责人和粮食行政管理部门、农业发展银行、粮食行业协会、粮食经济学会等单位的负责人共 300 多人参加了论坛。中国粮食行业协会会长白美清、国家统计局总经济师姚景源、国家发展改革委农经司副司长方言、商务部外贸司副司长江帆、国家粮食局发展司司长何毅、国家粮油信息中心主任尚强民、中粮粮油有限公司副总经理王印基、郑州商品交易所研究发展部总监施利敏等有关单位领导、专家先后作了报告。论坛紧紧围绕“我国粮食‘六连丰’后的新形势和后金融危机时期粮油市场展望”的主题，分别从我国宏观经济形势、粮食调控政策、进出口政策、国内外粮油市场形势、粮油加工业“十二五”发展规划等方面进行研讨，高层次、多角度、全方位地透视和剖析粮油企业当前及“十二五”期间所面临的新形势，为企业了解粮食形势、掌握粮食政策、分析市场行情、搞好经营决策提供新视角，拓展新视野，传递新信息。

25 日　商务部姜增伟副部长主持召开“生猪定点屠宰企业分级管理立法工作座谈会”，听取部分省市商务主管部门、企业及行业协会代表对生猪定点屠宰厂（场）分级管理立法工作的意见和建议。会议讨论了生猪定点屠宰厂（场）分级管理的必要性、可行性及实施效果，重点就定点屠宰企业分级级别的确定依据、分级管理实施可能产生的问题及对淘汰落后产能的作用进行了论证。姜增伟副部长强调，要严格落实《生猪定点屠宰管理条例》，做好生猪定点屠宰企业审核换证工作。在做好审核换证工作基础上，进一步完善《生猪定点屠宰厂（场）分级管理办法》，为开展生猪定点屠宰厂（场）分级做好准备。与会代表一致认为推行分级管理制度十分必要，当前要抓紧落实相关配套政策，逐步推进。

28 日　国家食品药品监督管理局和教育部在北京 101 中学联合举行“全国学校食堂食品安全专项整治行动推进会”。国家食品药品监督管理局副局长边振甲和教育部党组成员、部长助理林蕙青出席会议并讲话。国务院食品安全委员会办公室王小岩副司长出席会议。边振甲指出，学校食堂食品安全关系广大师生身心健康，关系社会和谐与稳定，关系国家和民族的未来。近年来，随着我国教育事业的快速发展，教育投入的不断加大，学校食堂无论从硬件改造还是软件建设上都有了显著进步，食品安全管理水平正在稳步提高。但由于我国经济社会发展不均衡，部分学校食堂食品安全风险意识不强，管理制度不健全，责任落实不到位，食品安全事件仍时有发生。边振甲强调：一是要切实加强组织领导，全面落实安全责任。各级食品药品监管部门要与各级教育行政部门密切配合，坚持统筹规划、科学安排、突出重点、综合治理的原则，把集中整治与日常监管、食堂自律与强化监管、全面推进与重点突破有机结合，将宣传教育贯穿始终，完善制度贯穿始终，落实责任贯穿始终，检查指导贯穿始终，确保学校食堂食品安全整治扎实推进。要坚持“地方政府负总责、监管部门各负其责、学校是食堂食品安全第一责任人”的责任要求，积极推动地方各级政府加大对学校食堂食品安全工作的投入，严格规范学校食堂餐饮服务许可，切实加强学校食堂日常监管。二是要认真排查安全隐患，及时堵塞管理漏洞。各类学校要围绕突出问题和薄弱环节，认真组织开展八个方面的严查，及时堵塞管理漏洞，不留盲点、不留死角，同时鼓励各类学校食堂采用先进的管理技术和管理方法，不断提高食品安全水平。三是要广泛开展教育培训，推进示范工程建设。要加强食堂食品安全培训，组织从业人员学习《食品安全法》及其实施条例、《餐饮服务许可管理办法》和《餐饮服务食品安全监督管理办法》以及学校食堂食品安全管理制度，不断提高食品安全责任意识和法治意识。同时，要在各地高等院校、中小学和托幼机构创建一批食品安全示范学校，充分发挥示范学校食堂的引领和辐射作用，促进全国学校食堂食品安全水平的稳步提高。四是要加大监督检查力度，确保整治取得实效。在各级各类学校全面自查的基础上，加大对专项整治工作的监督检查，尤其要对农村学校食堂、托幼机构食堂、量化分级等级较低的学校食堂、日常检查发现安全隐患较多的学校食堂，加大监督检查力度，确保整治工作取得实效。林蕙青结合教育工作实际，提出整治工作要求。各地教育行政部门、各类学校，要将本次专项整治工作与学习贯彻《食品安全法》及其实施条例结合起来，进一步增强法治观念，增强食品安全意识，依法完善食品安全管理制度，落实食品安全管理责任，规范加工制作行为，防控食物中毒事件发生，使学校食堂食品安全保障水平得到显著提高。要结合本地区实际，抓住存在的突出问题和薄弱环节，尽快提出本地本校的具体整治任务，制定操作性强的工作方案，增强整治行动方案的执行力，提高有效性。对每一所学校食品安全工作的每一个环节都要进行拉网式排查，认真做好检查记录，不放过、不漏过每一环节，每一处隐患。对排查发现的每一处安全隐患进行登记，并采取有效措施尽快解决。各地教育行政部门要会同食品药品监管部门组织力量对学校自查情况进行复查复核，检查中发现的违法行为要坚决予以处理，不符合规定的要限期整改，整改情况要进行跟踪检查，做到边检查、边总结、边整改、边落实。各地各级教育行政部门和学校必须以高度负责的精神，加强对本次专项整治行动的组织领导，要把专项整治列入重要议事日程。教育行政部门主要负责人和学校校长要亲自过问，分管负责人要直接抓，落实以校长为第一责任人的学校食堂食品安全责任制；落实食品安全岗位管理制度；建立完善从业人员健康档案管理制度；建立落实从业人员食品安全知识和技能培训制度；建立落实承包经营学校食堂的规范管理制度；完善落实食物中毒事故信息报告制度及责任追究制度。

6月

11日 “2010中国食品安全高层论坛”在京举行。国务院食品安全委员会办公室主任张勇出席论坛并讲话，工业和信息化部、农业部、商务部、卫生部、国家工商总局、国家质检总局、国家食品药品监管局等部门领导同志出席论坛并致辞。张勇指出，食品行业诚信自律是保障食品安全的重要基础，要通过规范食品生产经营活动和提高质量安全控制水平，来提升我国食品安全水平。促进食品企业诚信守法，提高食品质量安全水平，必须做到以下几点：一是完善各项规章制度，使企业诚信经营有据可依。有关部门依据《食品安全法》正在清理修订现有规章制度，制定配套法规规章，并加强食品安全标准体系建设，以尽快解决目前标准缺失、重复和矛盾问题，为企业按照统一标准组织生产经营活动提供依据。二是加大整顿治理力度，为企业诚信守法提供良好的市场环境。有关部门将继续严厉打击违法违规行为，坚决取缔无证照、无资质生产经营单位，为守法企业、优质产品保驾护航，使违法企业、假冒伪劣产品无立足之地。三是建立健全激励约束机制，提高企业诚信建设的自觉性。有关部门正在深入推进食品行业诚信体系建设试点工作，加快诚信信息征集和披露体系建设，建立企业诚信评价制度。这尤其需要新闻界一方面加强舆论监督，另一方面做好宣传引导，促使企业诚信守法，履行社会责任。四是研究完善扶持政策，为企业诚信经营创造良好的政策环境。国务院食品安全办将和有关部门一起，进一步研究制定有关规划和政策措施，加大扶持力度，促进食品产业转变发展方式，不断提高食品安全生产经营规模化、集约化水平，提升质量安全管理能力，从源头上消除安全隐患。

21～22日 农业部农产品加工局在辽宁省朝阳市举办“农产品加工技术对接活动”。农业部农产品加工局张天佐局长、王秀忠副局长、农业部规划设计研究院崔明副院长、辽宁省农村经济委员会刘长江主任、朝阳市政府张铁民市长出席活动。来自辽宁省

14个市县的300多名农产品加工企业代表参加了此次活动。张天佐局长作了重要讲话，讲话首先强调了加快发展农产品加工业对于解决我国“三农”问题的重要作用。同时指出解决农产品加工企业的技术瓶颈，提升产业技术水平是促进我国农产品加工业发展的必要手段。随后介绍了农业部在农产品加工技术研发体系建设、农产品加工技术推广等方面的工作进展。最后他指出此次农产品加工技术对接活动，针对辽宁省的农产品资源优势，一定能为农产品加工企业和相关科研单位建立一个“产学研”合作平台，解决加工企业技术创新力量不足问题，加速科研单位、大专院校科研成果的转化。针对辽宁省农产品加工业的特色及优势，活动设立粮油加工、果蔬加工、畜产品加工、水产品加工4个分会场。邀请8位相关农产品加工行业知名专家在分会场做主题报告。各位专家从相关行业技术发展趋势、行业发展建议等方面展开讲座，既有宏观层面的全行业技术发展现状，又结合微观加工企业实际，参会企业开拓了眼界、提高了认识。

28日 农业部和河南省人民政府在驻马店市联合召开了“2010年全国农产品加工业投资贸易洽谈会”，全国政协副主席陈宗兴出席大会并宣布大会开幕，农业部副部长高鸿宾致辞。高鸿宾副部长在致辞中指出，举办农产品加工业经贸洽谈会，是农业部落实国家西部大开发和中部崛起战略的重要举措，为推进我国乡镇企业和农产品加工业结构调整、产业转移和区域协调发展做出了积极的贡献。2010年的会议以“开放合作、互利共赢、科学发展”为主题，以项目合作、技术成果转化和展示展销为主要任务，着力打造我国农产品加工业合作交流和投资贸易一流平台，全面提升我国农产品加工业发展水平。河南是我国农业大省，也是农产品加工业强省。经过多年发展提升，全省农业基础更加稳固、结构不断优化，农业规模化、标准化、专业化、产业化发展势头强劲，农产品加工业发展迅猛，培育了一大批知名企业和名牌产品。高鸿宾强调，2010年是“十一五”收官之年，也是谋划“十二五”发展规划的关键之年，农产品加工业面临新的机遇和挑战。各级农业部门要坚持以科学发展观为指导，进一步解放思想，理清思路，求真务实，科学规划，采取切实有效措施，加快推进农产品加工业转变发展方式，为农业和农村经济的持续协调发展作出更大的贡献。来自全国27个省（自治区、直辖市）的120个代表团、16 700多人及中储粮总公司、中国牧工商（集团）总公司、中国轻工业对外经济技术合作公司等4 500多个国内知名企业和来自英国、荷兰、日本、孟加拉等国客商参会。大会共设78个特装展位，230个标准展位和820个产品贸易展位，是历年参展规模最大、参展企业最多的一年。据悉，洽谈会重点签约项目157个，投资总额335.3亿元，其中亿元以上项目92个，项目涉及农副产品深加工、农业生态综合开发、种植养殖、农业资源综合利用等领域。洽谈会期间还举办了重点项目签约仪式、农产品加工科研成果转化项目发布会、产品评奖和大型文艺演出等丰富多彩的活动。会议期间，还举办了“农产品加工科研成果发布与合作洽谈活动”。该活动以解决农产品加工企业的技术难题和需求为目标，以搭建农产品加工业科研成果转化平台为基础，加强构建大专院校、科研院所与农产品加工企业的科技合作为对接桥梁，进一步增强企业科技创新能力，促进农产品加工技术成果转化、推广和应用，成果转化涉及粮食制品、油料加工、畜禽及水产、果蔬加工、酒及饮品等行业。农业部高鸿宾副部长、河南省刘满仓副省长、农业部农产品加工局张天佐局长、卢永军副局长等领导参加了科研成果项目转化签字仪式。

7　月

1日 “全国饲料和生鲜乳质量安全监管工作会议”在广州召开，农业部副部长高鸿宾出席会议并讲话。公安部、监察部、商务部、卫生部、国家工商总局、国家质检总局等6部委的代表应邀出席了会议。各省（自治区、直辖市）畜牧饲料管理部门及新疆生产建设兵团畜牧兽医局、黑龙江农垦畜牧局分管饲料和生鲜乳质量安全的厅（局）长和处长参加了会议。会议由国家首席兽医师于康震主持。高鸿宾指出，目前饲料工业和畜牧业都处于转型提升的关键时期，各级畜牧饲料部门既要立足当前、突出重点，也要着眼长远、攻坚克难，全面加强饲料和生鲜乳质量安全监管工作。一是严格准入门槛，卡住不达标企业；二是强化日常监管，淘汰不合格企业；三是加强示范引导，提升一批企业；四是加大日常监督检查力度，严防不法收购站点反弹；五是督促已获证收购站继续改善条件，改进管理，提高水平；六是加强生鲜乳购销合同备案管理，规范生鲜乳收购行为；七是做好《生乳》国家标准的宣贯工作，严厉打击各种违禁添加行为。据介绍，目前奶站清理整顿工作已全面完成。全国现有奶站13 503个，比清理整顿前减少6 890个，减幅达34%，并且全部获得生鲜乳收购许可证。奶站机械化挤奶率达到87%，比清理整顿前提高36个百分点。2009年4月份以来，全国奶牛存栏稳步回升，年底达到1 219万头，全年牛奶产量3 554万t，乳制品企业利润总额是2008年的两倍多，100头以上奶牛规模养殖比例达到23.1%，比2008年底提高3.3个百分点，奶业基本恢复到婴幼儿奶粉事件之前的水平。饲料企业整合淘汰步伐明显加快，全国饲料生产企业数量减少近2 000个，年产50万t以上的饲料企业和企业集团达30个，其饲料产量占全国的比例达43%。2009年，饲料产品质量抽检合格率90.9%，同比提高2.3个百分点；饲料中三聚氰胺检测合格率99.3%，同比提高3.3个百分点。

13日 卫生部会同工业和信息化部等部门在京召开"乳品安全国家标准座谈会"。会议提出，在标准贯彻实施工作中，要始终坚持"三个依靠"：一要依靠广大食品生产经营单位讲诚信，落实食品安全主体责任，依法按照标准组织生产。二要依靠各级政府特别是政府的各基层监管部门进一步强化监管，严肃查处不符合标准的违法行为。三要依靠社会监督，广泛动员人民群众积极参与乳品安全工作，及时举报违法行为，曝光违法案件，营造人人参与的良好社会氛围。会议要求，认真做好以下工作：一是各级卫生行政部门要在前期宣传学习乳品安全国家标准的基础上，在2010年7月份集中宣传乳品安全国家标准，为标准的贯彻实施营造良好的舆论氛围。二是各级食品安全监管部门要按照乳品安全国家标准的实施时间，督促乳品生产经营者严格执行新的乳品标准，依法查处违法行为，并及时将实施情况和执行过程中存在的问题向当地卫生行政部门通报。三是各级卫生行政部门要依法加强食品安全标准的跟踪评估，积极探索建立跟踪评估的工作制度和机制，明确跟踪评估的重点和工作要求，有针对性地开展跟踪评估，并将跟踪评估情况向各相关部门通报，适时公布跟踪评估的结果。四是各级卫生行政部门要加强对食品安全标准工作体系建设，在组织机构、人员、设备和经费保障等方面加大投入力度，满足食品安全地方标准制定、企业标准备案、宣传培训、跟踪评价等各项工作需要，做好标准免费查阅工作。

16日 农业部农产品加工局在京组织召开了"我国部分农产品产地加工技术研讨会"。会议由农业部农产品加工局副局长王秀忠主持，局长张天佐、科教质量处处长杨泽钊等出席研讨会。张天佐局长首先就本次会议的由来、目的、内容、预期效果进行了全面阐述；随后，各位专家分别就我国西北地区马铃薯、苹果贮藏、果蔬干燥技术装备等情况，从产业现状、当前存在的问题，该地区该产业应用广泛、推广成效显著的技术设施与装备，论证其技术标准化与集成化的可行性等做了精彩的报告。通过互动交流形成了广泛的共识。张天佐局长最后指出，本次研讨会意义重大，成果显著。通过专家汇报与共同的讨论，对我国西北地区重点产业的贮藏加工技术装备现状有了较全面的了解，确定了农业部农产品加工局今后的一个工作重点。即本着设施装备简单实用、性价比高、能耗低让农民买得起、也用得起等原则，分区域、分产业筛选出真正适用于农民的技术和装备，在技术上实现标准化和规范化。通过国家财政资金的补贴大力推广，切实做到使农业增产增收、农民减损增效的目的，开创我部农产品产地加工与贮藏工作的新局面。

8 月

1日 "全国食品药品监管工作座谈会"在浙江省宁波市召开。国家食品药品监管局党组书记、局长邵明立作了题为《坚定不移地树立和实践科学监管理念》的工作报告。邵明立强调，在目前深化食品药品监管体制改革的关键时刻，实践科学监管理念需要把握三个重要问题：一是坚持把确保公众饮食用药安全作为一切工作的出发点和落脚点。一切工作都必须立足"安全"，围绕"好字优先"，努力推动实现产业结构好、产品质量好、市场秩序好和监管自身发展好。坚持用强有力的"安全"保障，推动实现食品药品产业"又好又快"发展。不论什么时候，监管工作在经济社会发展中的定位不能变，必须把确保公众饮食用药安全作为最基本的标准，用它来评价监管工作的得失，确定监管工作的取舍。只有"严"，才会有"安全"，才能实现食品药品安全的长治久安。规范的企业不怕严，整治市场秩序需要严，广大人民群众盼望严。做不到"严"，就是对违规违法行为的放纵，就是对合法企业的伤害。因此，必须坚持"严"字当头，尽最大可能增加食品药品生产经营的违法违规成本，坚决反对以任何借口放松监管，坚决防范监管失之于宽、失之于软的倾向。二是坚持把依法行政作为实践科学监管理念的基本要求。食品药品监管系统实行分级管理体制之后，必须更加强调保持执法统一，维护系统权威。各级食品药品监管部门要增强大局意识、系统观念和法制精神，坚持"全国一盘棋"，做到法令统一，令行禁止。旗帜鲜明地反对自行其是，反对地方保护、市场分割，反对形形色色的不作为和乱作为。实行分级管理以后，要更加注重执法的公平公正，各级监管部门要做到知法善用、执法有度、普法为民。要努力提升执法的效能，积极探索科学高效的监管机制，充分发挥主观能动性，充分发挥基层首创精神。三是坚持把能力建设作为实践科学监管理念的基本保障。能力建设要把重点放到基层。监管的基础在基层，基础不牢，地动山摇。要支持基层监管工作，关心基层监管队伍，为那些想干事、能干事、干实事的地方提供更多政策和经费支持。能力建设要以科技为依托。技术和人才是能力建设的两翼，互为支撑，不可偏废。邵明立指出，这次大会之所以强调实践科学监管理念的若干重大问题，是因为全系统仍处于体制改革的关键时期，“十二五”规划编制的关键时期，深入推进医改的关键时期，也是强化队伍思想作风建设的关键时期。在这样的形势下，必须保证思想不动摇，工作不走样，要求不放松。要达到这样的目标，当务之急是自觉运用科学监管理念，去认识新形势，把握新机遇，破解新难题。

16 日 “国务院食品安全委员会全体会议”在京召开，国务院食品安全委员会主任李克强主持会议并讲话，国务院食品安全委员会副主任回良玉、王岐山出席会议并讲话。会上，国务院食品安全办、卫生部、农业部、国家质检总局、国家工商总局等有关部门负责同志作了汇报。李克强指出，随着人民生活水平提高，食品安全已成为关系群众健康和保护消费者权益的重要内容，成为维护改革发展稳定大局的重要任务。近年来，各地、各有关部门大力推进食品安全整顿工作，取得了一定效果。但要清醒地看到，食品安全涉及面广、情况复杂，解决这一问题需要下更大的力气，持之以恒地抓下去。他要求各地、各有关部门：一是对食品生产经营中的违法违规行为，要依法处置，并加大曝光力度；二是对食品监管中的失职渎职行为，要严肃追究有关负责人和监管人员的责任；三是对接连发生问题的地区，要追究政府有关负责人的责任；四是对乳品、食用油等重点产品、行业和环节，要强化整顿措施，并建立长效监管机制。据了解，目前我国有食品生产经营企业几百万个，每天生产加工的食品达 110 多万 t，企业质量安全管理和政府食品安全监管的任务十分繁重。为保障食品安全、维护人民群众身体健康，2009 年国务院决定在全国集中开展为期两年的食品安全整顿工作；2010 年国务院进一步明确了深入推进食品安全整顿工作的具体任务和责任分工。目前，食品安全整顿工作正在紧张有序进行。

18 日 国务院总理温家宝主持召开国务院常务会议，研究部署进一步促进蔬菜生产，保障市场供应和价格基本稳定。会议确定了六项政策措施：一是切实强化“菜篮子”市长负责制。制定完善蔬菜市场供应应急预案，建立蔬菜储备制度，确保重要的耐贮存蔬菜品种 5～7 天消费量的动态库存。二是加强蔬菜生产基地建设。支持蔬菜标准园创建工作，建立健全发展高产、高效、优质、安全的蔬菜产业约束机制和标准园质量安全检测及追溯机制。三是改善蔬菜流通设施条件。加快实施《农产品冷链物流发展规划》，加强产地蔬菜预冷设施、批发市场冷藏设施、大城市蔬菜低温配送中心建设。加快产地农产品批发市场建设，升级改造一批大型蔬菜批发市场，支持城市菜市场建设改造。四是落实和完善“绿色通道”政策。在全国范围内对整车合法装载运输鲜活农产品的车辆免收车辆通行费。五是提高蔬菜产销组织化程度。引导大型零售流通企业和学校、酒店等最终用户与产地蔬菜生产合作社、批发市场、龙头企业等直接对接，促进蔬菜产区和销区建立稳定的产销关系。六是强化蔬菜信息体系建设。抓紧建立覆盖主要蔬菜品种生产、流通、消费各个环节的信息监测、预警和发布制度，严肃查处捏造、散布虚假价格信息行为。会议要求各地区、各有关部门：一是要高度重视，加强督促指导，确保各项措施落到实处。二是要建立健全“菜篮子”市长负责制的考核评价体系。三是要在做好蔬菜生产供应的同时，统筹抓好肉蛋奶和水产品等“菜篮子”产品的生产供应。四是要支持菜地大棚、畜禽圈舍和池塘网箱等洪涝灾害损毁设施的修复重建，帮助尽快恢复生产。

9 月

21 日 “食品工业企业诚信体系建设工作第一次部门联席会议”在京召开。国家发展和改革委员会、科技部、人力资源和社会保障部、农业部、商务部、卫生部、人民银行、国家工商总局、国家质检总局、国家食品药品监管局、国家认监委、中国轻工业联合会、中国食品工业协会等 15 个部门和单位的领导参加了会议。国务院食品安全委员会办公室的领导应邀莅临会议。会议由工业和信息化部党组成员、总工程师朱宏任主持。会上通报了工业和信息化部会同有关部门推进食品工业企业诚信体系建设工作开展情况及下一步工作考虑；宣读了《食品工业企业诚信体系建设工作部门联席会议制度》；审议了《2010—2012 年食品工业企业诚信体系建设工作实施方案》。联席会议制度由工业和信息化部、国家发改委、科技部、财政部、人力资源社会保障部、农业部、商务部、卫生部、人民银行、国家工商总局、国家质检总局、国家食品药品监管局、国家认监委、中国轻工业联合会、中国食品工业协会等 15 个部门（单位）组成。联席会议制度作为部门协同工作的平台，主要职责是：负责组织推动食品工业企业诚信体系建设工作，审定年度工作计划，协调工作推进中的问题，研究提出相关措施建议等。参会部门原则同意《2010—2012 年食品工业企业诚信体系建设工作实施方案》，同时结合各部门职责讨论提出了修改意见。朱宏任在会议总结时指出：保障食品安全，是深入贯彻落实科学发展观、维护人民群众根本利益的必然要求。食品工业企业诚信体系建设是保障食品质量安全长效机制的重要内容，是食品安全的治本之策。食品工业企业诚信体系建设工作既是一项复杂、艰巨而又长期的任务，又是一项带有管理探索和机制创新的工作，需要充分发挥部门协同机制作用，要加强协作，合力推动；要抓住关键，加快推进；要依法行政，共享信息；要制定措施，惩戒激励。他建议：联席会议制度成员单位要在国务院食品安全委员会的领导下，携手并肩，共同努力，持之以恒，共同推动食品工业企业诚信体系建设工作的落实。

26日 “中国食品工业协会第六次全国会员代表大会”在北京举行。国务院领导发来贺信：食品工业是永恒产业，直接关乎亿万群众身心健康，在促进增长、增加就业、提高人民生活水平等方面具有重要作用。贺信中提出，希望中国食品工业协会深入贯彻落实科学发展观，加强行业自律，强化自身建设，提高服务水平；希望食品工业企业切实履行食品安全第一责任人的职责，严格依法经营，共同为促进我国食品产业健康发展、保障食品安全而持续努力，作出更大贡献。国务院食品安全委员会办公室张勇主任出席了会议，政协第十届全国委员会副主席、中国企业联合会和中国企业家协会会长王忠禹向大会发来贺信，大会由中国食品工业协会常务副会长刘治主持。会上，全国人大常委会委员、财经委主任委员石秀诗宣读了第八届全国人大常委会副委员长田纪云、第十届全国人大常委会副委员长顾秀莲、政协第九届全国委员会副主席陈锦华、原中顾委委员和中国食品工业协会名誉会长袁宝华等领导为本次大会所作的题词。国务院国资委副主任黄淑和在会上作了重要讲话。他指出，市场经济发展到今天，正是行业协会要发挥大作用的时候。在这种情况下，中国食品工业协会选举产生新一届理事会以后，在新一届理事会的带动和领导下，希望中国食品工业协会大显身手、大力作为，能够取得骄人的成绩。会上，中国食品工业协会第五届理事会会长王文哲向大会作了题为《实践科学发展观，坚持“三服务”方针，推动食品工业持续稳定发展》的工作报告。报告肯定了食品工业的持续、快速、健康发展，指出了我国食品工业目前存在的主要问题。报告中还对第五届理事会工作进行了全面回顾，并对新一届理事会及今后主要工作提出了建议。中国食品工业协会常务副会长刘治向大会做了《中国食品工业协会章程》的修改说明，第五届理事会秘书长沈篪向大会做了《关于调整会费标准的说明》并提请代表审议。出席本次大会的嘉宾还有国家发改委、工业和信息化部、农业部、商务部、卫生部、国家工商总局、国家质检总局、国家统计局、国家食品药品监督管理局等有关司局领导。来自中国食品工业协会和全国各省、自治区、直辖市及计划单列市的食品协会负责人、全国食品骨干企业代表300多人参加大会。

28日 国家认监委在北京召开了“全国食品农产品认证工作会议”。国家认监委副主任王大宁出席会议并讲话，来自地方质检部门、认可机构、认证认可协会、研究所及全体食品农产品认证机构的100多名代表参加了会议。王大宁副主任全面总结和回顾了认监委成立以来我国食品农产品认证认可事业发展历程和取得的成绩，分析了当前面临的形势，并对下一步工作进行了部署，指出食品农产品认证关系广大消费者利益，关系“三农”和食品产业健康发展，各相关部门和单位要以对人民群众身体健康高度负责的精神，以及深入贯彻落实科学发展观要求的高度，切实提高认证有效性。为确保认证有效性，不断提高认证食品农产品的质量水平，国家认监委在食品农产品认证监管方面将着重建立三个体系即，监管体系、责任体系和认证有效性验证体系；打造一个平台，即食品农产品认证推广平台。为保证这些目标的实现，国家认监委还将针对认证制度运行环节建立风险分析和风险预警机制，健全食品农产品认证标准规范体系，大力加强食品农产品认证信息化建设。王大宁副主任还要求各级质检部门、认可机构、认证认可协会要充分发挥我国“法律规范、行政监管、认可约束、行业自律、社会监督”五位一体的认证认可监督体系优势，建立监管联动机制，加强对有机产品认证活动的监管；各有机产品认证机构要本着高度负责的精神，严把认证质量关，牢固树立认证评价主体责任意识，严格遵守有机产品认证各项制度、规范和标准。会上，各食品农产品认证机构还签署了诚信宣言，郑重承诺以质量为生命，以诚信为根本，严格执行法律法规和认证规范规则，严把食品农产品认证质量关，恪守诚信，严格自律，自觉接受社会监督。

10 月

14～16日 “第十届中国国际粮油产品及设备技术展览会”在浙江宁波举办，来自国内28个省（自治区、直辖市）、计划单列市以及香港、意大利、瑞士、法国、英国等国家和地区的700余个粮油粮机企业参加了展会。展会共实现粮油产品交易总量100.59万t，交易金额38.57亿元。来自全国29个省、自治区、直辖市的60余名厅局级领导以及国内外5 000余名粮油粮机专业观众参观了展览，3天的展期累计共有5万人次参观了展览。开幕式由国家粮食局副局长张桂凤主持，国家粮食局副局长郄建伟代表国家粮食局在开幕式上致辞。郄建伟在致辞中说，十多年来，粮油展一届比一届办得好，一年比一年影响大，为连接产销、调剂余缺、搞活流通、活跃市场发挥了积极作用；为加快粮油产业发展，满足城乡居民粮油消费需求，普及绿色、营养、安全、健康的消费理念发挥了积极作用；为国内外粮油界同行交流经验，沟通信息，开拓市场，增进了解和友谊发挥了积极作用；为宣传推广行业新品牌、新技术、新理念，加快科技成果转化发挥了积极作用；为实现国内粮油市场顺畅流通，保障国家粮食安全，推动行业科学发展，发挥了积极作用，作出了重要贡献。2010年爱粮节粮公益展览、新疆粮食产业项目推介暨对口援疆签约会及首届粮库摄影比赛作品暨仓储规范化管理优秀企业图片展等活动也和展会同期举行。

21日 “商务部全国肉菜流通追溯体系建设试点工作会议”在上海召开。上海等第一批10个试点城市政府及商务、财政部门负责人以及大型肉类蔬菜批发市场的企业领导，各省、自治区、直辖市、计划单列市、新疆生产建设兵团以及石家庄等21个省会城市商务部门主要负责人等共200多人参加了会议。商务部陈德铭部长出席会议并讲话。此次会议是商务部在推动“菜篮子”和“放心肉”建设工作中，总结上海、青岛等部分城市的做法和经验的基础上，开展全国肉类蔬菜流通追溯体系建设试点的工作部署会。肉类蔬菜流通追溯体系建设试点的主要内容是以发展现代流通方式为基础，运用信息技术手段，实现肉菜商品流通的索证索票、购销台账的电子化，从而形成来源可追溯、去向可查证、责任可追究的质量安全追溯链条。主要目的是提高生产经营者的责任意识和保障能力；改善消费者预期，促进放心消费；支持和帮助地方更好的落实“菜篮子”市长负责制。这项工作得到了财政部的大力支持，中央财政专门安排资金用于支持追溯体系建设。2010年，商务部和财政部共同确定了大连、上海、南京、无锡、杭州、宁波、青岛、重庆、昆明、成都等10个城市作为试点。会上，商务部负责同志与10个试点城市政府负责同志签订了肉类蔬菜流通追溯体系建设试点协议书，陈德铭部长作了重要讲话。陈德铭表示，建设肉菜流通追溯体系，要以信息技术为手段，兼顾信息采集手段的多样性与内容的统一性；完善法规标准，加强市场准入管理；抓住蔬菜批发市场电子化统一结算、提高屠宰行业集中度两个关键环节，夯实流通基础。考虑到城市是商品肉菜的主要销区市场，流通基础设施相对比较完善，并具有“菜篮子”市长负责制的体制优势，追溯体系建设将从城市先行试点，逐步铺开。陈德铭指出，建设肉菜流通追溯体系，是一项民心工程，有利于提高肉菜质量安全水平，保障和改善民生，促进明白放心消费；有利于完善和落实索证索票和台账管理等制度，为监管部门提高执法监管效率创造条件，增强食品安全保障能力；有利于利用物联网等信息技术，改变农产品落后的流通方式，更好的发挥市场和消费对农业生产的引导作用，促进肉菜生产流通的包装化、标准化、品牌化，推动我国农产品进入国际市场，帮助农民增收。希望各试点城市把追溯体系建设作为“一把手”工程全力推进，进一步完善落实试点工作方案，大力推进现代流通体系建设，坚持政府推动与市场化运作相结合，调动各方的积极性。

29日 “中国乳制品工业协会第四届理事会理事长扩大会议”在京举行，协会所属18家副理事长单位全部参加会议，此外还有部分常务理事、地方协会等共30余人出席了会议。工信部消费品工业司食品处巡视员郭翔出席会议。会议由理事长宋昆冈主持。宋昆冈首先阐述召开此次会议的目的和意义。他指出，此次会议的主要议题就是加强行业自律、规范企业行为、创造和谐发展的环境。他说，乳业近些年来一直处于超常规速度发展阶段，积累了很多问题。虽然三聚氰胺爆发之后，一些不规范的现象得到了遏制，问题得到了初步解决，但是并没有完全好转，特别是在行业竞争方面的企业行为，在市场竞争中有许多不规范的地方。宋理事长指出，行业不规范竞争主要表现在两个方面：一是奶源方面。两年前引发的三聚氰胺事件，奶源大战是罪魁祸首，在事件之后企业有所自律，但是随着市场的恢复，奶源竞争的无序又有所抬头，导致奶价大幅度提升，在国际和国内市场都失去竞争力。奶源无序的结果是奶价提升、质量下降，给行业造成了巨大的危机和隐患。二是在市场秩序方面，2010年以来许多企业开发了新的产品，但是企业的传统产品在市场上的竞争仍然十分激烈，价格的大战，广告宣传的大战尤为突出，导致一方面奶源提价，一方面销售降价，企业利润不容乐观，这些都与行业不规范的行为和恶性竞争都有巨大的关系。宋理事长还说，早在2001年中国乳制品工业协会就发布了乳制品行业职业道德规范，2004年发布了乳制品市场竞争规范，但是对企业来说约束力不强，协会在这方面工作也不到位。宋理事长指出，行业不规范的竞争一直都严重影响着行业的正常发展，导致最近发生的恶意中伤事件，影响非常恶劣和巨大，在国内和国际都造成了严重的后果，国内外媒体大幅度进行报道。宋昆冈理事长在现场分别宣读了《京华时报》、《时代周刊》和《香港华联早报》等著名的媒体对于此次事件的评论，可以看到中国乳业确实处于一个高度关注的时刻，任何小的事件都有可能引发行业的危机。所以就需要建立行业公约，大家共同遵守，企业加强自律。中国乳制品工业协会秘书长刘美菊在会上宣读了《中国乳制品工业协会行业公约》（讨论稿），与会代表对《公约》进行了热烈的讨论，并对其内容进行了认真的修改和补充。三元、圣元、佳宝、雀巢和得益等企业负责人对当前行业的不正当竞争行为给予严厉的谴责，指出大企业要负大责任，不仅产品销售的好，在企业文化建设、在遵守行规行约等方面都要起模范带头作用。与会者一致认为，《公约》制定非常必要，但是公约的执行需要制度和法制的保障。同时行业协会和政府有关部门也应对《公约》的执行起到监督管理作用，对不遵守《公约》的企业，应予以通报批评，必要时通过媒体的力量对不合法的行为进行曝光，以促进企业的自律。

11 月

3～5日 “中国食品科学技术学会第七届年会”在北京召开。本次年会以“反思、前瞻与发展”为主题，是中国食品科技界的重要交流，国内25个食品科研院所、62个食品高校、58个食品企业、29个其他相关行业的领导及国外食品界专家共400多人参加了会议。国家发展改革委产业协调司贺燕丽副司长出席了会议并致辞。她指出，中国食品工业在过去几年中获得了快速发展，取得了令人瞩目的成就，成为国民经济发展中的重要力量。“十二五”期间，随着城市化进程的加快，食品工业仍将继续保持稳步增长，但发展方式将面临重要调整：食品安全将越来越得到社会的重视，食品工业对科技的依赖将进一步加大，食品企业将加强全产业链建设。在致辞中，她充分肯定了食品科学技术学会在我国食品工业“十二五”发展战略研究及政策制定中发挥的重要作用。本次会议举行了2010年食品界最隆重的颁奖活动—2010年度中国食品科学技术学会科技创新奖的颁奖仪式。本届年会开启了中日食品科技界大规模交流的序幕，两国专家学者、企业科研负责人，首次在年会的平台上进行了交流，来自日本企业界的代表，结合各自企业发展特点，与中国同行分享成功经验。会议还举行了“中国食品科技学会第三届研究生论坛”、“食品科研院所新时期发展论坛”、“科技与企业对接论坛”、“中日食品研讨会”、“食品安全与检测”、“食品营养与健康评价”、“新产品与新技术”等专题论坛与学术研讨会，吸引了各地食品工作者共同探讨我国食品产业发展之路。

4日 “中国食品科学技术学会食品机械分会第二届理事会成立大会”在北京召开，会议选举产生了中国食品科学技术学会食品机械分会第二届理事会，中国农业机械化科学研究院院长李树君当选为理事长，中国包装和食品机械总公司总经理李子明、中国食品科学技术学会副秘书长郭勇等8人当选为副理事长，中国食品和包装机械工业协会秘书长楚玉峰当选为秘书长，大会代表就机械分会今后的工作进行了热烈的讨论。食品机械是食品科技得以发展的重要载体和保障，中国食品科学技术学会一直注重发挥食品机械在食品产业发展中的重要功能。新当选的中国食品科学技术学会食品机械分会第二届理事会理事长李树君指出，食品机械工业是食品工业发展的重要物质和技术支撑，是为食品工业提供技术装备的重要产业，是高科技食品制造的载体，是食物安全的重要保证，它肩负着拉动农产品增值、促进农民增收和食品工业产业升级的重要使命，对食品工业的发展、加速农村工业化进程发挥着举足轻重的作用。李树君理事长分析，从2000年到2009年，食品和包装机械工业的发展一直呈现良好的发展态势，产品销售收入直线上升，每年以平均18%的增长率递增，到2009年达到1484亿元。同时在国家政策的引导和支持下，食品机械科学技术领域的研究取得了丰硕成果，一些成果已经在产业发展中获得了应用，并取得较好的经济效益。但是，我们还必须清醒地认识到，我国食品机械行业发展还存在很多的不足。基础工业薄弱、先进设计方法和机加工手段的匮乏影响了产品质量；科研水平低下、科研投入不足、科研结构不合理、科研人员力量薄弱影响了食品机械行业的创新能力；低水平重复建设、标准国际化程度低、品牌意识薄弱、国际化进程缓慢、管理水平低下等依然是制约食品机械行业发展的主要瓶颈。李树君理事长指出，“十二五”期间，随着中央和各级政府的高度重视和支持、13多亿人口食品工业市场需求的拉动、国民经济和社会发展的需求以及人民生活水平的提高，需要大量高质量、高水平食品机械的快速发展。为顺应时代发展和社会发展的需求，食品机械行业需要加强食品机械专业人才的引进和培养；加强共性关键技术的研究开发；加强重大成套装备研究开发；加强食品工程信息化技术研究开发；加强食品和包装机械标准与检测技术研究；加强食品安全与溯源技术装备研究开发；推进产学研战略联盟的构建；同时还需要加强构建国际合作研发和交流平台。大力发展我国食品机械工业，将先进的食品科学技术和装备制造技术有机结合，是实现我国食品工业自动化、智能化与现代化，提升食品工业整体水平和国际竞争力的必由之路。

23日 中国食品和包装机械工业协会在京组织召开了“中国食品和包装机械行业‘十二五’发展规划专家座谈会”。来自全国各地的骨干企业、大专院校和科研院所的代表出席了会议。在中国食品和包装机械工业协会秘书长楚玉峰的主持下，专家们围绕食品和包装机械行业国内外发展现状、行业存在的主要问题、行业发展环境、发展思路、发展重点、发展目标等进行了探讨，同时对食品和包装机械行业未来5年该发展什么和不该发展什么提出了建议。会上，中国食品和包装机械工业协会李树君理事长指出，讨论“十二五”规划要以科学发展观为指导思想，围绕转变发展方式、创新发展模式的总体要求，从实际出发，真实反映行业“十二五”发展时期的重点、难点及关键性问题，提出我国食品和包装机械行业“十二五”发展规划的思路，努力提高规划的战略性、前瞻性、指导性、针对性和可行性。就目前行业的发展看，食品和包装机械行业技术进步比较慢，自动化、智能化成套设备研发速度跟不上欧美等发达国家，直接影响我国食品的安全性和科技进步，在一定程度上成为我国食品工业发展的制约因素。在专家发言中，多位专家都提出我国食品和包装机械的标准化工作需要加强。实践证明，没有高标准，就没有高品质产品，就没有大品牌。当前应该按照市场发展需求，完善食品和包装机械基础标准、方法标准、安全标准、卫生标准、管理标准等，提升产品标准数量和质量。另一方面，要积极采用国外先进标准，在科学研究和新产品设计中，鼓励采用ISO系列标准、EN系列标准以及发达国家的先进标准，推进食品和包装机械更多的技术装备符合安全卫生、节能减排、环境保护等国际惯例。此外，还要加强先进标准的实施和推广力度，筛选对企业的技术和产品有重要提升作用的标准，通过培训班、技术讲座等形式组织企业进行宣贯，以提升企业的科研水平和产品的技术含量。参加此次座谈会的专家大都围绕食品和包装机械行业“十二五”发展规划中应该优先发展的内容提出了宝贵的意见和建议。

12月

8日 “中国包装联合会七届四次理事会”在海南召开。来自全国各地包装理事单位的企业家、地方协会负责人，以及特邀的地方政府领导，相关行业的专家、学者近800人出席了会议。世界包装组织主席基斯·皮尔森也应邀出席理事会并致辞。本次会议是在全党、全国认真贯彻五中全会精神的热烈气氛中，在“十一五”与“十二五”规划交替的关键时刻，在中国包装联合会创立三十周年之际，召开的一次继往开来、总结提高、把握机遇、动员奋进的重要会议。会议意义深远、内容丰富充实，是我国包装行业2010年的一次盛会。世界包装组织副主席、亚洲包装联合会主席、中国包装联合会会长石万鹏在会上做了重要讲话。他指出，最近召开的党的十七届五中全会，全面总结了“十一五”时期我国经济社会发展的巨大成就和宝贵经验，科学分析了当前和今后一个时期面临的新形势、新机遇、新挑战，明确提出了未来5年我国经济社会发展的指导方针、奋斗目标、主要任务和重大举措，对于全党全国继续抓住和用好发展的重要战略机遇期，促进经济长期平稳较快发展，夺取全面建设小康社会新胜利，推进中国特色社会主义事业，具有十分重要的意义。他提出，结合我国包装行业实际，认真贯彻五中全会精神、着力推进行业转型发展需要做好以下四个方面的工作：一是认清国家发展新形势，把握包装行业新定位。二是紧扣主题主线新目标，攀登“五个发展”新高地。三是制定行业发展新规划，迈向包装强国新里程。四是适应政府职能新转变，开拓协会工作新局面。石会长强调，每位包装行业的企业家和工作者，必须要齐心协力，以党的十七届五中全会精神为指针，沿着国家“十二五”规划铺设的金光大道奋力前进，为高水平地实现包装强国的战略目标谱写新的光辉篇章。在理事会上，中国包装联合会常务副会长兼秘书长葛江河作了题为《继往开来，再创辉煌，为建设包装强国而努力奋斗》的工作报告。报告简要回顾了中国包装联合会成立三十年来的光辉历程，概述了联合会在“十一五”时期所取得的突出成绩，并总结了振兴包装行业的经验和体会。理事会还依照《中国包装联合会章程》的有关规定，调整、增补了一批理事和常务理事，同时举行了2010中国包装颁奖盛典；举办了2010中国包装科技成果展、2010中国包装文化艺术展、中国包装企业投融资战略论坛。中国包联金属容器委员会、包装教育委员会也同期召开了工作会议。海南省人民政府召开了“海南包装产业发展座谈会”。在理事会上，包装业界精英为夺取“十二五”包装工业新胜利，一致倡议发布了“全面贯彻科学发展的理念，努力开拓绿色发展的道路，坚持实施创新发展的战略，积极打造循环发展的模式，自觉恪守和谐发展的责任，为建设包装强国与和谐社会而奋斗”的中国包装行业《博鳌宣言》，表达了全国包装行业追求行业健康和谐和可持续发展的共同企盼。这次会议内容丰富、意义重大，必将为我国包装行业“十二五”时期的更好更快发展，产生积极而深远的影响。

9 日 工业和信息化部与黑龙江省人民政府共同召开了“食品工业企业诚信体系建设试点工作阶段总结暨黑龙江省现场交流会”。工业和信息化部党组成员、总工程师朱宏任出席会议并讲话。朱宏任同志回顾了一年多来工信部会同相关部门落实国务院对食品安全工作的部署，大力推进食品工业企业诚信体系建设开展的主要工作。一是建立工作机制，大力开拓食品企业诚信建设新局面。10 部门联合印发了《食品工业企业诚信体系建设工作指导意见》，15 部门（单位）共同建立了部门联席会议制度，初步形成协同指导和推动诚信体系建设落实的工作机制。二是制订工作方案，扎实推动食品企业诚信建设有序展开。制订并下发了《食品工业企业诚信体系建设工作实施方案》，把 3 年中要开展的诚信建设工作重点归纳为 8 个方面，细化为 48 条具体任务，分解到部门（单位），提出了工作进度要求。三是加强制度建设，积极拟定食品企业诚信建设规范标准。发布了两项诚信管理行业标准，组织编写了乳制品和肉类食品生产企业实施指南两本培训教材。四是推动试点工作，积极探索食品企业诚信建设正确路径。选择黑龙江省乳制品行业、河南省肉类加工行业作为第一批试点省份和试点行业。研究试点方案，组织专家对试点企业开展培训和指导。五是采取配套措施，努力提供食品企业诚信建设保障条件。实施国家重点技术改造专项；安排中小企业专项资金支持地方诚信信息平台建设，开展了全国食品工业企业诚信信息平台建设前期工作。六是积极宣传引导，大力营造食品企业诚信建设社会舆论环境。组织中央电视台、新华社、经济日报、中国工业报等媒体开展了诚信建设相关宣传。朱宏任要求，要按照国务院食安委的工作部署，继续加大工作力度，进一步全面推进食品工业企业诚信体系建设。一是确立工作目标。2011 年要重点指导一批试点企业建立诚信管理体系；组织一批企业开展诚信管理体系认证试点；在所有婴幼儿配方乳粉生产企业全面建立诚信管理体系；在北京、河北、福建、广东等 4 省、直辖市分别选择调味品、葡萄酒、罐头和饮料等行业开展诚信试点；继续支持地方公共服务平台建设。二是制订工作计划。黑龙江、河南省要进一步总结试点工作，提炼出可供借鉴推广的经验；北京、河北、福建、广东等 4 省、直辖市要抓紧制定本地区食品企业诚信建设实施方案；其他地区要结合本地实际，尽快制订推进食品企业诚信建设工作计划。三是加强工作指导。充分发挥部门联席会议制度作用，加强对地方工作的指导。四是开展培训交流。继续组织开展对诚信建设两项标准的培训，加大标准宣贯力度；总结推广地方、企业工作中的好做法和经验，组织开展企业诚信建设工作交流。五是夯实工作基础。组织制定《食品工业企业诚信信息征集与披露管理办法》；组织编写调味品、葡萄酒、罐头和饮料等重点行业诚信管理标准实施指南；研究制定诚信激励惩戒措施；进一步抓好乳品行业清理整顿工作。六是加强诚信宣传。继续大力营造诚信建设的舆论氛围，开展诚信建设主题宣传，巩固社会舆论监督的成果。国务院食品安全办公室有关负责同志到会指导。国家发展和改革委员会、农业部、商务部、卫生部、人民银行、国家工商总局、国家认监委、中国轻工业联合会、中国食品工业协会等食品工业企业诚信体系建设工作部门联席会议成员单位负责同志，部内有关司局同志，中国乳制品工业协会、中国肉类协会等行业协会负责人，31 个省（自治区、直辖市）、新疆生产建设兵团工业和信息化主管部门负责同志以及食品工业企业代表等近 300 人参加了会议。中央电视台、中央人民广播电台、新华社、经济日报社、光明日报社、中国工业报社等媒体记者参加了会议。

23 日 “全国乡镇企业与农产品加工业工作会议”在北京召开，提出了以加快转变经济发展方式为主线，推动乡镇企业和农产品加工业科学发展的工作思路。农产品加工业以“优化布局、创新发展”为核心，继续做大做强。2010 年我国规模以上农产品加工业产值预计突破 10 万亿元，比“十五”末增长约 1.5 倍。加工产值与农业产值比例从“十五”末的 1.1∶1 提高到 1.6∶1。企业从业者达 2 500 多万人，吸纳农村劳动力 1 500 万人以上，数万个领军企业按照公司加农户、龙头带基地等多种形式，建设了一大批规模化、标准化、专业化农产品生产基地，辐射带动 1 亿多农户。展望“十二五”时期，会议认为随着经济全球化深入发展，国际产业分工将进一步细化，科技创新孕育更多的突破，我国经济社会发展呈现新的阶段性特征，农村二三产业发展既面临难得机遇，也面对新的挑战。从机遇看，国家出台了加强宏观调控、扩大国内需求和强农惠农等一系列政策，加大了国民收入分配的调整力度，实施了区域发展战略、放宽了中小企业、民营经济的市场准入限制，为农村二三产业发展提供了政策推力；全球经济逐步回暖，出口恢复性增长，农业农村经济持续发展，农民收入稳步增加。这些都为农村二三产业的发展提供了巨大的市场空间。从挑战看，则是环境资源约束增强，严格的节能减排指标，要求农村工业特别是低端制造业必须调整提升；融资、用地、能源等生产要素供给趋紧，企业缺资金、缺技术、缺人才的问题尤为突出，生产成本上升的压力增大；后金融危机时期，国际贸易的不确定性反而增多，受汇率波动和贸易保护主义抬头等因素影响，产品出口难度加大。会议认为，“十二五”时期既是农村二三产业大有作为的重要战略机遇期，也是转型提升、创新发展的攻坚克难期。在这一大背景下，加快转变经济发展方式，就成为有效应对挑战、增强市场竞争力，突破资源环境约束、实现可持续发展的必由之路。“十二五”期间，农产品加工业产值翻一番，与农业产值比例达到2.2∶1。

第七部分 附　录

附录简要说明

1. 本部分统计资料数据主要包括：香港、澳门特别行政区和台湾省相关统计数据；世界和部分国家主要农产品收获面积、单产和总产量；禽畜产品产量；主要国家农业与农产品加工业生产指数；农产品加工业主要经济指标；世界主要国家农、林、畜、禽产品进出口情况；按营业额排序的世界最大500个企业中农产品加工业企业。

2. 本部分统计资料数据主要来源于国家统计局、农业部、2009年联合国粮农组织数据库、2009年联合国工发组织出版的《国际工业统计年鉴》、2010年版《国际统计年鉴》、世界银行统计数据。未注明“资料来源”的数据，均采用国家统计局公布的数据。

3. 本部分统计资料中符号使用说明：“空格”表示该项统计指标数据不详或无该项数据；“*”、“①”、“△”表示本表下面有注解。

表 1 部分国家（地区）农业生产指数（2007 年）

（1999—2001 年＝100）

国家或地区	农 业	食 品
世界总计	**115.0**	**114.0**
埃 及	115.0	116.0
南 非	107.0	109.0
加拿大	107.0	107.0
美 国	107.0	108.0
巴 西	132.0	131.0
中 国[①]	122.0	122.0
印 度	121.0	119.0
日 本	98.0	98.0
韩 国	96.0	97.0
法 国	92.0	92.0
德 国	96.0	96.0
意大利	94.0	94.0
俄罗斯	118.0	118.0
英 国	94.0	94.0
澳大利亚	75.0	79.0

资料来源：表中数据出自 2010 年版《中国统计年鉴》。

表 2 我国台湾省农业生产指数（2006—2008 年）

（2006 年＝100）

年 份	总指数	种植业	林 业	畜牧业	渔 业
2006	100.0	100.0	100.0	100.0	100.0
2007	97.5	93.5	68.5	97.6	105.1
2008	92.5	93.0	63.4	92.7	91.4

表 3 部分国家（地区）主要粮食作物总产量（2009 年）

单位：kt

国家或地区	小麦	稻谷	玉米	谷子	高粱
世界总计	**689 945**	**685 013**	**822 713**	**35 651**	**65 534**
埃 及		7 253			
南 非			11 597		
加拿大	28 611		10 592		11 998
美 国	68 026	9 240	307 384	337	1 966
巴 西		12 100	59 018		2 503
中 国	112 463	193 354	166 035	1 801	7 926
印 度	78 570	148 260	19 290	11 340	
日 本		11 029			
韩 国		6 919			
法 国	39 002		15 819		
德 国	25 989				
意大利	8 855		9 491		
俄罗斯	63 756		71	711	
英 国	17 227				
澳大利亚	21 397				3 072

资料来源：表中数据出自 2010 年版《世界农业》杂志第 8 期和 2009 年版《农业展望》杂志第 4 期。

表 4　2007/2008—2009/2010 年度世界粮食生产、消费、贸易、库存情况

单位：百万 t

世界粮食生产情况				
品　种	2007/2008 年度	2008/2009 年度	2009/2010 年度	同比增长（%）
粮食合计	**2 148.6**	**2 281.2**	**2 234.2**	**−2.10**
其中：小麦	625.5	681.4	678.0	−0.50
粗粮	1 081.9	1 140.7	1 107.0	−2.90
大米	441.2	459.1	448.6	−2.30
世界粮食消费情况				
品　种	2007/2008 年度	2008/2009 年度	2009/2010 年度	同比增长（%）
粮食合计	**2 156.3**	**2 186.9**	**2 224.7**	**1.70**
其中：小麦	644.9	647.8	665.5	2.70
粗粮	1 074.8	1 093.1	1 107.9	1.40
大米	436.6	446.0	451.3	1.20
世界粮食贸易情况				
品　种	2007/2008 年度	2008/2009 年度	2009/2010 年度	同比增长（%）
粮食合计	**273.0**	**283.3**	**258.1**	**−8.90**
其中：小麦	112.1	139.1	115.5	−17.00
粗粮	130.8	113.7	112.0	−1.50
大米	30.1	30.5	30.6	−0.50
世界粮食库存情况				
品　种	2007/2008 年度	2008/2009 年度	2009/2010 年度	同比增长（%）
粮食合计	**426.7**	**505.1**	**509.1**	**0.80**
其中：小麦	143.3	172.3	182.8	6.10
粗粮	172.6	208.7	205.0	−1.80
大米	110.8	124.1	121.3	−2.20

资料来源：表中数据出自于 2010 年版《世界农业》杂志第 7 期。

表 5　世界植物油年均生产、贸易状况（2005/2006—2009/2010 年度）

单位：万 t

植物油品种	生产量	出口量	进口量
植物油（总计）	**12 747**	**5 241**	**5 045**
棕榈油	4 031	3 131	307
大豆油	3 639	996	945
菜籽油	1 899	212	209
葵花籽油	1 085	400	339
4 种植物油小计	10 654	4 739	4 564
4 种植物油所占比率（%）	84	90	90

资料来源：表中数据出自于 2010 年版《中国油脂》杂志第 8 期。

表 6　部分国家（地区）主要油料作物总产量（2009 年）

单位：kt

国家或地区	大　豆	油菜籽	花　生	芝　麻
世界总计	**230 953**	**57 856**	**38 201**	**3 603**
埃　及	39		209	37
南　非	323	32	85	
加拿大	3 336	12 643		
美　国	80 536	660	2 335	
巴　西	59 917	170	297	16
中　国	15 545	12 102	14 341	586
印　度	9 045	5 833	7 228	666
日　本	227			
韩　国	133			18
法　国	63	4 719		
德　国		5 155		
意大利	346	33		
俄罗斯	746	752		
英　国		1 973		
澳大利亚	35	1 615		

资料来源：表中数据出自 2010 年版《国际统计年鉴》。

表 7　美国主要农作物收获面积、单产、总产量（2005—2009 年）

单位：万 hm^2、t/hm^2、万 t

年份	项目	玉米	高粱	棉花	小麦	大麦	大豆	燕麦	水稻
2005	收获面积	3 041	636	548	2028	132	2885	74	136
	单产	9.28	4.30	0.93	2.63	4.60	2.88	2.68	7.42
	总产	28 200	998	324	5 729	538	8 315	198	1 011
2006	收获面积	2 860	559	502	1 895	119	3 020	63	114
	单产	9.35	3.52	0.90	2.42	3.83	2.87	2.54	7.73
	总产	26 700	703	207	4 925	458	8 663	161	883
2007	收获面积	3 503	623	413	2 065	142	2 579	61	111
	单产	9.45	4.59	0.97	2.52	3.76	2.79	2.55	8.09
	总产	33 100	1 264	161	5 587	534	7 255	156	900
2008	收获面积	3 184	586	307	2 255	153	3 022	57	120
	单产	9.65	4.08	0.93	2.82	3.99	2.65	2.71	7.67
	总产	30 700	1 200	236	0 807	610	8 019	153	924
2009	收获面积	3 210	559	313	2 019	126	3 079	56	127
	单产	10.22	4.01	0.88	2.78	4.58	2.94	2.87	7.94
	总产	32 800	924	229	6 036	577	9 084	160	997

资料来源：表中数据出自 2010 年版《世界农业》杂志第 6 期。

表 8 世界植物油主要国家（地区）年均生产、贸易状况

世界棕榈油主要国家年均生产贸易状况（2005/2006—2009/2010 年度）

国 家	生产量（万 t）	国 家	出口量（万 t）	国 家	进口量（万 t）
世界总计	**4 031**	**世界总计**	**3 131**	**世界总计**	**3 071**
印度尼西亚	1 808	马来西亚	1 445	中 国	555
马来西亚	1 682	印度尼西亚	1 348	印 度	501
泰 国	110	巴布亚新几内亚	38	欧 盟	461
尼日利亚	81	贝 宁	36	巴基斯坦	212
合 计	3 681	合 计	2 867	合 计	1 729
所占世界比率（%）	91	所占世界比率（%）	92	所占世界比率（%）	56

世界大豆油主要国家年均生产贸易状况（2005/2006—2009/2010 年度）

国 家	生产量（万 t）	国 家	出口量（万 t）	国 家	进口量（万 t）
世界总计	**3 639**	**世界总计**	**996**	**世界总计**	**945**
美 国	902	阿根廷	546	中 国	231
中 国	697	巴 西	215	印 度	117
阿根廷	638	美 国	103	欧 盟	83
巴 西	594	欧 盟	29	伊 朗	48
合 计	2 831	合 计	892	合 计	479
所占世界比率（%）	78	所占世界比率（%）	90	所占世界比率（%）	51

世界菜籽油主要国家年均生产贸易状况（2007/2008—2009/2010 年度）

国 家	生产量（万 t）	国 家	出口量（万 t）	国 家	进口量（万 t）
世界总计	**2 019**	**世界总计**	**230**	**世界总计**	**226**
欧 盟	836	加拿大	151	欧 盟	38
中 国	450	欧 盟	14	中 国	33
印 度	212			加拿大	7
加拿大	182			日 本	3
合 计	1 680	合 计	165	合 计	81
所占世界比率（%）	83	所占世界比率（%）	72	所占世界比率（%）	36

世界葵花籽油主要国家年均生产贸易状况（2007/2008—2009/2010 年度）

国 家	生产量（万 t）	国 家	出口量（万 t）	国 家	进口量（万 t）
世界总计	**1 094**	**世界总计**	**400**	**世界总计**	**345**
俄罗斯	239	乌克兰	181	欧 盟	104
乌克兰	225	阿根廷	103	土耳其	40
欧 盟	218	俄罗斯	59		
阿根廷	142	欧 盟	13		
合 计	825	合 计	356	合 计	144
所占世界比率（%）	75	所占世界比率（%）	89	所占世界比率（%）	42

资料来源：表中数据出自 2010 年版《中国油脂》杂志第 35 卷第 8 期。

表 9 俄罗斯主要农产品生产情况（2009 年） 单位：百万 t

品 种	2009 年 1～10 月	农业生产	家庭农场	居民经济	2008 年 1～10 月
谷 物	101.3	78.9	21.5	0.9	112.4
向日葵	5.9	4.2	1.7		6.8
甜 菜	22.5	20.0	2.3	0.2	25.9
马铃薯	20.3	3.8	1.7	24.8	28.3
蔬 菜	12.4	2.2	1.3	8.9	12.2

资料来源：表中数据出自 2010 年版《世界农业》杂志第 4 期。

表 10 部分国家（地区）籽棉、麻类收获面积、单产、总产量（2009 年）

国家或地区	籽 棉			麻 类		
	收获面积（khm^2）	单产（kg/hm^2）	总产量（kt）	收获面积（khm^2）	单产（kg/hm^2）	总产量（kt）
世界总计	**31 432**	**2 099**	**65 985**	**1 578**	**2 026**	**3 198**
埃 及	240	2 333	560	1	2 316	2
南 非	14	1 877	26	1	1 000	1
孟加拉国	17	2 294	39	423	2 016	854
美 国	3 128	2 250	7 038			
巴 西	1 057	3 757	3 971	16	1 551	25
中 国	4 952	1 288	6 377	160	2 433	388
印 度	9 373	1 206	11 305	957	2 115	2 024
缅 甸	300	640	192	32	937	30
巴基斯坦	2 820	2 046	5 770	2	560	1
土库曼斯坦	674	1 261	850			
土 耳 其	495	3 678	1 820			
哈萨克斯坦	175	1 818	442			
乌兹别克斯坦	1 452	2 560	3 716	2	10 000	20
伊 朗	120	2 500	300			
澳大利亚	630	4 825	304			

表 11 部分国家（地区）烟叶、茶叶收获面积、单产、总产量（2009 年）

国家或地区	烟 叶			茶 叶		
	收获面积（khm^2）	单产（kg/hm^2）	总产量（kt）	收获面积（khm^2）	单产（kg/hm^2）	总产量（kt）
世界总计	**3 698**	**1 881**	**6 881**	**2 806**	**1 688**	**4 736**
印度尼西亚	199	852	170	107	1 411	151
南 非	9	2 222	20	2	2 100	4
加 拿 大	16.5	2 667	44			
巴 西	431	1 971	850	3	1 673	4
中 国	1 328	2 203	3 066	1 328	1 023	1 359
印 度	370	1 405	520	474	1 699	805
日 本	19	2 105	40	48	1 952	94
韩 国	15	2 367	36	1	1 107	2
法 国	6	2 610	16			
德 国						
意 大 利	35	2 857	100			
土 耳 其	121	827	100	76	14 510	1 100
伊 朗	14	1 333	180	34	1 765	60
巴基斯坦	51	2 097	108			
美 国	142	2 537	360			

表 12 部分国家（地区）甘蔗、甜菜收获面积、单产、总产量（2009 年）

国家或地区	甘蔗			甜菜		
	收获面积（khm^2）	单产（kg/hm^2）	总产量（kt）	收获面积（khm^2）	单产（kg/hm^2）	总产量（kt）
世界总计	**24 375**	**71 512**	**1 743 093**	**4 386**	**49 626**	**227 585**
埃及	136	121 103	16 470	108	47 528	5 133
南非	425	48 235	20 500			
加拿大				7	49 286	345
美国	374	73 805	27 603	407	65 939	26 837
巴西	8 141	79 710	648 921			
中国	1 709	73 094	124 918	232	43 293	10 044
印度	5 055	68 880	348 188			
日本				67	64 134	4 297
韩国						
法国				349	86 837	30 306
德国				369	62 339	23 003
意大利				71	53521	3 800
俄罗斯				800	36 244	28 995
英国				120	62 500	7 500
澳大利亚	390	87 110	33 973			

资料来源：表中数据出自 2010 年版《国际统计年鉴》。

表 13 部分国家（地区）蔬菜、水果和坚果产量（2009 年） 单位：kt

国家或地区	蔬菜	水果	坚果
世界总计	**916 102**	**572 407**	
埃及	13 751	9 601	
南非		6 077	
加拿大			
美国	36 432	28203	
巴西	10196	38988	
中国	457 730	107 838	
印度	78 886	62 672	
日本	12 700	3 483	
韩国	11 256	2 907	
法国		8 508	
德国			
意大利	13 687	17654	
俄罗斯	14 058	5 265	
英国			
澳大利亚		2 823	

资料来源：表中数据出自 2010 年版《世界农业》杂志第 12 期与 2010 年版《国际统计年鉴》。

表 14 部分国家（地区）苹果、梨、橙等水果产量（2009 年） 单位：kt

国家或地区	苹 果	梨	橙	葡 萄	香 蕉
世界总计	**69 603**	**20 998**	**67 696**	**67 709**	**90 706**
埃 及			2 138	1 531	1 062
南 非		345	1 436	1 792	
加拿大					
美 国	4 431	790	9 139	6 745	
巴 西	1 121		18 390	1 403	7 117
中 国	29 851	13 676	3 454	7 285	8 043
印 度	2 001	200	4 397	1 677	23 205
日 本	840	326			
韩 国		471			
法 国	1 940	162		5 664	
德 国	1 047			1 429	
意大利	2 208	770	2 527	7 793	
俄罗斯	1 467				
英 国					
澳大利亚				1 957	

资料来源：表中数据出自 2010 年版《世界农业》杂志第 12 期。

表 15 世界葡萄栽培面积前 10 位国家（2008 年）

国家或地区	栽培面积（万 hm^2）	占世界栽培面积比例（%）
西班牙	120.0	16.2
法 国	81.3	11.0
意大利	77.0	10.4
土耳其	48.3	6.5
中 国	43.8	5.9
美 国	37.9	5.1
伊 朗	31.5	4.3
葡萄牙	22.3	3.0
阿根廷	22.0	3.0
罗马尼亚	19.4	2.6

资料来源：表中数据出自 2010 年版《世界农业》杂志第 6 期。

表 16 世界葡萄主产国前 10 位国家（2008 年）

国家或地区	产量（万 t）	占世界葡萄产量的比例（%）
意大利	729.3	11.5
中 国	728.5	10.8
美 国	674.5	10.0
西班牙	605.3	8.9
法 国	566.4	8.4
土耳其	391.8	5.8
伊 朗	290.0	4.3
阿根廷	290.0	4.3
智 利	235.0	3.5
澳大利	195.2	2.9

资料来源：表中数据出自 2010 年版《世界农业》杂志第 6 期。

表 17　世界葡萄酒 10 强企业排名（2008 年）　单位：百万美元

排　名	企　业　名　称	年度销售额
1	Constellation Brands（美国星座集团）	3 358.8
2	E & J Gallo（美国嘉露集团）	3 080.0
3	Foster's Group（福斯特集团）	1 667.9
4	Pernod Ricard（法国保乐力加集团 ）	1 587.6
5	Castel - Freres（法国卡斯特集团）	980.0
6	The Wine Group（美国葡萄酒集团）	910.0
7	Changyu（中国张裕集团）	890.0
8	Diageo（英国帝亚吉欧集团）	868.8
9	Grand Chais de France（法国吉赛福集团）	830.0
10	Concha Y Toro（智利甘露集团）	520.0

资料来源：表中信息出自 2010 年版《中外葡萄与葡萄酒》杂志第 1 期。

表 18　世界主要葡萄酒生产国家（地区）出口状况（2006—2008 年）

单位：亿 L

国家或地区	2006 年		2007 年		2008 年	
	出口量	占有率（%）	出口量	占有率（%）	出口量	占有率（%）
总　计	**79.4**	**94.00**	**84.6**	**94.00**	**83.8**	**94.00**
法　国	14.7	17.00	15.2	17.00	13.6	15.00
意大利	18.4	22.00	18.5	21.00	17.2	19.00
德　国	32	4.00	3.5	4.00	3.6	4.00
葡萄牙	2.9	3.00	3.5	4.00	3.1	3.00
中东欧①	2.1	2.00	2.2	2.00	1.9	2.00
南　美②	7.7	9.00	9.7	11.00	10.0	11.00
美　国	3.8	4.00	4.2	5.00	4.5	5.00
南　非	2.7	3.00	3.1	3.00	4.1	5.00
马格里布③	0.4		0.4		0.4	
大洋洲④	8.2	10.00	8.6	10.00	7.9	9.00
摩尔多瓦	1.0	1.00	0.6	1.00	1.0	1.00
西班牙	14.3	17.00	15.1	17.00	16.5	19.00

注：①包括保加利亚＋匈牙利＋罗马尼亚；②包括阿根廷＋智利；③包括阿尔及利亚＋突尼斯＋摩洛哥；④包括澳大利亚＋新西兰。

资料来源：表中数据出自驻法国大使馆商赞处。

表 19　中国葡萄酒进口量前 5 位国家分布情况（2008 年）

规　　格	国　　家	进口量（kL）
2L 以下包装的	法　　国	22 944
	澳大利亚	11 628
	意 大 利	5 053
	智　　利	4 206
	美　　国	3 867
2L 以上包装的	智　　利	47 980
	阿 根 廷	25 170
	西 班 牙	10 792
	法　　国	5 413
	意 大 利	5 017

资料来源：表中数据出自中国酿酒工业协会葡萄酒分会。

表 20 世界主要葡萄酒消费国的消费量（2007—2008 年） 单位：亿 L

国家或地区	消费量	
	2007 年	2008 年
总 计	**244.90**	**242.90**
法 国	32.17	31.75
意大利	26.70	26.00
美 国	26.50	27.25
德 国	20.15	20.00
中 国		
西班牙	13.27	12.79
英 国	13.70	13.48
阿根廷	11.17	10.67
俄罗斯		
罗马尼亚		
葡萄牙	4.81	4.80
澳大利亚	4.77	4.91

资料来源：表中数据由驻法国大使馆商赞处提供。

表 21 世界食糖供求状况（2005—2009 年） 单位：百万 t

产量与消费量	2005 年	2006 年	2007 年	2008 年	2009 年
产 量	141.15	151.38	167.43	167.85	155.30
消费量	143.97	146.10	152.96	158.78	164.80

表 22 我国台湾省主要农产品产量（2006—2008 年） 单位：万 t

年 份	稻 谷	槟 榔	菠 萝	芒 果	甘 蔗	茶 叶	花 生	香 蕉
2006	155.8	14.2	49.2	19.1	65.1	1.9	7.2	21.4
2007	136.3	13.4	47.7	21.5	72.1	1.8	5.2	24.2
2008	145.7	14.4	45.2	17.7	70.7	1.7	5.5	20.7

表 23 部分国家（地区）肉类产量（2008—2009 年） 单位：kt

国家或地区	2008 年	2009 年	同比增长（%）
世界总计	**283 818**	**279 953**	**−1.36**
埃　及		1 431	
南　非		2 110	
加拿大	4 416	4 494	1.05
美　国	41 809	43 172	3.26
巴　西	20 082	22 832	13.69
中　国	88 681	74 539	−19.97
印　度	6 322	6 796	7.50
日　本		3 145	
韩　国		1 852	
法　国	5 064	5 471	8.04
德　国	7 053	7 687	8.99
意大利	3 977	4 134	3.95
俄罗斯	5 602	6 136	9.53
英　国	3 411	3 367	−1.29
澳大利亚	4 164	4 284	2.88

资料来源：表中数据出自 2010 年版《国际统计年鉴》。

表 24 部分国家（地区）猪肉产量（2005—2009 年） 单位：kt

国家或地区	2005 年	2006 年	2007 年	2008 年	2009 年
世界总计	**48 867**	**49 570**	**51 707**	**52 323**	**51 736**
中　国	45 553	46 505	42 878	46 205	48 500
欧盟 27 国	21 676	21 791	22 858	22 596	22 000
美　国	9 392	9 559	9 962	10 599	10 446
巴　西	2 710	2 830	2 990	3 015	3 123
俄罗斯	1 735	1 805	1 910	2 060	2 205
越　南	1 602	1 713	1 832	1 850	1 850
加拿大	1 765	1 748	1 746	1 786	1 790
日　本	1 245	1 247	1 250	1 249	1 285
菲律宾	1 175	1 215	1 250	1 225	1 225
墨西哥	1 195	1 158	1 152	1 161	1 150
韩　国	1 036	1 000	1 043	1 056	1 016
其　他	5 336	5 504	5 714	5 726	5 646

表 25 部分国家（地区）猪肉消费量（2005—2009 年） 单位：kt

国家或地区	2005 年	2006 年	2007 年	2008 年	2009 年
世界总计	**94 048**	**95 842**	**94 434**	**98 357**	**100 022**
中 国	45 139	46 051	42 726	46 412	48 300
欧盟 27 国	20 632	20 632	21 507	21 025	20 800
美 国	8 660	8 643	8 965	8 806	8 925
俄罗斯	2 486	2 639	2 803	3 112	2 954
巴 西	1 949	2 191	2 260	2 390	2 478
日 本	2 509	2 452	2 473	2 487	2 494
越 南	1 583	1 731	1 855	1 880	1 894
墨西哥	1 556	1 538	1 523	1 605	1 664
韩 国	1 311	1 420	1 502	1 519	1 415
菲利宾	1 198	1 239	1 275	1 270	1 267
中国台湾	944	928	926	945	958
其 他	6 081	6 378	6 619	6 906	6 873

表 26 部分国家（地区）猪肉进口量（2005—2009 年） 单位：kt

国家或地区	2005 年	2006 年	2007 年	2008 年	2009 年
世界总计	**4 740**	**4 921**	**5 087**	**5 915**	**5 323**
日 本	1 314	1 154	1 210	1 267	1 210
俄罗斯	752	835	894	1 053	750
墨西哥	420	446	451	535	600
韩 国	345	410	447	430	375
美 国	464	449	439	377	373
中国香港	263	277	302	346	345
乌克兰	62	62	82	238	240
加拿大	139	145	171	194	170
澳大利亚	105	109	141	152	170
中 国	88	90	198	430	150
新加坡	85	98	97	91	99
其 他	703	846	655	802	841

表 27 部分国家（地区）猪肉出口量（2005—2009 年） 单位：kt

国家或地区	2005 年	2006 年	2007 年	2008 年	2009 年
世界总计	**5 006**	**5 224**	**5 162**	**6 147**	**5 465**
美 国	1 209	1 359	1 425	2 217	1 887
欧盟 27 国	1 143	1 284	1 286	1 726	1 250
加拿大	1 084	1 081	1 033	1 129	1 130
巴 西	761	639	730	625	645
中 国	502	544	350	223	230
智 利	128	130	148	142	142
墨西哥	59	66	80	91	86
澳大利亚	56	60	54	48	45
韩 国	16	14	13	11	20
越 南	19	20	19	11	10
克罗地亚	1	2	2	3	5
其 他	28	25	22	21	15

表 28 部分国家（地区）猪、牛、羊、禽肉产量（2009 年） 单位：kt

国家或地区	猪 肉	牛 肉	羊 肉	禽 肉
世界总计	**103 190**	**65 722**	**13 174**	**91 699**
埃 及	2	590	61	664
南 非	150	805	155	981
加拿大	1 941	1 288	16	1 229
美 国	10 462	12 236	106	20 141
巴 西	3 015	9 024	109	10 661
中 国	47 208	6 152	3 806	15 814
印 度	497	2 755	781	2 563
日 本	1 249	520		1 366
韩 国	1 056	246	2	542
法 国	2 029	1 479	97	1 610
德 国	5 111	1 210	26	1 246
意大利	1 606	1 059	60	1 118
俄罗斯	2 042	1 769	174	2 044
英 国	740	862	326	1 430
澳大利亚	384	2 300	714	859

资料来源：表中数据出自 2010 年版《国际统计年鉴》。

表 29 世界主要贸易国肉类生产、消费及贸易情况（2005—2009 年）单位：万 t

产品类别	2005 年	2006 年	2007 年	2008 年	2009 年
一、产量					
牛肉	5 628	5 754	5 836	5 805	5 678
猪肉	9 442	9 608	9 459	9 853	10 024
禽肉	6 806	6 926	7 340	7 674	7 889
总计	**21 876**	**22 287**	**22 635**	**23 332**	**23 380**
二、消费量					
牛肉	5 583	5 680	5 795	5 745	5 612
猪肉	9 405	9 584	9 443	9 836	10 002
禽肉	6 736	6 907	7 310	7 581	7 611
总计	**21 724**	**22 171**	**22 548**	**23 161**	**23 225**
三、进口量					
牛肉	679	684	723	693	644
猪肉	474	492	509	592	532
禽肉	672	687	759	829	797
总计	**1 826**	**1 863**	**1 991**	**2 113**	**1 974**
四、出口量					
牛肉	732	750	757	749	711
猪肉	501	522	516	615	547
禽肉	744	712	797	907	872
总计	**1 976**	**1 985**	**2 070**	**2 271**	**2 129**
五、美国出口					
牛肉	316	519	650	856	785
猪肉	1 209	1 359	1 425	2 117	1 887
禽肉	2 618	2 609	2 926	3 464	3 232
总计	**4 143**	**4 487**	**5 001**	**6 437**	**5 904**
六、美国份额					
牛肉	4	7	9	11	11
猪肉	24	26	28	34	35
禽肉	35	37	37	38	37
总计	**21**	**23**	**24**	**28**	**28**

资料来源：表中数据出自 2010 年版《中国畜牧杂志》第 2 期。

表 30 俄罗斯主要畜牧业产品生产情况（2009 年） 单位：万 t

品 种	2009 年 1～10 月产量	相比增长（%）
牲畜和家禽	100	107.0
牛 奶	250	100.3
鸡 蛋（亿个）	33	104.1

资料来源：表中数据出自 2010 年版《世界农业》杂志第 4 期。

表 31　部分国家（地区）鱼类产品产量（2007 年）　单位：万 t

国家或地区	鱼类产品产量	其中	
		海　域	内陆水域
世界总计			
埃　及	98.2	11.4	86.8
南　非	65.8	65.6	0.2
加拿大	69.3	64.8	4.4
美　国	410.9	379.1	31.8
巴　西	92.2	47.5	44.6
中　国	2 811.7	900.5	1 911.1
印　度	660.6	263.5	397.0
日　本	361.6	354.8	6.7
韩　国	133.2	130.9	2.3
法　国	46.0	41.6	4.3
德　国	26.6	21.0	5.6
意大利	24.7	20.3	4.4
俄罗斯	342.5	309.4	33.0
英　国	61.9	60.3	1.6
秘　鲁	670.7	665.5	5.2

资料来源：表中数据出自 2010 年版《国际统计年鉴》。

表 32　世界鱼粉产量前 10 位国家（2009 年）　单位：kt

排　名	主要国家	产量
1	秘　鲁	1 490
2	智　利	800
3	泰　国	470
4	美　国	305
5	日　本	305
6	中　国	300
7	冰　岛	195
8	挪　威	180
9	俄罗斯	95
10	南　非	84

表 33　中国鱼粉进口主要国家和地区情况（2008—2009 年）

单位：万 t、亿美元

国家或地区	占进口总额比例（%）	2009 年		2008 年		同比增长（%）	
		数量	金额	数量	金额	数量	金额
俄罗斯	23.6	75.9	12.40	78.0	13.0	−2.6	−4.2
秘　鲁	14.9	85.7	7.86	99.9	9.9	−14.2	−20.5
美　国	12.7	38.5	6.70	33.5	6.4	14.8	4.9
智　利	9.9	41.0	5.20	29.7	4.1	37.6	27.4
东　盟	7.2	28.1	3.80	33.8	3.9	−16.7	−1.6
挪　威	5.3	14.8	2.80	8.8	1.9	69.7	47.8
日　本	4.2	12.0	2.20	11.5	1.9	4.9	13.9
欧　盟	3.8	13.3	2.00	20.4	3.2	−34.6	−36.3
加拿大	3.0	6.1	1.60	7.1	1.9	−13.9	−12.6

表 34 部分国家（地区）牛奶产量（2008—2009 年）

单位：kt

国家或地区	2008 年	2009 年	同比增减（%）
世界总计	**435 600**	**440 826**	**1.20**
埃及	2 200		
南非	3 000		
加拿大	8 270	8 250	—0.24
美国	86 179	85 366	—0.94
巴西	10 814	11 030	2.00
中国	10 100	10 400	2.97
印度	28 890	30 335	5.00
日本	134 346	134 300	—0.03
韩国	32 500	32 830	1.02
法国	11 070	10 350	—6.50
德国	36 700	38 630	5.26
意大利	44 100	45 140	2.36
俄罗斯	7 990	8 010	0.25
英国	15 141	16 400	8.32
澳大利亚	9 500	9 785	3.00

资料来源：表中数据出自 2010 年版《国际统计年鉴》。

表 35 部分国家（地区）乳饮料、酸奶和其他发酵乳产量（2006—2008 年）

单位：kt

国家或地区	2006 年	2007 年	2008 年
欧盟 27 国	10 052	10 251	10 142
瑞士	234	236	251
乌克兰	523	534	530
美国	1 498	1 577	1 633
加拿大	244	252	274
阿根廷	474	576	583
智利	172	177	192
墨西哥	569	636	631
以色列	164	167	170
中国	2 115	2 450	2 593
日本	2 726	2 779	2 656
韩国	504	485	455

资料来源：表 35～表 46 中数据出自 2009 年版《中国奶业年鉴》。

表 36 部分国家（地区）奶油产量（2006—2008 年） 单位：kt

国家或地区	2006 年	2007 年	2008 年
欧盟 27 国	2 053	2 065	2 075
瑞　　士	37	37	46
白俄罗斯	88	86	101
俄 罗 斯	230	245	258
乌 克 兰	104	99	85
澳大利亚	133	128	153
新 西 兰	420	390	400
加 拿 大	79	82	86
美　　国	657	695	749
阿 根 廷	47	47	51
巴　　西	78	82	84
中　　国	25	30	37
印　　度		108	114
日　　本	81	75	72

表 37 部分国家（地区）干酪产量（2006—2008 年） 单位：kt

国家或地区	2006 年	2007 年	2008 年
欧盟 27 国	8 156	8 222	8 376
挪　　威	83	84	85
瑞　　士	173	176	179
俄 罗 斯	405	434	429
乌 克 兰	319	346	352
加 拿 大	387	404	396
墨 西 哥	143	146	150
美　　国	4 673	4 755	4 793
阿 根 廷	467	487	491
巴　　西	528	580	630
中　　国	13	18	15
日　　本	125	125	118
以 色 列	113	115	119
澳大利亚	364	359	348
新 西 兰	308	314	345

表 38 部分国家（地区）炼乳产量（2006—2008 年） 单位：kt

国家或地区	2006 年	2007 年	2008 年
欧盟 25 国	1 120	1 080	1 080
俄罗斯	199	197	
白俄罗斯	88	88	
乌克兰	97	108	112
加拿大	48	44	41
美国	230	234	260
阿根廷	7	8	7
智利	44	45	42
秘鲁	279	281	
中国	120	150	173
日本	42	45	44
新加坡	252	253	
泰国	82	82	
南非	43	43	

表 39 部分国家（地区）全脂和半脱脂奶粉产量（2006—2008 年） 单位：kt

国家或地区	2006 年	2007 年	2008 年
欧盟 25 国	779	764	838
瑞士	19	21	22
白俄罗斯	35	36	
俄罗斯	76	75	84
乌克兰	25	30	30
美国	14	14	23
墨西哥	184	202	191
阿根廷	260	185	225
巴西	465	526	580
澳大利亚	135	142	138
新西兰	653	651	710
中国	1 100	1 300	1 200
印度	172	167	170
日本	14	14	14
南非			

表 40 部分国家（地区）脱脂奶粉产量（2006—2008 年） 单位：kt

国家或地区	2006 年	2007 年	2008 年
欧盟 27 国	1 015	986	972
瑞士	24	22	28
白俄罗斯	55	55	
俄罗斯	123	132	131
乌克兰	81	95	65
加拿大	72	75	85
美国	689	685	861
阿根廷	23	11	14
巴西	117	128	140
澳大利亚	209	177	221
新西兰	304	265	290
印度	151	162	180
日本	181	173	158

表 41 世界乳制品主要生产国家（地区）出口情况（2006—2008 年） 单位：kt

主要出口国家（地区）	2006 年	2007 年	2008 年
全脂奶粉			
世界合计	**1 700**	**1 580**	**1 680**
欧盟	434	364	491
美国	10	12	29
阿根廷	215	115	101
巴西	17	42	82
澳大利亚	143	125	163
新西兰	645	680	607
中国	15	58	62
新加坡	30	42	62
脱脂奶粉			
世界合计	**1 150**	**1 100**	**1 250**
欧盟	88	201	177
加拿大	13	14	10
美国	292	266	403
澳大利亚	173	127	178
新西兰	316	281	248
白俄罗斯	54	60	61
乌克兰	64	58	44
印度	36	32	43
黄油			
世界合计	**840**	**800**	**750**
欧盟	243	211	150
美国	11	40	89
澳大利亚	64	70	59
新西兰	391	364	330
其他国家	118	119	122
干酪			
世界合计	**1 480**	**1 530**	**1 400**
欧盟	582	594	555
瑞士	56	59	61
乌克兰	49	61	77
白俄罗斯	83	92	102
澳大利亚	212	202	132
新西兰	309	309	247
美国	71	100	131

表 42　世界乳制品主要进口国家（地区）情况（2006—2008 年）　单位：kt

主要产品进口国家（地区）	2006 年	2007 年	2008 年
全脂奶粉			
世界合计	**1 700**	**1 580**	**1 680**
俄罗斯	82	25	28
阿尔及利亚	182	160	170
委内瑞拉	44	47	50
中国	67	58	46
印度尼西亚	27	27	84
沙特阿拉伯	75	70	62
新加坡	60	61	73
马来西亚	59	64	50
菲律宾	40	42	45
脱脂奶粉			
世界合计	**1 150**	**1 100**	**1 250**
俄罗斯	5	42	63
中 国	62	41	55
印度尼西亚	86	91	77
日 本	32	35	32
菲律宾	95	98	80
沙特阿拉伯	53	42	35
新加坡	60	62	54
墨西哥	111	121	152
阿尔及利亚	68	91	105
黄油			
世界合计	**840**	**800**	**750**
欧 盟	82	92	65
俄罗斯	112	129	140
埃 及	40	26	33
摩洛哥	36	20	30
墨西哥	49	42	29
伊 朗	26	40	50
干酪			
世界合计	**1 480**	**1 530**	**1 400**
欧 盟	105	94	84
俄罗斯	218	330	350
美 国	206	198	165
墨西哥	78	86	68
日 本	207	225	187
韩国	45	49	47
沙特阿拉伯	103	98	70
澳大利亚	60	64	70

表 43 部分国家（地区）液体乳消费量（2006—2008 年）

国家或地区	消费总量（kt）			人均消费量（kg）		
	2006 年	2007 年	2008 年	2006 年	2007 年	2008 年
丹　麦	759	754		139.7	138.0	
德　国	7 829	7 791	7 730	94.4	95.0	94.0
法　国	5 670	5 721	5 567	89.4	89.7	86.8
爱尔兰	568	557	578	134.0	128.4	130.7
意大利	3 868	3 764	3 833	65.7	63.4	64.1
荷　兰	2 020	2 020	1 964	123.6	123.3	119.4
西班牙	5 104	5 060	5 005	114.2	112.0	108.6
英　国	6 352	6 405		104.8	105.1	
欧　盟	42 993	44 300	44 200	93.1	89.5	89.3
挪　威	537	543	551	116.7	118.0	116.2
瑞　士	610	612	617	81.1	79.0	79.9
加拿大	3 027	3 051	3 068	92.8	92.5	92.1
墨西哥						
美　国	25 010	24 987	25 011	83.8	83.0	82.6
阿根廷	1 724	1 729	1 762	44.2	43.9	43.9
巴　西						
澳大利亚	2 435	2 271	2 312	116.8	107.2	107.2
新西兰						
中　国						
日　本	4 574	4 464		35.8	34.9	
韩　国	2 181	2 177	2 152	45.2	44.9	44.3
南　非	1 630	1 680		37.9	39.1	

表 44 部分国家（地区）乳饮料、酸奶和发酵乳制品消费量（2006—2008 年）

国家或地区	消费总量（kt）			人均消费量（kg）		
	2006 年	2007 年	2008 年	2006 年	2007 年	2008 年
丹　麦	272	263		50.0	48.2	
德　国	2 514	2 532	2 510	29.8	30.8	30.5
法　国	2 037	2 058	1 915	31.6	31.0	29.9
荷　兰	706			45.0		
西班牙	1 300			29.1		
欧　盟	9 750	10 200	10 050	21.1	20.6	20.3
挪　威	109	117	121	23.7	25.4	25.5
瑞　士	234			31.4		
加拿大	243	251	273	7.5	7.6	8.2
墨西哥	568			5.3		
阿根廷	467	507	510	12.0	12.9	12.8
伊　朗	2 882	3 348	3 480	40.9	46.8	47.3

表 45 部分国家（地区）奶油消费量（2006—2008 年）

国家或地区	消费总量（kt）			人均消费量（kg）		
	2006 年	2007 年	2008 年	2006 年	2007 年	2008 年
丹 麦	9	10	11	1.6	1.7	2.0
德 国	538	523	515	6.5	6.4	6.2
法 国	499	504	502	7.9	7.9	7.8
爱尔兰	11	11		2.7	2.6	
荷 兰	54	56	54	3.3	3.3	3.3
意大利	170	157	154	2.9	2.6	2.6
英 国	226	195		3.7	3.2	
欧 盟	1 940	1 959	1 938	4.2	4.0	3.9
挪 威	20	18	19	4.3	4.0	4.0
瑞 士	42	44	45	5.6	5.7	5.7
俄罗斯	394	374	399	2.7	2.6	2.8
加拿大	86	91	90	2.6	2.8	2.7
美 国	645	687	772	2.2	2.3	2.5
阿根廷	29	28	29	0.7	0.7	0.7
澳大利亚	81	87	89	3.9	4.1	4.1
日 本	90	92		0.7	0.7	
西班牙	22	23	25	0.5	0.5	0.5

表 46 部分国家（地区）干酪消费量（2006—2008 年）

国家或地区	消费总量（kt）			人均消费量（kg）		
	2006 年	2007 年	2008 年	2006 年	2007 年	2008 年
芬 兰	102	104		19.1	19.1	
法 国	1 501	1 524	1 574	23.7	23.9	24.6
德 国	1 813	1 824	1 815	22.0	22.2	22.1
爱尔兰	28	31	27	6.7	7.1	6.1
意大利	1 280	1 249	1 280	21.7	21.0	21.4
荷 兰	289	295	285	17.7	18.0	17.3
西班牙	320	334	345	7.2	7.3	7.5
瑞 典	166	166		18.5	18.4	
英 国	734	744		12.1	12.2	
欧 盟	8 490	8 723	8 814	18.3	17.7	17.9
挪 威	70	71		15.2	15.4	
瑞 士	165	172	177	22.1	22.2	22.7
俄罗斯	705	764	779	4.9	5.4	5.5
加拿大	398	417	410	12.2	12.6	12.3
美 国	4 461	4 565	4 575	15.3	15.1	15.0
阿根廷	415	442	457	10.7	11.2	11.5
墨西哥	229	233	238	2.2	2.2	2.2
澳大利亚	249	250	254	11.9	11.8	11.8
日 本	254	263		2.0	2.1	
韩 国	72	74	72	1.5	1.5	1.5

表 47 世界乳品工业排名前 20 强企业（2009 年）

排序	企业名称	国别	销售收入（亿美元）
1	雀巢	瑞士	272.0
2	达能	法国	147.9
3	拉克塔利斯集团	法国	126.8
4	费里士兰坎皮纳公司	荷兰	111.7
5	恒天然	新西兰	102.0
6	德安食品公司	美国	97.4
7	阿拉乳品公司	丹麦/瑞典	86.4
8	美国奶农合作社	美国	81.0
9	卡福食品	美国	67.9
10	联合利华食品	爱尔兰/英国	63.8
11	明治乳业	日本	51.3
12	萨普托公司	加拿大	49.7
13	帕玛拉特	意大利	49.3
14	森永	日本	48.1
15	保健然食品有限公司	法国	45.7
16	蒙牛	中国	37.7
17	伊利	中国	35.4
18	蓝多湖	美国	32.1
19	贝勤集团	法国	31.0
20	格勒	挪威	30.2

资料来源：表中数据出自 2010 年版《中国乳品工业》杂志第 9 期。

表 48 部分国家（地区）蛋类产品产量（2009 年） 单位：万 t

国家或地区	蛋类产量		其中：鸡蛋产量	
	产量	占世界比重（%）	产量	占世界比重（%）
世界总计	**6 558.6**	**100.00**	**6 067.8**	**100.00**
中国	2 673.4	40.76	2 274.9	37.49
美国	533.9	8.14	533.9	8.80
日本	255.4	3.89	255.4	4.21
墨西哥	233.7	3.56	233.7	3.85
俄罗斯	213.5	3.26	211.9	3.49
印度	274.0	4.18	274.0	4.52
巴西	190.4	2.90	182.5	3.01
印度尼西亚	148.5	2.26	126.7	2.09
法国	87.9	1.34	87.9	1.49
德国	78.7	1.20	78.7	1.30
意大利	70.0	1.07	70.0	1.15
荷兰	62.7	0.96	62.7	1.03
土耳其	82.4	1.26	82.4	1.36
乌克兰	86.9	1.32	85.5	1.41
英国	61.4	0.94	60.0	0.99
泰国	87.2	1.33	56.2	0.93
伊朗	71.1	1.08	71.1	1.17

资料来源：表中数据出自 2010 年版《国际统计年鉴》。

表 49 世界主要鸡蛋生产国市场占有率情况（2008 年）

国家或地区	平均市场占有率（%）	市场占有率变化趋势
中 国	11.36	平 稳
美 国	33.75	平稳有所下降
印 度	5.43	上升幅度大
日 本	0.06	上 升
墨西哥	0.20	下 降
俄罗斯	1.42	波动上升
巴 西	2.87	近年呈上升
印度尼西亚	0.58	平 稳
法 国	18.61	逐年下降
乌克兰	0.64	近年快速上升
德 国	22.45	波动缓慢上升
意大利	2.64	近年比较平稳

资料来源：表中数据出自 2010 年版《农业展望》杂志第 5 期。

表 50 部分国家（地区）蜂蜜产量（2008—2009 年） 单位：t

国家或地区	2008 年	2009 年	同比增减（%）
世界总计	**1 073 000**	**1 496 000**	**39.42**
中 国	400 000	367 000	−8.25
印 度	52 000	52 000	
美 国	71 000	73 000	2.82
阿根廷	81 000	81 000	
墨西哥	56 000	55 000	−1.79
土耳其	87 000	81 000	−6.90
乌克兰	80 000	75 000	−6.25
澳大利亚	18 000	18 000	
巴 西	34 000	35 000	2.94
法 国	16 000	16 000	
德 国	25 000	16 000	−36.00
俄罗斯	56 000	57 000	1.79
西班牙	31 000	31 000	
加拿大	28 000	28 000	
伊 朗	36 000	36 000	
韩 国	25 000	27 000	8.00

资料来源：表中数据出自 2010 年版《国际统计年鉴》。

表 51 部分国家（地区）羊毛产量（2008—2009 年） 单位：kt

国家或地区	2008 年	2009 年	同比增减（%）
世界总计	**2 173.0**	**2 191.0**	**0.83**
埃及	8	7.6	−5.00
南非	45	45	
加拿大			
美国	18	17.5	2.78
巴西	11	11	
中国	412	395	−4.13
印度	46	46.4	0.87
日本			
韩国			
法国	22	22	
德国	15	15	
意大利	9	9.2	2.22
俄罗斯	51	53.5	4.90
英国	62	62	
澳大利亚	465	465	

资料来源：表中数据出自 2010 年版《国际统计年鉴》。

表 52 我国农业主要产品产量居世界位次（1949—2008 年）

项目	1949 年	2006 年	2007 年	2008 年
谷物		1	1	1
肉类	3	1	1	1
棉花	4	1	1	1
大豆	2	4	4	4
花生	2	1	1	1
油菜籽	2	1	1	2
甘蔗		3	3	3
茶叶	3	1	1	1
水果①		1	1	1

注：①不包括瓜类。

表 53 中国对日本农产品出口情况（2009 年） 单位：亿美元、%

类别	出口额	与 2008 年相比	占对日出口额比重	比重增减
水产品及制品	26.0	−3.6	33.8	−1.2
食品蔬菜	9.0	4.9	11.7	0.6
畜产品及制品	8.1	−1.4	10.6	−0.1
杂项食品	1.8	3.5	2.3	0.1
食用油籽	1.5	23.7	2	0.4
食用水果及坚果	1.4	−9.3	1.7	−0.2

资料来源：表中数据出自 2010 年版《国际农产品贸易》杂志第 1 期。

表 54 2009 年中国与东盟各国农产品贸易情况 单位：万美元、%

国家	出口		进口		贸易差额
	出口值	占比	进口值	占比	
东盟	535 984	100.00	876 784	100.00	−340 801
马来西亚	122 820	22.91	307 052	35.02	−184 233
印度尼西亚	105 097	19.61	228 016	26.01	−122 919
泰国	85 818	16.01	180 054	20.54	−94 235
越南	94 609	17.65	74 901	8.54	19 709
新加坡	44 610	8.32	42 894	4.89	1 717
菲律宾	72 592	13.54	23 394	2.67	49 198
缅甸	7 648	1.43	16 889	1.93	−9 241
老挝	628	0.12	2 939	0.34	−2 311
柬埔寨	1 426	0.27	640	0.07	785
文莱	735	0.14	6		730

资料来源：表中数据出自 2010 年版《世界农业》杂志第 6 期。

表 55 2009 年中国—东盟主要农产品进出口情况 单位：万美元、t

中国对东盟出口			中国从东盟进口		
产品	出口额	出口量	产品	出口额	出口量
农产品	535 984	6 515 686	农产品	876 784.1	19 164 381
蔬菜	135 353	1 953 122	植物油	465 102.1	7 078 297
水果	108 452	1 926 408	水果	92 994.9	1 931 712
水产品	77 122	356 620	薯类	88 877.7	6 107 207
粮食制品	22 331	401 972	水产品	38 095.2	282 656
畜产品	18 369	103 663	粮食制品	27 067.2	845 405
糖料及糖	18 315	240 894	谷物	23 366.6	457 431
油籽	16 756	165 254	糖料及糖	8 127.7	767 173
饼粕	14 124	410 976	饼粕	3 043.3	397 877

资料来源：表中数据出自 2010 年版《世界农业》杂志第 6 期。

表 56 2009 年中国与东盟各国主要农产品进出口品种情况

出口品种	主要出口国家	进口品种	主要进口国家
蔬菜	马来西亚、印度尼西亚 、泰国、越南	植物油	马来西亚、印度尼西亚
鲜冷冻大蒜头	印度尼西亚、马来西亚、越南、菲律宾、泰国、新加坡	棕榈油	马来西亚、印度尼西亚
鲜冷冻葫萝卜、萝卜	马来西亚、泰国、越南	水果	泰国、越南、菲律宾
鲜冷冻马铃薯	马来西亚、越南	香蕉	菲律宾
水果	印度尼西亚、越南、泰国、马来西亚、菲律宾	龙眼、榴莲、荔枝、猕猴桃	泰国
柑橘	印度尼西亚、越南、马来西亚、菲律宾	干木薯	泰国、越南
苹果	印度尼西亚、泰国、菲律宾、越南、马来西亚、新加坡	水产品	泰国、印度尼西亚、缅甸、马来西亚、越南
梨	印度尼西亚、越南、泰国、马来西亚	谷物	泰国
水产品	马来西亚、菲律宾、泰国	大米	泰国
鲜冷冻对虾	马来西亚	食糖	泰国

资料来源：表中信息出自 2010 年版《世界农业》第 6 期。

表 57　俄罗斯主要农产品进出口情况（2008—2009 年）

单位：亿美元、万 t、%

农产品进出口	2009 年 1～10 月	2008 年 1～10 月	同期相比（%）
农产品出口额	81.81	74.51	109.8
谷物出口	1 838	995.70	184.6
其中：小麦	1 391.8	883.70	157.5
大麦	319.1	99.72	320.0
油菜籽	10.6	2.30	460.0
葵花籽	10.7	2.97	360.0
农产品进口额	236.38	130.10	81.7
其中：肉类	111.60	62.40	78.8
禽肉	74.70	42.40	76.0
鱼类	62.60	32.72	91.3
奶制品	37.70	19.64	92.0
其中：奶粉	5.23	3.14	66.8
黄油	8.72	4.74	84.0
奶酪	23.70	11.47	106.6
蔬菜	220.50	117.73	87.3
葵花籽油	3.73	2.74	36.1
糖	121.70	75.97	60.2

资料来源：表中数据出自 2010 年版《世界农业》杂志第 4 期。

表 58　美国主要农产品进出口情况（2009 年）　　单位：亿美元

进口情况	
主要农产品	进口金额
畜产品	106.88
谷　物	45.22
油籽及其他产品	53.52
园艺产品	330.13
糖及热带产品	153.19
出口情况	
主要农产品	出口金额
小　麦	59.97
大　米	22.58
玉　米	93.12
大　豆	139.04
乳制品	22.64
棉　花	35.81
糖及热带产品	38.78

资料来源：表中数据出自 2010 年版《世界农业》的 5 期。

表 59 中国对新西兰农产品贸易情况（2004—2008 年）

单位：千万美元、%

年份	农产品出口	出口比重	农产品进口	进口比重
2004	3.49	3.20	87.83	76.00
2005	4.77	3.50	84.75	76.80
2006	6.41	4.00	92.05	75.80
2007	8.51	3.90	114.41	79.50
2008	9.90	3.94	143.47	79.44

资料来源：表中数据出自 2010 年版《世界农业》杂志第 7 期。

表 60 中国与拉丁美洲及加勒比地区农产品进出口情况（2005—2009 年）

单位：亿美元

年　份	2005 年	2006 年	2007 年	2008 年	2009 年
出　口	5.2	8.1	8.9	13.1	10.8
进　口	75.3	76.8	115.3	194.8	142.2
平衡情况	−70.1	−68.7	−106.4	−181.7	−131.4
中国从拉丁美洲及加勒比地区主要国家进口农产品情况					
拉丁美洲及加勒比地区	75.3	76.8	115.3	194.8	142.2
巴　西	30.1	38.0	48.2	87.9	84.4
阿根廷	29.9	24.1	51.8	84.2	34.9
秘　鲁	7.5	6.3	6.1	10.0	8.1
智　利	3.2	3.2	4.0	5.5	7.3
乌拉圭	1.0	2.0	2.6	3.9	4.3
古　巴	1.2	2.0	1.3	1.9	1.7
中国向拉丁美洲及加勒比地区主要国家出口农产品情况					
拉丁美洲及加勒比地区	5.2	8.1	8.9	13.1	10.8
墨西哥	2.2	2.8	3.1	4.0	3.4
巴　西	0.7	0.8	1.2	2.7	2.1
委内瑞拉	0.2	0.4	0.3	1.9	0.8
古　巴	0.6	0.5	0.8	0.6	0.7
智　利	0.1	0.2	0.4	0.7	0.6

资料来源：表中数据出自 2010 年版《世界农业》杂志第 7 期。

表 61 世界饲料加工业 30 强企业（2008 年） 单位：万 t

排 名	企 业 名 称	国 别	产 量
1	正大（卜蜂）集团 Charoen Pokphand（CpGroup）	泰 国	2 210
2	嘉吉/农标 Cargill/Agribrands	美 国	1 710
3	新希望 New Hope Group	中 国	1 300
4	蓝雷普瑞纳 Land o'lakes Purina	美 国	1 160
5	巴西食品 Brasil Foods	巴 西	1 020
6	泰森食品 Tyson Foods	美 国	1 010
7	泰高 Nutreco	荷 兰	900
8	全农 Zen-Nohco-Operative	日 本	740
9	东方新希望 East Hope Group	中 国	610
10	英国联合营养集团 ABAgri	英 国	470
11	唐人神 Hunan Tangrenshan Group	中 国	430
12	UcaabUcaab Co-Operatives	法 国	400
13	DLG DLG	丹 麦	370
14	广东温氏 Guangdong Wen's Group	中 国	370
15	普乐维美 Provimi	荷 兰	360
16	斯密斯菲尔德 Smithfield Foods	美 国	360
17	格伦山德 Glon Sanders	法 国	337
18	ADM ADMAlliance Natrition/AHSN	美 国	320
19	Bachoco Bachoco	墨西哥	310
20	Frangosul	巴 西	300
21	Invivo NSA	法 国	300
22	De Heus	荷 兰	291
23	大成 Dachan/East AsiA Group	中 国	290
24	Agravis Raiffeisen	法 国	270
25	塞黑维兰堡贝朗 Cehave Land Bonw Belang	荷 兰	270
26	维罗尼斯 Veronesi	意大利	268
27	普渡农场 Perdue Farms	美 国	260
28	Dentsche Tiernahrung Cremer	德 国	240
29	金吉斯 Gold Kisi	美 国	240
30	JD荷斯维尔 JD Heis Kell	美 国	240

资料来源：表中数据出自 2010 年版《中国畜牧》杂志第 10 期。

表 62　世界主要农畜产品最大生产国（2009 年）

农畜产品	第一位国家	产量（kt）	第二位国家	产量（kt）	第三位国家	产量（kt）
谷　物	中　国	481 008	美　国	403 772	印　度	26 582
小　麦	中　国	112 463	印　度	78 570	美　国	68 026
稻　谷	中　国	193 354	印　度	148 260	印度尼西亚	60 251
玉　米	美　国	307 384	中　国	166 035	巴　西	59 018
谷　子	印　度	11 340	尼日利亚	9 064	尼日尔	3 889
高　粱	美　国	11 998	尼日利亚	9 318	印　度	7 926
马铃薯	中　国	57 060	印　度	34 463	俄罗斯	28 874
甘　薯						
木　薯						
大　豆	美　国	80 536	巴　西	59 917	阿根廷	46 232
甘　蔗	巴　西	648 921	印　度	348 188	中　国	124 918
甜　菜	法　国	30 306	俄罗斯	28 995	美　国	26 837
油菜籽	加拿大	12 643	中　国	12 102	印　度	5 833
棉　花	中　国	22 500	印　度	11 305	美　国	7 038
茶　叶	中　国	1 257	土耳其	1 100	印　度	805
水　果	中　国	107 838	印　度	62 672	巴　西	38 988
花　生	中　国	14 341	印　度	7 338	尼日利亚	3 900
肉　类	中　国	74 539	美　国	43 172	巴　西	22 832
蛋　类	中　国	26 734	美　国	5 339	印　度	2 740
奶　类	印　度	109 000	美　国	86 179	中　国	40 130
禽　肉	美　国	20 141	中　国	15 814	巴　西	10 661
蜂　蜜	中　国	367	土耳其	81	阿根廷	81

表 63　香港特别行政区工业生产指数（2006—2009 年）（2008 年=100）

工　业　组　别	2006 年	2007 年	2008 年	2009 年
所有制造行业	108.7	107.2	100.0	91.7
其中：食品、饮品及烟草制品业	85.6	97.5	100.0	99.1
纺织制品业	122.5	112.5	100.0	77.8
成　衣	151.9	128.2	100.0	70.2
纸制品及印刷业	98.0	100.2	100.0	92.0

表 64　香港特别行政区主要加工食品及饮料出口与转口情况（2007—2008 年）

单位：亿港元

产　品	出　口			转口		
	2008 年	2007 年	同比增长（%）	2008 年	2007 年	同比增长（%）
奶制品	0.63	0.52	21.2	5.59	4.44	25.9
糖、糖制品及蜜糖	0.76	0.87	−12.6	10.14	8.81	15.1
杂项食品及配制食品	9.27	8.68	6.8	8.86	8.81	0.6
饮料	3.31	3.77	−12.8	38.93	35.43	9.9

资料来源：表中数据由中国轻工业信息中心提供。

表 65 我国台湾省农产品加工业主要产品产量（2005—2009 年）

年 份	食 品（万 t）	饮 料（万 L）	饲 料（万 t）	各种成衣（万打）	纸 板（万 t）	合成纤维（万 t）
2005	43.1	38 379.6	521.8	1 135.9	337.8	266.7
2006	43.9	34 478.9	518.3	1 039.9	335.1	246.4
2007	45.4	33 652.0	510.9	920.6	340.6	238.8
2008	43.8	31 211.5	516.5	744.5	291.0	193.7
2009	46.8	34 126.9	523.0	606.0	277.5	200.1

表 66 我国台湾省农业生产及稻米产量情况（2004—2008 年）

单位：人、户、hm^2、kg

年 份	农业从业人员	农户家庭总数	常用耕地面积	稻谷收获面积	稻谷均产
2004	3 392 676	759 716	237 351	237 015	6 049
2005	3 400 036	767 316	269 120	269 023	5 454
2006	3 232 592	756 366	263 194	263 188	5 920
2007	3 050 483	751 338	260 159	260 116	5 242
2008			252 321	252 292	5 776

资料来源：中国台湾省“农委会”《农业统计年报》。

表 67 我国台湾省出口与进口商品分类（2006—2009 年） 单位：亿美元

年 份	出 口				进 口			
	出口额	农产品	农产加工品	工业产品	进口额	资本设备	原材料	消费品
2006	2 240.2	3.5	18.5	2 218.2	2 027.0	345.2	1 527.9	153.9
2007	2 466.8	4.1	18.7	2 444.0	2 192.5	355.7	1 677.6	159.3
2008	2 556.3	5.4	21.7	2 529.2	2 404.5	326.9	1 908.5	169.1
2009	2 036.7	5.0	18.5	2 013.3	1 743.7	257.2	1 325.0	161.5

表 68 世界主要国家（地区）棉花产量（2009 年） 单位：万 t

年份	全 球	中 国	美 国	印 度	巴基斯坦	巴 西	乌兹别克斯坦	中国占（%）
2009	2 222	680	270.0	510.0	213.0	124.0	95.0	30.60

资料来源：表中数据出自 2010 年版《中国棉花加工》杂志第 3 期。

表 69 世界和中国纺织纤维产量（2005—2007 年） 单位：万 t

年 份	世界纤维产量				中国纤维产量			
	总 计	天然纤维	化学纤维		总 计	天然纤维	化学纤维	
			小计	其中：合成纤维			小计	其中：合成纤维
2005	6 961.5	2 679.7	4 081.8	3 822.4	2 323.6	665.8	1 657.8	1 527.3
2006	7 068.9	2 800.4	4 389.2	4 127.6	2 780.2	755.8	2 024.4	1 906.9
2007	7 613.7	2 862.1	4 751.6	4 452.1	3 231.7	838.6	2 393.1	2 233.7

资料来源：表中数据出自《2008/2009 年中国纺织工业发展报告》。

表 70 世界主要国家（地区）化纤产量（2005—2007 年） 单位：万 t

年份	全球	中国	美国	西欧	中国台湾	韩国	日本	印度	中国占（%）
2005	4 246.0	1 817.7	410.0	461.9	287.4	182.9	120.2	225.2	42.8
2006	4 389.2	2 024.4	379.2	452.8	270.4	162.6	117.5	257.9	46.1
2007	4 751.6	2 393.1	367.4	447.2	269.1	162.6	116.7	295.9	50.4

资料来源：表中数据出自《2008/2009 年度中国纺织工业发展报告》。

表 71 世界主要国家（地区）合成纤维产量（2005—2007 年） 单位：万 t

年份	全球	中国	美国	西欧	中国台湾	韩国	日本	印度	中国占（%）
2005	3 998.4	1 712.1	405.1	411.3	275.9	182.1	113.5	195.7	42.8
2006	4 127.6	1 906.9	376.1	402.8	257.2	161.7	110.9	226.9	46.2
2007	4 452.1	2 233.7	362.4	394.4	255.5	160.8	108.2	256.4	50.2

资料来源：表中数据出自《2008/2009 年度中国纺织工业农展报告》。

表 72 世界棉花供求情况（2008/2009—2009/2010 年） 单位：万 t

年 度	总产量	进口量	出口量	消费量	期末库存
2008/2009	2 340	655	658	3 079	1 326
2009/2010	2 310	734	734	3 222	1 126

表 73 世界主要国家棉花耗用量（2005—2008 年） 单位：万 t

国家	耗用量	2005 年	2006 年	2007 年	2008 年
全球	耗用量	2 392.1	2 621.5	2 603.5	2 616.1
	占总（%）	100.0	100.0	100.0	100.0
中国	耗用量	859.9	1 049.8	1 049.9	1 089.9
	占总（%）	35.9	40.0	40.3	41.7
美国	耗用量	129.3	106.7	100.2	95.1
	占总（%）	5.4	4.1	3.8	3.6
印度	耗用量	346.4	398.9	389.0	401.0
	占总（%）	14.5	15.2	15.3	15.3
巴基斯坦	耗用量	241.5	259.2	259.3	257.4
	占总（%）	10.1	9.9	10.0	9.8
土耳其	耗用量	155.0	150.0	155.0	135.0
	占总（%）	6.5	5.9	6.0	5.2
日本	耗用量	16.7	13.0	13.0	12.5
	占总（%）	0.7	0.5	0.5	0.5
巴西	耗用量	90.0	86.0	99.6	94.6
	占总（%）	3.8	3.3	3.8	3.6

资料来源：表 73～表 75 中数据出自《2008/2009 年度中国纺织工业发展报告》。

表 74 中国纺织品、成衣出口额占全球出口份额（2005—2007 年）

单位：亿美元

年 份	纺织品出口			成衣出口		
	全 球	中 国	中国占（%）	全 球	中 国	中国占（%）
2005	2 029.7	410.5	20.2	2 756.4	741.6	26.9
2006	2 185.9	486.8	22.3	3 114.1	953.9	30.6
2007	2 381.3	559.7	23.5	3 453.0	1 152.4	33.3

表 75 世界纺织品、成衣出口国（地区）前 10 强（2007 年） 单位：亿美元

排 序	国家或地区	合 计	纺织品	成 衣	占世界（%）
	世界总计	5 834.3	2 381.3	3 453.0	100.0
1	中 国	1 712.1	559.7	1 152.4	29.3
2	欧盟（27）	1 053.9	806.2	247.7	18.1
3	中国香港	421.9	134.2	287.7	7.2
4	土耳其	227.3	87.3	140.0	3.9
5	印 度	191.1	94.5	96.6	3.3
6	巴基斯坦	185.5	111.8	73.7	3.2
7	美 国	166.9	123.9	43.0	2.9
8	韩 国	122.8	103.7	19.1	2.1
9	中国台湾	109.7	97.2	12.5	1.9
10	孟加拉国	107.8	7.2	100.6	1.8

表 76 中国纺织品服装出口前 5 位的主要市场（2009 年）

国家或地区	出 口 额（亿美元）	占纺织品服装出口总额比重（%）
欧 盟	370.79	21.64
美 国	278.37	16.25
日 本	220.80	12.89
中国香港	139.98	8.17
东 盟	109.15	6.37
合 计	1119.09	65.32

资料来源：表中数据由中国纺织工业协会统计中心提供。

表 77 中国等 4 国纺织品、服装产品占欧盟进口的份额（2005—2009 年）

单位：%

年份	中国等 4 国纺织品占欧盟进口份额				中国等 4 国服装占欧盟进口份额			
	中 国	印 度	巴基斯坦	土耳其	孟加拉国	中 国	印度	土耳其
2005	23.40	11.60	7.14	18.73	6.71	35.32	6.76	15.69
2006	25.58	11.41	7.27	18.79	7.80	35.00	6.98	14.21
2007	27.18	11.58	7.68	18.58	7.13	38.34	6.77	14.67
2008	29.85	11.23	7.70	17.51	7.47	42.84	6.82	12.70
2009	30.99	10.96	8.24	17.49	8.40	44.77	7.43	11.72

资料来源：表中数据出自 2010 年版《纺织导报》杂志第 7 期。

表 78 2009 年 5 国 4 种产品占欧盟进口总额中的比重 单位：%

进口来源国	装饰类纺织品	针织或钩织类织物	女式针织或钩编类服装	男式针织或钩编类服装
中 国	40.54	30.73	41.18	38.44
土耳其	14.95	37.85	18.03	10.86
印 度	11.84	0.77	8.94	11.00
孟加拉国	3.51	0.01	6.82	12.62
巴基斯坦	12.99	0.15	0.81	2.85

资料来源：表中数据出自 2010 年版《纺织导读》杂志第 7 期。

表 79 世界 20 大纸与纸板生产国家或地区（2008 年） 单位：kt

名 次	国家或地区	产 量
1	美 国	79 952
2	中 国	79 800
3	日 本	30 627
4	法 国	22 842
5	加拿大	15 756
6	芬 兰	13 126
7	瑞 典	11 663
8	韩 国	10 642
9	意大利	9 481
10	法 国	9 418
11	巴 西	9 334
12	印度尼西亚	9 203
13	印 度	8 405
14	俄罗斯	7 684
15	西班牙	6 414
16	奥地利	5 151
17	英 国	4 982
18	墨西哥	4 665
19	中国台湾	4 143
20	泰 国	4 129

资料来源：表中数据出自 2010 年版《中外食品和包装机械》杂志第 2 期。

表 80 世界与中国纸浆、纸及纸板生产与消费情况（2007—2008 年）

单位：万 t

项 目		2007 年	2008 年	同比（%）
世 界	纸浆总产量	18 835		
	纸浆总消费量	19 619		
	纸和纸板总产量	39 430		
	纸和纸板总消费量	39 418		
	纸和纸板人均年消费量（kg）	59.2		
中 国	纸浆总产量	5 935	6 415	8.09
	纸浆总消费量	5 769	7 360	27.58
	纸和纸板总产量	7 350	7 980	8.57
	纸和纸板总消费量	7 290	7 935	8.85
	纸和纸板人均年消费量（kg）	55	60	9.09

资料来源：表中数据出自 2009 年版《中国造纸年鉴》。

表 81 我国台湾省主要纸品产销量情况（2008 年） 单位：t

主要产品	产 量	同比增长（%）	销售量	同比增长（%）	内销量	同比增长（%）	外销量	同比增长（%）
1. 纸张总计	1 233 063	－0.1	1 180 742	－11.0	904 821	－12.7	275 921	－4.8
印刷书写纸	698 109	－9.0	648 750	－17.5	436 267	－21.3	212 483	－8.6
其中：铜版纸	361 957	－4.9	345 330	－10.8	177 210	－15.1	168 120	－5.9
道林纸	247 340	－9.9	220 132	－21.6	186 977	－23.3	33 155	－10.5
模造纸	57 479	－16.3	53 593	－26.0	42 933	－25.0	10 660	－29.7
新闻纸	1 042	33.8	1 041	21.8	1 041	21.8		
生活用纸	206 163	3.6	204 501	1.6	196 782	－1.1	7 719	232.9
2. 纸板总计	2 909 620	－14.6	2 847 471	－16.9	1 901 880	－14.9	945 591	－20.7
其中：纸箱用纸板	2 111 693	－17.2	2 057 748	－19.9	1 457 471	－15.7	599 777	－28.4
牛皮纸板	1 050 141	－20.1	1 024 709	22.3	723 490	－17.1	301 229	－32.5
瓦楞原纸板	981 423	－14.9	955 960	17.8	674 357	－14.3	281 603	－25.1
白纸板	559 309	－6.7	558 634	－6.5	233 033	－12.3	325 601	－1.8
纸与纸板总计	4 142 683	－12.0	4 028 213	－15.2	2 806 701	－14.2	1 221 512	－17.6

资料来源：表中数据出自 2009 年年版《中国造纸年鉴》。

表 82 世界纸和纸板产量排名前 10 位的国家（2008 年）

排 序	国 家	产量（万 t）	同比增长（%）
1	美 国	7 995.2	−4.4
2	中 国	7 980.0	8.6
3	日 本	3 061.7	−2.1
4	德 国	2 284.2	−2.0
5	加拿大	1 575.6	−8.9
6	芬 兰	1 312.6	−8.4
7	瑞 典	1 166.3	−1.7
8	韩 国	1 061.0	−3.0
9	意大利	948.1	−6.4
10	德 国	941.8	−4.6

资料来源：表中数据出自 2009 年版《纸和造纸》杂志第 12 期。

表 83 世界纸浆产量排名前 10 位的国家（2008 年）

排 序	国 家	产量（万 t）	同比增长（%）
1	美 国	5 148	−3.7
2	加拿大	2 030	−9.3
3	中 国	1 976	3.0
4	巴 西	1 280	6.6
5	瑞 典	1 207	−2.7
6	芬 兰	1 172	−5.4
7	日 本	1 067	−1.3
8	俄罗斯	743	1.9
9	印度尼西亚	644	10.6
10	智 利	498	5.8

资料来源：表中数据出自 2009 年版《纸和造纸》杂志第 12 期。

表 84 世界纸浆主要净进口和净出口前 5 位的国家（2008 年） 单位：万 t

纸浆主要净进口国			纸浆主要净出口国		
排 序	国家	净进口量	排 序	国 家	净出口量
1	中 国	892.9	1	加拿大	932
2	德 国	402.7	2	巴 西	671
3	意大利	372.5	3	智 利	405
4	韩 国	246.4	4	瑞 典	294
5	日 本	167.4	5	芬 兰	192

资料来源：表中数据出自 2010 年版《国际造纸》杂志第 1 期。

表 85 世界纸和纸板消费量与人均消费量前 5 位的国家（2008 年）

纸和纸板消费量（万 t）			纸和纸板人均消费量（kg/人）		
排　序	国　家	消费量	排　序	国　家	净出口量
1	美 国	8 169	1	比利时	345
2	中 国	7 935	2	芬 兰	342
3	日 本	3 069	3	美 国	266
4	德 国	2 037	4	奥地利	252
5	英 国	1 130	5	瑞 典	248

资料来源：表中数据出自 2009 年版《纸和造纸》杂志第 12 期。

表 86 世界部分国家废纸回收量及进出口量（2008 年）

单位：万 t、%

国　家	回收量	回收率	利用率	出口量	进口量	废纸用量
美 国	4 758.9	58.3	36.2	1 823.7	71.6	2 889.9
日 本	2 243.7	73.1	62.1	349.2	6.1	1 900.6
德 国	1 561.7	76.7	67.8	329.2	316.4	1 548.9
英 国	876.7	77.6	80.2	488.0	7.4	399.3
法 国	688.5	64.1	60.3	212.5	93.8	567.7
意大利	631.6	60.0	56.2	150.7	52.0	532.9
中 国	3 127.7	39.5	69.5		2 421.0	5 548.7

资料来源：表中数据出自 2010 年版《国际造纸》杂志第 1 期。

表 87 世界部分国家或地区纸和纸板净出口量和净进口量（2008 年）

单位：万 t

纸和纸板净出口量			纸和纸板净进口量		
排　序	国家或地区	净出口量	排　序	国家或地区	净进口量
1	芬 兰	1 133	1	英 国	632
2	瑞 典	941	2	土耳其	199
3	加拿大	876	3	墨西哥	196
4	印度尼西亚	329	4	美 国	174
5	奥地利	308	5	比利时	166
6	德 国	248	6	意大利	161
7	韩 国	179	7	印 度	153
8	俄罗斯	126	8	中国香港	130

资料来源：表中数据出自 2010 年版《国际造纸》杂志第 1 期。

表 88 我国台湾省印刷业基本情况（2005—2009 年）

单位：百万新台币

年份	印刷产值	同比增长（%）	外销值	同比增长（%）
2005	74 025	4.33	7 424	−0.07
2006	71 098	−3.95	7 578	2.07
2007	70 174	−1.30	7 565	−0.17
2008	70 700	0.74	8 700	13.04
2009	67 100	−5.19	7 400	−11.50

资料来源：表中数据出自 2010 年版《今日印刷》杂志第 6 期。

表 89 我国香港特别行政区印刷业基本情况（2004—2008 年）

单位：个、百万港币

年 份	企业数量（个）	从业人数（个）	生产总值	工业增加值
2004	3 866	34 561	28 773	11 270
2005	3 814	35 490	29 307	12 063
2006	3 777	39 032	30 106	11 954
2007	3 585	39 106	32 749	13 689
2008	3 583	36 965	31 654	13 126

资料来源：表中数据出自 2010 年版《今日印刷》杂志第 6 期。

表 90 世界主要国家天然橡胶产量（2007—2009 年） 单位：万 t

国家或地区	2007 年	2008 年	2009 年
泰 国	305.6	309.0	308.6
印度尼西亚	275.5	275.1	253.5
马来西亚	119.9	107.2	85.6
印 度	81.1	88.1	81.7
中 国	59.0	56.0	63.0
越 南	60.6	66.0	72.4
科特迪瓦	18.3	19.4	20.6
斯里兰卡	11.7	12.9	13.3
利比里亚	10.6	8.1	7.7
巴 西	11.6	12.3	10.4
其 他	5.5	6.1	6.3
世界合计	9 801.0	10 031.0	9 602.0

资料来源：表中数据出自 2010 年版《中国橡胶》杂志第 13 期。

表 91 世界主要国家（地区）合成橡胶产量（2007—2009 年） 单位：kt

国家或地区	2007 年	2008 年	2009 年
世界总计	**13 430**	**12 784**	**12 168**
加拿大	93	96	74
美 国	2 697	2 314	1 962
巴 西	425	392	385
中 国	2 215	2 325	2 856
中国台湾	600	552	555
印 度	103	99	102
日 本	1 655	1 651	1 264
韩 国	1 010	970	1 149
法 国	655	645	514
德 国	803	791	655
意大利	235	220	200
俄罗斯	1 210	1 139	1 032
英 国	318	268	171
墨西哥	204	198	160
比利时	107	94	104

资料来源：表中数据出自 2010 年版《中国橡胶》杂志第 13 期。

表 92 世界天然橡胶和合成橡胶产量、消费量（2005—2009 年） 单位：kt

年 份	天 然 橡 胶		合 成 橡 胶	
	产 量	消费量	产 量	消费量
2005	8 907	9 073	12 160	11 899
2006	9 701	9 251	12 710	12 380
2007	9 801	10 224	13 430	13 308
2008	10 031	9 885	12 784	12 339
2009	9 602	9 547	12 168	11 878

资料来源：表中数据出自 2010 年版《中国橡胶》杂志第 13 期。

表 93 世界主要国家（地区）橡胶消耗量（2009 年） 单位：万 t

国家或地区	2009 年 橡 胶 消 耗 量		
	天 然 橡 胶	合 成 橡 胶	总 量
世界总计	**954.7**	**1 187.8**	**2 142.5**
斯洛文尼亚	1.4	3.6	5.0
马来西亚	47.0	13.0	59.9
斯洛伐克	2.8	4.8	7.5
捷 克	4.6	9.6	14.3
日 本	63.7	83.4	147.1
韩 国	33.0	27.8	60.8
比利时	2.5	8.0	10.6
芬 兰	0.9	1.5	2.4
德 国	17.0	45.0	62.1
西班牙	12.4	16.0	28.4
瑞 典	0.5	6.4	6.9
加拿大	10.3	15.8	26.1
俄罗斯	2.5	44.5	47.0
美 国	68.7	144.8	213.5
法 国	10.9	27.9	38.8
泰 国	36.0	23.2	59.2
葡萄牙	2.1	4.0	6.1
意大利	8.9	17.0	25.8
波 兰	6.9	14.3	21.3
荷 兰	0.8	8.0	8.8
奥地利	2.4	1.3	3.7
中 国	366.9	426.6	793.5
中国台湾	9.1	21.2	30.3
英 国	4.2	12.4	16.6
巴 西	25.5	44.5	70.0
澳大利亚	1.6	3.5	5.1
南 非	5.2	5.8	11.0
印度尼西亚	40.4	14.7	55.1
印 度	90.4	31.2	121.6

资料来源：表中数据出自 2010 年版《中国橡胶》杂志第 13 期。

表 94 我国台湾省天然橡胶和合成橡胶消费量（2007—2009 年） 单位：万 t

名 称	2007 年	2008 年	2009 年
合 计	**39.7**	**30.9**	**30.3**
天然橡胶	11.5	9.7	9.1
合成橡胶	28.2	21.2	21.2

资料来源：表中数据出自 2010 年版《中国橡胶》杂志第 13 期。

表 95 我国台湾省橡胶工业产值情况（2005—2007 年）

单位：亿新台币

年 份	轮 胎	其他橡胶制品	总 产 值	增长率（%）
2005	379.2	390.9	770.2	−1.55
2006	393.8	400.5	794.2	3.12
2007	434.7	420.7	855.4	7.71

资料来源：表中数据出自 2009 年版《中国橡胶工业年鉴》。

表 96 世界橡胶机械生产厂商前 10 名排序（2009 年） 单位：百万美元

排序	企 业 名 称	国 别	销 售 收 入	增长率（%）
1	H－F 公司	德 国	289.7	−3.2
2	神户制钢	日 本	261.2	37.4
3	飞 迈	荷 兰	204.0	28.1
4	青岛软控	中 国	168.7	42.4
5	德斯玛	德 国	123.9	6.8
6	三菱 重工	日 本	108.8	8.8
7	中田工程	日 本	92.5	82.9
8	大陆机械	德 国	91.1	−15.8
9	天津赛象科技	中 国	90.2	−26.8
10	桂林橡机	中 国	87.7	−4.8

资料来源：表中数据出自 2010 年版《橡胶科技市场》杂志第 12 期。

表 97 世界各区域市场橡胶机械销售收入情况（2007—2009 年）

单位：万美元

国家或地区	2007 年	2008 年	2009 年		
			销售收入	占世界份额（%）	增长率（%）
世界总计	**295 805**	**311 394**	**295 200**	**100.00**	**−5**
西 欧	54 370	45 410	43 300	15.00	−5
中 欧	40 630	40 980	32 100	11.00	−22
中东及非洲	7 500	7 680	5 200	2.00	−32
北美洲	33 800	33 480	32 000	11.00	−4
南美洲	11 840	15 370	15 200	500.00	−1
南亚洲	34 030	46 640	52 200	18.00	12
印 度	18 580	27 560	29 700	10.00	8
中 国	69 610	73 880	73 500	25.00	0
日 本	22 980	18 670	10 000	3.00	−48
澳大利亚	2 460	1 730	1 800	1.00	6

资料来源：表中数据出自 2010 年版《橡胶科技市场》杂志第 12 期。

表 98 2009 年中国农产品进出口市场排序情况 单位：万美元

中国农产品出口市场排序

排　名	市　场	出口金额
1	日本	768 000
2	欧盟	575 000
3	东盟	354 000
4	美国	470 000
5	中国香港	353 000
6	韩国	283 000
7	德国	149 000

中国农产品进口市场排序

排　名	市　场	出口金额
1	美国	1 400 000
2	东盟	857 000
3	巴西	844 000
4	阿根廷	349 000
5	欧盟	338 000
6	加拿大	265 000
7	澳大利亚	249 000

资料来源：表中数据由海关总署提供。

表 99 中国农村居民与部分发达国家消费结构情况比较（1990—2007 年）

单位：%

国家	年份	食品	衣着	住房	家庭设备用品	医疗保健	交通通讯	文教娱乐	其他
中国	1990	58.80	7.77	17.34	5.29	1.44	5.37	3.25	0.74
	1996	56.33	7.24	13.95	5.36	3.71	3.00	8.43	2.02
	2000	49.13	6.75	15.47	4.52	5.58	11.18	5.24	3.14
	2007	43.08	6.00	17.80	4.63	10.19	9.48	6.52	2.30
美国	1990	12.00	6.10	18.30	5.90	17.50	13.60	10.20	16.31
	1996	10.60	5.70	18.60	5.40	18.00	14.40	10.80	16.50
	2000	9.30	5.30	16.80	5.10	16.40	13.30	11.40	22.40
	2007	6.88	4.51	17.51	4.67	19.10	11.88	12.78	22.67
日本	1990	24.12	7.21	10.03	4.66	2.99	12.10	11.58	27.31
	1996	16.13	5.32	23.30	5.04	3.08	11.06	12.28	16.07
	2000	17.30	6.00	25.40	4.60	3.50	12.70	11.90	18.60
	2007	14.36	3.64	24.61	3.75	4.20	14.41	13.23	21.78
韩国	1990	32.02	8.33	9.15	5.70	5.24	8.40	12.84	18.32
	1996	28.51	7.34	7.27	4.49	4.64	12.76	15.12	19.87
	2000	17.27	4.15	17.36	4.66	6.42	16.78	12.73	19.63
	2007	14.77	4.42	16.87	4.22	5.37	16.54	13.49	24.32
英国	1990	18.13	6.49	20.53	8.33	1.78	19.41	8.63	16.70
	1996	19.90	5.79	19.57	6.53	1.62	17.01	10.48	19.10
	2000	17.41	6.31	18.03	6.62	1.25	16.67	13.49	20.22
	2007	8.94	5.84	19.76	5.84	1.62	17.32	13.99	26.69

资料来源：表中数据出自 2010 年版《世界农业》杂志第 8 期。

表 100 按营业额排序的世界最大 500 个企业中农产品加工企业（2010 年）

企业名称	国家或地区	营业额位次	营业额（百万美元）
食品业			
雀巢	瑞 士	44	99 114
CVSCarermarK	美 国	45	98 729
麦德龙	德 国	57	91 152
特易购	英 国	58	90 234
克罗格	美 国	70	76 733
阿彻丹尼尔斯米德兰公司	美 国	88	69 207
沃尔格林	美 国	106	63 335
永旺	日 本	127	54 092
邦基	美 国	172	41 926
西夫韦	美 国	176	44 104
SuperValu	美 国	178	40 597
卡夫食品	美 国	179	40 386
皇家阿霍德	荷 兰	184	38 814
Wesfarmers	澳大利亚	192	37 466
西斯科	美 国	194	36 853
沃尔沃斯	澳大利亚	198	36 523
森宝利（桑斯博里）	英 国	236	31 828
艾德卡	德 国	261	29 976
联合博姿	瑞 士	262	29848
乔治威斯顿	加拿大	285	28 009
德尔海兹集团	比利时	291	27 732
泰森食品	美 国	297	27 165
中粮集团	中 国	312	26 098
CHS	美 国	317	25 730
来德爱	美 国	319	25 669
Publix. supermarkees	美 国	339	24 515
威廉莫里斯超市	英 国	344	24 263
丰益国际	新加坡	353	23 885
MIGROS	瑞 士	374	22 976
麦当劳	美 国	378	22 745
达能集团	德 国	422	20 824
COOP 集团	瑞 士	493	17 238
JBS	巴 西	496	17 161
饮食服务			
金巴斯集团	英 国	424	20 747

（续）

企业名称	国家或地区	营业额位次	营业额（百万美元）
索迪斯	法　国	437	19 818
饮料业			
百事公司	美　国	171	43 232
百威英博	比利时	196	36 758
可口可乐公司	美　国	245	30 990
可口可乐企业	美　国	404	21 645
麒麟公司	日本	429	20 503
喜力公司	荷兰	430	20 491
服装业			
克里斯汀迪奥	法　国	338	24 665
耐克	美　国	453	19 176
造纸纸制品印刷出纸业			
国际纸业	美　国	362	23 366
金柏利公司	美　国	455	19 115
橡胶和朔料制品业			
布里奇斯通	日　本	289	27 750
米其林	法　国	426	20 581
烟草业			
菲里浦曼里斯	美　国	331	25 035
帝国烟草	英　国	377	22 760
英美烟草	英　国	387	22 157
日本烟草	日　本	416	21 335
肥皂与化装品业			
宝 洁	美　国	66	79 697
欧莱雅	法　国	342	24 286
综合			
沃尔玛公司	美　国	1	408 214
家乐福	法　国	22	121 452
联合利华	英国/荷兰	121	55 352
欧尚	法　国	122	55 141

资料来源：表中数据出自 2010 年版《国际统计年鉴》。

图书在版编目（CIP）数据

中国农产品加工业年鉴.2010/科学技术部农村科技司等编.—北京：中国农业出版社，2011.7
ISBN 978-7-109-15943-3

Ⅰ.①中… Ⅱ.①科… Ⅲ.①农产品加工—加工工业—中国—2010—年鉴 Ⅳ.①F326.5-54

中国版本图书馆CIP数据核字（2011）第151978号

中国农业出版社出版
（北京市朝阳区农展馆北路2号）
（邮政编码 100125）
责任编辑 孟令洋

中国农业出版社印刷厂印刷 新华书店北京发行所发行
2011年8月第1版 2011年8月北京第1次印刷

开本：787mm×1092mm 1/16 印张：29.75
字数：1000千字
定价：240.00元
（凡本版图书出现印刷、装订错误，请向出版社发行部调换）

ISBN 978-7-109-15943-3